Lecture Notes in Computer Science 9176

Commenced Publication in 1973
Founding and Former Series Editors:
Gerhard Goos, Juris Hartmanis, and Jan van Leeuwen

More information about this series at http://www.springer.com/series/7409

Margherita Antona · Constantine Stephanidis (Eds.)

Universal Access in Human-Computer Interaction

Access to Interaction

9th International Conference, UAHCI 2015
Held as Part of HCI International 2015
Los Angeles, CA, USA, August 2–7, 2015
Proceedings, Part II

 Springer

Editors
Margherita Antona
Foundation for Research and Technology –
   Hellas (FORTH)
Heraklion, Crete
Greece

Constantine Stephanidis
University of Crete
Heraklion, Crete
Greece

and

Foundation for Research and Technology –
   Hellas (FORTH)
Heraklion, Crete
Greece

ISSN 0302-9743   ISSN 1611-3349 (electronic)
Lecture Notes in Computer Science
ISBN 978-3-319-20680-6   ISBN 978-3-319-20681-3 (eBook)
DOI 10.1007/978-3-319-20681-3

Library of Congress Control Number: 2015942616

LNCS Sublibrary: SL3 – Information Systems and Applications, incl. Internet/Web, and HCI

Springer Cham Heidelberg New York Dordrecht London

Printed on acid-free paper

Springer International Publishing AG Switzerland is part of Springer Science+Business Media
(www.springer.com)

Foreword

The 17th International Conference on Human-Computer Interaction, HCI International 2015, was held in Los Angeles, CA, USA, during 2–7 August 2015. The event incorporated the 15 conferences/thematic areas listed on the following page.

A total of 4843 individuals from academia, research institutes, industry, and governmental agencies from 73 countries submitted contributions, and 1462 papers and 246 posters have been included in the proceedings. These papers address the latest research and development efforts and highlight the human aspects of design and use of computing systems. The papers thoroughly cover the entire field of Human-Computer Interaction, addressing major advances in knowledge and effective use of computers in a variety of application areas. The volumes constituting the full 28-volume set of the conference proceedings are listed on pages VII and VIII.

I would like to thank the Program Board Chairs and the members of the Program Boards of all thematic areas and affiliated conferences for their contribution to the highest scientific quality and the overall success of the HCI International 2015 conference.

This conference could not have been possible without the continuous and unwavering support and advice of the founder, Conference General Chair Emeritus and Conference Scientific Advisor, Prof. Gavriel Salvendy. For their outstanding efforts, I would like to express my appreciation to the Communications Chair and Editor of HCI International News, Dr. Abbas Moallem, and the Student Volunteer Chair, Prof. Kim-Phuong L. Vu. Finally, for their dedicated contribution towards the smooth organization of HCI International 2015, I would like to express my gratitude to Maria Pitsoulaki and George Paparoulis, General Chair Assistants.

May 2015

Constantine Stephanidis
General Chair, HCI International 2015

HCI International 2015 Thematic Areas and Affiliated Conferences

Thematic areas:

- Human-Computer Interaction (HCI 2015)
- Human Interface and the Management of Information (HIMI 2015)

Affiliated conferences:

- 12th International Conference on Engineering Psychology and Cognitive Ergonomics (EPCE 2015)
- 9th International Conference on Universal Access in Human-Computer Interaction (UAHCI 2015)
- 7th International Conference on Virtual, Augmented and Mixed Reality (VAMR 2015)
- 7th International Conference on Cross-Cultural Design (CCD 2015)
- 7th International Conference on Social Computing and Social Media (SCSM 2015)
- 9th International Conference on Augmented Cognition (AC 2015)
- 6th International Conference on Digital Human Modeling and Applications in Health, Safety, Ergonomics and Risk Management (DHM 2015)
- 4th International Conference on Design, User Experience and Usability (DUXU 2015)
- 3rd International Conference on Distributed, Ambient and Pervasive Interactions (DAPI 2015)
- 3rd International Conference on Human Aspects of Information Security, Privacy and Trust (HAS 2015)
- 2nd International Conference on HCI in Business (HCIB 2015)
- 2nd International Conference on Learning and Collaboration Technologies (LCT 2015)
- 1st International Conference on Human Aspects of IT for the Aged Population (ITAP 2015)

Conference Proceedings Volumes Full List

1. LNCS 9169, Human-Computer Interaction: Design and Evaluation (Part I), edited by Masaaki Kurosu
2. LNCS 9170, Human-Computer Interaction: Interaction Technologies (Part II), edited by Masaaki Kurosu
3. LNCS 9171, Human-Computer Interaction: Users and Contexts (Part III), edited by Masaaki Kurosu
4. LNCS 9172, Human Interface and the Management of Information: Information and Knowledge Design (Part I), edited by Sakae Yamamoto
5. LNCS 9173, Human Interface and the Management of Information: Information and Knowledge in Context (Part II), edited by Sakae Yamamoto
6. LNAI 9174, Engineering Psychology and Cognitive Ergonomics, edited by Don Harris
7. LNCS 9175, Universal Access in Human-Computer Interaction: Access to Today's Technologies (Part I), edited by Margherita Antona and Constantine Stephanidis
8. LNCS 9176, Universal Access in Human-Computer Interaction: Access to Interaction (Part II), edited by Margherita Antona and Constantine Stephanidis
9. LNCS 9177, Universal Access in Human-Computer Interaction: Access to Learning, Health and Well-Being (Part III), edited by Margherita Antona and Constantine Stephanidis
10. LNCS 9178, Universal Access in Human-Computer Interaction: Access to the Human Environment and Culture (Part IV), edited by Margherita Antona and Constantine Stephanidis
11. LNCS 9179, Virtual, Augmented and Mixed Reality, edited by Randall Shumaker and Stephanie Lackey
12. LNCS 9180, Cross-Cultural Design: Methods, Practice and Impact (Part I), edited by P.L. Patrick Rau
13. LNCS 9181, Cross-Cultural Design: Applications in Mobile Interaction, Education, Health, Transport and Cultural Heritage (Part II), edited by P.L. Patrick Rau
14. LNCS 9182, Social Computing and Social Media, edited by Gabriele Meiselwitz
15. LNAI 9183, Foundations of Augmented Cognition, edited by Dylan D. Schmorrow and Cali M. Fidopiastis
16. LNCS 9184, Digital Human Modeling and Applications in Health, Safety, Ergonomics and Risk Management: Human Modeling (Part I), edited by Vincent G. Duffy
17. LNCS 9185, Digital Human Modeling and Applications in Health, Safety, Ergonomics and Risk Management: Ergonomics and Health (Part II), edited by Vincent G. Duffy
18. LNCS 9186, Design, User Experience, and Usability: Design Discourse (Part I), edited by Aaron Marcus
19. LNCS 9187, Design, User Experience, and Usability: Users and Interactions (Part II), edited by Aaron Marcus
20. LNCS 9188, Design, User Experience, and Usability: Interactive Experience Design (Part III), edited by Aaron Marcus

Universal Access in Human-Computer Interaction

Program Board Chairs: Margherita Antona, Greece, and Constantine Stephanidis, Greece

- Gisela Susanne Bahr, USA
- João Barroso, Portugal
- Jennifer Romano Bergstrom, USA
- Margrit Betke, USA
- Rodrigo Bonacin, Brazil
- Anthony Brooks, Denmark
- Christian Bühler, Germany
- Stefan Carmien, Spain
- Carlos Duarte, Portugal
- Pier Luigi Emiliani, Italy
- Qin Gao, P.R. China
- Andrina Granić, Croatia
- Josette F. Jones, USA
- Simeon Keates, UK
- Georgios Kouroupetroglou, Greece
- Patrick Langdon, UK
- Barbara Leporini, Italy
- Tania Lima, Brazil
- Troy McDaniel, USA
- Ana Isabel Paraguay, Brazil
- Helen Petrie, UK
- Michael Pieper, Germany
- Enrico Pontelli, USA
- Jaime Sánchez, Chile
- Vagner Santana, Brazil
- Anthony Savidis, Greece
- Hirotada Ueda, Japan
- Gerhard Weber, Germany
- Fong-Gong Wu, Taiwan

The full list with the Program Board Chairs and the members of the Program Boards of all thematic areas and affiliated conferences is available online at:

http://www.hci.international/2015/

HCI International 2016

The 18th International Conference on Human-Computer Interaction, HCI International 2016, will be held jointly with the affiliated conferences in Toronto, Canada, at the Westin Harbour Castle Hotel, 17–22 July 2016. It will cover a broad spectrum of themes related to Human-Computer Interaction, including theoretical issues, methods, tools, processes, and case studies in HCI design, as well as novel interaction techniques, interfaces, and applications. The proceedings will be published by Springer. More information will be available on the conference website: http://2016.hci.international/.

General Chair
Prof. Constantine Stephanidis
University of Crete and ICS-FORTH
Heraklion, Crete, Greece
Email: general_chair@hcii2016.org

http://2016.hci.international/

Contents – Part II

Visual and Multisensory Experience

Gesture-Based Interaction

Intelligent Intent-Aware Touchscreen Systems Using Gesture Tracking with Endpoint Prediction

Bashar I. Ahmad[1]([⊠]), Patrick M. Langdon[1], Robert Hardy[2], and Simon J. Godsill[1]

[1] Department of Engineering, University of Cambridge, Cambridge, UK
{bia23,pml24,sjg30}@cam.ac.uk
[2] Jaguar Land Rover, Whitley, Coventry, UK
pb404@cam.ac.uk
rhardy@jaguarlandrover.com

Abstract. Using an interactive display, such as a touchscreen, entails undertaking a pointing gesture and dedicating a considerable amount of attention to execute a selection task. In this paper, we give an overview of the concept of intent-aware interactive displays that can determine, early in the free hand pointing gesture, the icon/item the user intends to select on the touchscreen. This can notably reduce the pointing time, aid implementing effective selection facilitation routines and enhance the overall system accuracy as well as the user experience. Intent-aware displays employ a gesture tracking sensor in conjunction with novel probabilistic intent inference algorithms to predict the endpoint of a free hand pointing gesture. Real 3D pointing data is used to illustrate the usefulness and effectiveness of the proposed approach.

Keywords: Interactive displays · Finger tracking · Bayesian inference · Target assistance · Endpoint prediction

1 Introduction

The proliferation of touchscreen technology and its use in wide range of consumer products, such as hand held devices and control modules in vehicles, is motivated by the ability of such displays to effectively accommodate large quantities of information, facilitate intuitive interactions via pointing gestures, particularly for novice users, and offer additional design flexibility through a combined display-input–feedback module [1–3]. The display can easily be adapted to the context of use via a reconfigurable Graphical User Interface (GUI). For example, in modern vehicles, there has been a notable move towards replacing conventional control units in cars (e.g. buttons, knobs and switches) with interactive displays [2, 3] and thereby minimising clutter in the vehicle interior due to mechanical controls; e.g. see the Volvo concept car in [4].

However, using an interactive display, such as touchscreen, entails undertaking a pointing gesture and dedicating a considerable amount of attention to successfully select the intended icon on the touchscreen. Additionally, with situational impairments, such as using a touchscreen on a moving platform (e.g. cars and boats), the user input

© Springer International Publishing Switzerland 2015
M. Antona and C. Stephanidis (Eds.): UAHCI 2015, Part II, LNCS 9176, pp. 3–14, 2015.
DOI: 10.1007/978-3-319-20681-3_1

can be perturbed leading to erroneous selections [1, 5, 6]. Adapting to the noisy environment or repeatedly undertaking the same selection task ties up even more visual-cognitive-manual attention that might be otherwise available to perform a primary task, such as driving or maintaining adequate level of situational awareness. This can have serious safety implications and undermine the user experience.

In this paper, we give an overview of the concept of intent-aware interactive displays that can determine, early in the free hand pointing gesture, the item a user intends to select, e.g. a GUI icon displayed on a touchscreen, by employing suitable Bayesian prediction algorithms. This yields significant reductions in the pointing time and therefore effort (visual, cognitive and manual) required to accomplish the selection task, helping the user to remain focused on the primary task and improve the overall user experience. Here, we consider the scenario where the touchscreen is placed within a reaching distance from the user, e.g. an in-vehicle touchscreen mounted to the car dashboard. We do not treat applications that involve selecting a target on the display of a handheld device where the pointing distance/time is minimal and intent inference can have limited benefits, if any. In noisy environments, such as pointing in a vehicle driven over harsh terrain, the correlation between the accelerations and vibrations experienced by the touchscreen and the movements of the recorded pointing hand/finger is weak-ambiguous as shown in [7]. This is attributed to the human complex nonlinear behavior in perturbed environments, user seating, screen position, etc. Hence, vibration-acceleration-compensation routines and stabilizing the display to aid the interactive display usability, e.g. see [5], can be ineffective.

Figure 1 depicts the proposed intent-aware interactive display system (for more details on the system and the various introduced prediction models see [7–11]). It uses a gesture tracker, which captures, in real-time, the pointing hand/finger location(s), in conjunction with probabilistic inference algorithms to determine the intended destination on the touchscreen. The prediction results for each of the GUI selectable icons are subsequently used to decide on the intended endpoint and accordingly alter the GUI to assist the selection process. The Inertia Measurement Unit (IMU) is employed to establish whether the user input is subject to perturbations due to situational impairments. The objective of the prediction module is to infer the user intentionally as early as possible, i.e. well before the user's pointing finger touches the display, given the available partial pointing trajectory. Due to the notable recent interest in gesture-based interactions in the gaming industry and the Human Computer Interaction (HCI) community, several 3D vision sensory devices have emerged, such as Microsoft Kinect and Leap Motion (LM) controller that allow accurate gestures tracking and recognition [12]. In this paper, a LM sensor is utilised to record trajectories of a free hand pointing gestures [13]. Figure 2 shows 3D pointing trajectories collected in a vehicle under various conditions. It can be noticed from the figure that perturbations due to the harsh terrain are clearly visible in the pointing gesture compared with the smooth tracks recorded whilst the vehicle is stationary.

A pointing task can be simplified and expedited by using a pointing facilitation technique, such as increasing the size of the target icon, altering its activation area, dragging the cursor closer to the target [14], etc. However, such strategies can be effectively applied only if the intended GUI item is known a priori. Thus, the advantages of predicting the destination of a pointing task are widely recognised in the HCI

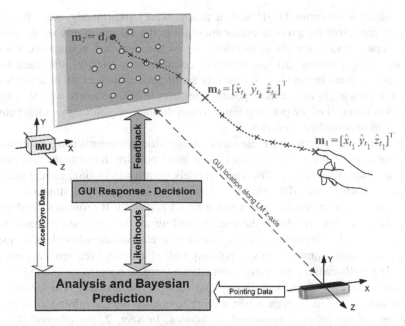

Fig. 1. The proposed intent-aware touchscreen system; gesture-tracker and IMU data are processed by the analysis/prediction module. The *GUI Response* module dynamically alters the display to facilitate the selection task, based on the prediction results.

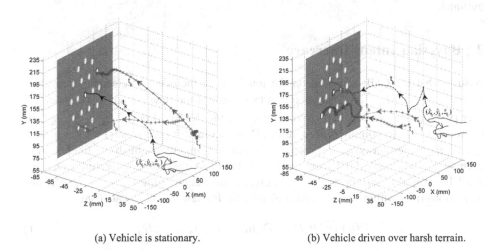

(a) Vehicle is stationary.   (b) Vehicle driven over harsh terrain.

Fig. 2. Full pointing finger-tip trajectory during several pointing gestures aimed at selecting a GUI item (white circles) on the touchscreen interface surface (blue plane) [9]. Arrows indicate the direction of travel over time, starting at $t_1 < t_k$ (Color figure online).

field, e.g. [14–21]. Such studies focus on pointing via a mouse or mechanical-device in a 2D set-up to select a GUI icon(s); a common mode of human computer interaction over the past few decades. In this paper, however, we consider free hand pointing gestures based interactions in 3D with a touchscreen. Additionally, majority of the destination predictors for a mouse cursor endpoint in the 2D set-up rely on the premise that the cursor always travels in the direction of the intended destination. Possible endpoints of the pointing task are therefore collinear and inferring the track length predicts the intended destination. Whilst this assumption makes intuitive sense for 2D GUIs, it does not apply to free hand pointing gestures in 3D as shown in [7–9]. Instead, the direction of travel of the pointing finger varies dramatically throughout the pointing task, even in unperturbed scenarios.

The introduced intent-aware displays utilise destination-reverting probabilistic models that capture the characteristics of free hand pointing movements and thereby provide superior prediction results. These models permit calculating, in real time, the likelihood of each of the GUI selectable icons being the intended destination. Hence, the proposed Bayesian prediction is a belief-based approach. It promotes flexibility in relaying the prediction results to the user depending on the application requirements and requested level of prediction certainty, unlike the classification-based techniques. It is noted that a small improvements in pointing task efficiency, even reducing pointing times by few milliseconds, will have substantial aggregate benefits on the overall user experience since interactions with displays are very prevalent in a typical scenario, e.g. using the in-vehicle touchscreen whilst driving to control the car infotainment system.

The rest of the paper is organized as follows. In Sect. 2, the adopted Bayesian inference framework is described and the modelling problem is highlighted. In Sect. 3, a concise overview of a number of prediction models are described. They are subsequently tested in Sect. 4. Conclusions are drawn in Sect. 5 and planned future work is outlined.

2   Bayesian Intent Inference

Assume that the GUI displayed on the touchscreen includes N selectable items, i.e. $\mathbb{D} = \{\mathcal{D}_i : i = 1, 2, \ldots, N\}$. The pointing task starts at the time instant t_1, i.e. when the user pointing finger/hand starts moving towards the display. Let $\mathbf{m}_k = [\hat{x}_{t_k} \ \hat{y}_{t_k} \ \hat{z}_{t_k}]^T$ be the location of the pointing finger-tip in 3D as recorded by the gesture-tracker at time $t_k > t_1$; $\mathbf{x}^T$ is the transpose operation. The predictor aims to establish the likelihood of each of the selectable GUI icons being the intent of the pointing gesture given the available partial trajectory $\mathbf{m}_{1:k} = \{\mathbf{m}_1, \mathbf{m}_2, \ldots, \mathbf{m}_k\}$ captured at $t_1, t_2, \ldots, t_k$. The primary objective, within the adopted probabilistic framework, is to calculate

$$\mathcal{P}(t_k) = \{P(\mathcal{D}_i = \mathcal{D}_I | \mathbf{m}_{1:k}), i = 1, 2, \ldots, N\} \tag{1}$$

at the arrival of each new observation of the pointing finger location. The intended destination, which is unknown a priori, is notated by $\mathcal{D}_I$ such that $\mathcal{D}_I \in \mathbb{D}$. It is noted that the 3D Cartesian coordinates of the items in $\mathbb{D}$ are known to the inference module where $\mathbf{d}_i = [d_{x_i} \ d_{y_i} \ d_{z_i}]^T$ denotes the location of $\mathcal{D}_i$. However, no assumptions are made on the distribution-layout of the GUI. Both $\mathbf{m}_k$ and $\mathbf{d}_i$ are defined with respect to the gesture-tracking sensor position and orientation (see Fig. 1).

After evaluating $\mathcal{P}(t_k)$ in (1), a simple intuitive approach to establish the intended destination at t_k is to select the most probable endpoint via

$$\hat{I}(t_k) = \arg\max_{\mathcal{D}_i \in \mathbb{D}} P(\mathcal{D}_i = \mathcal{D}_I | \mathbf{m}_{1:k}), \tag{2}$$

which is the Maximum a *Posteriori* (MAP) estimate. A more general decision framework is discussed in [8]. Assuming that the total duration of the pointing task is t_T (i.e. from the start of the pointing gesture at t_1 until the user finger reaches the intended destination displayed on the touchscreen), a successful intent inference at t_k can achieve a total reduction of $t_T - t_k$ in the pointing time. Clearly, an early correct prediction that maximizes such savings is pursued here.

Following (1) and using Bayes' rule, we have

$$P(\mathcal{D}_i = \mathcal{D} | \mathbf{m}_{1:k}) \propto P(\mathcal{D}_i = \mathcal{D}_I) P(\mathbf{m}_{1:k} | \mathcal{D}_i = \mathcal{D}_I) \tag{3}$$

for each of the selectable GUI items. The priors $P(\mathcal{D}_i = \mathcal{D}_I)$, $i = 1, 2, \ldots, N$, which are independent from the current pointing trajectory/task, can be learnt from contextual information, usage history, GUI layout, etc. Henceforth, all possible endpoints are presumed to be equally probable, i.e. $P(\mathcal{D}_i = \mathcal{D}_I) = 1/N$ for $i = 1, 2, \ldots, N$. Given the Bayesian nature of the adopted framework, if priors become/are available, they can be easily incorporated to guide the inference process as per (3). Therefore, determining $\mathcal{P}(t_k)$ and $\hat{I}(t_k)$ depends solely on calculating

$$\mathcal{L}(t_k) = \{P(\mathbf{m}_{1:k} | \mathcal{D}_i = \mathcal{D}_I), i = 1, 2, \ldots, N\}. \tag{4}$$

To summarize, the proposed Bayesian approach consists of the following four steps:

Step 1:   Wait for a new gesture-tracking measurement to arrive, i.e. $\mathbf{m}_k$,

Step 2:   With the new measurement at t_k, calculate $P(\mathbf{m}_{1:k} | \mathcal{D}_i = \mathcal{D}_I)$, for $i = 1, 2, \ldots, N$, depending on the utilised probabilistic model

Step 3:   Determine $P(\mathcal{D}_i = \mathcal{D} | \mathbf{m}_{1:k})$, for $i = 1, 2, \ldots, N$, given the available priors, if any, using (3) followed by normalisation to ensure that $\sum_{i=1}^{N} P(\mathcal{D}_i = \mathcal{D} | \mathbf{m}_{1:k}) = 1$

Step 4:   Infer the intended destination using the MAP estimate in (2)

The system repeats Steps 1 to 4 as long as it is operational.

In the next section, we outline a class of probabilistic models, dubbed destination reverting models, that allow the sequential calculation of $P(\mathbf{m}_{1:k} | \mathcal{D}_i = \mathcal{D}_I)$, for $i = 1, 2, \ldots, N$, using the available partial pointing trajectory at t_k. The performance of such predictors along with other benchmark methods is assessed in Sect. 4 using real pointing data collected in an unperturbed environment, i.e. pointing at the in-vehicle touchscreen whilst the car is stationary.

3 Linear Destination Reverting Prediction Models

Destination-reverting-based predictors model the pointing gesture movements as a stochastic process that is driven by the intended destination on the touchscreen; it has a dominant endpoint-reverting term. The utilized stochastic differential equations capture the salient features and characteristics of a pointing gesture, e.g. velocity profile. In this approach, we assume that the observation $\mathbf{m}_k$ at t_k, is derived as a noisy measurement from a true, but unknown, underlying pointing finger position $\mathbf{c}_k = [x_{t_k}\ y_{t_k}\ z_{t_k}]^T$ and $\dot{\mathbf{c}}_k = [\dot{x}_{t_k}\ \dot{y}_{t_k}\ \dot{z}_{t_k}]^T$ is the true finger velocity vector; higher order motion dynamics such as accelerations along each axis can be similarly represented. This true state is defined by the following linear Gaussian dynamic model

$$\mathbf{s}_{i,k} = \mathbf{F}_{i,k}\mathbf{s}_{i,k-1} + \mathbf{\kappa}_{i,k} + \mathbf{w}_k, \qquad\qquad i = 1, 2, \ldots, N \qquad (5)$$

where $\mathbf{s}_{i,k\text{-}1}$ and $\mathbf{s}_{i,k}$ are the hidden model state vectors at two consecutive time instants $t_{k\text{-}1}$ and t_k. The state $\mathbf{s}_{i,k}$ can include the true pointing-finger location and other higher order motion dynamics, e.g. $\mathbf{s}_{i,k} = \mathbf{c}_k$ or $\mathbf{s}_{i,k} = \left[\mathbf{c}_k^T\ \dot{\mathbf{c}}_k^T\right]^T$. Whereas, $\mathbf{F}_{i,k}$ is the state transition and $\mathbf{\kappa}_{i,k}$ is a time varying constant; both are with respect to the ith destination $\mathcal{D}_i$. The Gaussian motion model dynamic noise is $\mathbf{w}_k \sim \mathcal{N}(0, \mathbf{Q}_k)$.

The state in (5) is dependent on the endpoint and thus N such models are created, one for each nominal destination. The model that best matches the observed pointing movements produces the highest probability of its endpoint $\mathcal{D}_i$ being the intended destination and vice versa. On the other hand, the linear observations model that relates the hidden state to the measurements collected by the gesture-tracker is given by

$$\mathbf{m}_k = \mathbf{H}_k\mathbf{s}_{i,k} + \mathbf{n}_k \qquad\qquad (6)$$

where $\mathbf{H}_k$ is the observation matrix and $\mathbf{n}_k \sim \mathcal{N}(0, \mathbf{R}_k)$ is the measurement noise. Dimension of $\mathbf{H}_k$ depends on the dimensions of $\mathbf{s}_{i,k}$.

Two such linear destination reverting models are described below:

- **Mean Reverting Diffusion (MRD):** models the pointing hand movement as being attracted to the intended destination $\mathcal{D}_i$ such that $\mathbf{s}_{i,k} = \mathbf{c}_k$. This can be expressed in continuous-time by

$$d\mathbf{s}_{i,t} = \mathbf{\Lambda}\big(\mathbf{d}_i - \mathbf{s}_{i,t}\big)dt + \sigma d\mathbf{w}_t, i = 1, 2, \ldots, N, \qquad\qquad (7)$$

where $\mathbf{\Lambda} \in \mathbb{R}^{3\times 3}$ and σ are the reversion rate and noise variance matrices, respectively. Whereas, $\mathbf{w}_t$ is a Wiener process representing the dynamic noise.
- **Equilibrium Reverting Velocity (ERV):** models the pointing movement as moving/heading towards destination with an attraction force that is proportional to the distance away from the destination such that $\mathbf{c}_t = [x_t\ \dot{x}_t\ y_t\ \dot{y}_t\ z_t\ \dot{z}_t]^T$. Each endpoint has a gravitational-force-like field and the one that exerts the higher attraction on the current position of the pointing finger is designated a higher probability. The ERV model can be expressed by

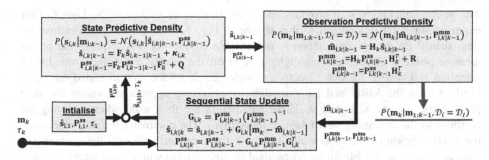

Fig. 3. Kalman filter implementation for destination-reverting-based predictors [8, 9]. It produces $P(\mathbf{m}_k|\mathbf{m}_{1:k-1}, \mathcal{D}_i = \mathcal{D}_I)$ for the endpoint $\mathcal{D}_i$ and N such filters are used.

$$d\mathbf{s}_{i,t} = \mathbf{\Gamma}(\boldsymbol{\mu}_i - \mathbf{s}_{i,t})dt + \tilde{\sigma}d\hat{\mathbf{w}}_t, i = 1, 2, \ldots, N, \qquad (8)$$

where the mean is $\boldsymbol{\mu}_i = \begin{bmatrix} d_{x_i} & 0 & d_{y_i} & 0 & d_{z_i} & 0 \end{bmatrix}^T$ and $\mathbf{\Gamma} = \mathrm{diag}\{\mathbf{\Gamma}_x, \mathbf{\Gamma}_y, \mathbf{\Gamma}_z\}$ represents the reversion such that $\mathbf{\Gamma}_x = \begin{bmatrix} 0 & -1 \\ \eta_x & \rho_x \end{bmatrix}, \mathbf{\Gamma}_y = \begin{bmatrix} 0 & -1 \\ \eta_y & \rho_y \end{bmatrix}$ and $\mathbf{\Gamma}_z = \begin{bmatrix} 0 & -1 \\ \eta_z & \rho_z \end{bmatrix}$; η_x, η_y and η_z set the reversion strength along the corresponding axis. Each of ρ_x, ρ_y and ρ_z is the damping factor in each direction, they are essential components in modelling the pointing gesture velocity profile [8]. The model dynamic noise is set by $\tilde{\sigma}$ where $\tilde{\mathbf{w}}_t$ is a Wiener process.

Upon integrating (7) and (8) over the time interval $\mathcal{T} = [t, t + \tau]$ and then discretizing the outcome, both MRD and ERV can be represented by (5); each produce a distinct expressions for $\mathbf{F}_{i,k}$ and $\boldsymbol{\kappa}_{i,k}$ (please refer to [8] for detailed derivations).

The linear destination reverting models can be implemented using a bank of N Kalman filters, i.e. each Kalman filter is dedicated to a particular nominal destination. The sought probabilities in (4) are calculated sequential with the arrival of new observation $\mathbf{m}_k$ at t_k according to

$$P(\mathbf{m}_{1:k}|\mathcal{D}_i = \mathcal{D}_I) = P(\mathbf{m}_k|\mathbf{m}_{1:k-1}, \mathcal{D}_i = \mathcal{D}_I), \ldots, P(\mathbf{m}_2|\mathbf{m}_1, \mathcal{D}_i = \mathcal{D}_I)$$
$$\times P(\mathbf{m}_1|\mathcal{D}_i = \mathcal{D}_I).$$

Thus, the *Prediction Error Decomposition (PED)*, at t_k, i.e. $P(\mathbf{m}_k|\mathbf{m}_{1:k-1}, D_i)$, suffices to establish $P(\mathbf{m}_{1:k}|\mathcal{D}_i = \mathcal{D}_I)$ in (4). A pictorial representation of the Kalman filter implementation is shown in Fig. 3; N such filters are needed to assess the likelihood of all the nominal destinations in $\mathbb{D}$.

4 Experimental Results

In this section, we demonstrate the performance of the intent-aware touchscreen system using 52 typical pointing tasks from 23 participants pointing at a touchscreen mounted to the dashboard of a stationary vehicle, i.e. unperturbed environment.

The gesture-tracking sensor provides an observation every $\approx$ 20 *ms*. The layout of the experimental GUI is identical to that shown in Fig. 1, with 21 nominal destinations (less than 2 *cm* apart) simultaneously present. Each pointing task requires the participant to point at a specified (highlighted) icon on the interface (i.e. the ground truth intention is known). Sample trajectories (under 20 % of the overall tested ones) are used to train the MRD and ERV models by choosing appropriate values for their parameters, e.g. σ, Λ, Γ and $\tilde{\sigma}$. These parameters are then used when applying the methods to the remaining out of sample trajectories. The parameter training criterion is the maximization of the model likelihood for the true destination in the training set. This procedure is suitable for an operational on-line system where parameter training is performed off-line. For example, a "*training-stage*" is introduced where the user is asked to undertake a set of pointing tasks when using the system for the first time.

In addition to the destination reverting models, we examine the following two benchmark methods that allow calculating $P(\mathbf{m}_{1:k}|\mathcal{D}_i = \mathcal{D}_I)$, $i = 1, 2, \ldots, N$, according to

- **Nearest Neighbour (NN):** measures the distance to the nearest neighbour and allocates the highest probability to the icon closest to the pointing finger current position. Therefore, $P(\mathbf{m}_k|\mathcal{D}_i = \mathcal{D}_I) = \mathcal{N}(\mathbf{m}_k|\mathbf{d}_i, \sigma^2 \mathbf{I})$ obeys a normal distribution with a mean equal to the location of the ith nominal destination.
- **Bearing (BA):** measures the change of angle to the target, hence $P(\mathbf{m}_k| \mathbf{m}_{k-1}, \mathcal{D}_i = \mathcal{D}_I) = \mathcal{N}(\theta_{i,k}, 0, \sigma^2 \mathbf{I})$. It assumes that the intended item is along the heading direction of the pointing finger, i.e. icons that are along the direction of travel of the pointing finger are allocated higher probability and vice versa.

Prediction performance is assessed based on the ability of the algorithm to successfully establish the true intended destination $\mathcal{D}_I$, i.e. the prediction success is $S(t_k) = 1$ if true destination is predicted and $S(t_k) = 0$ otherwise. Figure 4 displays the classification success versus the percentage of completed pointing time $t_p = 100 \times t_k/t_T$ to illustrates how early in the pointing gesture the predictor can correctly infer $\mathcal{D}_I$. Whereas, Fig. 5 depicts the *aggregate prediction success, i.e.* proportion of the total pointing gesture (in time) for which the algorithm correctly predicted the true endpoint. It can be noticed from Fig. 4 that the proposed Bayesian algorithms can infer the intended destination remarkably early in the pointing gesture. MRD and ERV notably outperform the NN, especially in the first 15 %-70 % of the pointing task (in time). This is the critical time period for which enabling pointing facilitation regimes can be most effective. Destination prediction towards the end of the pointing gesture (e.g. in the last third of the pointing time) has limited benefit, since by that stage the user has already dedicated the necessary visual, cognitive and manual efforts to execute the task. For example, the ERV model has a successful prediction rate two to three times that of NN for $t_p \in [15, 40]\%$. The performance gap between the ERV and NN diminishes towards the end of the pointing task as the pointing finger becomes inherently close to the endpoint on the touchscreen. The equilibrium reverting velocity model consistently outperforms the NN and BA. However, NN prediction success surpasses that of the MRD algorithm for $t_p \geq 65$ %, after which changes in the pointing position become minimal rendering the reverting effect in (7) ineffective. Additionally, the bearing angle

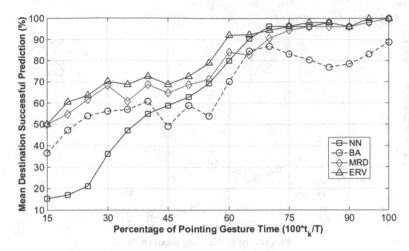

Fig. 4. Mean percentage of destination successful prediction as a function of t_p.

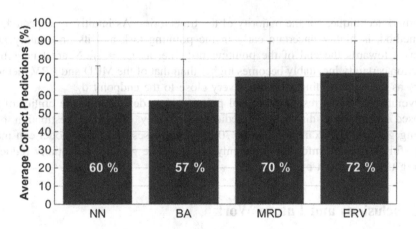

Fig. 5. Gesture portion (in time) during which the correct destination is inferred.

performance drastically deteriorates with the increase of t_p since the reliability of the heading angle as a measure of intent declines as the pointing finger gets closer to the touchscreen. In terms of overall prediction success, Fig. 5 demonstrates that the linear destination reverting models deliver the highest overall correct predictions across the pointing trajectories; ERV has the highest aggregate correct predictions exceeding 70 % of the pointing time. Both NN and BA deliver comparable performance.

In Fig. 6, we display the log uncertainty, $\varepsilon(t_k) = -\log_{10}(P(\mathcal{D}_i = \mathcal{D}_I|\mathbf{m}_{1:k}))$ as a function of the pointing movement duration where $\mathcal{D}_i$ is the true intended destination. It should be noted that the inference success metric does not necessarily imply high prediction certainty. Nonetheless, a reliable prediction will have $\varepsilon(t_k) \rightarrow 0$ as $t_k \rightarrow t_T$. This figure shows that the destination reverting models successfully predict the pointing gesture endpoint with substantially higher confidence levels compared to

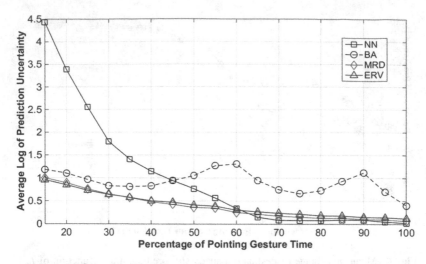

Fig. 6. Average log prediction uncertainty.

benchmark techniques for the majority of the trajectories. As intuitively expected, the NN method, is highly uncertain early in the pointing task and its uncertainty $\varepsilon(t_k)$ decreases towards the end of the pointing task, i.e. as $t_k \rightarrow t_T$. Nearest neighbour prediction certainty inevitably becomes higher than that of the MRD and ERV methods near t_T as the pointing finger becomes very close to the endpoint $\mathbf{d}_l$.

Overall, the above results from real pointing data demonstrate the ability of the proposed intent-aware displays to predict, remarkably early, the destination of a pointing gesture. For example, in over 70 % of the cases, the ERV model can make successful destination inference after only 30 % of the gesture, potentially reducing pointing time and effort by 70 %.

5   Conclusions and Future Work

Intelligent intent-aware displays can notably expedite and simplify interacting with touchscreens whose use is very prevalent nowadays, i.e. small improvements, in pointing task efficiency, even reducing the pointing time by few milliseconds, will have substantial aggregate benefits on the overall user experience. Such technology is particularly beneficial for users who are performing another primary safety critical task whilst interacting with a touchscreen, e.g. vehicle drivers. The introduced Bayesian framework constitute an effective approach to the endpoint inference problem where various state-space models of the 3D pointing movement can be devised and any known priors on the selection pattern-preference-frequency can be easily incorporated.

For scenarios where the user pointing gesture is mildly perturbed due to situational impairments, the results of the N Kalman filters utilised in the destination-reverting-based predictors can be combined to remove any unintentional noise-generated movements in the pointing finger track as shown in [8]. Hence, the introduced inference methodology combines the prediction and pointing trajectory online filtering or smoothing operations.

However, this approach is not applicable to highly perturbed scenarios, e.g. using a touchscreen in a mobile platform that is subject to high accelerations and/or vibrations. The unintentional perturbations-generated pointing hand movements in such cases take the form of jumps that cannot be captured by a linear model, see Fig. 2b. In [10], a pre-processing stage is proposed to remove any perturbations generated movements in the pointing trajectory using a variable rate particle filter [22] with a jump diffusion model. The filtered pointing track is then utilised to achieve superior prediction results, i.e. smoothing followed by prediction. Further work is currently being carried out to devise novel sequential Monte Carlo filtering techniques that merge the filtering-smoothing operation with the endpoint prediction for highly perturbed pointing tasks.

An important aspect of the intent-aware display system is the form of feedback offered to the user based on the prediction results. As depicted in Fig. 1, the prediction results are employed to alter the GUI on the touchscreen to assist the successful selection of the intended destination. Various pointing facilitation techniques can be applied, e.g. changing the sizes of the selectable GUI items depending on their likelihoods or selecting the most probable icon on behalf of the user (i.e. prior to the user pointing finger reaching the touchscreen); many other assistive strategies exist in the open literature. A full human trial is currently underway to identify the most effective feedback scheme based on the impact of the intent-aware touchscreen concept on the overall user experience in a number of usage cases.

References

1. Wu, F.G., Lin, H., You, M.: Direct-touch vs. mouse input for navigation modes of the web map. Displays 32(5), 261–267 (2011)
2. Burnett, G.E., Mark Porter, J.: Ubiquitous computing within cars: designing controls for non-visual use. Int. J. Hum Comput Stud. 55(4), 521–531 (2001)
3. Harvey, C., Stanton, N.A.: Usability evaluation for in-vehicle systems. CRC Press, London (2013)
4. Volvo Cars, Volvo car group unveils concept estate at Geneva motor show 27th February 2014. Accessed on: 14 October 2014 from https://www.media.volvocars.com/global/engb/media/pressreleases/139220/volvo-car-group-to-unveil-conceptestate-at-geneva-motor-show
5. Goel, M., Findlater, L., Wobbrock, J.: Walktype: using accelerometer data to accomodate situational impairments in mobile touch screen text entry. In Proceedings of the SIGCHI Conference on Human Factors in Computing Systems, pp. 2687–2696. ACM (2012)
6. Jaeger, M.G., Skov, M.B., Thomassen, N.G., et al.: You can touch, but you can't look: interacting with in-vehicle systems. In Proceedings of the SIGCHI Conference on Human Factors in Computing Systems, pp. 1139–1148 (2008)
7. Ahmad, B.I., Langdon, P.M., Godsill, S.J., Hardy, R., Dias, E., Skrypchuk, L.: Interactive displays in vehicles: Improving usability with a pointing gesture tracker and Bayesian intent predictors. In: Proc. of International Conference on Automotive User Interfaces and Interactive Vehicular Applications (AutomotiveUI 2014), pp. 1–8. ACM (2014)
8. Ahmad, B.I., Murphy, J., Langdon, P.M., Godsill, S.J., Hardy, R., Skrypchuk, L.: Intent Inference for Pointing Gesture Based Interactions in Vehicles. IEEE Transactions on Cybernetics (2015)
9. Ahmad, B.I., Murphy, J.K., Langdon, P.M., Godsill, S.J.: Bayesian target prediction from partial finger tracks: Aiding interactive displays in vehicles. In: Proceedings of the 17th International Conference on Information Fusion (FUSION 2014), pp. 1–7 (2014)

10. Ahmad, B.I., Murphy, J.K., Langdon, P.M., Godsill, S.J.: Filtering perturbed in-vehicle pointing gesture trajectories: Improving the reliability of intent inference. In: Proceedings of IEEE International Workshop on Machine Learning for Signal Processing (MLSP 2014) (2014)
11. Ahmad, B.I., Murphy, J., Langdon, P.M., Godsill, S.J.: Destination Inference Using Bridging Distributions. In: Proceedings of the 40th IEEE International Conference on Acoustics, Speech and Signal Processing (ICASSP 2015) (2015)
12. Garber, L.: Gestural technology: moving interfaces in a new direction [technology news]. Comput. IEEE **46**(10), 22–25 (2013)
13. Leap Motion Website. https://www.leapmotion.com/
14. McGuffin, M.J., Balakrishnan, R.: Fitts' law and expanding targets: Experimental studies and designs for user interfaces. ACM Trans. Comput.-Hum. Interact. **12**(4), 388–422 (2005)
15. Murata, A.: Improvement of pointing time by predicting targets in pointing with a PC mouse. IJHCI **10**(1), 23–32 (1998)
16. Lane, D., Peres, S., Sandor, A., Napier, H.: A process for anticipating and executing icon selection in graphical user interfaces. IJHCI **19**(2), 241–252 (2005)
17. Wobbrock, J.O., Fogarty, J., Liu, S., Kimuro, S., Harada, S.: The angle mouse: target-agnostic dynamic gain adjustment based on angular deviation. In: Proceedings of the SIGCHI Conference on Human Factors in Computing Systems, pp. 1401–1410 (2009)
18. Ahmad, B.I., Langdon, P.M., Bunch, P., Godsill, S.J.: Probabilistic intentionality prediction for target selection based on partial cursor tracks. In: Stephanidis, C., Antona, M. (eds.) UAHCI 2014, Part III. LNCS, vol. 8515, pp. 427–438. Springer, Heidelberg (2014)
19. Asano, T., Sharlin, E., Kitamura, Y., Takashima, K., Kishino, F.: Predictive interaction using the Delphian desktop. In: Proceedings of the ACM Symposium on User Interface Software and Technology, pp. 133–141. ACM (2005)
20. Lank, E., Cheng, Y.-C.N., Ruiz, J.: Endpoint prediction using motion kinematics. In: Proceedings of the SIGCHI Conf. on Human factors in Computing Systems, pp. 637–646 (2007)
21. Ziebart, B., Dey, A., Bagnell, J.A.: Probabilistic pointing target prediction via inverse optimal control. In: Proceedings of the 2012 ACM International. Conference on Intelligent User Interfaces, pp. 1–10 (2012)
22. Godsill S., Vermaak, J.: Models and algorithms for tracking using trans-dimensional sequential Monte Carlo. In: Proceedings of the IEEE International Conference on Acoustics, Speech, and Signal Processing (ICASSP 2004), vol. 3, pp. 973–976. IEEE (2004)

A Comparison of Gaze-Based
and Gesture-Based Input
for a Point-and-Click Task

Dominic Canare, Barbara Chaparro$^{(\boxtimes)}$, and Jibo He

Wichita State University, Wichita, KS, USA
{dominic.canare,barbara.chaparro,jibo.he}@wichita.edu

Abstract. Alternative input devices to the computer mouse are becoming more affordable and accessible. With greater availability, they have the potential to provide greater access to information for more users in more environments, perhaps while also providing more natural or efficient interaction. However, most user interfaces are built to be mouse-driven, and the adoption of these new technologies may depend on their ability to work with these existing interfaces. This study examined performance with gesture-control and gaze-tracking devices and compared them to a traditional mouse for a standard Fitts' point-and-click task. Both gesture-controlled and gaze-tracking proved to be viable alternatives, though they were significantly slower and more taxing than the familiar mouse. In order to make effective use of these devices, researchers, designers, and developers must find or create control schemes which take advantage of the alternative devices' benefits while curtailing the drawbacks.

Keywords: Gaze · Gesture · Mouse · Leap motion · Eyetribe · Fitts' law

1 Introduction

The ever-present computer mouse has been a staple of computing for many years. This remains true even as the number devices grows to unprecedented levels. Cisco (2014) reports that 526 million mobile devices and connections were added in 2013, with smartphones accounting for 77 % of the growth. They predict that by the end of 2014, the number of mobile connected devices will start to exceed the number of people, and by 2018 there will be 1.4 mobile devices per capita. As more devices are added and integrated into work and play, more data is being generated as is the need to access it. Alternatives to the mouse have been created and suggest the possibility of more intuitive interfaces to provide better access for a variety of populations. Other devices solve more specific problems, such as allowing access to data in sterile environments, overcoming physical handicaps, and exploring big data [1]. Sterile environments exist for users in surgical settings, where accessing a keyboard and mouse would require rescrubbing, a process that can take significant time and is critical to patient safety [2]. Alternate input devices such as vision-based interfaces, have the potential to create more accessible devices for users living with disabilities [3].

M. Antona and C. Stephanidis (Eds.): UAHCI 2015, Part II, LNCS 9176, pp. 15–24, 2015.
DOI: 10.1007/978-3-319-20681-3_2

The success of a new input device depends on many different factors. The longevity of the computer mouse has led to the development of user interfaces which are largely mouse-driven (e.g., a considerable amount of human-computer interaction can be described as simply pointing and clicking). The success of a new device may depend on its ability to transition users from these point-and-click interfaces to new control schemes, and part of that transition will require retrofitting new devices to point-and-click interfaces. This study examines the viability of new input devices using a point-and-click Fitts' Law task [4].

Performance is not the only factor contributing to the success or failure of a new device. Wachs et al. describe several requirements for gesture-based input devices - some of which can be generalized to all input devices [1]. As is often the case, cost is a factor, as the adoption of a new device is only plausible if the masses can afford it. Intuitiveness is another important factor to consider in a new input device. While the mouse has enjoyed many years as the preferred device without being the most intuitive, new input devices must now compete with users' experience, expertise, and preference for the computer mouse. Devices lacking intuitive control schemes are unlikely to compete. Requiring users to modify their appearance, wear special equipment, or alter their environment in order to use a new device will likely be seen as cumbersome and hinder a device's adoption.

The Leap Motion Controller is one alternative input device that relies on hand gestures as a means of input. The controller is sold as a stand-alone device and has been integrated into some laptop designs [5]. It is intuitive for users to physically manipulate tangible objects, and many of these physical manipulations have or approach one-to-one translations to a gesture-controlled interface. Depending on the sensing technique, gesture-based devices have the potential for a much larger bandwidth than a standard computer mouse [6]. The Leap Motion controller uses a depth-sensing camera with a high frame rate and level of detail. The depth-sensing method allows the device to detect gestures without the need for special markers or contrasting backgrounds. Because these gestures are performed in the air, the device is touchless, making it ideal for sterile environments.

The Eye Tribe gaze-tracking device is another alternative input device that is capable of approximating the location of a user's gaze using a high-power LED light source and high-resolution camera. The device is sold as a development kit for a price comparable to some computer mice [7]. Gaze-tracking has the potential to improve human-to-computer data transmission by opening an entirely new channel of communication. A person's gaze naturally indicates the area of their attention, and gaze-tracking equipment can help systems realize this data in meaningful ways [8]. One minor disadvantage with the Eye Tribe device is that it requires calibration for individual users. However, the calibration process is usually brief, and there are no other requirements for the user to begin using the device. Lastly, gaze-tracking is naturally touchless.

Gaze-tracking and gesture-control input devices have been studied by various researchers in the past. Zhai used gaze-tracking to provide context for actions [8]. More specifically, gaze information was combined with statistical analysis of the user interface to place the cursor in a predicted area of the user's intention. A study of this system found that, with just ten minutes of training, performance was similar to standard mouse usage. Wachs et al. developed a gesture-controlled interface through which surgeons could browse radiological images in a sterile environment while avoiding many of the typical drawbacks (rescrubbing, change in focus of attention, etc.) [1]. Their usability tests indicated that users found the system to be "easy to use, with fast response and quick training times" [1, 323].

The aim of this study was to determine how well gesture-control and gaze-tracking devices could be used for point-and-click tasks using Fitts's Law performance measures when compared to the traditional computer mouse.

2 Method

2.1 Participants

Twenty-two college students were recruited for this study. Of those, 3 were used for pilot data to modify and optimize parameters for gesture control, gaze control, and testing procedure. Of the remaining 19 participants, 4 could not be properly calibrated to the gaze-tracking equipment, and their data for all devices was discarded. The remaining 15 participants (5 female, 10 male) aged 18–56 (M = 25.6, SD = 10.8) reported that they owned either a laptop or desktop computer and used a computer regularly throughout the day. Participants were compensated with course credit for their participation.

2.2 Materials

The primary hardware components of this study included a standard computer mouse, a Leap Motion Controller for gesture control, and an Eye Tribe for gaze control. An ASUS Zenbook Prime connected to an LCD monitor (1280x1024) was also used. Participants sat at a desk with an adjustable chair, and the monitor was raised to eye-level, approximately 2 feet away from the participant.

Software was created to control the mouse cursor using the gesture and gaze-tracking devices. For gesture control, participants moved the on-screen cursor by pointing a finger and moving it about in the space in front of them, above the desk, and parallel to the monitor. X-Y air space was translated to X-Y screen coordinates absolutely, so that a pointing finger positioned on the left of the desk would relocate the mouse to the left side of the screen. The angle of the pointing finger relative to the palm was also tracked and used as an adjustment to the final cursor location in all directions. A pilot test was performed to determine the best gesture for selection between poking, tapping, and looping. Drawing a loop was found to be the easiest gesture to perform consistently, but accuracy was a challenge. To overcome this, the system was modified so that when the participants were required to first hover over the location where a click was desired for 50 ms within a 3 pixel radius, followed by gesturing a loop or circle. Upon detecting a hover event, a small red circle was displayed to provide feedback to the user, with the center marking the location where the selection would occur if the hover event was followed by a loop gesture.

Gaze location was sampled at approximately 30 Hz, and the cursor was positioned to the location of the participant's gaze. A selection event (mouse-click) was generated whenever the gaze was fixated on a 25 pixel area (approximately 0.59 visual degrees) for 500 ms, with the selection occurring at the average location of the fixation.

2.3 Procedure

Each participant was informed that the study was designed to evaluate the viability of alternative input devices to a traditional computer mouse. Prior to performing the experiment, participants completed a consent form and brief survey about their experience with computers and pointing devices.

The experiment itself consisted of 100 trials for each of the three devices (mouse, gesture, gaze). The order of devices was randomized for each participant. The trials were separated into 10 blocks with 10 trials in each. At the start of a trial, a circular target (the start target) was presented to the user with a 40 pixel radius in a random location on the screen. Once the subject selected the target, it disappeared and a new target (the stop target) appeared elsewhere on the screen for the user to select. Between trials there was a 1.5 s delay, and between blocks the experiment paused until the participant selected an area of the screen to indicate that they were ready to resume.

Within each block, the stop targets were one of ten combinations of sizes and distances. The size of the stop target was either large (120 pixel radius) or small (40 pixel radius), and the distance between the start and stop target was either 100, 250, 375, 500, or 750 pixels. The order of these 10 combinations was randomized within each block, and the angle between the targets was generated randomly. After completing the 100 trials for a device, participants completed the NASA Task Load Index survey to collect workload measures.

The index of performance, as defined by Fitts' Law [4], was the focal data for analysis. For an individual trial, the index of performance was calculated as a ratio of the difficulty of a trial to the amount of time required to complete it. More specifically, the time was measured between selecting the start target and selecting the stop target. Having a shorter movement time or a higher difficulty raised the index of performance, while a longer movement time or lower difficulty decreased the index of performance:

$$performance = difficulty/movementTime$$

The difficulty of a trial is a function of the stop target's size and distance from the start target. Targets which are further apart are more difficult than targets closer together. Likewise, smaller targets are more difficult to hit than larger targets:

$$difficulty = \log_2(2 * distance/size)$$

3   Results

3.1   Performance

A one-way repeated-measures ANOVA test was performed to compare the index of performance across all three devices. There was a significant difference in performance between all devices, $F(2, 28) = 196.49$, $p < 0.01$. Participants performed best with the mouse (M = 4.56, SD = 0.792), followed by the gaze-control (M = 2.321, SD = 0.352) and then the gesture-control (M = 1.56, SD = 0.20), and all of these differences were significant at $p < 0.05$ (See Fig. 1).

A 2-way (3x10) repeated-measures ANOVA was performed to determine whether participants improved with experience across the three input methods. There was a significant main effect of input method, $F(2, 28) = 199.41$, $p < 0.01$, experience, $F(9, 126) = 3.79$, $p < 0.01$, and a device x time interaction, $F(18, 252) = 1.86$, $p < 0.05$. Post hoc comparisons of the interaction showed that the mouse had a significant improvement in performance from the first block to the last, $F(1, 14) = 6.788$, $p < 0.05$, as did the gesture controlled device, $F(1, 14) = 7.196$, $p < 0.05$. The gaze-tracking device showed no significant change in performance amongst any of the blocks in this experiment.

Two types of errors were tracked during experimentation, and repeated-measures ANOVA tests were performed for these as well. A miss-click was counted anytime a participant performed a selection with the cursor outside of a target. The difference in miss-clicks was significant between all devices, $F(2, 28) = 41.238$, $p < 0.01$. The mouse had the fewest miss-clicks (M = 4.800, SD = 4.507), followed by gesture-control (M = 9.867, SD = 6.379), and then gaze-tracking (M = 69.533, SD = 35.377). Post hoc analysis indicates a significant difference between mouse and gesture, $p < 0.05$; mouse and gaze-tracking, $p < 0.01$; and between gesture and gaze-tracking, $p < 0.01$ (See Fig. 2).

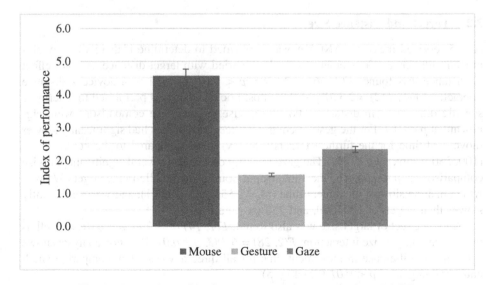

Fig. 1. Comparison of performance across input methods (± 1.0 SE)

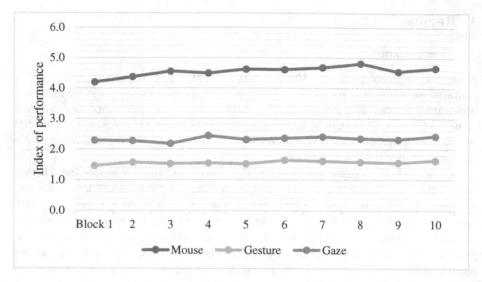

Fig. 2. Performance over time

A failure was counted whenever a participant could not successfully select a target within 10 s. The difference between devices for failures was also significant, $F(2, 28) = 8.966$, $p < 0.01$. No participant recorded any failures with the mouse. Gesture-control did yield some failures (M = 1.133, SD = 1.598), but was again eclipsed by gaze-tracking (M = 4.267, SD = 4.803). Post hoc analysis indicates a significant difference between mouse and gesture, $p < 0.05$; mouse and gaze-tracking, $p < 0.01$, and between gesture and gaze-tracking, $p < 0.05$ (See Fig. 3).

3.2   Target and Distance Size

A 3x5 repeated-measures ANOVA was performed to determine if there was any significant difference in movement time which varied with target distance. A main effect of distance was found, $F(4, 56) = 23.285$, $p < 0.01$, as well as a device x distance interaction, $F(8, 112) = 2.350$, $p < 0.05$. Post hoc analysis was performed to determine specific differences in distances. For the mouse, all pairwise comparisons were significant at $p < 0.01$. For the gesture-control device, participants had significantly slower movement time for the furthest targets (750 px) when compared to the nearest three (100, 250, 375px) at $p < 0.01$. The gaze-tracking device had several significant pairwise comparisons at $p < 0.05$. The most interesting point is the middle-range target (375 px), which had the slowest movement time (M = 1.551, SD = 0.091), and was significantly slower than targets at 100, 500, and 750 px (See Fig. 4).

A main effect of target size was also found, $F(1, 14) = 72.209$, $p < 0.01$, as well as the device x target size interaction, $F(2, 28) = 6.183$, $p < 0.01$. Post hoc analysis shows a significant difference in movement time for all three devices when comparing small and large targets at $p < 0.01$ (See Fig. 5).

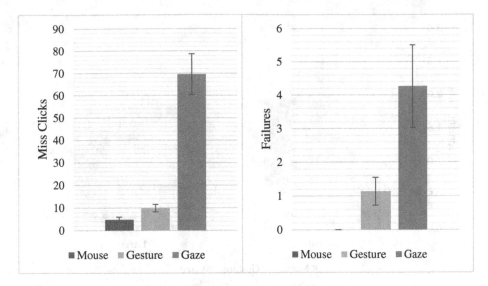

Fig. 3. Errors encountered for each input method (± 1.0 SE)

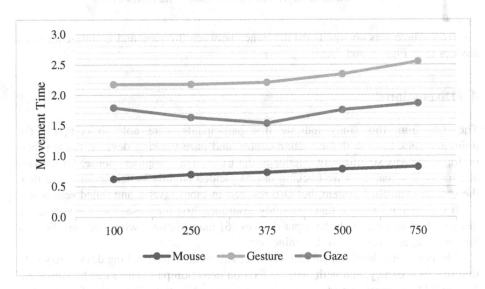

Fig. 4. Effect of target distance on movement time

3.3 Workload

A repeated-measures ANOVA was performed to compare the perceived workload using the weighted NASA Task Load Index across input methods. There was a significant difference between devices, $F(2, 28) = 10.02, p < 0.01$, with the mouse having lower perceived workload (M = 48.88, SD = 9.64), than both gaze-tracking (M = 60.95, SD = 15.37), $p < 0.05$, and gesture-control (M = 62.36, SD = 10.23),

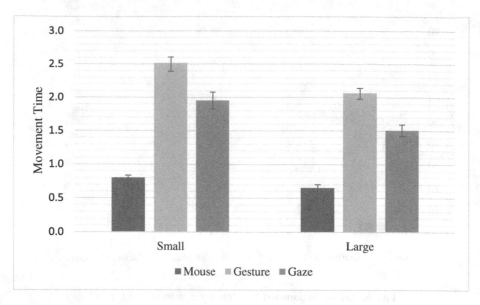

Fig. 5. Effect of target size on movement time (± 1.0 SE)

$p < 0.05$. There was no significant difference between the gaze and gesture-controlled devices (See Figs. 6 and 7).

4 Discussion

The data from this study indicate that participants were able to complete the point-and-click tasks with the gesture-control and gaze-tracking devices, though their performance was significantly inferior to the traditional computer mouse. Of the two alternative devices, the gaze-tracking device yielded slightly better performance than the gesture-controlled system, but also resulted in more invalid and failed selections.

It is important to note that this study examined first-time usage of the alternative devices. Performance with the input devices [6] may improve with more practice - a longer study is necessary to determine this.

The continued development and improvement of the gaze-tracking device may help improve its accuracy, and with that, the fixation detection parameters can be narrowed. This will likely improve performance and accuracy while reducing errors. Some participants reported difficulty when adjusting for the inaccuracies with the gaze-tracking equipment. The targets were presented on an otherwise blank screen, and participants struggled to fixate on a blank region offset from the target to adjust for inaccurate tracking.

There are many configurable parameters and different control schemes for a gesture-controlled interface, and the best settings will likely vary between individuals. The best implementation may require an adaptive control scheme or training period, or take into account hand velocity and acceleration to create a non-linear mapping of physical-space to screen space (like mouse-acceleration).

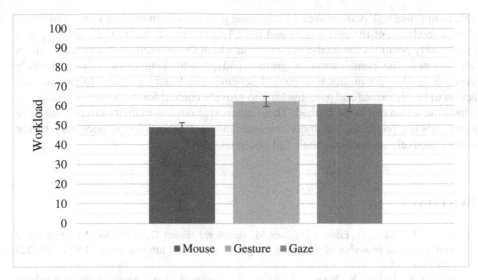

Fig. 6. NASA task load index (± 1.0 SE)

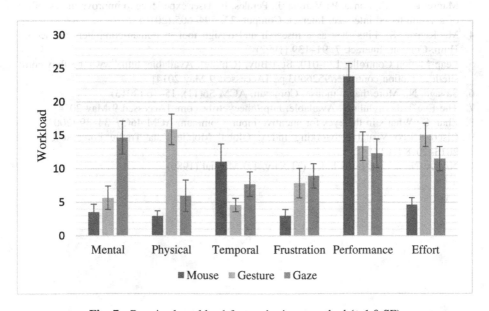

Fig. 7. Perceived workload factors by input method (± 1.0 SE)

While the results of this study are not in favor of the quick and easy adoption of these alternative input devices, they do not preclude the need for these devices or their potential. Rather, the results of this study should serve as motivation for further research exploring new user interfaces and control schemes which capitalize on the strengths of these devices while minimizing their drawbacks. This may involve multimodal input, combining data from multiple input devices [6]. For example, Zhai was able to improve task performance by capturing gaze data as an implicit input source [8]. With knowledge of the user's gaze and the UI topology, his MAGIC Pointing system predictively positions the mouse cursor, from which the user only needs to make minor adjustments. The combination of gesture and gaze-tracking devices is particularly interesting. One possibility is a control scheme which uses gestures to provide the action to be performed and gaze-tracking to provide context for the action or a target on which the action can be performed. These alternative devices in their current state solve some existing problems, but more research and experimentation is necessary to use them effectively and achieve their full potential.

References

1. Wachs, J.P., Stern, H., Edan, Y., Gillam, M., Handler, J., Feied, C., Smith, M.: A gesture-based tool for sterile browsing of radiology images. J. Am. Med. Inform. Assoc. **15**(3), 321–323 (2008)
2. O'hara, K., Harper, R., Mentis, H., Sellen, A., Taylor, A.: On the naturalness of touchless putting the "interaction" back into NUI. ACM Trans. Comput.-Hum. Interact. **20**(1), 5 (2013)
3. Manresa-Yee, C., Ponsa, P., Varona, J., Perales, F.: User experience to improve the usability of a vision-based interface. Interact. Comput. **22**, 594–605 (2010)
4. MacKenzie, S.: Fitts' law as a research and design tool in human-computer interaction. Hum.-Comput. Interact. **7**, 91–139 (1992)
5. Leap Motion Controller LM-010, Best Buy, [Online]. Available: http://www.bestbuy.com/site/leap-motion-controller/9526603.p/. [Accessed 9 May 2014]
6. Savage, N.: More than a mouse. Commun. ACM **56**(11), 15–16 (2013)
7. The Eye Tribe, [Online]. Available: http://theeyetribe.com. [Accessed 9 May 2014]
8. Zhai, S.: What's in the eyes for attentive input. Commun. ACM **46**(3), 34–39 (2003)
9. Cisco, Cisco Visual Networking Index: Global Mobile Data Traffic Forecast Update, 2013–2018 (2014)
10. NASA, Nasa Task Load Index (TLX) v. 1.0 Manual (1986)

Understanding, Evaluating and Analyzing Touch Screen Gestures for Visually Impaired Users in Mobile Environment

Vikas Luthra[✉] and Sanjay Ghosh

Samsung Research and Development Institute-Bangalore, Bangalore, India
{vikas.luthra, sanjay.ghosh}@samsung.com

Abstract. Smartphones usage among visually impaired users is growing in prominence and mobile phone providers are continuously looking for solutions to make touch screen interfaces more accessible to them. Key accessibility features for vision related impairment includes assistive screen reading applications like Voiceover (https://www.apple.com/in/accessibility/ios/voiceover/) in iOS or Talkback (https://support.google.com/accessibility/android/answer/6007100?hl=en) in Android which supports a variety of touch gestures for performing basic functions and commands. Our preliminary interactions with users from this community revealed that some of these existing gestures are ambiguous, difficult to perform, non-intuitive and have accuracy and detection issues. Moreover there is lack of understanding regarding usage of these accessibility features and existing gestures. In this paper, we address these challenges through set of three experimental exercises-*task based comparative evaluation, gesture elicitation and gesture performance* done with a group of 12 visually impaired users. Based on experimental evidences we pinpoint the exact problems with few existing gestures. Additionally, this work contributes in identifying some characteristics of effective and easy gestures for the target segment. We also propose design solutions to resolve users pain points and discuss some touch screen accessibility design guidelines keeping in mind different type of visually impaired users - *fully blind, extremely low vision and low vision.*

Keywords: Accessibility · Gestures · Assistive technologies · User centered design · Mobile user interfaces

1 Introduction

Touch based interfaces are extremely visually demanding and visually impaired users face difficulty in locating on-screen object in these phones. Absence of tactile feedback and physical buttons also plays a major deterrent for such users. Hence all smartphones currently provide assistive screen reading software as a prime accessibility solution to locate and read items on touch screen. These applications have inbuilt gestures to perform a given set of useful commands. However there are major challenges and issues with these screens reading software especially with the existing set of gestures. Some of these gestures are inconsistent and vary widely across platforms. For e.g. Talkback in Android uses mostly single finger swipe or circular gesture for a given

© Springer International Publishing Switzerland 2015
M. Antona and C. Stephanidis (Eds.): UAHCI 2015, Part II, LNCS 9176, pp. 25–36, 2015.
DOI: 10.1007/978-3-319-20681-3_3

function while Voiceover employs multi-finger gestures for same set of commands. This high inconsistency makes it difficult to develop consistent interaction language and gesture vocabulary for these users. Secondly, few of these existing gestures are highly ambiguous, non-intuitive and difficult to learn. Our initial interaction with some of the visually impaired users indicated that most of them were not using a large set of useful commands as they found gestures for those commands to be extremely difficult to remember and non-intuitive. The third major issue observed for the existing set of gesture was performance, accuracy and detection. For instance, gestures like circular movement for quick navigation in Talk back and two finger press hold in Voiceover were found complex to be performed by the users efficiently. Similarly, L-shape angular gesture in Talkback have poor detection due to high variation in angles and action speed, while some multi-finger gestures in Voiceover had finger detection issues by system because of difference in finger sizes or lifting of fingers. Apart from these challenges, few research work have been done to understand the accessibility and usability issues for such users and there is still lesser understanding regarding the usage of touch based phones by different segments of visually impaired users. Considering these challenges the following research questions were under exploration in this study –

- How effective are the existing touch phone gestures in terms of performance and intuitiveness for the users?
- Which are the most common errors that users commit while performing touch gestures and how can the gestures be designed to avoid those?
- What are the criteria for designing effective touch phone gestures for visually impaired?
- To what extent the visually impaired users rely on the haptic, sound and also partial visual feedbacks?

In this paper, we try to address these questions through a set of three experimental sessions done with a group of twelve users.

2   Related Works

Researchers in past have tried to work on improving interaction for *non-sight and non-visual browsing* of touch interfaces. Talking finger technique [5], Talking tactile Tablet [6], Touch 'n Talk [7] were some of the earlier solutions which involved exploring touch screens through touch and providing feedback through speech. However these solutions were visually demanding as they required users to remember layout of the screens. Then there were few *eyes free interaction* methods been proposed which employed gestures to improve exploration of screen and performing basic functions. Sánchez and Maureira [8] developed a subway assistant for visually impaired users on desktop system which involved using directional gestures to perform basic operations. Shiri et al. [9] developed a gesture based accessible authentication method for visually impaired which used multi-tap gestures sequences as a password. Kane et al. [10] used accessible multi-touch interaction techniques for non-visual browsing which consisted of four basic gestures -single finger click, a second finger tap, multidirectional flick and L-select gesture for touch screen interfaces.

Researchers in the past have also tried to identify accessibility issues with the assistive screen readers. McGookin et al. [3] investigated the accessibility of touch screens for visually impaired people in which they revealed problems on the use of buttons as well as gestures. Leporini et al. [4] investigated the usability of Voiceover in IPad and pointed issues with gestures involved. Kane et al. [2] compared and identified the differences in preferences and performances of touch gestures among blind and sighted users.

Past research by Morris et al. [11] showed that gesture generated by user being more effective and preferred than those designed by designers. So, it is imperative that users are made part in the process of designing gestures. Our methodology is inspired from referent based elicitation technique suggested by Wobbrock et al. [1] and slightly modified by Kane et al. [2]. In this approach users are shown the outcome of the action and are asked to invent gesture if they want to execute that action.

3 User Study

The main objectives for designing the user study were

- To gain deeper understanding regarding performance and intuitiveness of existing gestures in assistive screen readers.
- To evaluate performance of new gestures as well as explore intuitive gestures for current and new set of command.
- Understanding the usage of current touch screens accessibility features among different types of visually impaired users-*mainly extreme low vision, low vision and fully blind.*

Based on our objectives, we conducted three different exercises with our target users. We started with an observation based exercise: *task based comparative evaluation* between two prominent assistive screen readers *Voiceover* in iOS and *Talkback* in Android. Based on insights regarding issues with existing gestures, next we conducted two experimental exercises: *Gesture Elicitation and Gesture Performance.*

Participants. All the experiments were conducted at three different computer training centers for visually impaired users. A total of 12 participants (2 female and 10 male, Mean Age = 31, S.D. = 9.56) were part of the overall study. All the users considered were computer literate and have the experience of using screen based reader application like JAWS, NVDA. 8 of participants had experience of using touch based smartphones and 4 of them used keypad based feature phones.11 of the participants were right handed while 1 was left handed. The duration of blindness also varied among participants with 3 being birth by blind, 5 early blind and 4 late blind(blind for 6–8 yrs.).

4 Task Based Comparative Evaluation

The key motivation behind this exercise was to observe and gather insights of two popular assistive screen readers: Voiceover and Talkback with regards to issues with existing gesture and other accessibility functions. It was a qualitative exercise and thus observations were made while users performed tasks and unforced errors were noted. Participants performed four representative tasks-*Opening an application (Navigation Task), Opening phonebook and making a call (Navigation task), Scrolling through messages and reading a particular message (editing task), Composing a message,* using Talkback in Samsung Galaxy S4 Device and Voiceover in IPhone 5S. A custom background application was developed to capture user's trails and measure gesture speed. Post these tasks, the participants were asked to answer a qualitative questionnaire based on their experience during the session to gather feedback and understand the issues faced.

4.1   Observations and Insights from Task Based Evaluation

Performance of angular gestures: Talkback in android uses nine shortcut angular gestures for a given set of commands in which we observed few performance issues. On several instances the gesture performed by users were not identified by the system. In one particular instance, a user performed the L-gesture for nine times to activate global context menu and an inverted L gesture five times before being finally recognized by system. The major reason was the flexibility system had for the angles of these gestures. Another reason was the speed of performing gesture. Many users felt irritated and mentioned the need for relaxation in angle detection.

Need for Gestures for important function: The current user interface is highly driven by visual metaphors and icons. It becomes very difficult for visually impaired users to interact with the overall interface through these iconic metaphors. A lot of difficulty was faced by users in performing some of the frequent tasks like calling or picking up a call, sending a message, selecting and deleting an item, cancelling an action, searching an item etc. For e.g. to pick a call in talkback user first has to locate the call icon and then do swipe gesture, for sending a massage user has to locate the send icon and then double tap. Users also mentioned the need for shortcut gestures of useful functions like controlling of speech rate, frequently used punctuation marks etc. Based on these insights we identified some of the commands which could be executed through set of gestures and these commands were included for gesture elicitation exercise conducted later.

Errors and Ambiguity within Existing Gestures: As part of the task based observation few major unforced errors were observed. For e.g., there were lot of instances where two finger swipes got recognized as single finger double tap action which resulted in opening of random application by the user unintentionally. One of the users mentioned how he locates a blank space on screen and then double taps to avoid his double taps getting recognized as single tap and corresponding undesired event. There was another conflict found between the single finger double tap which is used for opening an application and single finger triple tap which is used for magnification for low vision users.

5   Gesture Elicitation and Performance

The second exercise done with the users was *command based gesture elicitation.* As part of the experiment protocol users were asked to invent 2 different gestures to execute the given command. Afterwards we asked users to perform each gesture they

Fig. 1. Experimental setup

invented thrice. A custom recording application on Android was developed with a blank screen for drawing gesture on which users' trails were recorded and gesture speed was measured. The haptic feedback was provided to make users aware of the area in which they need to perform their gesture. A Bluetooth client application was built to run on another device which helped experimenter in capturing screenshots for each of the user trials. List of twenty five commands including both the existing and new set was selected for elicitation. Commands were divided into five different contexts: Editing (*cut, copy, paste, save, select, enter, read from top*), Error prevention (*cancel, back, delete, undo*) Navigation (*open, close, next/previous, scroll, pause/play, search*) Calling Functions (*make a call, reject, accept, put on hold*) and General Actions (*go to home screen, recent apps, show, unlock*). After each trial users were asked the reason behind inventing each of the two gestures. Through the gesture elicitation we tried to answer questions regarding intuitiveness and easiness of gestures. To measure these variables user were asked to rate the two gestures they invented on scale of 1 to 7 (with 1 = strongly disagree, 7 = strongly agree) in terms of easiness (The gesture I invented is easy to perform) and intuitiveness (The gesture I invented is good for its intended function) (See Fig. 1).

The third experiment was *gesture performance*. This exercise aimed to answer questions related to ease of performance of existing and new gestures, and identify characteristics of effective and easy gestures for visually impaired users. We included set of different shapes, symbols and characters for evaluating the gesture performance. As part of the protocol [1, 2] users tried the gesture once for training and they repeated each gestures thrice and screenshots were captured. After each category trials users were asked to comparatively rate gestures in a given category. We tried to measure the ease of performance of the gesture user performed (the gesture I did is easy to perform) scale of 1–7 (with 1 = strongly disagree, 7 = strongly agree).

5.1   Results from Gesture Elicitation

Each participant invented 2 gestures for each of the 25 commands. We collected a total number of 300 gestures from the six users. In terms of easiness user rated the overall

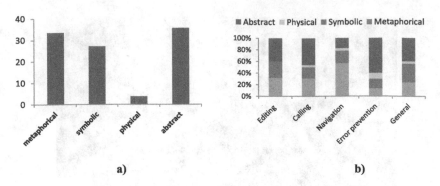

Fig. 2. (a) Percentage of gestures in each nature category as defined by Wobbrock [1] (b) Percentage of each gestures type in the given context of commands

gestures as [mean = 6.39, S.D. = 1.1], while for good match users rated their gestures as [mean = 6.12, S.D = 1.09].

Nature of Gestures: Wobbrock [1] has defined the gesture taxonomy based on the nature of the gesture. According to his definition a gesture could be divided into four different categories based on its nature: *Metaphorical, Symbolic, Physical and Abstract.* For grouping our gestures we took into account the user rationale behind each of the invented gestures. Most of the gestures elicitated belonged to abstract, metaphorical and symbolic categories (Fig. 2a). Extremely less gestures belong to physical category as touch gestures doesn't give freedom for the user to perform real world physical actions which is more in case of the air and motion gestures. Most abstract gestures included lot of characters suggested by users for performing a given command. As observed from Fig. 2b users preferred more metaphorical gestures for navigation commands which could be due to large set of users preferring swipes, taps for frequently used navigational actions. A large number of abstract gestures and symbolic gestures were part of general context commands (like going to home screen, read notifications etc.) as they had less frequent usage and were of specific and complex nature. So users might find difficult to comprehend metaphors for these actions.

Easiness and intuitiveness. User rated the metaphorical gesture they invented highest both on easiness [mean = 6.49, S.D. = 1.01] and good match [mean = 6.52, S.D. = .74] while symbolic gestures were rated lowest on easiness [mean = 5.68, S.D. = 1.5] and physical gestures lowest on intuitiveness [mean = 5.71, S.D. = 1.38]. However it was interesting to note that user rated the same symbolic gestures good on intuitiveness [mean = 6.17, S.D. = 1.43]. The reason could be since these gestures were derived from mental imagery they felt highly intuitive to them but they could have faced the difficulty while drawing the symbols and representing them. For abstract gestures user rated equally well both on intuitiveness [mean = 6.38, S.D. = .82] and easiness [mean = 6.42, S.D. = .94].There was also significant difference found in terms of easiness ($p < .05$, $n = 178$) between metaphorical and symbolic gestures.

Role of user's Cognition for Elicitated gestures: Gestures suggested by users were based on visual imagery, alphabets, braille characters, abstract metaphors etc. For e.g. in case of editing commands many users suggested drawing letter V for pasting (inspired from Ctrl + V paste command), X for cutting (inspired from Ctrl + X cut command) etc. Many of the users also suggested using the first letter of command name as gestures. For e.g. some users suggested using letter H for hold function, letter D for delete, letter N for reading notifications etc. One of the reasons behind the abstract nature of gestures suggested could be result of user being able to think more analytically than metaphorically. Role of cognition could also be understood from differences in gesture suggested by people blind by birth and late blind. People who were late blind suggested many symbolic gestures driven from visual imagery and symbolic learning while people who were early blind suggested mostly metaphorical or abstract gestures like swipes, taps, flicks etc. Less amount of symbolic gesture by former could be attributed to their lack of visual imagery formed because of their early blindness. Some users also suggested using *braille characters* as gestures for few commands. This was also relevant as early blind users were unaware of the forms of roman characters.

Agreement Scores. An agreement score, A_t, reflects in a single number the degree of consensus among participants. Wobbrock [1] provides a mathematical calculation for agreement, where:

$$A_t = \sum_{Pi} \left(\left| \frac{Pi}{Pt} \right| \right) \qquad (1)$$

In Eq. 1, t is a task in the set of all tasks T, Pt is the set of proposed gestures for t, and Pi is a subset of identical gestures from Pt. The range for A is [0, 1]. Figure 3, illustrates the agreement for the gesture set developed by our participants.

In general there wasn't any influence of the context of commands on user's consensus for gestures. There was more consensus for few general actions commands (notifications and home screen) and navigation commands (open, next scroll etc.) while very little consensus for error prevention commands (cancel and delete).

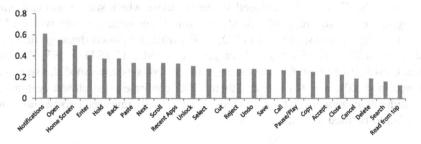

Fig. 3. Agreement scores for all the 25 commands

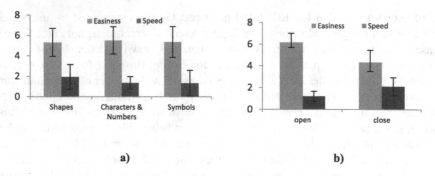

Fig. 4. a) Participants' easiness and speed ratings of shapes, characters and symbols. b) Participant average easiness and speed ratings of open and closed gestures. Error bars indicate +SD to - SD

5.2 Performance Evaluation of Gestures

Six users were part of the gesture performance study. A total of 19 gestures (including all shapes, symbols and characters) were evaluated for gesture performance. Some of the characters and symbols were unfamiliar for two participants who were birth by blind. Total number of gestures collected from 6 users was 318. Overall users rated all shapes, characters and symbols equally on easiness ratings with average being 5.34{S.D = 1.36},5.53{S.D = 1.33} and 5.35{S.D = 1.49} respectively (Fig. 4a). However there was difference in terms of gesture speed with user taking more time in drawing shapes [mean time = 1.96 s, S.D. = 1.2] than characters [mean time = 1.36 s, S.D. = .603] and symbols [mean time = 1.32 s, S.D. = 1.25] (Fig. 4a).The high standard deviation for gestures speed for symbolic gestures could be because some blind users taking more time to learn and draw few symbols with which they were not familiar. Based on the instances collected we evaluated the performance of gesture in terms of openness, continuity and curvature.

Open V/s Closed. For our comparison we considered open gestures as those where the initial starting point and end point doesn't meet for e.g. an arc, greater or less than symbol, letter S. We considered closed shapes as those where staring and end points meet together e.g. a square, circle, 8. Mean easiness for open gestures was 6.17 (S.D. = .84) and for gesture speed 1.214 (S.D. = .46) while for closed shape gesture mean easiness was 4.33 (S.D. = 1.11) and for gesture speed 2.12 (S.D. = .83).The independent t-test between both factors (easiness and speed) sets confirmed the significant difference ($p < .001$, $n = 80$) between them. This confirmed that closed gestures are indeed difficult in comparison to open shapes for a visually impaired person and should be avoided to be used as gestures.

Continuous V/s Discontinuous: During our qualitative discussion some users mentioned that they find drawing gestures where they need to lift their finger extremely difficult as they could lose track of reference point from where they need to restart drawing. Based on these statements we considered comparing discontinuous gestures in comparison to continuous gestures. For our comparison we considered continuous gestures as those where user could draw the complete gesture without lifting their finger e.g. letter N, S etc. We considered discontinuous shapes as those where user need to lift their finger for drawing the complete gesture e.g. letter A, E etc. Mean easiness for continuous gestures was 5.64 (S.D = 1.45) while for discontinuous gesture mean easiness was 5.1 (S.D. = 2.09).However the independent t-test didn't indicate the significant difference between the two data sets.

Angular Gestures: We considered all the L shapes, greater and less than symbols as part of evaluation of angular gestures. The mean easiness score for these gestures was 5.98 {S.D. = .95}.while average gesture speed was 1.17 s {S.D. = .338}.These results showed that these gestures are extremely easy to perform. We also analyzed all sets of gestures through MATLAB analysis which clearly showed the large variation in angles and sizes of these gestures.Thus the problem doesn't lie in the performance of these gestures but in the recognition of these gestures. Hence it is important that system model the large variations that are possible in these angular gestures for effective implementation of these gestures.

Multi-finger Gesture Evaluation. We evaluated the performance of multi-finger swipes, taps etc. in comparison to same gestures performed with single finger. Our results indicated that there was no significant difference found between the easiness of multi-finger gestures and the single finger gestures. Mean easiness score for multi-finger gesture was 5.47{S.D. = 1.2} while mean easiness score for single finger was 5.68{S.D. = .96}.One of the users mentioned multi-finger gestures sturdier than single finger gestures. However some performance issues were observed with multi-finger gestures like lifting of fingers, some finger not being detected because of differences in heights of the fingers. Thus one of the key insights was that though multi-finger gestures are easy to perform there are accuracy and detection issues as number of finger increases. So, one should prefer avoiding multi-finger gestures for frequently used commands.

6   Discussion

The three experimental studies discussed has helped us in gathering lot of insights regarding the use of assistive screen readers in case of touch based smartphones. We have discussed some of these insights that we gathered below:

6.1   Location of Gestures

We performed MATLAB image analysis on the user screenshots gathered from gesture performance to understand the preferred gestures location for drawing gestures by the users. The analysis indicated the user preference tending towards left top portion and all edges of the screen (which could be attributed to most users being right handed).The reason behind preference for edges could be due to the hard tactile cues the sharp edges of the smartphones provides from which these users can draw some reference. Another insight that we gathered was the user preference for performing gesture in particular location of screens. For e.g. one of the user suggested tapping in left and right corners to perform a given command. These insights could be really helpful in positioning visual elements on screens for the visually impaired users.

6.2 Gesture and User Type

Duration of Blindness: The duration of blindness had an impact on both gesture performance and elicitation. During gesture performance most users who very early blind couldn't draw many symbols or characters. They even faced difficulty in drawing one or two shapes. In gesture elicitation users who were blind by birth mostly preferred gestures like swipe, taps, flicks etc. and very less gestures influenced by visual imagery as it was difficult for them to imagine different visual shapes. Contrary users who were late blind came out with gestures inspired from lot of visual imagery which was easy for them to visualize. These insights provide pointers while deciding a uniform gesture vocabulary for the target segment.

Low Vision V/s Fully Blind: Most of the current assistive applications cater to fully blind situation or eyes free interactions and ignore how extremely low vision users uses them. The current user interface (UI) for most of the applications has smaller fonts, bad visual contrast and lot of small visual icons which makes difficult for low vision users to use them. During our exercises with extreme low vision users who could slightly make out difference in elements on screen it was observed that accessing and inter-acting with the UI was extremely difficult for them because of high visual demands. Thus it becomes imperative that designers understand these issues and build simplified UI with minimal visual demands for these users to access them easily.

6.3 Design Suggestions

Effective gestures for visually impaired users: Gestures which require users to come back to the starting point or lift their fingers should be avoided. One should consider gestures with open shapes and which are continuous in nature. Designers should avoid gestures which require some particular angles to be made by user as there could be performance and implementation challenges. Otherwise system should be modelled such that it allows large variation in sizes and angles.

Customizable gesture sets: Designing a uniform gesture vocabulary for visually impaired users would be an ideal solution but not seems feasible because of large variation in terms of easy and intuitive gestures among types of visually impaired users. Therefore one needs to build a customizable set of gestures which could cater these differences and would allow users to be able to choose gestures based on their preferences.

Use of corners and edges for positioning UI element: Since the edges and the corners of screen are easily accessible because of strong tactical cues, one should use them for positioning essential UI element while designing touch screen applications for visually impaired. This would actually allow exploring and skimming contents quickly without unforced errors.

Quick and Easy navigation: The current navigation and exploration in touch screens is sequential in nature which could be unnecessary tedious and irritating for users. The problem is more prevalent in case of interacting through web pages. Thus need for the designers is to device a system of non-sequential ways of navigation and shortcuts for skimming content quickly for touch based smartphones.

Designing touch applications for extreme low vision and low vision: The new challenge for designers is to make their applications accessible to extreme low vision and low vision. The accessibility features need to provide flexibility with regards to change of UI for making it more accessible to these users. Large target sizes, simplifying the UI by removing unnecessary functions, replacing small icons with large buttons, high visual contrast to differentiate between elements etc. are some of the ways designers could try to make their application more accessible to these users.

7 Conclusion and Future Work

This research started with open ended discussions with the visually impaired users to understand their pain points in using various features of smartphone. We received few direct feedbacks from these users such as their difficulties in accessing the UI elements on the screen, speed of talk back responses etc.. They also suggested including few gestures for certain task that they perform very frequently. Based on the evaluation study, we proposed the design suggestions for few existing gestures as well as suggested new gesture for certain commands. We also made touch screen accessibility design guidelines keeping in mind different types of users - fully blind and extremely low vision. As part of the next step in research we have already implemented few prototypes of the proposed gestures. The plan is to perform the comparative evaluation of these new gestures and modified gestures through experiments. We would plan to report the improvements in terms of accessibility for the target user group through use of our solutions.

References

1. Wobbrock, Jacob O., Meredith Ringel Morris, and Andrew D. Wilson. User-defined gestures for surface computing. In: Proceedings of the SIGCHI Conference on Human Factors in Computing Systems, pp. 1083–1092. ACM (2009)
2. Kane, S.K., Wobbrock, J.O., Ladner, R.E.: Usable gestures for blind people: understanding preference and performance. In: Proceedings of the SIGCHI Conference on Human Factors in Computing Systems, pp. 413–422. ACM (2011)

3. McGookin, D., Brewster, S., Jiang, W.: Investigating touchscreen accessibility for people with visual impairments. In: Proceedings of the 5th Nordic conference on Human-computer interaction: building bridges, pp. 298–307. ACM (2008)
4. Leporini, B., Buzzi, M.C., Buzzi, M.: Interacting with mobile devices via VoiceOver: usability and accessibility issues. In: Proceedings of the 24th Australian Computer-Human Interaction Conference, pp. 339–348. ACM (2012)
5. Vanderheiden, G.C.: Use of audio-haptic interface techniques to allow nonvisual access to touchscreen appliances. In: Human Factors and Ergonomics Society Annual Meeting Proceedings, vol. 40, no. 24, pp. 1266–1266 (1996)
6. Landau, S., and Wells. L: Merging tactile sensory input and audio data by means of the Talking Tactile Tablet. In: Proceedings of Eurohaptics, vol. 3 (2003)
7. Hill, D.R., Grieb, C.: Substitution for a restricted visual channel in multimodal computer-human dialogue. IEEE Trans. Syst. Man Cybern. **18**(2), 285–304 (1988)
8. Stephanidis, C., Pieper, M. (eds.): ERCIM Ws UI4ALL 2006. LNCS, vol. 4397. Springer, Heidelberg (2007)
9. Shiri, A., Rector, K., Ladner, R., Wobbrock, J.: Passchords: secure multi-touch authentication for blind people. In: Proceedings of the 14th international ACM SIGACCESS conference on Computers and accessibility, pp. 159–166. ACM (2012)
10. Kane, S.K., Bigham, J.P., Wobbrock, J.O.: Slide rule: making mobile touch screens accessible to blind people using multi-touch interaction techniques. In: Proceedings of the 10th international ACM SIGACCESS Conference on Computers and Accessibility, pp. 73–80. ACM (2008)
11. Morris, M.R., Wobbrock, J.O., Wilson, A.D.: Understanding users' preferences for surface gestures. In: Proceedings of graphics interface 2010, pp. 261–268. Canadian Information Processing Society (2010)

Touchless Text Entry for All: Initial Design Considerations and Prototypes

Alexandros Mourouzis[✉], Giorgos Arfaras, Vassilis Kilintzis,
Ioanna Chouvarda, and Nicos Maglaveras

Lab of Medical Informatics, School of Health Sciences, Aristotle University,
Thessaloniki, Greece
{mourouzi,maglaveras}@med.auth.gr

Abstract. In this paper, the foundations for a new *touchless text entry method* are set. The method in question is based on hand tracking for interacting with a novel virtual keyboard that has been designed to support *adaptive text entry* for all, including for users with disabilities or users of various assistive technologies. The virtual keyboard in question, which can be graphical or even imaginary (i.e., implied, but not visualised), implements a hierarchical selection approach for the *act of writing,* which involves character selection, text navigation and text modification. The proposed structure guarantees minimum *keystrokes per character,* and allows for user-friendly adaptations for offering accessibility, personalisation and increased performance rates for diverse input settings or display preferences. An implementation of the text entry method in question, using the LEAP, a novel 3D motion controller, is introduced here. Along with the fundamental specifications of the proposed keyboard and the required functionality of a software mechanism for initialising, personalising and interacting with it in any given context, this paper presents two prototypes currently under development for one- and ten-finger touchless text entry with LEAP, which are considered in view of developing a *universal text input solution* that could overshadow all past technologies.

Keywords: Text entry · Soft keyboard · 3D interaction · Universal access · LEAP

1 Introduction

Today, when it comes to the communication of text to computer systems, humans rely mostly on *manual methods*[1] and on various types of keyboards. In comparison to both *voice* and *brain* computer interfaces, which have been recently explored as potential alternative solutions, manual entry remains predominant for a variety of good reasons that have much less to do with technology than with how people work. Manual methods are not used just because they are more efficient (accurate and fast), but because they let people work without disturbing others, and without letting everyone else know every little thing that they are doing. As a result, despite the technological leaps in all other aspects of human-computer interaction and against all predictions, for

---

[1] i.e., controlled with the hands.

© Springer International Publishing Switzerland 2015
M. Antona and C. Stephanidis (Eds.): UAHCI 2015, Part II, LNCS 9176, pp. 37–49, 2015.
DOI: 10.1007/978-3-319-20681-3_4

decades now, in terms of text entry, the typical typewriter-like keyboard appears unbeaten and still far from being surpassed. A significant disadvantage of the typical keyboard that is seriously considered in our days is its big size and limited portability. Because of this, and as today we rely more and more on mobile devices and our needs for ubiquitous access to text entry are constantly increasing, we are often forced to leave our keyboards back home and compromise with less powerful, text entry solutions, such as smaller keypads, onscreen keyboards, speech-to-text systems, etc.

To this end, we argue that nowadays text entry has turned into a bottleneck in the communication process between humans and modern computer systems. In fact, we believe that the user performance (*speed* and *accuracy*[2]) is degrading significantly when it comes to mobile and on-the-move text entry. Furthermore, each time a developer needs to integrate a text input method into a new product (e.g., into a new smart TV, ATM, car-navigator system, medical machine, etc.), in the end the user is often confronted with a whole new input model that suffers from poor performance rates, serious accessibility issues, and unbalanced user satisfaction levels. Clearly, this blocks to a certain degree the overall potential of ICT and the realization of the disappearing computer vision. One could therefore argue that a major leap to text entry that would overcome such barriers, could revolutionize the interaction between humans and computers and release a huge technology and human potential, especially in the emerging cloud computing and ambient intelligence era.

This work aims at contributing to current research towards identifying modern text entry solutions that will unblocking the human potential, achieve better performance rates, and will make the dominant keyboard lose its throne held for so many years now.

2   Text Entry in Brief

Manual text entry, as the human process of communicating text to computer-based systems, is in essence an alternative way of *writing*. In other words, an alternative way of storing text into a tangible medium. The main difference is that the storage medium now used is the computer memory, rather than paper. Naturally, the new medium posed itself a whole new set of affordances and limitations. For instance, computers now require users to select among a set of pre-encoded characters,[3] whereas paper, as a flat surface, implies the use of 2D symbols. As a whole, the new medium brought along new options that changed writing, among others, forever. For instance, it enabled authors to act on transcribed texts without imposing restrictions for modifications, and to reproduce texts parts very easily (e.g., through copy-paste).

Manual text entry to computer systems is merely a *selection process* that can be defined as the human process T that involves choosing from a set of computer encoded characters C and modifying options M,[4] by means of a total number i of discrete, machine-detectable, user actions, such as key taps, gestures, etc.

---

[2] Two primary performance metrics for text entry [1].

[3] Graphemes, symbols, etc., or a set of encoded strings of characters, i.e., words or sentences.

[4] Mainly of two types: navigation / selection (back, forward, home, select all, etc.) and modifying / processing functions (delete, backspace, copy-paste, etc.).

Typing, originally introduced by mechanical typewriters, has been a diachronic manual text entry method since the early emergence of computers and command line interfaces. This method involves the correspondence of characters and modifiers with a set of keys spread across a device. Keyboards with different numbers of keys exist, but the 101/105-keys keyboard, like QWERTY, is still predominant. With the emergence of graphical user interfaces, *menu-based text entry* was introduced as a supplement of *typing*, allowing users to enter additional characters not found on the keyboard through menus. Such menus are now perceived as the ancestors of the later forms of *soft* or *onscreen keyboards*. The later, are features of a program or operating system that generate graphically a keyboard on screen that is then operated through mouse, stylus, etc. Soft keyboards are particularly useful in two cases: (a) for making text entry accessible to people with manual dexterities - e.g., they can be combined with *scanning techniques* and allow operation through few special switches; (b) for removing keypads from mobile devices and reducing their physical size – e.g., characters can be selected through tapping on a touch display. In both cases, soft keyboards are most usually a representation of a full-size QWERTY keyboard. With the emergence of mobile devices, typing and menu-based methods were fused to allow text entry through few keys [1]. Soon, the success of SMS messaging on mobile phones brought attention to 12-key keypads, with the letters A-Z being traditionally encoded on eight keys,[5] and a number of 12-key entry methods emerged for assigning more than one letters to each key [2], with *multi-tap* and *dictionary-based disambiguation* being the most common among them.

3   Background and Previous Related Work

The work presented here was originally motivated from previous research experiences of the lead author and his former colleagues on text entry methods for users with limited motor functionality of upper limbs. Out of those efforts, the basic concept of the *AUK keyboard* emerged [3]. That is basically a multi-tier 3x3 menu system, consisting of a primary menu, where eight cells are used for the alphabet letters and one cell is reserved for entering into additional, again 3×3, menus that accommodate additional characters C and modifying options M. Through this strict hierarchical structure, *AUK* supports: (a) minimum keystrokes per character (KSPC) in average, (b) entry through for the widest possible range of input devices, including keypads, indication devices, joysticks, etc., and (c) various layout configurations for achieving even lower KSPC values [1].

Back then, during the early development stages of the *AUK concept* as a text entry solution for disabled users, we also saw behind it the possibility to develop an ambient and ubiquitous text entry solution for all, for instance through optical tracking of the user fingers [3]. A novel *virtual keyboard*,[6] not necessarily visible, was conceived for

---

[5] See ITU E.161 international recommendation for telephone keypads.

[6] Although the term *virtual keyboard* (VK) is often used interchangeably with that of "soft keyboard", VKs are defined as touch-typing keyboards that do not have physical manifestation of the sensing areas, and thus should be perceived as different from onscreen keyboards.

10-finger text entry, thus replacing the traditional keyboards. By mapping each finger to one of the virtual keys of the *AUK*'s 10-key mode (ibid.), if, for instance, the user makes a discrete move of the small finger of the left hand, then the character 'a' is to be entered (see Fig. 1).

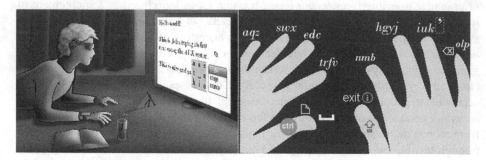

Fig. 1. Towards ambient ten-thumbs text entry (reprinted from [3]).

Given that few successful tracking solutions exist today, we now see a great opportunity to proceed in this direction and work on the development of a *universal text entry solution*. But let's first identify the desired quality characteristics of such a solution.

4   Guidelines for Universal Text Entry Solutions

After several years of research in text entry and hands on experience with hundreds of methods, we have listed a number of features that we would expect to find in an ideal, universal, manual text entry method that, ultimately, could 'show the exit' to the traditional keyboard. More specifically, we argue that an ideal method shall:

1. *Prevent user errors and allow for easy error recovery.* An ideal method shall minimise the frequency of user errors, such as typos due to wrong character selection, and shall allow for rapid error identification and recovery.
2. *Support fast typing.* The new method shall offer better typing rates than previous methods. Anything below the entry rates with today's solutions on smartphones and tablet would be a complete a failure.
3. *Be easy to learn and use.* Ideally, an ideal new method would allow for a smooth transition from the current ways and would introduce progressively various tips and adjustments to help users master the new method.
4. *Support WYSIWYG.*[7] An ideal method shall display the exact letters and words that are in the mind of the writer and avoid cluttering the display with rough text and words guesses (like with Dasher or T9 for instance).

---

[7] WYSIWYG is an acronym for "What You See Is What You Get".

5. *Support blind typing.* An ideal text entry needs to be *target-less* and potentially *eyes-free*. The user should not have to search for, and achieve physical contact with, a specific area (physical or virtual, e.g., a key), as this can eliminate performance delays related to time spent (a) in visual scanning for target identification (Hick and Human's method), and (b) in selecting the target (Fitt's Law). In that case, the user is free to focus on the transcribed text and the task at hand.

6. *Support minimal hand and finger movement and travelling.* For instance, during typing on a typical keyboard, finger and hand movements are quite intense, due the need to travel across a keyboard (and the mouse) to reach different keys, which is both time and energy consuming.

7. *Accommodate functionality for indication.* Ideally, both keyboard and mouse functionality shall be integrated into a single interaction concept. For instance, employ fingers tracking both for typing and for controlling the mouse cursor.

8. *Support entry through any desired number of detectable user actions* i. An ideal method needs to allow flexible configuration to any number of distinct user actions i, depending on each user's ability and preferences. In other words, it is desired that the method can be easily set or switched to $i = 10$ mode (two hands), or $i = 5$ (one hand), or $i = 3$ (special assistive switches), or $i = 1$ (one finger), etc.

9. *Support multi-device compatibility* (if not full device independence). An ideal method shall work equally well with any existing device type. The user needs to have a single model regardless if he is working with finger tracking, mouse alone, special switches, joystick, or the arrow keyboard keys.

10. *Be smart and adaptable.* An ideal text entry system shall be able to propose specific optimisations for options and functions used very often by the user and the process of writing shall be easily or even automatically adapted to various usage conditions, such as in switching to one-hand mode, typing in the dark, etc.

11. *Support additional special characters.* An ideal method would offer easy and rapid access to numbers and special characters.

5 Refining the AUK Concept

Here the reader is briefly introduced to the basics of the *AUK* concept, according which *everything must be organised in sets of nine (3 × 3) options*. As mentioned earlier, in text entry the user, in order to transcribe the text in mind, chooses repeatedly among a finite set of supported characters C and modification/control options M. *AUK* is nothing more than multi-tier menu system for organising all these options. The proposed structure (*keyboard*) consists of multiple levels of sets of strictly nine options (*menus*), starting with a *primary menu* (home menu), where eight "keys" are used for entering letters and one is reserved for switching between other similar 9-options *basic menus* in which extra characters and modification options are accommodated. Each 9-options menu can be visualised as a 3 × 3 grid that can accommodate *option keys* and at least one *menu switch key* for entering or exiting alternative menus. Up to nine *basic menus* are foreseen and these can be interchanged sequentially through a consistent *menu switch key* (see Fig. 2). Each individual *option key* can itself accommodate up to nine options. Typically, only a part of these options is to be used, leaving the rest empty (see Fig. 3).

The *home menu* (primary menu) shall typically accommodate the letters A-Z placed on eight *option keys*, and the *menu switch key* can be used for switching to the next basic menu and for *timeout kill*. Letters can be placed alphabetically, similarly to a phone keypad (see Fig. 4 - left). The *multi-tap technique* can then be used for character disambiguation (i.e., for selecting among the 9 sub-options on each *key*), and *system timeout* for entering consecutive letters from the same key. The main benefit of such an approach is clear: familiarity. However, there are also some disadvantages recorded: (a) timeouts slow down users; (b) with an alphabetic layout, some frequent letters require more keystrokes than some less frequently needed letters; (c) some very common characters or modifiers need to be pushed down to deeper level menus. Taking into account that several studies (e.g., [4]) have indicated that an alphabetic order is not critical for user experience, more effective layouts can be created by disregarding the alphabetical order all together. Thus, alternative arrangements of the letters and characters are considered (see [3]) for achieving less *keystrokes per character* (KSPC [5]). For instance, the apostrophe, SPACE (SP), BACK (BK), and SHIFT (SH)[8] can be added on the option keys of the home menu, and letters can be re-arranged (see Fig. 4 - middle), so that (a) letters on each key have the lowest possible *digraph frequencies* [6] in an *English text corpus* in order to have consecutive letters on the same key (and thus timeouts) less frequently,[9] and (b) the letters on each key are arranged in decreasing letter frequency in the English Language[10] – thus ensuring less 'taps' for most frequent letters.

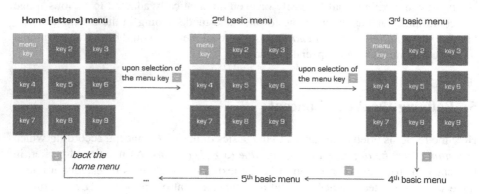

Fig. 2. Navigating through consecutive basic menus in the proposed 3 × 3 multi-tier structure.

---

[8] SP, BK, and SH are very common; in AUK, SP, being the most common key, is always the most easy to reach; the apostrophe, indicates missing letters, and thus is included here.

[9] The most frequent diagrams account for over 80 % of text in a language [6].

[10] E.g., see http://en.wikipedia.org/wiki/Letter_frequencies.

Home (letters) menu

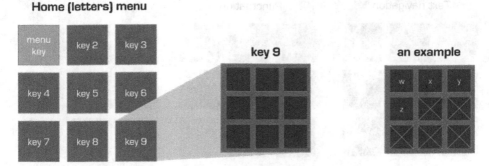

Fig. 3. Each *option key* (grey) on a menu is able to accommodate 1 to 9 input options (e.g., characters). For instance, in this example (*right*), "key 9" hosts the letters "w", "x", "y" and "z", thus selecting this particular key three times in the row, shall produce the character "y").

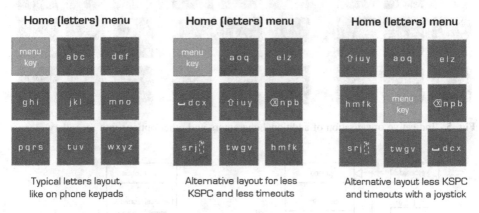

Fig. 4. The home menu (letters) based on the typical phone keypad layout (*left*) and on alternative layouts (Frequency order used for generating this layout is: SP BS e t a SH o i n s h r d l c u m w f g y p b v apostrophe k j x q z) for reaching less KSPC and timeouts with 9-keys (*middle*) or joystick (*right*)

In addition to the *home menu* (the "letters menu"), several additional menus (always as sets of nine options) can be introduced as described above, i.e., either as *basic menus* reached through the main *menu switch key* or as *secondary menus* that can be reached through *secondary switch keys* (a kind of link) that can be placed one any other menu, instead of an *option key*. Such menus can include: *navigation options*, *numerals*, *special characters*, *brackets*, *numeric operators*, etc. (see Fig. 5).

The class diagrams in Fig. 6 summarise the proposed structure. As discussed in [3], using this menu structure for arranging all text entry options, we achieve to deliver a universal model that works in an optimum way with any number of i between 1 and 9. For instance through this structure, the average KSPC is lower than in any other arrangement (e.g., in a QWERTY-like arrangement), even in 1-button mode, or 5-keys mode, joystick mode, etc.

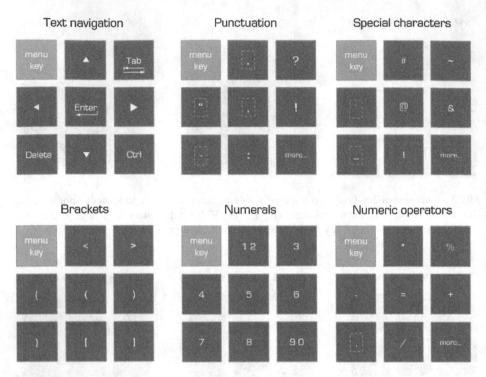

Fig. 5. Indicative organisation of additional characters and other options into secondary menus

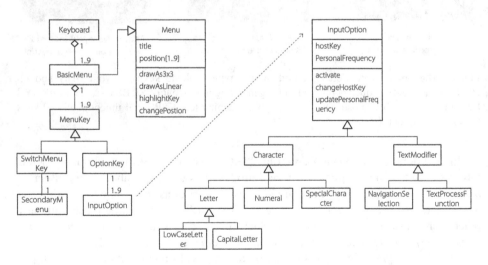

Fig. 6. Class diagrams for the proposed multi-tier structure

It should be stated here that the proposed structure can be visualised or not and presented in multiple ways. For instance, it can be presented in parts as consecutive 3 × 3 menus or simple lists of the 9-options presented horizontally or vertically. One could even represent all menu levels simultaneously, in a 2D or 3D representation. What needs to be made clear is that the allocation of input options to keys and menus is one thing, and the visualisation of menus and keys is another. For each unique allocation of options to menus and keys one can produce multiple *display versions*.[11] On the other hand, the allocation of options to menus and keys can be altered at any moment upon demand (e.g., for optimising performance rates as mentioned above), which means that for any finite set of options C and M, we can specify multiple versions of allocation. Such optimisations can be identified on a personal base, after for example calculating the use frequencies of individual options, keys or menus. Further discussion on possible layout rearrangement strategies is provided in [3]. In that same work, we also discussed a potential adaption for supporting 10 thumbs entry (i = 10) through finger tracking.

The last part of this paper, focuses on describing how proposed concept can lead to the development of a touchless text entry solution for writing with one finger up to ten fingers.

6 Towards Touchless Text Entry for All

As mentioned above, a number of successful tracking methods are made available today and the authors started working on implementing various proof-of-concept prototypes with one of them. That is *Leap Motion Controller,*[12] a novel 3D motion controller that uses infrared to detect the user hands and specify user gestures and interactions with virtual elements. The LEAP controller, now available as a USB device, supports a 150-degree field of view using infrared (IR) to detect the user hands and specify if the user points, waves, reaches, or grab virtual elements, such as a button on the user interface. This controller is already small enough to be embedded to portable devices, inspiring a huge leap in traditional HCI. Notably, there is an open programming API offered that has attracted the attention of hundreds of researchers from all over the world who turned into it to explore new ways to improve the user experience of their applications and systems. What is interesting, especially for the work presented in this paper, is that among the top 5 most viewed and liked projects at the LEAP community area, one can find two projects that aim at using LEAP for text entry. This is supporting the argument that text entry is emerging as major challenge today, and that we are all in search of new solutions and new paradigms of interactions.

6.1 LEAP for Text Entry: Previous Works and Their Limitations

Let's first have a quick insight in these text-entry related works from the LEAP community. One of them is that of *Dasher,*[13] an input method and computer accessibility tool that enables users to write without using a keyboard, by entering text on a

---

[11] Even auditory or tactile.

[12] Official site: www.leapmotion.com.

[13] http://www.inference.phy.cam.ac.uk/dasher/DasherSummary2.html

screen using a pointing device. Another method, which shares some common characteristics with that of Dasher, is that of the *Minuum keyboard* for LEAP,[14] which was
originally aimed to improve touchscreen typing, replacing the onscreen QWERTY-like
keyboards, through a minimal keyboard with a specialized auto-correction algorithm
that allows highly imprecise typing. *8pen*[15] takes a completely different tack to the
keyboard problem, by eliminating it altogether. 8pen arranges the most used letters and
characters in 4 sectors around a central ring. To "type" the user places the finger on the
center ring and draw loops through the sectors. The starting sector and the number of
sectors passed determine the character produced. A limitation seen in all the approaches, is that the only one finger is used, resulting in relatively slow rates. Furthermore,
only *8-pen* supports blind typing (subject to the user being able to memorise the
position of each letter). Another key issue, is that of ease of learning, and only *Minuum*
scores well on that.

Our vision is to deliver an advanced solution based on hand tracking (e.g., through
LEAP), that will overcome such limitations and conform to most if not all of the
guidelines set in Sect. 4. Towards this direction, we have conceived an approach that
builds on the *AUK* concept and makes use of the LEAP functionality in order to
implement 10-thumbs writing. As part of this effort, we have started working on the
development of various prototypes with LEAP based on the *AUK* concept for one up to
ten fingers writing. These are developed with *Unity*, a cross-platform game creation
system, including a game engine and integrated development environment (IDE), since
the Leap Motion SDK can be used as a Unity plugin to access Leap Motion tracking
data in a Unity application. Here, we are introducing two basic models based on the
AUK concept: one for one-finger input (like Dasher, 8pen, etc.) and one for 10-fingers
input as an alternative to typing with a standard desktop keyboard.

6.2   Writing with One Finger

The basic concept behind using *AUK* with LEAP for writing with one finger involves
placing within the interaction space (the area in which LEAP can detect the movement
of hands and individual fingers) the *menus* and *option keys* of the proposed 3 × 3 menu
structure and using finger tracking for interacting with them. A simple way of doing
this is by simply placing in the interaction zone nine virtual keys, applying to them any
desired arrangement according to the AUK concept, and then allow the user by
pointing in and out of them to type letter-by-letter. This approach shares some similarities with the *Minuum* and Dasher as it uses LEAP for *indication* (pointing).

An alternative approach that is closer to the gesture based approach of *8pen*,
involves splitting the interaction zone into nine vertical zones, as presented in Fig. 7.
Splitting the interaction space into 9 areas in order to support one-finger typing. In such
case, a potential arrangement for the home menu is that in Fig. 4 – right (which in fact
is a rearrangement of that shown in middle of the same figure), so that the user can

---

[14] http://minuum.com

[15] http://www.8pen.com

write by moving his finger around the eight directions N, NE, E, SE, S, SW, W, and NW and returning back to C for switching to other menus. For character disambiguation among letters on the same key, there are at least 4 possible options: (a) use a kind of multi-tap approach; (b) use gestures; (c) use dictionary-based disambiguation; or (d) split the zones to individual sub zones for each letter (e.g., see Fig. 8).

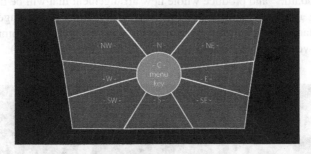

Fig. 7. Splitting the interaction space into 9 areas in order to support one-finger typing

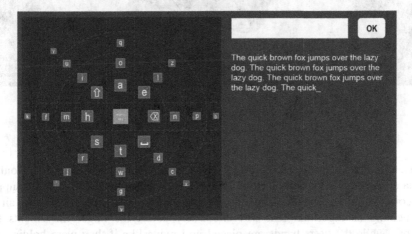

Fig. 8. Splitting the interaction space into individual subzones for each letter

6.3 Writing with 10 Fingers

In [3], an early discussion on a potential adaption of *AUK* for supporting 10 thumbs entry ($i = 10$), even through finger tracking, was included. This is important since it may enable reaching fast writing (close if not better than rates achieved with a desktop keyboard), and at the same time enable the detachment of the writing process from any kind of physical keyboard. With 10-fingers in mind, a 9 + 1[16] version of the multi-tier

---

[16] One can introduce a 10th key in order to use it as modifier (for CTRL or SHIFT) and /or for assigning to it the "Space" (SP) as a means for even faster typing.

structure is used, which may be visualised as a 10×1 horizontal grid. Then we can map each finger to one of these 10 virtual keys, and use LEAP to detect the movement of each individual finger and produce characters accordingly. One way, seeking familiarity, is to group and allocate the letters in the 10 keys in question by taking into account the way that the letters are placed on a QWERTY layout. However, we strongly believe, that one needs to detach the arrangement of letters from that of the QWERTY keyboard,[17] and produce whole new arrangement that will be designed from scratch for the new medium (hands tracking). An alternative arrangement would involve for instance assigning the most frequent keys to the more dominant fingers, ensuring the lowest possible digraph frequencies, etc. (e.g., see Fig. 9).

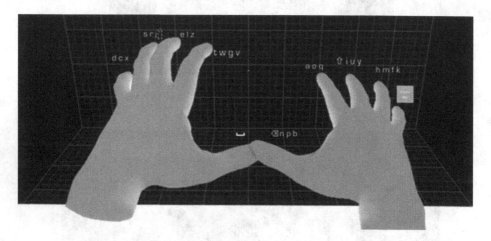

Fig. 9. Indicative *AUK* arrangement for 10-fingers typing with LEAP

Yet, in order to respect the physiology of the human hands and fingers and avoid the "gorilla arm" effect induced by uncomfortable placement of hands, we wish to support more comfortable placement of the hands while writing with LEAP. Thus, we aim at implementing an algorithm that will effectively detect the finger movements (i.e. key-taps), while the users hands are placed and move like if they were holding and playing with a virtual 3D ball, having their elbows resting on the table in front of them [7].

7   Conclusions & Future Work

The proposed text entry method is touchless, allows for blind typing, and supports various entry modes and multiple adaptations for diverse user skills and conditions of use.

---

[17] QWERTY arrangement was originally introduced for typewriting mechanical ma-chines back in 1867, as an alternative to the alphabetic placing in order to slow down fast typists and avoid key jamming.

Clearly, one can implement this technique with LEAP without conforming to the presented 3 × 3 multi-tier structure of *AUK*, but in that case all the benefits of that approach (device-independence, easy switch to any i < 10 mode, adaptations for improved performance and accessibility, etc.) would be lost for good. Overall, the concept of combining *AUK* with hand tracking shows a number of benefits and the potential to meet the majority, if not all, of the requirements of an ideal text entry method as presented earlier in Sect. 4. Nonetheless, there are substantial problems still with the use of the LEAP system for hand tracking. For example, IR reflections, finger occlusions and moving outside the detection space are all capable of halting the process. All these, shall be tested and validated in pilot tests using the developed prototypes.

Regarding our future plans: (a) the KSPC of each proposed mode and character layout will be calculated using public corpora, and detailed comparison results with other techniques will be collected; (b) user performance will be estimated and predicted using theory-based methods such as Hick and Human's method and Fitt's Law; (c) user trials will be conducted with the interactive prototypes; (d) a mechanism for employing personalised user corpora will be developed and integrated; (e) best possible arrangement for 10 fingers typing with LEAP will be proposed after studying hand and fingers kinematics and dynamics, and (f) research will be conducted to identify the frequency of all input options and the *dioption frequencies* (term used in analogy to digraph frequency) for optimising the tree structure of the menus, especially for the 10-key mode.

Acknowledgments. Part of the work reported here has been carried out in the framework of the project WELCOME (Grant Agreement No: 611223) funded by the EC.

References

1. MacKenzie, I.S., Soukoreff, R.W.: Text entry for mobile computing: models and methods. Theory Pract. Hum.-Comput. Interact. **17**, 147–198 (2002)
2. Oniszczak, A., MacKenzie, I.S.: A comparison of two input methods for keypads on mobile devices. In: Proceedings. of NordiCHI 2004, Tampere Finland, 23–27 October, pp. 101-104 (2004)
3. Mourouzis, A., Boutsakis, E., Ntoa, S., Antona, M., Stephanidis, C.: An Accessible and Usable Soft Keyboard. In: Stephanidis C. (ed.) Universal Access in HCI – PART II of the Proceedings of 4th International Conference UAHCI, Beijing, China, 22–27 July, pp. 961-970 (2007)
4. Norman, D.A., Fisher, D.: Why alphabetic keyboards are not easy to use: keyboard layout doesn't much matter. Hum. Factors **24**(5), 509–519 (1982)
5. MacKenzie, I.: KSPC (Keystrokes per Character) as a characteristic of text entry techniques. In: Paternó, F. (ed.) Mobile HCI 2002. LNCS, vol. 2411, pp. 195–210. Springer, Heidelberg (2002)
6. Zhai, S., Hunter, M., Smith, B.A.: Performance optimization of virtual keyboards. Hum.-Comput. Interact. **17**, 89–129 (2002)
7. Mourouzis, A., Kilintzis, V., Chouvarda, I., Maglaveras N.: Using the LEAP 3D motion controller for implementing text entry for all. In: Proceedings EMCIS 2014, 27th – 28th October 2014, Doha, Qatar (2014)

A Proposed Dynamical Analytic Method for Characteristic Gestures in Human Communication

Toshiya Naka[1,2(✉)] and Toru Ishida[1,2]

[1] Kyoto University, Kyoto, Japan
[2] Panasonic Advanced Research Lab, Kyoto, Japan
naka.tosiya@jp.panasonic.com

Abstract. In human communication, nonverbal information such as gestures and facial expressions often plays a greater role than language; and some gesture-driven operations of the latest mobile devices have proved to be easy-to-use and intuitive interfaces. In this paper we propose a method of analyzing gestures that focuses on human communication based on the dynamical kinematic model. We have extended the analysis method of our proposed approach to take into account additional effects, such as those exerted by external forces, and we analyze the effects over the entire body of forces generated by gestures. We found that the degree of exaggeration could be quantified by the value of, and changes in, torque values. Moreover, when calculating them taking into account external forces and the moment of drag that is acting on both feet, it is possible to determine the twisting torque of the main joints with a high degree of precision. We also noted "preparation" or "follow-through" motions just before and after the emphasized motion, and found that each behavior can be quantified by an "undershoot" or "overshoot" value of changes in torque.

Keywords: Nonverbal · Communication · Gesture · Virtual reality · Dynamics

1 Introduction

In face-to-face human communication, nonverbal information, such as gestures and facial expressions, often plays a greater role than language [1]. However, few studies of conventional cognitive psychology have quantitatively analyzed the roles and effects of nonverbal information of this type. We investigated the importance of nonverbal cues in human communication via the following approach, to quantify the function of characteristic gestures [2]. There is a wide range of types of nonverbal information that vary according to the context of a conversation, so we focused on the study of gestures, which are an important channel of human communication. Our initial studies revealed certain gestures that were used in Japanese Kabuki, in dance, and in Disney animation. We analyzed the effects of these special gestures, and examined whether they would fit into our proposed exaggerated-gesture model. By collecting dozens of characteristic gestures and applying them to our model, we found we were able to represent the degree of exaggeration in a quantitative manner. We also discovered our proposed

© Springer International Publishing Switzerland 2015
M. Antona and C. Stephanidis (Eds.): UAHCI 2015, Part II, LNCS 9176, pp. 50–57, 2015.
DOI: 10.1007/978-3-319-20681-3_5

model to be applicable to the speaker's exaggerated/emphasized movements in speeches and presentations that held the audience's attention. We regard these commonalities as being of great interest.

Most people accompany verbal information with exaggerated gestures when wishing to emphatically communicate their message. In our previous research, we defined these basic dynamics using an analytic model of certain characteristic behaviors. Some special gestures were quantified in terms of torque values of elements of a human skeletal model. We tend to apply force to the required portion of the arms and body for the action to be emphasized, so it is possible to quantify those effects in terms of the torque applied to each joint. There is a close correlation between gesture and torque applied. Although the use of dynamics as analytical technique for motion is used in sports kinematics [3, 4] and robotics [5, 6], there has been little research that mathematically analyzes communicative gestures [7]. In our previous studies, we proposed several basic mechanisms for analyzing and representing exaggerated gestures, but some problems remained because it was only an initial approach. In this paper, we attempted to develop our proposed model to resolve these problems. In the section below, we set out an overview of the exaggerated-gesture model suggested so far, and its drawbacks. We follow this with our proposal for a new analytical model designed to solve these problems by taking into account the overall effect on the human body. Finally, we summarize some typical experiments and their results.

2 Definition of Gesture Analytic Model

In previous studies of human gesture, social psychological approaches, which generate many observations and subjective evaluations, have usually been adopted. However, although this approach can give a general picture, it does not allow for a precise numerical evaluation of the role of gesture. We therefore focused on special gestures that are frequently used in human communication, and preceded with research to analyze their effects quantitatively. In general, human gesture can be expressed using a skeletal structure that follows a hierarchical link model, such as that shown in Fig. 1.

2.1 Mathematical Analysis of Gestures

Use of the skeletal hierarchical structure shown in Fig. 1 makes it possible to quantitatively define reproducible gestures in terms of the rotational angles around the x, y, and z axes (local coordinate system) of each joint. This method is termed *kinematics* and has hitherto been used chiefly in the field of robotics. Once we define the structure of a human as in Fig. 1, any gesture can be expressed using the following dynamical Eq. 1. In this equation, θ is each joint's rotational angle as a time-series data set such as $[\theta_1, \theta_2, \ldots \theta_n]$, M is the *inertia matrix*, C is the *Coriolis force*, g is the *gravity* term. Further, θ' and θ'' represent the *angular velocity* and *angular acceleration* of each joint respectively.

$$\tau = M(\theta)\theta'' + C(\theta, \theta')\theta' + g(\theta) \tag{1}$$

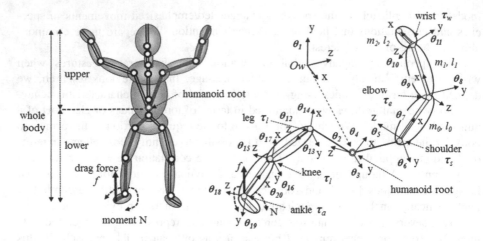

Fig. 1. Hierarchical skeletal model and definition of links

Using this dynamical equation, we can express the relationship between gestures expressed by θ and the torque variation τ of each joint. This equation is a general formula for the dynamical model, and torque τ can be calculated by using the following *Lagrange function L* [2, 8].

$$Q_i = \frac{d}{dt}\left(\frac{\partial L}{\partial \theta'_i}\right) - \frac{\partial L}{\partial \theta_i} \qquad \text{where i } = 0 \sim \text{n} \qquad (2)$$

In this equation, Q_i is the equation of motion, specifically the *Lagrange equation*, and for rotational force, Q_i represents the torque value. We can quantitatively analyze the basic mechanism of the enhancement or exaggeration of characteristic gestures using Eq. 2 [2]. In our previous studies, to simplify the problem, we focused chiefly on movement of the upper body while making these special gestures. For the purposes of the generalization of our proposed method, we then extended our analysis to the entire body, including all links from wrist to ankle, via the humanoid root shown in Fig. 1. Generally, humans have to support their upper body and balance their motion using their legs, so it is necessary to consider all the links from foot to hand, shown as solid colored links in Fig. 1, to be able to precisely analyze gestures that are made by the entire body [9]. The feet also need to be regarded as external forces, such as drag and friction forces f and N, from the floor.

$$\tau = J(\theta_i)^T \begin{pmatrix} f \\ N \end{pmatrix} \qquad (3)$$

In Eq. 3, f is the drag force acting on the feet, and N represents the moment around the legs. Furthermore, J is the *Jacobian matrix* for θ_i in the general coordinate system. The above equation is the general formula for numerical analysis of extended gestures.

In the following sections, we attempt to parse exaggerated gestures for the whole body using these definitions.

2.2 Target of Our Studies

In this section, we summarize our approach to these problems and the solutions we arrived at. As we have mentioned, in our previous studies it was not possible to analyze gestures while considering their effect on the entire human body and that of other influences such as external forces. The main targets of our studies are as follows.

1. As our newly proposed analysis model of the characteristic gestures, we will extend our original mathematical model to develop a dynamical analysis model that includes the whole body and takes into account all external forces [8].
2. Secondly, we plan to improve the accuracy of identification of the transition point between an ordinary gesture and an exaggerated gesture. This is the most important problem to solve in conventional gesture analysis.

For these two issues and objectives, we devised new strategies and carried out the following verifications.

3 Approach and Experiments

With respect to the first target, listed in Sect. 2.2, we carried out the following experiments to verify our hypothesis. The basic idea is that when reproducing a gesture, we need to take into account all external forces, such as f and N, which will be acting on the links from the hands to the feet. This calculation will be executed using Eq. 3 of the previous section. Regarding the second target, we examined the changes in the joints' torque to be able to precisely determine any enhancement or exaggeration of motion and thus identify the transition point between an ordinary motion and an exaggerated gesture. We named this method the *non-continuous search method*. We will describe the experimental results in more detail in the following sections.

3.1 A Precise Model that Takes into Account the Influence of the Whole Body

In our preliminary experiments, we collected about a hundred characteristic gestures made using the whole body, and classified them into five groups, in a way that resembles the proposal for comparison with our proposed method [2]. Figure 2 shows a typical analysis result for joint torque changes. In this figure, (a) shows the exaggerated gestures in a group of Japanese comedy actions, and (b) the upper graph shows the torque changes, but taking into account only the upper body. The lower graph shows body torque that takes into consideration the entire body, that is, with all external forces calculated using Eq. 3. In this typical example, $\tau 7$ indicates the twisting torque of the elbow joint, and $\tau 9$ shows the twisting torque of the shoulder joint.

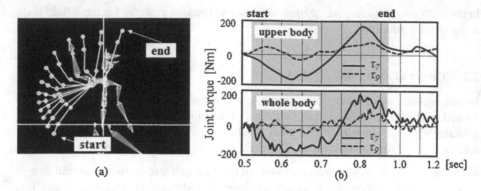

Fig. 2. Comparison of joint torque taking whole body into account (right hand)

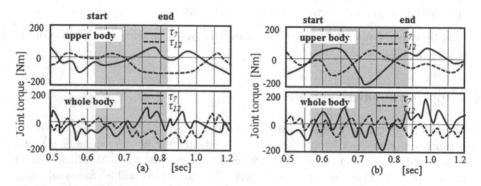

Fig. 3. Comparison of joint torque taking into account the whole body (a) Disney animation and (b) impassioned speech

The entire body needs to be supported with both legs, so we have to take into account the torque due to torsion and drag from the floor. These results reflect the high-frequency component that was applied to the torque due to torsion of the main joints. On the other hand, the changes in the extrapolation of torque curves (low frequency) are maintained.

These patterns were replicated in all the other five gesture groups (fifty-two gestures in all), which we used in our experiments. More analysis results are shown in Fig. 3, in which (a) shows gesture exaggerations which are often used in Disney animations, and (b) shows gestures which are used during impassioned speech. In these figures, the regions marked in gray indicate the torque change of gestures, with $\tau 12$ indicating the twisting torque of the right leg joint. From these experimental results, it is possible to quantify the degree of emphasis in terms of the torque change in the twist direction of the main joints when taking into account the whole body, similarly to our conventional approach.

3.2   Improving the Accuracy of Gesture Analysis

Next, we examined the potential for improving the accuracy of identification when there was a transition between ordinary motion and the exaggerated part of characteristic gestures. In the previous section, we showed that exaggerated gestures could be quantitatively evaluated by their torque value, as could changes that were generated at the main joints like the gray regions in Figs. 2 and 3. Moreover, we thought that the start and end points of exaggerated gestures could be accurately determined using the following method. The key point noted in our proposed model was that a "preparation" or "follow-through" motion was added just before or after the main part of the gesture [2]. When qualitatively described, these motions correspond to the concept of an "undershoot" or "overshoot," just before or after the main motion, in the variation of the torque curve.

The challenge here is to identify a method of accurately defining the start and end positions of the exaggerated motion. Our response to this problem was to focus on the synchronicity of verbal information, represented by voice intensity, with the exaggerated gestures. We named this method the *non-continuous search method*. The results of our preliminary experiments showed some human motions to be closely and synchronously correlated with voice intensity. The experimental results of monitoring the relationship between major torque variations and the voice variation of typical exaggerated gestures are shown in Fig. 4. The upper graph shows the changes in torque of the elbow, shoulder, and wrist joints respectively, and the lower graph shows the variation in sound data with which they are mutually synchronized. These data show the results for exaggerated gestures during an impassioned address by a famous public speaker. In the following section, we would like to show an example of a new mobile application environment that takes advantage of these methods.

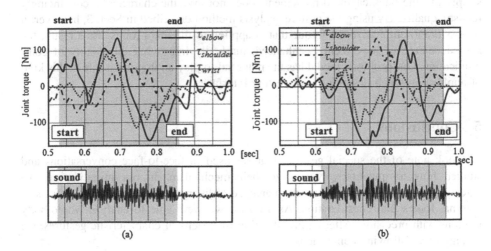

Fig. 4. Typical examples of exaggerated gesture torque (upper) and speech (lower)

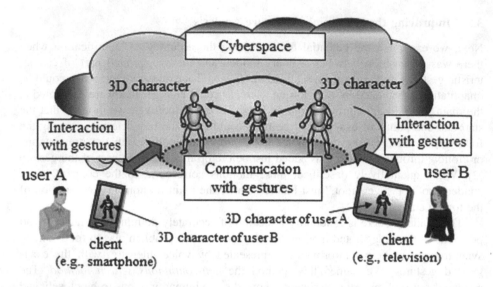

Fig. 5. Overview of mobile communication using 3D characters with realistic gestures

4   Application Using Gestures in Cyberspace

A new mobile communication system which uses 3D characters who make realistic gestures is shown in Fig. 5. Assisted by the 3D character of her or his agent, we are able to engage in natural interactions with multiple other users in 3D over cyberspace. To improve the quality of this communication via 3D characters, it is necessary to reproduce the reality of the appearance and expression of actual gestures. Some user gestures can be captured in real time using cameras on mobile devices. However, simply playing back captured movements does not give the characters a convincingly realistic quality. By using the gesture analysis method described in Sect. 3, however, it is possible to emphasize the torque that is applied to the main joints. As a result, the realistic nature of movement is enhanced, markedly improving the quality of communication. Our proposed model has the potential to play an important role in this kind of application when designing user-gesture interfaces.

5   Conclusions

We took note of the special gestures that are used in face-to-face conversations and studied how to quantitatively analyze their mechanism. In our investigation, we extended our conventional approach to analyze ordinary gestures, taking the effects of external forces into consideration. As a result, we were able to analyze whole-body motions with precision. After an investigation of dozens of characteristic gestures, we obtained the following conclusions.

1. The degree of exaggeration of human motion can be quantified by the total value and the extent of changes in torque value that are acting on the major joints of the

skeletal structure. By taking into consideration, during the calculation, the external forces and moments acting on both feet, it is possible to determine the torque of the main twisting components of joints with a high degree of precision. Generally, the more a speaker wants to emphasize his or her message, the greater the additional changes in rate of torque and torque value applied to the joints.

2. Just before or after the exaggerated or emphasized motion, there is a pattern of addition of "preparation" or "follow-through" motions. Each gesture can be quantified as an "undershoot" or "overshoot" value of torque. Furthermore, there is a high correlation of 0.87 between an exaggerated gesture and simultaneous volume of speech, making it possible to accurately identify and measure the start and end of exaggeration of a main motion.

Using these results makes it possible to quantitatively analyze gesture interactive mechanisms, making this technique widely applicable to processes such as the design of new interactive user interfaces using anthropomorphic agents.

References

1. Mehrabian, A.: Silent Messages: Implicit Communication of Emotions and Attitudes, 2nd edn. Wadsworth, Belmont (1981)
2. Naka, T., Ishida, T.: Proposal of the effective method of generating characteristic gestures in nonverbal communication. HCI **2**, 102–112 (2014)
3. Uno, Y., Kawato, M., Suzuki, R.: Formation and control of optimal trajectory in human multijoint arm movement-minimum torque-change model. Biol. Cybern. **61**, 89–101 (1989)
4. Putnam, C.: Sequential motions of body segments in striking and throwing skills: descriptions and explanations. J. Biomech. **26**(1), 125–135 (1993)
5. Badler, N., Allbeck, J., Zhao, L., Byun, M.: Representing and parameterizing agent behavior. In: Proceedings of Computer Animation, pp. 133–143. IEEE Computer Society (2002)
6. Kanda, T., Miyashita, T., Osada, T., Haikawa, Y., Ishiguro, H.: Analysis of humanoid appearances in human-robot interaction. IEEE Trans. Rob. **24**(3), 725–735 (2008)
7. Cassell, J., Pelachaud, C., Badler, N., Steedman, M., Achorn, B., Becket, T., Douville, B., Prevost, S., Stone, M.: Animated conversation: rule-based generation of facial expression, gesture and spoken intonation for multiple conversational agents. In: ACM SIGGRAPH (1994)
8. Mochizuki, Y., Inokuchi, S., Omura, K.: Generating artificially mastered motions for an upper limb in baseball pitching from several objective functions. IEEE Trans. Syst. Man Cybern. B Cybern. **30**(3), 373–382 (2000)
9. Kudoh, S., Komura, T., Ikeuchi, K.: Stepping motion for a human-like character to maintain balance against large perturbations. In: IEEE International Conference on Robotics and Automation (2006)

Collection and Classification of Gestures from People with Severe Motor Dysfunction for Developing Modular Gesture Interface

Ikushi Yoda[1(✉)], Kazuyuki Itoh[2], and Tsuyoshi Nakayama[2]

[1] National Institute of Advanced Industrial Science and Technology (AIST),
Tsukuba, Japan
i-yoda@aist.go.jp
[2] Research Institute, National Rehabilitation Center for Persons with Disabilities
(NRCD), Tokorozawa, Japan
{itoh-kazuyuki-0923,nakayama-tsuyoshi}@rehab.go.jp

Abstract. This study explores gesture controlled user interfaces for people with severe motor function disabilities stemming from cerebral palsy, quadriplegia, and traumatic brain injury. As a result of their disabilities (involuntary movement and spasticity), it is nearly impossible for these individuals to use conventional interface switches and other input devices to access and use a computer. The ultimate objective of this work is to provide these users with user-friendly, cost-effective gesture controlled interfaces that will enable them to comfortably operate a personal computer. We have now succeeded in developing a non-contact, non-restraining interface based on an off-the-shelf image range sensor that recently became available. In addition, we surveyed a large number of disabled subjects and compiled a fairly exhaustive collection of gestures that these users are capable of making, and classified these voluntary movements in terms of the body part involved. Finally, a series of recognition modules have been developed that are optimized to recognize the gestures associated with each body part (hand, head, leg, etc.). This paper provides an overview of the gesture data collection and classification processes, and discusses the development of the recognition modules.

Keywords: Gesture interface · Gesture recognition · Alternative input device · Persons with motor dysfunction

1 Introduction

There is a significant number of people who, due to disabilities of one kind or another, are unable to send and receive email or surf the web using a computer. More specifically, we refer to individuals with severe motor function disabilities who find it difficult or impossible to use conventional input devices due to spastic or involuntary motion, or limited range of motion or muscular weakness in the lower limbs. Currently, no convenient interface exists, and those who are stuck using the increasingly limited specially customized switch type interface find it extremely cumbersome to use for operating a computer [8]. Especially for those who are unable to freely venture

© Springer International Publishing Switzerland 2015
M. Antona and C. Stephanidis (Eds.): UAHCI 2015, Part II, LNCS 9176, pp. 58–68, 2015.
DOI: 10.1007/978-3-319-20681-3_6

outdoors, an environment that allows them to exchange email, surf the web, make online purchases, and other net-based activities really holds the key to a more enjoyable, fulfilling life. Yet for the disabled who are only able to use a simple switch type input device, these more sophisticated operations are all but impossible, not to mention the enormous costs involved in adapting these devices to the user's evolving disability or condition as the user gets older. The information gap will only continue to widen as the information society evolves and the disabled are left further behind.

The goal of this research is to develop a robust gesture controlled user interface that makes it relatively simple to operate a computer (including character input) for the motor function disabled who are uncomfortable or unable to use a keyboard or a mouse. Specifically, we developed a non-contact, non-restraining interface based on a common off-the-shelf range image sensor that provides a cost-effective interface within the budget of almost everyone. Most importantly, the technology must be customizable so it can be readily tailored to the various stages and conditions of the disabled population at low cost. This we achieved by surveying and collecting the widest possible range of movements that might be exploited as gestures, categorizing the movements based on part of the body, and developing modular recognition engines that recognize and identify the movements.

In pursuing work on a gesture controlled interface for IT purposes that involves enormous freedom of movement yet is very difficult to standardize, our objective is to focus first on the most severely disabled where the need is greatest and move toward a standardized gesture interface in the future that is both versatile and essential for categorizing the full range of movements that can serve as gestures.

This paper details our efforts to collect and classify gestures obtained from people with severe motor function disabilities, then develop a basic prototype recognition module capable of recognizing and identifying the gestures.

As part of an earlier project to aid people with severe disabilities, the authors developed a head gesture interface system for individuals with severe cerebral palsy who are unable to operate a wheelchair [1]. The project exploited high-end technology to finally give handicapped users for whom no input devices had been available with an interface they could actually use. This was a groundbreaking development for it brought together intelligence information experts with expertise in cutting-edge intelligence research in collaboration with rehabilitation experts. While this involved state-of-the-art technology, it had to be implemented within the framework of the practical equipment used within the disabled community. So, in terms of actual clinical practice, we gave highest priority to:

- Carefully consulting and listening to the views of patients themselves and their families from the very beginning and every step of the way all through the development.
- Mounting sensors near the joystick, and otherwise conforming to the actual settings of typical electric wheelchairs.
- Ensuring operability indoors or outdoors, in direct sunlight and under tree cover.
- Autonomous self-reliant operation once the caregiver turns the switch.

The work was carried out with these realistic objectives in mind. As a result, the project gave users the ability to move about safely and autonomously within pubic parks.

Yet two major hurdles remained. First, the unique stereo vision sensor hardware that we developed for generating range images in real time is simply too expensive (cost could be brought down if mass produced, but initial justification for mass production is problematic), and second, it is too costly to tailor the device to accommodate the full range of symptoms and conditions of the disabled population.

At least for indoor use, the first challenge has now been resolved with the availability of several off-the-shelf range image sensors featuring active pattern projection—Xtion PRO [9], Xtion PRO LIVE [10], KINECT for Windows [11], Leap Motion [12], and others—that can be readily obtained by virtually anyone at a modest cost of around 200US$. We are now starting to see accurate consumer-oriented devices on the market that work just fine over relatively short distances when not exposed to direct sunlight. If we could come up with a solution to the second challenge of tailoring the system to different user conditions, we could provide the viable interface that is so earnestly sought by the disabled community. For indoor environments at least, the only remaining barrier was to figure out how to adapt the technology to various individual conditions and disabilities.

This motivated the authors to develop an image range sensor-based cerebral palsy interface [3] for disabled who are unable to use the common input devices (aside from a caregiver or other familiar attendant or friend who can interpret some spastic movement or a particular bodily movement). Based on the notion of "harmony between man and machine," we devised an agile scheme over a one-year allotted time frame tailored for a particular subject, a man disabled with typical cerebral palsy who was unable to use conventional input devices. The interface mainly involved finger movements, supported by gyrations of the neck and opening and closing the mouth.

In a similar vein, the authors exploited Microsoft's Kinect sensor in developing observation and access with Kinect (OAK) [4] as a solution for assisting the activities of the severely disabled. The idea was to enable disabled users to directly or more intuitively operate a computer by combining our scheme with software developed using the Kinect software development kit (SDK) for Windows. Note that this project was primarily intended for the children of disabled parents, and was never really intended as a scheme for organizing and classifying adaptable gestures for the disabled community as a whole. We would also note that this scheme is based on libraries of existing games, which raises a fundamental problem: if you haven't previously captured the person from the front, then there is no corresponding library in the first place. Finally there is the problem that this device does not work without a particular type of sensor.

For the purposes of this work, we assume that all of the modules for recognizing gestures could be implemented using any of the stereo vision (range image)-based human sensing technologies available including real-time gesture recognition systems [5], shape extraction based on 3D information [6], data extraction based on long-term stereo range images [7], and so on. We also assume that exchanging or swapping out the range sensor should not affect the usability of interface. Our ultimate objective is automatic adaptation of the system to the widest applicable range of parts of the body that might be used to make gestures and long-term shifts in how users make gestures.

2 Collecting and Classifying Subject Data

Collecting Subject Data. Using the range image sensor, we recorded voluntary gestures for the interface from a range of disabled participants affiliated with the National Rehabilitation Center for Persons with Disabilities and a number of other agencies and organizations that deal with disabled individuals in the community. The participants had a range of different disabilities including:

- Children and adults with cerebral palsy (Spastic, athetoid, mixed types).
- Spinocerebellar degeneration, Parkinson's disease, and other neurodegenerative conditions.
- Muscular dystrophy and other muscular disorders.
- Survivors of traumatic brain injury (wounds, injury, stroke).
- Quadriplegics exhibiting spastic or involuntary motion due to genetic factors, syndromes, or unknown causes.
- High quadriplegics.

All of these subjects exhibited spasticity, spastic involuntary movement, or were quadriplegics with severe motor function disabilities. Even though they might have the ability to voluntarily move some part of the body, all subjects had severe motor function disabilities and were extremely limited in the body parts they could move voluntarily; they were significantly hindered by spasms and involuntary movements, and all found it extremely difficult to use existing switch type or other input devices. With this group of severely handicapped quadriplegics and other disabled individuals, we used the range image sensor to collect the full range of gestures they thought they might be able to use.

For these subjects who have great difficulty using an ordinary keyboard or mouse, the following parts of the body showed promise for making gestures that could be used for input:

- Hand and arm (arm, elbow, forearm, hand, finger).
- Shoulder.
- Head (motion of entire head, sticking out/retracting the tongue, eye movement).
- Leg movement (exaggerated movement of the foot or leg).

We collected a wide range of gestures from these four basic regions of the body over an eighteen month period using 33 subjects, while carefully consulting and listening to the views of the disabled users themselves and their caretakers. Counting gestures that could be made using multiple sites or regions of the body, we assembled gestures produced by a total of 104 parts or combinations of body features.

We obtained the consent of the subjects to undertake this work after explaining the nature of this project and had the approval of the Ergonomic Experimental Committee of the National Institute of Advanced Industrial Science and Technology and the Ethical Review Committee of the National Rehabilitation Center for Persons with Disabilities.

Classification of Gestures for Each Part of the Body. 3D movements collected from the disabled subjects are systematized as they are classified, assuming that they can be

Table 1. Classifications of gestures

Hand	Move 1 finger		15
	Move wrist		12
	Move hand		13
Shoulder			6
	Up/down	5	
	Forward/backward	1	
Head	Move entire head		17
	Stick out/retract tongue		1
	Eyes		15
	Blinking	10	
	Movement of eyes	3	
	Open eyes wide	2	
Legs	Point foot from ankle		3
	Move one leg from knee down		1
	Extend/retract knee		1
Other	Currently unclassified		12
	Total body sites		104
	Total sites including alternative forms		112

recognized from the range images. By systemization, we mean essentially the same kind of motion, a gesture classification that can be recognized by a recognition module that serves as a base. In other words, we assume that a module can be created that can recognize gestures for each and every region of the body based on the data that was collected. With this approach, since we are focusing on the operation of a computer in a quiet indoor environment with no movement [2], assuming that high-resolution range images are available, the body region of interest can be captured with excellent accuracy without having to use an advanced object model or image features that require significant computational resources. The results are shown in Table 1.

Based on the data collected from the 33 subjects in this project, we classified 3 areas of the body for hand, 3 areas for head, 1 area for shoulder, and 3 areas for the legs. The camera is set up in such a way that is doesn't disturb the subjects and is ideally located to recognize gestures, so the classification is done on the assumption that gestures can be recognized with a single model.

Only 33 subjects were recruited for the study, but we shot the same subject several times on different days to increase the number of regions or parts of the body that were filmed. We found that by reshooting the same subject on different dates, we were able to capture a number of different variations or alternative forms. This proved to be invaluable data for assessing day-to-day variation in the movement of the subjects. Counting these variations, we came up with a total of 112 gesture sites including the alternative forms, as shown in Table 1.

3 Recognition Modules for Different Parts of the Body

In order to recognize or identify the gesture movements that have been assembled so far, a series of prototype recognition modules was developed on the assumption that a single module can accommodate multiple subjects by manually tweaking parameters and other adjustments.

Finger Gesture Recognition Module. For finger gesture recognition, we adopted the following specifications to determine whether a single finger was bent or not and to apply a colored finger cot (single finger of a colored glove).

- Determine if a finger is bent or not.
- Apply finger cot to any 1 of 5 fingers.
- Select red, green, or blue finger cot (choose color that contrasts with clothing).

The prototype implemented for this project is built with recognition parameters set for a particular user, but as one can see from the screenshot shown in Fig. 1, the parameters can be manually tuned for a different user (eventually, this feature will be automated so day-to-day fluctuations are handled automatically).

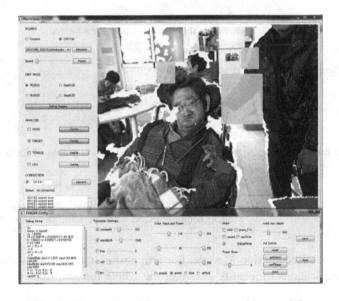

Fig. 1. Screenshot of finger gesture recognition module

The parameters that can be manually adjusted are listed in Table 2.

The recognition algorithm first detects a finger in the specified range space, then extracts a hand based on the position of the finger, and finally calculates the degree the finger is bent from the relationship between finger and hand. Basic steps of the algorithm are as follows:

Detect a finger

- Set 3D space that includes hand
- Extract 3D texture image
- Extract same color as the finger cot from texture image
- Label range of extraction
- Finger is recognized as portion marked by maximum label

Detect a hand

- Extract skin colored region from 3D extracted texture image adjacent to the finger
- Label range of extraction
- Object closest to the finger is recognized as the hand

Determine degree finger is bent

- Calculate moment of finger and hand. Calculate point group for both finger and hand as a 3D moment. Since facing the screen, next, calculate 2D screen
- Calculate 2 axes angle from the moment
- Calculate difference between angles of finger and hand; determine finger is bent when difference exceeds the threshold

Table 2. Parameters that can be manually adjusted

Setting	Description
Parameter settings	Feature to be recognized
• min-depth	Min range image setting
• max-depth	Max range image setting
• hue	Hue
• bright	Brightness
Hue hand and finger	Specify min and max saturation values of hand
	Specify color of finger cot
Finger base	Threshold for determining finger is bent
Check	Specify action to take when finger is bent
	(click; sound is made when pressing the 'a' key)

Arm Gesture Recognition Module. For arm gesture recognition, we adopted the following specifications to identify swinging the whole forearm from the elbow (see Fig. 2).

- Determine if forearm of one hand is swinging
- Set up camera so the arm to be recognized fits easily within the angle of view

Basic steps of the algorithm are set forth as follows:

Detect arm

- Set 3D space that includes arm
- Extract arm range image against 3D base

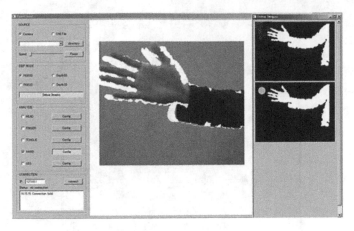

Fig. 2. Screenshot of arm gesture recognition module

Track arm

- Track with particle filter
- Determine likelihood of particle from inter-frame difference
- Now possible to track moving body part (the arm)

Determine swing of arm

- Estimate state of the arm from length of shifts on sway of center of gravity of set of particles
- Classify based on "exaggerated swinging of the arm" and "no movement"

4 Head Gesture Recognition Module

For head gesture recognition, first the normal direction is derived from the range image area centering on the nose, then this orientation is used as the orientation for the face. The user can employ any motion or movement he or she wants to trigger the switch.

- Estimate direction of face in real time
- Operate as switch when setup is oriented toward the face in a particular direction
- Facing to the right generates a click event

The light blue bar near the eyebrow of the subject in Fig. 3 shows the normal direction of the face. By changing the normal direction for turning on the switch, this can be used to describe an action.

The sequence of algorithm steps for estimating head orientation is as follows: face tracking, nose tracking, then calculate the normal area of the face.

Head tracking

- Calculate approximate area of head based on distance information
- Extract just face label using labeling

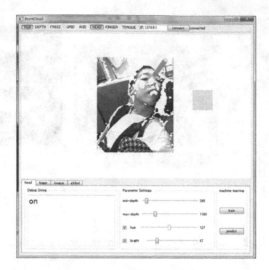

Fig. 3. Screenshot of head pose recognition module

Nose tracking

- Normalize zoomed, rotated, positioned extracted face image
- Nose is closest point to the camera

Calculate normal area of face

- Calculate face normalization (orientation) from the range image area centering on the nose.

Tongue Gesture Recognition Module. For tongue gesture recognition, we simply determine whether the subject is sticking out her tongue deliberately or not; the switch is turned on when the tongue remains out for more than a certain number of seconds. Moreover, the user can assign any motion or movement to trigger the switch. Currently, in setting the color threshold to match the color of individual's tongue and lighting environment, the individual and the lighting environment are highly dependent.

Tongue Gesture Recognition Algorithm

- As with the head recognition algorithm, this algorithm also starts by tracking the face
- Convert RGB information to HSV information in the face label
- Perform filtering based on the tongue hue threshold setting
- Tongue is recognized when the label exceeds a certain size

Knee Gesture Recognition Module. The finger, head, and tongue gestures can all be recognized simultaneously by camera settings, but the camera is set up differently to recognize knee gestures. For recording knee gestures, an extension arm is used to mount the camera up above the display looking down so the knees are caught at the center of the image (see Fig. 4)

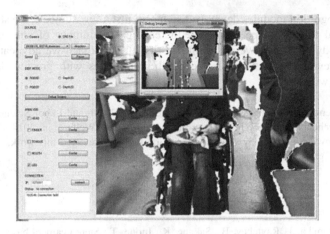

Fig. 4. Screenshot of knee gesture recognition module

- Estimate position of knees in real time
- Switch is triggered by moving the knees together or closing the knees

Basic steps of the knee position estimation algorithm essentially consist of first extracting the knee region, then estimating the knee position on the left and right sides with the hill-climbing method. This particular user defined the act of holding both knees together beyond a certain interval as triggering the switch.

5 Conclusions and Future Work

We began this project with the idea of developing gesture controlled user interfaces to enable people with disabilities to freely access and use information devices using simple gestures. To achieve this goal, the first stage is to compile and classify a collection of 3D actions or gestures that disabled users are capable of making using an economical off-the-shelf image range sensor. In this work, we gathered gesture data from 33 subjects, based on 104 different sites or parts of the body. We systematically categorized this data in terms of 10 total parts of the body that disabled users can employ to make voluntary movements that could be exploited as gestures: 3 areas of the body for hand, 3 areas for head, 1 area for shoulder, and 3 areas for the legs.

In addition, we constructed a series of prototype recognition modules and demonstrated their ability to recognize 5 types of movement among these 10 parts of the body: hands and arms (finger bending and arm waving), head (head swinging and sticking out and retracting the tongue), and legs (opening and closing the knees). Parameters are adjusted manually on the prototype modules, but ultimately we assume such adjustments will be done automatically to easily accommodate a wide range of disabled users.

For this current project we dealt with 33 subjects and 104 parts of the body, but a somewhat larger scale initiative involving around 50 subjects is needed to build a more robust modular gesture recognition platform that we envision. Since we have only tested the recognition modules developed so far on just a few subjects, we still have not gotten beyond the prototype stage. By increasing the number of subjects and the number of body part sites, we are confident that the approach we advocate here will lead to the development of gesture recognition modules with greater classification accuracy and wider scope.

Acknowledgment. Part of this work was supported by a Health and Labor Sciences Research Grants: Comprehensive Research on Disability Health and Welfare in 2014. The authors gratefully acknowledge the many who have supported and encouraged this work.

References

1. Yoda, I., Tanaka, J., Raytchev, B., Sakaue, K., Inoue, T.: Stereo camera based non-contact non-constraining head gesture interface for electric wheelchairs. In: Proceedings of International Conference of Pattern Recognition ICPR 2006, vol. 4, pp. 740–745 (2006)
2. Tanikawa, T., Yoda, I., et al.: Home environment models for comfortable and independent living of people with disabilities. J. Hum. Life Eng. **12**(1), 23–27 (2011) (in Japanese)
3. Yoda, I., Nakayama, T., Ito, K.: Development of Interface for Cerebral Palsy Patient by Image Range Sensor. Grant Program Report of Tateishi Science and Technology Foundation, vol. 22, pp. 122–125 (2013) (in Japanese)
4. Iwabuchi, M., Guang, Y., Nakamura, K.: Computer vision for severe and multiple disabilities to interact the world. ITE Tech. Rep. **37**(12), 47–50 (2013) (in Japanese)
5. Monekosso, D., Remagnino, D., Kuno, Y.: Intelligent environments: methods, algorithms and applications. In: Yoda, I., Sakaue, K. (eds.) Ubiquitous Stereo Vision for Human Sensing, Chapter 6. Advanced Information and Knowledge Processing, pp. 91–107. Springer, London (2009)
6. Hosotani, D., Yoda, D., Sakaue, K.: Wheelchair recognition by using stereo vision and histogram of oriented gradients, in real environments. In: IEEE Workshop on Applications of Computer Vision 2009, pp. 498–503 (2009)
7. Sato, N., Yoda, I., Inoue, T.: Shoulder gesture interface for operating electric wheelchair. In: IEEE International Workshop on Human-Computer Interaction in Conjunction with ICCV 2009, pp. 2048–2055 (2009)
8. Survey on persons with physical disability 2006, Department of Health and Welfare for Persons with Disabilities, Social Welfare and War Victims' Relief Bureau, MHLW (2006)
9. http://www.asus.com/Multimedia/Xtion_PRO/
10. http://www.asus.com/Multimedia/Xtion_PRO_LIVE/
11. http://www.microsoft.com/en-us/kinectforwindows/
12. http://www.softkinetic.com/

Touch-Based and Haptic Interaction

Reading Comprehension Issues and Individuals with Visual Impairments: The Effects of Using 8-dot and 6-dot Braille Code Through a Braille Display

Vassilios Argyropoulos[1(✉)], Aineias Martos[1,2], Georgios Sideridis[3],
Georgios Kouroupetroglou[2], Magda Nikolaraizi[1],
and Maria Papazafiri[1]

[1] Department of Special Education, University of Thessaly, Volos, Greece
vassargi@uth.gr
[2] Department of Informatics and Telecommunications,
National and Kapodistrian University of Athens, Athens, Greece
koupe@di.uoa.gr
[3] Boston Children's Hospital, Harvard Medical School, Boston, MA, USA
Georgios.sideridis@childrens.harvard.edu

Abstract. The purpose of the present study was to evaluate the effects of 6-dot and 8-dot braille code on the reading comprehension ability of individuals with severe visual impairments and/or blindness when the latter receive typographic meta-data (bold and italic) by touch through a braille display. Also, patterns of hand movements were investigated and related to issues of comprehension. The most important finding related to the superiority of the 8-dot braille code in predicting reading comprehension in individuals with severe visual impairments. It was also found that reading comprehension was particularly predicted from the negative relationship between participants' fluency and comprehension. It was conjectured that all comparisons between conditions were significant suggesting that the present findings were likely robust and not reflective of idiosyncrasies in the sample. The focus of the discussion was placed on the importance of conducting additional research increasing the sample size with more extensive training for those who will constitute the extended sample.

Keywords: Typographic meta-data · 6-dot braille · 8-dot braille · Braille display · Blindness · Patterns of hand movements · Linear regression

1 Introduction

Nowadays children with visual impairments have the opportunity to use various media for accessing information. The preference of the medium usually depends on teachers' instruction and students' comprehension [1]. For example, using synthetic speech is no-time consuming procedure but does not lead to deep comprehension of a text [2]. On the other hand, it seems that when individuals with visual impairments read by touch (i.e. through print braille or through refreshable braille display) they end up with better

© Springer International Publishing Switzerland 2015
M. Antona and C. Stephanidis (Eds.): UAHCI 2015, Part II, LNCS 9176, pp. 71–81, 2015.
DOI: 10.1007/978-3-319-20681-3_7

comprehension rates in conjunction with lower reading rates [3]. It is also worth mentioning that blind people's hands motions when reading braille by touch have been considered as a critical parameter in braille reading and comprehension [4, 5] The main research aim of the present study focuses on issues of reading comprehension, when users with blindness receive typographic meta-data (bold and italic) by touch through a braille display. This type of information (meta-data or meta-information) is the information that sighted readers get from documents at their typographic layer (such as, type, size, etc.) or/and font style such as bold, italics, underline [6]. In addition, levels of reading comprehension were investigated towards the 6-dot and the 8-dot braille code through a braille display.

The purpose of the present study was to evaluate the effects of the medium, that is, 6-dot and 8-dot braille codes on the reading comprehension ability of individuals with severe visual impairments and/or blindness. Specifically, the present study was designed to answer the following Research Questions (R.Q.).

R.Q.1. Are there differences in reading comprehension as a function of using 6-dot and 8-dot braille code of reading?
R.Q.2. Is fluency of bold and italic elements differentially predictive of reading comprehension using 6-dot and 8-dot braille code of reading?
R.Q.3. How is hand movement related to each of the two experimental conditions, the 6-dot and the 8-dot braille code of reading?

All research objectives refer to typographic meta-data and specifically to bold and italic. The reason of choosing these specific typographic signals is their frequency of use in Greek print materials [7].

2 Method

2.1 Participants

Participants were twenty individuals with severe visual impairments participated in a series of experiments using braille displays. All participants knew to read and write braille, had no other additional disabilities and their age range was from 19 to 44 years (mean = 31.35, SD = 3.57).

2.2 The Research Design

The participants were asked to read from a braille display different scripts within which meta-information was included (i.e. bold and italic). The scripts were divided into two categories. The first one consisted of texts in which bold and italic were rendered by the 8-dot braille code, and the second one consisted of an equivalent number of texts rendered by the 6-dot braille code. The rendition of meta-information "bold" and "italic" in the 8-dot and 6-dot braille codes was based on the results of the study which was conducted by Argyropoulos et al. [3]. In specific, when the meta-information in the first category of scripts was in bold then it was rendered by raised pins 7 and 8 constantly, whereas when these pins were raised intermittently (i.e. at the first, middle and last letters of a word or phrase) then the meta-information was meant to be in italic. For the rendition of "bold" and "italic" in the 6-dot braille code, the researchers used the tags which are specified by the Nemeth code with slight modifications because dots 4 and 6 constitutes the indicator for capitals in the 6-dot Greek Braille code [3]. The selected texts were aligned with all facets of the reading process (such as word length, content, level of difficulty). In turn, the participants were asked to answer comprehension questions without any time limit. The experimental procedure was video-recorded because it was the only way to describe with accuracy all participants' hand movements on the braille display when they were reading in 6-dot and the 8-dot braille code respectively.

All participants were invited to read aloud every single script and mention all the meta-information (bold and italic) they met. In total, each of the twenty participants was invited to read through a braille display four expository texts (two texts through 6-dot braille code and two other equivalent texts in the 8-dot braille code) and then they were asked to answer five comprehension questions for each text. The answers to these questions were based on the key-words or key-phrases which were rendered in bold or in italic (in each text there were three typographic meta-information in bold and three typographic meta-information in italic). All participants were given appropriate time to familiarize themselves with the use of a braille display. Also, all experiments were conducted with the same braille display and a training period preceded the experimental procedure to assure that all participants had the same baseline regarding renderings for bold and italic by a braille display.

2.3   Measures

Reading fluency comprises three basic constituents: the first one refers to accurate reading; the second one to the reading rate, and the last one to the appropriate prosody or expression of the reading process [8]. Hence, the authors in order to fully describe the reading fluency had to take into account the previous three constituents. Because the participants of the study were individuals with severe visual impairments it was conjectured that the element of the prosody could not be taken into account due to the lack of the holistic "view" of the text [9]. In other words, automatic decoding [10] which leads to appropriate prosody seems to be very hard for individuals with severe visual impairments because it has been reported that *"Fluent readers are better at seeing a word in a single eye fixation and do not need as many refixations or regressions"* (p. 702) [8]. Hence, reading fluency in the present work was determined by (a) rate or reading overall time, and (b) accuracy. The quantification of accuracy was defined in terms of the participants' recognition or identification of the typographic meta-data (bold and italic) within the four texts when using 6-dot braille and 8-dot braille respectively. In total, there were 12 typographic meta-information in italic and 12 typographic meta-information in bold. All correct identifications were scored with "1" while all incorrect identifications were scored with "0" (lowest score: 0 & highest score: 24). Also, it was decided to quantify reading rate in terms of the length of time that it would take for each participant to read a text (LTR – Length Time Reading).

Comprehension was measured through five comprehension questions corresponded to each text. The researchers constructed questions according to the three types of reading comprehension questions taxonomy of Pearson and Johnson [11]. All correct responses were scored with "1" while all incorrect responses were scored with "0". The scores that participants could achieve for all texts were from 0 up to 20.

2.4   Data Analysis

For the first research question, and in order to evaluate differences between 6- and 8-dot codes of reading, a paired samples t-test was employed. Power for Student's t-statistic was equal to 80 % for a two-tailed test using an alpha level of 5 % and a large effect size (equal to .8 of a standard deviation) [12]. The above configuration was associated with a pair of observations equal to n = 16. Thus, the current sample size would suffice to inferentially evaluate effects (Fig. 1).

With regard to the second research question, the critical value of the F-distribution for a linear regression model was equal to 4.279 units, for power levels equal to 80 %, an alpha level equal to 55 and a large effect size defined with a semi-partial correlation f^2 equal to 0.35. For this configuration, the required sample size equaled 25 participants, so the current analysis was slightly underpowered with the present sample size of n = 20 (see Fig. 2). Thus, the regression model was likely conservative and reflective of potential Type-II errors. For that reasons, evaluations using effect size metrics would be implemented over and above the inferential statistical findings.

For the third research question and in order to describe in detail the participants' hand movements when reading the texts by touch, a hand movement pattern was adopted [13]. According to this pattern six main characteristics of blind persons' hand movements may be determined when they read braille: (a) Scrubbing (Sc), involves the motion that the finger makes when it moves up and down over a braille character, (b) Regression (R), involves motions such when the finger(s) is/are moving back across the page to reread or check something, (c) Searching (Se), when the hands are looking for information but without reading, (d) Pausing (P), when the hand rests on the page, (e) Erratic movements (EM), when the movements include all type of motions except

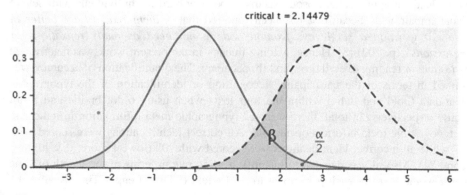

Fig. 1. Power estimates for a paired samples t-test as a function of an alpha level of 5 %

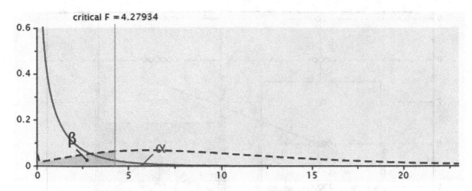

Fig. 2. Power curve for the linear regression model with one predictor

reading, and (f) Normal Braille Reading (NBR), when fluid movements take place on the paper by the user's hands.

2.5 Results

The results are presented as answers per research question and are shown below:

R.Q.1. Are there differences in reading comprehension as a function of using 6-dot and 8-dot braille code of reading?

Results using a paired samples t-test indicated that there were significant differences between the two conditions [$t(19) = 3.222$, $p = .0045$], with reading comprehension being favored in the 8-dot braille code (see Fig. 3). The mean in reading comprehension was equal to 6.0 units in the 6-dot braille code (C.I.$_{95\%}$ = 5.182-6.818) compared to 7.45 in the 8-dot braille code (C.I.$_{95\%}$ = 6.730-8.170). Inspection of the confidence intervals suggests that it is very unlikely that this difference is due to chance.

R.Q.2. Is fluency of bold and italic elements differentially predictive of reading comprehension using 6-dot and 8-dot braille code of reading?

A linear regression analysis model was fit to the data to predict reading comprehension from the ratio of time and accuracy (i.e., fluency). Results are shown graphically in Figs. 4 and 5. With regard to the bold elements the coefficient of determination was equal to 14.6 % for the overall sample, suggesting a medium effect size [12]. The respective regression equation was equal to $y = 8.1099 + -4.3748\ x$. The omnibus findings, when split to the two experimental conditions were associated with predictions equal to 5.9 % for the 6-dot condition and 4.9 % for the 8-dot condition, none of which reflecting an effect size that would approach meaningful estimates. Figure 4 shows the scatterplot and predicted regression lines for each experimental condition. The parallel lines are suggestive of approximately equal predictions and the sign of the fact that fluency was a negative predictor of reading comprehension.

For the italic elements, the findings were significantly more pronounced with the overall prediction being associated with an R-square equal to 16.8 %, exceeding a medium effect size per Cohen [12]. The prediction in the 6-dot condition was equal to

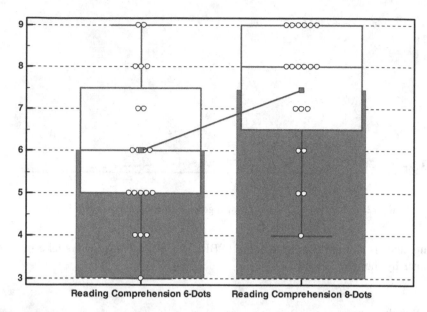

Fig. 3. Differences in reading comprehension between 6-dot and 8-dot conditions. The solid line indicates differences at the mean level and the boxed lines interquartile ranges.

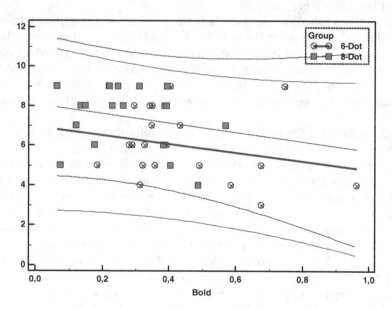

Fig. 4. Fitted regression lines for the prediction of reading comprehension from fluency of the bold elements in the 6-dot and 8-dot braille code.

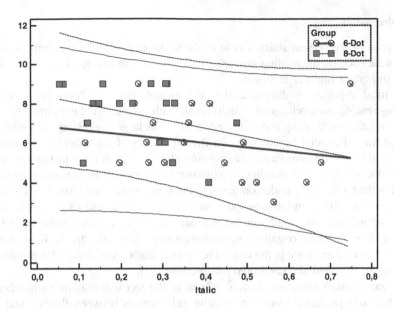

Fig. 5. Fitted regression lines for the prediction of reading comprehension from fluency of the italic elements in the 6-dot and 8-dot braille code.

Table 1. Braille Code and Hand Movements

	R	R-Sc	Sc	NBR
6-dot				
	142	37	10	50
8-dot				
	138	58	5	35

Note: R = Regression, R-Sc = Combined Regression & Scrubbing, S = Scrubbing, NBR = Normal Braille Reading

4.9 % but for the 8-dot condition equal to 10.6 %, suggesting a significant differentiation between the two conditions. This significantly more salient relationship in the 8-dot condition, paired with the significance differences in level between the levels of fluency in the two conditions (see Appendix A) is partly responsible for the higher achievement of reading comprehension in the 8-dot condition.

R.Q.3. How is hand movement related to each of the two experimental conditions, the 6-dot and the 8-dot braille code of reading?

For the type of the participants' hand movement, the findings indicated that more fluid movements took place when they used the 6-dot braille code (50NBR) compared to the 8-dot braille code (35NBR). Also it is worth noting that the pattern of regression was found to be more frequent under the 8-dot condition (138R & 58R-Sc) compared to the 6-dot condition (142R & 37R-Sc). Table 1 describes the type of the participants' hand movement according to Write, Wormsley and Kamei-Hannan study [13].

2.6 Discussion

The purpose of the present study was to evaluate the effects of the medium, 6-dot and 8-dot braille code on the reading ability of individuals with severe visual impairments. Several important findings emerged.

The most important finding related to the superiority of the 8-dot braille code in predicting reading comprehension in individuals with severe visual impairments. Albeit having a relative small sample size, the effect size was large suggesting the presence of robust findings. Potential explanations for the superiority of the 8-dot braille code may be related to issues of sensitivity and exposure to haptic stimuli since tactile movements on the 8-dot cell was more dominating compared to the 6-dot braille (more regression patterns in the 8-dot braille code compared to the 6-dot braille code, see Table 1) and as a result participants' attention was more intense in the first case (R.Q.1 & R.Q.3). It may be argued that this condition led the participants to a more elaborating tactile process enhancing their cognitive operations using more effectively their working memory. Working memory is the cognitive system that is responsible for holding and processing of new and already stored information [14].

The second most important finding related to the fact that reading comprehension was particularly predicted from the negative relationship between fluency and comprehension (R.Q.2). In the literature, the relationship between reading fluency and reading comprehension has been largely positive with some exceptions in which negative effects have also been documented. As Paris and Paris [15] noted, the relationship between fluency and comprehension for low achievers is expected to be positive as the prerequisite skill of decoding reading units is important to comprehend text. In other words, there can be no comprehension if words cannot be meaningfully read. In fact Paris and Paris [15] went one step further to posit that at low levels of reading accuracy (floor levels) this relationship is spuriously high there is a high degree of non-independence between decoding and other reading-related variables (e.g., vocabulary, prior knowledge, passage genre and test format-see Paris & Paris, 2001).

However, for higher ability individuals this relationship has been challenged as fluency is not even considered a necessary and prerequisite condition of reading comprehension as both fast rates and slower rates are associated with high reading ability. The fact that the relationship between fluency and reading comprehension was negative for the present high achieving group agrees with the findings from previous studies with again high achievers [16, 17]. In the present study point estimates of decoding were high, suggesting that the present sample was comprised of high decoders (e.g., point estimates of 5.0 with maximum values of 6.0). The fact that the relationship between high decoding ability and reading comprehension is negative largely explains the superiority of the 8-dot braille code as the levels of fluency were lower within this condition compared to the 6-dot braille code under evaluation.

The present study is limited for several reasons. First, sample size was relatively small and potentially some of the findings could be reflective of Type-II errors as large error variances could potentially mask true effects. However, in the present study, all comparisons between conditions were significant suggesting that the present findings were likely robust and not reflective of idiosyncrasies in the sample.

In the future it will be important to take the present methodology large scale. That is, implement the newly developed 8-dot braille code to a larger sample and with more extensive training so that issues of familiarity and automaticity would be more prevalent. That will allow for a more full evaluation of the pros and cons of the 8-dot braille code and its effects on reading and comprehension.

Acknowledgements. This research has been co-financed by the European Union (European Social Fund – ESF) and Greek national funds through the Operational Program "Education and Lifelong Learning" of the National Strategic Reference Framework (NSRF) under the Research Funding Project: "THALIS-University of Macedonia- KAIKOS: Audio and Tactile Access to Knowledge for Individuals with Visual Impairments", MIS 380442.

Appendix A

Box-plots with mean values showing differences in level between rates of accuracy (i.e., fluency) using the bold elements (upper panel) and italic elements (lower panel). All differences exceeded conventional levels of significance at p < .05.

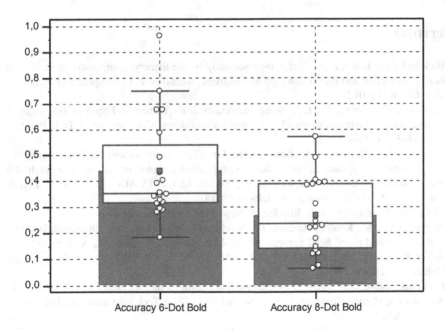

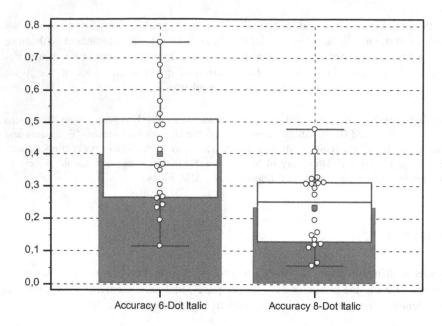

References

1. Bickford, J.O., Falco, R.A.: Technology for early braille literacy: comparison of traditional braille instruction and instruction with an electronic notetaker. J. Vis. Impairment Blindness **106**, 679–693 (2012)
2. Edmonds, C.J., Pring, L.: Generating inferences from written and spoken language: A comparison of children with visual impairment and children with sight. Br., J. Dev. Psychol. **24**, 337–351 (2006)
3. Argyropoulos, V., Martos, A., Kouroupetroglou, G., Chamonikolaou, S., Nikolaraizi, M.: An experimental approach in conceptualizing typographic signals of documents by eight-dot and six-dot braille code. In: Stephanidis, C., Antona, M. (eds.) UAHCI 2014, Part II. LNCS, vol. 8514, pp. 83–92. Springer, Heidelberg (2014)
4. Millar, S.: Reading by touch. Routledge, New York (1997)
5. Argyropoulos, V., Kouroupetroglou, G., Martos, A., Nikolaraizi, M., Chamonikolaou, S.: Patterns of blind users' hand movements. In: Miesenberger, K., Fels, D., Archambault, D., Peňáz, P., Zagler, W. (eds.) ICCHP 2014, Part I. LNCS, vol. 8547, pp. 77–84. Springer, Heidelberg (2014)
6. Kouroupetroglou, G., Tsonos, D.: Multimodal accessibility of documents. In: Pinder, S. (ed.) Advances in Human-Computer Interaction, pp. 451–470. I-Tech Education and Publishing, Vienna (2008)
7. Fourli-Kartsouni, Florendia, Slavakis, Kostas, Kouroupetroglou, Georgios, Theodoridis, Sergios: A Bayesian Network Approach to Semantic Labelling of Text Formatting in XML Corpora of Documents. In: Stephanidis, Constantine (ed.) HCI 2007. LNCS, vol. 4556, pp. 299–308. Springer, Heidelberg (2007)
8. Hudson, R.F., Lane, H.B., Pullen, P.C.: Reading fluency assessment and instruction: what, why and how? International Reading Association, pp.702–714 (2005) doi:10.1598/RT.58.8.1

9. Heller, M.A.: Picture perception and spatial cognition in visually impaired people. In: Heller, M., Ballesteros, S. (eds.) Touch and Blindness, pp. 49–71. Lawrence Erlbaum Associates, New Jersey (2006)

10. Torgesen, J.K.: Computers and cognition in reading: a focus on decoding fluency. Except. Child. **53**, 157–162 (1986)

11. Pearson, P.D., Johnson, D.: Teaching reading comprehension. Holt, New York (1978)

12. Cohen, J.: A power primer. Psychol. Bull. **112**, 155–159 (1992)

13. Wright, T., Wormsley, D.P., Kamei-Hannan, C.: Hand movements and braille reading efficiency: data from the alphabetic braille and contracted braille study. J. Vis. Impairment Blindness **103**, 649–661 (2009)

14. Cohen, H., Scherzer, P., Viau, R., Voss, P., Lepore, F.: Working memory for braille is shaped by experience. Communicative Integr. Biol. **4**, 227–229 (2011)

15. Paris, S.G., Paris, A.H.: Classroom applications of research on self-regulated learning. Educ. Psychol. **36**, 89–101 (2001)

16. Fujita, K., Yamashita, J.: The relations and comparisons between reading comprehension and reading rate of Japanese high school EFL learners. Reading Matrix **14**, 34–49 (2014)

17. Smith, J.L., Cummings, K.D., Nese, J.F.T., Alonzo, J., Fien, H., Baker, S.K.: The relation of word reading fluency initial level and gains with reading outcomes. Sch. Psychol. Rev. **43**, 30–40 (2014)

Making Blind People Autonomous in the Exploration of Tactile Models: A Feasibility Study

Francesco Buonamici, Rocco Furferi[✉], Lapo Governi,
and Yary Volpe

Department of Industrial Engineering of Florence, University of Florence (Italy),
Via Di Santa Marta 3, 50139 Florence, Italy
{francesco.buonamici,rocco.furferi,lapo.governi,yary.
volpe}@unifi.it

Abstract. Blind people are typically excluded from equal access to the world's visual culture, thus being often unable to achieve concrete benefits of art education and enjoyment. This is particularly true when dealing with paintings due to their bi-dimensional nature impossible to be explored using the sense of touch. This may be partially overcome by translating paintings into tactile bas-reliefs. However, evidence from recent studies suggests that the mere tactile exploration is often not sufficient to fully understand and enjoy bas-reliefs. The integration of different sensorial stimuli proves to dramatically enrich the haptic exploration. Moreover, granting blind people the possibility of autonomously accessing and enjoying pictorial works of art, is undoubtedly a good strategy to enrich their exploration. Accordingly, the main aim of the present work is to assess the feasibility of a new system consisting of a physical bas-relief, a vision system tracking the blind user's hands during "exploration" and an audio system providing verbal descriptions. The study, supported by preliminary tests, demonstrates the effectiveness of such an approach capable to transform a frustrating, bewildering and negative experience (i.e. the mere tactile exploration) into one that is liberating, fulfilling, stimulating and fun.

Keywords: Cultural heritage · Blind people · Hand tracking · Human-computer interaction

1 Introduction

Promoting, protecting and ensuring the full and equal enjoyment of all human rights and fundamental freedoms by all persons with disabilities is a worldwide high priority issue. Enjoying the Cultural Heritage makes no exception! This is particularly true for blind people (BP) since they are inevitably disadvantaged in enjoying artworks usually created for sighted people. In fact, for BP, the accessibility to cultural or artistic areas is affected not only by mobility impairment but rather by the inability to sense the artworks themselves. Moreover, when dealing with paintings, the inherently bi-dimensional structure of such artworks considerably complicates the experience of BP, practically excluding them in enjoying such kind of art.

© Springer International Publishing Switzerland 2015
M. Antona and C. Stephanidis (Eds.): UAHCI 2015, Part II, LNCS 9176, pp. 82–93, 2015.
DOI: 10.1007/978-3-319-20681-3_8

This may be partially overcome by translating paintings into 3D models i.e. into tactile bas-reliefs to be explored by using the sense of touch. Not coincidentally, renowned institutions such as the Omero Tactile Museum (Bologna), the Art Institute of Chicago and the Tactile Gallery at the Welcome Gallery of London, created a collection of famous paintings translated in the form bas-relief-like representations, oriented to the aesthetic education of blind people.

Unfortunately, the manufacture of tactile bas-reliefs is a complex task and, to date, entails the work of appositely trained artists (sculptors), thereby drastically increasing the cost and reducing both the production rate and the total number of available reproductions. With the aim of speeding up the manufacture of tactile bas-reliefs, in recent years a number of significant studies have been carried out making use of Computer-Aided techniques dealing with bas-relief reconstruction from images [1–3].

Authors themselves, recently, introduced a number of Computer Aided techniques for semi-automatic translation of paintings appositely devised to improve blind people's accessibility to bi-dimensional artworks [4–8]. The developed methodology, integrating perspective-based scene reconstruction with shape from shading-based shape retrieval, allows the virtual bas-relief reconstruction that can be converted into a physical tactile model possibly by means of Rapid Prototyping techniques (see Fig. 1).

Even though the scientific literature is moving towards the development of high quality 3D models from paintings, evidence from recent studies performed with blind people accessing this kind of reproductions suggests that the mere tactile exploration is often not sufficient to fully understand and enjoy them; therefore blind and visually impaired people often require to be specifically (though briefly) trained and assisted by a sighted accompanying person [9, 10] (see Fig. 2a). This is often perceived as a limitation for the blind who increasingly demand for autonomous accessibility to the world of cultural heritage.

From this point of view, the use of a hand-tracking system able to determine which area of the bas-relief is touched and to provide a real-time verbal description and/or other kinds of audio feedback could dramatically improve the blind people understanding and enjoyment during un-assisted exploration of artworks.

Fig. 1. From painting ("Madonna with Child and Angels" by Niccolò Gerini di Pietro, Villa La Quiete, Firenze, Italy) to bas-relief using the semiautomatic procedure developed by the authors.

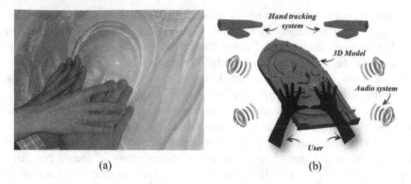

Fig. 2. (a) Typical exploration of artworks where skilled persons guide the hands of blind people [11] – (b) Conceptual framework of the exploration performed by the supposed system.

Accordingly, the main aim of the present work is to assess the feasibility of a new system consisting of a physical bas-relief (obtained using for instance authors' 3D modeling approach), a vision system tracking the blind user's hands during "exploration" and an audio system providing verbal descriptions (see Fig. 2b).

Such a novel system requires at least (1) a 3D acquisition device + software package to track the user hands; (2) a number of algorithms capable of detecting the position of the bas-relief in the same reference frame defined by the acquisition sensor; (3) a number of algorithms aiming at detecting the position and the distance of the user hand/finger with respect to the model; (4) the complete knowledge of the digital 3D bas-relief model and (5) an appropriate verbal description linked to relevant objects/subjects in the scene. As a consequence, the definition of a system capable of assisting BP in autonomous exploration of a bas-relief should take into account relevant issues such as hand tracking, point cloud registration and distance evaluation between user's fingertip and bas-relief model.

2 Background

Since, as mentioned in the introductory section (and deeply investigated in the Sect. 3), the proposed system encompass a number of methods for hand tracking, point cloud registration and distance evaluation, a brief reminder of the current state of the art related to these issues is provided below.

2.1 Hand Tracking

The term "hand tracking" encloses a number of techniques of the "human motion capture" family sharing with them the common purpose of locating the position of a human hand. This area of study offers massive possibilities to applications in the field of human-computer interaction [16], for example gestural interfaces to improve easiness of use of computer systems, or to interact with virtual environments, as in [17, 19, 20].

Furthermore, hand tracking techniques are widely implemented to help impaired people with everyday life in multiple situations [18, 21, 22].

The problem of tracking a human hand is tackled in literature through different approaches, which distinguish themselves by the hardware or the algorithm used. Wearable devices, visual markers, electromechanical sensors and actuators are some examples of the hardware used in various strategies.

The focus of the present work is on vision-based techniques, using an optic sensor observing the scene in order to get the data required to perform the tracking. In fact they allow maximum haptic sensitivity and gestural freedom to the user (essential requisite for BP).

Vision-based techniques can be classified into appearance - and model-based approaches [16, 23].

Appearance-based methods typically establish a mapping from a set of image features to a discrete, finite set of hand model configurations [12]. Such methods, as described in [18, 24], are computationally efficient and "well suited for problems such as hand posture recognition where a small set of known target hand configurations needs to be recognized. Conversely, such methods are less suited for problems that require an accurate estimation of the pose of freely performing hands" [12].

Model-based approaches [12, 24] use a digital model of a hand to simulate and estimate the position of the user hand in the observed scene. This is usually performed by solving an optimization problem whose objective function measures the discrepancy between the visual cues that are expected due to a model hypothesis and the actual ones. Even if these methods require costly algorithms (and accordingly the achievement of satisfying frame rate values during tracking is reached only by means of high-end computer hardware) they prove to be effective for a more refined estimation of hand position. Consequently, in this work model-based methods are investigated with particular reference to the model proposed by [12] and further developed in [25–27]. In such a model, 3D data provided by a Microsoft Kinect® are used to isolate the user hand in 2D and 3D by means of a skin color detection followed by depth segmentation. The hand model (palm and five fingers) is described by geometric primitives and parametrized encoding 26-DOF (i.e. is represented by 27 parameters). The optimization procedure is carried out by means of a Particle Swarm Optimization technique [13]. The procedure contemplates temporal continuity of subsequent frames, searching for a solution in the neighborhood of the one found for the last frame analyzed. Some examples of the results obtained with this method are shown in Fig. 3.

2.2 Point Cloud Registration

Point cloud registration techniques aim at minimizing the distance between two given sets of points usually by performing a rigid roto-traslation.

According to [28], where a review of the most relevant registration methods is provided, two distinct consequent phases are usually carried out: coarse registration and fine registration.

Coarse registration performs a rough estimation of the alignment between the two point clouds. Typically, this is achieved through iteration algorithms aiming at

Fig. 3. Snapshots from a hand tracking sequence from [12], the hand model in the hypothesized solution is placed upon the real hand RGB image taken by Kinect® (Color figure online).

matching common features in the two point clouds in order to obtain a set of correspondences. A number of algorithms can be used to perform the coarse registration: Point Signature, Spin Image, RANSAC-based (RANdom SAmple Consensus), PCA (Principal Component Analysis) and genetic algorithms [28]. As described in the next section, in the present work coarse registration is performed by means of an appositely devised interactive procedure based on the hand tracking system.

Fine registration performs a more accurate solution by using the coarse registration as an initial guess. In recent years, some methods have been presented in scientific literature: (a) iterative closest point (ICP); (b) Chen's method; (c) signed distance fields; and (d) genetic algorithms, among others [28].

Devised by Besl & McKay [29], the ICP method minimizes the distance between point-correspondences (i.e. closest points). Let A and B be the two point sets to be aligned; for each of the N_A points a_i belonging to the point cloud A the closest point b_i in the point cloud B is found using nearest neighbor search techniques (see Sect. 2.3). Using a mean squared error cost function (see Eq. 1) the combination of rotation (matrix R) and translation (vector t) that best align each point a_i to its match found in B is then computed.

$$f = \frac{1}{N_A} \sum_{i=1}^{N_A} \left\| \vec{a}_i - (R \cdot \vec{b}_i + t) \right\|^2 \tag{1}$$

This process is iterated, using the new set of point A rotated and translated according to R and t, until a convergence criterion is satisfied.

Differently from ICP approach, Chen's method uses point-to-plane distance in the optimization (rather than point-to-point distance). Distance-to-plane evaluation is more laborious, but the algorithm is more robust to local minima and less sensible in the presence of non-overlapping regions [28] thus allowing to obtain better results. As described in Sect. 3, in the present work fine registration is performed by implementing both methods.

2.3   Distance Evaluation

One of the more known methods to evaluate a distance between two 3D points is the Nearest Neighbor algorithm, an optimization problem for finding closest (or most similar) points. Among the huge number of methods proposed in literature, the most frequently used and reliable one is the so called "KD Tree" [14]. This approach relies upon an efficient organization of the data set; a tree-like structure is built to organize points in a k-dimensional space thus allowing to quickly computing the "nearest neighbor" of a given point.

In particular, KD Tree performs recursive binary partitions of the dataset (tree structure), creating regions circumscribed by K-dimensional hyper-planes. In a 3D tree the planes are usually created following the axis directions, allowing for particularly convenient computation of the distances. The points are, therefore, enclosed in well-defined regions that are usefully mapped to avoid redundancy in the computation of the nearest neighbor.

3 Feasibility Analysis

In this section the development of the prototypal system, sketched in Fig. 2a, is discussed. The main effort has been to build a first working prototype (although rudimentary) of the system to help BP in enjoying artworks. The effectiveness of the prototype would demonstrate the feasibility of such a system to be, once improved, installed in museums in the next future.

For developing the feasibility study, as already mentioned, the starting point consists of a high resolution digital 3D bas-relief and its physical counterpart. By a way of example, in the following description the tactile reproduction of the "Madonna with Child and Angels" of Niccolò Gerini di Pietro (in exposition at "Villa la Quiete", Firenze, Italy) is used to explain the overall process (see Fig. 1). The digital model, created using the approach described in [8], has a resolution of about 0.17 mm per pixel (depending on the resolution of the acquired image); the physical prototype is sized approximately 87 mm × 47 mm x 9 mm.

Let, accordingly, assume that the physical prototype (1) is conveniently arranged to a support allowing the user to easily touch it (e.g. bas-relief positioned at 0.8 m height and tilted by 20° with respect to the horizontal plane) and (2) the bas-relief falls inside a 3D acquisition device field of view.

With reference to the 3D acquisition device, in this feasibility analysis a Microsoft Kinect® is chosen as preferred hardware. As widely known, such a device consists of a projector-camera triangulation sensor able to obtain a streaming of 3D data of the observed scene with a maximum resolution of 1.3 mm per pixel inside an angular field of view of 57° horizontally and 43° vertically and through a range of approximately 0.7-6 m. The preferred frame rate used for the acquisition is in the range 15-20 fps. Frame rate is a key factor in hand tracking, and is indeed directly related to the quality of tracking achievable from the point of view of both stability and hand movement speed traceable by the method.

To track user's hand movement, the method proposed in [12] is adopted and the "Hand Tracking Library" proposed in [15] is used as a basis for implementing the proposed approach. This choice is motivated by the good performances obtained during introductory tests carried out by authors of the present paper. Such tests demonstrated both good overall performances (in terms of frame rate, accuracy and stability) and consistent results with reference to data available in literature.

Hand tracking is limited in this work, due to its conceptually nature, only to the right index fingertip; therefore, a custom algorithm to trace its position in the Kinect® reference system, based on the hand tracking library data, was implemented into MATLAB® environment. Moreover, to optimize hand tracking the 3D sensor has been placed at a distance of approximately 1 m from the hand, according to the suggestions provided in [12] and preliminary tests carried out by the authors.

Once the position of the user's finger is tracked in real time, it's necessary to know the position of the bas-relief relatively to the same reference system. This problem is tackled taking advantage of the Kinect®, using it as a 3D scanner to obtain, with a single placement, a 3D model of the bas-relief correctly referenced to the Kinect® reference frame system. This procedure allows the detection of the forefinger position with respect to the digital and physical models at the same time. This is a prime issue in order to identify what the user is touching and to provide the necessary information.

Unfortunately, Kinect® sensor provides low definition (LD) and highly noisy scans which are not optimal to be used in the subsequent phase where the contact between the user forefinger and the physical model needs to be precisely detected. For this reason the (available) high definition (HD) virtual model of the bas-relief is used in order to retrieve more accurate information. In other words, if on one side the LD model is useful to refer the physical prototype to the user finger (in the Kinect reference frame), the availability of the HD model is crucial for a better discrimination of the touched area. Moreover, since each significant area (e.g. the face of Virgin Mary in Fig. 4.(a) of the model has to be associated to a verbal description to be provided to the user, the HD model should be appropriately segmented. The 3D segmentation of the model, whose description falls outside the scope of the present paper, can be practically performed using dedicated software packages such as Rapidform® and the choice of the number of segments strictly depends on the information to be delivered to the user.

To refer the HD point cloud to the Kinect reference frame, a point cloud registration of the HD and LD models is required. Such a registration process, as mentioned in the previous section, is achieved in two steps: first, a coarse registration is carried out to roughly align HD and LD point clouds; then, a fine registration allows to properly refer the HD model to the reference frame.

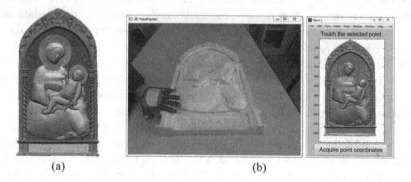

(a)   (b)

Fig. 4. (a) Segmented 3D digital model of the "Madonna with Child and Angels", by Niccolò Gerini di Pietro. – (b) GUI for coarse registration between the HD and LD models.

Coarse registration is performed using an interactive "custom-built" approach that takes advantage of the hand tracking system. The user is asked to touch with the tracked finger a number N (e.g. 6) of non-aligned areas on the physical bas-relief; the Nx3 matrix of coordinates C_{LD} locating the N finger-bas-relief contact points are then memorized.

Subsequently, using an appositely devised GUI, the user is required to select the HD model points roughly corresponding to the ones actually touched in the physical model. The result of this phase is to retrieve a matrix of coordinates C_{HD} describing the N points in the HD model (see Fig. 4b).

The general relationship between matrices C_{LD} and C_{HD} is described as follows:

$$C_{LD} = R * C_{HD} + t \tag{2}$$

To achieve the coarse registration, the rotational matrix R and translational vector t have to be evaluated from Eq. 2. This may be easily done using a SVD-based procedure [29, 31].

The coarse registration is used as an initial guess for the subsequent fine registration. In order to identify the best method (among the ones identified at the state of the art) to perform such a fine registration, a number of tests have been carried out implementing both the ICP and Chen's algorithms.

Despite according to literature Chen's method is usually most stable with respect to ICP one, the use of such algorithm to this specific application lead to unsatisfactory registration results. On the other hand, the ICP method turned out as the most reliable, although it proves to be less computationally efficient. Average time for convergence of ICP is in the range of 5−8 min with a RMS error between 2−3 mm; such an error value is comparable with the Kinect scan accuracy. On the basis of the above mentioned tests, the ICP method is used for fine registration. An example of final results obtained after the registration phase is depicted in Fig. 5.

Once the registration phase is performed, a real time computation of the distances between the user finger and the points of the HD model (correctly referenced in the Kinect frame system) is required. This step is carried out using the KD Tree algorithm into MATLAB® environment with increasing dataset dimension and increasing query

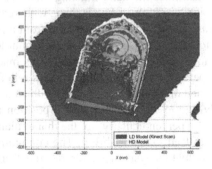

Fig. 5. LD and HD models of the "Madonna with Child and Angels" by Niccolò Gerini di Pietro after coarse and fine registration.

point number (this is made to forecast future implementations using information from multiple fingers touching the model at the same time). The results of the application of such an algorithm are compared, in terms of computational time, with other known methods such as N-D nearest point search [30] and brute force.

KD Tree proves to be the faster method, performing at about 0.02 s for a dataset comparable with the model dimensions and with a single query point. This means that the distance evaluation is performed with a 50 Hz frequency that is higher than the hand tracking fps acquisition (equal to maximum 20 fps). In evaluating the computational time it has to be noticed that the time required to create the tree-structure for performing the KD-tree algorithm is in an "offline" operation and, therefore, does not affect the real-time evaluation.

Finally, for every frame, the distance of the nearest neighbor to the query point (the right index fingertip) is compared to a threshold value (empirically set) that establishes the fulfillment of the touching condition. If the distance is smaller than the threshold, an algorithm searches for the segmented area in the 3D HD model corresponding to the actually touched region of the physical bas-relief. Since each segment is associated to a file containing the desired verbal description, this procedure allows the user to retrieve the information about the touched area.

The description provided above proves the feasibility from a technical point of view taking into account how to merge together all frameworks (hand tracking, registration, distance evaluation, etc.) to build an assistive system for BP. Obviously, in the hypothesis of a potential museum collocation of an improved system, the study of a possible final layout is required in order to maximize technical performances of the system together with accessibility and easiness for BP.

One of the most relevant parameters affecting the hand tracking performance is the sensor position; therefore, some tests are carried out to analyze the influence of the Kinect® position on the performance of the hand tracking algorithm, taking into account also the possible optical occlusions during the user-exploration phase. Prior to define the optimal position of the 3D sensor, it is necessary to decide the final disposition of the bas-relief to be explored by BP. To maximize the user ergonomics during tactile exploration (hypothetically placed into a museum environment), a preferred solution consists of positioning the bas-relief on a plane with a 45° inclination (with respect to the horizontal plane) and a height of approximately 1.2 m. As mentioned above, in order to maximize the hand tracking system performance, the sensor can be located in any point lying into a hemisphere with radius equal to 1 m (see Fig. 6a) centered in the bas-relief barycenter. Actually, from a practical point of view, this area can be reduced to a spherical sector with bevel equal to 60° (see Fig. 6b). In fact, this configuration allows reducing possible occlusions made by the user. On the basis of a series of tests performed using 4 different bas-reliefs, good hand tracking performance is obtained when the sensor is positioned with an angle β equal to 40° (see Fig. 6c). This is probably due to the fact that such a position allows the Kinect® to "observe" the hand mostly perpendicularly to the hand plane. Quite the reverse, positions with low β values lead to low stability. The configuration shown in Fig. 6c allows also to perform a virtual analysis of visible bas-relief areas. For each possible position described by varying angles α and β, the visible percentage of the bas-relief is

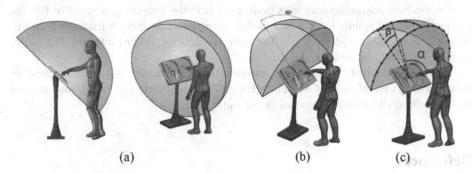

Fig. 6. Possible collocation surface of the sensor: (a) hemisphere with radius 1 m. (b) spherical sector with bevel of 60° (considering user-caused occlusions). – (c) α & β reference system for the collocation surface.

evaluated. The position with α = 0° and β = 50° results the best solution since it provides averagely for the 4 case studies analyzed a visibility equal to 86 %.

Considering the performance of the hand tracking system together with the visibility analysis, the ideal position for the sensor turns out to be the one with α = 0° and β = 40° corresponding to a visibility equal to 73 %.

4 Conclusion

In this work, the feasibility study of a new system consisting of a physical bas-relief, a vision system tracking the blind user's hands during "exploration" and an audio system providing verbal descriptions was provided. The hand tracking issue was tackled using the approach provided by [12], so that the position of the forefinger during the exploration of a tactile bas-relief is tracked in real time using Microsoft Kinect®. Then, the device was used as a 3D scanner to build a rough 3D model of the bas-relief correctly referenced to the Kinect reference frame system.

Since Kinect® sensor provides low definition and highly noisy scans which are not suitable to be used in the subsequent phase (where the contact between the forefinger and the model needs to be detected) the use of a high definition (HD) and less noisy virtual model was suggested. Being such a model already available as an outcome of author's previous works [8], an appositely devised procedure was used in order to register the HD model with the LD one.

Afterwards, using the KD Tree algorithm the region of the HD bas-relief nearest to the forefinger was determined so that the corresponding verbal description of the subject/object can be provided. Finally, the study of a possible final layout was performed in order to maximize technical performances of the system together with accessibility and easiness for BP.

Early tests demonstrated that the conceptual layout of the systems is quite sound even if a few limitations still subsist mainly due to the robustness of the tracking system which, from time to time, loses the target (hand) when it is moving too fast.

On the basis of preliminary tests performed with the support of a panel of BP, the proposed method results to be a first useful attempt to transform a frustrating, bewildering and negative experience (i.e. the mere tactile exploration) into one that is liberating, fulfilling, stimulating and fun.

Future work will be addressed to increase the performance and the robustness of hand tracking system (using for instance Kinect® 2.0 together) and to take into account multiple fingers touching the model at the same time.

References

1. Li, Z., Wang, S., Yu, J., Ma, K.L.: Restoration of brick and stone relief from single rubbing images. IEEE Trans. Vis. Comput. Graph. **18**(2), 177–187 (2012)
2. Reichinger, A., Maierhofer, S., Purgathofer, W.: High-quality tactile paintings. J. Comput. Cult. Heritage (JOCCH) **4**(2), 1–13 (2011)
3. Reichinger, A., Neumüller, M., Rist, F., Maierhofer, S., Purgathofer, W.: Computer-aided design of tactile models. In: Miesenberger, K., Karshmer, A., Penaz, P., Zagler, W. (eds.) ICCHP 2012, Part II. LNCS, vol. 7383, pp. 497–504. Springer, Heidelberg (2012)
4. Governi, L., Furferi, R., Volpe, Y., Puggelli, L., Vanni, N.: Tactile exploration of paintings: an interactive procedure for the reconstruction of 2.5D models. In: Proceeding of 2014 22nd Mediterranean Conference on Control and Automation (MED), Palermo, Italy (2014)
5. Volpe, Y., Furferi, R., Governi, L., Tennirelli, G.: Computer-based methodologies for semi-automatic 3D model generation from paintings. Int. J. Comput. Aided Eng. Technol. **6**(1), 88–112 (2014)
6. Governi, L., Furferi, R., Volpe, Y., Vanni, N.: Tactile 3D bas-relief from single-point perspective paintings: a computer based method. J. Inf. Comput. Sci. **11**(16), 1–14 (2014)
7. Governi, L., Carfagni, M., Furferi, R., Puggelli, L., Volpe, Y.: Digital bas-relief design: a novel shape from shading-based method. Comput.-Aided Des. Appl. **11**(2), 153–164 (2014)
8. Governi, L., Furferi, R., Volpe, Y., Carfagni, M., Puggelli, L., Vanni, N.: From 2D to 2.5D i.e. from painting to tactile model. Graph. Models **76**(6), 706–723 (2014)
9. Hayhoe, S.: An enquiry into passive and active exclusion from sensory aesthetics in museums and on the Web: two case studies of final year students at California school for the blind studying art works through galleries and on the web. Brit. J. Visual Impairment **32**(1), 44–58 (2014)
10. Hayhoe, S.: Arts, Culture and Blindness: Studies of Blind Students in the Visual Arts. Teneo Press, Youngstown (2008)
11. http://www.cavazza.it/sites/default/files/images/immagini_museo/fotoletturatattile1.jpg
12. Oikonomidis, I., Kyriazis, N., Argyros, A.A.: Efficient Model-Based 3d Tracking of Hand Articulations Using Kinect. BMVC, Dundee (2011)
13. Kennedy, J., Eberhart, R.: Particle Swarm Optimization. In: International Conference on Neural Networks, vol. 4, pp. 1942–1948. IEEE (1995)
14. Bentley, J.L.: Multidimensional binary search trees used for associative searching. Comm. ACM **18**(9), 509–517 (1975)
15. http://cvrlcode.ics.forth.gr/handtracking/
16. Pavlovic, V.I., Sharma, R., Huang, T.S.: Visual interpretation of hand gestures for human-computer interaction: A review. IEEE Trans. Pattern Anal. Mach. Intell. **19**(7), 677–695 (1997)

17. Malik, S., Laszlo, J.: Visual touchpad: A two-handed gestural input device. In: ICMI 2004 - Sixth International Conference on Multimodal Interfaces, pp. 289–296 (2004)
18. Imagawa, K., Lu, S., Igi, S.: Color-based hands tracking system for sign language recognition. In: Proceedings - 3rd IEEE International Conference on Automatic Face and Gesture Recognition, pp. 462–467 (1998)
19. Wang, R.Y., Paris, S., Popovic, J.: 6D hands: Markerless hand tracking for computer aided design.In: UIST 2011 - Proceedings of the 24th Annual ACM Symposium on User Interface Software and Technology, pp. 549–557 (2011)
20. Menelas, B., Hu, Y., Lahamy, H., Lichti, D.: Haptic and gesture-based interactions for manipulating geological datasets. In: Conference Proceedings - IEEE International Conference on Systems, Man and Cybernetics, pp. 2051–2055 (2011)
21. González-Ortega, D., Díaz-Pernas, F.J., Martínez-Zarzuela, M., Antón-Rodríguez, M.: A Kinect-based system for cognitive rehabilitation exercises monitoring. Comput. Methods Programs Biomed. 113(2), 620–631 (2014)
22. Boccanfuso, L., O'Kane, J.M.: CHARLIE: an adaptive robot design with hand and face tracking for use in autism therapy. Int. J. Soc. Robot. 3(4), 337–347 (2011)
23. Erol, A., Bebis, G., Nicolescu, M., Boyle, R.D., Twombly, X.: Vision-based hand pose estimation: a review. Comput. Vis. Image Underst. 108(1–2), 52–73 (2007)
24. De La Gorce, M., Paragios, N., Fleet, D.J.: Model-based Hand Tracking With Texture, Shading and Self-occlusions. In: CVPR, pp. 1–8, June 2008
25. Oikonomidis, I., Kyriazis, N., Argyros, A.A.: Markerless and efficient 26-DOF hand pose recovery. In: Kimmel, R., Klette, R., Sugimoto, A. (eds.) ACCV 2010, Part III. LNCS, vol. 6494, pp. 744–757. Springer, Heidelberg (2011)
26. Oikonomidis, I., Kyriazis, N., Argyros, A.A.: Full DOF tracking of a hand interacting with an object by modeling occlusions and physical constraints. In: ICCV, pp. 2088–2095, November 2011
27. Oikonomidis, I., Kyriazis, N., Argyros, A.A.: Tracking the articulated motion of two strongly interacting hands. In: Proceedings of IEEE Conference Computer Vision Pattern Recognition, pp. 1862 – 1869 (2012)
28. Salvi, J., Matabosch, C., Fofi, D., Forest, J.: A review of recent range image registration methods with accuracy evaluation. IVC 25, 578–596 (2007)
29. Besl, P., McKay, N.: A method for registration of 3-d shapes. IEEE Trans. Pattern Anal. Mach. Intell. 14(2), 239–256 (1992)
30. Barber, C.B., Dobkin, D.P., Huhdanpaa, H.T.: The Quickhull Algorithm for Convex Hulls. ACM Trans. Math. Softw. 22(4), 469–483 (1996)
31. http://nghiaho.com/?page_id=671

Finding Favorable Textures for Haptic Display

Hee Jae Hwang and Da Young Ju[✉]

School of Integrated Technology, Yonsei Institute of Convergence Technology,
Yonsei University, Incheon, Republic of Korea
{sit1219,dyju}@yonsei.ac.kr

Abstract. Haptic display is a powerful sensory medium to transfer information that gives a sense of haptic. We argue that giving haptic information positively affects only when the haptic makes a good impression. We examine the best materials that people feel pleasant to touch. Consequently, people prefer textures with uniform grain of brush, cotton clothes and silk. Throughout this paper, we propose a new approach to design of haptic display using tactile preference.

Keywords: Haptic display · Textures · Design for all methods · Emotional and affective interaction for universal access · User experience

1 Introduction

Recently, haptic technology is regarded as a strong medium that delivers the sense of emotion effectively to the users [1]. The existing research focus on the materialization of realistic haptic interaction. For example, TeslaTouch reproduces different textures using electro-vibration [2]. However, haptic technology is not advanced enough to represent every single texture.

This paper contains hypothesis, experiments, and conclusion of three-step research. The first introduces 'visual tactility' and shows the importance of the correspondence between two different sensory feedbacks. The next explores the conditions that make people dislike haptic display in depth. The last suggests some guidelines on prioritization of haptic display development. In conclusion, we suggest a new approach about haptic display based on these findings.

2 Correspondence Between Haptic and Visual Information

Since haptic display enables multimodal communication, some researchers have interest in the integrated sensory experiences. Looking at the surface, people can imagine the texture of the surface without touching it actually; this virtual texture is called 'Visual tactility' [3]. Previous works show that the visual tactility significantly affects the perceived tactility [4]. We hypothesize that user's satisfaction is related to the correspondence of visual and haptic information. Thus, we design a sequence of experiments to verify this.

M. Antona and C. Stephanidis (Eds.): UAHCI 2015, Part II, LNCS 9176, pp. 94–102, 2015.
DOI: 10.1007/978-3-319-20681-3_9

Table 1. Four type of the experimental conditions. (A and B be any source)

Condition	Haptic info.	Visual info.	Agreement
H	A		–
V		B	–
H + V	A	A	Agree
H-V	A	B	Disagree

Fig. 1. Sample materials for Exp.1 (from the left, Grass mat, E.V.A., Cork, Acryl, Rubber, Cotton, and Air cap).

2.1 Experiment

Feigyn et al. were interested in a training method using haptic and visual stimulus [8]. Therefore, they experimented to compare the performance of participants with either existent or nonexistent haptic and visual sources. Similarly, we measured the sensory and emotional responses of the participants so that we could verify how each conditions effect on user experience. There are four types of experimental conditions (Table 1). H and V are abbreviations of 'Haptic Source' and 'Visual Source'. We vary the existence of each sensory information. The 18 sample boxes contain haptic sources and visual sources of seven materials (Fig. 1). Although reconstructed texture might be slightly different from the original texture as Lee told [9], here we are assuming that reconstructed texture would be as precise as the original texture. We have 18 participants (twelve males and six females) whose ages range from 17 to 43 (average: 23.3) (Tables 2, 3).

Sensory Evaluation: Choe suggested these adjectives [5] to measure haptic senses. Sensory response is measured using Korean adjective pair evaluation (1-10 scale) using six aspects of haptic sense - roughness, hardness, dryness, coldness, stickiness, and thickness.

Emotional Evaluation: For emotion evaluation, the participants selected associated adjectives for the given experiences in the sensory evaluation. After, the adjectives were classified into positive, negative, and neutral groups. For example, 'pleasure', 'intimacy' and 'cozy' were classified in the positive group, while 'uncomfortable', 'dizzy', and 'nervous' were in the negative group. Some adjectives such as 'artificial' and 'slippery' were classed in the neutral group, because they do not give neither positive nor negative feelings. We compare the frequencies of the positive and the negative adjectives in order to objectify the emotional responses for the given condition.

Table 2. Result of emotional responses, the number of each adjective

Condition	Positive adj.	Neutral adj.	Negative adj.
H	25	9	12
V	28	9	14
H + V	38	12	14
H-V	14	13	14

Table 3. Result of emotional responses, the percentage of adjectives by the conditions

Condition		Positive adj. (%)	Negative adj. (%)
Haptic source	Exist	51.0	26.5
	Not Exist	54.9	27.5
Visual source	Exist	51.3	26.9
	Not Exist	54.3	26.1
Correspondence	Agree	59.3	21.9
	Disagree	48.6	29.0

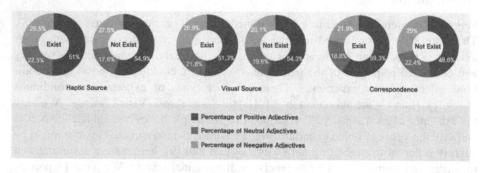

Fig. 2. The effect of existence and correspondence of haptic and visual information to the emotional response.

2.2 Results

The correlation between H and V is 0.06, between H and H + V is 0.63, and between V and H + V is 0.25. If two stimuli are given simultaneously, they both effect on the integrated tactile. When we compare H + V and H-V, H-V gives median of H and V scores. Although the haptic gives the larger effect, the visual information can easily mutate the integrated tactile. The mere existence of visual and haptic information have no positive effect on the emotional response. Resultantly, their correspondence is the unique factor to increase positive emotion (See Fig. 2).

Fig. 3. Image sources for Exp.2 (from the left, Air cap, blank, window, blurred air cap, and E.V.A.).

3 When Do People Dislike Haptic Display?

The first experiment shows that people sometimes dislike haptic display. Subsequently, we design following research that includes an experiment and discussion to figure out when people dislike haptic display.

3.1 Experiment

We examine whether the positive emotion is directly related to the user's satisfaction. Six participants (3 male and 3 females with average age 22 years) evaluated their emotional responses by marking points in the quadrant of two axes (likeness and naturalness) on -3-3 scales. We choose haptic sources as Air cap and E.V.A, which brought the most distinct and the haziest results in the first experiment. Glass, a general surface of devices is another haptic source. The visual sources are given as Fig. 3.

Afterwards, the participants answer to question about haptic display and the human factors based on their experiences.

3.2 Results

The emotional responses are categorized as 'agreement', 'neutral', and 'disagreement' groups. There are eight agreements, seven neutrals, and 15 disagreements. The naturalness condition is clearly distinct depend on the experimental conditions. The likeness condition has less distinction.

3.3 Interview

What they expect before manipulating haptic display? Imaging the Air cap, users expected round face (Visual), soft surface (Haptic), crisp sound (Auditory), tension and enjoyable feeling (Emotional), some changes after the burst (Interaction) in common. This implies the needs for multi-sensory communication.

What is that they feel about the discord between haptic and visual information? Among six participants, all of them agreed that the discord decreases the naturalness. Three participants mentioned that the discordance can disturb the understanding of the visual information. Three of them agreed that the disagreement brings unpleasant feelings. Two of them regarded that the texture is most important while the other participant regarded as expectation to be the most important.

When do people dislike haptic display? People expect to haptic display in visual, auditory, haptic, and interactive ways. Users' satisfaction decreases with their unfulfilled expectation. Users expect that visual and real tactility be well matched. Until and unless haptic and visual information correspond well, haptic device is better off without the haptic information. According to the first experiment, haptic information with discordance is disturbing rather than helping users to communicate. Even if visual and haptic information is well matched, users would hate the experience if the given texture is uncomfortable or unwanted.

4   Finding Favorable Textures

From the previous experiments with 32-participants, we observe that people do not satisfy with haptic display when expectation failed visually, auditory, haptic, and interactively (especially when there is discordance between haptic and visual feedback, and when the given texture is unwanted).

According to a clinical psychologist Anzieu, D. [6], touch is a basic primal sense and he defines the concept of the 'skin ego', which means that the skin is the psychological border that distinguishes oneself from others. Based on this theory, we can understand the phenomenon that people usually touch with their intimate people with affection. Unlike the other sensory communication, the users must directly contact their skin with the haptic display to feel the tactile sensation, thereby the preference for the texture is reflected with satisfaction for the haptic display. Accordingly, we explore which texture gives a positive feedback on users to make haptic display more attractive.

On-line Survey. Jani Heikkinen, T.O. et al. found that people expect familiar textures that we can easily find in the daily life in haptic communication [10]. Therefore, we conducted an on-line survey about the daily materials. Total 406 participants (210 males, 196 females, age: 41.7 years on average) answered to the question, "Please select from the list of all materials that provide positive feelings to you". This survey had been conducted for 15 days, while the nationalities of the participants are Korea, China, U.S.A., and Europe (Germany and France). They answered through the Internet, and we gave every participant the same choices. We referenced this survey result to choose the experimental materials, because the most likable materials globally supposed to be chosen.

Pre-experiment. We had to do pre-experiment to choose the representative texture and to examine the questionnaires. We asked ten people to rank the preference for twenty materials.

4.1   Experiment

We assert that asking the preference of individuals is valuable in the HCI field, because haptic experience is essential and subjective. Besides, we use AHP (Analytic Hierarchy Process), a tool that determines the importance of several factors using a matrix to order the materials used in this experiment [7], to objectify people's preferences. We selected

01	02	03	04	05	06	07	08	09	10

Silk	AirCap	Brush	Wood	Leather	Paper	Cotton Fabric	Sand	Cotton	Felt

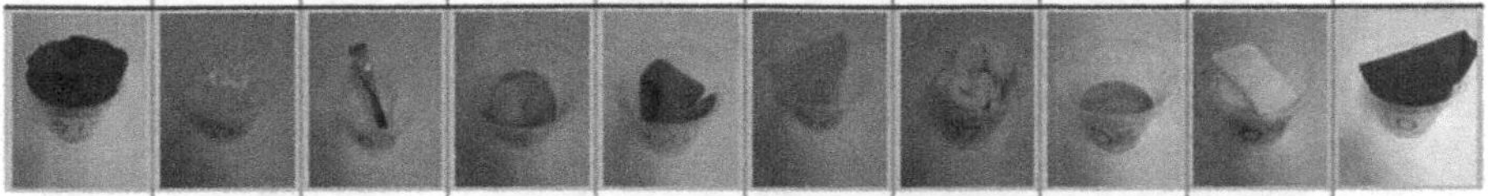

Fig. 4. Experimented materials selected by the survey and the pre-experiment

Fig. 5. Experiment 3 Environment

10-materials which are likely to be preferred from the result of the survey and the pre-experiment (See Fig. 4). These materials are Silk, Air cap, Brush, Wood, Leather, paper, Cotton Fabric, Sand, Cotton, and Felt which we can easily use in daily life. Twenty-five participants (age range of 19 to 40, 11 females and 14 males) responded after touching the 10-materials arranged in transparent vessels. They were asked to compare all pairs among the ten in 5-scale based on their personal preferences (Fig. 5).

4.2 Results

As a result, we obtain weights for the materials. (See Fig. 6) Because the consistency index is 0.0035 (acceptable level is < 0.100), this result is acceptable. Subsequently, brush, cotton fabric, and silk are most highly weighted. Indeed, these highly-ranked materials provide emotional satisfaction to individuals. Since we have chosen 10-materials to be likely to represent favorable feeling based on multiple experiment, we also infer that these materials would be highly ranked in the other experiments.

5 Discussion

This research is different with the presented studies which based on the technology, focusing on the human senses and investigating what users would feel when they experience through haptic devices.

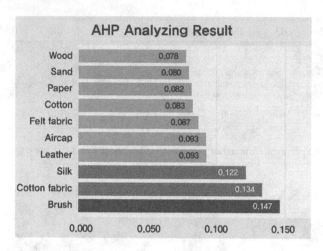

Fig. 6. AHP analyzing results

5.1 Correspondence

If we only take technical issue into the consideration, technology by itself may be developed. However, this research considers that consumers do not ensure that they would use the technology. According to the result, users are more cautious about haptic display. First, they are unpleasant when the visual and haptic stimulus discord. Also, they take an umbrage at the display that present a bad tactile. It is an important fact that people do not feel better even if the present display adds haptic technology. Agreement between haptic and visual sources is required condition for positive haptic display. Previously, it was found that two senses interfere each other when they are concurrently provided [4]. Nevertheless, our finding stands alone with the point of emotional differentiation.

5.2 Textures

In order to develop a positive haptic display, we argue that technology should allow user to feel transmitted texture with pleasure. Also, the textures of 'silk' and 'brush' are the most significant textures. The high ranked textures have some features of softness, fine-grained and familiarity in common. Despite of individual differences, there clearly exists some textures that please most people. Developing haptic display, such an overwhelming texture has a priority to be implemented. To sum up, we need to reproduce likable textures more delicately than unlikable textures in order to attract people to feel friendly about haptic display.

5.3 Future Haptic Display

Engineers work out various methods of actuators in haptic display such as electrotactile and vibrotactile. Even though present technology is rapidly growing, it requires more time to reproduce an exact texture in haptic display. In particular, 'sand' and 'soft cotton fabric' are too detailed to be implemented, although people prefer such textures. However, favorable texture should accompany delicate technology that represents temperature, z-force, and the softness. Conversely, the mere rough haptic display would not give users any reason to purchase.

Eventually, ideal display will be affective and has emotional relations with us, not just a rigid plastic and metal. As mentioned above, expansions of haptic will equal to expansions of oneself. To overcome the boundary between 'myself' and 'other', true ubiquitous beginning would come from haptic technology. Therefore, it is ponderable that haptic display, which is representing ourselves, has to give us 'good feeling'.

6 Conclusion

High-technology does not always give pleasure to people. Indeed, there was an important observation by experiments that users are not always favorable to haptic technology although it is an advanced technology. We argue that developed haptic display must be loved by people. To do so, we should aim to reproduce the likable texture first on haptic display. Considering that haptic display is one of the fundamental technology that will be applied in the future, we investigate haptic display that provides pleasant and familiar feeling to human individuals. Herein, this paper finds what kinds of materials gives positive feedback to the users.

Attractive haptic also gives several ways to think. For example, the preference would depend on the mode of haptic experience. Currently, we investigated only one form of haptic experience using fingertips. However, each of the body parts including facial skin, palm, lips, and foot would give totally different preference. The mechanism of human haptic is too complex to be defined in a simple manner. For that reason, the possibilities of the further research are unlimited in this area. Of course, there are also still a few loose ends to reproduce texture technology. However, we want to emphasize that studies on the human preference are essential as well as the technologies themselves in order to construct a technology system related to human-computer interaction.

Acknowledgement. This work was supported by the MSIP (Ministry of Science, ICT and Future Planning) under the "IT Consilience Creative Program" support program supervised by the NIPA (National IT Industry Promotion Agency) (NIPA-2014-H0201-14-1002).

References

1. Yohanan, S., MacLean, K.: The role of affective touch in human-robot interaction: human intent and expectations in touching the haptic creature. Int. J. Soc. Robot. **4**(2), 163–180 (2012)
2. Bau, O., Poupyrev, I., Israr, A., Harrison, C.: TeslaTouch: electrovibration for touch surfaces. In: Proceedings of the 23rd annual ACM Symposium on User Interface Software and Technology, pp. 283–292. ACM (2010)
3. Fröhlich, J., Wachsmuth, I.: The visual, the auditory and the haptic – a user study on combining modalities in virtual worlds. In: Shumaker, R. (ed.) VAMR 2013, Part I. LNCS, vol. 8021, pp. 159–168. Springer, Heidelberg (2013)

4. Konyo, M., Tadokoro, S., Hira, M., Takamori, T.: Quantitative evaluation of artificial tactile feel display integrated with visual information. In: 2002 IEEE/RSJ International Conference on Intelligent Robots and Systems, vol. 3, pp. 3060–3065. IEEE (2002)
5. Choe, D.: A Study on sensory and emotional responses according to tactile attributes of surface texture - With Emphasis on the application of surface texture on mobile devices - Department of Industrial Design, Master's thesis, KAIST (2010)
6. Anzieu, D., Turner, C.T.: The skin ego. Yale University Press, New Haven (1989)
7. Saaty, T.: Analytic hierarchy process. In: Gass, S., Fu, M. (eds.) Encyclopedia of Operations Research and Management Science, pp. 52–64. Springer, US (2013)
8. Feygin, D., Keehner, M., Tendick, F.: Haptic guidance: experimental evaluation of a haptic training method for a perceptual motor skill. In: 2002 Proceedings of the 10th Symposium on Haptic Interfaces for Virtual Environment and Teleoperator Systems, HAPTICS 2002, pp. 40–47. IEEE (2002)
9. Lee, J., Hwand, J.: Physical surface roughness and perceived roughness. Arch. Des. Res. **27** (2), 157–169 (2014)
10. Jani Heikkinen, T.O., Väänänen-Vainio-Mattila, K.: Expectations for user experience in haptic communication with mobile devices. In: MobileHCI 2009. ACM, Bonn (2009)

Improving Touchscreen Accessibility in Self-Service Technology

Elina Jokisuu$^{(\boxtimes)}$, Mike McKenna, Andrew W.D. Smith, and Phil Day

Consumer Experience, NCR Corporation, Dundee, UK
{elina.jokisuu,mike.mckenna,andrewWD.smith,phil.day}
@ncr.com

Abstract. There is a growing trend towards touchscreens in self-service terminals, such as ATMs and airport check-ins. However, these touchscreen-based
interfaces pose significant accessibility challenges, particularly for people with
visual impairment. This paper presents two research and development projects
aimed at improving touchscreen accessibility of self-service technology: one
describing the development of a physical input device and another investigating
gesture-based input techniques. These two projects are used to illustrate the key
challenges of accessibility in self-service technology.

Keywords: Self-service technology · SST · Touchscreen · Accessibility ·
Visual impairment

1 Introduction

Touchscreens proliferate in modern life driving the expectation to use touchscreens in
self-service terminals (SSTs), such as automated teller machines (ATMs), supermarket
self-checkouts and airport check-ins. This trend has been evident for the last decade,
and shows no sign of diminishing [1]. For example, a survey in 2004 of 18-34 year olds
in the US found that 82 % had used a touchscreen at a self-checkout system, and 70 %
had used a touchscreen at an ATM. The majority of respondents (89 %) reported that
they expected touchscreens to become the standard way of interacting with self-service
devices. [2] This is borne out by our experience; sales of touchscreen ATMs increased
from 16.9 % in 2010 to 24.7 % in 2011.

Self-service technology itself is becoming more widespread and increasing in
importance [3]. Through the use of self-service, consumers are being empowered to
conduct increasingly complex transactions at a time and in a location that is convenient
for them.

This trend, however, particularly when combined with the trend to use touchscreens
as the main interaction channel, can lead to considerable accessibility barriers.
Touchscreens can be extremely difficult, particularly for people with visual impairment,
to use. The expectation to use self-service technology, in addition to or instead of
service provided by humans, can severely limit the possibilities for a disabled person to
independently manage their daily activities, such as finances, shopping, and travel, if
care is not taken to make SSTs accessible. As one of the world's largest providers of
self-service technology, NCR takes its responsibility in integrating accessibility into its

© Springer International Publishing Switzerland 2015
M. Antona and C. Stephanidis (Eds.): UAHCI 2015, Part II, LNCS 9176, pp. 103–113, 2015.
DOI: 10.1007/978-3-319-20681-3_10

products very seriously. In this paper we describe the development of two touchscreen input methods and their applicability to self-service in the domains of travel and financial services. Furthermore, by using the two projects as case studies, we discuss the process of applying accessibility research in practice and the particular challenges of integrating accessibility into self-service technology. We also discuss the benefits of integrating accessibility solutions into mainstream products, along with a brief discussion as to the merits of accessibility solutions that are designed from a universal design perspective; namely to bring benefit to multiple groups of people and not just designing for a single type of physical or cognitive impairment.

2   Accessibility in Self-Service Technology

One of the biggest benefits of self-service is the convenience and availability of services to anyone, anywhere, anytime [4]. However, this is also one of the main challenges of making self-service accessible. SSTs must be accessible to anyone, without instructions, personalization or assistive technologies.

What makes an SST accessible is in major part defined in international and country-specific laws, standards and guidelines. These requirements include features such as making input options tactilely discernible without activation, and offering speech output to guide the user through the transaction (e.g. [5]). The benefit of these regulations is that they provide measurable details, for example the optimal angle for a keypad, which tell us that by meeting these requirements, accessibility will be improved.

On the other hand, there are certain disadvantages to having the laws and standards regulate so much of the product specifics. Firstly, some requirements, such as height and reach, vary significantly across the world. Secondly, the regulatory process sometimes lags behind technological development, which might mean that we cannot take full advantage of new technologies because they are not yet allowed by law. Thirdly, the regulatory framework is expanding continuously, which makes it a challenge to monitor: existing regulations are updated, new countries are developing their own accessibility laws and standards, and the regulations are expanding onto new domains, such as airport check-in kiosks. In addition to accessibility regulations, certain aspects of the transactions performed on SSTs, for example entering the Personal Identification Number (PIN) are very tightly controlled by security standards (e.g. [6]).

While the regulatory framework sets quite specific parameters to accessibility, we know very little about the actual user; the user can be anyone, anywhere, anytime. This further emphasizes the importance of integrating user research and usability testing in the development process to make sure users' needs are understood.

3   Developing a Physical Input Device

Although touchscreens on personal mobile devices have improved greatly in terms of their accessibility to people with visual impairment, these accessibility features do not necessarily scale well to a large screen, particularly on a device that must be usable without any training or learning as is the case for any self-service terminal. In addition, larger touchscreens can pose accessibility problems in terms of the required physical reach (a person must be able to reach across the expanse of the touchscreen); and this can be difficult for smaller people, particularly those in wheelchairs [7]. A solution is therefore required that offers additional tactile features both for locating and activating on-screen elements, and also offers reach benefits over a large touchscreen.

To address these challenges, a team of industrial designers, usability and accessibility specialists, and interaction designers embarked on a project to develop a physical input device that could be attached to a touchscreen-based SST. Overall, the development entailed three rounds of testing and gradual refinement of the concept based on user feedback. The development started with concept ideation to explore different input techniques, such as sliders, rotations, and buttons. Five of these concepts were developed into testable prototypes: a 4-way keypad, a capacitive touch-wheel, a scroll wheel, a pre-production sample of a tactile touchscreen and a commercially available navigation keyboard EZ Access. These were then evaluated with 25 participants to identify which of the physical movement modes offered the most benefit as input technique (reported in [8]). Although the tactile touchscreen performed best, it was not a feasible solution: it only gave feedback when an on-screen option was selected, not when the user was attempting to locate and identify the options, a key legal requirement in many countries. Therefore, the next preferred concept – the 4-way keypad – was taken for further development.

The resulting concept was a physical input device called the Universal Navigator (uNav) that provides tactile keys that allow the user to navigate through on-screen options. It has four direction keys arranged around a central select button, and an audio socket and volume button to enable private audio output (Fig. 1). The concept was later refined after an expert review with RNIB (Royal National Institute of Blind People), the leading UK support and research organisation for people with visual impairment. The expert review was particularly useful in giving direction on the auditory interaction that would best support the use of the device.

To test the uNav, two further rounds of usability evaluations were conducted: one in the UK with RNIB which involved 48 people with different levels of visual

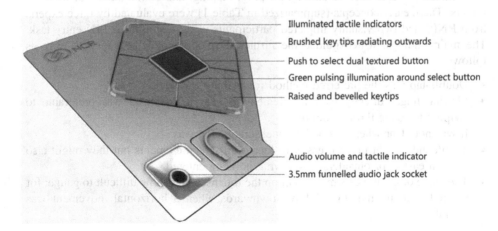

Fig. 1. The Universal Navigator (uNav)

impairment (reported in [9]); and another in the US with the Center for Visually Impaired (CVI) and disABILITY Link in the Atlanta metropolitan area which involved 20 people with physical and/or visual impairment (reported in [10]). An existing airline check-in application was used to test the concepts. This was chosen for two reasons: firstly it required complex interaction such as using an on-screen alphanumeric keyboard and the spatial task of seat selection. Secondly, by using an existing application we were able to validate how well a device like this could be retro-fitted to existing self-service technology with minimal impact to the existing infrastructure. In a repeated-measures experiment, participants completed the same flight check-in task twice: with the uNav in both horizontal (13° from horizontal tilted towards user, commonly found in keyboards) and vertical (65° from horizontal, in line with the display) orientations. Those who wanted to also attempted the task a third time with a conventional touchscreen; thus allowing for a comparison with the current method of interaction.

In terms of the main considerations for the accessibility of touchscreen-based SSTs, the project highlighted the importance of involving users and incorporating their feedback continuously throughout the development. The results from the usability evaluations showed high success rates and acceptance for the concept, both by people with visual impairment as well as people with physical impairment. This was a good example of how accessibility improvement in one area benefits others as well: the concept was shown to improve accessibility for people who use wheelchairs or have upper body mobility impairment, as it eliminated the need to reach across a touchscreen.

4   Developing Gesture-Based Input Techniques

As gesture-based touchscreen interaction has become more familiar through personal mobile devices, we wanted to investigate the possibility of using touchscreen as the only input mechanism. This would remove the need for a physical keypad altogether. In a similar manner to the uNav project, the first stage was to create several concepts that utilized gestures such as sliding, swiping, tapping, and combinations of multiple fingers. These early concepts (summarized in Table 1) were evaluated by three experts from RNIB and two visually impaired participants using a simplified PIN entry task. The main findings, which guided the further development of the concepts were as follows:

- Double-tap was the preferred method for making a selection.
- Moving finger directly over an element to hear it vocalized was preferable to swiping to rotate through options.
- It was not clear where the active touchscreen area was.
- Tactile aids might make it easier to locate on-screen elements but they might also make it easier for outsiders to see what is being entered.
- The angle of the finger's movement on the touchscreen can be difficult to gauge; for example end up moving slightly downwards when a horizontal movement was intended.

Table 1. Early concepts evaluated in the expert review

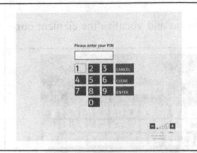	**Concept 1: Grid** User swipes left or right, up or down anywhere on the screen to move the focus around a numeric keypad on screen (with a layout similar to the current ATM keypad), then taps to select a number.
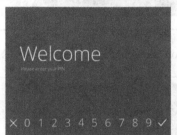	**Concept 2: Slider** User slides finger along the bottom of the screen to bring the focus to each number in turn, then swipes upwards to select a number.
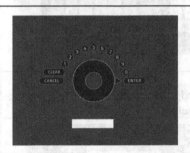	**Concept 3: Radial Controller** User drags finger around a circular shape to bring focus to each number in turn, then touches the screen with another finger to select a number.

After refinement of the concepts, a usability evaluation with 49 participants with varying levels of visual impairment was conducted in collaboration with RNIB. The concepts were tested using a 10" capacitive touchscreen which was attached to a pedestal simulating the actual height and angle of an ATM. Each participant completed three tasks: first task was to enter a Personal Identification Number (PIN), the second was to select a specific item on a menu, and the third was to enter the word 'SAVE' using an on-screen keyboard. The latter two tasks were similar in terms of their interaction gestures: there were three different concepts for both, each demonstrating a different interaction technique (summarized in Table 2). The concepts varied in terms of the method of moving the focus between elements, but the method of making a selection was the same in each: double-tap. In both tasks, the user was able to hear the option in focus, and get an auditory (and visual) confirmation of the selection they had

Table 2. Concepts evaluated in the usability test

Concept 1: Talking fingers
User drags a finger around the screen to bring focus to and vocalize the element currently under the finger. Double-tap to select.

Concept 2: Virtual grid
User swipes left or right, up or down anywhere on the screen to move the focus through the options. Double-tap to select.

Concept 3: Slider
User drags a finger horizontally along the bottom edge of the touchscreen to bring the focus to each of the options in turn. Double-tap to select.

---

made. Each concept provided audio instructions, similar to the audio instructions currently available at many ATMs. Using a repeated-measures experimental design, each participant used each of the concepts in a randomized order.

The research is still ongoing; therefore the focus here is to give a general overview of the work so far. Overall, the participants found touchscreen gestures an acceptable method of interacting with an ATM: 10 participants (21 %) said gestures would be an acceptable method of interaction and 33 participants (69 %) thought they would be acceptable but would require some changes. The most requested changes related to changing the keyboard to a QWERTY layout, and improving the color contrast to support access for the partially sighted users. There were five participants (10 %) who said gestures would not be an acceptable solution at all. The main reason for this was the difficulty of entering the PIN, rather than using touchscreen gestures per se.

Although the initial results were promising for the menu selection and text entry tasks, the PIN entry task was extremely challenging, with very low success rates. In the test, four different PIN entry concepts were evaluated, each with a different method for entering the numbers. Due to the stringent security requirements to ensure the privacy of the PIN [6], no feedback that distinguishes individual numbers can be given; the only feedback the user gets is a beep to indicate a number has been entered. The difficulty of this task further highlights the importance of appropriate voice guidance and audio feedback. More detailed research to develop a PIN entry method that is both accessible and secure is currently being conducted.

To improve our understanding of the difficulties people with visual impairments encounter when using touchscreens on self-service terminals, we analyzed the video recordings of the test sessions. We categorized these difficulties as follows:

Lack of feedback: The user needs auditory and/or tactile feedback firstly to locate and identify each interface element without activating them; and secondly to get confirmation that the desired element has been activated. For certain transactions, such as entering the PIN, the security requirements severely limit the feedback the system is allowed to give. Further research is required to better understand how these limitations can be overcome. We also continue to explore the possibilities of haptic feedback in SST touchscreens.

Disorientation/Reorientation: Since touchscreens often have smooth edge-to-edge glass surface without any distinguishable tactile features for reference, it is very easy to get disoriented. It requires a continuous effort to maintain an accurate mental model of the layout and elements on the screen. Without a permanent tactile reference point, the user is forced re-orientate themselves every time the content on the screen changes. Based on our observations, many participants used the physical edge of the touchscreen as their reference point, but this often lead to further difficulties. Typically a participant would keep one (non-dominant) hand on the edge of the screen and move the other (dominant) hand on the touchscreen in relation to the reference hand. However, the hand resting on the edge of the screen could easily activate an interface element by accident. Alternatively, the participant would be unaware of the fact that the active touch area does not extend all the way to the physical edge of the screen, as the touch-sensitive area is surrounded by a non-active frame which is not tactilely discernible. As a design consideration for self-service touchscreens, it is very important to make the active touch area tactilely discernible from the non-active frame. Because of the severity of the problems caused by disorientation, we will incorporate a tactile landmark, a permanent reference point in further development of the concepts (Fig. 2).

Fig. 2. Touchscreen interaction is made easier by having tactile markers along the bottom edge of the screen.

Fig. 3. Touchscreen gestures, such as double-taps and swipes, are unfamiliar to some users, which leads to accidental activation of functions; this picture illustrates a typical problem of knuckles accidentally grazing the screen surface.

Unfamiliarity with touchscreen gestures: Although many people with visual impairment use touchscreens on their personal mobile devices, there are those who do not. Half of our participants had very little or no experience of touchscreens, and for them it was very difficult to understand what was expected when the audio guidance instructed them to "swipe" or "double-tap" (Fig. 3).

Physical ergonomics: When the SST is designed primarily for touchscreen interaction, the height and angle of the display are often optimized for visual access, rather than tactile access. This can lead to awkward postures and uncomfortable hand movements (Fig. 4).

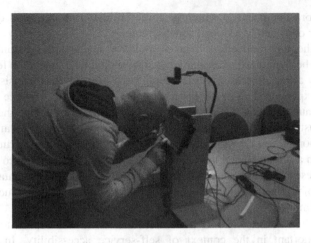

Fig. 4. A display designed for visual access can be less than ideal for visually impaired users

Situational awareness: The accessibility of an ATM encompasses much more than making the input and output accessible to the visually impaired users. Many participants commented on the particular concerns that they would have, were they to use this type of an ATM in the real world. Two key factors were raised by the participants: firstly, the longer a transaction takes, including the time needed to listen to the audio instructions, the more vulnerable they will feel. They will feel like they are holding up the people waiting behind them, or feel like they are drawing unwanted attention to themselves by taking longer to complete a transaction. Furthermore, to use the private audio they would need to have their headphones on, which would make them feel exposed and leave them dangerously unaware of their surroundings.

5 Conclusions

In this paper we have described the development of two touchscreen input methods: a physical input device called the Universal Navigator (uNav) and our early research into gesture-based interaction techniques. We presented these two projects as case studies to highlight some of the characteristics of accessibility for self-service technology.

There are four considerations to draw from this work, of particular concern in the self-service environment but also more widely applicable to accessibility research. Firstly, we should make no assumptions about the user's prior knowledge and experience. In the case of touchscreen technology, we should not assume that everyone who walks up to a self-service terminal will be familiar with touchscreen technology and know what is meant by a tap or a swipe. Even if they were familiar with touchscreen gestures on their personal mobile devices, the experience will not necessarily be transferable to the experience of using touchscreen gestures on SSTs. The SST touchscreen is bigger in size, which makes disorientation a constant challenge. Furthermore, whereas personal mobile devices can be personalized, and the user can spend time learning the features, this is rarely possible on a public SST. Further research is needed to explore the extent to which gestures familiar from personal device touch-screens transfer onto public terminal touchscreens.

Secondly, the time and effort it takes to learn a new interface and interaction technique must be minimized. A primary concern should be to make the features easily discoverable by a first-time user, while keeping the user interface consistent to allow for the more experienced users to learn and use shortcuts. To reduce the required learning effort, audio guidance is critically important. The wording and the sequence of instructions must be carefully considered and tested with users. We cannot overemphasize the importance of providing clear, precise and timely audio instructions to help the user form an accurate mental model of the system and how to use it to achieve their goals. Further research is indicated to discover how to help the user maintain the spatial understanding of a primarily visual user interface on a relatively large touchscreen with few tactile landmarks.

Thirdly, both hardware and software contribute to the user experience, and this is particularly important in the context of self-service accessibility. In the case of touchscreen-based SSTs, a primary design consideration is often to ensure optimal visual access to the display. In terms of the height and angle of the display, this might not be the ideal solution for tactile access. This is an issue that is not adequately addressed by current laws and standards, which most often recommend or require the display angle to be optimized visually, e.g. 55-70° from the horizontal, and a keypad angle optimized for tactile access, e.g. 10-30° from the horizontal.

Fourthly and finally, the core tenet of user-centered design – to know the user – is vitally important in the context of self-service accessibility. In self-service technology, the most common use case is "anyone, anywhere, anytime", which makes user research both a challenge and a necessity. For certain aspects of accessibility, such as height and reach measurements, we can – and have to – refer to the formal regulations, but this is still only the baseline of accessibility. As we have described in this paper, the goal of our research and development process is to integrate accessibility into mainstream products. In both projects, we applied a similar approach: early ideation followed by rapid testing of the underlying interaction principles to focus the development on the most promising ideas, followed by refinement using feedback from user research, expert reviews and usability testing. The process is based on inclusive design: making mainstream technology accessible to as wide an audience as possible. In the uNav project, for example, the physical input device was helpful both for people with visual impairment as it enabled tactilely discernible input, and for people with physical impairment as it removed the need to reach across a relatively large touchscreen. The gestural input research, on the other hand, further highlighted the need to support both the visual and auditory interfaces simultaneously and in synchronicity. Although the prototype used in the test was designed to assess a blind person's auditory-only experience, we acknowledge that it is a key requirement to provide an accessible experience for all levels of visual ability, not forcing users to choose between a visual interface and an auditory one.

Future work will continue to address the issues identified so far. We will continue to explore the constraints set by accessibility and security regulations, particularly in the context of PIN entry. This also extends to the concerns of privacy more generally: users are often asked to handle very personal and sensitive data using a very public terminal. In addition to the technical and legal requirements of handling personal data, the perceived privacy is equally important: the user, whoever, wherever, whenever they use a self-service terminal, must be made to feel confident and empowered.

References

1. Digital Trends European McDonald's to replace human cashiers with touch screen computers (2011). <http://www.digitaltrends.com/computing/european-mcdonalds-to-replace-human-cashiers-with-touch-screen-computers>. (Accessed on 26 February 2015)
2. Penn, S., Berland E.: TouchSystems In Touch Survey (2004). <http://www.elotouch.co.uk/AboutElo/PressReleases/040617.asp>. (Accessed on 26 February 2015)
3. Castro, D., Atkinson, R., Ezell, S.: Embracing the Self-Service Economy. ITIF The Information Technology and Innovation Foundation (2010)
4. James, B., Dunne, G., Peter, A., Glynn, W.J.: Handbook of Services Marketing and Management, pp. 89–101. SAGE Publications, Inc (1999)
5. Department of Justice 2010 ADA Standards for Accessible Design, 15 September 2010, as referenced in Americans With Disabilities Act of 1990, Pub. L. No. 101–336, 104 Stat. 328 (2010). <http://www.ada.gov/regs2010/2010ADAStandards/2010ADAstandards.htm>. (Accessed on 26 February 2015)
6. PCI Security Standards Council Payment Card Industry PIN Transaction Security Point of Interaction Security Requirements v4.0. PCI Security Standards Council LLC, June 2013
7. Summerskill, S.J., Marshall, R., Case, K., Gyi, D.E., Sims, R.E., Day, P.N., Rohan, C., Birnie, S.: Validation of the HADRIAN system using an ATM evaluation case study. Int. J. Hum. Factors Model. Simul. (IJHFMS) 1(4), 420–432 (2010). Special Issue on Application of Digital Human Modelling Tools in User Centred Design Processes
8. Day, P.N., Chandler, E., Colley, A., Carlisle, M., Riley, C., Rohan, C., Tyler, S.: The universal navigator: a proposed accessible alternative to touchscreens for self-service. In: Anderson, M. (ed.) Contemporary Ergonomics and Human Factors 2012, pp. 31–38. Taylor and Francis, London (2012)
9. Day, P.N., Carlisle, M., Chandler, E., Ferguson, G.: Evaluating the Universal Navigator with blind and partially sighted consumers In: Anderson, M. (ed.) Contemporary Ergonomics and Human Factors 2013, Proceedings of the International Conference on Ergonomics & Human Factors 2013, Cambridge, UK, 15–18 April 2013, pp. 355–362. CRC Press, Taylor & Francis Group (2013)
10. Day, P.N., Johnson, J.P., Carlisle, M., Ferguson, G.: Evaluating the Universal Navigator with consumers with reduced mobility, dexterity & visual acuity In: Sharples, S., Shorrock, S.T. (eds.) Contemporary Ergonomics and Human Factors 2014, pp. 183–190. CRC Press, Taylor & Francis Group (2014)

Transparent Touch – Interacting with a Multi-layered Touch-Sensitive Display System

Andreas Kratky[✉]

Interactive Media Division, School of Cinematic Arts,
University of Southern California, 3470 McClintock Ave.,
SCI 201Q, Los Angeles, CA 90089-2211, USA
akratky@cinema.usc.edu

Abstract. *Transparent Touch* explores interaction with a display system with two spatially distinct layers. A transparent touch screen is overlaid in front of another information layer, which can be a 3-dimensional object or second screen. Both layers are optically aligned and offer the advantage to provide distinct semantic contexts while optically and cognitively integrating them. The system is explored in three use-case scenarios in which the transparent screen serves as an augmentation layer, as an annotation layer, and as a control layer. The concept is known from HUD displays in airplanes or cars and integrates features of augmented reality systems, mid-air interaction systems and touch screens. Our study collects an initial set of user responses.

Keywords: Mid-air interaction · Augmented reality · Touch-screen · Gestural interaction · Museum interface · Heads-up display · Collaboration tools

1 Introduction

For approximately the last 40 years the combination of keyboard, mouse and a screen was the mainstay of human computer interaction. Since the demonstration of Douglas Engelbart's augmentation research this combination of technologies has dominated how we operate computers. As Engelbart describes it in his famous demo from 1968, the interaction with the mouse as a pointing device to control a tracking spot on the screen has always been somewhat indirect: "…as it moves up and down or sideways, so does the tracking spot. […] The way we use it continuously and conclusively is to watch the screen and to follow it around, and we use this […] device to move that tracking spot. And when you have your eye on the tracking spot you really don't care if it follows exactly this or not." [1] What used to be a strange procedure in 1968, the use of the mouse and the indirect control of its on-screen representation has become second nature to most computer users – but it had a learning curve as for example the "Mouse Skills" Introduction that shipped with every new Macintosh computer still in 1991 [2], indicates. The same introduction also shows that the management of different windows used to organize the different tasks and contexts on the screen needed some explanation and was not a straight-forward and easily grasped technique. Nevertheless, this form of

M. Antona and C. Stephanidis (Eds.): UAHCI 2015, Part II, LNCS 9176, pp. 114–126, 2015.
DOI: 10.1007/978-3-319-20681-3_11

directness was a large improvement compared to command-based interaction, and it prepared the way for direct manipulation interfaces as described by Shneiderman in 1982 [3, 4]. A core aspect of the so called "display editors" described by Shneiderman was the interaction with on-screen visual representations by way of a pointing device such as the mouse or a joystick. The idea of direct manipulation interfaces was to reduce the cognitive load and the time needed to carry out tasks on the computer. Despite the indirectness of the mouse control and the windowing systems, the overall system performance was superior for many task domains [5].

Other, more direct interaction devices, that did not require the negotiation of a dissociated pointing device and on-screen representation had their debuts already in 1963 with Ivan Sutherland's Sketchpad application, which used a light-pen to interact with visual on-screen representations directly by touching the screen and carrying out manipulations on those objects [6]. Light-pen systems never garnered a wide-spread distribution but since 2006 there has been a significant increase in touch screen devices, which arguably deliver a more direct interaction with on-screen representations [7]. Since their early stages in 1977 [8], touch screen devices have enabled a new stage of direct manipulation, allowing the direct "grabbing" and manipulating of on-screen representations with a finger or hand. But also touch screens come with their own problems. The most pronounced of those problems is the obscuring of the content that is being interacted with by the finger(s) of the user [9]. With stylus operations the obscuring problem is reduced, but still existent.

Equally since 2006, with the introduction of the Nintendo WII controller, gestural interfaces have seen a wider distribution and acceptance [10]. The range of different implementations of gestural interfaces is comparatively wide, but numerous implementations allow for direct pointing and manipulation of objects with a finger or the entire hand. In this sense gestural interfaces have the benefit of getting rid of the dissociation between pointing device and the cursor's on-screen representation, while avoiding the problem of obscuring the objects that are being manipulated with the pointing tool that impedes touch screen interaction.

With *Transparent Touch* we are exploring a different approach, which addresses several of the problems seen in the techniques discussed above. The core of the *Transparent Touch* system is a transparent touch screen superimposed in front of the objects that are being interacted with. These objects can be on-screen representations, rendered on a second screen behind the transparent screen, or actual 3-dimensional objects set up behind it. Interaction is carried out on the transparent screen, which is mounted in such a way that the interaction gestures optically coincide with the screen or object behind it. The display system can thus be classified as combination of augmented reality and spatial display. The use-case scenarios for this screen arrangement are targeted for interactive installations in public or semi-public spaces such as museums or collaborative group-work environments. The display set-up can be used in several different constellations for example as a control-layer for complex interaction patterns, an augmentation layer to display added information superimposed on real objects or as an annotation layer superimposed on a second screen presenting information that can easily be related to the second screen but is kept in a separate context. In the following we will elaborate and exemplify these different use-case scenarios.

2 Related Work

The three approaches of mouse, mid-air, and touch interaction described in the introduction are the main implementations of human computer interaction in both, the office and home use as well as the use in public or semi-public spaces. While for single person use the dominant interaction model is still the keyboard and mouse combination, for collaborative settings this combination has been replaced by other models. In semi-public spaces, in the realm of collaborative group-work environments the touch screen, and in particular the touch table design, is established as the most conducive model to foster collaboration [11–13]. Also in semi-public and public spaces such as museums touch screens have become a popular medium to enable interaction and collaboration [14], but lately a lot more attention has gone to augmented reality solutions [15–17]. The augmented reality solutions are credited to deliver a strong sense of realism and allow detailed information about specific characteristics of objects explored with added information overlay [18]. Besides some exceptions that use custom-made display settings [19], most of these implementations use the personal mobile devices of museum visitors as additional screens on which to display content that is overlaid on top of museum exhibits [20]. The video camera of the mobile device is used to scan the museum space or point it to specific exhibits and as the object appears on the screen of the mobile device additional information is displayed on the device. By optically registering the image captured by the camera and the additional information a relationship between the two units of information is established. While this implementation has certain popularity, it also has several disadvantages. Museum visitors are required to have their own device ready to use and mostly download specific software that enables the experience. The screen of the mobile device is generally rather small and does not lend itself easily to interaction. Most systems are used to add extra, non-interactive information on top the captured scene, while interaction is difficult due to fingers obscuring the image and due to difficulties of registering the interaction gestures correctly [21]. Furthermore the small screen size of the mobile devices used for many augmented reality applications does not lend itself to collaborative interaction. As a personal device the phone or tablet is intended to be handled by one person only.

Some of these problems have been addressed by the recent category of mid-air systems, which use tracking tools such as the Microsoft Kinect or the Leap Motion to enable gestural interaction. Interaction in this scenario is carried out in the empty air in front of the object or display that is being interacted with. Users have to stand in a defined area where they can be tracked; generally this area is large enough to accommodate collaborative interaction of several people. Among mid-air systems two categories have to be distinguished, the first consisting of one display screen in conjunction with gesture-tracking [22]. The second category has a transparent display such as a fog screen which is situated in the same space as the gesture tracking. The transparent screen allows to establish a close connection between the interaction gestures and their results, without obscuring the display and while providing the opportunity for collaborative interaction [23]. Hybridizations of these two categories exist, in which the mid-air display is used to augment a real object [24]. The difficulty with mid-air systems is a generally a lack of precision in the interaction. Due to the missing tactile feedback, which makes touch screens perform well, mid-air systems suffer from reduced performance in even simple target acquisition tasks [25]. Solutions to this lack of precision have been explored in employing stereoscopic displays, which support the depth-axis estimation of users and indeed reduce the error rate in several target-acquisition tasks [26].

3 The *Transparent Touch* System

3.1 System Configuration

The core of the *Transparent Touch* system is a glass panel suspended in space. The glass panel is equipped with a holographic back-projection film, which allows to project onto the glass in an angle and produce a visible image on the glass surface. The film has embedded micro-prisms refracting the light from the projector in such a way that the user can see the image when standing in front of the screen. The image has see-through qualities, enabling the user to at the same time look through the glass at an object or image behind the screen. Both images are superimposed but spatially separated. The system can be set up either as a combination of the glass panel and a real object, such as a museum artifact, or in combination with a second screen behind it. In both cases the transparent screen and the second object or display have to be arranged in such that they align optically with the user's viewing axis (Fig. 1). Since the angled projection creates a distorted image we are using a custom keystone correction to correct the images of the projection(s).

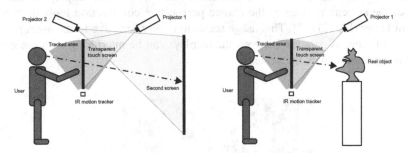

Fig. 1. Set-up variants of the *Transparent Touch* system: set-up with dual screens (left) and set-up with real object (right).

The area around the transparent touch screen is tracked by an IR sensor (Leap Motion) in order to capture interactions close to and on the surface of the screen. The option to use gestural input close to the screen rather than purely limiting the input to the surface of the screen is desirable in order to avoid possible occlusion and to distinguish more states of interaction than only presence or absence of contact. Earlier implementations of such a system have used a similar set-up with a holoscreen on a glass panel but resorted to tracking with the help of two cameras, treating the screen solely as a touch screen [27].

The *Transparent Touch* system builds on several paradigms of perception and human computer interaction and leverages them to make its operation intuitive and easy to understand. As an optical see-through system *Transparent Touch* uses the method of optically superimposing several layers of content that has been developed for heads-up displays (HUDs) [28]. HUDs have been developed for situations in which the fast and effortless perception of a scene with additional information is essential, such as in a airplane where pilots have to be able to see the exterior and the essential information about their vehicle together without having to look at different displays and cognitively integrating the two display contexts [29]. For similar reasons as heads-up displays are used in airplanes they are now being used also in cars in order to closely bring together the two viewing contexts of the car exterior and interior car controls. Through this form of optical coupling of the display contexts an increased precision and cognitive ease in working across both contexts is achieved [30]. In the *Transparent Touch* system optical coupling is used to work across two different display contexts and easily establish relationships between them while keeping them cognitively separate. This form of interaction is equally familiar from layer-organization in software interfaces, which has become a popular design characteristic of software such as Adobe Photoshop. The transparent superimposition of display layers enables the user to negotiate focus on one context and paying attention to several contexts [31]. Working with content layers and additional annotation layers is now widely established in document interfaces for example for PDF annotation or document review and can thus be assumed as a paradigm familiar to a large number of users.

Through the spatial layering of the display contexts our system can also be used to produce 3-dimensional perspectival characteristics between the display layers. The set-up of the screens is close to the classic perspective construction tools devised by Albrecht Dürer (Fig. 2) [32]. This usage scenario is very sensitive to the users position and point of view as parallax between the displays can be interfering with the correct spatial registration across the screens.

Fig. 2. Albrecht Dürer, method of perspective construction, in *Underweysung der Messung* (1525).

As augmented reality applications have become a popular and wide-spread tools with popular applications such as "Layar" [33] and others, our implementation can leverage this familiarity among a large number of users, which eases the accustomization and operation of the *Transparent Touch* system (see Fig. 3).

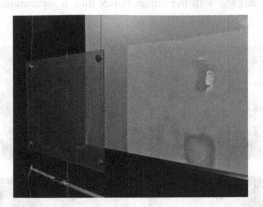

Fig. 3. Set-up with transparent touch screen, IR-tracking and secondary screen

3.2   Operation and Use-Case Scenarios

Our system is intended for situations such as museum exhibits or information kiosks, where several people interact with a defined information context for a limited amount of time. It is not intended for open-ended task solving. The vertical arrangement and the gestural interaction make it susceptible to the same problems of fatigue that is seen in mid-air-displays in general [34]. Nevertheless, for tasks with limited time of engagement it seems that the benefits outweigh the disadvantages. The presence of the screen immediately communicates the opportunity to interact and the availability of additional information about an artifact. Through the visibility of the display and the obvious relationship to the object or display behind it the information offer is easily discerned and understood [35], in this sense it provides a significantly better engagement opportunity than for example the markers that are often used with smart-phone-based augmented reality displays. Users do not have to scan the exhibition space for small and abstract markers, instead they can easily see upon entering the room where opportunities for interactive in-depth information are available. An additional benefit of the larger interaction surface compared to the small individual screen is the opportunity for collaborative interaction, which in the museum setting is highly welcome as it not only creates a communicative exchange among visitors about the object, it also stimulates an interest in the real object and focuses the interaction on the object rather than inserting a self-contained information context like a smart-phone app between visitor and object. The size of the transparent touch screen of *Transparent Touch* is designed to foster both, collaborative engagement as well as individual exploration. It gives the user the privacy to experience the information at an individualized pace, while still providing the opportunity for other users to see the same object and to be invited by an over-the-shoulder glimpse they might get from seeing some-body else interact with the system. For small visitor groups like families the display provides enough space to explore the content together. The system uses the fact that museum objects are for security and preservation reasons often displayed behind glass or somehow out of the direct reach of the visitor. The glass layer in this case can be used as a surface to engage with the object rather than a separation (see Fig. 4).

Fig. 4. Two variants of the first use-case scenario: transparent touch screen combined with real object, displaying general information (left), and information with specific references to object features (right).

As a first test we are observing three different types of use-case scenarios: The first is a museum exhibit scenario, which combines the transparent touch screen with a real 3-dimensional object. The two components are installed so that they accommodate a view-point height within a range of 1.65 to 1.75 m for best alignment between the transparent screen and the object behind it. If users have view-point heights beyond this range the registration of information on the transparent screen with the object will be misadjusted to a degree that is the function of the view-point height difference from the calibrated range. This is clearly one of the difficulties of the display arrangement and future iterations will address this problem. In this first iteration, though, our aim is to evaluate the efficiency of the set-up on a more fundamental level. The transparent screen measures 50 by 70 cm and is mounted in a distance of 1.5 m from the object. It displays general information about the object behind it and offers detail descriptions of appearance aspects of the object. Our aim is to compare the efficiency of the display for information that is referring to the object on a general level without making reference to specific surface features, and information that does make those references. The references to surface features are indicated by lines and circles, highlighting the feature in a way that view-point height differences within the specified range can be accommodated.

A second use-case scenario is intended for a group-collaborative environment with a dual-screen set-up. The transparent touch screen is combined with a second screen behind it. The transparent screen serves as an annotation layer to the second screen. The second screen displays dynamic content, which is being discussed and annotated by the users. The scenario emulates the practice of using tracing paper overlays in the discussion of architectural plans and design sketches; it also facilitates the workflow that is familiar from document annotation though symbols, text, highlights etc. By keeping the annotation layer physically separate from the information layer, different annotation complexes can easily be changed, swapped and compared. The complexity of the annotation layer can be reasonably high and contain interaction tools without obscuring or obstructing the readability of the main information layer. In this scenario we are interested if the display system brings any changes in efficiency compared to single display systems or whether users intuitively respond differently.

A third use-case scenario looks at the transparent screen as a control layer in complex interaction tasks. It uses the same dual screen set-up as described above. In this scenario we are interested if the additional information layer can be used to facilitate more complex interaction patterns that would be difficult to achieve in purely gestural systems, where users do not have any kind of tactile or visual feedback (some visualizations such as the Leap Motion Visualizer exist, but deliver visual representations that are complex and hard to decipher and therefore difficult to use to support interaction with a different focus), or with touch screens, where users have tactile feedback but no visual feedback. The additional information layer allows us to provide the same tactile feedback as touch screens provide but through the distance and optical parallax we can mostly avoid finger-occlusion of the content. By separating the control layer from the main information layer, it becomes possible to also provide visual feedback on the interaction gestures without obstructing the content on the main information layer. Items displayed on the control layer can range from tool display in the style of the "marking menu" of Autodesk's "Maya" modeling program [36], over temporal tracking of gestures and the display of past and possible future gestures, all the way to surrogate objects that provide targeted and simplified interaction opportunities [37]. As part of our first iteration we are exploring two of these examples: the temporal gesture tracking and surrogate object interaction.

One test set-up in this scenario is a game experience in which the interaction gestures are used to slowly reveal aspects of a story. Players use their fingers in order to reveal images, text, and video elements, which as a whole amount to a loose narrative about travel. Different elements require different gestures from the player and the temporal development of these gestures is logged and kept as history that determines the further outcome of the game. The second test set-up is a digital representation of a 3-dimensional object from a museum collection that has been 3-d scanned and is rendered on the second screen. Users can navigate and explore the object by rotating it and enlarging parts of it with the help of manipulator tools displayed on the control layer on the transparent touch screen. The main image of the object remains uncluttered by the interaction tools and can be observed by other people while somebody is exploring it. This form of presentation may be increasingly important as more and more museum collections are digitized and require an appropriate form of display for digital object representations.

While the use-case scenarios are targeting rather different situations, they all share the potential benefit of related, but physically separated contexts, while providing a very direct form of interaction with the represented information (see Fig. 5).

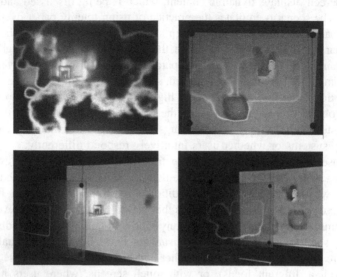

Fig. 5. Examples of the third use-case scenario: transparent touch screen combined with second screen displaying information about the interaction process.

4 Conclusions and Future Work

This paper covers the first iteration of the *Transparent Touch* system. The purpose was to analyze the potential benefits of a layered display system and get a better empirical understanding of the efficiency and user responses pertaining to this kind of set-up. We implemented three different use-case scenarios to analyze both, the combination of the transparent touch screen with real objects as well as with a second screen. For all scenarios we observed a group of ten people (graduate students) interacting with the set-up. All scenarios were installed in a lab environment. For the first scenario, the museum exhibit of a real object, we implemented two categories of additional information to be displayed on the transparent screen: general information that does not refer to specific visible features of the object, and targeted information about visible features, referring to the part in question through visual indicators (lines and circles). Our observations for this scenario can be summarized as follows: Users felt positive about the direct accessibility of the interactive experience. All users felt that the installation was easily seen and intuitive to operate. Compared to a cellphone-based augmented reality experience, which we used as a control experiment, they found that it took significantly less effort to enter the experience since they did not have to launch a specific app, scan a code and then operate the experience on a small screen. Visibility and ease of use of the large touch screen was generally seen as positive. The main negative criterion was that the registration of the transparent screen with the object behind it was significantly off for 50 % of the users, slightly off for 30 %, and only 20 % found the registration was good. All users noted that the registration is sensitive and strongly dependent on the users position. Not only view-point height but also movement have an influence on the quality of registration. While these issues were not as strongly noticeable and did not lead to explicit remarks by the users in the case of general information display, the specifically targeted information suffered from registration problems.

The second use-case scenario, the group collaborative environment was analyzed with document annotation tasks of a text and design variant comparisons of an architectural plan. The benefit that the *Transparent Touch* system provided was not particularly salient. While most users (80 %) found that the physical separation of the annotation layer encouraged annotation and comparison more than a situation in which the annotation is done on an interactive whiteboard, it was not considered a significant improvement. Users stated they would have been equally fine with the whiteboard. In comparison with the interactive whiteboard the spatial distinction of the displays was seen as a negative quality as it introduces parallax issues for members of the group who are not located in range of ca. 45° in front of the display. The user responses were different and significantly more in favor of the transparent touch screen, when compared to the annotations carried out on a laptop projecting the main image and the annotations on one screen.

The third use-case scenario, the control layer interaction, was implemented with the game described above as one variant and with a digitized representation of the same object, a wooden sculpture of a stylized monkey figure, we used for the first scenario, as a second variant. Users were able to rotate the figure and explore animations of arm movements of the figure. The reactions to the game were unanimously positive and the interactive gestures were seen as an inherent part of the experience. The comments indicated that the set-up was experienced as a custom interface to leverage specific aspects of the experience. The exploration of the monkey sculpture was seen as pleasurable but again a significant distinction between the layered display system and single touch screen interaction was not obvious. Most users stated that they would have been equally satisfied with a single touch screen.

As future work we are planning to run a larger study in a public space. It became obvious that the lab situation of this first study did not produce some of the characteristics the system is supposed to address: visual salience of the set-up does not play a role in the lab environment nor did the aspect that users can interact in a personal annotation layer while other visitors can still observe the same object play a role in the lab.

The main goal for the next iteration of the system will be to address the registration issues stated in most of the tests. One of the promising avenues to address this problem will be to implement eye tracking for the user and to adjust the registration according to the eye position and its relation to the object/second screen.

References

1. Engelbart, D.: Demo, clip 12, at ca. 33 minutes (1968). http://web.stanford.edu/dept/SUL/library/extra4/sloan/MouseSite/1968Demo.html
2. Apple system 7 Macintosh Basics Demo. https://www.youtube.com/watch?v=3ScS4OYDfHE
3. Shneiderman, B.: Direct manipulation: a step beyond programming languages. Computer 16 (8), 57–69 (1983). IEEE
4. Shneiderman, B.: The future of interactive systems and the emergence of direct manipulation. Behav. Inf. Technol. 1, 237–256 (2007). Taylor & Francis Group
5. Hutchins, E.L., Hollan, J.D., Norman, D.A.: Direct manipulation interfaces. Hum. Comput. Interact. 1, 311–338 (1985). L. Erlbaum Associates Inc.
6. Sutherland, I.E.: Sketch pad a man-machine graphical communication system. In: DAC 1964 Proceedings of the SHARE Design Automation Workshop, pp. 6.329–6.346. ACM (1964)
7. Walker, G.: A review of technologies for sensing contact location on the surface of a display. J. Soc. Inf. Disp. 20, 413–440 (2012). Wiley-Blackwell
8. Stumpe, B.B.: A New Principle for X-Y Touch Screen, CERN SPS-AOP-BS-jf, pp. i–17. CERN, Geneva (1977)
9. Hsiao, C.-Y., Liu, Y.-J., Wang, M.-J.J.: Usability evaluation of the touch screen user interface design. In: Yamamoto, S. (ed.) HCI 2013, Part I. LNCS, vol. 8016, pp. 48–54. Springer, Heidelberg (2013)
10. Kortum, P.: HCI Beyond the GUI Design for Haptic, Speech, Olfactory and Other Nontraditional Interfaces. Elsevier/Morgan Kaufmann, Amsterdam, Boston (2008)
11. Masoodian, M., McKoy, S., Rogers, B.: Hands-on sharing: collaborative document manipulation on a tabletop display using bare hands. In: CHINZ 2007 Proceedings of the 8th ACM SIGCHI New Zealand Chapter's International Conference on Computer-Human Interaction: Design Centered HCI, pp. 25–31. ACM (2007)
12. Maciel, A., Nedel, L.P., Mesquita, E.M., Mattos, M.H., Machado, G.M., Freitas, C.M.D S.: Collaborative interaction through spatially aware moving displays. In: SAC 2010 Proceedings of the 2010 ACM Symposium on Applied Computing, pp. 1229–1233. ACM (2010)
13. Bachl, S., Tomitsch, M., Kappel, K., Grechenig, T.: The effects of personal displays and transfer techniques on collaboration strategies in multi-touch based multi-display environments. In: Campos, P., Graham, N., Jorge, J., Nunes, N., Palanque, P., Winckler, M. (eds.) INTERACT 2011, Part III. LNCS, vol. 6948, pp. 373–390. Springer, Heidelberg (2011)
14. Arroyo, E., Righi, V., Tarrago, R., Blat, J.: A remote multi-touch experience to support collaboration between remote museum visitors. In: Campos, P., Graham, N., Jorge, J., Nunes, N., Palanque, P., Winckler, M. (eds.) INTERACT 2011, Part IV. LNCS, vol. 6949, pp. 462–465. Springer, Heidelberg (2011)
15. British Museum - Augmented Reality: Beyond the Hype. http://www.museum-id.com/idea-detail.asp?id=336
16. Augmented reality livens up museums. http://www.smithsonianmag.com/innovation/augmented-reality-livens-up-museums-22323417/?no-ist
17. Ultimate dinosaurs: Augmented reality. http://www.cincymuseum.org/exhibits/ultimate-dinosaurs/app

18. Noll, C., Häussermann, B., von Jan, U., Raap, U., Albrecht, U. -V.: Demo: mobile augmented reality in medical education: an application for dermatology. In: MARS 2014 Proceedings of the 2014 Workshop on Mobile Augmented Reality and Robotic Technology-Based Systems, pp. 17–18. ACM (2014)
19. Hornecker, E.: Interactions around a contextually embedded system. In: TEI 2010 Proceedings of the Fourth International Conference on Tangible, Embedded, and Embodied Interaction, pp. 169–176. ACM (2010)
20. Angelopoulou, A., Economou, D., Bouki, V., Psarrou, A., Jin, L., Pritchard, C., Kolyda, F.: Mobile augmented reality for cultural heritage. In: Venkatasubramanian, N., Getov, V., Steglich, S. (eds.) Mobilware 2011. LNICST, vol. 93, pp. 15–22. Springer, Heidelberg (2012)
21. Chun, W.H., Höllerer, T.: Real-time hand interaction for augmented reality on mobile phones. In: IUI 2013 Proceedings of the 2013 International Conference on Intelligent User Interfaces, pp. 307–314. ACM (2013)
22. Drossis, G., Grammenos, D., Birliraki, C., Stephanidis, C.: MAGIC: developing a multimedia gallery supporting mid-air gesture-based interaction and control. In: Stephanidis, C. (ed.) HCII 2013, Part I. CCIS, vol. 373, pp. 303–307. Springer, Heidelberg (2013)
23. Rakkolainen, I., Höllerer, T., DiVerdi, S., Olwal, A.: Mid-air display experiments to create novel user interfaces. Multimed. Tools Appl. **44**(3), 389–405 (2009). Springer US
24. Kim, H., Takahashi, I., Yamamoto, H., Kai, T., Maekawa, S., Naemura, T.: MARIO: mid-air augmented realityinteraction with objects. In: Reidsma, D., Katayose, H., Nijholt, A. (eds.) ACE 2013. LNCS, vol. 8253, pp. 560–563. Springer, Heidelberg (2013)
25. Chan, L. -W., Kao, H. -S., Chen, M. Y., Lee, M. -S., Hsu, J., Hung, Y. -P.: Touching the void: direct-touch interaction for intangible displays. In: CHI 2010 Proceedings of the SIGCHI Conference on Human Factors in Computing Systems, pp. 2625–2634. ACM (2010)
26. Bruder, G., Steinicke, F., Sturzlinger, W.: To touch or not to touch?: Comparing 2D touch and 3D mid-air interaction on stereoscopic tabletop surfaces. In: SUI 2013 Proceedings of the 1st Symposium on Spatial User Interaction, pp. 9–16. ACM (2013)
27. Wilson, A.D.: TouchLight: an imaging touch screen and display for gesture-based interaction. In: ICMI 2004 Proceedings of the 6th International Conference on Multimodal Interfaces, pp. 69–76. ACM (2004)
28. Normand, J. -M., Servières, M., Moreau, G.: A new typology of augmented reality applications. In: AH 2012 Proceedings of the 3rd Augmented Human International Conference, pp. 18:1–18:8. ACM (2012)
29. Edgar, G.K.: Accommodation, cognition, and virtual image displays: a review of the literature. Displays **28**(2), 45–59 (2007). Elsevier BV
30. Lauber, F., Follmann, A., Butz, A.: What you see is what you touch: visualizing touch screen interaction in the head-up display. In: DIS 2014 Proceedings of the 2014 Conference on Designing Interactive Systems, pp. 171–180. ACM (2014)
31. Harrison, B.L., Ishii, H., Vicente, K.J., Buxton, W.A.S.: Transparent layered user interfaces: an evaluation of a display design to enhance focused and divided attention. In: CHI 1995 Proceedings of the SIGCHI Conference on Human Factors in Computing Systems, pp. 317–324. ACM Press/Addison-Wesley Publishing Co (1995)
32. Dürer, A.: In: Underweysung der messung, mit dem zirckel und richtscheyt, in linien, ebenen unnd gantzen corporen. Hieronymus Andreae, Nüremberg (1525)
33. Augmented reality: layar. https://www.layar.com/

34. Hincapié-Ramos, J.D., Guo, X., Moghadasian, P., Irani, P.: Consumed endurance: a metric to quantify arm fatigue of mid-air interactions. In: CHI 2014 Proceedings of the SIGCHI Conference on Human Factors in Computing Systems, pp. 1063–1072. ACM (2014)
35. Müller, J., Walter, R., Bailly, G., Nischt, M., Alt, F.: Looking glass: a field study on noticing interactivity of a shop window. In: CHI 2012 Proceedings of the SIGCHI Conference on Human Factors in Computing Systems, pp. 297–306. ACM (2012)
36. Kin, K., Hartmann, B., Agrawala, M.: Two-handed marking menus for multitouch devices. ACM Trans. Comput. Hum. Interact **18**(3), 161–1623 (2011)
37. Kwon, B.C., Javed, W., Elmqvist, N., Yi, J.S.: Direct manipulation through surrogate objects. In: CHI 2011 Proceedings of the SIGCHI Conference on Human Factors in Computing Systems, pp. 627–636. ACM (2011)

A Haptic Knob as an Innovative User Interface for Visually-Impaired

Maura Mengoni[✉], Lorenzo Cavalieri, and Damiano Raponi

Polytechnic University of Marche, Ancona, Italy
{m.mengoni,lorenzo.cavalieri,d.raponi}@univpm.it

Abstract. The present work describes an early research activity on a haptic user interface to assist visually impaired in using a multi-experience shower that saves energy and water and informs the user about current consumptions. The user interface aims to joint visual, tactile and kinesthetic feedbacks to improve digital contents accessibility. The knob is applied both to interact with the graphic interface by able-bodied persons and to emboss Braille text to drive the blind in navigating the menu items. The developed prototype is then illustrated.

Keywords: Haptic feedback · Assisted living · Inclusive design · Interaction design

1 Introduction

Literature overview in Human-Computer-Interaction suggests two challenging issues to be faced: firstly the views of individual users with particular limitations were traditionally not sought to inform the design process, causing fails in satisfying the needs of a large proportion of the populance and reluctance to engage with new Human-Machine-Interfaces [1]; sencondly actual high-fidelity prototypes used to assess sample end-user response are generally costly, leading companies to neglect participatory approaches [2].

The research goal is to study and develop a low-cost high-fidely prototype exploiting haptic feedback technologies to stimulate different sensorial channels according to the individual user abilities while interacting with the interface. In order to fulfill target users needs and create a prototype that is applicable, appropriate and accessible to many users as possible, the adoption of an inclusive design approch becomes imperative [3]. The research work intention is actually to provide a solution that works as effectively for less able users as they do for able-bodied ones.

Most user-centric design approaches, which inclusive design belongs to, involve sample end-users in product design through iterative cycles of requirement gathering, prototype development, implementation and evaluation [1]. The construction of interactive prototypes to conduct empirical testing at each design stage is difficult to achieve in short time and low cost [4]. In the last ten years the Virtual Reality (VR) technologies have been introduced to provide novel human-computer interfaces through which creating accurate prototypes that are less expensive than high-fidelity ones. According to [5], VR technologies can be classified according to the sensorial

© Springer International Publishing Switzerland 2015
M. Antona and C. Stephanidis (Eds.): UAHCI 2015, Part II, LNCS 9176, pp. 127–138, 2015.
DOI: 10.1007/978-3-319-20681-3_12

modalities they stimulate (i.e. vision, touch and hearing) respectively in visualization and sound displays and haptic devices. Haptic devices are of particular interest for this research as they stimulate the sense of touch, that is one of the substituting modalities adopted by blinded people [6]. Haptic devices provide both tactile and kinesthetic feedbacks [5]. They allow the simulation of some object features such as weight, shape, surface texture, etc. [7]. A set of haptic devices is the so-called tangible user interfaces (TUI). They adopt physical objects to translate user action into input events in the computer interface [8, 9]. The adoption of TUIs for creating a high-fidelity prototype for experiments with target end-users represents a good solution to provide an aesthetically satisfying as well as a functional handle onto elements of the digital world. Although a lot of studies have been carried out to analyze how different VR technologies is able to support blinded people in exploring virtual environments, in rehabilitation, in assisting mobility and in information access on mobile devices and web-based applications [10–12], any research have been conducted yet to develop a tangible interface that facilitate them in using household appliances. Moreover, researches on designing such interfaces did not describe if and how to build low cost high-fidelity prototypes to improve the involvement of end-users in the overall design process and then guarantee the success of the solution.

The above-mentioned issues also emerged in a real industrial design case, represented by a long-term project called "MEET: Multi-Experience for wellness of life EnvironmenT", funded by the Italian Marche Region, involving three Small and Medium-Sized Enterprises and two research centers. Its goal is the development of an innovative multisensory shower oriented to elderly and visually impaired able to save energy and water and inform the user about current consumptions. The product has to integrate an interactive human-computer interface to achieve this second objective.

In this context, the present paper describes the design method adopted for conceiving the user interface and building a high-fidelity prototype. The adopted inclusive design approach has lead to the development of a dedicated user interface that consists of a graphic display where digital contents are projected to create the visual feedback, and a tangible knob providing both kinesthetic and vibrotactile feedbacks to emboss Braille texts and enable information understanding both to visually impaired and sighted users. An Arduino board compatible with Intel Galileo is used to implement the whole prototype hardware and software architecture, that represents a novelty both for applicative and technological domains.

2 Related Work

2.1 Applying User Centric Design to Product Development

Traditional design approaches have been accused of failing in case of less-able persons (e.g. older people, children, visually impaired) due to the insufficient involvement of end-users in the design process, with a consequence of compromising commercial opportunities and making the interactional experience of users poorly attractive [13]. For this reason, in the last twenty years numerous user-centric design approaches have been developed to push the design focus on the thing being designed (e.g. artifact, communication media, space, interface, service) looking for ways to ensure that it meets the need of an individual user and at the same time to a proportion of population as large as possible. The common element among the different UCD approaches is the involvement of sample end-user at all stages of product development, from information gathering, to design requirements, till alternative solutions' evaluation and experiments with final prototypes. For instance, inclusive design is an approach that aims to create interfaces, artifacts and products that are applicable, appropriate and accessible to many users as possible within the constraints of the design specification [3]. Similarly, participatory design aims to develop systems with the close involvement of all process stakeholders and end-users through cycles of requirement gathering, prototype development, implementation and evaluation [14]. Experience Design aim is to design users' experience of things, events and places by studying the communication process between the user and the object/service/environment [15]. One of the main critical issues in adopting the above-mentioned approaches regards the construction of interactive prototypes to conduct empirical testing at each design stage in short time and at low cost. This task becomes more critical in case of involvement of people with some kind of impairment [12].

Two main prototyping techniques are known in literature: low-fidelity prototyping (e.g. paper sketches, cardboard mock-up) and high-fidelity prototyping (e.g. software-based and virtual prototypes, physical mock-up). The second is able to make users realistically appraise the aesthetic attributes and functionalities of the product [4] but is expensive and cannot be implemented at the early stages of design. To overcome this limitation, in the last ten years VR technologies have been introduced to intuitively manipulate ad explore virtual prototypes as well as to simulate product behavior in different working conditions. Some studies demonstrate how virtual prototype interaction via VR can be used to rapidly carry out usability testing while reducing evaluation costs and time [16]. However, VR shows several technological limitations as it is still characterized by low sense of immersion, poor physical interaction, high complexity, intrusiveness and non-intuitiveness. Mixed Reality represents a compromise solution in which real and virtual worlds are combined in various proportions and presented as a unified whole [17]. Mixed Reality environments often exploit TUI technologies (e.g. haptic and tactile displays) to reproduce the real contact with the object while manipulating the virtual prototype. Although a lot of studies have been carried out to analyze how VR and MR are able to support elderly and disabled people in numerous contexts [18] any research have been conducted yet to create a tangible virtual prototype to involve the blind in user interface design. The research interest for the development of a TUI to create a reliable high-fidelity prototype for usability testing is twofold: it can be used as a mean for sensory substitution in case of visually impaired and despite many other interfaces it has the advantage to provide a natural affordance in tangible objects coupling digital information to physical artifacts and environments [19].

2.2 Tangible User Interfaces as Means for Prototyping Design Solutions

A TUI is a type of human-computer interface that leverages physical representation to connect between physical and the digital worlds [8]. Their main potentialities are as follows: they support learning due to their hand-on nature, which allows physical manipulation of objects [20]; they demonstrate superior performance in terms of memory and learning enhancement once a haptic signal is added to the visual and audio ones [21] as well as in terms of sense of presence in the virtual environment; they are more inviting, engaging, enjoying and intuitive than traditional graphic interfaces [19] due to the rich feedback and realism they provide.

Haptic displays are a set of TUIs that are generally used to physically manipulate digital information. They can be divided in force feedback devices (FFDs), and tactile devices. FFDs allow point or multi-point contact with virtual objects to provide kinaesthetic cues [22], while tactile displays reproduce the shape and the contact effect of the object surface by stimulating the mechanoreceptors of the human fingertips by providing cutaneous cues [23]. Three types of most relevant FFDs are [22] point-based devices (e.g. the PHANToM, the MOOG-HapticMaster and the Haption-Virtuose), multi-point based devices (e.g. Haptex system), physical rendering systems based on vertical pin displacement. On the other side, the field of research on tactile displays is rapidly growing. They spread from miniature pin array tactile modules based on elastic and electromagnetic forces to stimulate the human's mechanoreceptors [24], to electrotactile displays where the finger mechanoreceptors are stimulated by a current flow or an electric potential, to electro-vibration-based friction displays able to modulate electrotactile or friction forces between the touch surface and the sliding finger [24, 25]. There are also some examples of integration of force and cutaneous feddbacks. Kim et al. [26] proposed a lightweight tactile display integrated into a haptic glove; Oshii et al. [27] developed a tactile display using airborne ultrasound. Although the numerous studies, most systems lack of usability and have limited capabilities [28].

Due to the lack of visual contact, people with reduced sight obtain information from the surroundings using the other perceptions, especially touch and hearing. Most of the interfaces developed for visually impaired people adopt two types of feedbacks: haptic and/or tactile and acoustic. Focusing on the first class of means for sensory substitution, several technologies have emerged which can be used to present information to the sense of touch [6] as follows:

- raised paper displays that imply the reproduction via embossing or heat-raised paper of Braille texts, pictorial information, maps, etc.
- vibrotactile displays that consist of a single element stimulator to encode information in temporal parameters of the vibration signal. They are used as non-audio-based indicators of an incoming call or a warning;
- force feedback displays via single-point interaction probes that render the contact with virtual objects;
- tactile displays that produce touch sensations through electrical, thermal or mechanical stimulations.

Applications of force and tactile displays can be found for the development of user interfaces to support blind and visually impaired people for medical or rehabilitation scopes [10]. They are also used for orientation and mobility purposes, where the haptic cues are used to translate some visual information gathered from sensors or other input devices into touch information. For instance, Brown et al. [29] investigated the use of multiple vibration motors on the user's arm to access calendar information, while Kammoun et al., [30] proposed the usage of two vibrotactile bracelets to aid blind people during orientation and navigation. However, in all cases the adopted design approach appears more technological-oriented than user-oriented. Moreover, none example of their application for creating high-fidelity prototypes to support inclusive design has been found in literature.

3 The Design of the User Interface

3.1 The Design Approach

The approach adopted to design the proposed user interface consists of the following steps:

Step1: Information gathering about user needs to define a set of design requirements. Both surveys and semi-structured interviews are used for this purpose;

Step2: Design of the user interface including graphics, dynamics, and the physical components that are used to set the product items and receive proper feedbacks about the selected options. This stage includes the creation of a flow diagram of the interface elements and the conceptual design of the physical components (i.e. screen, control knobs and buttons);

Step3: Prototyping of alternative solutions for user testing. It includes the creation of the proposed high-fidelity prototype exploiting haptic technologies;

Step4: Usability testing via task analysis with sample end-users on the developed high fidelity prototypes;

Step5: Creation of a document containing all design specifications and guidelines deriving from the elaboration of usability tests' results to detail the best design solution.

Step6: Implementation of the selected solution (embodiment design and detail design of the interface) and creation of a final working prototype for evaluation.

As mentioned before, the proposed approach derives from the state of art in inclusive design and from the issues emerged during the MEET project. The MEET project is actually based on the idea to research and develop a new innovative shower able to save energy (-30%) and water (-40 () and offer a multi-sensorial experience to elderly and visually impaired persons. The user interface has to: *(i)* make the user aware of water and energy consumptions and achieved savings; and *(ii)* enable the user to select a proper combination of product items to create a custom wellness treatment. The functions offered by the multisensory shower are listed as follows:

- water functions:
  - rain effect;
  - cascade;
  - adjustable hand shower;
  - upper/central/lower massage;
  - vertical jets;
  - lower jets;
  - vaporized;

It is also possible to set the water flow rate and adjust the temperature.

- color therapy functions:
  - RGB led and white lights;
- music functions:
  - select genre, artist, album and playlist.

According to the selected sound track the system combines the other functions to give a coherent multi experience.

The first step concerns the analysis of user needs and the creation of a proper set of design requirements to start with the conceptual stage. This study is carried out by a survey on traditional user interfaces adopted in wellness sector and by interviews on their current usability. A semi-structured interview is submitted to 50 sample end-users aged between 50 and 70 years, about which 40 % are visually impaired. The main identified drawbacks regard the limitations of adopted touch displays that do not provide an accurate visual feedback when positioned into a wet environment and of voice controls that are not reliable due to the noise produced by water and selected sound tracks. Finally there are not any systems with solutions appropriate for impaired users' needs.

Thanks to the outcomes of the information gathering stage and to the proved affordance of TUI, it has been chosen to develop a user interface consisting of a LCD graphic display, where the digital contents can be visualized, and a haptic knob to select the shower items with functionalities appropriate both for able-bodied and visually impaired users. In order to include both sighted and blind persons in the shower environment, the haptic knob is designed according to the following requirements:

- Providing an ergonomic grip;
- Enabling a complete control of the interface without never removing the hand;
- Embedding "ok" and "back" buttons to allow the user to advance or regress into the hierarchical menu;
- Providing a tactile feedback to emboss Braille text.

The graphics interface is developed adopting a hierarchical tree structure to be compatible with the physical interface (i.e. knob). The followings requirements drive the design of its graphics and dynamics:

- Clear layout made of two distinctive areas, one for navigation and for information to be input or output and one for status information;
- Using more texts than symbols to express the information in an easy way;
- Enlargement and careful placement of items in the interface structure;
- Creating a contrast between items and background to make the information easily readable;
- Adopting visual and/or audio and/or touch cues to inform the user about the current event or the selected item (feedbacks);
- Mapping between provided functions and icons.

The designed graphic interface consists of a static column, on the left side, where the shower status is displayed (e.g. on/off, water temperature, set program, selected sound track) and a dynamic area, where information changes according to the selected options in the main menu. The menu is represented as a circle where items are listed around it. A study is conducted on the hierarchical menu in order to reduce the number of interactions necessary to perform a task. A flow diagram is created for that purpose. When the user selects one of the item in the menu, the text is enlarged and a new section appears to control the related sub functions (Fig. 1).

The circle displayed in the graphic interface is also physically reproduced through a circular haptic knob whose rotation is associated to the scrolling functions of the graphic menu. Two buttons, corresponding to "ok" and "back" functions, are positioned at opposite knob sides. They allow the user to go over and back into the hierarchical menu. The knob is divided into two parts, a fixed one where the buttons are positioned and a mobile one that rotates to allow the user to select the menu items. A Braille pad is placed on the top surface of the rotating ring, that clearly remains fixed (Fig. 2).

Both rings of the haptic knob have a diameter of 8 cm. Some preliminary ergonomic studies have been conducted to set the dimensions. The knob is realized in Duralight®, an innovative acrylic-based material patented by one of the industrial project partners, characterized by a nice finishing, particularly when it is wet by water, and by a flexible manufacturing process that allows the creation of custom shapes. A soft touch coating is additionally used to cover the areas of the haptic knob where the user goes in touch to increase the pleasantness of touch and provide a better grip for people that have some impairments in hand movement control and finger grasping.

Fig. 1. Two screenshots of the graphic user interface

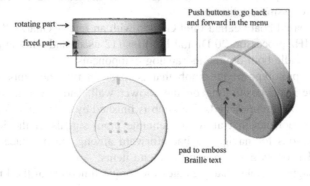

Fig. 2. Concept of the knob

4 Prototyping the User Interface: The Haptic Knob

The combination of different graphics of the user interface (e.g. dimensions and colors of icons), behaviors of the knob (e.g. hard or soft rotation) and shape, size and finishing of on-touch surfaces (e.g. coarse or smooth finishing) requires the building of low-cost prototypes to perform preliminary usability testing and select the most appropriate solution to develop the final one. Haptic technologies are then exploited to simulate the behavior of the knob while providing a tangible interaction to the user and visualizing the digital contents on the graphic display.

The proposed high-fidelity (Hi-Fi) prototype is composed of three basic elements: (i) the graphical user interface (GUI) for the reproduction of visual information; (ii) the control system to manage user interactions with the haptic knob and the coherent configuration of the GUI; (iii) the haptic knob with capacitive buttons and an electro-tactile pad. The prototype consists of both Hardware/Firmware and Software components that are integrated to guarantee system reliability and I/O synchronization.

The physical prototypes of differently sized knobs are realized by Rapid Prototyping techniques. A commercial LCD display is used to visualize the digital contents generated by the software prototype. The "ok" and "back" buttons have not physically prototyped because of their fragility in case of small dimensions of 3D printed shapes with respect to finger pressure. For that reason, two capacitive buttons are introduced to operate as pressure sensors to activate the same functions. The software prototype is developed in an Open-Source object-oriented programming language that is Processing. It manages the graphics and dynamics of the user interface. Arduino that is an Open-Source electronics platform based on easy-to-use hardware and software, is used to implement the Firmware (FM) to carry out data elaboration.

Figure 3 shows the overall system prototype and how the information flows across the HW and FW modules.

The Hardware architecture is composed by:

- A 7-inches LCD display connected to a laptop computer via VGA. It is used to visualize the screenshots of the graphical interface;
- A laptop with i7 processor at 2.2 GHz and 16 GB of RAM, to upload the interface manager FW on Arduino board and make the Processing application running. In addition, the laptop is used as a tool for serial communication between the Arduino board and Processing application;
- An Arduino-based board called Intel Galileo with an Intel® Quark ™ X1000 SoC, 32-bit 400 MHz processor, 20 Digital I/O Pins (12 used) and with an input voltage of 12 V, to handle both digital and analog components;
- The physical prototype of the knob that is made of two elements, one fixed to guarantee the knob positioning on the shower wall, and one rotating where the capacitive buttons are mounted. The knob is finished by different soft-touch paints;
- Hardware components that allow to generate input signals of the interface: two capacitive buttons for navigating back/forward among the interface pages and a rotary encoder to navigate through the menu items;
- An electromagnetic brake that regulates the torque functions of the knob to define its behavior and the number of clicks corresponding to the menu items. The brake is

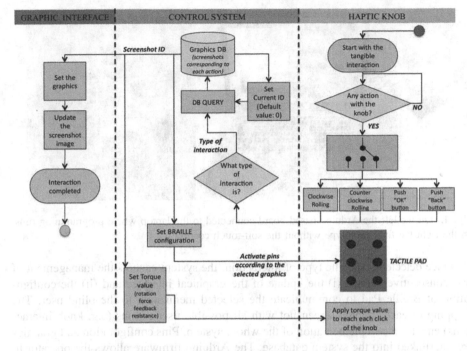

Fig. 3. Human-computer Interaction flow in the interface prototype

mounted on the rotation pivot of the knob and connected to a variable power supply circuit controlled by the Intel Galileo board;

- The tactile pad positioned on the top of the knob surface to emboss Braille texts. The pad is realized through a matrix of 2 × 3 pins connected to the six-pins of the board and a ground terminal - common to all the pins – used to the current back-flow. A Bare Conductive fluid is used to paint the output pins, the connections to the board (horizontal lines in Fig. 4) and the ground connections (vertical lines in Fig. 4). It is also applied inside the knob to create floating links to create the knob connections when the array is in the portrait mode. Two main advantages are achieved by the use of this electrically conductive paint: (i) there are no problems about tangled wires due to the knob rotation, (ii) the risk of inverted matrix and resulting wrong mapping pins is avoided, and (iii) it has not any performance degradation when covered by soft-touch paint to improve tactile sensations and grip effects.

Two programming platforms are used to implement the software as follows: (i) Arduino, that manages all electronic components and at the same time is used as a tool for communication with the GUI; and (ii) Processing, that controls the GUI through a serial communication with the Arduino-based Firmware. The choice of these two development systems is due to the strong integration between Arduino programming language and the Processing one. The software is implemented according to the flow chart developed in the conceptual design stage. It synchronizes the haptic interactions (i.e. pressure switch of the capacitive "ok" and "back" buttons, knob rotation) with the displayed graphics and the coherent reproduction of the Braille text.

Fig. 4. On the left the Arduino-based board connected to the laptop where programming runs; on the right the final prototype without the soft-touch coating.

Once detected a specific type of interaction, the system ensures the management of two consecutive events: (i) the update of the graphical interface and (ii) the configuration of Braille Pad to communicate the selected menu item to the blind user. The mapping of each graphic screenshot with all possible user actions (e.g. knob interactions) enables the implementation of the whole system. Pins configuration and graphics are interlinked into the system database. The Arduino firmware allows the operator to set the supply voltage of the electromagnetic brake in the setup phase, in order to control the torque function and hence the knob behavior.

5 Conclusion and Future Work

Learning from past research and development in the application of technology for the blind, this paper proposes an innovative user interface to assist visually impaired and sighted users in setting and customizing wellness treatments offered by a multi-experience shower. It consists of a graphic user interfaces coupled with a haptic knob embedding a refreshable Braille pad. As designing devices for the blind is more arduous than expected and requires a fully understand of their needs, an inclusive design approach has been applied. A high-fidelity prototype exploiting both force and electrotactile feedbacks displays is developed to conduct iterative evaluations of design solutions' usability and accessibility. The main proposed challenges regard:

- the application field of haptic technology for the blind. In literature it is generally used to create aids for orientation and rehabilitation. In this paper it is used both as a new interaction paradigm to create novel user interfaces for household appliances and as a tool to develop low-cost high fidelity prototypes for testing.
- the integration of a state-of art tactile pads [25] into an haptic knob to support the refreshment of Braille text to enable visually impaired in accessing information from the graphic user interface.

Future work will be focused on the experimentation of the developed haptic knob into the blind community in order to test the reliability of the adopted inclusive design method, the usability and acceptability of the developed user interface and finally the ability of the low-cost high fidelity prototype to accurately simulate the behavior of the designed interface.

References

1. Wilkinson, C., De Angeli, A.: Applying user centred and participatory design approaches to commercial product development. Des. Stud. **35**(6), 614–631 (2014)
2. Sauer, J., Sonderegger, A.: The influence of prototype fidelity and aesthetics of de-sign in usability tests: effects on user behaviour, subjective evaluation and emotion. Appl. Ergon. **40**, 670–677 (2009)
3. Keates, S., Clarkson, J.: Countering design exclusion – an introduction to inclusive design. Springer Verlag, London (2003)
4. Sade, S., Nieminen, M., Riihiaho, S.: Testing usability with 3D paper proto-types-case Halton system. Appl. Ergon. **29**(1), 13–61 (1998)
5. Burdea, G.C., Coiffet, C.: Virtual Reality Technology, 2nd edn. Wiley-IEEE Press, New York (2003)
6. Wall, S.A., Brewster, S.: Sensory substitution using tactile pin arrays: human factors, technology and applications. Sig. Process. **86**(12), 3674–3695 (2006)
7. Cavalieri, L., Germani, M., Mengoni, M.: Multi-modal interaction system to tactile perception. Lecture Notes in Artificial Intelligence in Computer Science – Part I. from the International Conference on Human Computer Interaction (HCI 2014), pp. 25–34. Heraklion, Crete (2014)
8. Ishii, H., Ullmer, B.: Tangible bits: towards seamless interfaces between people, bits and atoms. In: the International Conference on Computing System, 234–241, USA (1997)
9. Seichter, H., Kvan, T.: Tangible interfaces in design computing. Virtual Env. **2**, 159–166 (2004)
10. Levesque, V.: Blindness, technology and haptics. Center for Intelligent Machines. Technical report (2005)
11. Guerreiro, T., Oliveira, J., Benedito, J., Nicolau, H., Jorge, J., Gonçalves, D.: Blind people and mobile keypads: accounting for individual differences. In: Campos, P., Graham, N., Jorge, J., Nunes, N., Palanque, P., Winckler, M. (eds.) INTERACT 2011, Part I. LNCS, vol. 6946, pp. 65–82. Springer, Heidelberg (2011)
12. Ceccacci, S., Germani, M., Mengoni, M.: How to use virtual and augmented reality techniques to design high usable human-machine interfaces. In: Langdon, P., Clarkson, J., Robinson, P., Lazar, J., Heylighen, A. (eds.) Designing Inclusive Systems: Designing Inclusion for Real-World Applications, Universal Access and Assistive Technology, pp. 65–74. Springer-verlag, London (2012)
13. Hansen, J., Avons, S., Davidoff, J.: Attitude to telecare among older people, professional care workers and informal career: a preventive strategy or crisis management? Univ. Access Inf. Soc. **6**(2), 193–205 (2007)
14. Sharma, V., Simpson, R., LoPresti, E., Mostowy, C., Olson, J., Puhlman, J.: Participatory design in the development of wheelchair convoy system. J. NeuroEngineering Rehabil. **5**, 1–10 (2008)

15. Hassenzahl, M., Eckoldt, K., Diefenbach, S., Laschke, M., Lenz, E., Kim, J.: Designing moments of meaning and pleasure. Experience design and happiness. Int. J. Des. **7**(3), 21–31 (2013)
16. Wilson, J.R., D'Cruz, M.: Virtual and interactive environments for work of the future. Int. J. Hum Comput Stud. **64**, 158–169 (2006)
17. Bordegoni, M., Cugini, U., Caruso, G., Polistina, S.: Mixed prototyping for product assessment: a reference framework. Int. J. Interact. Des. Manufact. **3**, 177–187 (2009)
18. Mengoni M., Ceccacci C., Raponi D.: An inclusive approach for home environment design. In: the 10th IEEE/ASME International Conference on Mechatronic and Embedded Systems and Applications, Senigallia, Italy (2014)
19. Zuckerman, O., Gal-Oz, A.: To TUI or not to TUI: evaluating performance and preference in tangible vs. graphical user interfaces. Int. J. Hum Comput Stud. **71**(7-8), 803–820 (2013)
20. Marshall, P.: Do tangible interfaces enhance learning? In: the International Conference on Tangible and Embedded Interaction, pp. 163–170 (2007)
21. Hecht, D., Reiner, M., Karni, A.: Enhancement of response times to bi- and trimodal sensory stimuli during active movements. Exp. Brain Res. **185**, 655–665 (2008)
22. Hayward, V., Ashley, O., Hernandez, M.C., Grant, D., Robles-De-La-Torre, G.: Haptic interfaces and devices. Sens. Rev. **24**, 16–29 (2004)
23. Chouvardas, V., Miliou, A., Hatalis, M.: Tactile displays: Overview and recent advances. Displays **29**, 185–194 (2008)
24. Yang, T.-H., Kim, Y.-J., Park, Y.-K., Kim, S.-Y.: Design of a miniature integrated haptic device for cutaneous, thermal and kinaesthetic sensations. In: Auvray, M., Duriez, C. (eds.) EuroHaptics 2014, Part I. LNCS, vol. 8618, pp. 505–512. Springer, Heidelberg (2014)
25. Germani, M., Mengoni, M., Peruzzini, M.: Electro-tactile device for material texture simulation. Int. J. Adv. Manufact. Technol. **68**, 2185–2203 (2013)
26. Kim, S.C., Israr, A., Poupyrev, I.: Tactile rendering of 3D features on touch surfaces. In: the 26th annual ACM symposium on User interface software and technology, pp. 531 – 538, St. Andrews, UK (2008)
27. Hoshi, T., Takahashi, M., Iwamoto, T., Shinoda, H.: Noncontact tactile display based on radiation pressure of airbone ultrasound. IEEE Trans. on Haptics **3**(3), 155–165 (2010)
28. Bullion, C., Gurocak, H.: Haptic glove with MR brakes for distributed finger force feedback. Presence **18**(6), 421–433 (2009)
29. Brown, L.M., Brewster, S.A. Purchase, H.C.: Multidimensional tactons for non-visual information presentation in mobile devices. In: the 8th conference on Human-computer interaction with mobile devices and services, Espoo, Finland (2006)
30. Kammoun, S., Jouffrais, C., Guerriero, T., Nicolau, H., Jorge, J.: Guiding blind people with haptic feedback. In: Pervasive 2012 Workshop on Frontiers in Accessibility for Pervasive Computing, New Castle, UK (2012)

User-Acceptance of Latency in Touch Interactions

Walter Ritter[✉], Guido Kempter, and Tobias Werner

Vorarlberg University of Applied Sciences, Dornbirn, Austria
walter.ritter@fhv.at

Abstract. Nowadays direct input interfaces are nearly ubiquitous due to the advent of touch screen based smartphones, tablets, and computers. Latency in human-computer interfaces has been discussed since a long time, but established numbers have been questioned in recent research regarding their applicability for direct input interfaces like touch screens. This pilot study focuses on user-acceptable levels of latency in two distinct tasks: simple tapping on interface elements for invoking an action, and dragging tasks to control analog settings. Our results show acceptable latency levels around 300 ms for low attention tapping tasks and around 170 ms for dragging tasks, where visual feedback is essential. These findings are in accordance to previous findings and confirm the importance of considering the task to be fulfilled for drawing conclusions.

Keywords: Latency · Touch · Interaction · Acceptance · Gesture recognition

1 Introduction

Response times of technical systems have been a subject of debate since a long time [6]. Since the success and ubiquity of direct input devices like touch screens for smartphones, tablets, and computers, the question has been raised if findings for indirect input interfaces still apply (see [4,8]).

From a technical perspective, longer accepted response times would allow for example for more freedom regarding system design (e.g. network based architectures), or more reliable recognition of gestures. One recent example for this is the delay of 300 ms present in webviews of current smart phones and tablets to distinguish between a tap on a link and a double tap gesture to automatically zoom webpages to display the content tapped[1]. From a user's perspective, however, shorter response times allow for more efficient use of interfaces. Systems with longer response times might be considered less attractive than a more responsive one, or even prevent the user from successfully fulfilling tasks [12].

---

[1] A discussion of the 300 ms delay in webviews and efforts to work around it can be found at http://blogs.telerik.com/appbuilder/posts/13-11-21/what-exactly-is.....
-the-300ms-click-delay.

© Springer International Publishing Switzerland 2015
M. Antona and C. Stephanidis (Eds.): UAHCI 2015, Part II, LNCS 9176, pp. 139–147, 2015.
DOI: 10.1007/978-3-319-20681-3_13

Miller described these two aspects as technical needs and psychological needs for system response times [6]. Both need to be taken into account when designing systems.

In our research we use a definition of response time (latency) as the time between the moment a user performs an input action and the moment feedback is given by the system (so it's a combination of input-, processing- and output latency). In this paper we only consider visual feedback.

2   Related Work

Already in 1968 Miller pointed out that the needs for system response times vary heavily between different classes of human actions and outlined 17 different scenarios [6]. He proposed that longer delays may be accepted after closure of an activity than what would be accepted during an ongoing activity (clump), due to limitations of short term memory. Distractions for the short term memory would become even more of a problem, if an individual had an awareness of waiting, which usually happens after around 2 seconds according to Miller.

Shneiderman adds that expectations regarding response times are influenced by prior experiences made by users. If users can complete their tasks quicker than before they will be pleasantly surprised. However, if it would be too quick, they might be worried that they didn't perform the task correctly, or if it would be taking much longer they might become frustrated [9]. He also points out that time expectations vary greatly among individuals and across tasks, and that such expectations of people are highly adaptive. Therefore what used to be acceptable a few years ago, might now be considered unacceptable.

Even a small variation in response times might have effects on the perception of delays. Miller noted that 75 percent of test subjects recognized a variation of 8 percent in delays for durations of 2 s to 4 s [6]. Gallaway proposed a maximum variation of plus/minus 5 % for response times of up to 2s [3]. However, Shneiderman suggests that modest variations up to plus/minus 50 % are still tolerable [10].

Card et al. advocate the use of three different task classes for response times: 100 ms for perceptual processing, 1s for immediate responses, and 10 s for unit tasks [2]. Shneiderman mentions 50–150 ms for cursor movements, 1s for frequent simple tasks, 2s to 4 s for common tasks and 8 s to 12s for complex tasks [10].

Indirect input devices like trackpads or mice rely on feedback given on the screen in form of a cursor. This feedback is the only anchor point for a user to verify the correct input actions. In contrast to this, direct input devices like touch-screens would not need input feedback as the user's finger could directly act as zero latency feedback. This might have consequences for the perception of response times. Direct input devices might therefore be more forgiving regarding longer response times since they could simply be ignored.

Jota et al. addressed this question and found that latency in direct input devices still affects interaction. According to them, latency mostly affects movement times during the final stages of pointing. But more importantly in their research they also observed a significant increase of user performance with decreasing latencies down to 10 ms. They concluded that a reasonable time window to give feedback would be between 20 ms and 40 ms. For comparison, current touch screen devices feature response times between 50 and 200 ms [4].

In a previous study about perceptible levels of latency Ng et al. showed that during dragging operations users were able to perceive latencies down to 2.38 ms [8].

Anderson et al. performed a study about acceptable levels of latency for common tasks with touch screen devices. They reported that delays above 580 ms were considered unacceptable by their users [1]. However, as the experimental task were short, higher delays might be acceptable for more complex tasks.

While some studies confirm that latency can be perceived down to levels way beyond the capabilities of what is currently available on the market, and that those small latencies still affect performance of users, other studies show that user-acceptable levels of latencies are highly depending on the tasks performed by the users and might be well above the latency for cursor-feedback proposed by Shneiderman [10].

The broad range of findings for touch screen interactions, led us to perform a brief pilot study in the context of a concrete usage scenario to judge possible consequences for the technical requirements for the development of a specific device, balancing the technical and psychological needs.

3   Method

To find out about acceptable response times for our usecases in a specified context we conducted two pilot studies with ten test persons each (6 male, 4 female with an average age of 43 years). All of them already had experiences with touch screen devices. In the first study the acceptance level was rated by means of direct delay comparisons, in the second study delays were rated individually. Both studies should evaluate the acceptance levels for a simple tapping tasks as well as for dragging tasks, where visual feedback was required to be able to fulfill the tasks.

3.1   Delay Comparisons

In a first study participants were asked to tap consecutively on a row of buttons and after each tap wait for a glowing lamp feedback to appear on screen before they moved on. Once they completed a row, they were asked up to which button they found the delay acceptable. Then they had to perform a set of dragging tasks, moving a number over a line at the top of the screen (see Fig. 1 for an illustration of the task screens, and Fig. 2 for an illustration of the rating screen).

In this setup 4 sets of delays were used. Each set was used twice - one time ordered ascending, the other time ordered descending. All participants had to rate all 4 sets in both directions. The order in which test persons were presented with the different sets was randomized to compensate for order effects. The sets

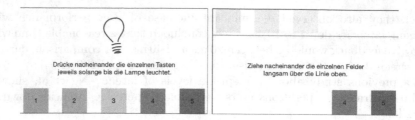

Fig. 1. On the left the user interface for the tapping tasks is shown, on the right side the one for the dragging tasks including the instructions for the test participants.

were comprised of delays between 70 ms (the native latency of the test device) up to 1000 ms.

```
S1: {70,100,150,200,250} ms
S2: {70,150,250,350,500} ms
S3: {70,200,350,600,1000} ms
S4: {70,300,400,700,800} ms
```

To further investigate the influence of the usage-situation on accepted response times, one half of the test persons were instructed to perform the tasks as quickly as possible, while the other half of the test persons were instructed to perform the tasks slowly. Also these instructions were assigned randomly.

Our hypotheses were that we should find differences in the acceptable delays between tapping and dragging tasks (H1a) and find differences in the acceptable delays between the groups with quick and slow instructions (H1b). This would confirm the dependence on the task and the situation for acceptable delay levels.

The tests were performed on an iPad Air with a native latency of 70 ms. Each person needed about 10 min to complete the test.

Fig. 2. The rating screen for the last acceptance level of latency. Note that the slider allowed to rate in between two delays too.

3.2   Absolute Delay Ratings

In a second study participants were asked to perform taps on buttons and observe the feedback given for 4 times, and then adjust the hue of one filled rectangle

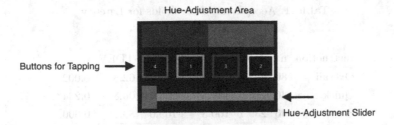

Fig. 3. Tapping and dragging elements for hue adjustments between the left and right rectangle on the top.

to match the hue of another filled rectangle (see Fig. 3 for an illustration of the tasks). This task required exact feedback and was not directly influenced by Fitts law (i.e. there was no direct mapping of the location of the users finger and the feedback given) in contrast to other studies performed (e.g. [4,5,11]).

After each delay time, users were asked to rate the acceptance level of the delay between 0 (best) and 10 (worst) for the tapping task as well as for the dragging task. A complete test consisted of delays of {100, 150, 200, 250, 300, 350, 400, 450, 500, 600, 700, 800, 900, 1100} ms where each delay was presented two times, one time in an ascending manner and the other time in a descending manner relative to the previous value. The order itself was randomized to account for order effects.

Our hypotheses was that ratings regarding acceptance levels should differ between the two task groups (H2).

The tests were performed on an Asus EeeTop Touch PC with a native latency of 100 ms. Each person needed about 30 min to complete the test.

4 Results

4.1 Delay Comparisons

To identify an acceptance threshold of latency among the different sets of comparisons we linearly transformed the values of the given ratings into ms values and calculated descriptive statistics. Then we first compared the overall difference between the groups of tap- and dragging tasks using a paired-samples t-test.

To see the effect of the instruction given, we then splitted the results by instruction type and again compared tap- and dragging tasks for differences in the threshold levels using a paired-samples t-test.

The analysis shows that there were differences in the acceptance threshold for latency between tapping and dragging tasks (Tap: avg=263.0 ms, sd=127.6; Drag: avg=212.7 ms, sd=162.8; p=0.002), supporting our H1a despite the high standard deviation for the dragging operation rating.

Comparing the differences regarding acceptance threshold for latency between tapping and dragging tasks considering the instructions given

Table 1. Acceptantce Thresholds for Latency

Instruction	n	Tap		Drag		
		AVG	STDEV	AVG	STDEV	p
Overall	80	263.0	127.6	212.7	162.8	0.002[*]
Quick	40	286.9	147.5	256.5	206.8	0.234
Slow	40	239.1	100.3	169.0	83.5	0.000[*]

(Tap: avg=286.9 ms, sd=147.5; Drag: avg=256.5 ms, sd=206.8; p=0.234 for the quick instruction; Tap: avg=239.1 ms, sd=100.3; Drag: avg=169.0 ms, sd=83.5; p=0.000 for the slow instruction) reveals significantly lower acceptable latency levels for slow dragging tasks than for tapping tasks. See Fig. 4 for a graphical representation and Table 1 for a detailed overview of the results. While H1b was not supported for simple tapping tasks, it was confirmed for slow dragging tasks.

4.2 Absolute Delay Ratings

To compare the given ratings for the tested touch latency times we calculated descriptive statistics for each latency and interaction for the interaction types tap and drag.

Results show negative ratings regarding acceptance for tap actions starting at 600 ms and 450 ms for drag actions, however, the confidence intervals overlap considerably in these ranges.

We then compared the two interaction types against each other using paired-samples t-tests to see if there were significant differences in ratings between the two interaction types among the tested latencies.

At latency times of 200 ms, 250 ms and interestingly 400 ms a significant difference between tap and drag interaction was found confirming our H2 for these latencies (see Table 2 for detailed results). Figures 5 and 6 show the ratings for the tested latency times for tap and drag actions.

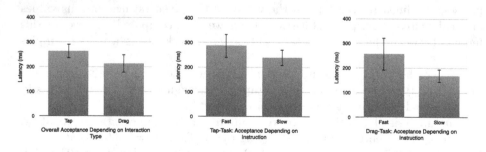

Fig. 4. Differences of acceptance levels depending on interaction type and instruction type. Error-bars show the 95 % confidence interval.

Table 2. Latency ratings for Tap and Drag actions

Tap		Tap		Drag		
Latency (ms)	n	AVG	STDEV	AVG	STDEV	p
100	20	0.6	0.7	1.2	1.8	0.078
200	20	1.3	1.3	2.9	2.7	0.006*
250	20	2.8	1.9	4.2	2.8	0.018*
300	20	2.3	1.7	3.5	2.8	0.079
350	20	4.6	2.4	4.5	3.0	0.875
400	20	3.1	1.7	4.6	3.1	0.027*
450	20	5.6	2.4	5.8	3.4	0.694
500	20	5.4	2.6	6.2	2.6	0.145
600	19	7.3	2.1	7.3	2.7	0.970
700	20	7.7	2.3	7.7	2.5	0.980
800	20	7.4	2.5	8.2	2.4	0.115
900	20	7.8	2.6	8.4	2.2	0.288
1100	20	9.2	1.4	9.2	1.4	0.949

5 Discussion

The results in our study on the one hand confirm findings by Anderson [1] with an absolute negative rating for acceptance starting at 600 ms latency for tap actions, and 450 ms for drag actions, but on the other hand also show the dependency of these levels on the task to be performed, which is inline with previous findings e.g. by [6,9].

The results of our comparison study show the influence of different usage contexts on the level of acceptable latency. In scenarios where not a lot of attention is needed to complete a task (in our case the quick tapping scenario) the accepted threshold is much higher (286.9 ms) than for interactions that involve more attention to detail (in our case the slow dragging scenario) (169 ms). For simple tapping tasks the influence of instructions could not be confirmed.

While our study for absolute delay ratings seemingly yielded much higher acceptable latency times (up to 600 ms) than our comparison study (286.7 ms), a closer look reveals, that the actual level might be in line with what our comparison study revealed. Significant differences between tap and drag tasks in the 200–250 ms range indicate, that the requirements for tap and drag actions are different at this stage. A possible explanation for this would be, that for tap actions these times are already pleasant enough for the users, whereas for drag actions there is still a desire for an improvement. At levels above 300 ms both could be beyond a comfortable levels, and thus not yield significant differences anymore. Interestingly a significant difference was also found at 400 ms. Here it would be interesting to perform additional tests to see if this was due to the

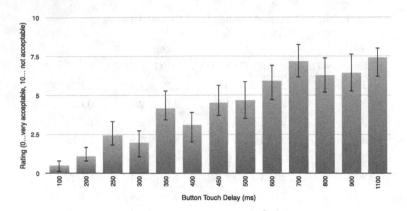

Fig. 5. Differences of acceptance ratings for the tested button touch latencies. Error-bars show the 95 % confidence interval.

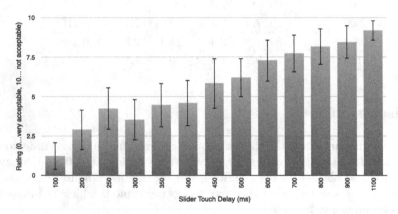

Fig. 6. Differences of acceptance ratings for the tested slider touch latencies. Error-bars show the 95 % confidence interval.

small sample size or if there might even exist something like an uncanny valley [7] for response times.

We are aware that these pilot studies can only be considered as an indication of what might be an acceptable amount of latency in touch interactions due to the small sample sizes. However, since the results are inline with previous research and the numbers are robust with different analysis methods we feel confident that within the narrow usage context we set out in our studies (we worked with very small movements (max. up to 10 cm) specific for our needs), values at around 170 ms for dragging tasks and around 300 ms for low attention tapping tasks are realistic acceptance levels for latency. Other dimensions might yield different requirements.

Shneiderman outlined the importance of prior experience for the judgement of latency [9]. This means that with more responsive technology evolving over the years, these acceptable levels might be subject to change considerably in future. Jota et al. already confirmed that productivity increases further with even lower latency levels [4], so if technically possible at a reasonable cost, we would recommend aiming for lower latency levels as currently found acceptable by users.

Acknowledgements. Financial support for this project was provided by the Austrian research funding association (FFG) under the scope of the COMET program within the research project "Easy to use professional business and system control applications (LiTech)" (contract # 843535). This programme is promoted by BMVIT, BMWFJ and the federal state of Vorarlberg. We also express our gratitude to WolfVision Innovation GmbH for their in-kind contributions.

References

1. Anderson, G., Doherty, R., Ganapathy, S.: User perception of touch screen latency. In: Marcus, A. (ed.) HCII 2011 and DUXU 2011, Part I. LNCS, vol. 6769, pp. 195–202. Springer, Heidelberg (2011)
2. Card, S.K., Robertson, G.G., Mackinlay, J.D.: The information visualizer, an information workspace. In: Proceedings of the SIGCHI Conference on Human Factors in Computing Systems, pp. 181–186. CHI 1991. ACM, New York, NY, USA (1991)
3. Gallaway, G.R.: Response times to user activities in interactive man/machine computer systems. Proc. Hum. Factors Ergon. Soc. Ann. Meet. **25**, 754–758 (1981)
4. Jota, R., Ng, A., Dietz, P., Wigdor, D.: How fast is fast enough?: a study of the effects of latency in direct-touch pointing tasks. In: Proceedings of the SIGCHI Conference on Human Factors in Computing Systems. CHI 2013, pp. 2291–2300. ACM, New York, NY, USA (2013)
5. MacKenzie, I.S., Ware, C.: Lag as a determinant of human performance in interactive systems. In: Proceedings of the INTERACT 1993 and CHI 1993 Conference on Human Factors in Computing Systems. CHI 1993, pp. 488–493. ACM, New York, NY, USA (1993)
6. Miller, R.B.: Response time in man-computer conversational transactions. In: Proceedings of the Fall Joint Computer Conference on 9–11 December 1968, Part I. AFIPS 1968 (Fall, part I), pp. 267–277. ACM, New York, NY, USA (1968)
7. Mori, M.: The uncanny valley. Energy **7**(4), 33–35 (1970)
8. Ng, A., Lepinski, J., Wigdor, D., Sanders, S., Dietz, P.: Designing for low-latency direct-touch input. In: Proceedings of the 25th Annual ACM Symposium on User Interface Software and Technology. UIST 2012, pp. 453–464. ACM, New York, NY, USA (2012)
9. Shneiderman, B.: Response time and display rate in human performance with computers. ACM Comput. Surv. **16**(3), 265–285 (1984)
10. Shneiderman, B., Plaisant, C.: Designing the User Interface: Strategies for Effective Human-Computer Interaction, 4th edn. Pearson Addison Wesley, Boston (2004)
11. Ware, C., Balakrishnan, R.: Reaching for objects in vr displays: lag and frame rate. ACM Trans. Comput.-Hum. Interact. **1**(4), 331–356 (1994)
12. Zhicheng, L., Heer, J.: The effects of interactive latency on exploratory visual analysis. IEEE Trans. Vis. Comput. Graph. (Proceedings InfoVis 2014) **20**(12), 2122–2131 (2014)

Towards Vibrotactile Direction and Distance Information for Virtual Reality and Workstations for Blind People

Simon Schätzle[(⊠)] and Bernhard Weber

German Aerospace Center (DLR), Oberpfaffenhofen, Germany
Simon.Schaetzle@dlr.de

Abstract. In the current paper psychophysical aspects of a vibrotactile feedback device were investigated and its potential of signal modulation was analyzed. We identified magnitude calibration factors for equal perceptions of the different stimulation locations of the device and determined the spatial acuity with which the user is able to correctly detect the stimulation's location. Furthermore we investigated different approaches of vibrotactile stimulation for communicating direction and distance information to the human arm (motion guidance) and also explored different approaches of signal modulation for the transmission of additional information content.

The knowledge of these vibrotactile perception aspects is a fundamental requirement in order to design and evaluate different parameters for the design and application-oriented optimization of vibrotactile stimulation patterns.

Keywords: Vibrotactile stimulation · Vibrotactile perception · Motion guidance · Distance coding · Virtual reality

1 Introduction

During the last years, vibrotactile displays are more and more subject of research for many different purposes [2, 7] such as human-machine-interfaces for virtual reality [10] and telerobotics [3], attention direction [6], sensory substitution [14] or navigation [4]. Vibrotactile stimulation has great potential as (1) it is an intuitive form of feedback (stimuli are directly mapped to body coordinates e.g. in motion guidance the user simply follows the direction of vibrotactile stimulation), (2) it can be used successfully in situations where auditory or visual presentation is not possible (e.g. noisy or visually cluttered environments), (3) it avoids overloading the usually involved auditory and visual perception channels, (4) information is displayed in an unobtrusive way without annoying others or drawing their attention to confidential matters, and (5) it is a possible modality for sensory substitution (e.g. vibrotactile presentation of inaccessible information due to visual occlusion).

Compared to the well-known and very simple forms of vibrotactile stimulation in cell phones, spatially- and direction-resolved information can be presented with devices designed for a distributed perception. At the German Aerospace Center (DLR), a vibrotactile feedback device has been developed for a broad range of applications.

M. Antona and C. Stephanidis (Eds.): UAHCI 2015, Part II, LNCS 9176, pp. 148–160, 2015.
DOI: 10.1007/978-3-319-20681-3_14

The so called VibroTac is a wrist band with six vibrotactile actuators and is described in Sect. 2. The device will be used - among other things – for motion guidance in virtual reality (and augmented reality) applications and in the context of workstations for blind people. Thus, relevant positions, objects or events to which the user should move the hand can be indicated through adequate stimulation patterns (e.g. a blind person can be guided to the correct shelf of a goods issue). Vibrotactile assistance should be realized as intuitive and effective as possible. Furthermore, prolonged use of the device has to be as comfortable as possible.

In order to evaluate and judge different parameters in the design and application-specific optimization of vibrotactile stimulation patterns, it is a fundamental requirement to have knowledge about certain aspects of perception. Therefore, in this paper we investigate psychophysical aspects such as the magnitude calibration for equal perceptions of different stimulation locations (Sect. 3) and the spatial acuity with which the user is able to correctly detect the stimulation's location (Sect. 4).

Furthermore we analyze the potential of signal modulation for distance coding in Sect. 5 (principal approaches of vibrotactile stimulation for communicating direction and distance information to the human arm are compared) and for the transmission of additional information content in Sect. 6.

2 The Vibrotactile Feedback Device VibroTac

At DLR, a battery driven and wireless controllable wrist band with six vibration motors (called tactors) has been developed. Its design with respect to the type of tactors, number of stimulation locations and their arrangement is based on the outcome of evaluations with a prototype reported in [12].

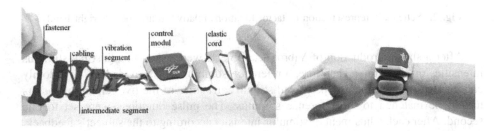

Fig. 1. The vibrotactile feedback device VibroTac

Due to the ergonomic concept, the device [13] can be worn on a wide range of arm or leg diameters while all tactors correctly self-align in equal distances independent from the circumference. Each tactor can be activated and controlled separately in frequency (0–190 Hz). The tactors are direct current (DC) cylindrical motors which generate vibrations by rotating an unbalanced mass. Therefore, in order to vary the perceived magnitude of stimulation, the drive voltage has to be changed. Different vibrotactile stimulation patterns such as impulses, ramps, waves, knocks, trembling etc. can be generated and displayed to the user.

3 Magnitude Calibration

Dependent on the tactors' locations e.g. on the lower arm, the stimulus magnitude of a certain frequency might be perceived differently. For instance, tactors that are placed on the ulna or the radius could produce different sensations of vibrotactile stimulation compared to tactors located on muscles or fatty tissues.

In applications such as collision feedback or motion guidance, information is not only coded with stimulation patterns but also with the signal strength itself. Thus, the knowledge of calibration factors is essential in order to be able to present stimuli at different tactor locations that are perceived with equal magnitude.

3.1 Method

Calibration factors for all tactors were determined using the magnitude estimation method [15]. The device was attached to the right wrist of eight sighted subjects (two females, six males, M_{Age} = 39.5 years; SD = 16.5; age range 23–67 years).

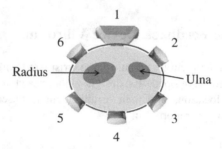

Fig. 2. Schematic representation of tactor locations relative to arm bones (right hand)

After a short introduction of VibroTac, subjects were asked to adjust the stimulus intensities of all tactors. Therefore, a reference stimulus was provided on a randomly chosen tactor. Subsequently, perceived stimuli intensities of the five remaining tactors had to be matched to the reference stimulus. The pulse durations were set to one second. After each adjustment of stimulus intensity according to the subject's feedback, the updated and the reference stimulus were repeated in quick succession for direct comparison.

The adjustment procedure was performed in randomized order with each tactor as reference and for two different frequencies (66 vs. 132 Hz). Altogether, twelve matching series had to be completed in random order.

After averaging the adjusted stimuli intensities for the lower and the higher frequency, the adjusted intensities of each tactor were divided by the adjusted intensity of tactor 1 as reference.

3.2   Results and Discussion

For both frequencies, we found that perceived stimuli magnitudes were higher for tactors 2, 3 and 6 compared to tactors 1, 4 and 5. Obviously, vibrotactile stimuli were perceived as more intensive at locations with a lower proportion of muscle, tendons or fatty tissue (see Fig. 2).

Table 1. Calibration factors at two different frequencies; Means (SD)

Tactor	Calibration factors at 66 Hz	Calibration factors at 132 Hz
1	1.00	1.00
2	0.85 (0.20)	0.72 (0.15)
3	0.86 (0.23)	0.81 (0.26)
4	1.12 (0.28)	0.90 (0.32)
5	1.06 (0.31)	0.89 (0.30)
6	0.90 (0.25)	0.72 (0.18)

Besides, in the case of reference stimuli with higher frequency (132 Hz), the calibration factors for tactor 2−6 are consistently smaller than that of tactor 1 (1.0). This means that the perceived magnitude of stimuli generated by tactor 1 is noticeable lower than that of the other tactors. This effect can be explained by the fact that tactor 1 is coupled with the control module which results in a higher mass compared to the other tactors that is set into vibration. Accordingly, participants reported that the per-ceived stimulus from tactor 1 was noticeably different compared to the remaining tactors. This effect was particularly evident for the higher frequency condition. Please note that the result pattern reported above was quite homogeneous across individuals.

Applying the calibration factors to the commanded intensities allows for similar perceptions of vibrotactile stimuli at the six different tactor locations (Table 1).

4   Spatial Acuity

As another basic feature of a vibrotactile system with several actuators, the spatial acuity with which the user is able to distinguish and localize the stimulation's position should be verified. Therefore, we determined the detection rate for the corresponding stimulated location as an indication of the user's performance that can be expected in applications such as motion guidance. In previous psychophysical studies, hardware issues such as type, number and alignment of vibration motors have been investigated. Experiments to determine the spatial acuity revealed that a configuration with six actuators distributed on the arm's perimeter in equal distances is a good compromise between the number of feedback locations and reliable detection of feedback locations when compared with configurations of four and eight actuators [12].

As the tactor size of the final VibroTac design has changed compared to the prototype of earlier studies, we determined the matching rate for VibroTac worn close to the wrist as this is the intended wearing position. Based on our earlier investigations

[12], we assume that the matching rate of the rest of the arm is better than that of the wrist due to the smaller arm circumference at this position compared to other positions of the arm.

4.1   Method

In order to familiarize subjects with the different stimulation locations, three clockwise sequential activations of the actuators were given with VibroTac worn close to the wrist. Afterwards two clockwise sequential activations with 0.4 s pulse length and 3.5 s pause duration were presented and positions were visualized by the investigator on a cross-section drawing of the arm. In the following training phase, subject had to point at the corresponding location of perceived stimulation on the drawing for a series of 32 impulses on randomly chosen tactors (on duration 0.4 s, off duration 3.5 s) and verbal feedback was given whether judgments were correct or not.

In the main study, three runs with 18 tactor activations (each tactor three times in randomized order with 0.4 s on-duration and 3.5 s off-duration) were presented to 16 sighted subjects (13 females, three males, M_{Age} = 33.7 years; SD = 7.2; age range 23–48 years; $M_{Arm\_circumference}$ = 18.5 cm; SD = 1.6) – resulting in 1152 impulses. The off-duration was set to 3.5 s to avoid any time pressure. Besides, this pause duration is intended to avoid a relative orientation to other tactors which is advantageous when determining the absolute spatial acuity.

We applied the 66 Hz calibration factors for equal perception of stimuli intensities. Except for the familiarization phase, subjects had to wear acoustic ear protection in order to avoid auditory influence of the low-level tactor noises. Subjects were not allowed to touch the device with their hands.

4.2   Results and Discussion

The detection rate of stimulated and recognized location is listed separately for all runs and for all tactors (T1 – T6) in Table 2.

There is no indication for any time effects (like learning or fatigue) across the four runs, as indicated by a one-way ANOVA performed on the hits in each trial ($F (3;1148)$ = .53; ns.). The correct detection rate across all subjects and runs (in total 1152 activations) was 95.2 %. This shows that tactor locations of VibroTac can be detected reliably - even with very little training.

Table 2. Matching rate of stimulated and recognized location (%)

	T1	T2	T3	T4	T5	T6	Average
Run 1	97.9	93.8	93.8	91.7	89.6	100.0	94.5
Run 2	97.9	93.8	97.9	93.8	95.8	97.9	96.2
Run 3	100.0	93.8	93.8	95.8	95.8	95.8	95.8
Run 4	100.0	89.6	93.8	95.8	91.7	95.8	94.5
Average	99.0	92.8	94.8	94.3	93.2	97.4	95.2

An explanation for the particular good detection rate for tactor 1 might be the different stimulation (despite magnitude calibration) that is generated by this segment due to its larger housing mass which is set into vibration compared to the other segments.

Table 3. Contingency table of activated and perceived tactors (%)

		Perceived					
		T1	**T2**	**T3**	**T4**	**T5**	**T6**
Activated	**T1**	99.0	1.0	0.0	0.0	0.0	0.0
	T2	0.5	92.7	6.8	0.0	0.0	0.0
	T3	0.0	1.0	94.8	4.2	0.0	0.0
	T4	0.0	0.0	3.1	94.3	2.6	0.0
	T5	0.0	0.0	0.0	0.5	93.2	6.2
	T6	0.5	0.0	0.0	0.0	2.1	97.4

Table 3 shows the relation between activated and perceived tactor locations based on the complete set of data (all runs of all subjects). Hit rates on the principal diagonal differ significantly from all other values in the corresponding line. In cases of wrong matching, only immediately adjacent tactors were identified. There is a significant (Z-test; $p < 0.05$) number of cases in which T2 is mistaken for T3 and in which T5 ismistaken for T6. Obviously it is more difficult to localize tactors that are located close to a bone (e.g. ulna or radius) than tactors that are located on soft tissue.

The interrelation between activated and recognized location of stimulation was analyzed with Goodman and Kruskals' Lambda [5] and shows a significant relation ($\lambda = .94$; $p < .001$).

5   Distance Coding

Vibrotactile cues can be used to convey movements in navigation [18] and for guiding human hands or arms [8, 9]. Although adding distance information to navigation tasks could not improve the performance (speed, time) for reaching a target [16, 18], distance information can be advantageous for intuitive and effective motion guidance for the hand [17]. In [11], different cues in order to convey the distance to a target are evaluated. Approaches with continuous and discrete stimulation and variations of the interstimulus interval (ISI) are compared. Stimuli intensities are kept constant in all cases.

In the present study we explore different vibrotactile cues with variations in intensity, ISI and pulse lengths for their suitability to convey distance information.

5.1   Methods

In a within-subjects design with randomized condition orders, ten blindfolded subjects (two females, eight males, $M_{Age} = 23.8$ years; $SD = 1.2$; age range 22–27 years) were spatially guided with eight different distance coding schemes. For each coding condition, fifteen pre-defined target positions at different distances located in the fronto-parallel plane had to be matched. The starting position was in the middle of the workspace of the human arm. There were three randomly chosen directions from the starting position (downward, upper left, upper right) that had to be followed until reaching the target positions at randomly chosen distances (with a minimum of 13 cm and a maximum of 33 cm). In all conditions, the vibrotactile stimulus is deactivated when reaching the target area and is re-activated when the target is overshot beyond a 2 cm distance threshold. The distance to the virtual target was calculated based on the subject's hand position which was tracked by an optical motion capture system (Vicon). Corresponding stimulation patterns were generated and commanded to the device wirelessly.

In Fig. 3, eight different distance codings for reaching near distance targets with the hand or arm are visualized. We compared three continuous distance codings (1–3) and four two-phases codings (4–7). The two-phases codings were implemented with an initial phase without any distance information and a subsequent phase with distance information (intensity or interval variation) after having reached the target area (one third of the start to target distance). Besides, we compared three codings with intensity codings (1, 4, 5) vs. four codings with pause/signal length variations (2, 3, 6, 7) and one coding combining both approaches (8).

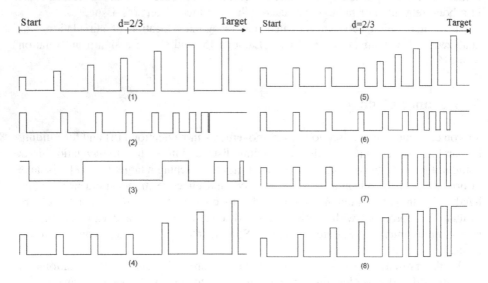

Fig. 3. Different approaches for distance coding (signal intensity plotted against target distance)

Coding schemes were evaluated by performance measures (completion time, i.e. the required time for matching the target position and holding it for one second; number of overshootings of the target position; relative path length: actual movement path length in relation to ideal path length) as well as subjective ratings (questionnaires) subsequent to each of the eight experimental trials.

5.2 Results

Performance Data. In a first step of analysis, the performance data (see Table 4) were explored using analysis of variance (ANOVA). Performing a repeated measures ANOVA, no significant differences between the codings were found for the number of overshootings (F (3;7) = 2.98; n.s.). Nevertheless, the number of overshootings were relatively high for the coding schemes providing distance information by varying intensity solely (i.e. codings 1 and 4). In conditions 7, the lowest number of over-shootings occurred. Analyzing completion times, ANOVA revealed a significant coding main effect (F (3;7) = 20.4; p < .05). In general, participants were faster when being supported by two-phases coding schemes, except for the continuous coding scheme 2 (variation of pause intervals). In condition 7, participants performed best. Next, a marginally significant coding main effect was evident for the relative path length (real path length/ideal path length) variable (F (3;7) = 8.64; p = .05). Similar to the over-shooting data, participants performed least accurately when being supported by coding schemes 1 and 4. Similarly, performances decreased with the distance-dependent var-iation of signal and pause intervals (3). The highest degree of precision was reached when working with coding scheme 7.

Table 4. Performance data of the different distance codings; Means (SD)

	Overshootings	Completion times (t)	Relative path length (%)
Coding 1	1.23 (0.55)	10.23 (1.06)	2.58 (0.71)
Coding 2	0.74 (0.39)	7.58 (2.04)	1.68 (0.35)
Coding 3	0.89 (0.53)	9.73 (3.13)	2.09 (0.45)
Coding 4	1.08 (0.50)	7.47 (1.87)	2.10 (0.66)
Coding 5	0.74 (0.31)	7.30 (1.8)	1.69 (0.26)
Coding 6	0.80 (0.30)	6.48 (0.93)	1.63 (0.18)
Coding 7	0.44 (0.19)	6.08 (1.45)	1.40 (0.16)
Coding 8	0.65 (0.38)	7.17 (1.40)	1.58 (0.30)

Subjetive Ratings. Next, subjective ratings in questionnaires (seven-point Likert scales ranging from 1 to 7) were analyzed. In a first question subjects were asked "How appropriate is the coding scheme for displaying distances" (1 = "not at all"; 7 = "very"). Coding schemes 2, 7, and 8 were rated as most appropriate for distance coding, with mean ratings far above the scale mean of 4 (see Table 5). Yet, no significant effect was found in ANOVA (F (3,7) = 4.2, n.s.). We also did not find significant effects (F (3,7) = 3.7, n.s.) for the following question ("I was able to estimate the current distance to the target at any time"; 1 = "does not apply at all"; 7 = "fully applies"). Not surprisingly, the both coding schemes with a continuous distance-dependent variation of pause intervals (2 and 8) were rated best. Relatively high ratings were also reported for both two-phases coding schemes with a discrete change of pause intervals (5) or intensity (7) when reaching the target zone. Finally, we asked subjects "How difficult was it to interpret the signals" (1 = "not at all"; 7 = "very"). A marginally significant was evident in ANOVA (F (3,7) = 5.5; p < .10). Coding schemes with distance-dependent signal intensity variation only (1 and 4) were rated worst.

Table 5. Subjective data for the different distance codings; means (SD)

	Appropriateness	Estimation of target distance	Interpretation difficulty
Coding 1	3.2 (1.0)	2.9 (1.3)	4.2 (1.7)
Coding 2	5.9 (0.9)	5.4 (1.0)	2.3 (0.8)
Coding 3	3.8 (1.8)	3.3 (1.7)	3.3 (1.8)
Coding 4	3.6 (1.4)	2.7 (1.6)	3.6 (1.7)
Coding 5	4.8 (1.6)	5.1 (1.4)	2.1 (1.0)
Coding 6	4.3 (1.9)	4.4 (1.6)	2.5 (1.4)
Coding 7	5.4 (1.6)	4.9 (1.6)	2.1 (1.1)
Coding 8	5.7 (0.9)	5.3 (1.3)	2.0 (0.9)

5.3 Discussion

Altogether, we found evidence that a distance-dependent variation of pause intervals only (coding 2) allows a higher performance than variations of signal intensity (coding 1), as mirrored by all objective and subjective data. This is in accordance with the findings of [1]. Obviously, signal frequencies can be distinguished much easier than signal intensity increments with an arbitrarily chosen intensity maximum.

This problem is also evident when implementing a two-phases approach, with intensity variations in the target area (coding 4). Shortening the pause intervals in the second phase (coding 5) had a positive effect, because it is much easier to recognize that the target zone has been entered. An even more successful approach is an abrupt intensity increase when having reached the target zone in combination with a distance-dependent signal pause interval (coding 7). Here, we obtained the best performance data and convincing subjective ratings.

6   Signal Shaping for Additional Information

So far, in applications such as collision feedback or motion guidance, we concentrated on the variation of patterns and intensity of vibrotactile stimulation in order to convey information.

Additional information might be transmitted by modulating the stimulation pulses themselves. In this study, we investigate whether signal shapes such as ramps, square-wave, saw tooth or e-function can be distinguished and examine their potential

Fig. 4. Modulated signal shapes: different stimuli classified into categories "increasing" (1–3), "decreasing" (4–6) and "symmetric" (7–8).

of communicating impressions such as acceleration, deceleration, warnings and the like.

6.1   Methods

In Fig. 4, eight different signal shapes categorized in three different types (increasing, decreasing and symmetric) are depicted. We are aware that the real signal shapes differ from these theoretical shapes particularly at steep flanks due to the time constant (T ≈ 30 ms) of the motor.

The signal duration above the perception threshold was set to 500 ms for all variations. Signals were presented in a rhythm with one second pause. The maximum intensity was set to 40 %.

In three training sessions, 15 subjects (two females, 13 males, M_{Age} = 33.0 years; SD = 6.4; age range 26–48 years) wearing ear protectors were familiarized with the different signals. In the first two sessions each shape was presented five times followed by a session with randomized order of signal presentation and visual feedback whether the correct signal was identified was given by the investigator. In the final run, each signal shape was presented three times in a sequence with randomized order. As soon as the subject assigned a signal to one of the eight shapes, the output was switched to the next signal. Afterwards, all signal shapes were presented again and subjects were asked to rate their subjective impressions (such as acceleration, deceleration etc.) they associate with the signal shapes.

6.2   Results and Discussion

Table 6 shows the interrelation between commanded and recognized signal shape. The number of correct assignment is low except for the signals 2, 6 and 7. These signals have been assigned correctly to the commanded signal significantly often.

Regarding the assignment of signals to the correct category (see Table 7. Interrelation of commanded and recognized category for signal shapes 2, 6 and 7 (%), we found a significant relation (Goodman and Kruskal's λ = .92; p < .001) for signal shapes 2, 6 and 7.

When imagining motion guidance with a pull-metaphor (moving towards the signal), subjects mostly associated -as intended- impressions like "Continue!" with signal shapes of the category "increasing" whereas impressions such as "Stop!" or "Slow down!" were mainly assigned to signal shapes of the category "decreasing". Signal shape eight was understood as a warning signal.

Table 6. Interrelation of commanded and recognized signal shapes (%)

	1	2	3	4	5	6	7	8
Shape 1	50.0	23.3	13.3	6.7	1.7	0.0	0.0	5.0
Shape 2	11.7	78.3	1.7	0.0	1.7	5.0	0.0	1.7
Shape 3	23.3	5.0	25.0	1.7	5.0	0.0	33.3	6.7
Shape 4	0.0	1.7	0.0	33.3	18.3	36.7	0.0	10.0
Shape 5	1.7	0.0	11.9	22.0	35.6	1.7	8.5	18.6
Shape 6	0.0	3.3	0.0	1.7	8.3	83.3	0.0	3.3
Shape 7	0.0	0.0	1.7	0.0	0.0	0.0	95.0	3.3
Shape 8	20.0	3.3	10.0	18.3	15.0	1.7	3.3	28.3

Table 7. Interrelation of commanded and recognized category for signal shapes 2, 6 and 7 (%)

	Increasing	Decreasing	Symmetric
Signals of category increasing	98.3	1.7	0.0
Signals of category decreasing	1.7	91.7	6.7
Signals of category symmetric	3.3	3.3	93.3

The results of this study show that signal shapes with an abrupt change of intensity can be distinguished reliably and have potential to transmit additional messages. These findings are consistent with our findings for distance codings where fine variations of intensities are detected less reliably.

7 Conclusion

The experiments presented in this paper are the second step in the development of a vibrotactile feedback device for motion guidance of the human hand. Aspects of fundamental relevance for the design and optimization of vibrotactile stimuli patterns used to convey direction and distance information have been investigated.

We determined calibration factors which allow for stimuli with equal perceived magnitudes despite of different tactor locations. Furthermore, the investigation of spatial acuity has revealed a very good detection rate which constitutes a promising basis for the presentation of directional cues. In the distance coding study we evaluated different approaches to convey distance information. We found evidence that a distance-dependent variation of pause intervals resulted in better performance than variations of signal intensity. Best performance was obtained with a two-phases approach characterized by an abrupt change of stimuli when distances to the target are below a certain threshold.

Besides coding distances, we successfully conveyed additional information by modulating the signal shapes of stimuli. Subjects were able to distinguish signal categories ("increasing", "decreasing", "symmetrical") and associated impressions such as "slow down", "continue" or "watch out" with the different categories.

Based on the findings of the conducted studies we will extend the vibrotactile motion guidance for targets in three-dimensional space. Furthermore, we will evaluate the proposed system with individuals who are blind.

References

1. Bosman, S., Groenendaal, B., Findlater, J.W., Visser, T., de Graaf, M., Markopoulos, P.: Gentleguide: an exploration of haptic output for indoors pedestrian guidance. In: Human-computer interaction with mobile devices and services (2003)
2. Elliott, L.R., Coovert, M.D., Prewett, M., Walvord, A.G., Saboe, K., Johnson, R.: A Review and Meta Analysis of Vibrotactile and Visual Information Displays. U.S. Army Research Laboratory, Aberdeen Proving Ground, Aberdeen, MD (2009)
3. Galambos, P.: Vibrotactile feedback for haptics and telemanipulation: survey, concept and experiment. Acta Polytech. Hung. 9(1), 41–65 (2012)
4. Gilson, R.D., Redden, E.S., Elliott, L.R.: Remote tactile displays for future soldiers, Technical. report. ARL-SR-0152. Aberdeen Proving Ground, Army Research Laboratory, MD (2007)
5. Goodman, L.A., Kruskal, W.H.: Measures of Association for Cross Classifications. Springer, New York (1979)
6. Ho, C., Tan, H.Z., Spence, C.: Using spatial vibrotactile cues to direct visual attention in driving scenes. Transp. Res. Part F Traffic Psychol. Behav. 8(6), 397–412 (2005)
7. Jones, L.A., Sarter, N.B.: Tactile displays: guidance for their design and application. Hum. Factors 50(1), 90–111 (2008)
8. Kapur, P., Jensen, M., Buxbaum, L.J., Jax, S.A., Kuchenbecker, K.J.: Spatially distributed tactile feedback for kinesthetic motion guidance. In: IEEE Haptics Symposium, pp. 519–526 (2010)
9. Lehtinen, V., Oulasvirta, A., Salovaara, A., Nurmi, P.: Dynamic tactile guidance for visual search tasks. In: Proceedings of the 25th annual ACM symposium on User interface software and technology, pp. 445–452. ACM (2012)
10. Lindeman, R.W., Yanagida, Y.: Empirical studies for effective near-field haptics in virtual environments. In: Proceedings of the IEEE Virtual Reality Conference, pp. 287–288. IEEE Computer Society, Los Alamitos, CA (2003)
11. Oron-Gilad, T., Downs, J.L., Gilson, R.D., Hancock, P.A.: Vibrotactile guidance cues for target acquisition. IEEE Trans. Syst. Man Cybern. Part C Appl. Rev. 37(5), 993–1004 (2007)
12. Schätzle, S., Hulin, T., Preusche, C., Hirzinger, G.: Evalution of vibro-tactile feedback to the human arm. In: Proceedings of EuroHaptics, Paris, Frankreich (2006)
13. Schätzle, S., Ende, T., Wüsthoff, T., Preusche, C.: VibroTac: an ergonomic and versatile usable vibrotactile feedback device. In: IEEE International Symposium in Robot and Human Interactive Communication (Ro-Man) (2010)
14. Schmidmaier, M.: Sensory substitution systems. In: Media Informatics Advanced Seminar on Multimodal Human-Computer Interaction (2011)
15. Stevens, S.S.: Psychophysics: Introduction to its Perceptual, Neural, and Social Prospects. John Wiley, New York (1975)
16. Straub, M., Riener, A., Ferscha, A.: Distance encoding in vibrotactile guidance cues, pp. 1–2. IEEE, MobiQuitous (2009)

17. Weber, B., Schätzle, S., Hulin, T., Preusche, C., Deml, B.: Evaluation of a vibrotactile feedback device for spatial guidance. In: IEEE World Haptics Conference, Istanbul, Turkey (2011)
18. Van Erp, J.B., Van Veen, H.A., Jansen, C., Dobbins, T.: Waypoint navigation with a vibrotactile waist belt. ACM Trans. Appl. Percept. 2(2), 106–117 (2005)

Improving Accessibility Design
on Touchscreens

Shuang Xu(✉)

Lexmark International, Inc., 740 West New Circle Road, Lexington,
KY 40550, USA
shxu@lexmark.com

Abstract. Touchscreen interfaces present critical accessibility concerns because they do not offer tactile cues for the visually impaired users to distinguish interaction controls. The recent advancement of interaction technology makes new design solutions possible. This research examines blind users' performance and perception of gesture and auditory feedback designs. Findings from this three-phase study indicate that pressing is the most accurate and slightly faster selection gesture, as compared to lifting finger, tapping, or double tapping on the screen. 12 blind participants were able to navigate touchscreens as first-timer users, if facilitated with instant auditory feedback. For text entry tasks, blind users need more advanced assistive tools such as speech recognition. Design guidelines to improve accessibility on touchscreens are discussed in this paper.

Keywords: Accessibility · Touch interaction · Gesture · Auditory feedback

1 Introduction

Touchscreens are becoming increasingly prevalent across a wide range of devices, including smartphones, computers, vehicles, kiosks, printers, and home appliances. Although these interfaces are intuitive and easy to use, the absence of tactile feedback presents critical accessibility concerns for the 285 million world-wide visually impaired people [1]. In addition, the location of interaction controls on touchscreens varies, which makes it impossible for blind users to learn or memorize how to navigate on touchscreens. With the exponential growth of the mobile devices market, touchscreen based interaction has quickly penetrated areas from education, government, to enterprises. This could significantly reduce the degree of independence and equal opportunities for the visually impaired community.

For accessibility improvement on touchscreens, current Human-Computer Interaction (HCI) research focuses on gesture designs and vibration or auditory feedback. However, the nature of the touchscreen technology may advance in the very near future with physical cues and pressure sensors. Tactus [2] provides a tactile solution by enabling application-controlled transparent physical buttons that dynamically rise up from the touch surface on demand. Neonode [3] introduces Z-force to allow accurate detection of different pressure on the touchscreen. Unfortunately, little is known about how this change would impact on blind users' touchscreen experiences.

© Springer International Publishing Switzerland 2015
M. Antona and C. Stephanidis (Eds.): UAHCI 2015, Part II, LNCS 9176, pp. 161–173, 2015.
DOI: 10.1007/978-3-319-20681-3_15

This paper discusses findings from usability evaluations of simple accessibility solutions on touchscreens, including the simulated "touch and press" interaction design that is not yet available on commercial products. The gesture designs selected in this investigation met the following criteria: (1) one-finger gesture (to enable thumb operation with one hand); (2) no prior knowledge or training is required; and (3) supporting common interaction needs such as navigation, selection, and text entry.

Data from this study reported that "touch and press" had 0 % error rate and was faster than the other gestures. This result encourages further investment on technological evolution to make touchscreen more inclusive, rather than focusing on complex gesture designs. In addition, participants' feedback and behavior patterns in the study confirmed a number of design guidelines, some of which were known to the accessibility community.

2 Related Work

A large body of research work has been carried out in the last decade to improve the accessibility of touch interfaces. These innovative techniques can be categorized in two areas: (1) gesture based interaction for input or selection, (2) screen overlays with tactile feedback such as texture or vibration, and auditory feedback such as earcons or speech. These approaches alleviate the accessibility concern, but not without problems.

VoiceOver is an accessibility feature introduced on iPhone since 2009. Users can receive auditory feedback by gliding finger over the screen content, and use a split-tap (i.e., touching an item with one finger while tapping the screen with another finger) to confirm selection. A single-finger swipe will move the readout focus to the next item, which matches blind users' mental model of navigation. But as Vidal and Lefevre report in their comparison study [4], users find it is difficult to discover and accurately reproduce certain gestures with VoiceOver.

Several Braille-based typing techniques were adopted on touchscreens to support eyes-free data entry (e.g., BrailleTouch [5], PerkInput [6], and TypeInBraille [7]). Although these methods have significantly improved typing efficiency and accuracy, they have limited application as fewer than 10 percent of the legally blind people in the United States can use Braille [8]. Meanwhile, it is difficult to generalize these accessible text entry methods for information browsing tasks on touchscreens.

To evaluate the effectiveness of gesture designs, Oliveira et al. [9] compared four methods: QWERTY, MultiTap, NavTouch, and BrailleType. They conclude that blind users with low spatial skills are unlikely to perform well with QWERTY and MultiTap. But NavTouch and MultiTap are more demanding regarding memory and attention. Multi-touch interaction such as split-tap is ineffective for users with low pressure sensitivity. Multi-touch gestures were not chosen in this investigation because they require two-hand operations for mobile users.

Various haptic overlay solutions have also been explored to compensate the absence of tactile feedback on touchscreens. Touchplates [10] uses inexpensive plastic guides on the touchscreen and can be recognized by the underlying software application. This approach is low-cost and easy to adapt, but it is unlikely that users will carry a set of static Touchplates for real-world uses.

MudPad [11] uses electromagnets combined with an overlay of magnetorheological fluid to create instant multi-point perceivable feedback, from different levels of surface softness to dynamically changeable textures. Similarly, Thermal signs [12] use Peltier micropumps as temperature dots to develop simple graphics to introduce dynamic tactile feedback to touchscreen interaction. Usability evaluation is not yet available for these methods. Further investigations are needed to examine their effectiveness, efficiency, and development cost.

Compared to texture or temperature based touch feedback, physical buttons provide more intuitive and effective tactile cues. To create physical buttons that can be dynamically controlled, Harrison and Hudson propose a technique [13] to raise, recess, or remove pre-defined buttons on touch interfaces. Following this approach, Tactus Tactile layer [2] uses dynamic microfluidic pressure to raise buttons on demand. Research in these areas has shed light to a promising future, where physical buttons on touchscreens can be shaped and located on the fly.

In summary, gesture interaction allows fast but less accurate input. It brings new challenges to the blind community as 82 % of the blind people are 50 years and older [1] and many have cognitive or motor disabilities [14]. It is difficult for them to remember, distinguish, and accurately reproduce the required gestures like sighted users [15]. Tactile feedback helps. However, the static or predefined physical overlays suffer from their inflexibility. Assistive reading software offers auditory feedback about the visual contents, but a great deal of navigational information is often lost in the readout.

3 Experiment Design

The main purpose of this study was to understand the key attributes that make accessibility solutions effective, efficient, and easy to use. It aimed to answer the following questions: (1) What are the needs and concerns blind users have regarding the assistive technologies available in their daily lives? (2) How do gesture designs affect blind users' task performance and satisfaction on touch interfaces? (3) How to improve auditory feedback in assistive solutions? A three-phase research study was carried out to answer these questions:

Phase I. One-on-one interviews with visually impaired participants to identify their needs and concerns with touch based interactions.

Phase II. Examination of five methods of gesture-based touchscreen interaction via blind participants' performance and perception.

Phase III. Prototypes were developed based on the findings from Phase II with additional auditory feedback and confirmation of selection, to evaluate perceived effectiveness and efficiency from blind participants.

Twelve participants were recruited in this three-phase study (see Table 1).

In Phase I, one-on-one semi-structured interviews were carried out with each participant to identify their needs and concerns of touch based interactions. All interviews focused on understanding how their everyday activities were supported (or limited) by technologies. The interview covered questions such as what devices they had required touchscreen interaction, what assistive tools or technologies were

Table 1. Participants information

Gender	Female: 6, Male: 6
Age	25 ~ 34: 3, 35 ~ 44: 3, 45 ~ 55 yrs: 3, 56 ~ 64 yrs: 3
Education	High School: 1, Some College: 3, College: 4, Graduate Scool: 4
Visual impairment	Legally Blind*: 6, Totally Blind: 6 (*Legally Blindness refers to central visual acuity of 20/200 or less)
Touchscreen devices	Cell phone: 10, Tablet: 6, ATM: 5, Printer: 5; Computer: 4, Home appliances: 3

Table 2. Gestures examined in phase II

	Method 1	Method 2	Method 3	Method 4	Method 5
Gesture for speech feedback	Touch[1]	Touch	Touch	Touch	Single tap
Gesture to perform selection	Press down[2]	Lift finger[3]	Single tap[4]	Double tap[5]	Double tap

Notes: 1. *Touch* refers to finger contacting the target on screen. 2. *Press down* refers to finger pressing down on the target. 3. *Lift finger* refers to finger lifting up and off the target. 4. *Single tap* refers to finger quickly touching on the target and lifting up. 5 *Double tap* refers to two continuous single taps on the same target.

available to them, what they needed or concerned about accessibility improvements on these devices.

In Phase II, five interaction methods (see Table 2) were selected to investigate users' task performance (speed and accuracy) and satisfaction.

In this within-subject experiment, each participant completed 15 tasks, 3 tasks for each gesture method. For each task, they were asked to start from a pre-defined screen position (one of the 16 circled spots in Fig. 1) to navigate to a pre-defined target (one of the 9 buttons in Fig. 1) as quickly and accurately as possible. Task assignments were randomized to reduce learning effect.

All tasks were performed on a 15" touchscreen interface. Performing a defined gesture would start the voice readout immediately. The current readout would stop as soon as a new readout was initiated. All voice readout indicated what the current target was and how to select it. E.g., "Tap to select [*target*]", "Press down to select [*target*]", etc. Participants' preferences on readout speed were measured, but voice readout was played at 156 words/minute (wpm) in this study for consistency.

Because pressure-sensing was not available on the touchscreen used in this study, the "press down" gesture was simulated via a Wizard of Oz approach – the moderator activated the selection when the participant performed an explicit press-down gesture.

The five methods were evaluated via the following dependent variables: (1) Task completion time, measured as the time elapses from navigation-starts to target-selected; (2) Error rate, measured as the number of incorrect selections divided by the number of tasks; (3) Perceived ease of use, (4) Perceived learnability, and (5) Perceived satisfaction were subjective ratings measured on a 7-point Likert Scale.

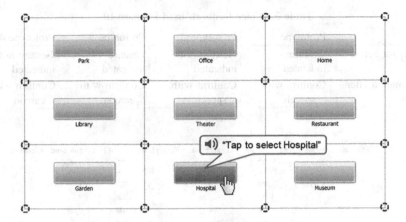

Fig. 1. Illustration of prototype used in phase II

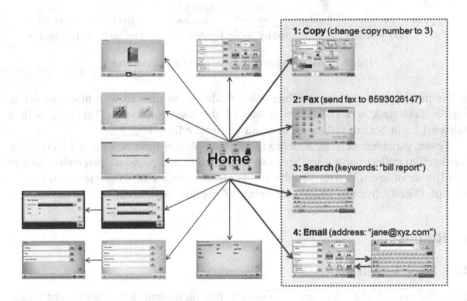

Fig. 2. Illustration of prototype used in phase III

In Phase III, the investigation focused on the effectiveness of auditory feedback. A prototype was developed to simulate the printer interaction experience because: (1) it offers a range of task complexity levels; and (2) no participant had seen or used this interface previously. The gesture design chosen for this prototype was based on the testing results from Phase II.

The evaluation in Phase III included four tasks (as shown in Fig. 2): Copy, Fax, Search, and Email. All tasks started from the Home screen. Participants were asked to follow the voice feedback to complete each task. The blue arrows in Fig. 2 mark the correct routes to complete each task. The incorrect navigation paths were also available

Table 3. Voice feedback used in phase III

	Prototype 1	Prototype 2	Prototype 3	Prototype 4
Prompt for action	Gesture indicated	Gesture not indicated	Gesture indicated	Gesture not indicated
Confirmation after action	Confirm with speech	Confirm with speech	Confirm with earcon	Confirm with earcon

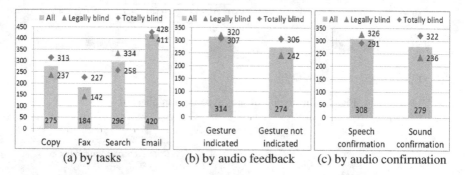

(a) by tasks   (b) by audio feedback   (c) by audio confirmation

Fig. 3. Task completion time in phase III (in seconds)

in this prototype, with corresponding voice feedback, as marked with black arrows in Fig. 2. Each task was coupled with one of the four prototypes (Table 3), with a balanced Latin Square task order to avoid learning effects Fig. 3.

Seven variables were measured: (1) task completion time, a 7-point Likert Scale was used to collect participants' pre-task expectation and post-task perception ratings on (2) ease of use; (3) error likelihood; (3) effectiveness and (4) efficiency of speech prompt, (5) effectiveness and (6) efficiency of confirmation, and (7) satisfaction.

4   Results

4.1   Phase I – Interview

The outcome of the interviews confirmed the increasing accessibility challenges introduced by touchscreen interaction. The following accessibility improvements were highly demanded by the 12 blind participants:

- *Equal opportunities to access information and technologies as sighted people.* Equal opportunity to education and employment has always been a major concern in the visually-impaired community. Many felt the situation has been worsened by the recent technological advancement that required visually-demanding interaction.
- *To use mainstream devices* via *effective yet inexpensive assistive technologies.* Although specialized devices or applications are more user-friendly, they are often much more expensive. Some mentioned that accessibility features such as Voice-Over were also needed by sighted users when driving. Accessibility solutions should be available on mass-market devices.

- *Adjustable speed for screen read-out to optimize efficiency.* For blind users, the auditory output is their main channel to receive information. They have often developed abilities to comprehend speech information at a much faster speed. Data from Phase II experiment shows that participants' preferred speech rate was 256 wpm (varied from 187 to 421wpm). Being able to personalize speech rate would most likely improve the efficiency of their information processing.
- *Auditory feedback on the touch interface of home appliances and office devices.* Participants emphasized their needs for independence and privacy. One totally blind participant asked her sighted friend to place Braille tags on the flat touch panels of all her home appliances, so that she could use them without additional help. Inclusive designs are in demand for office devices (e.g., printers) as well to allow blind user to live and work independently.
- *Simple and intuitive touch gestures that are easy to discover, remember, and use.* Similar to the findings reported by Kane et al. [15], participants suggested that gestures designed for blind users should (1) rely on physical orientation references such as screen edges and corners, (2) reduce requirements on accuracy, speed, and complexity. Successful gesture designs should work for blind users with a wide range of age difference, cognitive and motor capabilities, and educational levels.

4.2 Phase II – Gesture Design

Quantitative data collected in this research were analyzed with One-way Analysis of Variance (ANOVA). Findings are discussed in the following sections

4.2.1 Task Completion Time

Gestures had a significant impact on completion time ($F_{4,175} = 9.60$, $p < .001$), see Table 4. However, the speed difference amongst the touch-for-feedback gestures (touch-press, touch-lift, touch-tap, and touch-double tap) was not significant ($F_{3,140} = 0.19$, $p = .902$). The main contributors to task completion time are (1) navigation gestures (touch vs. tap), where $\text{Mean}_{touch} = 27.56$ s, $\text{Mean}_{tap} = 71.27$ s ($F_{1,178} = 38.63$, $p < .001$); and (2) selection gestures (non-double-tap vs. double-tap), where $\text{Mean}_{non\text{-}d\text{-}tap} = 27.46$ s, $\text{Mean}_{d\text{-}tap} = 49.58$ s ($F_{1,178} = 13.09$, $p <= .001$).

Participants' vision status also affected their task efficiency. In general, legally blind participants were able to complete tasks faster than totally blind participants:

Table 4. Task completion time (in seconds)

	Touch-Press	Touch-Lift	Touch-Tap	Touch-Double tap	Tap-Double Tap
All	24.57	29.64	28.17	27.88	71.27
Totally blind	37.24	37.46	40.15	36.63	108.52
Legally blind	11.89	21.82	16.19	19.13	34.03

$Mean_{LegalBlind} = 20.61$ s, $Mean_{TotalBlind} = 52$ s ($F_{1,178} = 29.86$, $p < .001$). A two-way ANOVA reports a signification interaction between Gesture and Vision ($F_{4,170} = 4.88$, $p = .001$).

4.2.2 Error Rates

The performance data showed that error rate was significantly affected by different gestures ($F_{4,175} = 6.21$, $p < .001$), see Table 5. Error rate with tap-for-feedback was about 6 times higher than touch-for-feedback: $Mean_{Touch} = 6.94$ %, $Mean_{Tap} = 50.00$ % ($F_{1,178} = 22.46$, $p < .001$). Double tapping for selection also had much higher error rate than other selection gestures: $Mean_{non-d-tap} = 6.48$ %, $Mean_{d-tap} = 29.17$ % ($F_{1,178} = 8.71$, $p = .004$). Error rate was not significantly affected by Vision ($F_{1,1718} = 2.10$, $p = .149$).

4.2.3 Subjective Ratings

A 7-point Likert Scale was used to collect perception ratings (1-lowest, 7-highest) and participants were also asked to rank their preference of the 5 methods (1-lowest, 5-highest) after the completion of all tasks. Significant difference was found in all subjective ratings (see Table 6), except perceived learnability ($F_{4,55} = 1.62$, $p = .182$).

Gestures had an impact on perceived Ease of use ($F_{4,55} = 5.02$, $p = .002$). Specifically, the ratings were heavily influenced by whether one could touch or tap for speech feedback: $Mean_{touch} = 5.9$, $Mean_{tap} = 3.8$ ($F_{1,58} = 20.02$, $p < .001$). Totally blind participants had lower ratings, $Mean_{LegalBlind} = 6.1$, $Mean_{TotalBlind} = 4.9$ ($F_{1,58} = 8.72$,

Table 5. Error rate

	Touch-Press	Touch-Lift	Touch-Tap	Touch-Double tap	Tap-Double Tap
All	0.00 %	2.78 %	16.67 %	8.33 %	50.00 %
Totally blind	0.00 %	5.56 %	27.78 %	16.67 %	55.56 %
Legally blind	0.00 %	0.00 %	5.56 %	0.00 %	44.44 %

Table 6. Subjective ratings and overall ranking

	Touch-Press	Touch-Lift	Touch-Tap	Touch-Double Tap	Tap-Double Tap
Ease of use (1 ~ 7) *	6.00	5.67	5.79	6.17	3.83
Easy to learn (1 ~ 7)	6.33	6.58	6.33	6.50	5.50
Satisfaction (1 ~ 7) *	5.83	5.79	5.88	6.04	4.17
Overall ranking (1 ~ 5) *	3.00	3.08	3.67	3.42	1.83

(*Statistically significant.)

p = .005), whereas younger participants seemed to have higher expectation, thus lower ratings, on Ease of Use, $Mean_{18\text{-}34yr} = 4.0$, $Mean_{35\text{-}54yr} = 6.3$, $Mean_{55\text{-}74yr} = 5.8$ ($F_{2,57} = 11.94$, $p < .001$).

Although participants commented that all five methods were fairly easy to learn, a closer look revealed that the perceived Learnability was impacted by age: $Mean_{18\text{-}34yr} = 5.0$, $Mean_{35\text{-}54yr} = 7.0$, $Mean_{55\text{-}74yr} = 6.4$ ($F_{2,57} = 20.09$, $p < .001$), and vision: $Mean_{LegalBlind} = 6.6$, $Mean_{TotalBlind} = 5.9$ ($F_{1,58} = 4.4$, $p = .040$). Being able to touch for feedback also made the gesture easier to learn, $Mean_{touch} = 6.4$, $Mean_{tap} = 5.5$ ($F_{1,58} = 6.37$, $p = .014$).

Similar to the ratings on Ease of Use, Satisfaction ratings were impacted by gestures ($F_{4,55} = 2.80$, $p = .035$), vision ($F_{1,58} = 8.71$, $p = .005$), age groups ($F_{2,57} = 10.41$, $p < .001$), and if participants used touch for speech feedback ($F_{1,58} = 11.60$, $p = .001$).

The overall ranking on Method 5 (tap for feedback, double-tap for selection) was significantly lower than the other four methods ($F_{4,55} = 3.41$, $p = .015$), as participants were frustrated by the tap-for-feedback gesture ($F_{1,58} = 11.89$, $p = .001$).

4.2.4   Discussion

In debriefing, participants explained why tap-for-feedback was particularly difficult for blind users: (a) it had no point of reference – for totally blind users, tapping to find target was like "taking a stab in the dark"; (b) it was very easy to miss the target – sometimes they tapped on a target but moved away too quickly and missed the voice feedback; (c) continuous tapping on the same target was registered as a double-tap, which resulted in a selection error rather than voice feedback; and (d) several participants were able to find the target quickly, but their selection was slightly off the target, and had to spend more time to re-find and select the target. In addition, individuals had various speeds of double-tap, which made it difficult for the system to distinguish a slow double-tap from two quick single-taps.

Data from the Phase II experiment indicate:

Touch-for-feedback allowed users to find a target significantly faster and more accurately than tap-for-feedback. This gesture would have worked more effectively if there had been tactile difference between target areas vs. non-target areas.

The selection gestures examined in this study had their pros and cons:

- Despite of users' familiarity, tapping or double tapping to select a target resulted in great frustration and higher error rate as they required the user to tap accurately on the target once it was found. Split-tapping may alleviate this concern, but it is not applicable for one-handed thumb operation.
- Lift-to-select was easy to use and learn. But users could easily make mistakes if they accidentally lifted finger off the wrong target. For typically compact mobile layout design on touchscreens, using this gesture can be stressful if the user must keep her finger on the screen to avoid unintentional selections.
- Press down-to-select was the fastest and most accurate method. But most participants were not yet customized to this new gesture. Because the prototype did no offer tactile feedback, a few participants were uncertain how hard they had to press. Participants' preferred force for Touch was 0.45 newton, and 5.50 newton for Press,

on average. Strength of this gesture will likely be fueled by emerging technologies [2, 13] that offer physical feedback on touchscreens instantly and dynamically.

Auditory feedback must be prompt in assistive designs for blind users. When users are relying on the auditory information to "see" the touch interface, any delay in feedback will lead them to either wander away or perform their selection again, which may result in errors.

4.3   Phase III – Auditory Feedback Design

In Phase II, Method 1 (Touch-Press) outperformed others gesture designs in efficiency and accuracy, therefore it was chosen for the prototype used in Phase III.

4.3.1   Performance

Unsurprisingly, participants' task completion time was significantly impacted by the nature of the tasks ($F_{3,44} = 4.37$, p = .009). But the auditory feedback in this study did not influence the performance as expected: whether gesture was indicated in prompts ($F_{1,46} = 0.60$, p = .443), or whether speech confirmation was used ($F_{1,46} = 0.32$, p = .573).

4.3.2   Perception

Participants' subjective ratings are summarized in Fig. 4.

The perception ratings were not statistically significant across the four treatments, but it is interesting to see that after trying out the prototypes, participants did not think mentioning gesture in the prompt was as helpful as they thought. In contrast, having speech confirmation was perceived more helpful to avoid errors, as earcons could be misunderstood. Overall, participants were able to use audio cues to complete the tasks, but the interaction experience was not as satisfactory as they had expected.

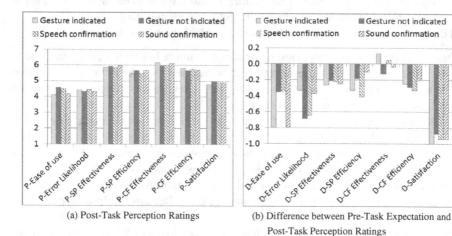

(a) Post-Task Perception Ratings

(b) Difference between Pre-Task Expectation and Post-Task Perception Ratings

Fig. 4. Subjective ratings in phase III (on a 7-point likert scale)

4.3.3   Discussion

The tasks in Phase III were selected based on their complexity levels (Level 1: easiest, Level 4: hardest), which was predefined by the steps required by each task:

- Level 1. From Home to Copy screen, change copy number to 3, click on "Copy It".
- Level 2. From Home to Fax screen, enter the 10-digit number, click on "Fax It".
- Level 3. From Home to Search screen, enter the search query, click on "Search".
- Level 4. From Home to Email screen, go to Recipient screen to enter the email address, return to the Email screen, click on "Send".

However, most participants were able to completed Fax faster than Copy. Because they were familiar with the standard numpad layout on the Fax screen, many were able to quickly enter any number once number "5" was located. The layout of the Copy screen was foreign to all participants and it took them a while to find where to enter the copy number, which is in the middle of the bottom of the screen. This finding indicates that familiarity with the screen layout critically affects blind users' task performance. Participants' behavior also suggested that the key action controls should be located near physical reference points such any corner of the touchscreen.

For tasks of Search and Email, participants did not think the auditory feedback was helpful when navigating a soft QWERTY keyboard. The challenges include:

- It was difficult to distinguish letters that are phonetically similar and located closely on the keyboard (e.g., C, V, and B). Context was needed such as "B as in Bob."
- Error correction was painful. For example, to correct "vill report", they had to erase all entries rather than to highlight and change "v" to "b". Immediate confirmation of what was entered reduces efforts on correction.
- All participants understood the layout of a QWERTY keyboard, but motor memory of typing with both hands did not help when typing with one finger.

In summary, for text entries on touchscreens, blind users would expect more sophisticated methods such as speech recognition or attached keyboard.

It is interesting that legally blind participants in the study were able to complete tasks faster when gesture was not mentioned (Mean$_{SayGesture}$ = 320 s, Mean$_{NoGesture}$ = 241 s, $F_{1,22}$ = .95, p = .339) and when earcon was used (Mean$_{Speech}$ = 326 s, Mean$_{Earcon}$ = 236 s, $F_{1,22}$ = 1.25, p = .276). All participants believed that if the gesture designs were consistent on a device, the gesture indication would only be necessary initially, or in a tutorial. But split opinions were reported about the use of earcons: some liked them because them were efficient and easy to understand, others had concerns because (1) "it only makes sense to tech savvy users"; (2) users with hearing disability may have difficulty hearing the "click"; (3) it was less effective in situations where explicit confirmation was desired (e.g., "Email was sent successfully.").

5   Conclusions

This paper has reported findings from a three-phase research study that aims to investigate the needs and concerns of accessibility improvement, as well as how gesture designs and auditory feedback designs affect blind users' touchscreen experience.

This investigation has confirmed the following guidelines to improve accessible designs on touchscreens:

1. Avoid gestures that require precision (e.g., "tap on the target"). Otherwise, allow error tolerance by making the touch area for selection larger than the touch area for audio cues.
2. For soft numpad or keyboard designs, use the standard layout and button size similar to the physical numpad or keyboard to match blind users' motor memory.
3. Use consistent gesture designs and offer tutorials for users to quickly familiarize themselves with the accessibility modes.
4. Use gesture design and auditory feedback to support navigation and selection, but automatically switch to speech recognition or other specialized typing methods for text entry.
5. Enable separate accessibility modes for low-vision vs. no-vision users. Totally blind users rely on prompt auditory feedback of the screen target they are touching. Visually impaired users could better benefit from features such as adjustable color contrast and zooming.
6. Provide adjustable speed and volume of speech output to satisfy individual needs.
7. Place critical interface elements (e.g., Home, Back, etc.) near physical reference points such as the screen corners or edges for easier orientation and faster access.

One limitation of this research is that all gestures required on-target selection, which resulted in poor performance and high frustration. Future experiments are under development to compare performance and perception amongst Touch-and-press, Touch and split-tap (as in VoiceOver on iPhone), and Touch and double-tap-anywhere (as in TalkBack on Android). It would be interesting to see if the inconvenience of multi-touch gestures is an acceptable tradeoff for speed and accuracy.

Whereas many research studies focus on gesture designs for accessible solutions on touchscreens, this paper reports positive findings on Touch-and-press interaction. Results of this research encourage further investment on the evolution of touchscreen technology. By satisfying user needs with new technological enablement, we can deliver intuitive and inclusive designs and offer equal opportunities to people with visual disabilities.

References

1. World Health Organization. New Estimates of Visual Impairment and Blindness (2010). http://www.who.int/blindness/estimates2011.pdf
2. Taking Touch Screen Interfaces into a New Dimension. http://www.tactustechnology.com
3. Neonode Technology. http://www.neonode.com
4. Vidal, S., Lefebvre, G.: Gesture based interaction for visually-impaired people. In: Proceedings of NordiCHI 2010, pp. 809–812. ACM Press, NewYork (2010)
5. Frey, B., Southern, C., Romero, M.: BrailleTouch: mobile texting for the visually impaired. In: Stephanidis, C. (ed.) Universal Access in HCI, Part III, HCII 2011. LNCS, vol. 6767, pp. 19–25. Springer, Heidelberg (2011)

6. Azenkot, S., Lee, N.L.: Exploring the use of speech input by blind people on mobile devices. In: Proceedings of SIGASSETS 2013, Article No. 11, ACM Press, New York (2013)
7. Mascetti, S., Bernareggi, C., Belotti, M.: TypeInBraille: quick eyes-free typing on smartphones. In: Miesenberger, K., Karshmer, A., Penaz, P., Zagler, W. (eds.) ICCHP 2012, Part II. LNCS, vol. 7383, pp. 615–622. Springer, Heidelberg (2012)
8. Fewer Blind Americans Learning to Use Braille. http://www.nbcnews.com/id/29882719
9. Oliveira, J., Guerreiro, T., Nicolau, H., Jorge, J., Goncalves, D.: Blind people and mobile touch-based text-entry: acknowledging the need for different flavors. In: Proceedings of ASSETS 2011, pp. 179–186. ACM Press, NewYork (2011)
10. Kane, S.K., Morris, M.R., Wobbrock, J.O.: Touchplates: low-cost tactile overlays for visually impaired touch screen users. In: Proceedings of ASSET 2013, Article No. 22, ACM Press, NewYork (2013)
11. Jansen, Y., Karrer, T., Borchers, J.: MudPad: tactile feedback and haptic texture overlay for touch surfaces. In: Proceedings of ITS 2010, pp. 11–14. ACM Press, Saarbrucken (2010)
12. Boron, K., Bratek, P., Kos, A.: Graphical touch screen of thermal signs for the blind people – clinic tests. Microelectron. Int. **24**(2), 23–27 (2007)
13. Harrison, C., Hudson, S.E.: Providing dynamically changeable physical buttons on a visual display. In: Proceedings of CHI 2009, pp. 299–308. ACM Press, Boston (2009)
14. Kane, S.K., Jayant, C., Wobbrock, J.O., Ladner, R.E.: Freedom to roam: a study of mobile device adoption and accessibility for people with visual and motor disabilities. In: Proceedings of ASSETS 2009, pp. 115–122. ACM Press, NewYork (2009)
15. Kane, S.K., Wobbrock, J.O., Ladner, R.E.: Usable gestures for blind people: understanding preference and performance. In: Proceedings of CHI 2011, pp. 413–422. ACM Press, NewYork (2011)

Visual and Multisensory Experience

Senses in Space: Mapping the Universe to the Human Body

J. Aguilera[1,2(✉)]

[1] Adler Planetarium, South Lake Shore Drive, Chicago, IL 60605, USA
jaguilera@adlerplanetarium.org
[2] Planetary Collegium, University of Plymouth, Plymouth, UK

Abstract. This paper articulates the challenges of the human senses in the experiencing of space at extreme scales. It surveys the issues astronomy simulations confront when attempting to make sense of the kinds of scales that are integrated in the same experience, especially if one is to interact with them so that the ranges of size make sense with each other. In some cases parameters are hidden, while in other cases they are proportionally altered to become noticeable. In other cases, senses can be swapped for the benefit of creating a multi-sensory space that the human body can relate to. This is where research of outer space, and the technologies developed for people with disabilities, have an interesting area of affinity. Whereas missing a sense such as hearing, smell, vision or proprioception has been incorporated into alternative ways of experiencing our own world, now some of those same approaches can be reflected upon to experience the universe that is beyond reach for human perception.

Keywords: Senses · Visualization · Space · Interaction · Astronomy · Perception · Body · Integration

1 Introduction

The distance we humans have extended our vision into space falls outside what we can see with our unaided eyes, as well as the sensory range of particular phenomena like sound, touch, and the many senses of the human body: the big and small, close and far, fast and slow, humid and dry, intense and soft, hot and cold, bright and dark… but we do, however, have the means to translate these non-experienceable things to the domain of our human senses through technologies and visualization. This is not that different from compensating for a missing capability within the human body. In the case of a disability, the need to interact with and navigate space may help adapt and compensate within the environment to orient and evaluate decisions and actions, yet the environment remains the same for people with and without disabilities.

Navigating and interacting with space to handle objects by changing place and position happens as a multimodal experience. Senses confirm and enhance each other to gain awareness and to reason and act on the information gathered by the senses. "Our world radiates out from our bodies, as perceptual centers from which we see, hear, touch, taste, and smell our world" [1]. From this perspective an experience is not about the senses themselves but rather the overall spatial construction of the experience

© Springer International Publishing Switzerland 2015
M. Antona and C. Stephanidis (Eds.): UAHCI 2015, Part II, LNCS 9176, pp. 177–185, 2015.
DOI: 10.1007/978-3-319-20681-3_16

enabled by the sensory signals that converge in the brain. Soundscapes, temperature variation, touch used to move about –to name a few–, all contribute to creating an internal model of the space, or objects in space around the body.

On the other hand, the natural experience of the world is the main referent to how we evaluate representation in any form: auditory, visual, tactile, and so on. Yet our representation devices have become such a big part of our daily lives that we forget how eerie they feel the first time we experience them with our senses, when the media used only partially recreates a multi-sensory experience: what the first people confronted with a silent film felt, for example, not having accurate sounds to accompany the images displayed on the screen, or even today, what people experiencing virtual reality devices describe as nausea, because of the contradictory information regarding motion being acquired by vision but not by the vestibular system: where the eyes see a landscape as if one was moving forward, yet the balance system in human ears do not sense any spatial displacement.

The difference between a purely visual printed piece or representation, and any experience that includes real time sensory input, calls attention to itself as a novelty. The challenge today is to evaluate sensory means of representation against natural experiences, where the senses' bias are taken into account, like virtual architecture tailored to the senses, to fully utilize the capacity of human perception and attention to be meaningful. This biased experience of "(...) the nature of our bodies, the constrains on our perception, and the structure of our consciousness give prominence to the CENTER-PERIPHERY organization of our experienced reality" [1].

Working at the Adler Planetarium informs the insights mentioned here, since the experience of the Universe, derived from data collected by devices that extend our senses, is being tailored to our perceptual system in different ways, just like issues of perceptual disability are tailored to compensate for a given limitation. This approach is also related to the connection to nearby Electronic Visualization Laboratory, and the Virtual Reality work produced there which has evolved to consider the creation of virtual experiences as enhancers of perception in matters of extension of the human senses in courses such as Human Augmentics.

2   Perception and Cognition as a Personal Experience

Perception does not work as an isolated system within a person, but is part of a continuum of understanding that may trigger preconditioned automated responses. Perception may also increase a person's awareness, prompting the need to elaborate new meaning from the experience. New meaning may be formed in order to produce a custom response, a future automated response, or even create new metaphorical constructs. In this continuum "Metaphor reaches down below the level of propositions into this massive embodied dimension of our being" [1]. The connection to the experience is thus not lost, but abstracted and revisited as needed.

When we think of the personal experience of space, whether it an experience of pose, displacement, or a motion pattern, perception works to acquire information to elicit a response that may be a physical action, or a concept, or both, that remains tied to that experience of space that allows us to "understand abstract purpose in terms of motion along a path" [1].

This relation to form connects to the posture of the person and is a way in which we internalize structures outside of our body, and bring the outside inside. But not all senses create the same separation between inside and outside. While visual perception is the main sense to negotiate decisions with the world outside of the body, sound, for one, has to come inside of the body to be acknowledged, and we can even hear the inside of our own body. In this manner, the "(…) sense of sight implies exteriority, whereas sound creates an experience of interiority" [2].

Taste may also suggest interiority, and other kinds of sensory input also have a conditioned assumption of spatial placement and distance as to how they can reach, besides a starting proximity that is located inside, in the boundary (i.e.: touch) or outside of the body as in the case of vision. The body, as the point of origin of perception, measures space and places an understanding of the structure of space in the experience. Memories of skiing, displacing the body at high speed in the soft snow, may be assembled from the perceived brightness, wind sensation including tempera-ture, and vestibular tilt, whereas the experience of an earthquake may be assembled from rambling sounds that come from colliding objects at various distances and from various directions simultaneously, together with the body's vestibular system strug-gling to aid in keeping balance against the moving floor.

3   Perception and Cognition as a Collective Experience

In contrast to personal experiences, what is standard about our perceptual system? Similar weight and reaction to gravity, similar leg height and arm's length? There is a range of functionality of the human body with its senses and its dependence on the environment that can be shaped onto a collective understanding of how such a body relates to space through the coordinated input from senses. In turn, there is difference between people who are better at certain modalities [3].

The evolution of senses in different species are all traceable to adaptations to different environmental variables that affect survival such as obtaining food, protection from dangerous conditions, and ensuring continuity [4]. As a species we align our senses into one process, and in doing so we develop interaction patterns for handling and navigating. We could say that there is no thought or action detached from the body and the mind is "(…) part of an ongoing evolutionary process in which organisms seek to survive, grow, and flourish within various environments." Moreover, mind is but an "emergent process, never separate from body. Thus, experience is a series of purposive bodily activities immersed in the ongoing flow of organism-environment interactions" [1].

It is in this series of interactions and emergence of the mind where there are no ontological gaps between various levels of functional complexity [1] From this per-spective, organisms "develop what we call mind when they achieve levels of functional organization that make communication and shared meaning possible for them, thereby opening up a host of unprecedented possibilities for dealing with the life problems they encounter." At this level the capability of shared meanings arise to "engage in various modes of inquiry and reasoning, and coordinate activities with other creatures who have minds, using symbols that have meaning for us" [1]. Thus, the mind is also externalized to connect with others as a collective mind or thinking process. But how similar is perception from one person to another? Perceptual development has been averaged in terms of defining learning disorders [5]. It is in those disorders that tracing missing meaning points to perception that is lacking or perhaps varies too much to fall within what constitutes collective understanding.

The design of interactive spaces that are tailored to an approximation of the collective understanding built from perception requires an understanding of this continuum. The collective understanding that emerges from the interaction of independent perceptual systems centered on emergent minds is required for the emergence of the collective. Automatic responses at the collective level are what we know as generic, that is, devoid of specific meaning that corresponds to a specific situation, but rather, a response that is general and remains hidden from consciousness.

A learning disability rooted in perceptual differences may also have parallels in social learning. What would account for a perceptual problem at that scale? The collective experience, average or not, may reflect back to the individual as a perceptual modifier of the understanding of space navigation and handling.

4 Disability and the Limits of Perception: A Comparison

We can learn about our capabilities from our limitations. Compensating for a loss may imply a translation of something usually sensed in a particular way to another available sense. In scientific visualization the translation of data to a perceivable form is a way to expand our existing perceptual system, and also a way of compensation. What part of one sense cannot be replaced by another sense? What is beyond the senses altogether? The translation of what is missing from the capabilities of the average person, or limited by the average set of senses, is nothing new. In both cases, a person needs to train her or himself to recognize the translated signal, correlate it with other sensory cues, and accept it as natural. In this regard the concept of Human Augmentics considers senses as an ecosystem where perceptual cues can communicate with each other to coordinate necessary assistance [6].

In the case of astronomy, the farther one sees, the more we see the same thing. Perception of distant phenomena causes the point of view of humans to converge, since we all humans are looking out from the same planet, albeit in different directions depending on where we are on the planet's surface. Our experience of the Universe is a collective experience, enabled by instruments such as ground and space telescopes. These instruments collect data that is then scaled and/or retimed to show forms where constitutive parts relate to each other, and change, and become part of our human experience.

There is also the question of whether vision is defined by the eyes or the brain. Research in sensory integration reveals that when there are issues regarding how the senses connect to each other, spatial perception can be impaired. When senses that work in tandem to assess space cannot relate to each other, neglect may result because of this impairment in integration. In a situation of neglect a person may not see things on the right side of the visual field, for example [7]. Another visual issue is the inability to see stereoscopically. It is common knowledge that about 12 % of the population have issues with binocular vision where the sight of both eyes does not get integrated into an understanding of visual depth, although other perceptual cues for visual depth such as motion parallax are still available.

Senses support each other to extend the experience. This is an important aspect of disability compensation where ultimately we seek to handle spatial interaction, no matter the combination of senses that inform it. A well-known issue with VR devices is that when a user moves through virtual worlds there may be a conflict with the vestibular system. As mentioned before, the vestibular system may not be able to match the speed at which the image is changing due to the lack of motion expected in the balance system located in the ears. Similarly, in planetarium domes, tilting imagery has to be done at a discrete speed so as to not unbalance viewers.

Lastly, information about the Universe that is being translated to visible light, to noticeable speed, and in a scale that matches the range of human perception, is not direct, but also a translated or mediated experience. We notice the edges of perception when we cannot sense anything anymore, but require aids such as telescopes, cameras, or filters that can capture what human vision, scale and timeframe cannot. Yet the need for this spatial and temporal translation is not perceived as a disability, but a gain, because by extending our senses, we are extending human understanding. This gain, however, may still reflect into an experience of spatial and temporal reasoning, just as a natural experience would.

5 Sensory Integration to Understand and Interact with Space

The perception and experience of reality and designed reality is multi-sensory, and there is a premise in that triggers of involuntary memory are produced by a minimum of two senses [8]. The design of graphical interfaces and visualization development relies, whether consciously or not, on saccadic eye motion (the way human eyes wander about an image to build a model of it in the mind) all the way to proprioception in literally navigating space, for the purpose of visual flow. Conditioned areas in the brain that are devoted to multimodal perception affect the integration of these kinds of motion since visual navigation is integrated with other senses for assessment. For example, parts of the brain triggered by multimodal perception are slightly different than the sum of the independent sensory modalities [3].

On the other hand, sensory integration relies on attentional modulation, that is, memory or conditioning from previous experiences that inform how worthy an event is of attention [9]. Senses interact with biases recorded from past experiences in the brain. So in a way, the human senses not only negotiate among each other to process what is perceived, but sensory information is itself processed against memories [10].

Ultimately, these experiences of managing visual flow in the actual world model the experience of interaction with visualization devices. In turn, devices are taking over part of the role of memory in dealing with the environment, which affects the decision on what is worth thinking about and what is just a cue for resource acquisition [11]. In scaling spatial and temporal data, the cues for understanding space and duration can be greatly enhanced by engaging as many senses as possible. Spatial depth already suggests the understanding on how proprioception would work if one were able to move around a given environment. There are connections among our senses that inform the understanding of what we see, and incorporating other senses, even those that have no current stimulus, would reinforce the existence of what is being perceived.

6 Ranges of the Scale in the Human Body

For the human body, our senses have evolved in particular ways to relate to space and time, and also to extend its spatial reaches and understand the passage of time, invest in memory and make predictions, based on information. This is the human Umwelt, the world as sensed by the human perceptual system [4].

Devices such as telescopes and microscopes extend human vision to the very distant and the very small, but in scientific visualizations that information can be stretched in terms of range in order to see the large and the small together, slowed down to see what happens too fast, and compressed in order to see what happens too slowly. In other words, in order to see patterns, not only size and speed matters but range. Some patterns are out of range because the things being connected may be too small and too far from each other to be seen at once. Not only things are bigger and smaller than human senses can experience, but the thresholds where they die off –if we assume that the perceptual human range is maintained– may result in nothing to be perceived. This because salient qualities may have become too small and their distance from each other too large, perhaps, to the point nothing is visible or perceived by other senses either.

The human body has evolved to structure imagination within the ranges of its senses, although imagination can extend those senses through associative and combinatorial means. As Johnson puts it, "Imagination is our capacity to organize mental representations (especially percepts, images, and image schemata) into meaningful, coherent unities" [1]. Johnson accounted from Kant's work on the role of functional imagination to achieve meaning, and being able to understand, reason and communicate. The development of scientific visualizations fits within this task like an operation as described by Aristotle, where imagination is more of a mechanical operation tied to the senses rather than a creative process [1].

Furthermore, besides association, "Kant describes this ultimate unifying structure of consciousness as an operation of imagination, because it is a synthesizing activity that gives the general structure of objective experience as such" [1]. This synthesizing activity used in the development of representations or scientific visualizations belongs to the discipline of an artist who can imagine multiple scales simultaneously, and understand structure at various scales and ranges: a composition at many levels where weight can also be distributed and modulated in all of them to converge in the human perceptual system.

7 Extending Ranges of Experience

We live in extended bodies today, from communication devices that allow us to reach distant people and places, and information from the past and the future, to air conditioned cars that enhance speed while keeping us in a comfortable climate bubble, and virtual experiences that allow us to explore what is beyond our natural ability to perceive what exists beyond our senses, sensory ranges, and our spatial and time constraints. Indeed any media extends: books as assistive memory devices, photography as visual record, film as spatial and temporal memory as well. Remote cameras extend real time presence. Virtual Reality devices and spaces for collaborative and remote endeavors are becoming more common as the need to coordinate and extend experiences involving scientific or fantastic data increase.

"Our lives are filled with paths that connect up our spatial world (...) certain paths exist, at present, only in your imagination, such as the path from Earth to the nearest star outside of our solar system" [1]. Interacting with multi-scale datasets creates new paths and new challenges for multisensory integration. The very action of changing scales is in itself non intuitive, either because a constant speed tends to appear too slow in the larger end of the scale, and too fast in the shorter end of the transformation. But increasing size and speed together help keep the experience consistent among the senses. Perhaps they work like "Preconceptual gestalt forces as constraint of coherence" [1] in the realm of visualization as well.

Representations of scale in science fiction cartoons or movies may make us forget that our perceptual system has limits. When giant monsters roam about, their ability to even pay attention to small humans tends to be over stated. In the movie "Monolith Monsters" there is no reason to run from rocks if they are not falling or even moving the slightest. What does that mean for metaphors of outer space? Of the unreachable? Of course movies seek to elicit emotions rather than spatiotemporal paths per se. This is where interaction capabilities have been utilized to fill in the evoking of cross-sensory relationships that fit a change of orientation or speed. Like target practice with arrows, the general orientation of the head serves to calibrate target. This requires multimodal integration. Multimodal relationship bias respond to tracking because space needs to be handled, especially space in the universe. Interaction is important in evoking senses other than visual, in this case, touch evoked by handling, since non-informative vision affects haptic performance [12]. Building a multi scalar visualization is an interesting process where what was presented before as a graph or an abstract model is now being designed as an immersive spatial experience bound to its own set of constraints both defined and evoked by the medium.

8 Reconfiguring the Perceptual System

Looking beyond our human senses has afforded humanity knowledge about phenomena that does not appear immediate to the human perceptual system. Extended senses still evoke the connection to other senses that have been conditioned by the life we live in the environment of our planet however, reconstructing a multimodal experience that reinforces existing structures of the mind or perhaps creates new ones. The ultimate goal remains the creation of a spatial model of being in space that 'makes sense' of all sensory information available. This model would rely not only on each sensory input, but on the synergy created over time by simultaneously triggered senses in such a way that they can reinforce each other. This synergy is what Mark Johnson described as where "there is an inferential structure in the epistemic domain that is tied to gestalt features of our experience of physical force and barriers" [1].

9 Conclusion

The experience of the Universe, derived from data collected from devices that extend our senses, is being tailored to our perceptual system in different ways, just like issues of perceptual limitations are tailored to compensate for missing capabilities.

Perception does not work as an isolated system within a person, but is part of a continuum of understanding that may trigger preconditioned automated responses. Perception may also rise to the person's awareness, prompting the need to elaborate new meaning from the experience. New meaning may be formed in order to: produce a custom response, a future automated response, or even create new metaphorical constructs. There is a range of functionality in the human body with its senses that can be shaped into a collective understanding of how the body relates to space through the coordinated input from various senses.

Perceptual development has been averaged in terms of defining learning disorders. The collective experience, average or not, may reflect back to the individual as a perceptual modifier of the understanding of space navigation and object handling. Senses also support each other to extend the experience. This is an important aspect of disability compensation where we ultimately seek to understand the environment, with any available senses.

Sensory integration relies on attentional modulation, that is, memory or conditioning from previous experiences that inform how worthy an event is of attention [9]. Senses interact with biases recorded from past experiences in the brain. In a way, senses not only negotiate among each other to process what is perceived, but sensory information is itself processed against memories [10]. Ultimately, these experiences of managing visual flow in the actual world model the experience of interaction with visualization devices.

For the human body, senses have evolved in particular ways to relate to space and time, and also to extend their spatial reaches. This evolution has shaped us up to understand the passage of time and invest in memory and manage prediction models based on this information. The human body has also evolved to structure imagination within the ranges of its senses, although imagination can extend those senses through associative and combinatorial means. This synthesizing activity used in the development of representations or scientific visualizations belongs to the discipline of an artist who can imagine multiple scales simultaneously, and understand structure at those various scales and ranges: a composition at many levels where weight can be distributed and modulated across all of these levels to converge in the human perceptual system.

We live in extended bodies today, from communication devices that allow us to reach distant people and places along with information from the past and the future, to air conditioned cars that enhance speed while keeping us in a comfortable climate bubble, and virtual experiences that allow us to explore what is beyond our natural ability to perceive what exists beyond our senses, sensory ranges, and our spatial and time constraints.

Cinematographic techniques seek to elicit emotions rather than spatiotemporal paths per se. Beyond movies, interaction capabilities have been developed to evoke relationships that fit a change of orientation or speed that can be used to enhance understanding of information. In designing interactive experiences, multimodal relationships respond to tracking because the act of maneuvering objects or the environment greatly aids in orienting ourselves in space, especially space in the universe. For example, the use of various interactive devices including 3D prints of asteroids changes the appreciation people have of models seen in movies. Interaction is also important in evoking senses other than vision, for example, touch evoked by handling, since non-informative vision affects haptic performance [12]. Building a multi scalar visualization of the Universe that we know about from data is a complex process where what was presented before as a graph or an abstract model is now being designed as an immersive sensory experience that compensates for our human constraints.

References

1. Johnson, M.: The Body in the Mind. University of Chicago Press, Chicago (1987)
2. Pallasmaa, J.: The eyes of the skin: architecture and the senses. Wiley, New York (2012)
3. Giard, M.H., Peronnet, F.: Auditory-visual integration during multimodal object recognition in humans: a behavioral and electrophysiological study. J. Cogn. Neurosci. **11**(5), 473–490 (1999)
4. von Uexküll, J.: A stroll through the worlds of animals and men. In: Schiller, C.H. (ed.) Instinctive behavior: The development of a Modern Concept. International Universities Press, New York (1934)
5. Norwood, K.W.: Reliability of 'the motor observations with regards to sensory integration': a pilot study. British J. Occup. Ther. **62**(2), 80–88 (1999)
6. Kenyon, R.V., Leigh, J.: Human augmentics: augmenting human evolution. In: Engineering in Medicine and Biology Society, EMBC, Annual International Conference of the IEEE. IEEE (2011)
7. Pouget, A., Driver, J.: Relating unilateral neglect to the neural coding of space. Curr. Opin. Neurobiol. **10**(2), 242–249 (2000)
8. Milligan, A. et al.: Drawing Sounds. A Grand Day Out: Empathic Approaches to Design (2008)
9. Andersen, R.A.: Multimodal integration for the representation of space in the posterior parietal cortex. Philos. Trans. R. Soc. Lon. Ser. B: Biol. Sci. **352**(1360), 1421–1428 (1997)
10. Bechara, A., et al.: Deciding advantageously before knowing the advantageous strategy. Science **275**(5304), 1293–1295 (1997)
11. Clark, A., Chalmers, D.: The extended mind. Analysis **58**, 7–19 (1998)
12. Sander, Z., et al.: Multisensory integration mechanisms in haptic space perception. Exp. Brain Res. **157**(2), 265–268 (2004)

Thinking Outside of the Box or Enjoying Your 2 Seconds of Frame?

Per Bækgaard[✉], Michael Kai Petersen, and Jakob Eg Larsen

Cognitive Systems Department of Applied Mathematics and Computer Science, Technical University of Denmark, Building 321, 2800 Kgs. Lyngby, Denmark
{pgba,mkai,jaeg}@dtu.dk

Abstract. The emergence of low cost eye tracking devices will make QS quantified self monitoring of eye movements attainable on next generation mobile devices, potentially allowing us to infer reactions related to fatigue or emotional responses on a continuous basis when interacting with the screens of smartphones and tablets. In the current study we explore whether consumer grade eye trackers, despite their reduced spatio-temporal resolution, are able to monitor fixations as well as frequencies of saccades and blinks that may characterize aspects of attention, and identify consistent individual patterns that may be modulated by our overall level of engagement.

Keywords: Eye tracking · Fixation Density Maps · Fixation duration

1 Introduction

Although we may visually perceive whatever attracts our attention as a static entity, our eyes process information from short fixations characterized by foveal acuity interspersed by rapid saccadic eye movements. Essentially the oculomotor plant can be modeled as a dynamic system which through contraction of muscles and elastic tendons continuously pulls and rotates the eye globe when directing our gaze towards an area of interest. These muscles are controlled by neural signals modulated by areas in the brain responsible for constantly engaging and relocating our visual attention [12], which at the same time reflect our cognitive state as fatigue and demanding tasks have been found to lower saccadic velocity, whereas higher peak saccadic velocity indicates increasing arousal [7]. It is also known that the frequency and duration of blinks can be indicative of fatigue or time-on-task [8,9,16,17]. However, fixation density patterns and saccadic movements differ highly across individuals [13,15] yet remain stable over a variety of viewing conditions due to systematic endogenous factors [3,10]. We would therefore expect that our current eye tracking study might reflect both unique individual traits as well as variations in fixation patterns due to varying levels of engagement. Applying a low cost eye tracker running at a low resolution [6], we explore whether we are able to distinguish stable individual characteristics when viewing suddenly appearing contrasting visual stimuli with uniform

© Springer International Publishing Switzerland 2015
M. Antona and C. Stephanidis (Eds.): UAHCI 2015, Part II, LNCS 9176, pp. 186–195, 2015.
DOI: 10.1007/978-3-319-20681-3_17

baseline metrics [5]. The experiment is repeated over a week in order to analyze how eye tracking parameters related to fixation density maps may vary due to changing levels of perceived fatigue.

2   Experiment

Being amongst the first eye-self-trackers, this experiment explores whether we can identify individual signatures reflecting levels of attention in eye tracking

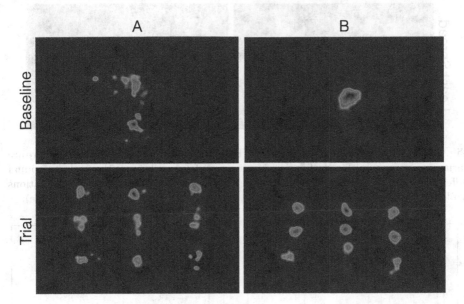

Fig. 1. Typical fixation density Maps, for A (left column) and B (right column), of fixations in the baseline examples (upper row) when observing solid colors only, and in trial (lower row) when the colored squares are presented against the complementary color background.

The Trial Fixation Density Maps (lower row) reflect the position of the visual stimuli, nevertheless there are clear differences between the test persons; B has a higher tendency to maintain focus within the frame of the squares. A appear less focused on the frame and is rather *thinking outside of the box*, while overall fixations appear less dense in the middle horizontal versus the lower and upper horizontal rows. Likewise for B the central square in the lowest horizontal row shows a larger spread and overall this row reflects a less dense focus, although we cannot rule out the possibility of calibration errors for the eye tracker in the lower screen area.

The Baseline Fixation Density Maps (upper row) depict a higher degree of difference between the subjects. Again, B has a higher tendency to maintain focus towards the center of the screen whereas A shows a tendency to focus at the middle vertical, with fixations skewed towards the left side of the screen. We speculate that this consistent offset for A, rather than being an artifact, could potentially be related to gaze direction rooted in right hemisphere dominance when processing spatial information [2] (Color figure online).

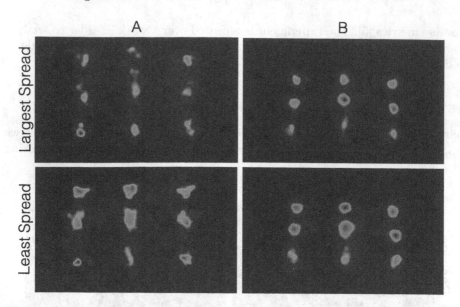

Fig. 2. Variations in fixation density maps (baseline/trial combined). Although there are variations in power within the fixation density maps for A and B over the week, individual differences are discernible, where the upper row shows the largest spread of fixations while the lower row represents more narrowly focused fixations (Color figure online).

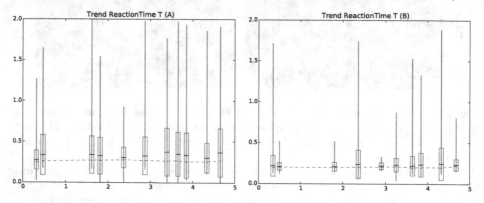

Fig. 3. Differences in *time to target* reaction time when fixating on the presented visual stimuli in trials throughout the week for A (left) and B (right); minimum, mean standard deviation, mean, mean+standard deviation, and maximum. The dashed line indicates the median.

This reaction time is measured from the presentation of the stimuli to the first fixation starts at, or close to the presented, square. This includes the reactive saccade between points. The saccade time cannot be accurately determined due to the 60 Hz sampling frequency of Eye Tribe tracker, but is estimated to be 30–50 ms. Fixations typically jump to adjacent positions in space, so the variation in distance is not large, as can be seen. The reaction time median, which best filters out any noise and accidental mis-calibrations, remains remarkably consistent throughout the entire week, and clearly differs between the test persons at around ~269 ms vs ~201 ms.

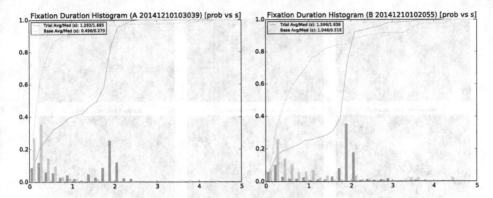

Fig. 4. Fixation duration histograms (bars) and cummulative histograms (lines), for both A (left) and B (right) during an experiment.

Fixation duration appears to be stimuli dependent with, in this case, a median time of 1.695 s vs 0.270 s for person A in Trials (blue) vs Baseline (yellow) and 1.936 s vs 0.516 s for person B. This indicates consistent differences in A and B's fixation durations. This stimuli-dependent difference when attending to the presented squares versus the solid color backgrounds is not only observed in fixation durations, but also to some extent in e.g. saccade frequencies and fixation patterns. No dependency on color of the presented squares were observed, despite the large self reported perceived differences related to the extreme complementary color contrasts such as green squares on top of a red background or yellow squares presented against a blue background.

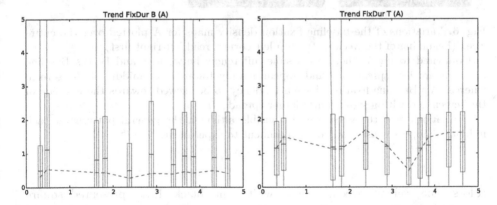

Fig. 5. Variations of the Fixation Duration for A across all experiments in the entire week. The Baseline fixation length when observing solid background colors shows less variation than when attending to the presented complementary colored squares.

data. During the experiment, eye tracking data has typically been collected twice a day over a week, each consisting of 24 trials where 8 colored squares (∼3 degrees wide) are sequentially presented on the screen, alternating between the

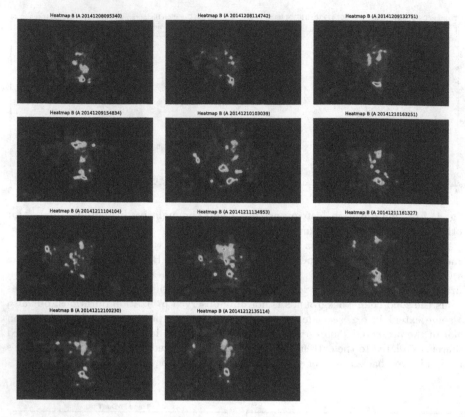

Fig. 6. Variations of the baseline fixation density maps for A plotted over the entire week (beginning of the week at the top left corner; read left-right first).

Compared to Fig. 7, there are visible differences between A and B: B's Baseline fixations are less spread out and appear mainly towards the middle of the screen, whereas A's Baseline fixations have a tendency to be skewed towards the left side of the screen and with a significantly larger spread.

Variations over the week are also visible although the general pattern for each individual appear consistent from experiment to experiment.

colors blue, yellow, green, yellow, white and black. Each presented square appeared for 2 s against their complementary color as screen background (referred to as *Trial* conditions), followed by 4 s of solid complementary color (referred to as *Baseline* conditions). In total, this constitutes 480 secs of visual stimuli for each of 11 experiments performed over a week.

After an initial calibration at the beginning of each experiment, stimuli was presented on a conventional MacBook Pro 13" in an ordinary office environment, running PsychoPy software [14]. The Eye Tribe mobile eye tracking device, connected via USB, retrieved the eye tracking data through the associated API [18],

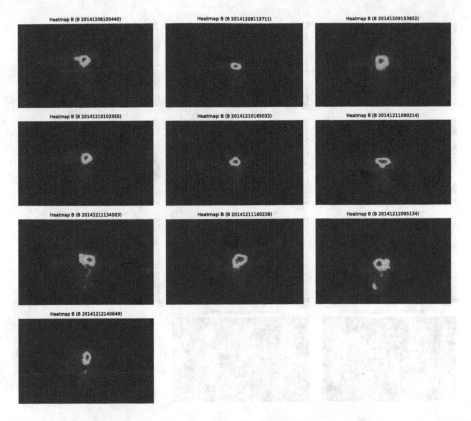

Fig. 7. Variations of the baseline fixation density maps for B plotted over the entire week (beginning of the week at the top left corner; read left-right first).

Compared to Fig. 6, there are visible differences between A and B: B's Baseline fixations are less spread out and appear mainly towards the middle of the screen, whereas A's Baseline fixations have a tendency to be skewed towards the left side of the screen and with a significantly larger spread.

Variations over the week are also visible although the general pattern for each individual appear consistent from experiment to experiment.

using PeyeTribe [1]. Subsequently a density based clustering approach to define fixations was applied. Two right-handed subjects (males, average age 55) participated in the experiments and were not instructed to follow any specific viewing patterns.

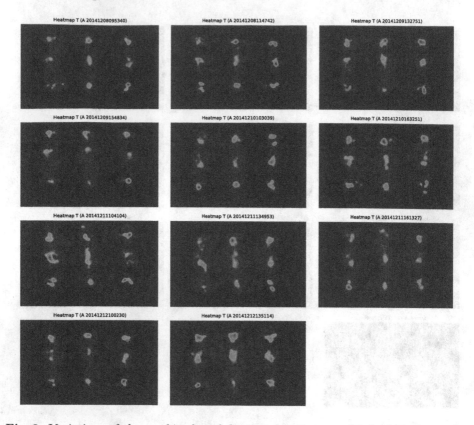

Fig. 8. Variations of the combined trial fixation density maps for A plotted over the entire week (beginning of the week at the top left corner; read left-right first).

Compared to Fig. 9 there are similar differences in these stimuli-driven Trial Fixation Density Maps as there are for the Baseline ones, although they are less pronounced. B has again less spread-out fixations compared to A, and it's likely that any random A and B Fixation Density Map could be compared and classified as belonging to either A or B based on their looks.

3   Results

Below, Figs. 1 and 2 compare typical Fixation Density Maps in Trial and Baseline for A and B, and variations in spread of the combined Fixation Density Maps. Figures 3, 4 and 5 show *time to target* reaction times and fixation durations. Figures 6, 7, 8 and 9 illustrate variations in the Fixation Density Maps for the entire week of experiments.

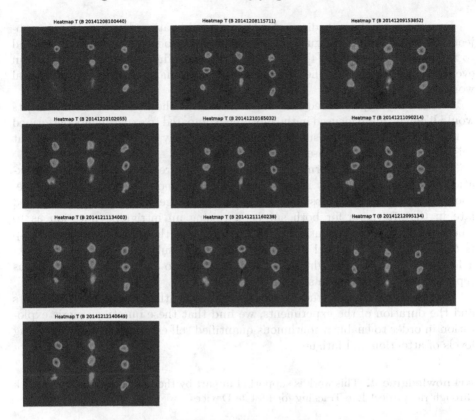

Fig. 9. Variations of the combined trial fixation density maps for B plotted over the entire week (beginning of the week at the top left corner; read left-right first).

Compared to Fig. 8 there are similar differences in these stimuli-driven Trial Fixation Density Maps as there are for the Baseline ones, although they are less pronounced. B has again less spread-out fixations compared to A, and it's likely that any random A and B Fixation Density Map could be compared and classified as belonging to either A or B based on their looks.

4   Conclusion

While the *time to target* reaction time, reaching first fixation on the presented visual stimuli, differentiates subject A from B, this eye tracking measure nevertheless appears constant within the two subjects during the whole week. This is not inconsistent with the reported findings of Wang and Stern [19], as cited by [17], which indicates *reactive saccades* to be invariant of time-on-task. It thus seems to reflect a personal signature neither affected by training nor the differing complementary color contrasts of the presented stimuli in the experiments, whereas the spread and length of fixations in response to the presented colored squares varies within subjects A and B during the experiments over the week.

Recent eye tracking studies indicate extended fixation duration time in subjects reporting feeling fatigued at non-optimal periods during the day related to their circadian rhythm [4], whereas shorter gaze duration has been found in eye tracking experiments when subjects read emotionally positive versus neutral words [11].

We initially hypothesized that the fixations on the presented visual targets would likely be more focused in the morning, compared to experiments performed in the afternoon where the subjects might presumably be feeling more tired, but this seems not to be the case.

During some of the morning experiments which resulted in less focused fixations the subjects actually reported that they felt more fresh and alert. Correspondingly, some of the most dense fixations on targets were actually recorded late in the afternoon for both subjects, raising an intriguing question as to whether the wider distribution of the fixations in the Fixation Density Map is correlated with the level of engagement of the subjects, or merely reflects a less agile focus that might be inversely related to the perceived fatigue, as reported by the subjects in some of the experiments.

Although the present study is clearly limited by the number of participants and the duration of the experiments, we find that these questions merit exploration in order to enable a continuous quantified self estimation of our changing levels of attention and fatigue.

Acknowledgment. This work is supported in part by the Innovation Fund Denmark through the project Eye Tracking for Mobile Devices.

References

1. Bækgaard, P.: Simple python interface to the eye tribe eye tracker. http://github.com/baekgaard/peyetribe/ (Accessed: 17 February 2015)
2. Carlei, C., Kerzel, D.: Gaze direction affects visuo-spatial short-term memory. Brain Cogn. **90**, 63–68 (2014)
3. Castelhano, M.S., Henderson, J.M.: Stable individual differences across images in human saccadic eye movements. Can. J. Exp. Psychol./Rev. Can. Psychol. Expérimentale **62**(1), 1 (2008)
4. Cazzoli, D., Antoniades, C.A., Kennard, C., Nyffeler, T., Bassetti, C.L., Müri, R.M.: Eye movements discriminate fatigue due to chronotypical factors and time spent on task-a double dissociation. PloS ONE **9**(1), e87146 (2014)
5. Corbetta, M., Shulman, G.L.: Control of goal-directed and stimulus-driven attention in the brain. Nat. Rev. Neurosci. **3**(3), 201–215 (2002)
6. Dalmaijer, E.: Is the low-cost eyetribe eye tracker any good for research?. Technical report. PeerJ PrePrints (2014)
7. Di Stasi, L.L., Catena, A., Canas, J.J., Macknik, S.L., Martinez-Conde, S.: Saccadic velocity as an arousal index in naturalistic tasks. Neurosci. Biobehav. Rev. **37**(5), 968–975 (2013)
8. Dodge, R.: The laws of relative fatigue. Psychol. Rev. **24**(2), 89 (1917)
9. Dodge, R., Cline, T.S.: The angle velocity of eye movements. Psychol. Rev. **8**(2), 145 (1901)

10. Kasprowski, P., Ober, J.: Eye movements in biometrics. In: Maltoni, D., Jain, A.K. (eds.) BioAW 2004. LNCS, vol. 3087, pp. 248–258. Springer, Heidelberg (2004)
11. Knickerbocker, H., Johnson, R.L., Altarriba, J.: Emotion effects during reading: influence of an emotion target word on eye movements and processing. Cogn. Emot. **29**(5), 784–806 (2015). doi:10.1080/02699931.2014.938023
12. Komogortsev, O., Holland, C., Karpov, A., Price, L.R.: Biometrics via oculomotor plant characteristics: Impact of parameters in oculomotor plant model. ACM Trans. Appl. Percept. (TAP) **11**(4), 20 (2014)
13. Komogortsev, O.V., Jayarathna, S., Aragon, C.R., Mahmoud, M.: Biometric identification via an oculomotor plant mathematical model. In: Proceedings of the 2010 Symposium on Eye-Tracking Research & Applications, pp. 57–60. ACM (2010)
14. Peirce, J.W.: Psychopy-psychophysics software in python. J. Neurosci. Methods **162**(1), 8–13 (2007)
15. Rigas, I., Komogortsev, O.V.: Biometric recognition via fixation density maps. In: International Society for Optics and Photonics. SPIE Defense+ Security, pp. 90750M–90750M (2014)
16. Schleicher, R., Galley, N., Briest, S., Galley, L.: Blinks and saccades as indicators of fatigue in sleepiness warnings: looking tired? Ergonomics **51**(7), 982–1010 (2008)
17. Sirevaag, E.J., Stern, J.A.: Ocular measures of fatigue and cognitive factors. In: Engineering psychophysiology: Issues and Applications, pp. 269–287 (2000)
18. TheEyeTribe: Api reference eyetribe-docs. http://dev.theeyetribe.com/api/ (Accessed: 17 February 2015)
19. Wang, L., Stern, J.A.: Oculometric evaluation of subjects performing a vigilance task: The bakan continuous performance task. Unpublished Manuscript (1997)

A Study on Within-Subject Factors for Visually Induced Motion Sickness by Using 8K Display

Through Measurement of Body Sway Induced by Vection While Viewing Images

Hiromu Ishio[1(✉)], Tatsuya Yamakawa[2], Akihiro Sugiura[2,3],
Kazuki Yoshikawa[2], Takehito Kojima[4], Shigeru Terada[2],
Kunihiko Tanaka[3], and Masaru Miyao[2]

[1] Department of Urban Management, Fukuyama City University,
2-19-1, Minatomachi, Fukuyama, Hiroshima 721-0964, Japan
h-ishio@fcu.ac.jp
[2] Department of Information Engineering, Graduate School of Information
Science, Nagoya University, Furo-cho, Chikusa-ku, Nagoya 464-8603, Japan
[3] Department of Health Science, Gifu University of Medical Science, 795-1,
Ichihiraga-aza-Nagamine, Seki, Gifu 501-3892, Japan
[4] Department of Nursing, Chubu Gakuin University, 2-1, Kirigaoka, Seki, Gifu
501-3993, Japan

Abstract. Visually induced self-motion perception (vection) is one of the phenomena related to human vision. It often emerges as a precursory symptom of motion sickness while viewing moving images. Employing a large number of subjects in a wide range of age groups and using a large-scale 8 K display, we investigated within-subject factors which can influence a sense of vection. We report some results of statistical analyses of vection-induced body sway which occurred when the subjects viewed rotating images on the display. Then we find that our fundamental study may provide useful information in order to set safety guidelines for large-scale ultra-high-definition displays such as 4K and 8K which are becoming popular in public use.

Keywords: Within-subject factor · Visually induced motion sickness · 8K display · Body sway · Vection

1 Introduction

Recent advances in image transmission and presentation technologies have brought us the benefit of increase in size and resolution of displays such as ultra-high-definition (UHD) 4 K (3840 × 2160) and 8 K (7680 × 4320). As a result, we have more and more opportunities to be exposed to virtually created but ultra-realistic environments [1]. The advantage is that those displays can present more dynamic and exciting information to

© Springer International Publishing Switzerland 2015
M. Antona and C. Stephanidis (Eds.): UAHCI 2015, Part II, LNCS 9176, pp. 196–204, 2015.
DOI: 10.1007/978-3-319-20681-3_18

viewers. On the other hand, the disadvantage is that one of the problems arising from such situations is visually induced motion sickness (VIMS). It is considered that, the larger the display size becomes and the more moving images of higher resolution are involved, the more easily VIMS arises. Symptoms of VIMS are in general (i) head spins, body sway, headache, sense of fatigue, feeling of drowsiness, facial pallor, etc. in the early stage, (ii) cold sweats, hypothermia, increased saliva production, stomach discomfort, etc. in the middle stage, and (iii) nausea, vomiting, etc. in the severe stage. Since the appearances of VIMS are similar to carsickness, seasickness, etc., VIMS is classified as kinesia [2].

The mechanism of kinesia is not yet fully understood in detail although several hypotheses are suggested. Let us refer to the most common hypotheses for the cause of motion sickness here. First is the "sensory discrepancy" hypothesis that the primary factor which develops motion sickness is the visual global motion which contradicts the actually static body, causing a sensory integrative discrepancy between visual and balance information [3]. Second is the "toxic" hypothesis that the presence of nausea is a part of our defensive function against intoxication [4, 5]. In the case that we have swallowed (ingested) poisons by mistake, we unconsciously make the functional interrelation in our visual and vestibular systems incommensurate each other in the brain, resulting in head spins, body sway, etc. leading to vomiting for forceful expulsion of contents of the stomach. It is considered that humans have acquired such physiological function to survive in the evolutionary process. Once we obtained the function, incommensurate functional interrelation induced for our visual and vestibular systems can cause head spins, body sway, etc. leading to vomiting not only when poisons are detected but also for any reason such as motion sickness. Third is the "postural instability" hypothesis that putting ourselves in an unfamiliar environment to keep our postural stability is the cause of motion sickness [6]. Naturally, we uncon- sciously keep ourselves in a stable position by using various kinds of sensory infor- mation. However, when we happen to put ourselves in an unstable situation and have difficulty keeping ourselves in a stable position, then we suffer from motion sickness. Unfortunately, there exist evidences both for and against each of the three hypotheses described above. They are merely hypotheses and there has been no definite proof provided for any of them so far.

Regardless of our poor understanding of the mechanism of motion sickness, there is an urgent need for safety evaluation in viewing moving images as is described at the beginning of this section. However, there is not so much progress not only in setting safety guidelines on VIMS [7, 8] but also in finding a standard method for safety evaluation from the viewpoint of prevention of VIMS [2, 9] or even identifying incentive factors [10].

Visually induced self-motion perception known as vection [11] is one of the phe- nomena related to human vision. In particular, rotational and translational self-motion perception is called circular and linear vection, respectively [11]. The vection is induced in the following way: When stationary observers are exposed to large-field one-way visual flow stimulating the retina with corresponding optic flow uniformly and con- tinuously in one direction, they often experience an illusory perception of self-motion in the opposite direction to the visual stimulus. It means that visual information has a significantly crucial influence on self-motion perception [12, 13].

Vection is deeply related with VIMS and often emerges as a precursory symptom of VIMS. Therefore, it has been used as a clue to verify and elucidate occurrence factors and mechanisms of VIMS in the past studies. Most of such studies are on VIMS-influencing "information factors" such as velocity [14–16], acceleration (vestibular sensory information supposed to be integrated with visual information) [17–19], direction (i.e., retinal, body, head and/or world coordinates) [20], frequency [21], depth feel [22], view angle [23, 24], etc. However, because of experimental difficulties, very little research has been done on "within-subject factors" so far except a report verifying a difference between children and adults [25, 26]. Vection is supposed to become prominent when we use a display of larder size with higher resolution because of the enhancement of reality of the presented image.

In this study, employing a large number of subjects in a wide range of age groups and using a large-scale 8 K display, we examined within-subject factors which might influence a sense of vection while viewing moving images. We evaluated the effect of vection through measurement of body sway. Candidates of within-subject factors for the verification experiment in this study are sex (SX), age (AG), physical condition (PC) of the day, pupil distance (PD), average cylindrical power (CYL) indicating the degree of astigmatism and average spherical power (SPH) indicating the degree of nearsightedness or farsightedness.

2   Method

2.1   Stimuli

Moving images used in the experiment were produced by using a digital 4 K video camera recorder (Sony FDR-AX100). Each of them consisted of small beads with different colors. Those beads were densely distributed at random on the frame. The images have two types in speed, i.e., slow moving (SM) and fast moving (FM): SM and FM images were produced such that they rotate clockwise at a constant angular velocity of 3 and 6 degrees per second around its own center, respectively. We also produced a green monochrome (GM) image by computer graphics as a static reference.

2.2   Apparatuses

The images were presented on an 8 K tiled-display of 185-inch (4×4 Sumsung UD46C, total 16 commercial FullHD LED-backlit LCD flat panels of 46-inch 1920×1080). It was operated by a supercomputer (SGI UV 2000 with 20 TB RAM and 4 GPU enabling to present 8 K images on the display) and installed as a part of the High-Definition Visualization System in Information Technology Center, Nagoya University. On the display, the luminance at the position of beads in the SM and FM images was an average of 235 cd/cm^2 while that of the GS image was 20.4 cd/cm^2.

The experiment was conducted in a dark chamber. At the position of subjects, the illuminance toward the display and overhead was an average of 110.2 lx and 42.2 lx, respectively, for the SM and FM images while 65.4 lx and 35.4 lx, respectively, for the GM image.

Body sway of each subject was measured by using Wii Balance Board (Nintendo) [27–29] together with a head-mounted three-axis acceleration sensor. The Balance Board plays the role of a stabilometer and can record the center of pressure (COP) displacement on the two-dimensional surface of the board (x and y-axis for horizontally parallel and perpendicular direction to the display surface, respectively, in the experiment). In the analyses below, we only used data collected by the Balance Board.

2.3   Participants

Total 88 naive volunteers, 43 males and 45 females, participated in this experiment. Their ages range from 18 to 76 years old. We classified the ages into four groups, i.e., young (Y) for ages 18–29 years, young-middle (YM) for ages 30–44 years, middle (M) for 45–64 years and elder (E) for more than equal 65 years. All the subjects reported either normal vision or vision corrected with glasses or contact lenses. They also reported no particular history of vestibular system disease and no fatigue at the beginning of the experiment. None of them was aware of the purpose of the experiment.

We obtained informed consent from all the subjects and the experiment in this study was approved by the Ethics Review Board in Graduate School of Information Science, Nagoya University.

2.4   Procedure

In advance, we carried out questionnaire investigation (SX, AG, PC, hours and quality of sleep, previous experience of motion sickness, etc.) as well as examination of visual functions (PD, visual acuity including SPH, refractivity including CYL, etc.) for each subject. Then the subject was asked to stand still on the Balance Board placed 2 m in front of the display, facing straight the display and maintaining the posture with the bilateral toes and heels together (Romberg's posture [30]). Stabilometry is generally performed in the Romberg's posture. It is because the posture with a small support area is unstable and body sway increases in inverse proportion to the area of the supporting base. Therefore, the Romberg's posture is appropriate to measure the degree of dis-equilibrium [31]. We should note that the SM and FM images correspond to so-called "roll" rotations around the front-to-back axis for the subject. Among roll, pitch and yaw, roll is considered to have the largest influence on VIMS [32]. We should also note that the length of the narrow side of each image (i.e., height of the screen of the display) is nearly equal to the width (diameter) of the field of view (FOV) of the subject because the central visual field (CVF) of Japanese people on average is within about 30 degrees (conical angle) around the direction of the line of sight [33, 34], so that the width (diameter) of CFV is about 2.3 m which nearly coincide with the height of the 185-inch screen of the display with aspect ratio 16:9. In the estimation, we ignored the peripheral visual field since it is considered to have much lower ability to perceive than the central visual field [33, 34].

200 H. Ishio et al.

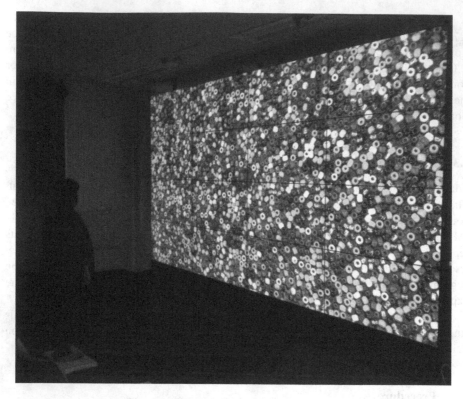

Fig. 1. Actual condition of the experiments

Protocol of the experiments was the following:

1. First, as a pre-test, each subject was instructed to concentrate on the central part of the GM image presented on the display and the body sway (i.e., center of gravity) was recorded for 60 s. Succeedingly, the subject was instructed to close the eyes and the body sway was recorded again for 60 s. Afterwards, the subject was required to answer Simulator Sickness Questionnaire (SSQ) [35] as a standard method for subjective evaluation of the degree of VIMS.
2. Next, as a 1st main test, the subject was instructed to concentrate on the central part of the SM image presented on the display and the body sway was recorded for 30 s. Then suddenly the rotation of the image was suspended. The subject was instructed to continue to keep the eyes open and the body sway was recorded for 60 s. Succeedingly, the subject was instructed to close the eyes and the body sway was recorded again for 60 s. Afterwards, the subject was required to answer SSQ.
3. Finally, as a 2nd main test, we repeat the same first main test but with the FM image.

The actual condition and sequence of the experiments are shown in Fig. 1 and Fig. 2, respectively.

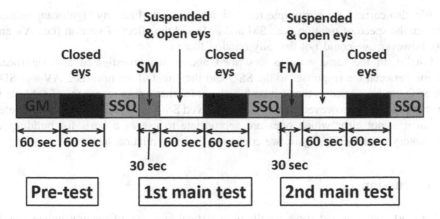

Fig. 2. Sequence of the experiments

3 Results

We first calculated average value (AV) and standard deviation (SD) of x and y components of COP for the entire subjects as statistical analyses in terms of time steps of the data in each task shown in Fig. 2. Then we have found that, especially while the subjects were gazing at the SM and FM images, the AV of x significantly deviates rightward, i.e., the bodies of the subjects were swaying toward the direction of rotation of the images before suspension while, after suspension, the value deviates leftward opposite to the rotation of the images. Correspondingly, SD of x was enhanced in both cases. On the other hand, AV and SD of y did not have much change in a series of the tasks. These effects are rather known in the past literatures. The braking of symmetry in the results may attribute to the Romberg's posture the subjects were forced to take. With the posture it is more difficult to keep their balance in the x-direction than in the y-direction [36]. Therefore, it is strongly recommended that, for safe viewing of moving images, we should take a posture more stable in the direction of x-axis.

We further investigated statistics on the AV and the SD. We considered each of them as an index of vection and hence an objective variable. Then, using a multiple regression analysis, we estimated factors (explanatory variables) which may have largest influences on the objective variable. Candidates of such factors in this study were SX, AG, PG, PD, CYL and SPH. We carried out a reliability test of the estimation by t-test, where we say that the explanatory variable with its significance probability (p-value) less than 0.05 has a significant relation to the objective variable. According to our calculation, p-value for each explanatory variable was around 0.05 or larger so that we report almost no statistically significant difference between the explanatory variables we chose. Only exception was that, while viewing the FM images, SX has a stronger significant relation with SD of both x and y: SD of x, $t = 2.0$ ($p = 0.05$); SD of y, $t = 1.9$ ($p = 0.06$). This means that males have larger SD of both x and y than females, which contradicts a belief that females are more "unsteady" than males. We need more detailed investigations to solve this contradiction.

We also carried out a multiple regression analysis to find any significant relation between the speed of rotation (i.e., SM and FM) and the effect of vection (i.e., AV and SD), however, we could not find any relation there.

Finally, in the same way as described above, we investigated any significant relation between the responses to the SSQ and the effect of vection (i.e., AV and SD). The SSQ has been used as the standard methods for measuring responses of subjects in the study of VIMS, however, many of the observed SSQ variables are highly correlated so that it is not clear which ones are appropriate to use as a basis for building an explanatory model [37]. Again, we could not find any relation here.

4 Discussion

In the work, we reported some results of statistical analyses of vection-induced body sway while viewing the rotating images on the 8 K display and discuss an effect of vection on motion sickness. Although our trials using a multiple regression analysis were not so successful, we find that our fundamental but pioneering study may provide useful information in order to set safety guidelines for large-scale UHD displays such as 4 K and 8 K which are becoming popular in public use. That is, our study may serve as a proof to say that it seems safe to show on such a display a rotating image of 6 degrees per second to people in wide range of generations. In the experiment, no one complained of headache, etc. as a symptom of VIMS. In this context, identification of a maximum speed limit value of rotation for preventing VIMS, if it exists, may be a future issue to be solved.

Another issue to be examined in detail is that, in the case of circular vection, it is not certain but said that the sense of vection increases in proportional to the speed of rotation until 10 degrees per seconds and then saturates.

As for statistical analysis of COP, we can further study stabilogram indices such as area of sway, total locus length, velocity of COP, etc. We can also apply a FFT analysis to the motion of COP.

Acknowledgements. This work was partially supported by JSPS KAKENHI (Grant-in-Aid for Scientific Research (B)) Grant Number 24300046.

References

1. For overview of researches and developments in ultra-realistic communication-related technologies, the home page of Ultra-Realistic Communications Forum (URCF). http://www.urcf.jp/english/
2. Standards for Image Safety to Be Studied by Advanced Industrial Science and Technology (AIST). http://www.aist.go.jp/aist_e/latest_research/2004/20040203/20040203.html
3. Reason, J.T., Brand, J.J.: Motion Sickness, pp. 103–128. Academic Press, New York (1975)
4. Treisman, M.: Motion sickness: an evolutionary hypothesis. Science 197, 493–495 (1977)
5. Nalivaiko, E., Rudd, J.A., So, R.H.Y.: Motion sickness, nausea and thermoregulation: the "Toxic" hypothesis. Temperature 1, 164–171 (2014)

6. Riccio, G.E., Stoffregen, T.A.: An Ecological theory of motion sickness and postural instability. Ecol. Psychol. **3**, 195–240 (1991)
7. Report of Feasibility Study on Development of Image Production Support System for Compliance with International Guidelines on Visually Induced Motion Sickness (in Japanese). http://home.jeita.or.jp/page_file/20120601142409_GSrKkoEYvZ.pdf
8. ISO/IWA 3:2005 "Image safety – Reducing the incidence of undesirable biomedical effects caused by visual image sequences" (Standards catalogue). http://www.iso.org/iso/catalogue_detail.htm?csnumber=43019
9. Ujike, H.: Developing an evaluation system of visually induced motion sickness for safe usage of moving images: fermentation of a social understanding to supply secure and comfortable images through integration of researches on human characteristics, image analysis technique and image production technique. Synthesiology **3**, 180–189 (2010)
10. Matsuda, T., Ohnaka, Y.: A note on the relation between trembling of pictorial image and visually induced motion sickness. Ritsumeikan J. Hum. Sci. **9**, 97–106 (2005)
11. Fischer, M.H., Kornmüller, A.E.: Optokinetisch ausgelöste Bewegungswahrnehmung und optokinetischer Nystagmus [Optokinetically induced motion perception and optokinetic nystagmus]. J. Psychol. Neurol. **41**, 273–308 (1930)
12. Howard, I.P.: Human Visual Orientation. Wiley, Chichester (1982)
13. Warren, W.H.: Self-motion: visual perception and visual control. In: Epstein, W., Rogers, S. (eds.) Perception of Space and Motion. Academic Press, San Diego (1995)
14. Sauvan, X.M., Bonnet, C.: Spatiotemporal boundaries of linear vection. Percept. Psychophys. **57**, 898–904 (1995)
15. de Graaf, B., Wertheim, A.H., Bles, W., Kremers, J.: Angular velocity, not temporal frequency determines circular vection. Vis. Res. **30**, 637–646 (1990)
16. Kawashima, Y., Uchikawa, K., Kaneko, H., Fukuda, K., Yamamoto, K., Kiya, K.: Changing driver's sensation of speed applying vection caused by flickering boards placed on sides of road. ITE (The Institute of Image Information and Television Engineers) J. **65**, 833–840 (2011)
17. Carpenter-Smith, T.R., Futamura, R.G., Parker, D.E.: Inertial acceleration as a measure of linear vection: an alternative to magnitude estimation. Percept. Psychophys. **57**, 35–42 (1995)
18. Harris, L.R., Jenkin, M., Zikovitz, D.C.: Vestibular cues and virtual environments: choosing the magnitude of the vestibular cue. In: IEEE International Conference on Virtual Reality, pp. 229–236 (1999)
19. Edwards, M., O'Mahony, S., Ibbotson, M.R., Kohlhagen, S.: Vestibular stimulation affects optic-flow sensitivity. Perception **39**, 1303–1310 (2010)
20. Seno, T.: Vection is not determined by the retinal coordinate. Psychology **5**, 12–14 (2014)
21. Golding, J.F., Finch, M.I., Stott, J.R.: Frequency effect of 0.35-1.0 Hz horizontal translational oscillation on motion sickness and the somatogravic illusion. Aviat. Space Environ. Med. **68**, 396–402 (1997)
22. Palmisano, S.: Perceiving self-motion in depth: the role of stereoscopic motion and changing-size cues. Percept. Psychophys. **58**, 1168–1176 (1996)
23. Brandt, T., Dichgans, J., Koenig, E.: Differential effects of central versus peripheral vision on egocentric and exocentric motion perception. Exp. Brain Res. **16**, 476–491 (1973)
24. Andersen, G.J., Braunstein, M.L.: Induced self-motion in central vision. J. Exp. Psychol. Human **11**, 122–132 (1985)
25. Shirai, N., Seno, T., Morohashi, S.: More rapid and stronger vection in elementary school children compared with adults. Perception **41**, 1399–1402 (2012)
26. Shirai, N., Imura, T., Tamura, R., Seno, T.: Stronger vection in junior high school children than in adults. Front. Psychol. **5**, 1–6 (2014)

27. Kawaida, Y., Fukudome, K., Uejima, A., Nishi, T., Matsushita, H.: Use of Balance Wii Board as a stabilometer. In: Proceedings of 44th Congress of the JPTA (Japanese Physical Therapy Association); 44th Annual Meeting of JPTA (Tokyo), B3P1321 (2009) (in Japanese). doi:10.14900/cjpt.2008.0.B3P1321.0
28. Clark, R.A., Bryant, A.L., Pua, Y., McCrory, P., Bennell, K., Hunt, M.: Validity and reliability of the Nintendo Wii Balance Board for assessment of standing balance. Gait Posture **31**, 307–310 (2010)
29. Hatsushika, S.-I.: A study on body sway by using a stabilometer: fundamental study and clinical significance. Nippon Jibiinkoka Gakkai Kaiho **90**, 598–612 (1987). (Tokyo) (For review of the significance of the body sway test using a stabilometer)
30. Romberg, M.H.: Manual of nervous diseases of man. Sydenham Soc. **2**, 395–401 (1853)
31. Browne, J., O'Hare, N.: A review of the different methods for assessing standing balance. Physiotherapy **87**, 489–495 (2001)
32. Ujike, H.: Aiming to create a viewing environment of human-friendly images (in Japanese). AIST Today **6**, 28–29 (2006). http://www.aist.go.jp/Portals/0/resource_images/aist_j/aistinfo/aist_today/vol06_03/vol06_03_p28_29.pdf
33. Masuda, C.: Three Dimensional Display, p. 49. Sangyotosho, Tokyo (1990). (in Japanese)
34. Mitsuhashi, T., Hatada, T., Yano, S.: Image and Visual Information Science. Corona, Tokyo (2009). (in Japanese)
35. Kennedy, R.S., Lane, N.E., Berbaum, K.S., Lilienthal, M.G.: Simulator sickness questionnaire: an enhanced method for quantifying simulator sickness. Int. J. Aviat. Psychol. **3**, 203–220 (1993)
36. Abe, T.: Examine of the effect higher-order visual information to self-motion sensation. Bachelor thesis, School of Information, Kochi University of Technology (2014) (Similar result obtained by analysis of the velocity of COP was reported)
37. Bruck, S., Watters, P.A.: The factor structure of cybersickness. Displays **32**, 153–158 (2011)

Seeing, Hearing and Feeling Through the Body: The Emerging Science of Human-Somatosensory Interactions

Maria Karam[1](✉) and Patrick Langdon[2]

[1] Department of Informatics, Kings College London, Strand Campus,
London, UK
maria.karam@kcl.ac.uk
[2] Engineering Design Centre, University of Cambridge, Cambridge, UK
pml@edc.cambridge.ac.uk

Abstract. Research involving the human skin and its potential to be used as a versatile, practical and highly effective communication channel for receiving information has been explored for over a century. But while the body's ability to perceive and process information is relatively well understood, touch is only one of the senses of the somatosensory system. Although the communication potential is great, the body is still not represented in the computer interactions we have come to accept in our everyday lives. In this paper, the domain of physical display systems and interactions are surveyed with a view to developing a framework that can offer a more principled and cohesive perspective of this multi-disciplined field of interaction research and development. The paper presents a brief survey of physical displays, and proposes a framework that combines critical parameters from four areas of research to help understand this field of somatosensory-based computer interactions: application, physiology, technology, and psychology.

Keywords: Somatosensory interactions · Tactile displays · Haptic interfaces · Sensory substitution · Framework development · Touch-based displays · Kinesthesia

1 Introduction

The human somatosensory system is a complex sensory channel comprised of many different subsystems including the skin, vestibular system, tendons, muscles, joints, and the cochlea, in addition to the cognitive processes behind the perception and response to physical sensations. The sensations available to the body include temperature, vibration, balance, position, and pain, stretching of the skin, movement, organs, joints, muscles, and all of the sensations we can feel. These sensations represent a lexicon of physical perceptions that can be considered the language of the body. But while the body can detect so many different types of stimuli, it remains underused as a communication channel for computer displays: even with the growing problem of sensory overload from the increasing numbers of devices competing for our auditory and visual attention. To address this problem, physical displays are reviewed and categorized

© Springer International Publishing Switzerland 2015
M. Antona and C. Stephanidis (Eds.): UAHCI 2015, Part II, LNCS 9176, pp. 205–216, 2015.
DOI: 10.1007/978-3-319-20681-3_19

along four axes based on application, physiology, technology, and psychology. This multidisciplinary approach to understanding interfaces for the physical and somatic (touch) senses may also provide the groundwork for developing a framework that can support greater cohesion within the disciplines towards increasing usability, accessibility, and development of display systems for the body.

2 Background

The concept of physical interactions refers to both input and output devices and interfaces that communicate through the body. In this work, the focus is on display systems that communicate to the body in the same way audio and visual displays present information to the ears and eyes.

It has been close to 100 years since the first sensory substitution system was developed to convert sounds into vibrations to help deaf children understand speech [1], yet, physical display systems are primarily used only for research. Classifications, frameworks, and toolkits can offer guidelines and help in making sense of specific areas of touch interactions, [4–6], but the discipline remains fragmented and dispersed across a vast network of researchers, systems, and devices that do not quite meet the requirements to make it to the consumer electronics market.

The study of display interfaces for the body draws on knowledge from different fields, including physiology, psychology, computer science, and engineering. Early works of E.H. Weber and Fechner, who pioneered research on the somatosensory system, and in particular, the somatic senses, or sense of touch, revealed much of what is currently understood about mechanoreceptors, psychophysics, and the different sensations the body can detect. More recently work by haptics researchers such as Klatsky and Ledermen have moved the field forward considerably [1, 3]. However, given the complexities of the sensory system, along with the perceptual, physical, and processing demands required to develop and use physical displays, it is not surprising that so few novel systems have made their way into everyday computing displays and interactions.

2.1 Making Sense of the Sense of Touch

An important problem to address is the disconnect that exists between the different disciplines, and the need to have a better understanding of these areas in order to improve the interfaces, applications, and devices that support physical interactions. While the sense of touch represents the most commonly referenced sense for physical interactions, tactile sensations relate primarily to the cutaneous system, and the receptors of the skin [2], In contrast, haptic sensations are the combined sense of both tactile and kinesthetic senses [3]. The human "feel" sense actually consists of three main senses, which are often difficult to distinguish: tactile or somatic senses, the kinesthetic sense, and haptic sense. This is an oversimplified representation of the physical senses, however, outlines sensations that can be leveraged for physical display interactions.

Touch. The tactile senses, or "touch senses," are based on the cutaneous system, and the mechanoreceptors located in the skin [2]. There are two types of skin on the human body: glabrous (non-hairy) and non-glabrous (hairy). Glabrous skin is positioned mainly along the ventral areas of the fingers, hands, feet, lips and genitalia, and is more sensitive to stimuli than non-glabrous skin covering the rest of the body [2, 3]. Tactile receptors include mechanoreceptors (pressure, vibration, stretch), thermoreceptors (temperature), and nociception (pain), and are primarily experienced through a 'passive' form of stimulation [8]. These receptors cover the skin, epithelia, skeletal muscles, bones, joints, internal organs, and cardiovascular system [2, 3]. Sensations are dependent on rapidly adapting and slow adapting mechanoreceptors (RA I, SA I, RA II, SA II), embedded in the skin. Touch sense has been identified with Pacinian Corpuscles; the RAII receptors, but in fact, is known to be associated with all the glabrous skin afferents, including Meissner corpuscles, Ruffinii corpuscles and the Merkel complex cells.

Kinesthesia. Kinesthesia or "body sense" is the result of a combined awareness of movement, position and orientation of parts of the human body. The human kinesthetic capability senses the position of the body parts. Limbs and movements are perceived as a single unified perception despite their origination in diverse sensory sources such a joint loads, muscle stretch, skin stretch and the vestibular balance and movement detections system. Kinesthesia includes the operation of mechanoreceptors, and proprioceptors (position, movement, tissue compression) that are sensitive to forces in the skin, muscles, tendons and joints, which are interpreted in conjunction with knowledge of efference or outgoing motor signals, visual feedback and muscle stretch receptors. This, and proprioception, are both remarkable and poorly understood, as they involve considerable sensory fusion problems combined with the integration of numerous incompatible spatial and temporal coordinate systems. Hence, hand space must be somehow mapped to end of arm location relative to the head coordinates and this is related to visual view-centered coordinates and vestibular acceleration information. Also, time course of the various sensors information differs, generating a difficult sensor fusion task. It is known that some visual information is required for accurate calibration of kinesthesia, and hence for localizing the position of a touch sensation.

Haptics. Haptic perception involves the active gathering of information about objects outside of the body through a combination of tactile and kinesthetic senses. Active perception requires exploratory movement control to communicate shape, texture, form, edge detection, force, or motion [2, 8, 9]. Active perception, like moving fingertips along a surface to determine its texture, is a different sensation than passive perception, which receives information that can be detected without exploration, like temperature or physical motion. Haptic perception incorporates sensations from the proprioceptors, mechanoreceptors, as well as the vestibular system (balance), to represent a broader range of potential interaction opportunities.

When a receptor is activated by some kind of device or stimuli, this results in the depolarization of sensor nerve endings, and leads to the initialization of an action potential that will travel up along the spinal cord and trigger a neurological process that initially occurs in parietal lobe. There are also secondary processing centers to consider, such as the cerebellum, which contribute to our sense of balance, in addition to the somatosensory processes within the parietal lobe. However, this can be explored further in the literature and related works to ensure there is a strong grasp of the physiological factors that relate to the specific physical interface intended to support an application when designing physical-displays [2–5].

2.2 Somatosensory Displays and Systems

While the existing human-machine interface (HMI) interaction paradigm relies principally on visual feedback, often supported by sound, the use of tactile or haptic displays are often restricted to the physical interactions with specific input devices such as feeling the mouse or a control wheel or basic vibratory stimulators. This leaves the skin under-utilized, and the lack of articulatory feedback [10] makes interaction more difficult and suggests a new potential carrier channel for information. In an attempt to clarify the different types of touch-based displays based on understanding the sense of touch and the somatosensory system, a brief review of somatosensory-based displays is presented and organized according to the three main somatic senses: touch, kinesthesia, and haptic.

Touch displays are commonly designed to provide messages to the body that can be simple notifications [11, 12], or complex images or sounds [13, 14]. Typically, the complexity of the information reflects in the number and positioning of the tactile display. For example, a tactile-vision sensory substitution system (TVSS) uses an array of 400 transducers to map images onto the back [15], while a notification in a mobile phone may use only a single vibration motor. Different sensations include vibrotactile, electro-tactile, ultrasonic, or gusts of air [16–18]. The fingers, back, arm, and tongue are most commonly used for touch-based displays, although most any part of the body can be targeted as a location for displaying information to the body using some form of technology given the correct display characteristics.

Kinesthetic displays are also costly and not accessible to everyone; however, they provide the user with a sense of motion and position that are essential to full body immersion or simulations. Movement, actuation, and orientation provide the user with a physical experience that replicates some of the sensations one would expect from driving, flying, or riding a roller coaster. Coupled with a VR display and stereo sound, one could achieve an incredible state of realism from a virtual experience. However, size and costs limit use of these systems, as does the need for content that can provide a realistic and effective experience for users to experience and adopt.

Haptic displays are also used in feedback, notification, and entertainment applications, leveraging both kinesthetic and cutaneous senses [19–21]. Haptic displays are commonly used in remote operations environments [5, 22], remote object detection and manipulation [23], and virtual and augmented reality [19]. Devices such as the Phantom Omni 6DOF Haptic device [24] create physical sensations that enable remote and virtual objects to display their physical characteristics to the user but are primarily used as research tools to support continuous or force-varying virtual haptic displays. Disney research demonstrates a haptic device driven by gusts of air [18], but like many of technologies, they are either too expensive, or still in the research phase.

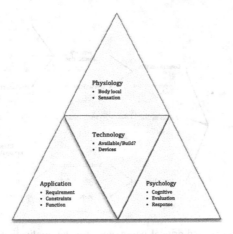

Fig. 1. Example categories and critical parameters for a perspective on somatosensory-based interactions.

3   A Framework for Somatosensory-Based Display Systems

To aid in promoting clarity in the study and development of physical display systems and interactions, a proposed framework is presented in an attempt to quantify and qualify the diverse interaction technologies, applications, physiological, and psychological factors within this field. One approach is to organize interfaces into categories that highlight critical parameters to support effective design and development of physical interactions and display systems. Critical parameters serve as useful tools for supporting cross-domain comparisons and evaluations of applications, designs, performance and technologies [26]. The categories proposed in this paper (Fig. 1) represent a high-level structure on which to build a framework that links the critical parameters from the different disciplines, to the system being designed or evaluated, and provides a method for using the parameters across different systems and applications.

3.1   Application

From the application perspective, the goals, functional requirements, and expected outcome of using a physical display serve as high-level critical parameters that define the interaction scenario. Goals may include communication, simulation, or augmentation, and within each of these parameters, further requirements and expectations that define the application can be derived and presented. The goals and specific functions can be determined, evaluated, and compared using each critical parameter, allowing systems to be assessed on the same axes. Communication may include sensory substitution, notification, or feedback as factors, with each of the critical parameters providing a clearer set of metrics to use when developing and designing applications that use physical displays (Fig. 2). Further levels can be included to drill down into a

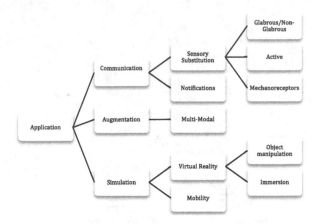

Fig. 2. Suggested critical parameters for the application factors

more detailed set of requirements for the interaction. All parameters can be weighted for importance and flexibility, and should reflect enough about the application requirements to support decisions involving the other categories that will best match the goals for the application interaction.

3.2 Physiology

Critical parameters describe interaction requirements, constraints and scenarios relating to the senses and the physical mechanics of presenting information to the right place on the body, using the right kind of stimuli. Parameters like body position, sensitivity, sense, and receptors represent some of the physical constraints to consider when designing the system interaction. In addition, understanding the interaction context of the application can also determine optimal placement of sensations on the body. This can also influence the type of form factor, and other ergonomic characteristics that the display system should support. For example, desktop applications imply the user will be seated, while mobile devices may not. Constraints of the physical state of the user during interaction will guide the placement, sensations, and form factors required to support the application goals. Critical factors will be based on the three types of physical sense, and defined by the specific type of effect that the application aims to produce for the user, and an example is presented in Fig. 3.

3.3 Technology

Technology represents one of the most constraining factors within the framework, supporting application goals and driving the physical sensations. In a pure research environment, it is possible to develop new devices that can create sensations for the body, but it is always easier to work with systems that already exist. Most physical displays are built using existing motors, transducers, or contactors, which are

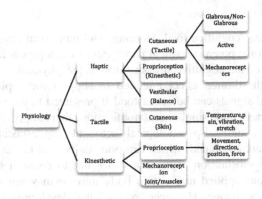

Fig. 3. Examples of critical parameters to describe the physiological factors of physical interfaces.

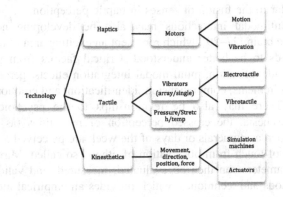

Fig. 4. An example of potential critical parameters based on the technology category

assembled into arrays or other configurations to provide the desired physical stimulation. However, from an end user's perspective, there are very few tactile, haptic, or kinesthetic systems that are easily accessible, usable, and affordable for most people. Outside of the direct force feedback systems, rumble pads, or vibration motors, most of the systems described in the literature are a long way from being available to consumers for everyday interactions (Fig. 4).

Again, even after so many systems have been designed, researched, and deemed valuable, there remains a problem in getting these to the people who want and need them. For example, pin-arrays, wayfinding systems, and tactile-vision display systems that could improve the lives of people with sensory disabilities are a long way from making a mark on the consumer electronics market. Simple devices such as vibration motors in gaming controllers are common, but are a low-end solution to delivering immersion and realism that touch-based systems have been shown to deliver in the literature.

3.4 Psychology

Perceptual processing, cognitive load, learning, and emotional effects of using touch displays represent some potential critical parameters from a psychological perspective. The end goal is to create cognitive impact through the physical sensing mechanisms that will produce the desired effect intended to support the application interaction design. Complicated signals can be understood if presented to the right location using the right signal, as can simple single-point notifications that simply aim to get the user's attention. There are additional psychological factors at play, especially when multiple sensory modalities are combined, which can potentially lead to the creation of a new sensations. Sensory substitution applications that aim to create a sense of an image through the vibrations applied to a user's body may or may not result in the same percept as seeing the image. However, part of the development process involves evaluating novel interfaces to determine what the user actually perceives, and how they can interpret, map, and process a physical-cognitive sensation. This is a new research field that has considerable potential. Cross-modal perceptions could even be viewed as new senses, similar to the fusion of senses in haptic perception.

Similarly, multimodal interactions may also be developing new perceptional mechanisms in the brain [27–29], which represent an exciting area of research in tactile displays that needs to be better understood. Critical factors from psychology thus include sensation identification, multi-modal integration effects, perceptual cognition, interpretation requirements, comprehension, identification, and emotional and affective responses [30]. There may also be relationships to the psychological processes involved in Synesthesia: the crossed perception of modalities (as when sound or abstract entities such as numerals or days of the week are perceived as having colour); or the perception of touch from observation of others, so called, Mirror-touch Synesthesia. These parameters can then be evaluated, measured, and validated using psychophysical methods and techniques, which provides an empirical means of studying the perceptual responses of users to touch-based sensations that can be in addition to self reporting data, or observations. The factors are shown in Fig. 5.

Evaluating Touch-Displays. Usability studies are essential for assessing the overall effects and affects of any interaction, and psychophysics provides the tools and

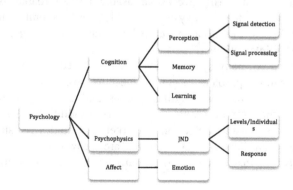

Fig. 5. Psychological factors relating to the design of physical interfaces

methods to enable empirical evaluations of stimuli and response across different applications, technologies, and information. Psychophysics is the study of quantitative relations between sensations and the stimuli that produce them. There are many texts that suggest methods and approaches to conducting psychophysical experiments, often based on the early works of Weber and Fechner [2, 3]. While there are many studies that have been conducted to evaluate interactive physical displays [31, 32], and new approaches can be developed to support the expanding range of sensations and perceptions that are being explored in the literature. A few examples illustrating the structure of the framework and the categories and parameters are presented next.

4 Applying the Framework

Sensory substitution applications represent one of the earliest examples of using the skin as a display technology. In 1929, Dr. Gault developed a 5-channel system that converted audio into physical vibrations. The device influenced many systems that followed in the next century, including the tactile Vocoder [17], and the Emoti-Chair [14]. However, Bach-y-Rita was one of the most innovative researchers in the field of touch-based displays, who developed several influential sensory substitution systems including the tactile vision sensory substitution system (TVSS) [15], a tongue display [33], and finger-displays [22]. Application goals may include communication of detailed information, with high demands on cognitive processing and comprehension. The interaction context for 'viewing' images on the body may be best implemented in a chair form factor however, different requirements will apply to mobile context.

Physical factors relating to the application goals include body location (large area to support image data), receptors (mechanoreceptors), sensory system (cutaneous), skin type (glabrous, non-glabrous) and intensity (must support cutaneous stimulation). These will vary, but ultimately, thinking along these lines can support decision matrices, and other methods that can allow the comparison and evaluation of different combinations of parameters to support more informed design decisions, leading to better displays. Tactile-stimulation is likely the best option for providing detailed information to the body, as a high level of resolution is required to translate detailed image information onto the body.

Changing the application parameters has led to a variety of alternative systems based on the TVSS, which explored the abdomen, thigh, and fingertips as display locations [22], but these represent common physical factors that enabled the solenoids to be used on different parts of the body. However, in a new scenario, the tongue was considered as a location for the TVSS, which led to different devices, namely electrotactile stimulators, arranged in a 49 point, 1.8×1.8 cm array, showing similar results to the TVSS system for the back [33].

In summary, all of the categories used to determine critical factors for any physical display system must be considered both individually, and as a whole. Each factor must reflect the goals, and requirements that motivate the use of physical displays, and will vary across different scenarios and interactions. However, these can also be applied to different systems in general, which can facilitate research, development, design, and evaluation activities in physical. This can apply to the current move to bring VR displays to the forefront of consumer products, with the introduction of several devices including the Oculus rift, where the need to increase immersion and realism of these devices can be addressed through the introduction of viable displays that can give the user a physical enhancement to the audio and visual experience.

5 Conclusions

Through the development of frameworks, different systems can be organized, understood, and compared to support a more cohesive community of researchers exploring the domain of touch-based display interactions. Using the same factors, we can compare different applications, technologies, and implementation techniques to enable the science of touch-based interactions to emerge. The goal of this paper is to stimulate discussions that will contribute to an evolving framework that will serve researchers and developers working the field of touch-based displays, and potentially help to bring these technologies to a more prominent position in our everyday computing interactions.

Perhaps it is the expense and size of tactile devices that are holding back uptake, possibly the lack of understanding of the somatosensory system, or even poor application choices. In any case, the research suggests that there is interest and valid application cases for the sense of touch to be used as an information display. From this discussion, the expectation is that more touch-based devices, system, and interactions may make their way into the public domain, supporting a more seamless and effortless move out of the research labs, and into the hands and bodies of those who need and want to leverage the body as a new medium of communication for computer interactions.

References

1. Popular Mechanics Magazine, Hearing through your fingers, vol 51, issue no 5, pp. 755–760, May 1929. http://books.google.ca/books?id=wN4DAAAAMBAJ&lpg=PP1&pg=PA3#v=onepage&q&f=false
2. Klatzky, R.L., Lederman, S.J.: Touch. In: Healy, A.F., Proctor, R.W. (eds.) Experimental Psychology ,vol. 4 in I. B. Weiner (Editor-in-Chief) Handbook of psychology, pp. 147–176. Wiley, New York (2002)
3. Gustav, T.F.: Elements of psychophysics, Sections VII ("Measurement of sensation") and XIV ("The fundamental formula and the measurement formula") (1860). (Trans. by Herbert S. Langfeld, first appearing in B. Rand (Ed.) (1912), The classical psychologists)
4. Ward, T.B., Foley, C.M., Cole, J.: Classifying multidimensional stimuli: Stimulus, task, and observer factors. J. Exp. Psychol. Hum. Percept. Perform. **12**, 211–225 (1986)
5. Pham, H.-P., Ammi, M., Fontaine, J.-G., Bourdot, P.: A framework for building haptic interactions for teleoperation systems. In: Proceedings of the 2008 Ambi-Sys workshop on Haptic user interfaces in ambient media systems (HAS 2008). ICST (Institute for Computer Sciences, Social-Informatics and Telecommunications Engineering), Brussels, Article 5, p. 10 (2008)

6. Ledo, D., Nacenta, M.A., Marquardt, N., Boring, S., Greenberg, S.: The HapticTouch toolkit: enabling exploration of haptic interactions. In: Stephen N. Spencer (ed.) Proceedings of the Sixth International Conference on Tangible, Embedded and Embodied Interaction (TEI 2012), pp. 115–122. ACM, New York, NY, USA (2012) doi:10.1145/2148131. 2148157. http://doi.acm.org/10.1145/2148131.2148157

7. Wall, S.A., Brewster, S.: Sensory substitution using tactile pin arrays: human factors technology and applications. Sig. Process. **86**, 3674–3695 (2006)

8. Loomis, J.M. Lederman, S.J.: What utility is there in distinguishing between active and passive touch. In: Talk presented at the annual meeting of the Psychonomic Society, San Antonio Texas, November 1984

9. Jones, L.A., Lederman, S.J.: Human Hand function. OU Press, Maidenhead (2006)

10. Hix, D., Hartson, H.R.: Developing User Interfaces: Ensuring Usability Through Product & Process. Wiley, New York (1993)

11. Brewster, S., Brown, L.M.: Tactons: Structured Tactile Messages for Non-Visual Information Display, 5th Australian User Interface Conference (AUIC2004). Dunedin, New Zealand (2004)

12. Van Erp, J.B.F., Van Veen, H.A.H.C., Jansen, C., Dobbins, T.: Waypoint navigation with a vibrotactile waist belt. ACM Trans. Appl. Percept. (TAP) **2**(2), 106–117 (2005). doi:10. 1145/1060581.1060585

13. White, B.W., et al.: Seeing with the skin. Percept. Psychophysics **7**(1), 23–27 (1970)

14. Karam, M., Russo, F.A., Fels, D.I.: Designing the model human cochlea: an ambient crossmodal audio-tactile display. IEEE Trans. Haptics **2**(3), 160–169 (2009). doi:10.1109/ TOH.2009. http://dx.doi.org/10.1109/TOH.2009.32

15. Bach-y-Rita, P.: Tactile vision substitution: past and future. Int. J. Neurosci. **19**(1-4), 29–36 (1983)

16. Kaczmarek, K.A., Webster, J.G., Bach-y-Rita, P., Tompkins, W.J.: Electrotactile and vibrotactile displays for sensory substitution system. IEEE Transactions on Biomedical Engineering **38**(1), 1–16 (1991). doi:10.1109/10.68204

17. Brooks, P.L., Frost, B.J.: Evaluation of a tactile vocoder for word recognition. J. Acoust. Soc. America **74**, 34–39 (1983). http://dx.doi.org/10.1121/1.389685

18. Sodhi, R., Poupyrev, I., Glisson, M., Israr, A.: AIREAL: interactive tactile experiences in free air. ACM Trans. Graph **32**(4), 10 (2013). doi:10.1145/2461912.2462007. Article 134. http://doi.acm.org/10.1145/2461912.2462007

19. Burdea, G.C.: Force and Touch Feedback for Virtual Reality. Wiley, New York (1996)

20. Hwang, F., Keates, S., Langdon, P., Clarkson, P.J.: Multiple haptic targets for motion-impaired computer users. In: Proceedings of the SIGCHI Conference on Human Factors in Computing Systems (CHI 2003), pp. 41–48. ACM, New York NY, USA (2003) doi: 10.1145/642611.642620. http://doi.acm.org/10.1145/642611.642620

21. Eid, M., Orozco, M., El Saddik, A.: A guided tour in haptic audio visual environments and applications. Int. J. Adv. Media Commun. **1**(3), 265–297 (2007). doi:10.1504/IJAMC.2007. 013918. http://dx.doi.org/10.1504/IJAMC.2007.013918

22. Bach-y-Rita, P., Webster, J.G., Tompkins, W.J., Crabb, T.: Sensory substitution for space gloves and space robots. In: Space Telerobotics Workshop, 20–22 1987, pp. 51–57. Jet Propulsio Lab, Pasadena (1987)

23. Yu, W., Brewster, S.: Comparing two haptic interfaces for multimodal graph rendering. In: IEEE VR2002, 10th Symposium on Haptic Interfaces for Virtual Environment and Teleoperator Systems, Orlando, FL (2002)

24. Sensable technologies LLC. Phantom OMNI haptic device. http://www.dentsable.com/ haptic-phantom-omni.htm

25. Metropolis Entertainment. 360 interactive flight simulator. http://www.metropolisav.com/

26. Newman, W.M.: Better or just different? on the benefits of designing interactive systems in terms of critical parameters. In: Coles, S. (ed.) Proceedings of the 2nd conference on Designing Interactive Systems: Processes, Practices, Methods, And Techniques (DIS 1997), pp. 239–245. ACM, New York, NY, USA (1997). doi:10.1145/263552.263615. http://doi.acm.org/10.1145/263552.263615

27. Jinnai, A., Otsuka, A., Nakagawa, S., Kotani, K., Asao, T., Suzuki, S.: Evaluation of somatosensory evoked responses when multiple tactile information was given to the palm: a meg study. In: Yamamoto, S. (ed.) HCI 2013, Part I. LNCS, vol. 8016, pp. 594–603. Springer, Heidelberg (2013). doi:10.1007/978-3-642-39209-2_66. http://dx.doi.org/10.1007/978-3-642-39209-2_66

28. Wu, Q., Li, X.R., Wu, G.S.: Interface design for somatosensory interaction. In: Marcus, A. (ed.) DUXU 2014, Part II. LNCS, vol. 8518, pp. 794–801. Springer, Heidelberg (2014). doi:10.1007/978-3-319-07626-3_75. http://dx.doi.org/10.1007/978-3-319-07626-3_75

29. Murphy, E., Moussette, C., Verron, C., Guastavino, C.: Supporting sounds: design and evaluation of an audio-haptic interface. In: Magnusson, C., Szymczak, D., Brewster, S. (eds.) HAID 2012. LNCS, vol. 7468, pp. 11–20. Springer, Heidelberg (2012)

30. Kayser, C., Petkov, C., Augath, M., Logothetis, N.: Integration of touch and sound in auditory cortex. Neuron **48**(2), 373–384 (2005)

31. McGuirl, J.M., Sarter, N.B.: Presenting in-flight icing information: a comparison of visual and tactile cues. Digit. Avionics Syst. DASC **1**, 2A2/1–2A2l/8 (2001)

32. Politis, I., Brewster, S.A., and Pollick, F.: Evaluating multimodal driver displays under varying situational urgency. In: CHI 2014, pp. 4067–4076. ACM Press (2014b)

33. Form perception with a 49-point electrotactile stimulus array on the tongue: a technical note. J. Rehabil. Res. Dev. vol. 35, pp. 427–430

Sensoriality and Conformed Thought

Silvia Laurentiz[✉]

University of Sao Paulo, Butantã, SP, Brazil
silvialaurentiz@gmail.com

Abstract. We live in a world permeated by signs that belong to multiple areas of knowledge. Signs that have been filtered and stored by our natural and artificial interfaces can determine our perceptions and conceptions about the complexities of the world. The proposal of this study is to present poetic experiments that sustain a consistency between what is real and what can be defined as *semiotically real*, and that sustain an efficient behavior but, in being poetic, exerts tension on this close relationship. The exercise of exploring the limits of conformed thought - understood here as a composition of codes, standards, patterns and cultural representations – expands and reveals a variety of settings that are not readily perceived in the world.

Keywords: Art · Signs · Semiotic · Poetic · Thought

1 Introduction

We live in a world permeated with signs that belong to multiple areas of knowledge. Signs which have been filtered and stored by our natural and artificial interfaces can determine our perceptions and conceptions about the complexities of the world. The proposal of this study is to present poetic experiments that sustain a consistency between what is real and what can be defined as *semiotically real* [1, 2], and that sustain an efficient behavior but, in being poetic, exert a degree of tension on this close relationship. The exploration of the limits of the conformed thought - understood here as a composition of codes, standards, patterns and cultural representations – expands and reveals a variety of settings that are not readily perceived in the world. It is important to note that we are referring to thought that is "conformed" and not "shaped". The two words can be synonymous in some cases but here we mean that we are not restricted to forms, appearances, expressions of patterns, and we include the sense of model, where form and content are indissoluble and conceptual characteristics are inseparable from the materials. Furthermore, conformed thought is the thought or

M. Antona and C. Stephanidis (Eds.): UAHCI 2015, Part II, LNCS 9176, pp. 217–225, 2015.
DOI: 10.1007/978-3-319-20681-3_20

action that is determined by the prevailing standards, attitudes, practices, etc., of society or a group.[1]

There must be consistency between the things of the world and "things" as we conceive of them (known as signs) that we define as reality; otherwise, we could not act in the world. Nothing would work if signs and things did not maintain a close relationship. It would not even be possible to cross a street if things and signs were not closely related.

Based on this assumption, we can presume that we will always reach a fragmentation of the real, as we are always accessing the things of the world through signs. In addition, signs become habits, converting themselves into states of affordable things – which we define as objects.

Our understanding of the world becomes conformed through a combination of irreducible relations between all that contributes to the physical environment where we live and the organisms that share the same environment, and the ways in which this physical and interpreted environment incorporates the same significant sphere of existence shared by all that therein has any sense [3]. We mean that signs are in themselves multiple layers of meanings shared within this sphere.

What we can say is that the ability of "human beings" to produce signs is fed back to the environment, which in turn forces the evolution of man to create increasingly complex systems of interpretation. Therefore, new signs are generated through feedback, making us look at and recognize the objects in the world in many different ways (i.e. targeted things).

According to John Deely, based on Jakob von Uexkull's Umwelt concept [3, 4], there is also

> a distinction between sensation (as the action of the environment upon the animal body objectifying certain aspects only of the surroundings) and the higher-level perceptual response to that stimulus (wherein the data of sensation, never atomic but already a complex and multiple network of naturally determined sign-relations, wherein differentiations of light reveal also shapes, positions, and movements, etc., are further structured into objects of experience) [5].

This study will identify some aspects of these reconstructed objects of our conformed thought into things that can engender new sensations and responses in perceptual terms, in the form of images, sounds, and haptic (tactile) feedback.

This can be easily illustrated by the classic effect generated by the figure below:

---

[1] This article posits that every conformed thought is a sign, but not every sign is a conformed thought. Every thought is formed by different kinds of signs (cf.Peirce, 1994; Sebeok, 2001). One type in particular, which we discuss here, is conformed thought, which relates to acquired habit(s) in a period. Hence, conformed thought is cultural and depends on context, and is related to a technology of its time. Another type of sign that composes our thinking (according to Peirce) is a vague composition of sensations, emotions and feelings. This type is governed by our sensorial system (including our sense of experience and of observation), which drives our thinking in semiotic developments, promoting changes in habits and giving rise to new signs. Amid the tension between sensing and conformed thought lies a fertile environment of conflicts, interferences, correspondences, tensions, settings and a mix of information.

The Stroop test was developed by J. Ridley Stroop [6] to evaluate the reading process automation. The task is to name the color of the printed words, and not actually read them, as the actual words do not denote the name of the color of the printed word. In general, the use of words strongly interferes with our ability to identify the actual colors. Thus, the interference generated in the processing of the divergent information (the word itself and the color of the word) by the brain creates a conflicting message. Neuroscience attempts to explain the reasons behind this phenomenon, but for us the important thing is to focus on the interference and the effort evoked here. The interference and the effort required demonstrate that we are invariably being guided by habits and beliefs, despite not always being aware of it. This entails that every abstract thought should create an interference of some sort in the way we perceive and act in the world (See Figs. 1, 2, 3 and 4)

The work by Janet Cardiff and George Miller entitled Alter Bahnhof Video Walk, presents another important example related to this matter:

> The Alter Bahnhof Video Walk was designed for the old train station in Kassel, Germany as part of dOCUMENTA (13). Participants are able to borrow an iPod and headphones from a check-out booth. They are then directed by Cardiff and Miller through the station. An alternate world opens up where reality and fiction meld in a disturbing and uncanny way that has been referred to as "physical cinema". The participants watch things unfold on the small screen but feel the presence of those events deeply because of being situated in the exact location where the footage was shot. As they follow the moving images (and try to frame them as if they were the camera operator) a strange confusion of realities occurs. In this confusion, the past and present conflate and Cardiff and Miller guide us through a meditation on memory and reveal the poignant moments of being alive and present. [7]

In this way, the habit of using a camera guides the experience and the way we interpret a place. Even though we are looking at pre-recorded images, we are able to navigate through different dimensions even as we stand in the same place, which results in a different sense of reality. The practice of "selfies" also conform to our present thought-process. Moreover, and this is precisely our point, the mediums conform our thinking, and the habit of this conformed thought becomes a unity of feeling for new signs and new thoughts that are formed in a continuous semiosis. Therefore, there evidently is a close relationship between feeling and thinking.

In order to achieve our goal we will base ourselves on the artwork developed by the Realities Research Group (www2.eca.usp.br/realidades), at the School of Communication and Arts of the University of São Paulo - SP.

This group explores concepts arising from the relationship between art and science. From virtual to augmented and mixed reality environments; from cybrid modalities to

Fig. 1. Image test to Stroop effect

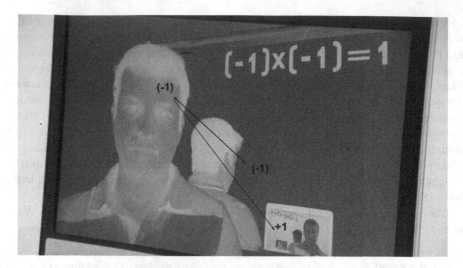

Fig. 2. Still of artwork installation "(-1) x (-1) = + 1 - An enigma for Flusser"

Fig. 3. Still of artwork installation "$f(\Delta t)$ – An enigma for Bergson"

ubiquitous computing; from representations to emulations and simulations, we can find a broad spectrum that contemplates games, websites, interactive art and installations, and that challenges and redefines the concept of reality.

In an era characterized by increasing complexity, we question how to coherently deal with the systems that grant us access to the *'semiotically real'* [1, 2, 8, 9] and which, for now, will be referred to as 'reality'. This research group periodically aims to:

a) Compile a significant number of documents and create a collection on this subject, with the intent of contributing to and supporting the development of several Master dissertations and Doctorate theses;

b) Produce primary research sources (interviews and testimonies of artists and those who are part of the artistic and cultural milieu, whose trajectories are relevant to art

Fig. 4. Still of artwork installation "Φ - An enigma for Gibson"

and technology studies), which will be released on the Internet or made available for the academic community under any other format that grants free access to these researchers;

c) Produce poetic experiments as a practical laboratory for research.

The exploration of this aspect of the sign has been the research goal of the Realities Group and we would hereby like to share our results and experiences. The members of the Realities Research Group have developed poetic experiments since 2012, questioning this conformed thought - such as representation by reflection, familiar recognition of faces in the mirror, the inversion generated by video cameras, webcams and by face recognition software programs, as well as in *"selfies"* used in social networks. One particular artwork also examines the habit acquired by the camera and by film and video. When using a webcam, we are guided by a distinct point of view, which nonetheless bears familiarity to the reflection in the mirror, acting upon us in ways that we may not be aware of.

2   Poetic Experiments of the Realities Research Group: Three Enigmas

2.1   "(-1) X (-1) = + 1 - an Enigma for Flusser" (2012)[2]

The artwork "(-1) x (-1) = + 1 - An enigma for Flusser" is an interactive installation with three different images overlaid in the same two-dimensional space: the image of a

---

[2] "(-1) x (-1) = + 1 - An enigma for Flusser' (2012), in http://www2.eca.usp.br/realidades/en/1-x-1-1-um-enigma-para-flusser/), Realities Research Group, Coordinator: Silvia Laurentiz, ECA-USP, Authors: Dario Vargas, Matheus Ramos, Paulo Angerami, Saulo Santos, Silvia Laurentiz, Viviane Sá.

mirror, the image captured by a camera, and the image calculated by the computer. The dialogue between camera and mirror makes the visualization of the three layers of images and their different contexts possible. A camera positioned above the monitor aims to simulate a mirror on the screen, but in this case, the mirror image is not reversed, and its colors have been altered (via software generation) in a negative way (-1).

When this reverse image is returned as a reflection in the mirror, it remains negative and mirrored (-1). This way, the camera acts as a false mirror; on the other hand, the mirror itself acts as a disguised camera.

In the third layer of the image, we can recognize ourselves due to the resemblance of the simulation of a mirror (+1). Added to this, the software is equipped with a system of facial recognition which also recognizes us, or rather, recognizes the human face.

Since childhood, we are taught that we are the image that we see reflected in the mirror, and that it is the representation of ourselves. That is, the representation of ourselves has always been reversed. When standing in front of a mirror, we suppose that as we raise our left hand, the right hand of the image that is reflected will be raised. This is exactly what happens, it has always been this way, and it is natural. Proof of this is that we find it strange when instead we see an image where the left hand is raised - because we expect the right to be raised.

In the feedback process, the image becomes positive and mirrored. At this point we recognize the "real" when we perceive the "(i) real" text which is now also mirrored. This is the point where the image acts like a mirror, in a way that is so familiar to us. These layers of images represent the process (-1) x (-1) = + 1.

Flusser [10] stated that the technical image is the result of a text. Here the text triggers the (i) reality of the image, at the time that (-1) x (-1) can be (+) and/or (-) 1. Therefore, the principle of reality is questionable, and the relationship between image and text demonstrates this conflict. The image with multiple layers challenges the precepts of exact truths. Thus, the system operates as a "meta-Flussean" apparatus.

We could ask: at present, is the mirror image our most familiar image? Webcams and cell phones are rendering pictures of ourselves that are being distributed by networks and stored in clouds, reaching more people and at greater distances than any mirror could ever achieve. Furthermore, *"selfies"* are superseding our pictures as representations of events and locations, in ways that no mirror could have done before. Therefore, today, a mirror image may not be the most familiar image of myself that I can actually have. This, in turn, generates a series of changes, including sensory changes.

2.2 "$f(\Delta T)$ – An Enigma for Bergson" (2013)[3]

The artwork "$f(\Delta t)$ – An enigma for Bergson" is an Interactive installation with a projection that is a feedback image from a camera, constituted by merging images with

---

[3] "$f(\Delta t)$ – An enigma for Bergson" (2013), in http://www2.eca.usp.br/realidades/en/%c6%92%ce%b4t-um-enigma-para-bergson/), Realities Research Group, Coordinator: Silvia Laurentiz, ECA-USP, Authors: Dario Vargas, Giovanna Lucci, Matheus Ramos, Saulo Santos, Silvia Laurentiz, Viviane Sá.

a transparency percentage according to the specific time they were captured. Every time an individual image is captured by the camera and exhibited in real time, the system saves it to a file, where it is immediately overlaid by the forthcoming image, and so on, in eternal circularity. Every captured image is displayed on the screen over the camera image, which is still capturing the screen - with a specific percentage of transparency. The overall effect is an apparent movement that also moves between volumes and transparencies generated by the overlays. That is a motion that occurs among the various layers of overlapping images captured and recorded. As a result of these marks of time, greater stability is achieved, and in turn, the greater the durability of the images in the system. Greater instability, on the other hand, inevitably leads to the disappearance of the image.

Delta-T is an abstract concept for calculating the time difference obtained by subtracting Universal Time (UT) from Terrestrial Time (TT). Universal Time is a timescale based on the rotation of the Earth, which is somehow irregular because there are forces that can change the rate of rotation of the Earth. This means that environmental factors should be taken into consideration, revealing a relationship between dependent systems, even though they are autonomous. The systemic dependence was used poetically in this artwork, because the transparency percentage applied to each overlaid image depends on the specific moment when it is exhibited. As a result, this creates an effect where the flows of duration and permanence of the image will appear to have different speeds during each passing hour. Feedback to the system with the location in the solar system creates a dependency between systems - artwork and its environment, which also generates perceptual changes from this relationship. On the other hand, this is another way to visualize changes in time we are not used to doing and this representation model suggests new experiments for the space-time dimension.

2.3   "Φ - An Enigma for Gibson" (2014),[4]

The artwork "Φ - An enigma for Gibson [11] " is an interactive installation that sets two video cameras in the same place, generating images that are captured by a computer in real-time and manipulated through Processing Software. The captured light is decoded in straight and curved monochromatic lines by the computer, creating an abstract representation of the physical space. The important point here is not the interpretation of shapes and colors but the image constructed by the variance and invariance of light in space. The luminous flux (Φ), measured in lumen (lm), is responsible for the variations of the image, causing the effect of another space, not the one we are used to, but the one that comes to us in a synthetic and rational way. One that uses different kinds of lines to build itself, immediately referring to the drawing, the design. By applying filters to the image captured by the cameras in real-time, the difference in brightness between each segment determines the changes that may occur

---

[4] "Φ - An enigma for Gibson" (2014), in http://www2.eca.usp.br/realidades/en/%cf%86-um-enigma-para-gibson/) Realities Research Group, Coordinator: Silvia Laurentiz, ECA-USP, Authors:Anita Cavaleiro, Cássia Aranha, Dario Vargas, Giovanna Lucci, Loren Bergantini, Silvia Laurentiz, Viviane Sá.

in the screen area and the system draws contours with lines of minor thickness, mapping spatial structures in time. The tracing creates maps that are intertwined, generating new representations and visualizations of three-space data.

We explore the representation of space through cameras, charts and graphs. They are traces that create mappings that interweave, bringing out new representations, rendering maps and scanning, and data visualization of these spaces. This is also a real-time data calculation experiment, and that generates a combination of drawings, diagrams and records of physical space lights, creating an effect of augmented reality, although not actually use apparatuses for this kind of representation as is understood today by the technological area.

3   Considerations

In conclusion, we can say that there are sensory elements in the conformed thought; all abstract thought has the power to generate an interference of some sort in the way we perceive the world; and that there is a close relationship between the things of the world and signs. Consequently, our relationship with the world depends on our relationship with our surroundings, an expanded Umwelt formed by a complex network of interlaced interpretations of things, objects and conformed thought. Finally, as the Umwelt acts as an interface that selects and filters information of the environment and internalizes it in encoded form, any material used by a living system to build knowledge has a representational condition, i.e., is formed by a myriad of 'somethings' that represent 'external somethings', which are rendered into 'particular somethings' of their cognitive system [12–14]. This feature interferes with our perception of the world, and transforms our senses, body and mind in an indissoluble way.

References

1. Merrell, F.: Semiosis in the Postmodern Age. Purdue University Press, USA (1995)
2. Merrell, F.: Peirce, Signs, and Meaning. University of Toronto Press, Canada (1997)
3. Deely, J.: Semiotics and Jakob von Uexkull's concept of Umwelt. Sign Syst. Stud. **32**(1/2), 11–34 (2004)
4. Von Uexküll, T.: A teoria da umwelt de jakob von uexküll. In:Revista Galáxia n 7, PUC-SP, pp. 19–48, April 2004
5. Deely, J.: Semiotics and jakob von uexkull's concept of umwelt. In: Sign Systems Studies 32.1/2, p. 15 (2004)
6. Stroop, J.R.: Studies of Interference in serial verbal reactions. In: Classics in the History of Psychology - An internet resource developed by Christopher D. Green, York University, Toronto, Ontario (first published in Journal of Experimental Psychology, 18, 643–662) (1935). http://psychclassics.yorku.ca/Stroop/. Accessed 05 March 2015
7. Cardiff, J., MILLER, G.: http://www.cardiffmiller.com/artworks/walks/bahnhof.html. Accessed 05 March 2015
8. Albuquerque Vieira, J.: Complexidade e Conhecimento Científico. In: Oecologia Brasiliensis, vol. 10, n. 1. Rio de Janeiro: PPGE/UFRJ, pp. 10–16 (2006)

9. Albuquerque Vieira, J.: Teoria do conhecimento e arte: formas de conhecimento – arte e ciência uma visão a partir da complexidade. Fortaleza: Expressão Gráfica e Editora (2008)
10. Flusser, V.: Língua e Realidade. Annablume, São Paulo (2004)
11. Gibson, J.J.: The ecological approach to the visual perception of pictures. Leonardo **11**, 227–235 (1978)
12. Peirce, C.S.: The electronic edition of the collected Papers of Charles Sanders Peirce.Utah: Folio Corporation (Vol. I-VI edited by Charles Hartshorne e Paul Weiss; vol. VIIVIII edited by Artur W. Burks), Harvard University Press (1994)
13. Sebeok, T.A.: Signs: An Introduction to Semiotics, 2nd edn. University of Toronto Press, Canada (2001)
14. Deely, J.: Umwelt. Semiotica 134 – ¼, pp. 125–135 (2001)

How Different Presentation Modes of Graphical Icons Affect Viewers' First Fixation and Attention

Hsuan Lin[1](✉), Wei Lin[2], Wang-Chin Tsai[3], Yu-Chen Hsieh[4], and Fong-Gong Wu[5]

[1] Department of Product Design, Tainan University of Technology,
Tainan, Taiwan
te0038@mail.tut.edu.tw
[2] Department of Interior Design, Hwa Hsia University of Technology,
Taipei, Taiwan
weilin@cc.hwh.edu.tw
[3] Department of Product and Media Design, Fo Guang University,
Yilan, Taiwan
forwangwang@gmail.com
[4] Department of Industrial Design, National Yunlin University of Science
and Technology, Yunlin, Taiwan
chester@yuntech.edu.tw
[5] Department of Industrial Design, National Cheng Kung University,
Tainan, Taiwan
fonggong@mail.ncku.edu.tw

Abstract. This study aimed to explore how different presentation modes of graphical icons affect the viewer's attention. The relevant experiment was designed to investigate three main variables: icon composition, polarity, and border. Through permutation and combination, six presentation modes were obtained as follows: line + positive polarity + border (M1), plane + positive polarity + border (M2), line + negative polarity + border (M3), plane + negative polarity + border (M4), line + positive polarity + no border (M5), and plane + positive polarity + no border (M6). Thirty-six participants were required to watch thirty stimuli, or graphical icons, presented concurrently in six abovementioned modes. The number of first fixations was recorded by eye-trackers; meanwhile, subjective evaluation of attention was conducted and analyzed. As indicated by the experimental results, the icons presented in M4 attracted the most attention; in contrast, the icons presented in M5 attracted the least attention. The findings herein can be used as a reference by interface designers while icons are being designed.

Keywords: Eye-tracking · Line composition · Plane composition · Positive polarity · Negative polarity · With border · Borderless

© Springer International Publishing Switzerland 2015
M. Antona and C. Stephanidis (Eds.): UAHCI 2015, LNCS 9176, pp. 226–237, 2015.
DOI: 10.1007/978-3-319-20681-3_21

1 Introduction

The booming market of applications (APP) has exerted a great influence on our daily lives. From the standpoint of marketing, icon shapes of applications play the same role as static salespersons, being highly valuable. Moreover, icon presentation is often the primary focus which attracts consumers' attention, induces consumers' interaction with applications, and leads to purchase as well as usage. Graphical interfaces are widely used in both computers and handheld devices, including overwhelmingly popular smartphones, information kiosks, automatic teller machines (ATM), tablet computers, and event data recorders (EDR) [1, 2]. Also, graphical interfaces are extensively used in a variety of specialized fields, such as cash registers, medical environments, and industrial machinery [3]. By clicking on-screen graphical user interfaces (GUI) to receive and process large amounts of numeric or graphical information [4], users can intuitively input instructions to be executed and interact with devices [5]. Therefore, icon design on the GUI becomes an important consideration in inter-face design.

Graphical icons may be standardized so that users can easily locate their desired instructions or programs in a number of different icons [6]. With good graphical icons presented in a relaxing way, users can not only handle lots of numbers or symbols effectively but also identify their required functions or targets smoothly on low-resolution screens, such as on smartphones [4]. Nevertheless, designers tend to make icons more and more complex so that icons may provide large amounts of information in a limited space and enhance users' attention [6]. Furthermore, the presentation modes of icons are currently rather diverse. As a result, while searching for an icon on the main menu, a user may not find the needed interface or function quickly, which causes operational problems. Well-designed icons can achieve such positive effects as reducing operational errors, shortening the time to finish a job, and improving customers' satisfaction [4]. Besides conveying correct messages to users adequately, well-designed icons will affect users' operation, recognition, and preference in accordance with different graphical designs [6]. Therefore, there were many re-searchers carefully studying the impact of icon operation on users. Through human operation, icons on the touchscreen were assessed in order to enhance operational efficiency [7, 8]. According to some studies, icon distances and sizes affected visual search when users watched the graphical interfaces; also, icons lying in the corner of the touchscreen affected operation directly [4]. In the field of icon interfaces and interface operation, many studies utilized eye-tracking systems to analyze as well as to enhance the interaction between users and interfaces. For example, the methods for studying user interfaces included assessing users' operational performance, oral analysis, and evaluation of interface browsing [9]. To further explore the arrangement and presentation of icons, Lindberg et al. took icon spacing and icon sizes as independent variables and visual processing time as a dependent variable, used an eye-tracker to record visual processing time, and investigated how fast the eye-tracking system processed icons [4]. The two researchers found that if the visual angle of an icon was less than $0.7°$, the speed of visual search would increase significantly. As for spacing between two adjacent icons, the distance equal to an icon was accepted and preferred while no spacing between two icons should be avoided.

Currently, research on icon observation mainly focuses on icon sizes and distances [6, 10–12], contrast [12], and users' subjective satisfaction levels [5, 7]. However, studies of the presentation modes of icons are rarely found. Good presentation modes attract consumers' attention, boost search speed, and reduce errors. Therefore, how presentation modes affect users' attention is the main concern of this study.

At present, concerning the characteristic elements and arrangement of icons, there are no definite guidelines for design. In such a situation, presentation modes cause a lot of problems to users, bringing much inconvenience. This study investigated the icons on the main menus in the Internet and digital systems, analyzed them, and identified the characteristic elements of presentation modes. The eye-tracker was employed to measure first fixations, and then subjective evaluation of attention was performed. In that way, the optimum presentation mode that could attract users' attention might be identified. Also, users' operational efficiency might be enhanced, and the guidelines for icon design might be established. The findings in this study can be used by UI designers as a reference in the future.

2 Investigation and Analysis of Icon Presentation Modes

2.1 Investigation of Icon Presentation Modes

While icons were being collected, those on the main menus served as the major sources, including the main menus of digital TV, online application stores, video game consoles, cellphones, tablet computers, and computers. In November, 2012, with the help of Google search engine, the author entered the following keywords in both Chinese and English: online music stores, digital TV, and online application stores. The top five websites were arranged in order of relevance, and then the main menus with icons were selected. Only one out of the similar websites was chosen, those websites with unstable connection were excluded, and if the same website used both English and Chinese, the official website was adopted. The main menus of video game consoles were based on the mainstream products on the market, with five consoles obtained. As to cellphones, tablet computers, and computers, there were numerous models available, so this study selected the main menus based on their operating systems (OS). One hundred and sixty-eight icons were collected and reorganized in the first stage.

2.2 Analysis of Icon Presentation Modes

To analyze the characteristic elements of icon presentation, the author invited six professionals to form a focus group. Two of the professionals were surface designers with three years of work experience, another two were interface designers with two years of work experience, and the others were industrial designers with four years of work experience. In compliance with the principles of icon design [13], the characteristics of icon presentation were analyzed. As indicated by the finding, current presentation modes consist of three main features: icon composition, polarity, and icon border. To be exact, icon composition is subdivided into line composition and plane composition, polarity is subdivided into positive polarity (white backgrounds and black

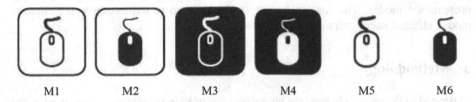

M1   M2   M3   M4   M5   M6

Fig. 1. Six presentation modes of graphical icons

characters) and negative polarity (black backgrounds and white characters), and icon border is subdivided into having borders and having no border. Through permutation and combination, six presentation modes were obtained as follows: line + positive polarity + border (M1), plane + positive polarity + border (M2), line + negative polarity + border (M3), plane + negative polarity + border (M4), line + positive polarity + no border (M5), and plane + positive polarity + no border (M6), as shown in Fig. 1. There were two nonexistent modes: line + negative polarity + no border and plane + negative polarity + no border. Table 1 shows the characteristics of various

Table 1. Composition of icon presentation modes

		Icon composition		Polarity		Border	
		Line	Plane	Positive polarity (white backgrounds and black characters)	Negative polarity (black backgrounds and white characters)	With border	No border
M1		X		X		X	
M2			X	X		X	
M3		X			X	X	
M4			X		X	X	
M5		X		X			X
M6			X	X			X

Note: X means having the kind of feature.

presentation modes. The finding herein would be used to explore how presentation modes affected users' attention in the next stage.

3 Methodology

Illustrated in the above chapter, the characteristics of icon presentation were used as the criteria for selecting stimuli. Concerning the experiment, eye-trackers were employed to measure the participants' first fixations while they were watching the icons. Additionally, their operational performances were compared, and subjective evaluation was conducted to explore how icon presentation modes affected users' attention.

3.1 Selecting Stimuli

In this study, a number of sample icons were selected for the experiment. As the stimuli were collected, nearly all chosen icons were based on two operating systems (Windows and OS). To reduce the impacts of those stimuli on the participants' recog-nition, commonly-used icons on 3C products were selected. Nevertheless, those icons too complex, blurred, or abstract to be judged immediately were rejected. If two or more icons were similar, only one of them got chosen. In the end, sixty-eight icons were collected. Based on the original icons, their contour drawings were produced. Next, thirty college students with some experience of product design were requested to rate all the icons on a scale of 1-7 with the help of the software E-Prime. Finally, the top thirty icons were picked out as the stimuli in the formal experiment.

3.2 Participants

For the purpose of the experiment, thirty-six college students were recruited as the participants, with males and females in equal numbers, whose ages ranged from eighteen to twenty-two. Because the participants were widely different in height, the location and height of each chair had to be adjusted to match its occupant. Besides, the height of each participant's head was fixed so that his or her sight line was parallel with the center of the screen right in front of him or her. The participant's eyes should be kept at 66 cm away from the screen; meanwhile, each participant had to feel relaxed in a sitting posture throughout the experiment. Immediately after entering the laboratory, each participant sat in front of the computer. After being properly seated, each participant started to read the instructions. When the visual fixation experiment was made with the help of an eye-tracker, the participant's vi-sion and attention would affect his or her judgment. Therefore, each participant had to pass the procedure called "correction of the visual fixation point." Moreover, his or her vision had to conform to the standard vision before or after correction. Another important thing was that each participant had to take care so as not to suffer from visual fatigue after a long experiment. This precaution was taken to prevent any errors in the experimental data. The thirty-six participants followed the design of within-subjects factors, and the sequence in which they performed the experiment was in compliance with the counterbalanced measures design. In other words, the order in which each participant operated the experimental interface varied with his or her sequence in the experiment. After an experiment was finished, its result was automatically recorded in the system. At the end of the whole experiment, each participant was rewarded with NT$300.

3.3 Stimuli

The colors, backgrounds, and decorative lines of the collected sample icons were removed so that such factors as color, brightness, contrast, and outer shadow might not affect attention levels and image recognition. After that, the sample icons were converted into contour drawings, with the line width of either icons or borders being 2 pixels. All the stimuli were made into contour drawings mainly presented in lateral views, for lateral views achieved the best performance. In this experiment, thirty representative stimuli were selected, with each stimulus presented in 6 different modes, or a group of six icons. In the group, the distance between the screen center and each icon was equal [14]; likewise, the distance between the centers of two adjacent icon stimuli was equal. Consequently, after being connected, the six icons formed a regular hexagon, as shown in Fig. 2. With the experimental results compared, it was determined which of the six presentation modes got the most first fixations. Through random permutation and combination, each of the six presentation modes appeared in six different positions for as many times. Each presentation mode of any icon was compared with the other five modes. The type of an icon shape could not be clearly defined based on the screen surface or on the visual fixation experiment, and neither could the detailed location or division of the icon. For the aforesaid reason, this experiment focused on the overall shape of an icon to make a judgment, without presenting its detailed features.

Fig. 2. Six presentation modes of an icon stimulus

3.4 Experimental Tools and Conditions

With a resolution of 1024*768 pixels, the 22-inch screen was employed and connected with an eye-tracker to record vision tracks. As for image presentation, the HP desktop computer was used to control graphical software. Further, GazeTracker (GT), a piece of interface software in the HP desktop computer, was responsible for detecting the number of first fixations measured by FaceLab v4, which is an eye tracking system produced by Dell Corp. The sampling frequency of FaceLab is 60 Hz; mean-while, the position of the head or eyes was monitored through FaceLab software to record the positions of the eyeballs as well as the number of first fixations.

3.5 Experimental Procedures for Attention

- The experimental goals, methods, and procedures were explained to all participants.
- Each participant started to write down his or her basic information, including name, age, gender, and college major.
- After reading the experimental instructions, each participant was requested to observe the graphical icons which attracted much attention.
- Vision examination and visual fixation point correction were per-formed.
- The participants started to be exposed to a gray screen for 6 s.
- The participants were exposed to a fixation plus sign ("+") for 2 s.
- As the participants went on to watch a target image, the contour drawings of an icon in six presentation modes appeared simultaneously for 6 s.
- The participants went on to experiment with the next icon to test first fixation, repeating steps 5 to 8 above until all the thirty icon stimuli were tested.
- The participants were required to fill out a subjective questionnaire of attention in accordance with a scale of seven levels, with level 1 meaning extremely negative, level 4 meaning neutral, and level 7 meaning extremely positive. The whole experiment lasted for about twenty-five to thirty minutes.

3.6 Analysis of the Collected Data

Thirty-six participants were requested to watch thirty icon stimuli presented simultaneously in six modes. In addition, eye-trackers were employed to measure first fixations. As each icon was observed repeatedly by the participants, thirty groups of first fixations as well as subjective evaluation of attention were obtained. Next, the different numbers of first fixations were analyzed through the chi-square test, while subjective evaluation of attention was analyzed through one-way ANOVA. Also, the statistical software, Windows SPSS 12.0, was used to analyze the results, with $p < .05$ taken as the standard of statistical significance.

4 Results

4.1 Analysis of First Fixation

The number of first fixations reached a significance level ($X2$ = 167.4, p<.001). Thirty-six participants were involved in the experiment, watching thirty icon stimuli presented simultaneously in six modes, which resulted in 1080 first fixations. The relationship between six presentation modes and first fixations is listed as follows: M1 = 141, M2 = 171, M3 = 257, M4 = 290, M5 = 90, and M6 = 131, as shown in Fig. 3. In other words, M4 got the largest number of first fixations while M3 ranked second; meanwhile, only M4 and M3 reached the expected value. By contrast, M2, M1, M6, and M5 all failed to reach the expected value, with M5 getting the smallest number of first fixations.

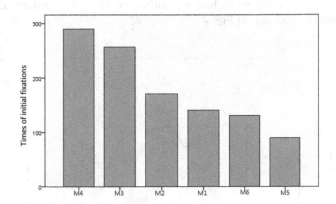

Fig. 3. Six presentation modes and their respective first fixations

4.2 Subjective Evaluation of Attention

Presentation modes of icons exerted a significant effect on subjective evaluation of attention ($F(5, 175)$ = 19.842, $p < 0.001$), as shown in Table 2. Analyzed through the LSD multiple range test, six presentation modes and their respective mean scores are listed in order of rankings as follows: M4 = 5.444, M2 = 4.111, M6 = 3.611, M3 = 3.306, M1 = 2.972, and M5 = 1.944, as shown in Table 3. In other words, the

Table 2. One-way ANOVA of subjective evaluation of attention

Source	df	SS	MS	F
Within subjects	35	2.759	.079	
Subject	5	247.593	49.519	19.842***
Subject within group	175	436.741	2.496	

Significant at *≦0.05; **≦0.01; ***≦0.001.

Table 3. Mean values of subjective evaluation of attention under each level of the independent variables and LSD multiple range tests on significant factors.

Source	n	Subjective evaluation	Std. Error	LSD
Icon Presentation Mode				
M1	36	2.972	1.341	M4>M2>M1, M3, M6>M5
M2	36	4.111	1.410	
M3	36	3.306	1.564	
M4	36	5.444	1.482	
M5	36	1.944	1.413	
M6	36	3.611	1.460	

participants subjectively considered that plane + negative polarity + border (M4) attracted the most attention, while line + positive polarity + no border (M5) attracted the least attention, as shown in Fig. 4.

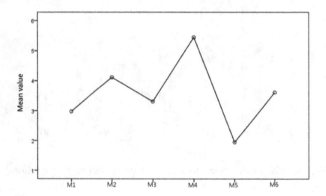

Fig. 4. Subjective evaluation of attention concerning six presentation modes

5   Discussion

5.1   First Fixation

Among the icon presentation modes evaluated in this study, M4 got the largest number of first fixations, M3 ranked second, M2 ranked third, M1 ranked fourth, M6 ranked fifth, and M5 got the least number. The reason why M4 performed the best of all is that its border is regarded as an integral part of an icon [15]. The icon with a border has a larger area than that with no border. When it comes to attracting visual attention, the larger icon has more advantages than the smaller one, being likelier to be noticed by the participants [16].

M3 got the second largest number of first fixations. Although negative polarity combined with borders makes the icon seem larger and apt to catch attention, still line composition is more complex than plane composition, which fact contributes to lower recognizability [17–19]. Further-more, the icon composed of lines tends to become blurred owing to fine lines. By contrast, the icon composed of planes is divided by planes, so it usually has a larger area [20], looking more vivid than the line-composed icon. As a result, M4 is likelier to be noticed than M3. In addition, M2, M1, and M6 got fewer first fixations than M4 or M3. The main reason is that negative polarity combined with line composition or plane composition has a black background and a white image, thus catching visual attention more easily. By contrast, as the icons in M1 and M2 have a white background and a black image, they are less likely to attract first fixation [21].

As indicated by the experimental results, M2, M6, and M1 showed no significant difference in terms of first fixation. This finding is similar to that reached by Fleetwood & Byrne, who explored icon borders [6]. According to the two researchers, having no border, round borders, and square borders showed no significant difference in their effects on users' search. This study discovered that the participants paid more attention to the icon composed of planes. Although the icon with borders and positive polarity was larger than the icon with no border, the participants paid too much attention to the icon itself to notice the fine lines in borders. In consequence, the icon with borders and positive polarity did not attract more attention than the icon with no border though the former was larger.

M5 is similar to M6 in that they both have no border. However, M6 is composed of planes while M5 is composed of lines. The plane-composed image has a larger area and looks more vivid than the line-composed image [20]. In contrast, the line-composed image tends to look blurred owing to quite fine lines. Thus, the line-composed icon with no border, or M5, is the likeliest to be ignored among the six icons.

5.2   Subjective Evaluation of Attention

As discovered by this study, graphical icons produce a significant influence on subjective evaluation of attention. The participants considered that M4 was the most attractive, followed by M2, M6, M3, and M1 in order of rankings; contrarily, M5 was viewed as the least attractive. Regarding M4, the results coming from subjective evaluation of attention agree with those coming from first fixation. With the largest number of first fixations, M4 was considered by the participants to attract the most attention. As for M3, its performance in first fixation does not correspond with its performance in subjective evaluation of attention. Concerning subjective evaluation of attention, M2 performs better than M3; contrarily, in terms of first fixation, M2 performs worse than M3. As indicated by the findings herein, it is mainly because the participants subjectively considered that plane composition is always better than line composition. Based on the author's speculation, the participants subjectively considered that the icon with line composition and negative polarity has many fine details, rendering the image more complex [17]. The more complex an image is, the worse recognition will result [19]. In addition, as a line is finer than a plane, the former used in an icon is less likely to be noticed than the latter. In the situation where the participants cannot identify images smoothly, the participants regarded M3 icons as more unnoticeable than M2.

On the other hand, although M1 and M3 both have borders, they show no significant difference from M6, which has no border, in subjective evaluation of attention. The above result is somewhat different from that found by Bullimore et al., who suggested that a lager image produced better recognition [15]. M1 and M3, which have borders, are larger than M6, which has no border. Even though M1 with borders and positive polarity has increased the icon size, the fine lines prevent it from looking as obvious as a plane-composed icon. As for M3, although it has negative polarity and borders, the icon is line-composed, thus not looking as obvious as a plane-composed icon.

6   Conclusion

This study explores the effects of icon presentation modes on users' attention. Through eye trackers, the participants' first fixations were measured while the icons were being observed; besides, subjective evaluation of attention was conducted. This study has discovered that plane + negative polarity + border (M4) attracted the most attention, while line + positive polarity + no border (M5) attracted the least attention. It is suggested that follow-up studies may probe into the characteristic elements of icons; thus, the impacts of those characteristic elements on viewers' attention may be determined. The findings herein can be used as a reference by interface designers to design icons.

References

1. Albinsson, P.-A., Zhai, S.: High Precision Touch Screen Interaction, pp. 105–112. ACM Press, New York (2003)
2. Wu, F.-G., Lin, H., You, M.: Direct-touch vs. mouse input for navigation modes of the web map. Displays 32(5), 261–267 (2011)
3. Huang, H., Lai, H.-H.: Factors influencing the usability of icons in the LCD touchscreen. Displays 29(4), 339–344 (2008)
4. Lindberg, T., Näsänen, R.: The effect of icon spacing and size on the speed of icon processing in the human visual system. Displays 24(3), 111–120 (2003)
5. Wu, F.-G., Lin, H., You, M.: The enhanced navigator for the touch screen: A comparative study on navigational techniques of web maps. Displays 32(5), 284–295 (2011)
6. Fleetwood, M.D., Byrne, M.D.: Modeling icon search in ACT-R/PM. Cogn. Syst. Res. 3(1), 25–33 (2002)
7. Beringer, D.B., Peterson, J.G.: Underlying behavioral parameters of the operation of touch-input devices: Biases, models, and feedback. Hum. Factors J. Hum. Factors Ergon. Soc. 27(4), 445–458 (1985)
8. Sears, A.: Improving touchscreen keyboards: design issues and a comparison with other devices. Interact. Comput. 3(3), 253–269 (1991)
9. Goldberg, J.H., Kotval, X.P.: Computer interface evaluation using eye movements: methods and constructs. Int. J. Ind. Ergon. 24(6), 631–645 (1999)
10. Legge, G.E., Pelli, D.G., Rubin, G.S.: Psychophysics of reading—I. Normal Vision Vision Res. 25(2), 239–252 (1985)
11. Legge, G.E., Rubin, G.S., Luebker, A.: Psychophysics of reading—V. The role of contrast in normal vision. Vision. Res. 27(7), 1165–1177 (1987)

12. Näsänen, R., Karlsson, J., Ojanpää, H.: Display quality and the speed of visual letter search. Displays **22**(4), 107–113 (2001)
13. Horton, W. K., The icon book: Visual symbols for computer systems and documentation. Wiley & Sons, New York (1994)
14. Huang, K.-C., Chiu, T.-L.: Visual search performance on an LCD monitor: effects of color combination of figure and icon background, shape of icon, and line width of icon border. Percept. Mot. Skills **104**(2), 562–574 (2007)
15. Bullimore, M., Howarth, P., Fulton, J.: Assessment of visual performance. In: Evaluation of Human Work: A Practical Ergonomics Methodology, pp. 804–839 (1990)
16. Mirzoeff, N.: The visual culture reader. Psychology Press, New York (2002)
17. Curry, M. B., McDougall, S. J., de Bruijn, O.: The effects of the visual metaphor in determining icon efficacy. pp. 1590–1594 (1998)
18. Dewar, R.: Design and evaluation of public information symbols. In: Zwaga, H.J.G., Boersma, T., Hoonhout, H.C.M. (eds.) Visual information for everyday use: Design and research perspectives, pp. 285–303. (1999)
19. Easterby, R.S.: The perception of symbols for machine displays. Ergonomics **13**(1), 149–158 (1970)
20. Wong, W.: Principles of Form and Design. Wiley & Sons, New York (1993)
21. Wolfe, J.M., Oliva, A., Horowitz, T.S.: Segmentation of objects from backgrounds in visual search tasks. Vision. Res. **42**(28), 2985–3004 (2002)

Numerical Analysis of Body Sway While Viewing a 3D Video Clip Without Perspective Clues

Yuki Mori, Yoshiki Maeda, and Hiroki Takada[✉]

Department of Human and Artificial Intelligent Systems, Graduate School of
Engineering, University of Fukui, 3-9-1 Bunkyo, Fukui 910-8507, Japan
takada@u-fukui.ac.jp

Abstract. Recently, with the rapid progress in image processing and
three-dimensional (3D) technology, stereoscopic images are not only seen on
television but also in theaters, on game machines, etc. However, symptoms such
as eye fatigue and 3D sickness are experienced when viewing 3D films on
displays and visual environments. The influence of stereoscopic vision on
human body has been also insufficiently understood; therefore, it is important to
consider the safety of viewing virtual 3D contents. The aim of this study is to
examine the effects of exposure to 2D/3D video clips on human equilibrium
systems. Stereoscopic video clips with complexly ambulated spheres and their
monocular (2D) vision were shown to subjects using binocular parallax smart
glasses. We compared stabilograms recorded during exposure to video clips
with/without depth cues on 3D images. The time-average potential function was
obtained from stabilograms using stochastic differential equations as a mathematical model for body sway to conduct a numerical analysis.

Keywords: Body sway · Stabilograms · Three-dimensional (3D) · Depth
cues · Time-average potential

1 Introduction

With the improvements in 3D image display technology, 3D images utilizing TV and
game devices have become commonplace. On the other hand, 3D images have adverse
effects, such as discomfort, dizziness, and eye strain, depending on the viewing condition [1]. However, knowledge of the influence of 3D images on the body is insufficient, and experimental studies should be conducted to investigate how to safely view
such images [2, 3].

Biological signals from the vestibular system, which may be the most frequently
referred to among the body balance systems, are also projected to the vestibular nuclei
present in the brainstem. Balance sense signals are transmitted to the higher centers,
such as the spinal motoneurons, oculomotor neurons, vestibulocerebellum, cerebral
cortex, and brainstem autonomic center, through the vestibular nuclei [4]. Vestibular
stimulation is transmitted to the vomiting center present in the medulla oblongata
through the vestibulo-autonomic nerve system, and motion sickness is induced through
the vestibulo-vegetative reflex. The vestibular and autonomic nerve systems are closely

© Springer International Publishing Switzerland 2015
M. Antona and C. Stephanidis (Eds.): UAHCI 2015, Part II, LNCS 9176, pp. 238–245, 2015.
DOI: 10.1007/978-3-319-20681-3_22

related anatomically and electrophysiologically [5], suggesting their close relationship with symptoms of motion sickness, and quantitative evaluation of motion sickness based on body sway, which is an output of the body balance system, is considered possible. The input into the vestibular system described above is controlled by the visual and somatosensory systems and parietal lobe. Regarding the developmental mechanism of visually induced motion sickness, the sensory conflict theory [6] is generally accepted, similarly to that of typical motion sickness.

Stabilometry performed as a balance test is useful to comprehensively evaluate the balance functions, such as the evaluation of the stability of a standing position and diagnosis of central disease-associated equilibration disturbance [7]. Stabilometry is a simple test in which a 60-s recording starts when a standing position is stabilized. To increase the diagnostic value of body sway, analytical parameters of stabilograms have been proposed, including the total distance of body sway and distance of body sway per unit area [7].

In this study, the influence of a 3D video of complex sphere movements in space on body sway was investigated, and changes in a mathematical model describing the body balance system were examined. In addition, whether or not perspective clues stabilize the standing position control system was investigated.

The Simulator Sickness Questionnaire (SSQ) is the best-known psychometric method to evaluate visually induced motion sickness. This questionnaire is comprised of 16 subjective items considered useful to evaluate simulator sickness [8]. In [9], the total distance of body sway significantly increased corresponding to the load in a high compared to low score group.

In this study, the influence of a 3D video of complex sphere movement in space on body sway was investigated using Smart glass. In addition, perspective clues were added to the 3D video and their influence was compared with the above, including the subjective evaluation using SSQ. Furthermore, time-average potential functions were calculated from stabilograms, and a mathematical model of body sway was constructed.

2   Materials and Methods

2.1   Experimental Method

The subjects were 19 healthy young persons (21.4 ± 4.1 years old (mean ± standard), 19 middle-aged persons (49.5 ± 6.3 years old), and 19 elderly persons (69.3 ± 5.6 years old) with no past medical history of diseases of the ear or nervous system. The experiment was sufficiently explained to the subjects and written consent was obtained before the experiment.

Stabilometry was performed while watching 2D and 3D videos. For the stabilometer, the gravicorder GS3000 (Anima Corp., Tokyo) was used. The sampling frequency was set at 20 Hz. The subjects watched 3D videos using Smart glass BT-200 (EPSON, Tokyo). Four videos (2D and 3D) were prepared by reconstituting Sky Crystal (Olympus Memory Works Corp., Tokyo) after approval by the company (Fig. 1). In the experiment, the video was presented during the test with open eyes. The

(a)   (b)

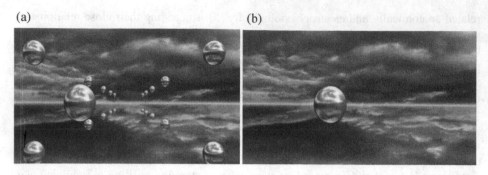

Fig. 1. Spheres are fixed at the 4 corners, giving perspective clues, and another sphere moves on the screen in a complex way (a). Video without spheres at the 4 corners, giving no perspective clue (b).

body sway was continuously measured during a 1-min test with open eyes and then a 1-min test with closed eyes, and the 4 videos were presented to all subjects. Measurement was performed in Romberg's posture, and the order of videos was randomized in consideration of the influence of the order effect. To exclude external stimulation other than the video, a blackout curtain was set in front of the subject to remove the influence of light penetrating the Smart glass.

2.2 Investigation Items

The x-y coordinates were recorded at each sampling time-point in the tests with open or closed eyes, and the parameters were calculated. The obtained data were converted to time series of the center of gravity position in the x- (right direction was regarded as positive) and y- (forward direction was regarded as positive) directions in each test, and the circumferential area, total distance of body sway, distance of body sway per unit area, and density were evaluated. The circumferential area, total distance of body sway, and distance of body sway per unit area are analytical parameters of stabilograms used in previous studies, and we used these based on the equations established by the Japan Society for Equilibrium Research. The density is a parameter of that of multiple points scattered on a plane proposed by Takada et al., and it is considered to be involved in the stability of a standing position [10]. The parameters are defined as follows:

Circumferential area: The area of the region surrounded by the circumference (envelop) of body sway on the x-y coordinate system. An increase in the value indicates the instability of sway.

Total distance of body sway: The total distance of movement of the center of gravity within the measurement time. An increase in the value indicates the instability of sway.

Distance of body sway per unit area: A value calculated by dividing the total distance of body sway by the circumferential area. A decrease in the value indicates the instability of sway.

Density: The stabilogram is divided into squares, and the frequency of passing over the center of foot pressure is determined in each square. As the sway narrows, i.e., the local density increases, the value becomes closer to 1. Inversely, the value decreases as the sway widens.

These 4 parameters were calculated in each stabilogram of the tests with both open and closed eyes, and 2-way layout analysis of variance with 2 factors out of 3-dimensionality of the video, the presence or absence of perspective clues, age, and persistence of the influence of watching the video was performed for each parameter, followed by multiple comparison, setting the significance level at 0.05.

2.3   Numerical Analysis

The equations below have been proposed as mathematical models describing the body sway [11]:

$$\dot{z} = -gradU(z) + \mu\omega(t) \tag{1}$$

$$U(z) = -\frac{1}{2}lnG(z) \tag{2}$$

μ represents the noise amplitude coefficient, and ω represents a pseudorandom number. The time-average potential functions in the x- and y-directions were calculated from the frequency distribution determined in the experiment using Eq. (2). The calculated time-average potential functions were approximated using the quadratic equation below:

$$\widehat{U}(z) = az^2 + b \qquad z = (x, y) \tag{3}$$

The mathematical model of the body sway shown below was established using Eq. (1):

$$\dot{z} = -grad\,\widehat{U}(z) + \mu\omega(t) \quad z = (x, y) \tag{4}$$

Numerical analysis was performed using this model. In Eq. (4), setting the initial values of (x,y) at (0,0), the pseudorandom number ω was prepared using white Gaussian noise (mean ± standard deviation: 1 ± 1). Setting the noise amplification coefficient μ at $1 \leq \mu \leq 20$ (1 step) and time step Δt at $0.001 \leq \Delta t \leq 0.01$ (0.001 step), 22,000 steps of a numerical solution were set using the Runge-Kutta 4th order method. Of the numerical solutions, the first 10,000 steps were discarded, and the remaining 12,000 steps were divided into 1,200-step increments. The total distance of body sway (Xs) and circumferential area (Ys) were calculated in these time series. Designating the measured total distance of body sway and circumferential area as (Xr) and (Yr), errors (E) between the numerical solutions of the mathematical model and measured values were calculated using the equation below:

$$E = \sqrt{\frac{\sqrt{Yr}}{Xr}(Xr - Xs)^2 + (\sqrt{Yr} - \sqrt{Ys})^2} \qquad (5)$$

3   Results

The 2D and 3D videos in which spheres giving perspective clues were fixed at the 4 corners and those in which spheres at the 4 corners were absent were presented in a random order, and the analytical parameters of stabilograms were compared. Typical stabilograms are shown in Fig. 2. No consistent tendency was noted among these stabilograms. The analytical parameters were calculated from the stabilograms. In the elderly subjects, the total distance of body sway, circumferential area, and density in the test with open eyes while watching the 3D video without spheres at the 4 corners significantly increased compared to those while watching the 2D video ($p < 0.05$) (Fig. 3). The distance of body sway per unit area while watching the 3D video without spheres at the 4 corners significantly increased in the test with open eyes compared to that with closed eyes ($p < 0.05$). No significant difference was noted in the other analytical parameters in the elderly subjects.

Stabilograms were measured while viewing video clips, 2D A, 2D B, 3D A, and 3D B that were corresponding to a 2D video with perspective clues by spheres at the 4

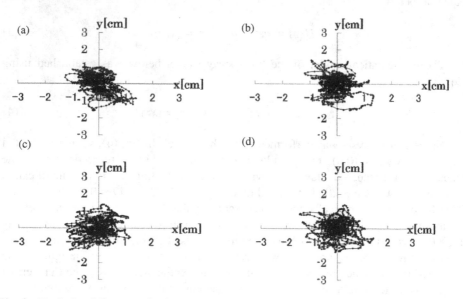

Fig. 2. Typical stabilograms (in the same subject): stabilograms while watching the 2D video showing the perspective clues (a), 3D video showing the perspective clues (b), 2D video showing no perspective clue (c), 3D video showing no perspective clue (d).

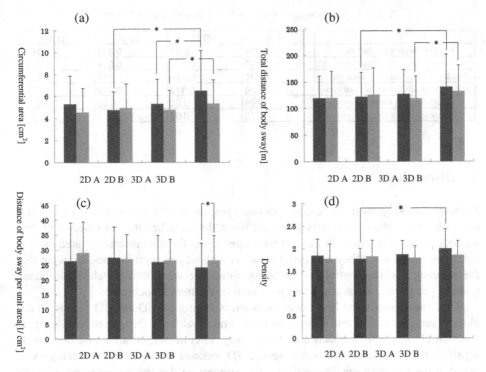

Fig. 3. Body sway in elderly subjects: circumferential area (a), Total distance of body sway (b), Distance of body sway per unit area (c), Density S_2 (d) (*$p < 0.05$).

corners, a 2D video without perspective clues, a 3D video with perspective clues, and a 3D video without the clues.

In the young subjects, the total distance of body sway while watching the 2D video without spheres at the 4 corners significantly increased in the test with closed eyes compared to that with open eyes ($p < 0.05$). No significant difference was noted in the other analytical parameters. In the middle-aged subjects, no significant difference was noted in any analytical parameter.

The time-average potential function of each measured data was calculated, and numerical analysis was performed using Eq. (4). The numerical solutions for the total distance of body sway and circumferential area were calculated, and errors (E) from the measured values were calculated. Regarding combination of the noise amplification coefficient μ and time step Δt of the numerical solution with the minimum E as the optimum value, scattering roughness of sway, $\mu * \Delta t$, was calculated (Table 1).

In the middle-aged and elderly subjects, the scattering roughness of sway was greater after viewing the 3D video without perspective clues by spheres at the 4 corners than that after viewing the videos with the perspective clues. Irrespective to their ages and the perspective clues, the scattering roughness was greater after viewing the 3D video than that after viewing the 2D video.

Table 1. Sparseness of sway ($\mu * \Delta t$) under each condition

	2D A	2D B	3D A	3D B
Young subjects with open eyes	0.064	0.06	0.072	0.06
Young subjects with closed eyes	0.068	0.072	0.076	0.072
Middle-aged subjects with open eyes	0.076	0.068	0.072	0.06
Middle-aged subjects with closed eyes	0.06	0.072	0.072	0.076
Elderly subjects with open eyes	0.08	0.09	0.09	0.095
Elderly subjects with closed eyes	0.095	0.09	0.08	0.095

4 Discussion

In the elderly subjects in the test with closed eyes, the total distance of body sway and circumferential area significantly increased when they watched the 3D videos with and without perspective clues. In the test with open eyes, the circumferential area significantly increased when they watched the videos without perspective clues, showing that the standing position control system became unstable when they watched the videos without perspective clues compared to watching them with such clues.

On comparison of the body sway between watching the 2D and 3D videos, in the elderly subjects in the test with open eyes while watching the videos without perspective clues, the total distance of body sway, circumferential area, and density S_2 significantly increased while watching the 3D video, but no significant change was noted in the young or middle-aged subjects, suggesting that the increases were due to aging-related reduction of the balance function, and elderly persons are more markedly influenced by 3D images.

In the numerical solutions of the mathematical model, the scattering roughness of sway increased while watching the 3D video without perspective clues compared to that while watching the 3D video with such clues in the elderly subjects. In the middle-aged and elderly subjects, the scattering roughness of sway was greater after viewing the 3D video without perspective clues by spheres at the 4 corners than that after viewing the 2D video with the perspective clues, suggesting that the characteristic of the measured body sway was reproduced by the mathematical model.

5 Conclusion

The influence of 3-D images on body sway was investigated using videos of complex sphere movement in space and Smart glass. In addition, perspective clues were added to the videos and the influence on body sway was compared. Significant changes in analytical parameters were noted when the videos without spheres at the 4 corners giving no perspective clue were presented, showing that the standing position control system became unstable while watching the video without perspective clues, compared to that while watching them with such clues.

On comparison between the 2D and 3D videos, significant changes were noted in the elderly group in the test with open eyes while watching the video without perspective clues, but no significant change was noted in the young or middle-aged subjects. The reason for the marked influence on the elderly subjects may have been an aging-related reduction of the body balance function, strongly reflected in the body sway while watching the 3D video.

We successfully developed a mathematical model describing the above findings. Values similar to the measured data were obtained using this model, suggesting that it is useful to clarify the influence of 3-D images on the body balance function.

Acknowledgements. This work was supported in part by the Ministry of Education, Culture, Sports, Science and Technology, through a Grant-in-Aid for Scientific Research (C) (Number 26350004).

References

1. International standard organization: IWA3:2005 image safety-reducing determinism in a time series. Phys. Rev. Lett. **70**, 530–582 (1993)
2. Yano, S., Ida, S., Thwaites, H.: Visual comfort and fatigue based on accommodation response for stereoscopic image. J. Inst. Image Inf. Telev. Eng. **55**(5), 711–717 (2001)
3. Yano, S., Emoto, M., Mitsuhashi, T.: Two factors in visual fatigue caused from stereoscopic images. Inst. Image Inf. Telev. Eng. **57**(9), 1187–1193 (2003)
4. Barmack, N.H.: Central vestibular system: vestibular nuclei and posterior cerebellum. Brain Res. Bull. **60**, 511–541 (2003)
5. Balaban, C.D., Poster, J.D.: Neuroanatomic substrates for vestibuloautonomic interactions. J. Vestib. Res. **8**, 7–16 (1998)
6. Reason, J.T., Brand, J.J.: Motion Sickness. Academic Press, London (1975)
7. Suzuki, J., Matsunaga, T., Tokumatsu, K., Taguchi, K., Watanabe, Y.: Q&A and a manual in stabilometry. Equilibr. Res. **55**(1), 64–77 (1996). (In Japanese)
8. Kennedy, R.S., Lane, N.E., Bardaum, K.S., Lilienthal, M.G.: A simulator sickness questionnaire(SSQ): a new method for quantifying simulator sickness. Int. J. Aviat. Psychol. **3**, 203–220 (1993)
9. Scibora, L.M., Villard, S., Bardy, B., Stoffregen, T.A.: Wider stance reduces body sway and motion sickness. Proc. VIMS **2007**, 18–23 (2007)
10. Takada, H., Kitaoka, Y., Ichikawa, S., Miyao, M.: Physical meaning on geometrical index for stabilometry. Equilibr. Res. **62**(3), 168–180 (2003)
11. Takada, H., Miyao, M.: Visual fatigue and motion sickness induced by 3D video. Forma **27** (Special Issue), S67–S76 (2012)

A Temporal Analysis of Body Sway Caused by Self-Motion During Stereoscopic Viewing

Akihiro Sugiura[1,2(✉)], Kunihiko Tanaka[1], Hiroki Takada[3],
Takehito Kojima[2], Tatsuya Yamakawa[2], and Masaru Miyao[2]

[1] Department of Radiology, Gifu University of Medical Sienese, Seki, Japan
{asugiura, ktanaka}@u-gifu-ms.ac.jp
[2] Graduate School of Information Sciense, Nagoya University, Nagoya, Japan
tkojima45@gmail.com, yamakawa.tatsuya@d.mbox.nagoya-u.ac.jp, mmiyao@is.nagoya-u.ac.jp
[3] Graduate School of Engineering, University of Fukui, Fukui, Japan
takada@u-fukui.ac.jp

Abstract. While continuously viewing objects in motion, humans may develop an illusionary sense of moving in the opposite direction as the objects, despite being quiescent. This phenomenon is termed as vection. In this study, we investigated the effect of long-duration viewing through binocular stereopsis on vection by measuring the body sway. Subjects watched a static movie for a minute, sinusoidal-motion movie at 0.3 Hz for 3 min, and the initial static movie for a minute, in sequence. We had three observations from the results of this study. First, the longer the viewing time, the higher the synchrony with direction of motion in the movie. Stoppage of the motion-movie and returning to viewing a static movie decreases the synchrony gradually. Second, synchrony is higher while viewing a 3D- than a 2D-movie. Third, the body sways in the anteroposterior direction in a cyclical manner by sensing self-motion in the horizontal direction.

Keywords: Self-motion · Vection · Stereoscopic movie · Sinusoid · Synchrony

1 Introduction

It is assumed that the mechanism of human posture control processes information about self-location, -posture, and -direction. This information is generated through integration of the visual system, vestibular-labyrinthine apparatus, and somatosensory system through a brain to whole body continuum. It has been reported that information from the visual system has the largest effect on human posture control with it constituting more than 50 % of the input [1, 2]. When continuously observing moving objects, humans may develop an illusionary sensation of moving in the opposite direction as the moving objects, which is a good example of posture control by the visual system. This phenomenon is termed as vection [3–6]. Vection is described as a sensation of self-motion in a person attributed to visual information despite the person being quiescent.

In previous studies on vection, three major approaches were followed. The first approach was to measure vection. Measurement methods can be classified as subjective and

© Springer International Publishing Switzerland 2015
M. Antona and C. Stephanidis (Eds.): UAHCI 2015, Part II, LNCS 9176, pp. 246–254, 2015.
DOI: 10.1007/978-3-319-20681-3_23

objective. The advantage of the subjective method is that it enables direct measurement of sensory phenomenon. In previous studies, orally answering questions about both the perceived direction of self-motion and its amplitude were mainstream. In particular, magnitude estimation, which is one of the methods in experimental psychology, has frequently been used in studies on vection. On the other hand, objective methods in vection studies evaluate bodily changes attributed to kinesthesis. In vection-measurement, correlation between bodily changes and the sense of self-motion is an important verification point. Previous studies, which included both oral-response and physiological measurements, indicate a correlation between body displacement, such as head movement, body sway or nystagmus, and answers on self-motion [1, 5, 7, 8]. Thus, objective methods in vection studies have been used extensively. Recent studies have utilized functional magnetic resonance imaging to identify active parts of the brain during vection [9].

The second approach was trend analysis for identifying human characteristics for easy perception of vection. Previous studies have reported that motion sickness is strongly linked to vection [10–12].

Third is the analysis of relationship between movie-characteristics and vection. Studies have investigated vection while viewing movies, which differ in the direction of optic flow in the foreground and background, or which change the velocity or acceleration of optic flow. In addition, the effects of interaction between central and peripheral vision and binocular stereopsis on vection have also been studied. These show that background motion, which is detected by the peripheral vision, wields influence over vection. Thus, spatial perception is important in vection. However, the longest viewing time utilized in previous studies was 1 min, which fails to describe the characteristics of vection in longer viewing durations. Therefore, in this study, we investigated the effect of long-duration viewing through binocular stereopsis on vection by measuring body sway.

2   Method

2.1   Creation of Movies

A screenshot of the movie used in this study is shown in Fig. 1. The movie was created using the computer graphics software 3dsMax 2015 (AUTODESK, USA). The movie shows a large number of balls at random position. We created four types of movies with the following features. Motion-direction in the movies followed two patterns: depth direction (Z-direction) and side direction (X-direction); and the kind of movies were 2-dimensional (2D) and 3-dimensional (3D), using horizontal image translation (H. I. T.) with binocular stereopsis. The motion in the movies was sinusoidal at 0.3 Hz in each direction generated by moving camera-simulated ocular globes (the balls did not move directly). Amplitude of the sinusoidal motion was same in all directions. The maximum dive distance and maximum pull distance from the ocular globes in the 3D movies were, respectively, 0.85 m (parallactic angle, 2.5 degree) and 2.961 (parallactic angle, 1.8 degree), when the viewing distance was 2 m.

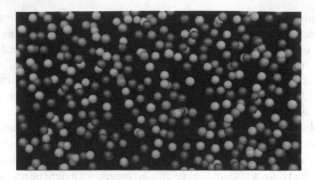

Fig. 1. Screenshot of the movie (2D image version). A large number of balls were placed at random positions in the movie space. Direction of motion in the movie followed two patterns: depth direction (Z-direction) and side direction (X-direction), and the movies were either 2-dimensional (2D) or 3-dimensional (3D) with binocular stereopsis. Sinusoidal motion at 0.3 Hz in each direction was generated by moving camera-simulated ocular globes (no direct motion of the balls).

Fig. 2. A scene of the study. The subject stands on a Wii Balance Board to measure body sway with a 2 m viewing distance to the screen. In 3D-movie viewing, subjects wear 3D-glasses.

2.2 Measurements

Nineteen students (12 male and 7 female, 21–24 years old) who did not have vision and equilibrium problems participated in this study which was approved by the Research Ethics Committee at Gifu University of Medical Science (approval number: 26-6). Written consent was obtained from participants after the purpose and significance of the study, and nature and risk of measurements were explained, both orally and in writing. Following this, the study was carried out in line with the Helsinki Declaration.

The setup utilized in the study is shown in Fig. 2. We performed measurements under a controlled environment (temperature: 29.5 degrees, illuminance: 13 lx), to avoid variations caused by visual stimuli. For presentation, the movie was projected on a white wall 2 m in front of the subject with a domestic version 3D projector (EH-TW5100, EPSON, Japan). Projected movie size was 155 cm × 274 cm, and the viewing distance was 2 m. Thus, the view angle was 68.8 degrees. In 3D movie viewing, subjects wore 3D-glasses (ELPGS03, EPSON, Japan) as a parallax barrier. In addition, to measure body sway during movie viewing, subjects stood on a Wii Balance Board (Nintendo, Japan) with a static erect position and toe opening at 18 degrees.

The following protocol was followed. First, subjects watched a non-moving movie (static movie: SM) for a min as pre-test. Next, subjects watched a sinusoidally-moving movie (motion movie: MM) for 3 min. Finally, the initial static movie was shown again for 1 min. During the entire duration, the body sway was recorded continuously. These 4-min tasks were treated as one trial, after which, four trials (2D-X-direction, 3D-X-direction, 2D-Z-direction, and 3D-Z-direction) were performed in random sequence to avoid the order effect. Trial-interval was set at more than 5 min.

2.3   Analysis Procedure

Each change in the voltage of four strain gauge sensors at the corners of the Wii Balance Board were output to a biological signal acquisition system (DC-300H, NIHON KOHDEN, Japan). These voltage data were recorded at 200 Hz using the biological signal recording software Lab Chart 7 (AD Instrument, USA). Next, voltage data were transformed to gravity point data using a reduction formula. Finally, the gravity point data underwent downsampling at 20 Hz following low-pass filtering at 10 Hz, which is the norm in studies on body sway using a stabilometer.

The continuous data on temporal change in body sway were separated by each 1-min of viewing time. Each separated data unit underwent a frequency analysis by fast Fourier transform using the Hamming window.

3   Results

A typical stabilogram result from one of the subjects (24 years old, female) viewing the 3D-Z direction movie is shown in Fig. 3a–e. Comparison of SM (Fig. 3a) and MM viewing (Fig. 3b–d) showed that the continuous change in gravity point in the direction of motion was bigger while viewing the MM than while viewing the SM. Moreover, the change in gravity point increased with an increase in the viewing time. The large change in body sway in the motion-direction while viewing the MM from 120 to 180 s (Fig. 3d) was drastically reduced in the following motionless SM (Fig. 3e). Thus, there was a gradual return to the initial state by viewing the SM. This phenomenon was seen in the viewing of movies with motion in all directions, and was regardless of the Z-direction.

Frequency analysis for body sway of the 19 subjects while viewing the SM (pre-test) and 3D-MM (120 to 180 s) are shown in Fig. 4a (3D-X-direction) and 4b (3D-Z-direction). The graphs show average magnitude values calculated from the Fourier analysis as the ordinate, and frequency as the abscissa. Both graphs showed

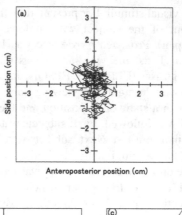

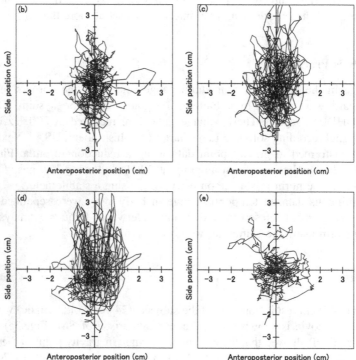

Fig. 3. Stabilogram of one subject (24 years old, female) viewing a 3D-Z direction movie. (a) Viewing the SM (pre-test), (b) viewing the MM for 0 to 60 s, (c) viewing the MM for 60 to 120 s, (d) viewing the MM for 120 to 180, and (e) viewing the SM (post-test).

peaks at 0.01 Hz and 0.3 Hz for MM viewing but the 0.3 Hz peak was missing for SM. Thus, only 0.3 Hz sway increased while viewing the MM. Frequency at 120 to 180 s while viewing the MM was analyzed (Fig. 4). The 0.3 Hz component was also detected in other Sects. (0 to 60 s or 60 to 120 s). In addition, while viewing the 2D-MM, a similar tendency was found.

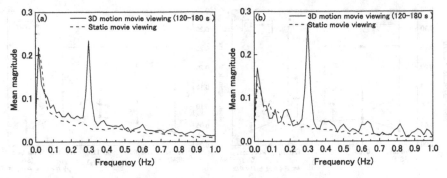

Fig. 4. Frequency analysis for body sway of 19 subjects while viewing the SM (pre-test) and viewing 3D-MM for 120 to 180 s. The both (a) and (b) show average magnitude value calculated from the Fourier analysis as the ordinate and frequency as the abscissa. (a) Shows data from viewing of 3D-X-direction MM, and (b) from viewing of 3D-Z-direction MM.

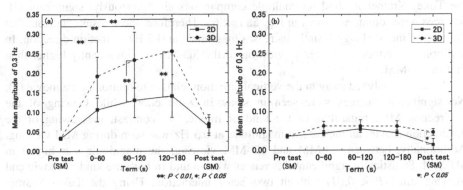

Fig. 5. Temporal change in the 0.3 Hz component in SM and Z-direction MM viewing. (a) Analysis result of sway in same direction as movie motion (Z-direction), and (b) analysis result of sway in the vertical direction relative to movie motion (X-direction).

Temporal change in the 0.3 Hz component while MM viewing was analyzed (Fig. 5, 6). Figures 5a, b show results from viewing of the Z-direction MM, and Fig. 6a, b, X-direction MM. (a) and (b) in each figure are analysis direction of the body sway: (a) is the same direction as the motion direction in the movie, and (b), the relative vertical direction.

Analysis of body sway in the motion direction of the movie (a) showed an increase of the 0.3 Hz component in the viewing of all direction motion MM, compared to the SM (pre-test). In addition, as viewing time increased, so did the 0.3 Hz component. However, we found an appreciable reduction of this component in SM viewing (post-test). Between 2D-MM and 3D-MM viewing, the magnitude at 0.3 Hz was higher in all time segments. To test for significance, two-way repeated measures ANOVA with viewing time and kind of movie (2D or 3D) as factors was performed. Significant differences were found in both the kind of movie and viewing time ($P < 0.01$) without two-factor interaction, and regardless of the motion direction. Moreover, when we used

252   A. Sugiura et al.

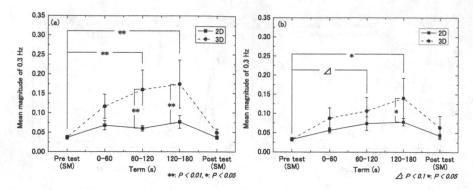

Fig. 6 Temporal change in 0.3 Hz components in SM and the X-direction MM viewing. (a) Analysis result of sway in same direction as movie motion (X-direction), and (b) analysis result of sway in vertical direction to movie motion (Z-direction).

the Tukey-Kramer method for multiple comparisons simultaneously, significant differences were found, as shown in Fig. 5a and 6a. Therefore, these results indicate that viewing of the MM significantly increases magnitude at 0.3 Hz in motion direction. In addition, magnitude at 0.3 Hz in viewing of the 3D-MM is significantly higher than that in 2D-MM.

Next, we analyzed sway in the vertical direction relative to motion in the movie (b). No significant changes were seen in sway in X-direction while viewing of the Z-direction MM, regardless of the kind of movie. By contrast, in viewing of the X-direction movie, an increase in magnitude at 0.3 Hz was seen during MM viewing. Additionally, between 3D-MM and 2D-MM viewing, the magnitude was higher in 3D-MM. Statistically significant differences were found in both the kind of movie and viewing time ($P < 0.01$) without two-factor interaction. Using the Tukey-Kramer method, significant differences were found (Fig. 6b).

4 General Discussion

In this study, we continuously measured body sway to investigate the effects of long-duration viewing on vection through binocular stereopsis. Using stabilograms, we found that changes in gravity point were in the same direction as that in the viewed movie (Fig. 3). Additionally, frequency analysis revealed a significant increase in the magnitude of 0.3 Hz sway component (Fig. 4). We inferred this specific change in body sway to be influenced by 0.3 Hz motion component in the MM. Vection is generally develop by continuous optic flow in one direction [13, 14]. However, similar to the findings of Ojima et al., we found that vection also occurs by viewing movies containing sinusoidal motion [15].

In frequency analysis, the component at 0.3 Hz in body sway increased with increase of viewing time, and decreased with the discontinuation of MM viewing (Fig. 5, 6). An increase of the 0.3 Hz component indicates an improvement in synchronization accuracy. There is a proportional relation between viewing time and synchronization accuracy of body sway in response to motion in the movie. Hence, The measurement of body sway might be effective in objectively evaluating the sensation of vection.

The 0.3 Hz component during 3D-MM viewing was significantly higher than while viewing the 2D-MM (Fig. 5, 6). This tendency was detected in each directional MM. Stereoscopic view by binocular parallax is a technique that provides humans with pseudo-depth perception. Additionally, vection is a phenomenon attributed to spatial movements. Thus, results in this study match those of previous studies and the theoretical mechanism for vection. However, during viewing of the X-direction MM, we noticed a significant cyclical swing at 0.3 Hz in the Z-direction. This swing could relate to the sole shape of humans. Postural maintenance is easier to disrupt in the horizontal than in the anteroposterior direction because feet are vertically positioned. The margin of change in gravity point in response to excessive moving in the anteroposterior direction is bigger than that in horizontal direction. Therefore, we conclude that the force of change in sway due to the sense of self-motion in the horizontal direction (X-direction) converts into an anteroposterior direction (Z-direction) to prevent a fall.

5   Conclusions

In this study, we investigated the effect of long-duration viewing by binocular stereopsis on vection using a continuous measurement of body sway. The following were demonstrated.

1. Longer the viewing time, higher is the synchrony with direction of motion in the MM. Stopping MM viewing decreases the synchrony in a gradual manner. The measurement of body sway might be effective as an objective evaluation tool for vection.
2. A 0.3-Hz component generated while viewing of the 3D-MM was significantly higher than that of 2D-MM because vection is attributed to spatial movement. Results in this study match the previous studies on theoretical mechanism behind vection.
3. By sensing self-motion in the horizontal direction, the body-sway significantly moves in a cyclical manner to the anteroposterior direction. This could be caused by conversion of the force of change in sway (due to vection) in the horizontal direction to the anteroposterior direction since center of gravity in humans is harder to disrupt in the anteroposterior direction.

References

1. Kawakita, T., Kuno, S., Miyake, Y., Watanabe, S.: Body sway induced by depth linear vection in reference to central and peripheral visual field. Jpn. J. Physiol. **50**, 315–321 (2000)
2. Edwards, A.S.: Body sway and vision. J. Exp. Psychol. **36**, 526–535 (1946)

3. Held, R., Dichigans, J., Bauer, J.: Characteristics of moving visual scenes influencing spatial orientation. Vision. Res. **15**, 357–365 (1975)
4. Schor, C.M., Lakshminarayanan, V., Narayan, V.: Optokinetic and vection responses to apparent motion in man. Vision. Res. **24**, 1181–1187 (1984)
5. Brandt, T., Dichgans, J., Koenig, E.: Differential effects of central verses peripheral vision on egocentric and exocentric motion perception. Exp. Brain Res. **16**, 476–491 (1973)
6. Zacharias, G.L., Young, L.R.: Influence of combined visual and vestibular cues on human perception and control of horizontal rotation. Exp. Brain Res. **41**, 159–171 (1981)
7. Allison, R.S., Howard, I.P., Zacher, J.E.: Effect of field size, head motion, and rotational velocity on roll vection and illusory self-tilt in a tumbling room. Perception **28**, 299–306 (1999)
8. Guerraz, M., Bronstein, A.M.: Mechanisms underlying visually induced body sway. Neurosci. Lett. **443**, 12–16 (2008)
9. Cardin, V., Smith, A.T.: Sensitivity of human visual cortical area V6 to stereoscopic depth gradients associated with self-motion. J. Neurophysiol. **106**, 1240–1249 (2011)
10. Stern, R.M., Hu, S., Anderson, R.B., Leibowitz, H.W., Koch, K.L.: The effects of fixation and restricted visual field on vection-induced motion sickness. Aviat. Space. Environ. Med. **61**, 712–715 (1990)
11. Smart, L.J., Stoffregen, T.A., Bardy, B.G.: Visually induced motion sickness predicted by postural instability. Hum. Factors **44**, 451–465 (2002)
12. Kiryu, T., Nomura, E., Bando, T., Kobayashi, N.: Time–frequency structure of image motion vectors around cybersickness intervals determined with biosignals. Displays **29**, 176–183 (2008)
13. Telford, L., Frost, B.J.: Factors affecting the onset and magnitude of linear vection. Percept. Psychophys. **53**, 682–692 (1993)
14. Andersen, G.J., Braunstein, M.L.: Induced self-motion in central vision. J. Exp. Psychol. Hum. Percept. Perform. **11**, 122–132 (1985)
15. Ojima, S., Yano, S.: Effect of depth sensation to body sway on binocular vision. IEICE Trans. Fundam. (J. Ed.) **J79-A**, 354–362 (1996)

Effect of Background Viewing on Equilibrium Systems

Hiroki Takada$^{(\boxtimes)}$, Yuki Mori, and Toshitake Miyakoshi

Department of Human and Artificial Intelligent Systems Graduate School of
Engineering, University of Fukui, 3-9-1 Bunkyo, Fukui 910-8507, Japan
takada@u-fukui.ac.jp

Abstract. Our previous study indicated an increase in the sway values that
were observed during peripheral viewing. Especially in the background, there
are large differences between human binocular images and artificial stereoscopic
images, to which our convergence corresponding to depth cues is not accommodated. This is why equilibrium functions are affected by peripheral viewing.
In the present paper, we examine the effect of the exposure to stereoscopic video
clips without the background on our equilibrium function. Fifteen healthy young
males voluntarily participated and maintained the Romberg posture in stabilometry. Their stabilograms were recorded during monocular vision or binocular
parallax vision using semipermeable smart glasses. We also measured the body
sway with the subjects' eyes closed 0–3 min after the exposure to the video
clips. A statistical comparison indicated that our equilibrium function is
significantly affected by video clips with the background 0–2 min after the
exposure to the video clips.

Keywords: Visually-induced motion sickness (VIMS) · Stabilometry ·
Stereoscopic video clips · Background

1 Introduction

When humans maintain an upright posture, the body always sways. The base supporting the body is a narrow area comprising the bilateral feet. To ensure a stable
posture, it is necessary to control the feet along a spatial perpendicular line from the
center of gravity within the narrow base of support [1]. Although the floor reaction to
actually support the body is provided by the bilateral legs, since the center of gravity of
the head, upper limbs, and trunk, accounting for 2/3 of the body weight, is present at
2/3 of the height from the floor surface, the center of gravity constantly sways in the
space, and balance is maintained by controlling the relationship with the center of
pressure, serving as a fulcrum to support the body, within the base of support [2, 3].
The reflex to return a swaying body to its original position is termed the righting reflex.
Physiologically, it is a body equilibrium function controlled by an involuntary regulatory system [4]. Elucidation of the function is essential to diagnose symptoms
accompanying equilibrium disorders, such as progressive cerebellar degeneration, basal
ganglia disorder, and Parkinson's disease [5].

© Springer International Publishing Switzerland 2015
M. Antona and C. Stephanidis (Eds.): UAHCI 2015, Part II, LNCS 9176, pp. 255–263, 2015.
DOI: 10.1007/978-3-319-20681-3_24

A body equilibrium function test, stabilometry, is considered useful to comprehensively evaluate the equilibrium function. Stabilometry is generally performed on standing in Romberg's posture in which the feet are together and the eyes open and closed, and for 60 s each, sways of the center of pressure (COP) are measured, which is regarded as a projection of the center of gravity. To increase the diagnostic value of stabilometry, measurement methods and analytical indices of stabilograms have been proposed [6]. The analytical indices include the total length of body sway and locus length per unit area. The latter is considered to represent micro changes in postural control and serve as a scale of proprioceptive postural control. Romberg's posture is an upright posture with the feet placed together. It is an unstable standing posture because the base of support is narrow, and so body sway becomes marked, and a reduced equilibrium function is likely to appear in stabilograms.

Stabilograms measured by stabilometry represent the process accompanied by irregular swaying components, and time-course sways in lateral and front-back directions in stabilograms can be independently assessed [7]. Stochastic differential equations (SDEs)

$$\frac{\partial x}{\partial t} = -\frac{\partial}{\partial x} U_x(x) + w_x(t), \tag{1.1}$$

$$\frac{\partial y}{\partial t} = -\frac{\partial}{\partial y} U_y(y) + w_y(t), \tag{1.2}$$

are used as mathematical models to describe sways of the center of gravity [8]. The described time-courses are considered to be generated through the Markov process, and when there is no anomaly, there is a relationship between the distribution in the measured direction, G_z, and temporally averaged potential constituting the stochastic differential equation, U_z, as follows: ($z = x, y$)

$$U_z(z) = -\frac{1}{2} \ln G(z) + const. \tag{2}$$

The stochastic differential equation describes minimum stable movement local of the potential surface, and a high density at the measurement point, z, is expected to be around the minimal points.

We focus on instability in the mathematical model of the body sway. In order to discuss metamorphism of the potential function U_z in the SDEs, it is important for us to take nonlinearity of the function into consideration. The degeneration in the function U_z would be lifted due to the perturbation actualized by the experimental load for our balance system. For instance, the alcoholic intake represses function of the cerebrum, and motor disturbance can be seen in the clinical observation.

To begin with, upright postures is considered to be instable. When humans maintain an upright posture, the body always sways. To ensure the posture, it is necessary to control the feet along a spatial perpendicular line from the center of gravity within the narrow base of support [1]. In the Romberg posture, the base supporting the body is the narrowest. The posture could become more instable on a tilting table [9].

Stereoscopic videos utilizing binocular stereoscopic vision often cause unpleasant symptoms of asthenopia, such as headache and vomiting, depending on the audiovisual condition [10]. Ataxia in simulator-induced sickness has been reported. The influence of visual induced motion sickness on the body has been measured employing subjective scales, such as the Simulator Sickness Questionnaire (SSQ) [11], and by quantitatively investigating the relationship between external factors and internal conditions using physiological indices [12–15], such as respiratory function, electro - cardiogram, skin electrical activity, electrogastrogram, and the body sway.

Although mechanism of the symptoms does not have been elucidated and been unclear, our previous study showed increase in sway values that were obsereved during peripheral viewing [16, 17]. Especially in the background, there are large difference between human binocular image and artificial stereoscopic image to which our convergence corresponding to depth cues is not accommodated. That is why equilibrium function affect from peripheral viewing. In this study, we examine effect of the exposure to stereoscopic video clips without the background on our equilibrium function.

2   Materials and Methods

Fifteen healthy young males (age, 21–24 years), who may have had any otorhinolaryngologic or neurological diseases in the past, voluntarry participated in this study. The experiment was sufficiently explained to the subjects, following which written consent was obtained from them.

In this experiment, the body sway was measured while viewing 2D/3D video clips with use of semipermeable smart glasses that displayed content in the Sky Crystal (Olympus Memory Works Ltd. Co., Tokyo), which was modified with permission from the company, and was used as the visual stimulus in this experiment. The stimulus includes spheres fixed in four corners, which supplies perspective. A sphere complexly ambulated in a video clip. The subjects stood on the detection stand of a stabilometer GS3000 (Anima Co. Ltd., Tokyo), without moving, with their feet together in the Romberg posture, for 30 s before the sway was recorded. Each sway of the COP was then recorded at a sampling frequency of 20 Hz. The subjects were instructed to maintain the Romberg posture during the trials. For the first 60 s, the subjects were asked to do the following:

 I. Gaze at a static circle with a diameter of 3 cm (Control).
 II. Peripherally viewing video clips without pursuing the ambulated sphere (Fig. 1a).
 III. Peripherally viewing video clips as same in II without the backgrounds (Fig. 1b)

We also measured body sway with eyes closed 0–3 min after the exposure to them, and the Post-stabilogram were composed every 1 min. We calculated sway values that were obtained from stabilograms during/after exposure to video clips with/without the background (i.e. clouds in the sky/plain gray background).

The circle (I) was placed before the subjects, 2 m away, at their eye level. Stereoscopic video clips (II)/(III) and their monocular (2D) vision were shown to subjects on the binocular parallax 3D display. We measured the body sway and the subjective

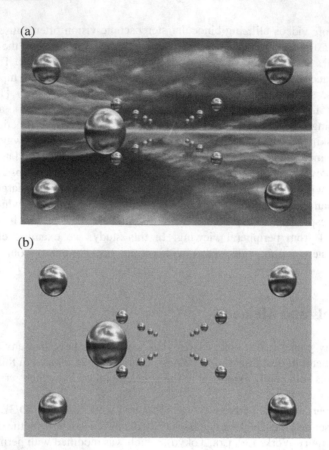

Fig. 1. One cut of the video clips with backgrounds (a) and without background (b)

evaluation for each vision (I) Control, (II)-2D, (II)-3D, (III)-2D, and (III)-3D situation randomly, according to the abovementioned protocol.

We conducted the stabilometry with eyes open/closed. The experimental periods with eyes open and closed was designed in our experimental protocol to evaluate the severity of the VIMS during and after viewing the video clips. In stabilometry, the COP on an x-y plane was recorded at each time step where x and y directions were defined as the right and the anterior planes on their faces, respectively. Stabilograms were obtained each experimental period from the time series of their COP. Finally, we calculated the new index sparse density (SPD) (See Appendix), and the previously stated sway values such as area of sway, total locus length, total locus length per unit area, defined in Suzuki *et al.* [6].

The aforementioned indices were calculated from each stabilogram recorded with the eyes open/closed. Any two of the following were assumed to be potentially important influencing factors: the solidity of the subjects' vision (2D/3D), existence of the backgrounds in the video clips, and persistency of the visual stimulus. A two-way analysis of variance (ANOVA) was conducted 15 times on these factors. In addition, the influence of the exposure to the video clips on our equilibrium system was investigated in comparison with the control data (I). The sway values during and after the viewing of the (I), (II)-2D, (II)-3D, (III)-2D, and (III)-3D stimuli were compared using Wilcoxon signed-rank tests for multiple comparisons.

3 Results and Discussion

Most stabilograms observed 0–2 min after viewing a 3D video clip with the background (II)-3D were dispersed compared with the control stabilograms. In contrast, no persistent tendency was observed in the stabilograms measured 2–3 min after the cutoff of the visual stimulus. However, most stabilograms observed 0–2 min after exposure to video clips without the background (III)-2D/3D were not dispersed compared with the control stabilograms. The stabilograms were dispersed three minutes after the cutoff of the visual stimulus.

The two-way ANOVA on the sway values did not reveal an interaction between any pair of two factors. According to the two-way ANOVA whose factors were set as the solidity and the persistency, the former primary effect was observed from the total locus length per unit area during/after viewing the video clips with the background. Furthermore, the main effect of the background presence was observed from the total locus length per unit area during/after exposure to a 2D video clip in accordance with two-way ANOVA, whose factors were set to be the presence of the background and the persistency of the visual stimulus. We also found the same main effect while calculating the SPD S_3 during/after exposure to a 3D video clip, in accordance with two-way ANOVA.

Post hoc tests of the total locus length indicated a significant difference between the control and (II)-3D stabilograms 1–2 min after viewing a 3D video clip with the background as shown in Post 1–2 in Fig. 2a. The latter was significantly greater than the control total locus length. One to two minutes after viewing the video clips, the total locus length for a stereoscopic video clip with the background (II)-3D was significantly greater than that for a 2D video (II)-2D (Figs. 2a, 3a).

As a result of post hoc tests of the SPD, the control equilibrium system was regarded to exhibit higher stability than that experienced after 0–1 min of exposure to a 3D video clip with the background (Fig. 2b). Moreover, the control equilibrium system was regarded to be more stable than that after 2–3 min of exposure to a 2D video clip without the background (Fig. 3b).

The other sway values, 0–2 min after the cutoff of the visual stimulus, also revealed that our equilibrium system was affected by the video clips with the background. The sway values 2–3 min after the cutoff of the visual stimulus suggested that our equilibrium system was affected by the video clips with/without the background (Fig. 3b). The persistency of the upright posture might deteriorate in our equilibrium function. Conversely, the effect of the exposure to the video clips on our equilibrium function can be continued for 0–2 min. In contrast, the sway values 0–2 min after the cutoff of

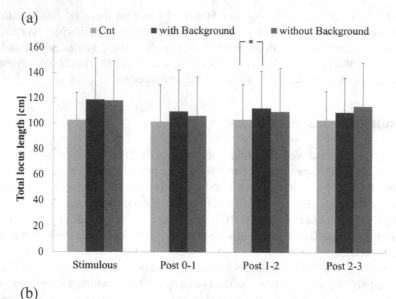

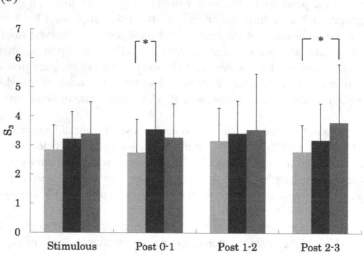

Fig. 2. Typical sway values during/after a 3D video clip: total locus length (a), SPD S_3 (b)

the visual stimulus suggested that our equilibrium system was not affected by the video clips without the background. Subjects tracked the sphere in the video clips owing to the absence of a background, and the VIMS did not occur by visual pursuit. Peripheral viewing could induce motion sickness, as our previous studies suggested. In future, we will discuss the metamorphism of the potential function (2) induced by this kind of VIMS.

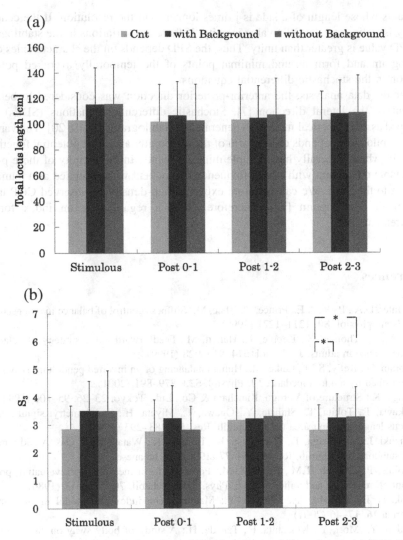

Fig. 3. Typical sway values during/after a 2D video clip: total locus length (a), SPD S_3 (b)

Acknowledgements. This work was supported in part by the Ministry of Education, Culture, Sports, Science and Technology, through a Grant-in-Aid for Scientific Research (C) (Number 26350004).

Appendix: Sparse Density

Herein, we describe the new quantification indices, sparse density (SPD) [18]. The SpD is defined as the average of the ratio $G_j(1)/G_j(k)$ for $j = 3, 4, \ldots, 20$, where $G_j(k)$ is the number of divisions with more than k measured points. A stabilogram is divided into quadrants whose length of a side is j times longer than the resolution. If the center of gravity is stationary, the SPD value is unity. If there are variations in the stabilograms, the SPD value is greater than unity. Thus, the SPD depends on the characteristics of the stabilogram and form around minimal points of the temporally averaged potential function in the stochastic differential equations.

For the data analysis, the anterior-posterior direction was considered to be independent of the lateral direction [7]. Stochastic differential equations (SDEs) were proposed as mathematical models to generate the stabilograms [8, 19, 20]. The variance in the stabilogram depends on the form of the temporally averaged potential function in the SDE, which generally has multiple minimal points. In the vicinity of these points, local stable movement with a high-frequency component was generated as a numerical solution to the SDE. We can therefore expect a high-density of observed COP in this area of the stabilogram [18]. Therefore, SPD is regarded as an index for this measurement.

References

1. Winter, D.A., Patla, A.E., Prince, F., Ishac, M.: Stiffness control of balance in quiet standing. J. Neurophysiol. **80**, 1211–1221 (1998)
2. Gatev, P., Thomas, S., Kepple, T., Hallett, M.: Feedforward ankle strategy of balance in quiet stance in adults. J. Physiol. **514**, 915–928 (1999)
3. Loram, D., Kelly, S.M., Laike, M.: Human balancing of an inverted pendulum: is sway size controlled by ankle impedance? J. Physiol. **523**, 879–891 (2001)
4. Kaga, K.: Structure of Vertigo. Kanehara & Co., Ltd., Tokyo, 23–26, 95–100 (1992)
5. Okawa, T., Tokita, T., Shibata, Y., Ogawa, T., Miyata, H.: Stabilometry: significance of locus length per unit area (L/A). Equilib. Res. **54**, 283–293 (1995)
6. Suzuki, J., Matsunaga, T., Tokumatsu, K., Taguchi, K., Watanabe, I.: Q & A and a manual in stabilometry. Equilib. Res. **55**, 64–77 (1996). (in Japanese)
7. Goldie, P.A., Bach, T.M., Evans, O.M.: Force platform measures for evaluating postural control: reliability and validity. Arch. Phys. Med. Rehabil. **70**, 510–517 (1986)
8. Takada, H., Kitaoka, Y., Shimizu, Y.: Mathematicha index and model in stabilometry. Forma **16**, 17–46 (2001)
9. Fukui, Y., Mori, Y., Kinoshita, F., Takada, H.: A study of body sway on slopes with tilt angles of 10° and 20°. IEICE Technical report 114 (361), 7–10 (2014)
10. Ukai, K., Howarth, P.A.: Visual fatigue caused by viewing stereoscopic motion images. Displays **29**, 106–116 (2008)
11. Kennedy, R.S., Lane, N.E., Berbaum, K.S., Lilienthal, M.G.: Simulator sickness questionnaire: an enhanced method for quantifying simulator sickness. Int. J. Aviat. Psychol. **3**, 203–220 (1993)
12. Holomes, S.R., Griffin, M.J.: Correlation between heart rate and the severity of motion sickness caused by optokinetic stimulation. J. Psychophysiol. **15**, 35–42 (2001)
13. Himi, N., Koga, T., Nakamura, E., Kobashi, M., Yamane, M., Tsujioka, K.: Differences in autonomic responses between subjects with and without nausea while watching an irregularly oscillating video. Auton. Neurosci. Basic Clin. **116**, 46–53 (2004)
14. Yokota, Y., Aoki, M., Mizuta, K.: Motion sickness susceptibility associated with visually induced postural instability and cardiac autonomic responses in healthy subjects. Acta Otolaryngol. **125**, 280–285 (2005)

15. Scibora, L. M., Villard, S., Bardy, B., Stoffregen, T. A.: Wider stance reduces body sway and motion sickness. In: Proceedings of VIMS, pp. 18–23 (2007)
16. Takada, M., Fukui, Y., Matsuura, Y., Sato, M., Takada, H.: Peripheral viewing during exposure to a 2D/3D video clip: effects on the human body. Environ. Health Prev. Med. (2014). doi:10.1007/s12199-014-0424-4
17. Takada, M., Miyao, M., Takada, H.: Subjective evaluation of peripheral viewing during exposure to a 2D/3D video clip. In: Proceedings of IEEE VR (2015) (to appear)
18. Takada, H., Kitaoka, Y., Ichikawa, M., Miyao, M.: Physical meaning on geometrical index for stabilometry. Equilib. Res. **62**, 168–180 (2003)
19. Newell, K.M., Slobounov, S.M., Slobounova, E.S., Molenaar, P.C.: Stochastic processes in postural center of pressure profiles. Exp. Brain Res. **113**, 158–164 (1997)
20. Collins, J.J., De Luca, C.J.: Open-loop and closed-loop control of posture: a random-walk analysis of center of pressure trajectories. Exp. Brain Res. **95**, 308–318 (1993)

Visual Pursuit of Two-Dimensional/Three-Dimensional Objects on Video Clips: Effects on the Human Body

Masumi Takada[1,2], Masaki Sakai[3], Masaru Miyao[4],
and Hiroki Takada[2,3(✉)]

[1] Chubugakuin University, Gifu, Japan
[2] Aichi Medical University, Aichi, Japan
takada@u-fukui.ac.jp
[3] Graduate School of Engineering, University of Fukui, Fukui, Japan
[4] Graduate School of Information Science, Nagoya University, Nagoya, Japan

Abstract. With the recent rapid progress in image processing and three-dimensional (3D) technology, stereoscopic images are visible on television and in theaters and game machines, etc. However, 3D sickness symptoms, such as intoxication and eye fatigue, have been observed when viewing 3D films, depending on display and visual environment conditions. Further, the effect of stereoscopic vision on the human body has not been explored sufficiently. Therefore, to clarify its effects on the human body in society at large, it is important to consider the safety of viewing virtual 3D content. This present study aimed to examine the effects of peripheral viewing on the human body, specifically during exposure to two-dimensional (2D)/3D video clips. We compared stabilograms recorded during exposure to video clips with or without visual pursuit of a 3D object using two-way analysis of variance. Using statistical analysis, we found that our equilibrium is significantly affected by the background after exposure to the video clips.

Keywords: Visually induced motion sickness (VIMS) · Visual pursuit · Peripheral viewing · Stabilometry

1 Introduction

In recent times, the familiarity towards three-dimensional (3D) images has increased greatly because 3D movie contents providing binocular parallax are loaded onto different sources of amusement, such as cinema, home television, and game machines. Although the visual presence has been enhanced by the progress in 3D technology, which enables portrayal of movie scenes more realistically, each merit has its demerit. In this case, motion sickness is induced while viewing stereoscopic video clips [1].

© Springer International Publishing Switzerland 2015
M. Antona and C. Stephanidis (Eds.): UAHCI 2015, Part II, LNCS 9176, pp. 264–272, 2015.
DOI: 10.1007/978-3-319-20681-3_25

Watching 3D movies, though, can produce certain adverse effects such as asthenopia and motion sickness [2]. It has been considered that this visually induced motion sickness (VIMS) is caused by the sensory conflict that results from the disagreement between convergence and visual accommodation while viewing 3D images [3]. Thus, stereoscopic images have been devised to reduce this disagreement [4, 5]. In this paper, we also examine whether the VIMS is caused by this kind of the sensory conflict.

However, it is still unclear how long the duration of the impact of the mild symptoms induced by peripherally viewing of the 3D video clips are remained on our equilibrium systems. In order to approach the mechanism, we investigated the relationship among the body sway, visual function, and head posture while viewing stereoscopic video clips. Until recently, it has been believed that our convergence adjusts to virtual depth popped up from 3D TV screen, whereas human beings focus on the surface of the display during stereoscopic vision. It is generally explained that, "During the stereoscopic vision, accommodation and convergence are mismatched, and this is the main reason for the visual fatigue caused by viewing 3D video clips". According to the findings presented in our previous report [6], however, such explanations are incorrect. We developed a new device that can simultaneously measure accommodation and convergence. As a result, lens accommodation is considered to be consistent with convergence because the accommodation does not adjust to the surface of the display, but adjusts to the virtual depth during the stereoscopic vision [7].

The recent widespread use of stereoscopic vision facilitates provision of virtual reality and sensation; however, as discussed, since long, there has been concern over the symptoms caused by stereoscopic vision. Accordingly, in the present study, we have examined whether our visual and equilibrium systems are affected by an hour-long session of stereoscopic viewing [8, 9]. In an earlier study by Yoshikawa et al. [9], the sway values measured after visual pursuit of the stereoscopic sphere in a video clip tended to become smaller than those after (peripheral) viewing without purposeful pursuit of the object. In addition, when the subjects were not allowed to fix the point of gaze as they wished, they looked at the objects with different virtual depth. Especially in the background, there are large difference between human binocular image and artificial stereoscopic image to which our convergence corresponding to depth cues is not accommodated. Each time subjects change their point of gaze, interaction occurs between systems to control accommodation and convergence. A state of non-equilibrium in the control system for visual information processing imposes additional load on the human body. Further, the intermittent inconsistency between accommodation and convergence is considered to cause imbalance in our autonomic nervous system. That is why equilibrium function affect from peripheral viewing. In this paper, we examine effect of the exposure to stereoscopic video clips without the background on our equilibrium function.

In order to examine this hypothesis, we measured the severity of the influence of peripheral viewing, which is expected to cause uncomfortable symptoms of motion sickness, and compare it with the influence of the visual pursuit of a virtual object on the equilibrium function.

2   Materials and Methods

Eight men (mean ± standard deviation, 22.6 ± 0.7 yrs.), who may have had any otorhinolaryngologic or neurological diseases in the past, participated in this study. The experiment was sufficiently explained to the subjects, following which written consent was obtained from them. The research was approved by the Ethics Committee in Graduate School of Information Science, Nagoya University.

In this experiment, the body sway was measured while viewing 2D/3D video clips. The subjects stood on the detection stand of a stabilometer GS3000 (Anima Co. Ltd., Tokyo), without moving, with their feet together in the Romberg posture, for 30 s before the sway was recorded. Each sway of the COP was then recorded at a sampling frequency of 20 Hz. The subjects were instructed to maintain the Romberg posture during the trials. For the first 60 s, the subjects were asked to do the following:

I.   Gaze at a static circle with a diameter of 3 cm (Control).
II. Follow a sphere which complexly ambulated in a video clip (Fig. 1).
III. Peripherally view the same video clip as shown in (II) without pursuing the sphere on the 40-inch display KDL 40HX80R (Sony, Tokyo).

That is, we categorized the visual sighting method as pursuit (II) and peripheral viewing (III). Subjects gazed at a point of fixation (I) or video clips (II)/(III) with their eyes open for the first 60 s, after which they closed their eyes for 60 s.

The circle (I) was placed before the subjects, 2 m away, at their eye level. Stereoscopic video clips (II)/(III) and their monocular (2D) vision were shown to subjects on the binocular parallax 3D display. The content in the "SkyCrystal" (Olympus Memory Works Ltd. Co., Tokyo) was modified, with permission from the company, and used as the visual stimulus in this experiment. The stimulus includes spheres fixed in four corners, which supplies perspective. We measured the body sway and the subjective evaluation for each vision (I) Control, (II)-2D, (II)-3D, (III)-2D, and (III)-3D situation randomly, according to the abovementioned protocol.

We conducted the stabilometry with eyes open/closed. The experimental periods with eyes open and closed was designed in our experimental protocol to evaluate the

Fig. 1. One cut of the video clips [10]

severity of the VIMS during and after viewing the video clips. In stabilometry, the COP on an x-y plane was recorded at each time step where x and y directions were defined as the right and the anterior planes on their faces, respectively. Stabilograms were obtained each experimental period from the time series of their COP. Finally, we calculated the new index SPD, and the previously stated sway values such as area of sway, total locus length, total locus length per unit area, defined in Suzuki et al. [11].

The abovementioned indices were calculated from each stabilogram recorded with the eyes open and closed. Two-way analysis of variance (ANOVA) was conducted for 8 repeated values and used to determine solidity of the subjects' vision (2D/3D) and their vision method (visual pursuit versus peripheral viewing), which were assumed to be important influencing factors. In addition, the influence of exposure to video clips on our equilibrium system was investigated and compared with the control data (I). The sway values during and after viewing the (I), (II)-2D, (II)-3D, (III)-2D, and (III)-3D stimuli were compared using Wilcoxon signed-rank tests for multiple comparisons.

3   Results

With the eyes open, most stabilograms observed during peripheral viewing of the 2D/3D video clips were widely scattered on the plane, compared with the control stabilograms. In contrast, there was no consistent tendency in the stabilograms taken when the subjects' eyes were closed. Moreover, most stabilograms taken during and after exposure to the video clips were dispersed in comparison to the control stabilograms. The sway values when the subjects' eyes were open were calculated from the stabilograms. Except for the total locus length per unit area, the control sway values were smaller than those obtained from stabilograms recorded during exposure to the 2D/3D video clips (Fig. 2).

The two-way ANOVA on sway values did not reveal any interaction between the two factors: solidity of the subjects' vision (2D/3D) and their vision method (visual pursuit/peripheral viewing), except for the total locus length per unit area. Therefore, the total locus length per unit area was excluded as an analytical index for stabilogram. No main effect resulted from stabilometry with the eyes open. However, the main effect of solidity of the subjects' vision was obtained from the SPD S_3, S_5 ($p < 0.1$) and the area of sway ($p < 0.05$) in stabilograms taken with the eyes closed.

The sway values during the exposure to the video clips (II)-2D, (II)-3D, (III)-2D, and (III)-3D were compared with the control (I) using the Wilcoxon signed-rank test. With the eyes open (Fig. 2a, b), the area of sway, total locus length, and SPD for the control were significantly smaller than those obtained from stabilograms during exposure to the video clips ($p < 0.05$). Further, there were no significant differences between any values for stabilograms taken during the exposure to the 2D and 3D video clips.

With the eyes closed (Fig. 3a, b), the abovementioned sway values obtained from stabilograms recorded during peripheral viewing of the stereoscopic video clip (III)-3D were also significantly greater than those obtained from the other conditions (I) and

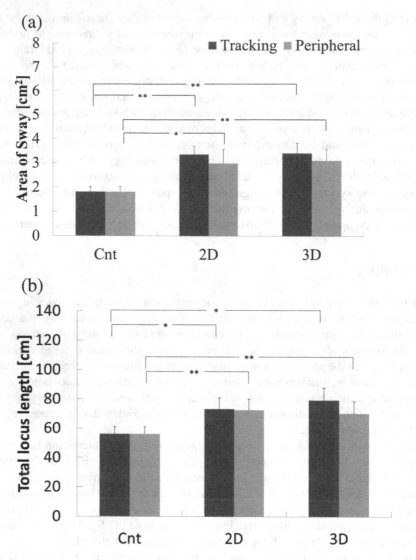

Fig. 2. Typical sway values with the eyes open: Area of sway (a), Total locus length (b)

(III)-2D. The sway values for visual pursuit of the 2D/3D sphere did not differ from those of the control, whereas a significant influence was seen when stabilometry was conducted with the subject's eyes open (Fig. 2a, b). The subjects' equilibrium after peripheral viewing of the 3D video clip was significantly less stable than that after peripheral viewing of the 2D clip. The control equilibrium system was more stable than that during peripheral viewing of the stereoscopic video clip.

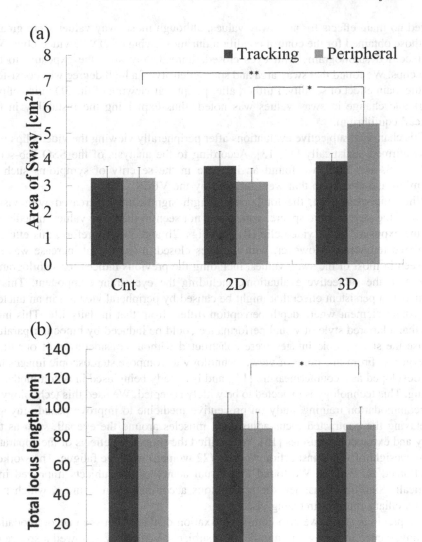

Fig. 3. Typical sway values with the eyes closed: Area of sway (a), Total locus length (b)

4 Discussion

In this paper, we examined whether exposure to stereoscopic video clips could induce motion sickness and could worsen according to the vision method. Solidity of the subjects' vision (2D/3D) and their vision method (visual pursuit/peripheral viewing) were assumed to be influencing factors for the equilibrium function and were examined using two-way ANOVA for the body sway. When eyes were kept open, these factors showed no main effects for any sway values, although most sway values were greater than those obtained for the control condition during viewing of 2D/3D video clips. We also recorded stabilograms with eyes closed, immediately after the exposure to the video clips. We found that sway area and sparse density of a high degree was consistent with the main effect of solidity. Further, after peripheral viewing of the 3D video clip, a remarkable change in sway values was noted, thus explaining the instability in the subjects' equilibrium.

This change in subjective evaluations after peripherally viewing the video clips was also confirmed statistically [12, 13]. According to the analysis of the SSQ sub-score N, OD, TS, and VAS, we found an increase in the severity of symptoms such as discomfort and eye strain that were induced by the VIMS.

When the eyes open, the total locus length significantly increased with visual pursuit of the stereoscopic sphere, which was not seen in the sway value immediately after the exposure to the video clip (II)-3D (Figs. 2b and 3b). Therefore, this effect is considered temporary. However, with the eyes closed, a significant increase was not only seen in most of the sway values, including the previous indices for stabilograms, but also in the subjective evaluations, including the eye strain component. This is regarded as a persistent effect that might be caused by peripheral viewing in an unclear background element where depth perception differs from that in daily life. This indicates that a labored style of visual performance could be induced by binocular parallax because the stereoscopic images were constructed without consideration of our finite convergence. From this point of view, technology to compose stereoscopic images has been developed as a countermeasure [14], and is already being used in accommodation training. This technology is expected to be widely accepted. We used this technology in an accommodation training study on preventive medicine to improve pseudo-myopia by relaxing the contracted focus-adjustment muscles around the eyeball, such as the ciliary and extraocular muscles [15]. We verified the short-term effects of the apparatus on the eyesight of visual inspection workers (22 women) with eye fatigue. The workers were trained for 3 days. We found that visual acuity of the subjects improved in a statistically significant manner after continuous accommodation training, which promoted a ciliary muscle-stretching effect.

In a previous study, we also compared fixation distances between accommodation and convergence in young and middle-aged subjects, while they followed a sphere on 2D/3D video clips used in the present study [16]. Both groups of subjects showed roughly similar results. Fixation distances among accommodation, convergence, and depth map (theoretical distance of the surfaces of objects) were compared while the subjects tracked on the sphere in the video clip (II)-3D on LCD, and measurements were repeated. There were no differences between visual accommodation and convergence for the first 60 s of continuously viewing 3D images. However, an inconsistency was gradually observed, and we found delay in accommodation variations of the middle-aged subjects, indicating that subjects' accommodation and convergence when viewing 3D images changed the diopter value, which is synchronous with the movement of the 3D images. However, lens accommodation was not consistent with convergence in the middle-aged subjects after gazing at the 3D video clips for 90 s, although subjects in this study did not follow the stereoscopic sphere for more than 90 s. The abovementioned inconsistency was not considerable, indicating that this inconsistency between the lens accommodation and convergence may not be the cause of 3D sickness.

In this study, the influence of the vision method, i.e., visual pursuit and peripheral viewing, on our equilibrium systems during and after viewing 2D/3D video clips was examined. We found that regardless of the vision method followed by the subject, sway values were greater during viewing of 2D/3D video clips than those during viewing in the controls. Systems that help control upright posture tended to become unstable during exposure to the video clips. In addition to deterioration in equilibrium, subjectively increased exacerbation of uncomfortableness was observed after peripheral viewing of the video clips compared with to that after viewing clips involving visual pursuit of the sphere. This is regarded as persistent influence that might be caused by peripheral viewing in an unclear background elements due to their depth perception that differ from those observed in daily life. VIMS might be caused by an overload of visual information.

Acknowledgements. This work was supported in part by the Ministry of Education, Culture, Sports, Science and Technology, Grant-in-Aid for Scientific Research (B) Number 24300046 and (C) Number 26350004.

References

1. Malik, A.S., Choi, T.S., Nisar, H. (eds.): Depth Map and 3D Imaging Applications: Algorithms and Technologies. Proc IGI Global, Hershey (2011)
2. Takada, H., Fujikake, K., Miyao, M., Matsuura,Y.: Indices to detect visually induced motion sickness using stabilometry. In: Proceedings of VIMS 2007, pp. 178-83 (2007)
3. Wann, J., Rushton, S., Williams, M.: Natural problems for stereoscopic depth perception in virtual environments. Vis. Res. **35**, 2731–2736 (1995)
4. Yasui, R., Matsuda, I., Kakeya, H.: Combining volumetric edge display and multiview display for expression of natural 3d images. In: Proceedings of SPIE, vol. 6055, pp. 0Y1–0Y9 (2006)
5. Kakeya, H.: MOEVision: simple multiview display with clear floating image. In: Proceedings of SPIE, vol. 6490, p. 64900 J (2007)
6. Miyao, M., Ishihara, S., Saito, S., Kondo, T., Sakakibara, H., Toyoshima, H.: Visual accommodation and subject performance during a stereographic object task using liquid crystal shutters. Ergonomics **39**, 1294–1309 (1996)
7. Shiomi, T., Uemoto, K., Kojima, T., Sano, S., Ishio, H.: Simultaneous measurement of lens accommodation and convergence in natural and artificial 3D vision. J. Soc. Inf. Disp. **21**, 120–128 (2013)
8. Takada, M., Murakami, K., Kunieda, Y., Hirata, T., Matsuura, Y., Iwase, S., Miyao, M.: Effect of hour-long stereoscopic film on equilibrium function. In: Proceedings of IMID Digest, pp. 737–738 (2011)
9. Yoshikawa, K., Takada, H., Miyao, M.: Effect of display size on body sway in seated posture while viewing an hour-long stereoscopic film. In: Stephanidis, C., Antona, M. (eds.) UAHCI 2013, Part II. LNCS, vol. 8010, pp. 336–341. Springer, Heidelberg (2013)

10. Yamaguchi, H., Sakai, M., Hirata, T., Takada, H.: Effects of Peripheral Viewing on Human body During Exposure to 2D/3D Video Clips. IEICE Technical report, MBE2013, 11–14 (2013) (in Japanese)

11. Suzuki, J., Matsunaga, T., Tokumatsu, K., Taguchi, K., Watanabe, I.: Q & A and a manual in stabilometry. Equilib. Res. **55**, 64–77 (1996) (in Japanese)

12. Takada, M., Fukui, Y., Matsuura, Y., Sato, M., Takada, H.: Peripheral viewing during exposure to a 2D/3D video clip: effects on the human body. Environ. Health Prev. Med. **20**, 79–89 (2014). doi:10.1007/s12199-014-0424-4

13. Takada, M., Miyao, M., Takada, H.: Subjective evaluation of peripheral viewing during exposure to a 2D/3D video clip. In: Proceedings of IEEE VR (2015) (to appear)

14. Nishihira, T., Tahara, H.: Apparatus for Recovering Eyesight Utilizing Stereoscopic Video and method for Displaying Stereoscopic Video. US Patent US7404693B2 (2002)

15. Takada, M., Miyao, M., Satoh, M., Yoshikawa, K., Matsuura, Y., Takada, H.: Effect of accommodation training on visual function of visual inspection workers and middle-aged people. J. Sports Med. Doping Study **2** (2012). doi:10.4172/2161-0673.1000112

16. Takada, M., Uemoto, K., Miyao, M., Matsuura, Y., Satoh, M., Takada, H.: Comparison of fixation distances in middle-aged subjects. Int. J. Biosci. Biochem. Bioinforma. **2**, 389–394 (2013)

Texture Recognition for Users with Color Vision Deficiencies

Fong-Gong Wu[✉], Erica Huang, and Chao-Yuan Tseng

Department of Industrial Design, National Cheng Kung University,
Tainan, Taiwan
Fonggong@mail.ncku.edu.tw

Abstract. In this study, we designed a new type of primary color recognition assistive system for this user group, adding (1) directly perceived labels (the label group), (2) shape and color related dots (the dot group), or (3) distinctive vein lines (the vein group) to help with the recognition of primary colors red, green, and blue. Verification and evaluation were done for each part of the results, in order to describe the accuracy and feasibility of each system. The study has been divided into two phases. The first phase is the preliminary experiment, in which the label group investigates and verifies the objects that represent each of the primary colors and transforms into representative labels. The second phase employs the results of the preliminary experiment from the three groups onto colored cards, forming experiment group through color vision deficiency simulators, then issue out questionnaires of performance evaluation and subjective preferences for each group. Experiment results show that regardless of group, there was significant help in color recognition, decreasing the recognition error rate and task completion time. In terms of subjective questionnaires, participants believe that the difficulty level of primary color recognition evidently decreased, with an average preference of 6 and above.

Keywords: Color vision · Color vision deficiency · Texture composition

1 Introduction

About $8 \sim 10$ % male and 0.45 % female are affected by certain level of color recognition disability [1, 2]. Unable to recognize the correct color would cause inconvenience or even danger in life, with examples of the recognition of traffic lights and labels on medication packages. Limitations exist at work too, such as occupations in medicine, chemistry, electric engineering, and painting.

Currently in clinical medicine, human color vision deficiency can only be detected but not treated. Supplementary instruments such as the color blind simulator, the color blind glasses [3]., and the appearance enhancement are used [4]. These supplementary technologies mainly reconstruct the information of the original image and color into color ranges able to be seen by the color vision challenged. This can act as supplementary reference for graphic and web designers while selecting colors. However, the help in solving the problems in everyday life is still limited.

© Springer International Publishing Switzerland 2015
M. Antona and C. Stephanidis (Eds.): UAHCI 2015, Part II, LNCS 9176, pp. 273–284, 2015.
DOI: 10.1007/978-3-319-20681-3_26

Masataka brought forward in 2002, that different background texture can be added to unrecognizable color ranges to allow users with mild color-blind symptoms to distinguish the boundary line between different color regions [5]. However, the above mentioned method is yet to be organized into a systematic color recognition related texture or label for designers to search. Hence, although the color vision challenged can successfully recognize the boundary between color regions, they can not systematically tell what color each texture represents. For example, to distinguish between red and green pills in a first-aid kit, if dots are added to the red ones while check patterns are added to the green ones, then the two could be distinguished. However, users still can not tell which is red and which is green, unless he knew in advance that the dots represent red and the checks represent the green.

The current design solution for the color vision challenged is mostly adjusting to the colors recognizable by them. However, this would affect the vision for the other users. Some employs different shapes to represent different messages or adding frames to text and icons with a background color. Changing shapes, which is adding shape as an identifying element, is the most commonly suggested solution. However, this can only be used in the graphic design field such as item connections [6].

In addition, adding frames is commonly used to colored texts since when only different colors are used to differentiate between text and background color, it causes the color vision challenged difficulty in reading.

The Color Universal Design Organization in Japan, CUDO in short [7] mainly aims at solving inconvenience for the color vision challenged. They reward designs on the market for the color vision challenged and bring forward design suggestions and color selection standards. Most of the CUDO approved designs commonly use (1) Changing colors to avoid the colors that cause confusion for the color vision challenged; (2) Increasing the brightness and the hue; (3) Changing the color combination or enhancing the frame; these are done to make identification easier. However, changing the colors would sometimes affect the visual for common users or the performance of the colors.

The aim of this research is to solve the confusion the color vision challenged have with the three primary colors, to proceed with experiment and analysis according to the problem descriptions, hoping to achieve the following goals:

- Under the precondition of not influencing the visual of common users, using the principle of color dithering, adding tiny color dots to construct a dithering ratio for the new three primary colors.
- Evaluate whether the new color recognition supplementary system reliably increase the color recognition level of the color vision challenged.

2   Methods

This study employs the principle of color dithering, adding tiny colored dots to the primary colors. These tiny dots are undetected by people with normal visions, hence does not significantly affect the presentation and recognition of colors. However, for the color-blind, they are able to tell the different in texture.

This study is divided into three main parts. The first part adds icons to the corner of each color chip as labels. This part employs the color association theory of color psychology, using the experiment procedures and confusion matrix brought forward by Kaneko to evaluate. Selecting icons related to each primary color, we then employ the selected icons to proceed with tests.

The second part uses the principle of visual dithering, adding tiny dots to primary colors. People with normal visions are able to use the shape of the dots to recognize the real color. The third part adds tiny colored dots on the picture, using repeated dot patterns to create different texture (veins), using the existence of distinctive veins as the supplementary assistance in color recognition.

This study employs ColorDoctor, the color blind simulator, to simulate the color cards for the experiment. People with normal color visions were selected to avoid the established impression the color vision deficient have towards colors after a long term of trial and error experience and hence the difficulty to measure the difference this new type of assistive system brings. People with normal visions have no obvious association towards the colors seen by the color blind. Hence in the experiment, regardless of which assistive method is used, the color itself would not affect the judgment of users. The development of this new type of system aims at helping the color vision challenged people of all ages and levels to achieve more convenience in life.

2.1   Label Group – Preliminary Test

- *Label Group – Collection of the associative objects of the three primary colors*

According to the previously mentioned theories, participants were free to associate the colors with any concrete objects, such as sun for yellow and heart for red. The test was done on participants between $20 \sim 40$ years old with the study procedure showing in Fig. 1. The first step of this experiment employed open questionnaire to collect all the concrete objects associated, then uses ranking method to select the 5 associated objects that come in the highest frequency. Participants of this step were selected to be designers or design students with at least a year of related background and were told in advance that the aim of the experiment and the use of these associative objects before asking them to write down five appropriate objects.

The results of the concrete object investigation are shown in Table 1. Since part of the participants were trained design-related workers and the aim and study goal were told, most of the objects of the highest frequencies were natural scenery objects without concepts of culture or habits. These concepts were developed and drawn into icons afterwards.

- *Label Group – Confirmation of concrete object and color association*

Through induction and arrangements, the icon selections of the associative objects were drawn. In order to increase experiment accuracy, different icons were drawn for each object for selection. The associative objects were proceeded with confusion matrix, asking participants to match the objects with the subjective associated color,

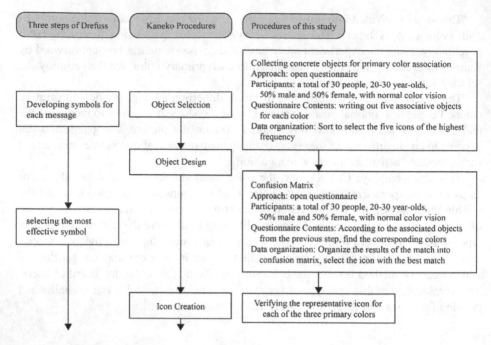

Fig. 1. Experiment parameters and procedures for the confirmation of associative objects of the three primary colors.

Table 1. Results of the concrete object investigation

Color	Associated concrete objects(with the highest frequency)
Red	Apple, heart shape, fire, blood, sun
Green	Tree, mountain, grass, leaf
Blue	Ocean, snow, wave, water

and evaluate the checked color and its icon for $0 \sim 10$ points showing the level of representation of each icon. In this experiment, the questionnaires contain only the answering instructions, questions, and black icons to avoid influence of colored icons.

- *Label Group – Confirmation of the representative icons for the three primary colors*

Descriptive statistics were done to the questionnaire results done in step two, selecting the icons with the most color-icon connections (most votes) and the highest points in the representative grading. Table 2 shows the icons and results of the questionnaire (only the five icons with the most votes). The selected icons for each color were heart for red, tree for green, and water drop for blue. We concluded these three icons to be the representative icon for each of the three primary colors as the basis for further experiments.

Table 2. Dot color selection direction

Background color	Dot color selection direction	Dot colors seen by the color blind	Dot shapes (Item)
Red	Purple-red	First and second color blind: blue	Square
Green	Blue-green	First and second color blind: blue	Triangle
Blue	Blue-purple	Third color blind: red	Circle

2.2 Dot Group – Preliminary Test

- *Dot Group – Constructing dot diagrams*

The second part of this study integrates concepts of color-icon association and dithering, constructing dotted diagrams for the three primary colors. The first step is the establishment of a program to construct dots. The contents of the program are as follow:

- Produces dot diagrams with assigned color backgrounds. The dot shapes include squares, rounded triangles, and circles.
- Adjustable dot colors, sizes, and densities.
- Output dot diagrams as picture files and keeps a record of the diagram parameters.

Color dithering I used to adjust the color of the dots to avoid influence on people with normal color visions while the color vision challenged can tell the colors according to the Fig. 2. The color selection directions are shown in Table 2 (Fig. 3).

Based on the dot selection direction described above, integrating with the color resemblance suggestions (mono mode) from the Color Scheme Designer website, selecting three dot colors for the dots corresponding to the three primary colors for further experiments. The size, density, and color selected for the dots are listed in Table 3. In order to find the most compatible arrangement without influencing people

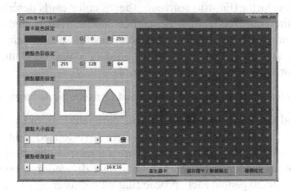

Fig. 2. Dot out program image (Color figure online)

Fig. 3. Dot diagram generated by the program (not the original size) (Color figure online)

Table 3. Dot Group Preliminary Test – Colored Cards Selection Combination

Chip color	Dot shape	Dot size (multiple)	Dot density (level)	Dot color (RGB)
Red	Square	3	8 × 8	210.0.137
		4	12 × 12	170.40.101
		5	16 × 16	212.91.148
		6	20 × 20	
Green	Rounded triangle			0.166.120
				48.191.152
				53.211.167
Blue	Circle			95.53.212
				120.48.191
				84.0.166

Note 1: The original color chip with dots output by the program is 8 cm^2.
Note 2: The dot size multiples are calculated by: Length of color chip (8 cm) ÷100 = diagonal length of square dot (1x) = distance of center to top vertex of rounded triangle dot (1x) = radius of round dot (1x).
Note 3: Dot density level calculation: 8 × 8 meaning dividing the color chipinto64 squares, where the center of the dots line up to define the center of the square. The same goes for 12 × 12, 16 × 16, and 20 × 20.

with normal color visions while the color blind can recognize the dot shapes, we use the program to produce 48 primary colored cards according to dot size, density, and color arrangements.

Using the ColorDoctor (Fujitsu) software, the 48 color cards described above were simulated under the color recognition deficiency mode. That is, red chip using first primary color blind mode simulation, green chip using second primary color blind mode simulation, and blue chip using third primary color blind mode simulation, producing 48 color cards after simulation (Fig. 4).

- *Dot Group – Dot diagram continuity interval approach clustering investigation*

In order to find the best combination of dots compatible to our goal, in this stage, the primary color and simulated color cards were investigated using the continuity interval clustering investigation. Participants were a total of 40 people between 20 ~ 30 years old with normal color visions. Participants were divided into original group and simulation group with 20 people each, proceeding with clustering of the 48 color cards. Since it is a large sample, in order to pursue the accuracy of clustering, we used two

Fig. 4. Dot diagram after ColorDoctor program simulation (Color figure online)

levels of hierarchical clustering, clustering the color cards into three groups first, then further cluster into three groups within each cluster, obtaining nine color cards in total, as shown in Fig. 5.

The original group of participants clustered following the principle of "dot influencing visual". The participants filled in group nine to group one following the order of most influence to the least. The simulation group of participants clustered following the principle of "clearly seeing dot shapes". They filled in group nine to group one following the order of the clearest shape to the least clear Fig. 6.

The clustering results were compared to our experiment goal, extracting group one to three from the original group, that is, the cards from the three groups of the least influence, giving 3 points, 2 points, and 1 point respectively. We also extracted cards from groups 7 to 9 of the simulation group, giving 1 point, 2 points, and 3 points respectively, as shown in diagram 3−9.The color cards with the heist points are shown in Tables 2, 3 and 4. We have obtained the best combination of dots for each color as the basis for further experiments.

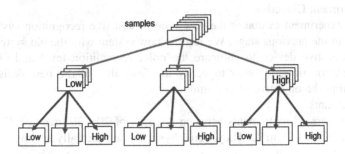

Fig. 5. Continuity interval clustering

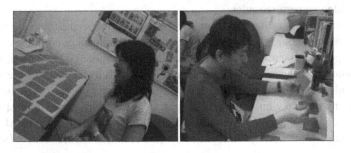

Fig. 6. Continuity interval clustering experiment scene

Table 4. Results of color chip clustering experiment

Color	Dot size (multiple)	Dot density (level)	Dot color (RGB)
Red	5	8 × 8	170.40.101
Green	4	8 × 8	0.166.120
Blue	4	8 × 8	84.0.166

2.3 Experiment Verification and Evaluation

Three indices were used to rate the performance of the results. They are

- Reaction time: the time required for users to complete a certain task.
- Accuracy rate: The rate of users completing a certain task accurately.
- Preference: user's preference during the operation process.

In this study, we employed the three performance indices mentioned above, applying individual results from the preliminary experiments onto color cards, evaluate the recognition error rate and time and feasibility. This section is the analysis of results, comparing the error rate and recognition time of the new primary color assistive system with the original system without any supplements as the verification of the advantage of the new design. The subjective questionnaire evaluation was also integrated to further evaluate the advantages, disadvantages, and user preference between groups as the reference for further designs.

- *Primary color recognition assistive system performance evaluation experiment.*

   (a) Experiment Objective
   This experiment evaluates the new type of assistive recognition system developed in the previous stage. We test the new system with the old system without any assistive device to compare the color recognition level and observe the recognition time, in order to verify the feasibility of the new design, further reaching the objective of our study.

   (b) Participants
   There were 30 participants between the ages of $20 \sim 30$ (average 22.87 years), 15 male and 15 female. They were physically and mentally healthy with normal visions.

   (c) Experiment equipment and location planning
   - Laptop (Sony VGN-SR15T)
   - Video camera recorder
   - Location: *Lighting*: Different light resources influence the color recognition reaction of our visual system. Therefore, under ideal conditions, color related experiments are required to be under the standard D65 (annotation) light source. Since this ideal light source is difficult to control, for the objectivity and enhance, we conducted the experiment in a steady experiment space, using normal white fluorescent lighting and a computer to minimize the error in color enhancing. *Annotation*: The definition of the standard D65 light source is the average sunlight two hours after and before sunrise (with a color

temperature of 6500 K). *Seating*: Adjustable seating is available according to requirement. *Distance to the screen*: As shown in the following figure, the steady visual distance is 60 cm.

(d) Experiment color cards preparation

Five groups of color cards were used and labeled as group A ~ E, containing six basic color cards including red, green, blue, and orange, yellow, purple have been added to increase experiment complexity to avoid memory effect. Group A (original group) uses original colors; Group B (simulation group) uses color cards of Group A simulated using ColorDoctor simulator; Group C (label group) uses color cards of Group B adding labels obtained in the previous stage in the bottom right corner. For unification purposes, the orange, yellow, and purple cards have used the sun, star, and grape icons; Group D (dot group) uses color cards of Group A adding dot combination results obtained from 3-3. For unification purposes, trapezoid, triangle, and oval dots have been added to orange, yellow, and purple cards. Dot colors were orange-yellow, yellow-green, and dark blue respectively. The size and density of the dots were based on the dots on the green card with minor adjustments. The six dot diagrams were further simulated using ColorDoctor; Group E (vein group) uses the green card produced from 3−4 and the five other cards from Group B. Of the simulated color cards of Groups B to E, the red cards were simulated using first primary color blind mode, the green cards the second primary color blind mode, the blue cards the third primary color blind mode. As for the three other colors, considering there is a higher ratio of color vision deficiencies in the second color blind group, were simulated using the second primary color blind mode.

(e) Experiment Variables

Independent Variable: The experiment is divided into five stages according to groups A ~ E. In which Group A is the testifying group, testifying unobstructed color recognition from the participants. Group B is the control group, and Groups C, D, and E are experimental groups. Therefore the experiment variables are the addition of the new types of assistive systems C ~ E.

Dependent Variable: Recognition error rate, recognition time length, subjective preference questionnaire

- *Experiment task design*

  In this experiment, every participant is required to do the tests from Group A ~ E with 30 questions each. The questions include 10 questions of "select red", 10 of "select green", and 10 of "select blue" randomly. Four colored cards are shown in each question. Besides the correct answer, the other three cards were randomly chosen from the other five colors. The sequence of the four colored cards is also randomly arranged.

  To avoid the learning memory effect of experiment groups C, D, and E, these three groups are required to proceed according to the order to retain objectivity. There are 30 s break times in between each experiment for all groups to reduce the influence of visual fatigue.

- *Subjective evaluation questionnaire*

   After the above experiment, participants were asked to write a subjective evaluation questionnaire. This questionnaire focuses on the evaluation of color recognition difficulty and feasibility of each group (including practical level, immediate level, learning level, application level, appearance, and preference).

3 Result and Analysis

This research uses color recognition to study the feasibility of three new types of assistive system, recording task completion time, error rate, and subjective evaluation questionnaire. In this section, we analyze the results by comparing the performances between using the three types of assistive system and with no assistive system. The three types of assistive system are (1) adding color related labels (label group); (2) adding shape and color corresponding dots (dot group); (3) adding color related distinctive veins (vein group) respectively.

   The original color group (A) is the testifying group, therefore has not been listed into the statistic range. The Vein group (E) focuses the test on only the green color. Hence only the results of the green color tests are included in the statistics and discussions of average error rate, task completion time, and subjective questionnaire on difficulty.

4 Discussion and Conclusions

This study focuses on the three assistive system designed for the people with color vision deficiencies. The experiments results proved to be different from color recognition dependent only on memory or speculations. The probability of confusion has evidently decreased, and the accuracy rate increased. In addition, due to the assistive reference in color recognition, thinking time has largely decreased too.

   Responding to the research objective described in the first section, we obtain the three following:

- Obtaining from experiment the intuitive representative icon of each color (label group)
- Application of geometric figures representing each color (dot group)
- Adding the use of veins, yet to be applied to all colors (vein group)

   The three major color recognition assistive plans have the following advantages compared to the original:

- Lowered error rate. Participants were able to accurately select the corresponding colors.
- Shortened color recognition time and increased reaction speed.

   For red, there was a significant difference in the lowering of error rate in both label and dot groups. However, the dot shapes were difficult to differentiate, therefore the task completion time was not significantly lowered as in the label group, but slightly increased. This shows that the dot group requires further investigation and improvement. In terms of recognition difficulty, participants believe that adding labels or dots both significantly decrease difficulty, showing practical assistance from these two groups of assistive system.

For green, the accuracy rate significantly increased with the addition of assistive system. However, since the dot on the green cards (rounded triangles) and the yellow cards (equilateral triangles) are very similar, it requires careful observation to tell the difference, the recognition time of the dot group has on the contrary increased. This same reason could also have been the cause of a low accuracy rate but short completion time in the simulation group test as participants guessed instead of observed. There were significant differences in the influence of difficulty between the three groups and the simulation group. This means the addition of any of the groups would significantly lower the difficulty level. There was significant difference between the dot group and the other two groups, showing that the assistance of the dot group is less than the other two groups.

For blue, since the simulated blue cards (simulation group) shows a blue-green color in the visual of the people with normal visions, it is easily differentiated and closer to the original hue when compared to the other colors of the simulation group (red, orange, yellow, green). Hence in the test of the simulation group, the error rate of selecting blue would be lower than the error rate of selecting red or green. This may be the reason that in terms of error rate, there was no significant difference between the simulation group and the other two experimental groups. In terms of recognition time, the label group has evidently lowered the recognition time, while the dot group, similar to the results of the green color, the similarity in shape and size has caused an increase in time. There was significant difference in difficulty level between the simulation group and the other two experimental groups. This shows a significant assistance from the two experimental groups in lowering the recognition difficulty of blue cards. In addition, the significant difference between the two groups also showed that the dot group did not perform as well as the label group in terms of lowering difficulty levels.

The label group has filtered the icons through the preliminary test and confusion matrix, obtaining the final icons that are highly representative, intuitive, and perceivable. This has been proved in the verification test where the participants do not need to spend extra time to memorize and are able to associate the icons with colors immediately. This has resulted in the best achievements and the highest scores in the seven subjective satisfaction indices. However, due to its characteristics, the application of the icons is not as expected. The suggested applications are the outlines light signals, label (such as cold and hot water indicators), or education purposes. In addition, the labels can also be used on annotations such as clothing tags to help people with color vision deficiencies to select the right colors.

The tiny shapes and the similarity between the colors have lead to a longer recognition time. In the performance indices, even though the assistance in color recognition still exists, the performance and subjective evaluation scores were lower when compared to label and vein groups. This shows a need of improvement. There were also suggestions that the dot group would be more compatible to large areas than the label group since the labels are only shown in a corner, while the dots can be evenly distributed and therefore easily observed. In addition, for people with normal visions, the dot group has a less influence on the visual of the picture, and can be applied on filling of areas.

The vein group has currently being tested on the color green. Participants believe the assistance is not extensive enough, and has influenced the scores on the subjective evaluation questionnaires. However, looking at the error rate and completion time of the vein group, it does achieve immediate results and essential help in color recognition. The application of the vein group has its limitations. On top of the age limitations mentioned earlier, it is also limited to plain areas. Areas with multiple texture and veins, such as knitwear or leather, are not compatible. Participants suggested supplementary tactile assistance in daily life applications to show its assistance. The construction of vein styles for other colors also needs to be further discussed.

In conclusion, the addition of the new color recognition assistive system does effectively help in the recognition of the correct primary color. Each group has its characteristics, advantages and disadvantages that need to be used in the correct way and appropriate scenes to display its maximum performance. The goal is to use them so they do not influence the visual of the people with normal visions nor cause visual burden to the people with color vision deficiencies, reaching the goal of universal design.

References

1. Simunovic, M.: Colour vision deficiency. Eye **24**(5), 747–755 (2009)
2. Birch, J.: Diagnosis of defective colour vision. Oxford University Press, New York (1993)
3. Muttaqin, G. F., Suwandi, I.S.: Simulation system of color blind glasses by image processing. In: Electrical Engineering and Informatics (ICEEI) (2011)
4. CUDO. Color universal design handbook. CUDO, Japan (2006)
5. Okabe, M., Ito, K.: Color Universal Design (CUD)-How to make figures and presentations that are friendly to Colorblind people. (2008). http://jfly.iam.u-tokyo.ac.jp/color/index.html
6. Beveren, T.v. We are colorblind.com. http://wearecolorblind.com/
7. CUDO. Color Universal Design Organization. http://www.cudo.jp/index.html
8. Steven, H.S.: Visual Perception: A Clinical Orientation, pp. 6–9. McGraw-Hill Medical, New York (2010)
9. Kolb, H., et al.: WebVision (2009). http://webvision.med.utah.edu/

Measurement of Lens Accommodation During Viewing of DFD Images

Tatsuya Yamakawa[1], Hideaki Takada[2], Munekazu Date[2],
Takehito Kojima[1], Ichizo Morita[1], Yuma Honda[1],
and Masaru Miyao[1(✉)]

[1] Graduate School of Information Science, Nagoya University, Furo-cho,
Chikusa-ku, Nagoya, Aichi 464-8601, Japan
{t.yamakawa0128, tkojima45}@gmail.com,
ichizo@dpc.agu.ac.jp, honda.yuma@f.mbox.
nagoya-u.ac.jp, miyao@nagoya-u.jp
[2] NTT Media Intelligence Laboratories, Nippon Telegraph and Telephone
Corporation, 1-1Hikari-no-oka, Yokosuka, Kanagawa 239-0847, Japan
{takada.hideaki, date.munekazu}@lab.ntt.co.jp

Abstract. Recently, a stereoscopic technology called DFD (Depth-fused 3D) developed in NTT. With this method two images are overlapped, displaying two planes with different depths. Humans usually perceive such overlapped two images as one image with one depth. When Humans perceive the depth of the DFD image, it is assume that they use factors of depth perception, such as lens accommodation, convergence and binocular parallax. Researchers have studied depth perception factors during the viewing of DFD images. However, studies have not clarified the effects of viewing of DFD images on accommodation. In this study, we measured lens accommodation in subjects who gazed at DFD images. We verified that a viewer's lens accommodation can adjust to DFD images.

Keywords: Depth-fused 3D (DFD) · Lens accommodation · Luminance ratio

1 Introduction

Recently, manufacturers have introduced many stereoscopic 3D (3-dimensional) technologies. Examples of stereoscopic 3D technology include the binocular 3D method, which makes stereoscopic vision possible with binocular parallax, the multi-viewpoint method that enables viewers to see multiple viewpoints, and holography, which records light waves and reconstructs them. Stereoscopic technology called DFD (Depth-fused 3D) developed in NTT [1, 2]. With this method two images are overlapped, displaying two planes with different depths. Humans usually perceive such overlapped two images as one image with one depth. As shown in Fig. 1, the viewer interprets the depth by the effects of luminance on a plane. For example, if the image is displayed only on the rear plane, the luminance of front image is 0 %, and the luminance of rear image is 100 %. If the image is displayed only on the front plane, the luminance of front image is 100 %, and the luminance of rear image is 0 %. Both the luminance of front and rear images are

© Springer International Publishing Switzerland 2015
M. Antona and C. Stephanidis (Eds.): UAHCI 2015, Part II, LNCS 9176, pp. 285–296, 2015.
DOI: 10.1007/978-3-319-20681-3_27

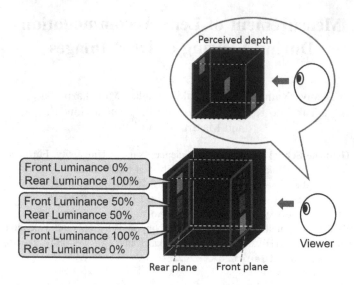

Fig. 1. Depth perception of DFD images

50 %, viewers perceive the DFD image with a depth perception just in the middle of the two planes. We can adjust the depth of the image by controlling the luminance ratio. These DFD images can be viewed without special glasses and is promising as a stereoscopic technology that is easy on the eyes [3, 4].

A DFD image is formed by a slight shift of the front and rear images. We can recognize the edge shift of the front and rear images as one virtual edge. When Humans perceive the depth of the DFD image, it is assume that they use factors of depth perception, such as lens accommodation, convergence and binocular parallax. Researchers have studied depth perception factors during the viewing of DFD images. However, studies have not clarified the effects of viewing of DFD images on accommodation. In this study, we measured accommodation in subjects who gazed at DFD images. We argue that the accommodation focus moves to the depth of the DFD images.

2   Method

2.1   Subjects

In this study, we measured subject's lens accommodation during the viewing of DFD images. We carried out experiments with 122 healthy subjects between the ages of 15 to 82 years. We gave detailed descriptions of the experiment to the subjects in advance to obtain their informed consent. The study was approved by the ethics committee of the Graduate School of Information Science, Nagoya University.

The subjects were divided into the following four groups: young subjects (n = 30, 29 years of age or younger), young middle aged subjects (n = 30, 30–44 years of age), middle aged subjects (n = 46, 45–64 years of age), and elderly subjects (n = 16, 65 years of age or older). This grouping was done because the crystalline lens loses elasticity with age and the changes of their refractive power also decreases [5, 6].

- Young subjects: The young group had sufficient accommodative power.
- Young middle aged subjects: The young middle aged group had somewhat weak accommodative power and did not suffer from presbyopia.
- Middle aged subjects: The middle-aged group had mild difficulty in seeing near objects because of presbyopia.
- Elderly subjects: The elderly group had severe presbyopia, and felt difficulty in seeing near objects.

2.2   Measurement Instrument

We used an auto ref/keratometer WAM-5500 made by Shigiya Machinery Works, Ltd. in this experiment., As shown in Fig. 2, this instrument can measure the refractive value (accommodation value) of a single eye when the subject gazes at a target at a given distance at a sampling frequency of 5 Hz.

Because the distance between two planes is very narrow (about 5–10 cm), it is difficult to detect the movement of accommodation focus with our instrument. Thus, we proposed the binocular DFD method to widen the distance between two planes [7].

2.3   Binocular DFD Method

If a edge shift becomes large, it is difficult to perceive the DFD image as a single image at one depth, as shown in Fig. 3 [8], and it is difficult to increase the interval between two planes. Thus, we combined the circular polarized 3D method and the DFD method to widen the distance between two planes. We defined this method as binocular DFD. This is a stereoscopic method to separate the left and right images using the filter through a different circularly polarized light, which allows for a binocular parallax.

There is no edge shift in the front and rear images displayed by binocular DFD for right eye, but there is a luminance ratio. The images for the left eyes are the same. These images were delivered to each eye through the circular polarized filter. This

Fig. 2. WAM-5500

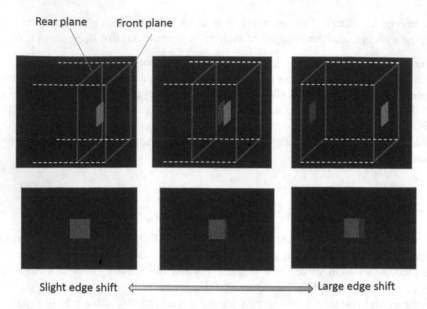

Fig. 3. Depth separation of DFD image

method is artificially possible and allows fort the appearance of the DFD images to fuse the images in the brain. In the case of binocular DFD method, it is necessary to consider that the edge of two images reflected in each eye does not increase. Hence, we must display the binocular DFD image with an appropriate parallax corresponding to the pupillary distance of the subject. Thus, we measured the pupillary distance of the subjects before taking the measurement of their lens accommodation. During a measurement of the pupillary distance, subjects gazed an image of a white spot on a black background displayed on the rear plane at 1.0 D.

2.4   Experimental Procedure

In this study, we measured the subject's eye accommodation during the viewing of DFD images. We argue that the accommodation focus moves to the depth of the DFD images.

We used a binocular DFD to display the image while taking the measurement of accommodation. Figure 4 shows a schematic diagram of the experimental apparatus, while specifications for stereoscopic display are shown in Table 1. In the experiment, the two planes were arranged at right angles with a half mirror at 45 degrees. By putting the half mirror in place, it is possible that the front plane is displayed on the virtual position. We set the front plane at the location of the 1.5 D (0.67 m), and the rear plane at the location of the 1.0 D (1.0 m). The rear image was 1.5 times larger than the front image. As shown in Table 2, we used five patterns images in the experiment. The DFD image moved in five steps between the two planes. As the DFD image moved, we measured the pupillary distance of the subjects before taking the measurement of

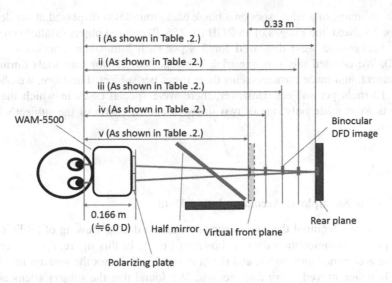

Fig. 4. Schematic diagram of experimental apparatus

Table 1. Specifications for stereoscopic display

Manufacturer	Mitsubishi Electric Corp.
Screen size	23 In.
Resolution	1920 × 1080
Refresh rate	60 Hz
3D data format	Top and bottom
Average of illuminance of the screen	27.5 cd/m^2

Table 2. Luminace and distance of DFD images

	i	ii	iii	iv	v
Luminance of the front image (%)	0	25	50	75	100
Luminance of the rear image (%)	100	75	50	25	0
Distance (m)	1.00	0.92	0.83	0.75	0.67
Distance (D)	1.00	1.09	1.20	1.33	1.50

accommodation. We chose the image by the pupillary distance of the subjects. In this experiment, we set a parallax which fixed convergence on the position of 1.0 D to exclude the influence of its stimuli. In other words, the subjects perceived the depth as a factor of the luminance ratio.

Before taking the measurement of accommodation, we made a fine adjustment of the parallel of the two planes and the horizontal and vertical position. We arranged the front and rear planes which displayed the five spot images arranged in a cross-like pattern for all subjects to perceive the DFD image as a single image at one depth.

First, an image of a white spot on a black background was displayed at the depth of 1.0 D for 5 s. Next, the images of an RGB (0, 255, 0) colored object (Maltese cross) on a black background were displayed for 5 s per each luminance ratio (as shown in Table 2). We decided this was one trial. We repeated this for four trials during one measurement, and made measurements three times per subject. Therefore, we obtained data of 12 trials per subject. However, there were special cases in which the measurements were made only one or two times in consideration of the subject's health condition.

3   Result

3.1   Typical Example of Accommodation Data

In this study, we acquired the data of accommodation during viewing of DFD images. First, typical accommodation data is shown in Fig. 5. In this figure, the vertical axis shows the accommodation focus, and the horizontal axis shows the measurement time. The DFD image moved every five seconds. We found that the subject's lens accommodation focus moved with a change of the depth of DFD image. The result indicated that the accommodation focuses on the DFD image, did not focus on each two plane.

3.2   Statistical Analysis

In this study, we statistically analyzed the data of accommodation. Incidentally, we executed data cleansing to remove any error value or missing data before the statistical analysis.

The WAM-5500 measured accommodation every 0.2 s because the sampling frequency was 5 Hz. First, we excluded accommodation values measured on the subject side of the position of a polarizing plate at 6.0 D. We excluded the data for missing

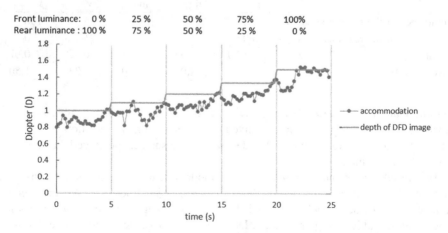

Fig. 5. Typical accommodation data (female, 35 years old)

Table 3. Number and age of subjects

	Number	Age (average ± standard deviation)
All subjects	78	39.40 ± 14.25
Young subjects	25	22.96 ± 2.79
Young middle aged subjects	23	38.65 ± 4.24
Middle aged subjects	27	51.30 ± 5.06
Elderly subjects	3	75.00 ± 1.00

ratios of over 50 % per the data for one trial. Furthermore, we also excluded the values that did not have an average ± 2.58 standard deviation (99 % confidence interval of a normal distribution) of the data for one trial. We calculated the average values by time at intervals of 0.2 s using the data of at most 12 trials per subject. This data set was the typical accommodation data set for each subject. In addition, we did not adopt the accommodation data of those subjects that had existed missing values in these data sets. Table 3 shows the accommodation data sets of the 78 subjects.

We calculated the group average of the accommodation data sets, as shown in Figs. 6, 7, 8, 9. Moreover, we employed a one-way ANOVA (analysis of variance) and the Tukey-Kramer test to the accommodation data set as the dependent variable and depth of the five steps as the independent variable (at 5 % significance level). Because there was a slight error between the start time of the moving image and the measurement instrument, we did not use the accommodation values of the first one second from the beginning and the last one second to the end in five seconds while the DFD image on each luminance was displayed. The results of the one-way ANOVA are shown in Tables 4, 5, 6, 7. The results of the Tukey-Kramer test are shown in Figs. 10, 11, 12, 13.

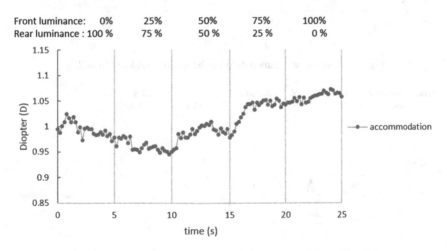

Fig. 6. Average accommodation of the young subjects (n = 25)

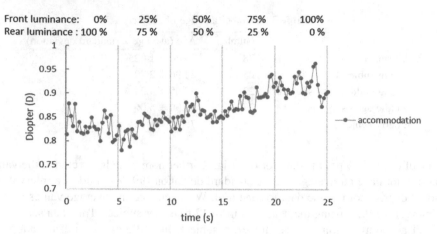

Fig. 7. Average accommodation of the young middle aged subjects (n = 23)

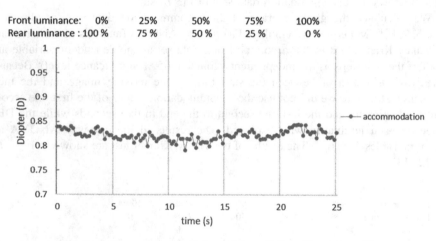

Fig. 8. Average accommodation of the middle subjects (n = 27)

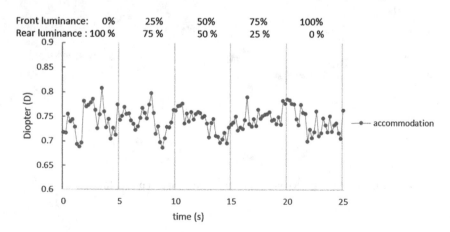

Fig. 9. Average accommodation of the elderly subjects (n = 3)

Table 4. Result of one-way ANOVA of the young subjects (n = 25)

	Df	Sum sq	Mean sq	F value	Pr(>F)
Factor	4	2.29	0.57	6.26	0.000
Residual	1870	171.15	0.09		

Table 5. Result of one-way ANOVA of the young middle aged subjects (n = 23)

	Df	Sum sq	Mean sq	F value	Pr(>F)
Factor	4	1.96	0.49	4.16	0.002
Residual	1720	202.80	0.12		

Table 6. Result of one-way ANOVA of the middle aged subjects (n = 27)

	Df	Sum sq	Mean sq	F value	Pr(>F)
Factor	4	0.2	0.04	0.16	0.961
Residual	2020	498.5	0.25		

Table 7. Result of one-way ANOVA of the elderly subjects (n = 3)

	Df	Sum sq	Mean sq	F value	Pr(>F)
Factor	4	0.01	0.00	0.03	0.998
Residual	220	13.07	0.06		

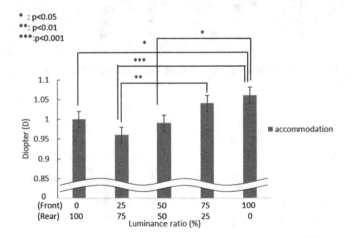

Fig. 10. Result of Tukey-Kramer test of the young subjects (n = 25)

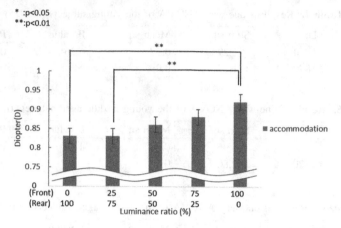

Fig. 11. Result of Tukey-Kramer test of the young middle aged subjects (n = 23)

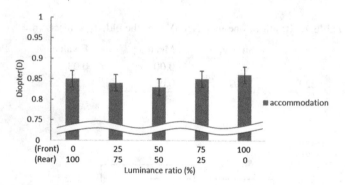

Fig. 12. Result of Tukey-Kramer test of the middle aged subjects (n = 27)

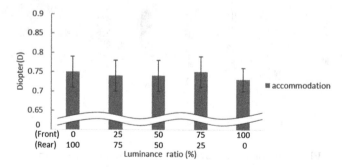

Fig. 13. Result of Tukey-Kramer test of the elderly subjects (n = 3)

4   Discussion

Previous studies have shown that when a person views stereoscopic images, a visual discrepancy occurs because convergence, which focuses at the position of the virtual object, and lens accommodation which is fixed on the screen. However, authors have not found such a mismatch in experiments with young subjects [6, 9]. In addition, studies have not clarified the effects of viewing of DFD images on accommodation. Thus, we investigated it.

As shown in Fig. 6, the accommodation focus of the young subjects clearly couldn't be seen the characteristic change when the luminance of front image was 0 % and the luminance of rear image was 100 %, and when the luminance of front image was 25 % and the luminance of rear image was 75 %. The accommodation focus of the young subjects approached the DFD image when the luminance of front image were 50 % or more. We inferred that subjects did not recognize that the DFD image was approaching them when the luminance of front image changed from 0 % to 25 % and the luminance of rear image changed from 100 % to 75 %. This indicates that the subjects perceived that the DFD image was approaching them when the luminance of front image were 50 % or more. As shown in Fig. 7, the accommodation focus of the young middle aged subjects approached the DFD image when the luminance of front image was 25 % or more. This indicates that the subjects perceived that the DFD image was approaching them. As shown in Figs. 8, 9, the accommodation focus of the middle aged and the elderly subjects did not change much. We presume that the changes of their refractive power decreases with age.

As shown in Tables 3, 4, 5, 6, and Figs. 10, 11, 12, 13, there were significant difference in the young and the young middle aged subjects. The accommodation focus was significantly moved toward the DFD image as the DFD image was approaching the subjects. There were no significant difference in the middle aged and the elderly subjects. The results suggest that the subjects perceived the DFD image was moving and they altered their lens accommodation because of the changes in luminance. In addition, this trend was seen in the young and the young middle aged subjects.

5   Summary

In this study, we verified that a viewer's lens accommodation can adjust to DFD images. We measured lens accommodation in subjects who gazed at DFD images. As a result, there were significant difference between the measurement data with depth of the five steps as the factor in the young and the young middle aged subjects. The young and young middle aged subjects perceived the approach of the DFD image. There were no significant difference in the middle aged and elderly subjects because with older individuals the crystalline lens loses elasticity with age and the changes of their refractive power also decreases. Hence, we concluded that lens accommodation was affected by the changes of luminance in the DFD image. Viewer adjusted their lens accommodation because of the changes in luminance.

References

1. Suyama, S., Takada, H., Ohtsuka, S.: A direct-vision 3-D display using a new depth-fusing perceptual phenomenon in 2-D displays with different depths. IEICE Trans. Electron. **E85-C** (11), 1911–1915 (2002)
2. Suyama, S., Ohtsuka, S., Takada, H., Uehira, K., Sakai, S.: Apparent 3-D image perceived from luminance-modulated two 2-D images displayed at different depths. Vision Res. **44**, 785–793 (2004)
3. Ishigure, Y., Suyama, S., Takada, H., Nakazawa, K., Hosohata, J., Takao, Y., Fujikado, T.: Evaluation of visual fatigue relative in the viewing of a depth-fused 3-D display and 2-D display. In: Proceedings of IDW 2004, VHFp-3, pp. 1627–1630 (2004)
4. Suyama, S., Ishigure, Y., Takada, H., Nakazawa, K., Hosohata, J., Takao, Y., Fujikado, T.: Evaluation of visual fatigue in viewing a depth-fused 3-D display in comparison with a 2-D display. NTT Tech. Rev. **3**(12), 82–89 (2005)
5. Fisher, R.F.: Presbyopia and the changes with age in the human crystallin lens. J. Physiol. **228**, 765–779 (1973)
6. Kojima, T., Shiomi, T., Kazuki, Y., Miyao, M.: Comparison of simultaneous measurement of lens accommodation and convergence in stereoscopic target with sine curve movement. Int. J. Adv. Intell. Syst. **6**(3-4), 318–328 (2013)
7. Date, M., Andoh, Y., Takada, H., Ohtani, Y.: Viewing zone connection of depth fused 3D (DFD) display. In: SID 2009 Digest of Technical Papers, P. 25, San Antonio, Texas, USA, pp. 1176–1179, June 2009
8. Takada, H., Suyama, S., Date, M.: Evaluation of the fusional limit between the front and rear images in depth-fused 3-D visual illusion. IEICE Trans. Electron. **E89-C**(3), 429–433 (2006)
9. Shiomi, T., Hori, H., Uemoto, K., Miyao, M., Takada, H., Hasegawa, S., Omori, M., Watanabe, T., Ishio, H.: Comparison of simultaneous measurement of lens accommodation and convergence in natural vision and 3D vision. In: SID 2012 (2012)

Effects of Two-Minute Stereoscopic Viewing on Human Balance Function

Kazuki Yoshikawa[1](✉), Fumiya Kinoshita[1], Koji Miyashita[2],
Akihiro Sugiura[1], Takehito Kojima[1], Hiroki Takada[3],
and Masaru Miyao[1]

[1] Department of Information Engineering, Graduate School of Information
Science, Nagoya University, Furo-Cho, Chikusa-Ku, Nagoya 464-8601, Japan
yoshikawa.kazuki@f.mbox.nagoya-u.ac.jp
[2] Department of Human and Artificial Intelligent Systems, University of Fukui,
3-9-1 Bunkyo, Fukui 910-8507, Japan
[3] Department of Human and Artificial Intelligent Systems, Graduate School
of Engineering, University of Fukui, 3-9-1 Bunkyo, Fukui 910-8507, Japan

Abstract. Recently, with the rapid progress in image processing and three-dimensional (3D) technologies, stereoscopic images are not only available on television but also in theaters, on game machines, and elsewhere. In contrast to two-dimensional (2D) films that project flat images, stereoscopic films elicit the feeling of being at a live performance. However, asthenopia and visually-induced motion sickness (VIMS) can result from the exposure to these films. Even though various hypotheses exist, the pathogenesis of VIMS is still unclear. There is not enough knowledge on the effects of stereoscopic images on the living body, and the accumulation of basic research is thus important. The aim of this paper is to accumulate information relevant to VIMS and to examine whether the exposure to 3D video clips affects the human equilibrium functions. We evaluated body sway by conducting stabilometry studies. As a result, we verified that 3D viewing effects on our equilibrium function depends on exposure time.

Keywords: Visually induced motion sickness (VIMS) · Stabilometry · Exposure time · Sparse density (SpD)

1 Introduction

Recently, with the rapid progress in image processing and three-dimensional (3D) technologies, stereoscopic images are not only available on television but also in theaters, on game machines, and elsewhere. Current 3D display mechanisms include stereoscopy, integral photography, the differential binocular vision method, volumetric display [1, 2], and holography [3]. Viewing stereoscopic images may elicit adverse effects, such as asthenopia or visually-induced motion sickness (VIMS) in some individuals [4]. While the symptoms of general motion sickness include dizziness and vomiting, the phenomenon of VIMS is not fully understood. Currently, there is not

© Springer International Publishing Switzerland 2015
M. Antona and C. Stephanidis (Eds.): UAHCI 2015, Part II, LNCS 9176, pp. 297–304, 2015.
DOI: 10.1007/978-3-319-20681-3_28

enough knowledge accumulated on the effects of stereoscopic images on the living body and basic research is thus important [5].

At present, VIMS is explained by the sensory conflict theory [6]. In humans, the standing posture is maintained by the body's balance function that is an involuntary physiological adjustment mechanism referred to as the "righting reflex". In order to maintain the standing posture in the absence of locomotion, the righting reflex that is initiated in the vestibular system and processed in the nucleus ruber is essential in the nucleus ruber is essential. Sensory receptors, such as visual inputs, auditory and vestibular functions, and proprioceptive inputs from the skin, muscles, and joints, are required to maintain the body's balance function [7]. According to the sensory conflict theory, motion sickness is a response to the conflict generated by a discrepancy between received and previously stored messages. Variations are thus expected that may arise from acquired experiences. Contradictory messages originating from different sensory systems, or the absence of a sensory message that is expected in a given situation, are thought to lead to the feeling of sickness. The human equilibrium system receives information input from the visual, vestibular, and somatosensory systems. The sensory conflict theory states that when the combination of information is inconsistent with previously established human experiences, spatial localization of self becomes unstable and produces discomfort. Visual input enters the brainstem from the visual and somatosensory systems and the cerebellum, in addition to the vestibular system, suggesting that the nuclei physiologically integrate this sensory information. Researchers generally agree that there is a close relationship between the vestibular and autonomic nervous systems both anatomically and electrophysiologically. This view strongly indicates that the equilibrium system is associated with the symptoms of motion sickness [8] and provides a basis for the quantitative evaluation of motion sickness based on body sway, an output of the equilibrium system.

Stabilometry is a useful test of body equilibrium for investigating the overall equilibrium function. Stabilometry methods are presented in the standards of the Japanese Society for Equilibrium Research and in international standards [9]. In Japan, devices to measure body sway are defined by the Japanese Industrial Standards (JIS) [10]. Stabilometry is a simple test in which 60 s recording starts when body sway stabilizes. Objective evaluation is possible by the computer analysis of the speed and direction of the sway, enabling diagnosis of a patient's condition [11].

In previous studies, viewing 3D images has been shown to affect body sway [12]. However, thus far, it has not been mentioned on whether it is dependent on the viewing time period. In this study, we examined the 3D viewing effect on our equilibrium function to determine whether it is dependent on the exposure time.

2 Materials and Methods

Sixteen healthy male subjects (mean age ± standard deviation: 22.4 ± 0.8 years) participated voluntarily in the study. We ensured that the body sway was not affected by environmental conditions. We used an air conditioner to adjust the temperature at 25°C in the exercise room. The experiment was explained to all subjects and written informed consent was obtained in advance.

Fig. 1. The image shown for the volunteer tests projected on a 3D display

In this experiment, we conducted a stabilometry test with subjects viewing 2D and 3D images. The device used was a Wii Balance Board (Nintendo, Kyoto). The sampling frequency of the Wii Balance Board was 20 Hz. The subjects stood upright on the device in Romberg's posture. We conducted two types of measurements: (I) after resting for 30 s, the body sway of each subject was measured for one minute with opened eyes and for three minutes with closed eyes consecutively, and (II) after resting for 30 s, the body sway of each subject was measured for two minutes with opened eyes and three minutes with closed eyes consecutively. However, in the two-minute measurement test with opened eyes, we also collected data for a period of one minute after the test. Experiments were performed in a dark room to avoid irritation from sources other than the video. The 2D or 3D images were shown on a 3D KDL 40HX80R display (SONY, Tokyo) placed two meters away from the subject. In the image used in the experiment, spheres were fixed at the four corners, while another sphere moved around the screen (Fig. 1). A comparison was then made with subjects who were asked to simply gaze at a point 2 m in front of them at eye level in the case where no image was displayed. The experiments were carried out in random order. Each experiment was carried out on a separate day.

The x-y coordinates were recorded for each sampled time point collected in the tests that were conducted with open and closed eyes, and the quantitative indices were calculated. The data were converted to time series and included the position of the center of gravity in the x (the right direction, designated as positive) and y (the anterior direction, designated as positive) directions in each of the open and closed eye tests, the area of sway, total locus length, locus length per unit area, and density, used for subsequent evaluation. The area of sway and total locus length are analytical indices of stabilograms that were used in previous studies. We used these based on the definitions established by the Japanese Society for Equilibrium Research [13].

- Area of sway: Area of a region surrounded (enveloped) by the circumferential line of sway on the x-y coordinates. An increase in the value represents a more unstable sway;
- Total locus length: Total extended distance of movement of the center of gravity within the measurement time period. An increase in the value represents a more unstable sway;
- Locus length per unit area: Value calculated by dividing the total locus length by the area of sway. A decrease in the value represents a more unstable sway;

- Sparse Density (SpD): Frequency of passage by the center of foot pressure at each fraction established by dividing the stabilogram into squares (See Appendix). The value gets closer to unity when sway is small, i.e., in a region with a high local density. Inversely, the value increases when the sway is scattered.

The area of the sway, the total locus length, and the SpD were obtained from stabilograms recorded when the volunteers had their eyes open and closed. Solidity of the subjects' vision (2D/3D) and persistency of this influence were assumed to be important affecting factors on which a two-way analysis of variance (ANOVA) was conducted accounting for the number of repetitions. In addition to this two-way ANOVA for each stabilogram index, post hoc comparisons were employed at a significance level of 0.05.

3   Results

We compared stabilograms measured before exposure to the stereoscopic film with those after the exposure (Fig. 2). We also calculated the area of sway, the total locus length, and the locus length per unit area for each subject studied (Fig. 3).

In accordance to the two-way ANOVA results, there was no interaction between the abovementioned two factors. When we viewed the video clips recorded over a period of one min, there was a main effect of the locus length per unit area on the solidity. Except for the locus length per unit area, there was no significant difference between the sway values estimated during the open eye test and those estimated during the closed eye test in terms of multiple comparisons.

On the other hand, when viewing a 3D video clip for two min, the total locus length for the open eye test was significantly larger than that for the closed eye test (after been viewed for two min) ($p < 0.01$). Moreover, when we viewed a 3D video clip for one min, the area of sway, the total locus length, and the SpD for the open eye test were significantly larger than those for the closed eye test (after been viewed for one min), respectively ($p < 0.01$). When viewing video clips for two min, the area of sway, the total locus length, and the SpD for the open eye test were significantly larger than those for the closed eye test (after been viewed for one, and two min, respectively) ($p < 0.01$). When a video clip was viewed for two min, the locus length per unit area for the open eye test was significantly smaller than that for the closed eye test (after been viewed for two min) ($p < 0.01$). When a 3D video clip was viewed for one min, the area of sway, the total locus length, and the SpD for the open eye test were significantly larger than those for the closed eye test (after been viewed for three min), respectively ($p < 0.05$). When a 3D video clip was viewed for one min, the locus length per unit area for the open eye test was significantly smaller than that for the closed eye test (after been viewed for three min), respectively ($p < 0.05$).

Furthermore, when a 2D image was viewed of two min, the area of sway and the total locus length for the open eye test were significantly larger than those for the closed eye test (after been viewed for 1 min), respectively ($p < 0.05$). The area of sway and the total locus length for the open eye test were significantly larger than those for the closed eye test (after been viewed for two min), respectively ($p < 0.01$). The area of sway and

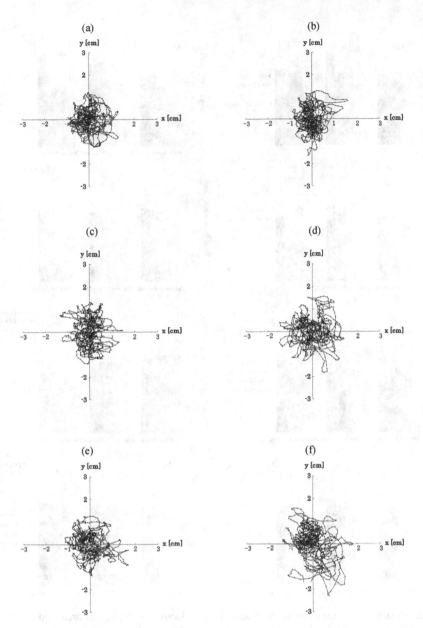

Fig. 2. Typical stabilograms (a, one min recordings with opened eyes, without viewing an image; b, one min recordings with closed eyes, without viewing an image; c, one min recordings with opened eyes, without viewing 2D images; d, one min recordings with closed eyes, without viewing 2D images; e, one min recordings with opened eyes, without viewing 3D images; f, one min recordings with closed eyes, without viewing 3D images).

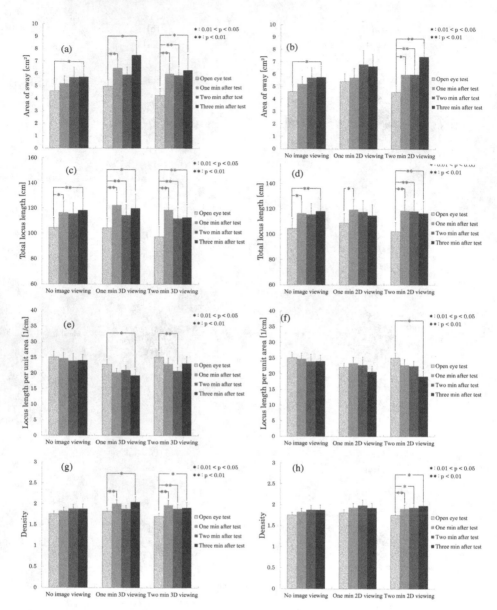

Fig. 3. Result of the area of sway, total locus length, locus length per unit area, and density (a, area of sway, viewing 3D image; b, area of sway, viewing 2D image; c, total locus length, viewing 3D image; d, total locus length, viewing 2D image; e, locus length per unit area, viewing 3D images; f, locus length per unit area, viewing 2D images; g, density, viewing 3D images; h, density, viewing 2D images).

the total locus length for the open eye test were significantly larger than those for the closed eye test (after been viewed for three min), respectively (p < 0.05).

4 Discussion

When viewing a 2D image, sway is increased depending on the viewing time. Moreover, when viewing an image for two min, the area of sway and the total locus length were significantly larger for the open eye test compared to the values elicited when the image had been viewed two min after the test. Therefore, we considered that after the image had been viewed, equilibrium function still remained. Moreover, regardless of the 3D or 2D images, the area of sway and the total locus length were significantly larger in the open eye test compared to the values elicited in the case where these images were viewed three min after the test. The results of the control were the same as these. Accordingly, the reason for the sway increase in the case when the images were viewed three min after the test is not attributed to the effects of VIMS but to the effects of fatigue. Therefore, we considered that the change in viewing time affected the equilibrium function system, and that viewing a 3D image for two min affected the equilibrium function system for a period of two min after the images had been viewed.

Acknowledgements. This work was supported in part by the Ministry of Education, Culture, Sports, Science and Technology, through a Grant-in-Aid for Scientific Research (B) (Number 24300046).

Appendix: Sparse Density

Herein, we describe the new quantification indices, sparse density (SpD) [13]. The SpD is defined as the average of the ratio $G_j(1)/G_j(k)$ for $j = 3, 4, ..., 20$, where $G_j(k)$ is the number of divisions with more than k measured points. A stabilogram is divided into quadrants whose latus is j times longer than the resolution. If the center of gravity is stationary, the SpD value is unity. If there are variations in the stabilograms, the SpD value is greater than unity. Thus, the SpD depends on the characteristics of the stabilogram and the minimal structure of the temporally averaged potential function.

For the data analysis, the anterior-posterior direction was considered to be independent of the lateral direction [14]. Stochastic differential equations (SDEs) were proposed as mathematical models to generate the stabilograms [15–17]. The variance in the stabilogram depends on the form of the temporally averaged potential function in the SDE, which generally has plural minimal points. In the vicinity of these points, local stable movement with a high-frequency component was generated as a numerical solution to the SDE. We can therefore expect a high-density of observed the center of pressure in this area of the stabilogram [17]. Therefore, SpD is regarded as an index for this measurement.

References

1. Dowing, E.: Development and Commercialization of a Solid State Volumetric Display. OSA Annual Meeting, ILS-XIII, WSS1 140 (1970)
2. Suyama, S., Date, M., Takada, H.: Three Dimensional Display System with Dual Frequency Liquid Crystal Varifocal Lens. Jpn. J. Appl. Phys. **39**(Part 1(2A)), 480–484 (2000)
3. Gabor, D.: A New Microscopic Principle. Nature 161, 777–779 (1948)
4. International standard organization: IWA3: 2005 image safety-reducing determinism in a time series. Phys. Rev. Lett. **70**, 530–582 (1993)
5. Sumio, Y., Shinji, I.: Visual comfort and fatigue based on accommodation response for stereoscopic image. Inst. Image Inf. Telev. Eng. **55**(5), 711–717 (2001)
6. Reason, J.T., Brand, J.J.: Motion Sickness. Academic Press, London (1975)
7. Okawa, T., Tokita, T., Shibata, Y., Ogawa, T., Miyata, H.: Stabilometry: significance of locus length per unit area (L/A) in patients with equilibrium disturbances. Equilib. Res. **55** (3), 283–293 (1995)
8. Barmack, N.H.: Central vestibular system: vestibular nuclei and posterior cerebellum. Brain Res. Bull. **60**, 511–541 (2003)
9. Japan Society for Equilibrium Research: Standard of stabilometry. Equilib. Res. **42**, 367–369 (1983)
10. Kaptyen, T.S., Bles, W., Njiokiktjien, ChJ, Kodde, L., Massen, C.H., Mol, J.M.: Standarization in platform stabilometry being a part of posturography. Agreessologie **24**, 321–326 (1983)
11. Hase, M., Ohta, Y.: Meaning of barycentric position and measurement method. J. Environ. Eng. **8**, 220–221 (2006)
12. Kato, H.: Effects of a Stereoscopic Film on Human Body. Department of Human and Artificial Intelligence. System, University. of Fukui (2013)
13. Takada, H., Kitaoka, Y., Ichikawa, M., Miyao, M.: Physical Meaning on Geometrical Index for Stabilometry. Equilib. Res. 62, 168–180 (2003)
14. Goldie, P.A., Bach, T.M., Evans, O.M.: Force platform measures for evaluating postural control: reliability and validity. Arch. Phys. Med. Rehabil. **70**, 510–517 (1986)
15. Collins, J.J., De Luca, C.J.: Open-loop and closed-loop control of posture: a random-walk analysis of center of pressure trajectories. Exp. Brain Res. **95**, 308–318 (1993)
16. Newell, K.M., Slobounov, S.M., Slobounova, E.S., Molenaar, P.C.: Stochastic processes in postural center of pressure profiles. Exp. Brain Res. **113**, 158–164 (1997)
17. Takada, H., Kitaoka, Y., Shimizu, Y.: Mathematicha index and model in stabilometry. Forma **16**, 17–46 (2001)

Sign Language Technologies

ASL-Pro: American Sign Language Animation with Prosodic Elements

Nicoletta Adamo-Villani[✉] and Ronnie B. Wilbur

Purdue University, West Lafayette, IN, USA
{nadamovi,wilbur}@purdue.edu

Abstract. Efforts to animate American Sign Language (ASL) are aimed at eliminating barriers preventing ASL-using Deaf children from achieving their full potential. These barriers result from reduced information accessibility and affect language, cognitive development, and general education. Deaf children receive limited input with which they are unable to interact. Digital learning materials with ASL translation in the form of realistic 3D character animations can provide a solution to this problem. However, existing ASL animations lack the characteristics of natural, intelligible signing, producing stilted, robot-like signing when signs are put into sentences. What they lack is linguistic "prosody": rhythmic phrasing, stress, and intonation. In ASL these markers are provided by timing and the face, head, and body. Our goal is to remedy this situation by adding predictable prosodic markers using algorithms that reflect the content and syntax of the signs in sequence. We refer to this new animation capability as ASL-pro, that is, ASL with pro(sody). Specifically, we describe (1) development of computational algorithms for inserting basic prosodic markers (e.g. facial articulations) and editing basic prosodic modifiers (e.g. lengthening sign duration in phrase-final position), and (2) design, development and initial evaluation of a new user interface allowing users to input English sentences in ASL-pro notation to automatically generate corresponding signing animations with prosodic elements.

Keywords: American Sign Language (ASL) · ASL animation · ASL prosody · Deaf education · Facial articulation

1 Introduction

As a general notion, prosody includes relative prominence, rhythm, and timing of articulations. Prosodic markers indicate which units are grouped together and serve as cues for parsing the signal for comprehension. Speech has a Prosodic Hierarchy [1]: (smallest to largest) Syllable <Prosodic Word <Prosodic Phrase <Intonational Phrase. The variables used to cue these groupings for parsing are pitch (fundamental frequency), intensity (amplitude), and duration. For example, phrase-final words are longer than non-final words (Phrase Final Lengthening). How phrases are constructed depends on syntax, information status (old vs. new),

© Springer International Publishing Switzerland 2015
M. Antona and C. Stephanidis (Eds.): UAHCI 2015, Part II, LNCS 9176, pp. 307–318, 2015.
DOI: 10.1007/978-3-319-20681-3_29

stress (affected by information status), speaking rate, situation formality (articulation distinctness), etc. [2, 3].

Over time, ASL has accommodated to the production and perception requirements of manual/visual modality, developing a prosodic system similar in function to spoken languages but different in means of expression. Thus, the signed signal variables are displacement, time, and velocity ($v=d/t$), and derivatives thereof. In addition, there is considerable simultaneous transmission of information in the signal, which makes traditional notions from parsing speech less useful to us [2]. The hands are not the sole articulators: multiple meaningful articulations are possible from parts of the face, positions of the head and body, collectively known as nonmanuals (NMs). ASL carefully coordinates hands and NMs so that NMs can perform intonational functions, pausing and sign duration changes can indicate phrasing and rhythmic structure, and phrasal prominence (stress) can be signaled by higher peak velocity than unstressed signs [5].

Despite differences, the role of prosody is as critical in signing as it is in speech, and there are many similarities between them. Like speech, ASL has Phrase Final Lengthening. In ASL there is also good correspondence between syntactic breaks and prosodic breaks [2]. Like speech, ASL syntax does not predict all prosodic domains [3, 7, 8], with information structure and signing rate [5] strong influences. Finally, the Prosodic Hierarchy holds for ASL [4, 9]. These functional similarities entail that absence of prosodic cues in animated signing will be as unacceptable and potentially as difficult to understand as robotic speech lacking cues to phrasing, stress, and intonation. We describe the newly-developed capacity to add prosody to animated signing which we call ASL-pro and the testing conducted, in progress, and planned. Animation algorithms must be sensitive to relative values of prosodic elements (pauses, sign lengthening), and not just absolute or local values.

2   ASL Prosody

Only a few of the articulators involved in speech production are visible, and except for speechreading, what is visible is generally not relevant. In contrast, the entire body is visible during signing, so the signal must cue the viewer that linguistic information is being transmitted and how to parse it. The complexity of the signal is reflected by the fact that there are 14 potential NM articulators with multiple positions which can occur simultaneously: body (leans, shifts), head (turn, nod, tilt, shake), brows (up/down, neutral), eyelids (open, squint, closed), gaze (up/down, left/right), nose (crinkle), cheeks (puff, suck), lips (round, flat, other); lip corners (up/down, stretched), tongue (out, touch teeth, in cheek, flap, wiggle), teeth (touch lip/tongue, clench), chin (thrust) [2]. The non-signing hand may be a phrasal prosodic marker. The NM system has evolved to avoid interference among articulations in production or perception. For example, facial articulations can be subdivided into upper face/head [2, 6], which occur with larger clausal constituents, and lower face, which occur with smaller phrasal (nouns, verbs) to provide adverbial/adjectival information. These articulations are under tight control: ASL negative headshakes begin and end precisely with the negated content (within

15–19 ms), showing that they are grammatical, not affective, in contrast to speakers, who start and stop headshakes without concern for English syntactic constituency.

Unfortunately, animators do not have the ASL linguistics information to add prosody. Worse, even if they did, they would have to manually modify the code for each articulator and movement for each sign. Thus, our interface represents a leap forward by combining findings on ASL prosody with algorithms for easily adding predictable prosody to animated signing. Figure 1 shows a comparison between a real signer, an animated avatar signing with prosody, and an animated avatar signing without prosody.

2.1 ASL Prosodic Elements We Predict with Certainty - Linguistic Rules on Which the Algorithms are Based

Linguistic work has provided some guidelines for predicting prosodic elements. Readers are referred to [5] for an overview.

Prosodic Constituency and Phrasing: For spoken English, longer pauses (above 445 ms) occur at sentence boundaries; shorter pauses (to about 245 ms) occur between conjoined sentences, noun or verb phrases; and the shortest pauses (under 245 ms) occur within phrasal constituents. For ASL, Longer pauses between sentences average 229 ms, between conjoined sentences 134 ms, between NP and VP 106 ms, and within the VP 11 ms [2]. Pause duration and other prosodic markers also depend on signing rate [5]. Ideally, algorithms can make adjustments across phrases within sentences, and possibly across sentences within narratives, without requiring users to enter markers other than commas and periods in the annotation [10]. Prosodic groupings show NM changes. Larger groups are marked with changes in head, body position, upper face, and periodic blinks [3]. The lowest relevant prosodic levels (Prosodic Word) are separated from each other by lower face tension changes [7].

Stress: ASL uses peak speed and higher location in the signing space to mark stress. Generally, ASL has sentence stress in clause-final position and on the first syllable in multisyllabic words that are not compounds [2,9].

Intonation for Sign Languages: Sandler [8] argues that intonation is represented by the NMs. However, there may well be a better as-yet-unidentified analogue to intonation (pitch), and the NMs may be showing morphemic layering [2]. For example, in addition to, or instead of, a negative sign (NOT, NEVER), a negative headshake starts at the beginning of the content that is negated and continues until the end of the negated phrase. Thus, our algorithm need only find a negative sign in the input to automatically generate the negative headshake at the right time. Similarly, brow lowering is a marker of questions with wh-words (who, what, when, where, why, how) [11]. Brow raising occurs with many structures: topics, yes/no questions, conditionals (if), relative clauses, among others. Unlike negative headshakes and brow lowering, there can be more than one grammatical brow raise in a

	NATURE.	HAVE	WHAT.	HURRICANE	FOREST-FIRE	return-to-neutral.
A	NATURE.	HAVE	WHAT.	HURRICANE	FOREST-FIRE	return-to-neutral.
B	nature-topic	have	what-end phrase	hurricane	forest fires	end of clause
C	"What nature has is hurricanes and forest fires."					
D	up-topic	up-wh-cleft ⟶		neutral	down-emphasis	neutral
E	back-topic	forward ⟶		down	back-emphasis	neutral
F	'na'	'ha...............ve'			'wow'-emphasis	neutral
G	topic	wh-cleft ⟶		list item₁ ... last list item₄-emphasis		
H	comma phrasal lengthening slower speed, add pause			period sentence final lengthening slower speed, add longest pause		

Fig. 1. Video, animation with prosody, and animation without prosody of the same sentence. Row A gives the gloss encoding, B the phrasing, C the English translation, D, E, and F the prosodic elements rendered with the brows, head, and mouth, respectively, G the ASL predictive structure, and H the ASL-pro notation mark and its effects. The animation with prosody was generated by an expert animator in several days using a professional-grade entertainment-industry computer-animation system. The goal of our research is to enable the generation of ASL animation with prosody automatically.

sentence; for this reason, the input to our computational algorithms includes commas to trigger brow raise (as well as phrase final lengthening), except for yes/no questions, which trigger brow raise with a question mark.

Weast [12] measured brow height differences to differentiate syntactic uses of brow height from emotional uses (anger, surprise). She reported brow height shows clear declination across statements and somewhat before sentence-final position in questions, parallel to spoken intonation pitch. Emotional uses set the height range (anger lower, surprise higher), into which syntactic uses of brow raising and lowering must be integrated.

A fourth example is use of eyeblinks. Of the three blink types (startle reflex, periodic wetting, and deliberate), both periodic and deliberate blinks serve linguistic functions in ASL. Periodic blinks (short, quick) mark the ends of higher prosodic phrases [6]. Deliberate blinks (long, slow) occur with signs for semantic/pragmatic emphasis. Our algorithms prevent over-generation of too many periodic blinks by requiring a minimum number of signs or elapsed duration between blinks at boundaries.

To recap, we can predict where pausing and sign lengthening occur, along with changes in brows, head, body, blinks, gaze, cheek and mouth. Now we can see the brilliance of the ASL prosodic system: hand movement marks syllables; lower face changes mark Prosodic Words; and upper face, head, and body positions mark largest Intonational Phrases. Emotions affect range of articulator movement. Everything is visible and tightly coordinated.

3   Prior Work on ASL Animation

Research findings support the value of ASL computer animation. Vcom3D [13] developed two commercial products: Signing Avatar and Sign Smith Studio. Their ASL animation is based on translating high-level external commands into character gestures and a limited set of facial expressions which can be composed in real-time to form sequences of signs. Their animation can approximate sentences produced by ASL signers but individual handshapes and sign rhythm are often unnatural, and facial expressions are not all coded due to the inability to represent ASL prosody effectively. Vcom3D also developed a system for creating animated stories using more realistic ASL (more facial expressions, improved fluidity of body motions, and some ASL prosodic elements) [14]. However, it was animation rendered off-line, derived from motion capture technology, and took a substantial amount of time to complete.

In 2005, TERC [15] collaborated with Vcom3D and the National Technical Institute for the Deaf on the SigningAvatar®accessibility software. TERC also developed a Signing Science Dictionary [16]. Both projects benefited young deaf learners, but did not advance state-of-the-art ASL animation as they used existing technology.

Purdue University Animated Sign Language Research Group led by Adamo-Villani and Wilbur, with the Indiana School for the Deaf (ISD), focuses on development and evaluation of innovative 3D animated interactive tools, e.g. Mathsigner, SMILE and ASL system [17,18]. Animation of ASL in Mathsigner and SMILE, although far from truly life-like, improved over existing examples. Signing adult and children's reactions to SigningAvatar and a prototype of Mathsigner rated Mathsigner significantly better on readability, fluidity, and timing, and equally good on realism.

In the U.S., English to ASL translation research systems include those by Zhao et al. [19] and continued by Huenerfauth [20] and by Grieve-Smith [21].

3.1   Prior Work Specifically Targeted at Animated ASL Prosody

Several studies have advanced animated signing beyond straightforward concatenation of hand/arm motions from individual signs. Huenerfauth has investigated the importance of ASL animation speed and timing (pausing) [22,23], based on earlier ASL psycholinguistics experiments. The model is encoded into two algorithms: one modulating sign duration based on sign frequency and syntactic context (e.g. subsequent occurrences of repeated verbs are shortened by 12 %, signs at a sentence or a clause boundary are lengthened by 8 % and 12 % respectively), and another inserting pauses at inter-sign boundaries in greedy fashion by selecting the longest span of signs not yet broken by a pause and by selecting the boundary within the span with the highest product between a syntactic complexity index and the relative boundary proximity to span mid-point. These algorithms created animations with various speeds and pausing, which were shown to native ASL signers to check comprehension and recall; viewers were asked to rank naturalness on a Likert scale. Animations produced with speed and timing algorithms scored significantly better. The study demonstrated that signed prosodic elements can be added algorithmically.

Zhao et al. developed a system for automatic English to ASL translation that renders ASL inflectional and derivational variations (i.e. temporal aspect, manner, degree) [19] using the EMOTE animation system [24]. EMOTE is procedural: animation is achieved from rules and algorithms, not user input; it is general purpose, i.e., not developed just for ASL, and it allows conveying Effort and Shape, two of the four components of the Laban Movement Analysis system. This shows the feasibility of applying general animation principles to ASL.

4   The ASL-Pro Algorithms

Why automatic generation of prosodic marking in animated signing? As mentioned, ASL prosodic elements are used to clarify syntactic structures in discourse. Research has identified over ten complex prosodic markers and has measured frequencies of up to seven prosodic markers in a two second span. Adding such number and variety of prosodic markers by hand through a graphical user interface (GUI) is prohibitively slow and requires animation expertise. Scalability to all age groups and disciplines can only be achieved if digital educational content can be easily annotated with quality ASL animation by individuals without technical background and computer animation expertise.

Our novel algorithms automate enhancing ASL animation with prosody. An overview of the pipeline is given in Fig. 2.

The **pipeline input** consists of:

1. *Humanoid 3-D character rigged for animation.* We use a character with 22 joints/hand, 4 joints/limb, 18 joints for the body (e.g. hips and spine), and 30 facial expression controllers.
2. *Database of signs.* The algorithm relies on a sign database. The animation of a sign is partitioned into 3 subsequences: in, middle, and out, which allows for smooth interpolation.

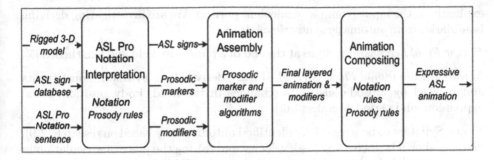

Fig. 2. Flowchart illustrating the ASL-pro pipeline

3. *Sentence encoded in ASL-pro notation.* Our project does not target automatic translation of English into ASL. The user provides translation in textual form using ASL-pro notation, which is an enhanced form of ASL gloss.

The **pipeline output** is ASL animation data for the character, with prosodic elements, corresponding to the input sentence. The output animation data consists of animation *elements* – units of animation such as "signing the number 3", or "tilting head forward"— and animation *modifiers* — associate to animation elements to set parameters, e.g. "translate joint on a Bezier arc between starting and ending positions", or " hold position for 0.7 seconds". The functionality of the three stages of the pipeline is as follows.

4.1   ASL-Pro Notation Interpretation

The ASL-pro notation of the input sentence is interpreted to identify the signs and prosodic markers and modifiers needed to animate the sequence. Some prosodic markers are included explicitly in the input sentence using ASL-pro syntax (a), and others are derived automatically using ASL prosody rules (b).

(a) Prosodic markers specified by the user are those that are not predictable from linguistic analysis of the sentence, such as affective markers and markers with hard-to-predict semantic/pragmatic functions (e.g., emphasis). Emotional aspect is known to play a decisive role in learning for deaf students [25] and Weast [12] has shown that emotion constrains grammatical markers, so affective markers are indicated by hand: Sad-Neutral-Happy, Angry-Neutral, Shy-Neutral-Curious, Scared-Neutral, Impatient-Neutral, Embarrassed-Neutral, and Startled. Each marker is encoded with a distinctive text tag (e.g. SadNHappy) followed by a numerical value ranging from -100 to 100 with 0 corresponding to neutral. The ASL-pro notation allows for modifying range and speed of motion to convey emotions. The modifiers are persistent, meaning that their scope extends until a marker for return to neutral (e.g. SadNHappy 0). The exception is the brief startled affect.

(b) Prosodic markers are derived automatically from prosody rules as follows:

Pausing. Pauses between and within sentences are added automatically according to research [2]. The current algorithm works with boundaries marked by the user explicitly in the input (comma, semicolon, period). We are investigating deriving boundaries from automatic syntactic analysis.

Phrase Final Lengthening. Signs at the end of a phrase are held and lengthened [5].

Marking Intonational Phrases (IPs). IPs are derived from syntactic constituents and marked by prosodic elements (changes in the head, body position, facial expression, and periodic blinks [3, 6]).

Stress. Syllables to be stressed are identified automatically based on research [2, 9]. Stress is shown by increasing peak velocity and raising the place of articulation in signing space [2]. At the word level, stress on two-syllable signs is equal, except for compounds which have stress on the second; signs with multiple syllables (repetitions) are stressed on the first. At the sentence level, one syllable, usually on the last sign, carries sentence stress.

Negation. Negative headshakes are added when a negative is identified from a negative word or [neg] marker in the notation (e.g. not, never) and go from the negative to the clausal end.

Content questions. These are identified by finding wh-words (e.g. who, what, when, where, why, how) not followed by commas and generate prosodic markers for brow lowering until a period. If followed by commas (wh-clefts - not true questions), such words generate brow raise.

Topic phrases, yes/no questions, conditional clauses, relative clauses. Such cases are identified from keywords (e.g. if, [cond]) and user provided or automatic syntactic analysis. The prosodic marker generated is brow raise until a comma or, for yes/no questions, a period is reached.

4.2   Animation Assembly

Animation elements are retrieved from the sign database for all the signs needed by the input sentence. The prosodic markers, explicit and derived, are translated into animation elements and modifiers using specific sub-algorithms. For example, the body-lean prosodic marker sub-algorithm takes a leaning amplitude parameter specified as a percentage of a maximum lean and generates the corresponding animation element. Similarly, the hand-clasp sub-algorithm generates the corresponding animation element using a combination of forward (e.g. for finger joints) and inverse kinematics (e.g. for elbow joints). The displacement prosodic modifier sub-algorithm takes as input a given fractional displacement amplitude and produces an animation modifier which can be applied to any element to achieve the desired effect. A multi-track animation timeline is populated with the resulting elements and modifiers. Most prosody markers are layered on top of the elements of a sign. Some prosody markers, such as e.g. hand clasp, are inserted between signs in phrases/sentences.

4.3 Animation Compositing

The animation layers, defined by the multiple animation tracks, are collapsed in the final animation. This stage has the important role of arbitrating between various animation elements and modifiers and reconciling conflicts. Physical constraint violations (collisions and excessive joint rotation amplitudes) are detected and remedied by computing alternate motion trajectories.

5 The ASL-Pro User Interface

The key components of the interface are the underlying algorithms (described in Sect. 4), the ASL-pro notation, and the editor. The interface allows users to input notation to generate animations with prosodic elements. Without a generally accepted system of written ASL, to write ASL signs and sentences, linguists use glossing, written in CAPITAL LETTERS, i.e. IX-1 LIKE APPLE I like apples. Gestures that are not signs are written in lower-case letters, i.e. go there. Proper names, technical concepts and other items without obvious ASL translation may be fingerspelled, which is written either as fsMAGNETIC or m-a-g-n-e-t-i-c. NMs are shown above the signs with which they co-occur, with a line indicating the start and end of the articulation. For instance,

wh-q

YOUR NAME?   or   YOUR NAME WHAT?
'What is your name?'   wh-q

where wh-q indicates a facial articulation with lowered eyebrows.

To animate ASL sentences, the user types the ASL-pro notation into the interface editor. The notation is interpreted and automatically converted to the correct sign animations with clearly identifiable prosodic elements. The ASL-pro notation is similar to, but not exactly the same as ASL gloss; Fig. 3 shows differences and similarities. Our goal is to allow any user with knowledge of ASL to create animation with prosody. Future work will develop and assess a tutorial, notation exam-

English	Nature can be unbelievably powerful.
ASL gloss	br bl lb, hu, bf bl lf bl NATURE SELF-1 WOW AWESOME POWER . br = brow raise; bl = blink; lb = lean back; hu=head up; bf=brow furrow; lf = lean forward
ASL-Pro notation	NATURE, SELF-1 WOW[emph] AWESOME POWER[focus].

Fig. 3. ASL-pro notation differs from ASL gloss: there are no lines above sign names; the comma after NATURE triggers brow raise, a blink and within-sentence phrase final lengthening; POWER triggers a lean forward for primary stress and sentence focus; a period triggers a blink and phrase final lengthening; the name of the sign SELF-1 calls a different sign from the lexicon than SELF. To be determined and evaluated for clarity and ease of use: how best to write in ASL-pro emphasis on WOW, primary focus on POWER. Here they are in brackets, but, for example, [emph] could be replaced by !.

ples, and a user-friendly editor with syntactic highlighting to help users learn the ASL-pro system.

To evaluate the quality of ASL-pro animations produced with the interface, we integrated the interface into our existing ASL system, which is a system generating 3D animations of ASL signs and sentences [for details, [26]]. A video of the system can be accessed at: http://hpcg.purdue.edu/idealab/asl/ASLvideo.mov

6   Initial Evaluation of the ASL-Pro Animations

We conducted a small-scale evaluation to determine the accuracy of the algorithms. Algorithms are considered accurate if, given a specific ASL-pro notation, they generate (1) prosodic elements perceived by users as accurate with correct intensity and timing with respect to the hands; (2) ASL animation perceived by users as intelligible and close to real signing; and (3) character motions and facial articulations perceived by users as fluid and life-like.

Judges: Validation of the algorithms relied on formative feedback from 8 ASL users (2 Deaf, 2 CODAs (Child of Deaf Adults), and 4 students in ASL with advanced ASL skills).

Stimuli: ASL-pro algorithmically generated animated ASL with prosodic elements based on the following text: *"Nature can be unbelievably powerful. Everyone knows about hurricanes, snow storms, forest fires, floods, and even thunderstorms. But wait! Nature also has many different powers that are overlooked and people don't know about them. These can only be described as FREAKY"*. (From National Geographic KIDS - August 2008). An ASL user translated the English into ASL-pro notation and entered it into the notation editor. The animation algorithms were applied to generate the ASL animation. A segment of the algorithmically generated ASL-pro animation can be viewed at: http://hpcg.purdue.edu/idealab/web/ASL-pro.htm.

Procedure: Judges viewed the video and completed an online survey rating the three areas of desired feedback on a 5-point Likert scale(1=highest rating; 5=lowest rating): accuracy of prosodic markers, intelligibility and closeness to real signing, and fluidity of motions and facial expressions.

Initial Findings: Results indicate that judges thought the prosodic elements were accurate and with correct timing (1.7/5); the signing was readable and fairly close to real signing (1.9/5); and the character motions and facial expressions were fairly fluid and realistic (2.3/5). Comments suggested that a more realistic-looking avatar could better convey prosodic elements (especially facial expressions) but that, despite the stylized look of the avatar, the animated signing was very close to real signing.

7   Conclusion and Future Work

In this paper we have presented a new sign language animation capability: ASL-pro, that is, ASL with pro(sody). We described the development of algorithms for inserting basic prosodic markers in animated ASL, and the design of a new user interface that allows users to input English sentences in ASL-pro notation to automatically generate the corresponding animations with prosodic elements. Findings of an initial study with 8 ASL users are promising, as they show that the algorithmically generated ASL-pro animations are accurate, close to real signing and fluid.

In future work we plan to conduct additional studies with larger pools of subjects to further validate the algorithms. We will also conduct an evaluation of the ASL-pro interface to examine its usability and functionality and to identify weaknesses, with the overarching goal of revising and improving its effectiveness and efficiency. Specifically, usability evaluation will assess educators'perceptions of the ease of using the ASL-pro interface, and their perceived benefits and challenges of using the interface in developing units/modules for their classes.

Our research addresses the need to enhance the accessibility of educational materials for deaf individuals by allowing ASL users with no animation and programming expertise to add accurate and realistic sign language animations to digital learning materials. While our initial objective has been to target the educational audience, we believe that facilitating creation of ASL translation is important beyond the education domain. For instance, ASL-pro animations could be used in entertainment and social networking to remove communication barriers between hearing and non-hearing members of our society.

References

1. Nespor, M., Vogel, I.: Prosodic Phonology. Foris, Dordrecht (1986)
2. Pfau, R., Steinbach, M., Woll, B. (eds.): Sign language. In: An International Handbook (HSK - Handbooks of Linguistics and Communication Science). Mouton de Gruyter, Berlin (2012)
3. Sandler, W., Lillo-Martin, D.: Sign Language and Linguistic Universals. Cambridge University Press, Cambridge (2006)
4. Brentari, D.: A Prosodic Model of Sign Language Phonology. MIT Press, Cambridge (1998)
5. Wilbur, R.B.: Effects of varying rate of signing on ASL manual signs and nonmanual markers. Lang. Speech. **52**(2/3), 245–285 (2009)
6. Wilbur, R.B.: Eyeblinks and ASL phrase structure. Sign Lang. Stud. **84**, 221–240 (1994)
7. Brentari, D., Crossley, L.: Prosody on the hands and face: evidence from american sign language. Sign Lang. Linguist. **5**(2), 105–130 (2002)
8. Sandler, W.: Prosody in Israeli sign language. Lang. Speech. **42**(23), 127–142 (1999)
9. Wilbur, R.B.: Sign syllables. In: Van Oostendorp, M., Colin, J.E., Elizabeth, H., Keren, R. (eds.) The Blackwell Companion to Phonology. Blackwell Publishing, Oxford (2011)
10. Wilbur, R. B., Malaia, E.: A new technique for assessing narrative prosodic effects in sign languages. In: Linguistic Foundations of Narration in Spoken and Sign Languages, Potsdam, Germany (2013)
11. Watson, K.: Wh-Questions in American Sign Language: Contributions of Nonmanual Marking to Structure and Meaning. MA thesis, Purdue University, IN (2010)
12. Weast, T.: Questions in American Sign Language: A Quantitative Analysis of Raised and Lowered Eyebrows. University of Texas, Arlington (2008)

13. Vcom3D. http://www.vcom3d.com
14. The Forest (2007). http://www.vcom3d.com/vault_files/forest_asl/
15. TERC (2006). http://www.terc.edu/
16. Signing Science (2007). http://signsci.terc.edu/
17. Adamo-Villani, N., Wilbur, R.: Two novel technologies for accessible math and science education. IEEE Multimed. Spec. Issue Accessibility **15**(4), 38–46 (2008)
18. Adamo-Villani, N., Wright, K.: SMILE: an immersive learning game for deaf and hearing children. In: ACM SIGGRAPH 2007 Educators Program, Article 17 (2006)
19. Zhao, L., Kipper, K., Schuler, W., Vogler, C., Badler, N.I., Palmer, M.: A machine translation system from english to american sign language. In: White, J.S. (ed.) AMTA 2000. LNCS (LNAI), vol. 1934, pp. 54–67. Springer, Heidelberg (2000)
20. Huenerfauth, M.: A multi-path architecture for machine translation of english text into american sign language animation. In: Student Workshop at the Human Language Technology Conference/North American Chapter of the Association for Computational Linguistics (HLTNAACL) (2004)
21. Grieve-Smith, A.: SignSynth: a sign language synthesis application using Web3D and Perl. In: Wachsmuth, I., Sowa, T. (eds.) Gesture and Sign Language in Human-Computer Interaction, 2298. Lecture Notes in Computer Science, pp. 134–145. Springer-Verlag, Berlin (2002)
22. Huenerfauth, M.: Evaluation of a psycholinguistically motivated timing model for animations of american sign language. In: 10th International ACM SIGACCESS Conference on Computers and Accessibility (ASSETS08), pp. 129–136 (2008)
23. Huenerfauth, M.: A linguistically motivated model for speed and pausing in animations of american sign language. ACM Trans. Access. Comput. **2**(2), 9 (2009)
24. Chi, D., Costa, M., Zhao, L., Badler, N.: The EMOTE model for effort and shape. In: ACM Computer Graphics Annual Conference, New Orleans, LA (2000)
25. Toro, J., Furst, J., Alkoby, K., Carte, R., Christopher, J., Craft, B., Davidson, M., Hinkle, D., Lancaster, D., Morris, A., McDonald, J., Sedgwick, E., Wolfe, R.: An improved graphical environment for transcription and display of american sign language. Information **4**(4), 533–539 (2001)
26. Hayward, K., Adamo-Villani, N., Lestina, J.: A computer animation system for creating deaf-accessible math and science curriculum materials. In: Eurographics 2010-Education Papers, Norrkoping, Sweden (2010)

Design and Development of an Educational Arabic Sign Language Mobile Application: Collective Impact with Tawasol

Abeer Al-Nafjan[1,2(✉)], Bayan Al-Arifi[2], and Areej Al-Wabil[2]

[1] Computer Science Department, College of Computer and Information
Sciences, Imam Mohammed Bin Saud University, Riyadh, Saudi Arabia
alnafjan@ccis.imamu.edu.sa
[2] College of Computer and Information Sciences, King Saud University, Riyadh,
Saudi Arabia
{bialarifi,aalwabil}@ksu.edu.sa

Abstract. This paper describes Tawasol, a multimedia system offering an innovative and engaging learning experience for people with hearing impairments. Tawasol is a project developed in collaboration between a university-based research group and a charitable foundation. We describe the novel system features specific to Arabic interfaces and signing conventions. Challenges that were faced in the design and development of the software are discussed.

Keywords: Arabic sign language ArSL · Deaf · Hearing impairment · Assistive technology · Education tool

1 Introduction

The prevalence of hearing impairments and the number of deaf/hard of hearing people in the Arab world is on the rise. According to the recent statistics by the Ministry of Economy and Planning in Saudi Arabia, there are 720,000 deaf in Saudi Arabia only. At the same time, there is a considerable insufficiency in deaf education. One important deficiency here is the absence of institutions and materials for sign language education [1].

Sign language (SL) is a visual-gestural language used by deaf and hard-hearing people for communication purposes. They use three-dimensional spaces and the hand movements (and other parts of the body) to convey meanings. It has its own vocabulary and syntax entirely different from spoken languages [2].

Even before they are one year old, both deaf and hearing children are capable of creating language. Hearing children learn the spoken language of their families. They also learn from media: TV, radio, movies, and computer programs with voice. Deaf children, unless they are born to deaf parents, frequently lack role models from whom to learn sign language. This may result in delayed language acquisition [3]. For many Arabic-speaking individuals who are deaf, Arabic text is a second language.

© Springer International Publishing Switzerland 2015
M. Antona and C. Stephanidis (Eds.): UAHCI 2015, Part II, LNCS 9176, pp. 319–326, 2015.
DOI: 10.1007/978-3-319-20681-3_30

People who are deaf/hard of hearing benefit from sign representations associated with text. Many studies show that using videos for representing signs has an important advantage over still images since movement plays an important role in sign language. A video image more accurately represents signs thereby providing students a greater understanding of the concept and method and increases their interest in learning [4, 5].

There is no consistency in the Arabic sign language. Although, two books were published about Arabic sign language; namely *The Arabic Sign Dictionary of Gestures for Deaf* published by the Arabic League in Tunisia in 2001, and *The Arabic Dictionary of Gestures for the Deaf II* which was a result of collaboration between The Arab States League, the Arab Union for Deaf, and the Arab Organization for Culture and Sciences along with the support of the Arab deaf. In both these books, it is clearly noted that there are different signs to the same word which often causes confusion and hinders those who speak these different Arabic sign languages from communicating [6, 7].

The sign language with the most published data is American Sign Language ASL, followed by British Sign Language BSL and German Sign Language. Studies on languages such as Arabic Sign Language and Indian/Pakistani Sign Languages are just beginning to emerge [8, 9]. Arabic speaking individuals with hearing impairments also lack interactive educational programs that help them to learn Arabic sign language.

Applications for Arabic sign language are limited. For example, after searching the AppStore using the keyword "sign language" in February 17, 2015, up to 342 applications were found under different categories; education, reference, and communication, and most of them were for American Sign Language ASL, British Sign Language BSL, and Japanese Sign Language JSL. However, only three Arabic sign language apps were found; 3D Arab Alphabet Sign Language, Palestinian sign language, and our app, namely Tawasol Arabic sign language.

For example, iSign [10] is an iOS-ASL application; this app contains up to 800 animated ASL phrases, ability to search within the app, and interactive quiz. Likewise, ASL Translator [11] is an iOS/Android-BSL application; This app is a text-to-sign generator and also contains ASL phrases; 30,000 + words; 1,400 + idioms and phrases; can translate up to 50 words at a time; 110 ASL phrases; video. Also, Japanese Sign Language [12] is an iOS-JSL application; this app contains basic JSL fingerspelling with Japanese and English text and shows images of hands for each letter.

In this paper, we present a mobile application that addresses the inadequate localized technology support for people who are deaf or have hearing impairments. Tawasol was designed as an iOS/Android application offering an attractive and engaging learning experience for deaf individuals, their parents and people around them who want to learn the Arabic sign language. Tawasol's main functions include a sign dictionary, tutorial activities, and fingerspelling.

2 Collective Impact in Collaboration with the Tawasol Center

Large-scale social change requires broad cross-sector coordination; the provision of bespoke assistive technologies for under-served populations often involves designers, developers, advocates, and funding organizations. Through carefully structured processes, several studies have reported collective impact in collaborations between non-profit charitable foundations and developers from both academia and industry [13–15]. In these collaboration models, both the organization and the process it helps facilitate, is an example of collective impact, the commitment of a group of key actors from different sectors (e.g. technology, research, healthcare providers) to a common agenda for solving a specific social problem.

In the context of assistive technologies, the Software and Knowledge Engineering Research Group at King Saud University (skerg.ksu.edu.sa) in Saudi Arabia, has been involved in collective impact initiatives. These initiative are characterized by a centralized infrastructure, a dedicated team of researchers and developers, and a structured process that leads to a common agenda, shared measurement, continuous communication between the stakeholders from non-profit organization and in healthcare delivery contexts.

The Princess Al-Anoud's charitable foundation has many projects; Tawasol Center is one that was founded in 2013. Tawasol Center is a private, non-profit organization dedicated to creating technologies and services that benefit deaf and hard of hearing individuals [16]. Tawasol Center's mission is to support and promote equal access and opportunities to education, employment and public services by individuals who are deaf or hard of hearing. In fact, many deaf and hard of hearing people face language, education, information and employment barriers and are unable to access other agencies providing essential services. Thus, Tawasol Center addresses an important need in the community.

Tawasol Center offers services addressing key issues facing the deaf and hard of hearing individuals. They provide information and referral, sign language training, free courses and community outreach. To help businesses and employers comply with the Saudi with disabilities by providing sign language interpreting and real-time captioning services. Moreover, they have Twitter account and YouTube channel in order to upload sign language videos.

3 Context-of-Use

Our research has revealed how there is a lack of educational resources that serve individuals who are deaf/hard of hearing and people around them. Furthermore, the lack of uniformity in Arabic sign language became an obstacle to the deaf community in communicating with people from other native Arabs. This has motivated us to develop an Arabic Sign Language education application to support the needs of deaf people and help them to effectively utilize their communication abilities and integrate them in society.

Tawasol was primarily designed as an educational tool. However, it can also be used in mediating communication between the user and others. Interaction with this application takes place when hearing people are trying to learn Arabic sign language or in the middle of a conversation that involves an individual with hearing impairments and another hearing individual that is not accustomed to the Arabic sign language where the application will act as a communicator.

4 System Description

Insufficient and inadequate support for Arabic-based sign language applications was the motivation for developing Tawasol in cooperation with Tawasol Center. Tawasol is an educational iPhone/iPad application that is developed in the area of assistive and educational technology to support adults with hearing impairments. The key contribution of this application is providing an Arabic sign language educational resource for Arabic-speaking populations, which is not available in the market today. Unlike the majority of available sign language systems, Tawasol supports other novel features. We use the Tawasol center's created Saudi sign language videos to build a mobile application. Tawasol app contains a dictionary, tutorial, and fingerspelling editor.

Dictionary. Consists of different categories representing Arabic words as shown in Fig. 1(a). Each category contains a number of words; when a word is selected, a corresponding video clip of the selected word sign appears with its pronunciation as shown in Fig. 1(b). Dictionary features: Search function that lets users look up a specific word, Repeat; Determine number of repeating the sign, Sound control; Determine with/without pronunciation, and Favorites allow the user to add favorites words on the (My words) list.

Tutorial. As a quiz; a player matches a presented sign language video to the correct word from a list of different words as shown in Fig. 2. The user has the ability to customize the quiz by selecting various difficulty levels; number of presented word options 2, 3 or 4.

Fingerspelling. The App will take a phrase entered by the user and then display the Sign Language symbol for each letter in the phrase as illustrated in Fig. 3.

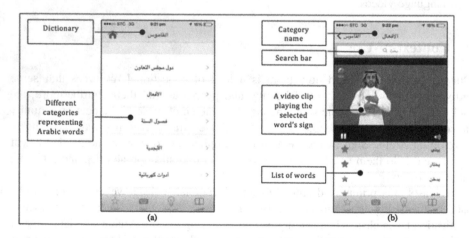

Fig. 1. (a) Category (b) Dictionary

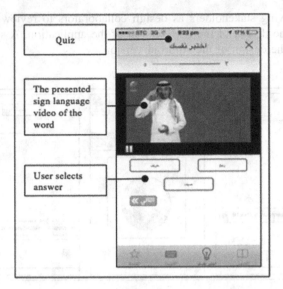

Fig. 2. The tutorial interface

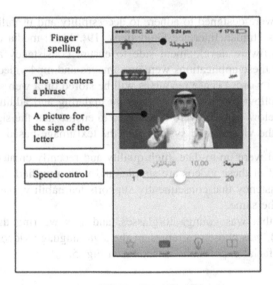

Fig. 3. The interface for fingerspelling

5 Design Considerations

As prior research has indicated (e.g. [17, 18]), portable electronic devices, in this case, tablets and smart phones are more engaging in learning contexts than printed material. In addition to that, their portability allows them to be used at anytime and anywhere.

The design approach followed the User-Centered Design framework [19]. Iterative cycles of review were conducted including low-fidelity prototypes as shown in

Fig. 4, and involving stakeholders as design collaborators to review mockups. This paper considers the design of the iOS version of the application. A similar approach was followed in the design of the Android version.

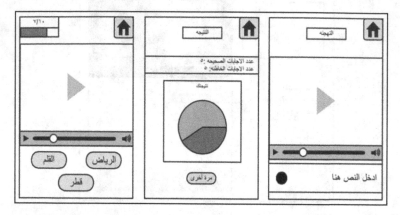

Fig. 4. Low-fidelity prototypes

The interfaces were designed to adhere to accessibility and usability guidelines, in addition to Apple's Human Interface Guidelines [19]. Multi-media editing was conducted from the software development side to ensure consistency and quality. The media used in both these applications were.png images and.mp4 videos of Arabic sign language letters and words. These recourses will be stored on a web server linked to a webpage/client to allow for easy and convenient updating and addition of recourses. Furthermore, the below features were considered to ensure that the signs' videos have the advantages of the video-based system over the text\image-based system:

- The videos used were up-to-date, high quality and recently created in late 2014.
- The background of these videos are simple, and with a unified theme.
- To ensure consistency that consequently supports learnability, the speed of all the sign videos is the same.
- An interpreter that was young, no-glasses, and was wearing the Saudi custom clothing (thobe), was chosen to represent the sign language videos to ensure clear presentation of facial expressions as shown in Fig. 5.

Fig. 5. Interpreter

6   Conclusion

In this paper we presented the Tawasol App [20] as an example of collective impact projects conducted in the context of research collaboration between non-profit organizations and academia. Tawasol aims to help people of the deaf group who need to communicate with others. Communication applications such as Tawasol would help to build and exchange knowledge and establish bases of mutual understanding for the individual with the community.

The design and development of such assistive technologies provide evidence to suggest that large-scale social change can stem better from cross-sector coordination between research and academia rather than from the isolated intervention of individual organizations. Evidence of the effectiveness of this approach is still emerging in our local context, but these examples suggest that considerable progress could be made in alleviating many of the serious and complex social and technological challenges if nonprofits and academia were brought together around a common agenda for developing effective technological solutions to create collective impact.

For future work, further improvements to the application will be carried on, more functions will be added, and new words and categories to the dictionary such as (Human Body, Science and Weather, Plants, School, Health and Safety, and Sports). In addition, user acceptance testing sessions will be conducted on the targeted population with focus on assessing the engagement of their learning experience.

Acknowledgements. The authors extend their appreciation to the Deanship of Scientific Research at King Saud University for funding the work through the research group project number RGP-VPP-157. Special thanks to the developers of Tawasol, Sarah bin Mahfoudh, Abrar Alsumayer, and Rana Alomar. In addition, the authors would like to acknowledge the support of Tawasol-Princess Al-Anoud call center services for the deaf for providing materials, data and suggestions for this project.

References

1. Ministry of Economy and Planning in Saudi Arabia: Statistical yearbook, vol. 49 (2013). http://www.cdsi.gov.sa/yb49/
2. Brill, R.G., Barbara, M., Lawrence, R.N.: Framework for appropriate programs for deaf children: conference of educational administrators serving the deaf. Am. Ann. Deaf **131**, 65–77 (1986)
3. Sahoo, A.K., Gouri, S.M., Pervez, A.: A proposed framework for Indian sign language recognition. Int. J. Comput. Appl. **5**, 158–169 (2012)
4. Abdel-Fattah, M.A.: Arabic sign language: a perspective. J. Deaf Stud. Deaf Educ. **10**, 212–221 (2005)
5. Al-Khalifa, H.S.: Introducing arabic sign language for mobile phones. In: Miesenberger, K., Klaus, J., Zagler, W., Karshmer, A. (eds.) ICCHP 2010, Part II. LNCS, vol. 6180, pp. 213–220. Springer, Heidelberg (2010)
6. The Arabic Sign Dictionary of Gestures for Deaf published by the Arabic League in Tunisia (2001)

7. The Arabic Dictionary of Gestures for the Deaf II which was a result of collaboration between The Arab States League, the Arab Union for Deaf, and the Arab Organization for Culture and Sciences along with the support of the Arab deaf (2007)
8. Al-Nafjan, A.N., Al-Ohali, Y.A.: A multimedia system for learning arabic sign language: tawasoul. World Conf. E-Learn. Corp., Gov., Healthc., High. Educ. **2010**, 2470–2473 (2010)
9. Al-Nafjan, A.N.: The design and development of labib: an arabic sign language educational tool. World Conf. Educ. Multimed. Hypermedia Telecommun. **2010**, 3231–3234 (2010)
10. iSign. https://itunes.apple.com/us/app/isign/id288858200?mt=8
11. ASL Translator. https://itunes.apple.com/us/app/asl-translator/id421784745?mt=8
12. Japanese Sign Language. https://itunes.apple.com/us/app/japanese-sign-language-american/id419118421?mt=8
13. Hoxmeier, J., Lenk, M.M.: Service-learning in information systems courses: community projects that make a difference. J. Inf. Syst. Educ. **14**, 91–100 (2003)
14. Leidig, P.M., Ferguson, R., Leidig, J.: The use of community-based non-profit organizations in information systems capstone projects. ACM SIGCSE Bull. **38**, 148–152 (2006)
15. Pinkett, R.D.: Bridging the digital divide: sociocultural constructionism and an asset-based approach to community technology and community building. In: 81st Annual Meeting of the American Educational Research Association (AERA), pp. 24–28, New Orleans, LA (2000)
16. Alanood. http://www.alanood.org.sa
17. Frutos, M., Bustos, I., Zapirain, B.G., Zorrilla, A.M.: Computer game to learn and enhance speech problems for children with autism. In: The 16th International Conference on Computer Games CGAMES, pp. 209–216. IEEE (2011)
18. Autism Society. http://www.autism-society.org/about-autism
19. iOS Developer Library-Apple Developer. https://developer.apple.com/library/ios/documentation/UserExperience/Conceptual/MobileHIG/index.html#//apple_ref/doc/uid/TP400065
20. Tawasol Arabic sign language. https://itunes.apple.com/us/app/tawasol-arabic-sign-language/id895600264?mt=

A Context-Based Collaborative Framework to Build Sign Language Databases by Real Users

Diego Roberto Antunes(✉), André L.P. Guedes, and Laura Sánchez García

Federal University of Paraná (UFPR), Curitiba, PR, Brazil
{diegor,andre,laura}@inf.ufpr.br

Abstract. Sign Languages (SL) are the main tools used by Deaf people for access to information (AI), an essential issue to allow their social inclusion. Information Systems (IS) have a key role in this AI, but in some cases they fail to work by not considering the needs of the Deaf, such as a Human-Computer Interaction (HCI) with communication by SL. The Automatic SL Recognition (ASLR) area has developed algorithms to solve technical problems, but there's still need to develop HCI tools for users in real contexts. This paper presents a context-based collaborative framework to create and upgrade SL databases by Deafs, to improve the development process of ASLR systems from the HCI perspective.

Keywords: Context-based framework · Tools for deafs · Collaborative methods · Sign language · Datasets · Real users · Automatic recognition

1 Introduction

The language is a powerful tool for the acquisition of cultural values, the inclusion of individuals in society, the exercise of their citizenship and their access to information and scientific knowledge [12,21].

The lack of access to information has been a serious problem faced by Deaf people that have tried for many years to conquer their inclusion in society and the exercise of their citizenship.

The Deaf have their own culture and identity that are characterized by a Sign Language (SL) as their main tool for the communication and interactions. However, because of poor knowledge of SL by society and of the lack of information in SL, the Deafs are excluded from the access to knowledge [6,21].

Information Systems (IS) play an essential role to break this barrier to accessibility. However, in many cases IS fail to provide a real access to information, mainly by not considering the real needs of the Deaf, such as features related to communication with the interface, namely natural input and information in SL.

Thus, the problem is the lack of a more natural Human-Computer Interaction (HCI) for the Deaf: an interaction based in the SL.

A research field that has tried to develop computational services based in SL is the Computer Vision (CV), which for over 30 years has developed algorithmic strategies for Automatic Sign Language Recognition (ASLR) systems - a computational basis necessary for building the HCI by SL [6].

© Springer International Publishing Switzerland 2015
M. Antona and C. Stephanidis (Eds.): UAHCI 2015, Part II, LNCS 9176, pp. 327–338, 2015.
DOI: 10.1007/978-3-319-20681-3_31

Regarding ASLR, CV studies have focused in the algorithms to solve the technical problem with discrete sets of signs domains, but the applying of these resources to design a HCI by SL in a real context of use is still far away [7]. The inclusion of a HCI approach can be considered to improve the development process of ASLR systems, among others, to clearly understand the needs of the Deafs and SL structure [6,7].

Antunes et al. (2011) [7] reviewed several CV studies providing an overview of the development process of ASLR systems, in order to identify some limitations related to the lack of a HCI approach, describing some categories and their problems, such as: object of research, approaches, SL databases and technologies.

Then, a framework to support the development process of ASLR systems was proposed, based on the HCI perspective [7]. This framework describes the needs of the Deaf, details the SL structure and the factors to be considered towards technology (e.g. not to use sensors that restrict the natural movements). In addition, Garcia et al. (2013) [22] presented a HCI architecture with a larger focus and methodological details to assist the development of tools for the Deaf.

However, the lack of a strategy to build SL databases, that considers a HCI approach, it is still a problem. The SL database is an initial step necessary for the ASLR development process, because it is the resource used to train and test the algorithms of pattern recognition, and their quality impacts the end solution. Therefore is important that the database also contemplates a HCI approach.

Thus, some factors should be considered, such as: involvement of real users (Deafs) and their common contexts (e.g. learning), low cost techonologies (e.g. webcams), an adequate methodology and criteria to define the signs and their descriptions, among others.

This paper presents a conceptual framework to support the building of SL databases based on contextual and collaborative activities of the Deaf communities, considering HCI factors, such as context, user needs, SL, Deaf culture. In this ways, ASLR systems can work with natural data from a real context of use.

The main contribution is the design of a framework to improve the development process of ASLR systems, providing a strategy for building or using SL databases from HCI perspective. This paper discusses the Deaf and SL, contextual activities, a methodology for choice and description of the signs and an algorithmic strategy to minimize the size of the database.

In addition, the framework includes an approach to adjust and use an existing SL database in the process. This proposed approach can also be used as a model to continuous and iterative training / testing of the ASLR system in real environments, improving the system with the collaboration of end users.

2   Theoretical Background

The goal of Human Computer Interaction is to develop systems that are easy to use and solve the real needs of the users in their contexts. In this sense, it is essential to involve the users in the process, in order to understand the real requirements, for building appropriate interactive systems [30].

Social, cultural and linguistics aspects should be part of the process of the interaction design. The focus on users is the key, for understanding how they performed their tasks, the ways of use, etc. [30].

2.1 Context, Collaboration and Framework

The context consists of understanding the users, their needs, their main activities, their knowledge and use of the technology, in a real environment [24].

The context involves the proper environment, the situation and the activities performed by a people group. When considering the context of use it is possible to improve the human-computer interaction and develop more useful applications [16]. However, determining of the context is not simple, because users interact in many social environments with different goals, technologies and results [5].

Context can be classified by four types: Activity, Identity, Location, and Time. These categories aim to assist in the description of the context, as the tasks and actions (activity), the environment (location), the time when this activities occur and the people involved (identity) [4].

Thus, an adequate understanding of the users activities in practice and their relationship with technology is crucial to build context-based applications [33].

Collaboration means working together with the intention of sharing goals and contribute to problem solving. The collaboration on local activity involves processes such as communication, negotiation, sharing, coordination, etc. [9].

The collaboration consists of coordinated activities to shared tools to perform a task continuously. This process of interaction enables the exchange of knowledge, the discussion of solutions and the building of consensus [37].

A framework consists of an conceptual schema or a specific domain model that describes its situations, its properties and its relationships. Thus, a framework can be used to communicate ideas, to define domains, to describe a context, to represent methods and processes in the development of a system [32,35].

2.2 The Deaf

In the context of this research, the Deaf is an individual who belongs to a minority community characterized with his own identity and culture defined by the use of a SL as the maternal language for communication and social interaction.

The Deaf encounters difficulties to perform even the simplest tasks of daily life: general access to information, medical appointments, in the purchase of medications at drugstores, finding educational materials in their language, etc.

In order to minimize the barrier to accessibility and provide inclusion, many Deaf communities use social gatherings to share information, local study groups, online collaborative activities due to geographical separation, etc.

2.3 Sign Language (SL)

SL is the natural language of Deaf people, a resource used for communication, education, etc. SLs are complete linguistic systems, characterized by the gestural-visual modality capable of allowing the Deaf to develop all their linguistic potentialities [12,20,21].

Since society has little knowledge about the SL and there is little knowledge available in the SL, the Deaf people are constantly excluded from society. Therefore, IS have an important role in the tools to provide resources in SL for a real accessibility of information and knowledge.

2.4 SL Phonology

The linguistic defense of SL as natural languages started with Stokoe (1960), who conducted a research about the signs used in the communication of Deafs and showed that SL had all the linguistic features of a natural language [31].

Then, the study showed that the American Sign Language (ASL) has three parameters that were used in a finite number of combinations to constitute the signs: the handshape, the location and the movement [36]. In subsequent studies another property was described: the orientation of the hand palm (OP) [10,20].

Later, Baker (1983) [8] and others described the Non-Manual Expressions (NME) as a distinctive unit: movements of face, eyes, torso and head.

From these surveys, which developed phonological models based on parameter classes, emerged a new branch of structures: the segment-based models.

The Movement-Hold (MH) model [27] states that signs were formed by two segments: Hold, which were signs without movement, and Movements.

Later, there were other models with more specific features for the phonological structure: Hand Tier (HT), Moraic (sub-units in moras), Dependency Phonology (concepts of locations and sub-spaces), Visual Phonology (geometric and mathematics features) and the Prosodic model [6,10].

3 HCI by Sign Language

3.1 Examples of Tools Without SL Interaction

ASL Browser [2] is a sign search tool that classifies the signs by their association with the letters of the oral language. When the user selects a word in english, a video of the sign and its meaning is presented. This IS leaves out those these potential users who don't know the language of their country, and is of little no use to find a sign the Deaf has never seen before.

The Spread the Sign [3] offers a free collection of terms in many languages. In order to use the system to search a synonymous or a equivalent sign, the user must input the keyword in the application, but this input is not in SL.

In the Acesso Brasil dictionary [1] there is a search by handshape, but, due to its lack of usability, the results are presented as a list of words in Portuguese, the same situation of no use within the ASL Browser.

3.2 Automatic SL Recognition Systems (ASLR)

The CV has developed several studies and produced strategies for the technical problem of recognition. However, these studies have not applied these resources to create tools for the end user. A literature review [7] presented an overview of the common limitations related to lack of a HCI approach in ASLR systems.

Inadequate Object of Research. Most methodological approaches have focused on computational techniques in which the Deafs were not included. If the purpose is to promote access to information, an approach focused on the Deaf is required to know their real needs, cultural aspects and conditions of use, aiming at an adequate computational treatment of SL.

Inadequate Methodological Approaches. The common approach *whole-word* consists of an isolated dataset of signs that are represented by matching signs to words in the spoken language. The system is trained to recognize this set. The problem is that the systems are limited by the set that were trained. As the language can produce infinite signs, this approach is inadequate for large vocabularies.

SL Databases. A factor in the development of an efficient ASLR system is the use of a robust database for training and testing the algorithms. In the studies reviewed, the databases were not built following a methodology from HCI perspective. The recurrent problems are showed in Table 1.

Table 1. Common problems in SL Databases [7].

Category	Problems
Not based on HCI	(a) not include the real context and use;
	(b) controlled environments;
	(c) use of special cameras (depth sensors);
	(d) use of sensors like data gloves;
SL Approach	(a) random signs without criteria;
	(b) few phonetic sub-units models;
	(c) sub-units repetition;
	(d) signs without similarity;

The Purdue RVL-SLLL [28] classified the ASL data by handshapes and movements, signs and sentences. The first classification (handshapes and movements) is important because the most adequate approach is to recognize the sub-units (phoneme model) before processing isolated signs or full sentences. The database consists of 2576 videos of 39 motion primitives, 62 handshapes, and sentences.

The RWTH-BOSTON-400 database has 843 sentences, several signers and subsets for training, development and testing [17]. This database also works on controlled environment and with whole-word model. For the authors, *"it is still unclear how best to approach recognition of these articulatory parameters"*.

The BSL project [34] uses a methodology related with sociolinguistics and corpus linguistics. The project includes native signers that told short personal stories (users grouped by age and location), but a software (not a computacional model) was used to annotate the signs.

The Dicta-Sign [18] is a project that involves database collection, ASLR and animation and translation for Internet. The prototype of the ASLR system use a depth sensor to recognition. The dataset was described in a computational model (helping to generate animations), but has a low level of details because it is based in a SL writing system.

The other databases found consist of SL corpus that contain a collection of videos conversations [15,19,25], isolated signs [11,25,26], isolated handshapes [19,26], special cameras and sensors [15], recordings with multiple synchronized cameras [15,25] or focused only on linguistic research [19,34]. Melnyk et al. (2014) [29] presented a review of other databases by ASLR perspective, but from HCI context there are the same limitations.

The problems of these databases are related either to the disconsidering of the context of use or to controlled environments that restrict the natural movements of the user. Another usual problem is related to the conceptual approach: (a) the use of the whole-word model, and (b) select signs randomly and without criteria.

In this case, a database with a large number of signs can not cover all the SL in relation to the sub-units. In addition, the use of the sets without similarity between the signs in the training and testing of the application, provides a system with low accuracy in the results and consequently a poorer user experience.

The lack of a computational model to describe the signs and their sub-units is evident. The use of the phoneme-based approach with a robust computational model in the development process of ASLR systems [7] can improve the user experience in real environments with more accurate and complete systems.

4   Context-Based Collaborative Framework

The framework (Fig. 1) describes: the **computational framework** (approach, storage, sharing, etc.) that assists all stages of the process, such as the **context of use and the activity**, the **collaborative approach**, the **SL database** and the **continuous improvement**. Each module of the framework assists the other modules, providing an integrated approach to build a SL database.

In subsequent sections each module is detailed, presenting some results of their application in a real context of the Deafs to validate the strategy.

4.1   Context and User Activities

This module is intended to describe a special context of a Deaf community. The description must specify: **(a)** the profiles, **(b)** the environment, **(c)** the activity worked in this context, and **(d)** the time. In the case study to validate this module, we instantiate the following way:

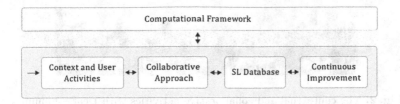

Fig. 1. The steps of the context-based collaborative framework

Profile. The users consist of Deaf students at an undergraduate course of Lilbras (Brazilian Sign Language). This profile was chosen due to the easy access to them inside of the university. However, any user profile can be chosen, if properly connected with the activity, the environment and the time.

Environment. We performed the activities in the classroom, a common room and daily used by the students. It is important to mention that due to the visual feature of the SL, it is common for classrooms to be organized in a way that facilitates the conversation and the view of the current "speaker" (usually an interpreter) by the students.

Activity. The discussion and the application of the concepts learned in the classroom; in this case, the SL Phonology. Any activity could be chosen. During activities (discourse), the isolated signs must be captured and saved by the coordinator.

Time. Meetings occurred as complementary activities, some days after the correspondent lessons. This brought benefits to the Deafs, who practiced the concepts and counted these meetings as extra activities for their course.

4.2 Collaborative Approach

The **collaborative** strategy can be local or online supported by a system. The key issue is to develop the contextual activity planned, saving the discourse and the generated signs. For the experiment we used local meetings. If the online is chosen, a platform as InCoP [38] is needed to support the collaboration.

The **coordination** is conducted by a mediator (tasks organization, activity description and control) and an assistant (operational tasks). In the case of at least one actor does not communicate in SL, an interpreter must attend. The interpreter must belong to the same community, to avoid communication problems due to regionalisms and slang.

In the **Cooperation** process, the mediator should supervise the discussion and when necessary help to create a consensus. During the activity, the discourse and the interactions must be recorded in the database as **discourse**.

We use the phonology context based on CCKC (Collaborative Consensus and Knowledge Creation) process [23] to define **isolated signs**. This approach interconnects the context, the collaboration and the computation to generate a

Fig. 2. The contextual and collaborative activities with Deaf community

robust, contextual and representative database. Some of the activities carried out along the process were show in Fig. 2.

4.3   SL Database

Approach. The *phoneme-based model* [7] consists of segmenting the signs in sub-units that are described in the SL structure: the phonetic sub-units (finite set used to create the signs). Thus, it is possible to build an ASLR system to recognize these parameters, obtaining a generic service, even with signs included later. This approach allows the generation of a representative database, since it can be built from a set of signs which covers all the subunits that compose the phonological tree leaves.

Description. Each isolated sign should be described trought a computational model that represents the structure and rules of the phonology of SL. This model must have a high level of details, because should differentiate the very similar signs with different meanings in SL.

For this task we used the CORE-SL (*Computational Representation Model of the SL*) [6], that defines each sub-unit, provides examples, has a high level of detail and is based on HCI approach for natural interaction by SL.

Storage and Retrieval. Each isolated sign should be stored in the database at the end of each activity with the video and the corresponding description, creating a reference to the sign used in the discussions.

For the storage we used the system presented in the CORE-SL [7], which allows the upload of the sign in video and their description. Additionally, the system has a search engine to retrieve the signs and groups based on sub-units.

For the experiment we used a conventional and low cost video camera, frequently used during the activities of the Deafs such as classroom video chat.

Min-Max Approach. The problem of the existing databases is the lack of a method to determine if the signs set is representative (cover the signs creation possibilities). The objective is to allow this completeness with a Minimum-Maximum Set of Signs (MMSS), that should minimize the number of signs, but should maximize the sub-units of the computational model, in order to reduce the complexity, the training cost and acquisition of the signs from new users.

The Min-Max approach is defined as: given as input a set $E = \{e_1, e_2, ..., e_n\}$ of CORE-SL sub-units, and a signs set (dictionary) $S = \{s_1, s_2, ..., s_m\}$ where

---

Algorithm 1. MMSS Greedy Strategy

1: **function** MMSS(E, S)
2:     $C \leftarrow []$ ▷ C initially empty
3:     **while** $E \neq []$ **and** $S \neq []$ **do**   ▷ repeat until cover all E sub-units
4:         $choice\ S' \in S, max(|S' \cap E|)$ ▷ S' should cover a maximum of E
5:         $E \leftarrow E - S'$ ▷ remove the sub-units of S' in E
6:         $C \leftarrow C \cup S'$ ▷ C gets the solution of this iteration
7:         $S \leftarrow S - S'$ ▷ remove S' of **S**
8:     **return** C ▷ return the solution

---

each sign is described by a combination of the E, find the set $C \subseteq S$ such that $|C|$ should be minimum and their elements should cover a maximum of E sub-units.

The MMSS can be modeled as the *Set Cover Problem* (SCP). Since the SCP does not have an algorithm to compute the optimal solution in polynomial-time, a solution is the use of an approximation algorithm which aims to find an approximate solution efficiently [14]. Then, a Greedy algorithm was used [13].

The MMSS can be applied to the CORE-SL system that controls the list of sub-units that not were instantiated by a sign. Thus, during the CCKC process, this feature can be used to select signs for the sub-units not yet instantiated.

4.4 Continuous Improvement

The database generated at one activity can be continuously improved. This can be done by: (a) applying the framework to other groups and activities (same database); (b) including the framework in the ASLR system, that can be provided as a service / tool for the end user (Deaf communities).

In the service, the system can use the collaboration of the users applying a continuous iterative testing for the improvement of the database and the system, iteratively building a better interaction experience for the Deaf.

For instance, after processing the user's search (in SL), the system can return a result and ask the user if its correct. If incorrect, the system:

1. can show a list of signs to the user and request the correct sign;
2. can allow the user to record a new example of this sign via webcam;
3. can allow the updating of a description in computational model;

Initially, the ASLR system is trained with the SL database. The MMSS can also be used to generate the training and the test set, for example, customizing the algorithm to include one or more signs by parameter in result. In the test step, the system receives a sign (training set), processes, generates the description (CORE-SL) and evaluates the similarity of the result with the SL Database. If not found, the system is trained again (iterative process), as showed in Fig. 3.

In the real environment, the user searches a sign in the system. This input is processed and the results evaluated. Then a list is returned with a solution of candidates signs (based on a similarity function). Then, through this list, the user can take actions to improve the system, as previously mentioned. Then, the human-computer interaction will be improved in use.

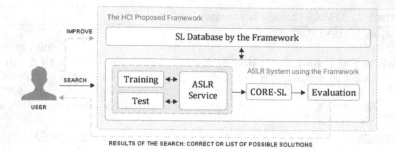

Fig. 3. The framework applied in the ASLR system as a service for the Deaf people.

4.5 Using Related Literature SL Databases

The framework also can be applied in related literature SL databases. In this case, the selected SL database should be incorporated into the CORE-SL system, and then, the framework can be applied with real users, for example, on a local or online activity to describe the signs. Since our hypothesis is that the use of an existing database to create new knowledge of phonology or even knowledge of other SL (sub-units are universal).

5 Conclusions

The present work describes the requirements for the appropriate development of SL databases regarding the correctness of the computational linguistic treatment and the attending to the real needs of Deaf users in associated applications or services. By our perspective, CV recognition protocols have to be adapted to this framework whenever the ASLR systems aim to support these communities (Deaf people) in their activities in the real world.

The framework has been proved to be an adequate method to create natural SL databases, from contextual and collaborative activities with Deaf people.

Since the phoneme-based approach requires that there are signs for all sub-units (ensuring completeness), a controlled human process would be costly and require a long time. Therefore, a collaborative approach (local or online) can minimize the time to create the database, as well as the size of the signs set of the database.

Furthermore, the context-based approach provides more robust insights than controlled environment, such as the real discourse situations, the regionalisms, the similar signs and the interpersonal variations.

These insights should be considered in the development process of the ASLR systems, in order to provide more quality and accuracy for the service, improving the user experience during the human-computer interaction through the SL.

The HCI approach supported by the framework aims to develop an end-user ASLR service. Thus, the service can be continually improved by its use in a real environments with the cooperation of the end users.

References

1. Acesso Brasil, May 2011. http://acessobrasil.org.br/libras
2. ASL Browser, May 2011. http://aslbrowser.commtechlab.msu.edu
3. Spread the sign. spreadthesign.com (2015). http://www.spreadthesign.com/gb/
4. Abowd, G.D., Dey, A.K.: Towards a better understanding of context and context-awareness. In: Gellersen, H.-W. (ed.) HUC 1999. LNCS, vol. 1707, pp. 304–307. Springer, Heidelberg (1999)
5. Ackerman, M., Darrell, T., Weitzner, D.J.: Privacy in context. Hum.-Comput. Interact. **16**(2–4), 167–176 (2001)
6. Antunes, D.R.: Um Modelo de Descrição Computacional da Fonologia da Língua de Sinais Brasileira. Master's thesis, Pós-Graduação em Informática, UFPR (2011)
7. Antunes, D.R., Guimarães, C., García, L.S., Oliveira, L.E.S., Fernandes, S.: A framework to support development of sign language human-computer interaction: building tools for effective information access and inclusion of the deaf. In: Proceedings of the Fifth IEEE International Conference on Research Challenges in Information Science, pp. 126–137 (2011)
8. Baker, C.A.: Microanalysis of the nonmanual components of questions in American Sign Language. Ph.D. thesis, University of California, Berkeley (1983)
9. Barros, L.: Suporte a ambientes distribuídos para aprendizagem cooperativa. Ph.D. thesis, COPPE/UFRJ, Rio de Janeiro (1994)
10. Brentari, D.: A Prosodic Model of Sign Language Phonology. A Bradford book - MIT Press, London (1998)
11. Bungerot, J., Stein, D., Dreuw, P., Ney, H., Morrissey, S., Way, A., van Zijl, L.: The atis sign language corpus (2008)
12. Chomsky, N.: Knowledge of Language: Its Nature, Origin and Use. Praeger Publishers, New York (1986)
13. Chvátal, V.: A greedy heuristic for the set-covering problem. Math. Oper. Res. **4**(3), 233–235 (1979)
14. Cormen, T.H., Leiserson, C.E., Rivest, R.L., Stein, C.: Introduction to Algorithms, 2nd edn. The MIT Press, Cambridge (2001)
15. Crasborn, O., Zwitserlood, I.: The corpus NGT: an online corpus for professionals and laymen. In: Workshop of Representation and Processing of Sign Languages (2008)
16. Dey, A.K.: Understanding and using context. Pers. Ubiquit. Comput. **5**(1), 4–7 (2001). http://dx.doi.org/10.1007/s007790170019
17. Dreuw, P., Neidle, C., Athitsos, V., Sclaroff, S., Ney, H.: Benchmark databases for video-based automatic sign language recognition. In: LREC 2008, ELRA (2008)
18. Efthimiou, E., Fotinea, S.E., Hanke, T., Glauert, J., Bowden, R., Braffort, A., Collet, C., Maragos, J., Goudenove, F.: Dicta-sign: Sign language recognition, generation, and modelling: a research effort with applications in deaf communication proceedings of the language resources and evaluation. In: Conference Workshop on the Representation and Processing of Sign Languages : Corpora and Sign Languages Technologies (2010)
19. Efthimiou, E., Fotinea, S.-E.: GSLC: creation and annotation of a Greek sign language corpus for HCI. In: Stephanidis, C. (ed.) HCI 2007. LNCS, vol. 4554, pp. 657–666. Springer, Heidelberg (2007)
20. Felipe, T.A.: Os Processos de Formação de Palavra na Libras. ETD - Educação Tematica Digital **7**(2), 199–216 (2006)
21. Fernandes, S.: Educação de Surdos, 2nd edn. Editora Ibpex, Curitiba (2011)

22. García, L.S., Guimarães, C., Antunes, D.R., Fernandes, S.: HCI Architecture for Deaf Communities Cultural Inclusion and Citizenship. In: Proceedings of the 15th International Conference on Enterprise Information Systems - ICEIS 2013, vol. 3, pp. 68–75. Angers, France, July 2013

23. Guimarães, C., Antunes, D.R., Fernandes, S., García, L.S., Miranda, A.J.: Empowering collaboration among the deaf: Internet-based knowledge creation system.In: IADIS WWW/Internet 2011 Conference. Proceedings of the IADIS International Conference on WWW/Internet, pp. 137–144 (2011)

24. Jacko, J.A., Sears, A. (eds.): The Human-Computer Interaction Handbook: Fundamentals, Evolving Technologies and Emerging Applications. L. Erlbaum Associates Inc., Hillsdale (2003)

25. Johnston, T., Schembri, A., Adam, R., Napier, J., Thornton, D.: Auslan Signbank: the Auslan Lexical Database (2015). http://www.auslan.org.au/

26. Kumar, E., Kishore, S.R.C., Kishore, P.V.V., Kumar, P.: Video audio interface for recognizing gestures of indian sign language. Int. J. Image Process. (IJIP) 5(4), 479–503 (2011)

27. Liddell, S.K., Johnson, R.E.: American sign language: the phonological base. In: Valli, C., Lucas, C. (eds.) (org.) Linguistics of American Sign Language: an introduction. Clerc Books/Gallaudet Press, Washington, D.C. (2002) (1989)

28. Martinez, A., Wilbur, R., Shay, R., Kak, A.: Purdue rvl-slll asl database for automatic recognition of american sign language. In: 2002 Proceedings of the Fourth IEEE International Conference on Multimodal Interfaces, pp. 167–172 (2002)

29. Melnyk, M., Shadrova, V., Karwatsky, B.: Towards computer assisted international sign language recognition system: a systematic survey. Int. J. Comput. Appl. 89(17), 44–51 (2014)

30. Preece, J., Rogers, Y., Sharp, H.: Interaction Design, 1st edn. John Wiley & Sons Inc., New York (2002)

31. de Quadros, R.M., Karnopp, L.B.: Língua de Sinais Brasileira: Estudos Linguísticos. Artmed, Porto Alegre (2004)

32. da Rocha, L.V., Edelweiss, N., Iochpe, C.: Geoframe-t: a temporal conceptual framework for data modeling. In: Proceedings of the 9th ACM International Symposium on Advances in Geographic Information Systems. GIS 2001, pp. 124–129. ACM, New York, NY, USA (2001)

33. Rodden, T., Cheverst, K., Davies, K., Dix, A.: Exploiting context in hci design for mobile systems. Workshop on HCI with Mobile Devices (1998)

34. Schembri, A., Fenlon, J., Rentelis, R., Reynolds, S., Cormier, K.: Building the british sign language corpus. Lang. Documentation Conserv. 7, 136–154 (2013)

35. Shehabuddeen, N., Buddeen, N., Probert, D., Phaal, R., Platts, K.: Representing and approaching complex management issues: part 1 - role and definition. Centre for Technology Management (CTM) (1999)

36. Stokoe, W.C., Casterline, D., Croneberg, C.: The Dictionary of American Sign Language on Linguistic Principles. Gallaudet College Press, USA (1965)

37. Tijiboy, A.V., Maçada, D.L., Santarosa, L.M.C., Fagundes, L.d.C.: Aprendizagem cooperativa em ambientes telemáticos. Informática na Educação: teoria & prática. Porto Alegre, vol. 1(2) (abr. 1999), pp. 19–28 (1999)

38. Trindade, D.F.G.: InCoP: Um Framework Conceitual para o Design de Ambientes Colaborativos Inclusivos para Surdos e Não-Surdos de Cultivo a Comunidades de Prática. Ph.D. thesis, UFPR, Informatics Program, Curitiba, PR (2013)

Prototyping and Preliminary Evaluation of Sign Language Translation System in the Railway Domain

Cristina Battaglino[1]([✉]), Carlo Geraci[2], Vincenzo Lombardo[1], and Alessandro Mazzei[1]

[1] CIRMA and Department of Informatics, University of Torino, Turin, Italy
battagli@di.unito.it
[2] CNRS, Institut Jean-Nicod, Paris, France

Abstract. This paper presents the prototype and the preliminary evaluation of an automatic translation system developed in the LIS4ALL project. The system domain is the corpus of railway station announcements in Italian. The output of the system is a 3D animated avatar that signs announcements in Italian Sign Language. The preliminary evaluation, which measures the accuracy of the translations at the sentence level, relies through the BLEU-RAC4 metric, a variant of the traditional BLEU metric used to evaluate Machine Translation, specifically designed for sentence level evaluation. The aim of the evaluation is to compare the LIS4ALL translation outputs with the human counterparts.

1 Introduction

Automatic translation from spoken into sign language (SL) is of growing interest for the scientific community. In fact, in addition to the traditional issues featured by the automatic translation for spoken languages, Sign Languages exhibit a new variety of challenges: dealing with under-studied languages (e.g., the absence of reference grammars), poorly understood linguistic phenomena (e.g., how to manage the signing space, where signs are performed), the lack of a suitable written form for SL that goes beyond the gloss level; the handling of the multichannel nature of SL articulators (namely, manual and non-manual articulators). Therefore, automatic translation into SL is an interdisciplinary research domain where linguistic, graphic and algorithmic skills are required.

Most of the current research on the automatic translation into sign languages features both symbolic [5,10] and statistical approaches [11]. Symbolic approaches adopt algorithms and knowledge bases that have a direct correspondence with traditional linguistics (grammar, vocabulary, etc.). Natural Language Processing tools are used for analysis and generation of morphological, syntactic and semantic features for both the spoken language input and the sign language output. Often, it is necessary to develop from scratch lexical resources, grammars and knowledge bases. In contrast, statistical approaches adopt algorithms based on alignment frequencies between texts in the source and target languages

© Springer International Publishing Switzerland 2015
M. Antona and C. Stephanidis (Eds.): UAHCI 2015, Part II, LNCS 9176, pp. 339–350, 2015.
DOI: 10.1007/978-3-319-20681-3_32

(sequences of glosses in the case of SL), respectively. Large resources (such as, e.g., parallel corpora) are needed to compute such frequencies. Both approaches have advantages and drawbacks in the specific context of the automatic translation into SL; both adopt avatar technology in order to visualize the translation output [5, 7, 11, 15].

This paper presents a symbolic Italian-LIS translation system for the Italian Sign Language (called LIS - Lingua Italiana dei Segni, the language of the Italian Deaf community), with an avatar animation output, and its preliminary evaluation using the BLEU-RAC4 metric [17].

The paper is organized as follows: in Sect. 2 we present the LIS4ALL architecture and describe how the LIS output is generated from an Italian text. In Sect. 3 we describe the application domain, based on railway station announcements. Section 4 presents the results of the evaluation by using the BLEU-RAC4 metric and discusses the results. Section 5 concludes the paper.

2   The Architecture of LIS4ALL

Current research projects on the automatic translation into SL investigate relatively small domains in which avatars show a good performance, such as, e.g., post office announcements [2] and drivers license renewal [15]. Project LIS4ALL does not make an exception, and its domain is the corpus of announcements broadcast in Italian railway stations.

The project approach relies on the experience, knowledge, and resources of the previous ATLAS project [10], a pioneering project on the automatic translation from Italian into LIS that set up the complete pipeline and focused on the weather forecasting domain. The LIS4ALL project extends the coverage of syntactic constructions and the lexicon built for ATLAS (about 2350 signs), by adding the signs that are specific to the railway domain (about 120).

The major innovations of LIS4ALL are: (1) the account of new linguistics issues that are typical of the domain addressed, and (2) the translation architecture that is partially modified with a parser based on regular expressions. This choice is motivated by the fact that the railway station announcements are based on pre-determined templates and by the particular linguistic structure internal to railway station announcements (see Sect. 3). This allows us to build a parser based on regular expressions that recognizes the correct template for each specific announcement.

Figure 1 illustrates the pipeline of the LIS4ALL architecture, which includes four modules (for further details about the system and the translation process see [4]):

1. Regular expression parser for Italian;
2. Filler/slot based semantic interpreter;
3. Generator for the LIS grammar;
4. Avatar performing the synthesis of the sequence of signs (i.e., the final LIS sentence).

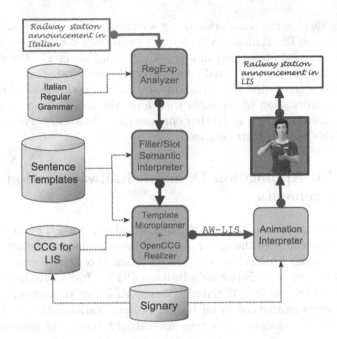

Fig. 1. LIS4ALL Translation Architecture.

The architecture of the LIS4ALL project employs a regular expression-based analyzer that produces a simple (non recursive) filler/slot based semantics to parse the Italian input. This has proven to be more effective because of the large number of complex noun phrases, with several prepositional phrases and nominal modifiers, resulting in degraded parser performance due to multiple attachment options (see Sect. 3).

The LIS4ALL generator consists of two sub-modules: a microplanner and a realizer [14]. The microplanner decides about the syntactic organization of the LIS sentence and about the signs to use in the generation. Following [3], the microplanner is based on templates, which exploit the filler/slot structure produced by the semantic analyzer. The output of the microplanner is a hybrid logic formula in a tree structure (XML), that encodes an abstract syntactic tree. Extending the *Combinatory Categorical Grammar* (CCG) grammar [18] designed in the ATLAS project [10] and using the parallel Italian-LIS corpus produced in LIS4ALL, we implemented a new CCG grammar for LIS that can be used by the OpenCCG realizer to produce LIS sentences in the railway domain [19]. The output of the realizer is an XML file specified with the AWLIS (Atlas Written LIS) language, i.e., a sequence of *lemmata*, accompanied by a description of the meaning of each lemma, its syntactic number and the link to the corresponding sign. The AWLIS language is an XML based language and is used for communication between the generator and the avatar. The Animation Interpreter (see Fig. 1) takes as input the AWLIS representation of the sentence and generates the animation of the virtual signer.

In order to display the translation using a virtual avatar, the following operations are necessary. The signs are collected (through motion capture or key-frame animation techniques) and stored in a repository, the "signary". The signs that create a sentence are then retrieved, concatenated, and synthesized, so that the animation player can guide the virtual avatar in the realization of the translation. The concatenation of the signs that form the LIS sentence is expressed through an animation language [8] that encodes the animation curves into tracks associated with the body parts engaged.

3   LIS4ALL Application Domain: Railway Station Announcements

Railway station announcements are the domain of application of the LIS4ALL project. The structure and the templates for these announcements are described in the Manuale degli Annunci Sonori (MAS – Manual of the Spoken Announcements), filled out by Rete Ferroviaria Italiana (RFI – Italian Railway Network company) [1]. MAS specifies 39 templates that RFI uses to automatically produce the messages announced in all Italian railway stations: 15 templates concern departures, 13 templates concern arrivals, 11 templates concern special situations, such as, e.g., strikes.

The templates have been designed by a group of linguists to yield concise and direct messages in Italian. Full relative clauses, sentential coordination and complex structures (e.g., ellipses) at the sentential level are avoided. As a consequence, the language domain is a controlled language. However, while the syntactic complexity is kept simple at the sentential level, the level of complexity of nominal expressions is considerably high. Consider the following example:

1. "Il treno straordinario Frecciabianca 9764, di Trenitalia proveniente da Roma Termini e diretto a Torino Porta Nuova, delle ore 13:57 è in arrivo al binario 5." ("*Trenitalia Frecciabianca 9764 special train, from Roma Termini, directed to Torino Porta Nuova, with scheduled arrival at 1:57pm is arriving at platform 5.*")

The syntactic structure of the entire clause simply involves a nominal subject ("il treno" / "*the train*"), an unaccusative predicate ("è in arrivo" / "*is arriving*"), and a prepositional complement ("al binario" / "*at platform*"). However, the internal structure of the subject is incredibly complex, involving the following six components:

1. an intersective adjective (e.g., "speciale" / "*special*");
2. an appositive nominal modifier encoding the category of the train (e.g., "Frecciabianca");
3. an appositive nominal modifier encoding the number of the train (e.g., "9764");
4. a prepositional phrase encoding the enterprise that owns the train (e.g., "di Trenitalia" / "*Trenitalia*");

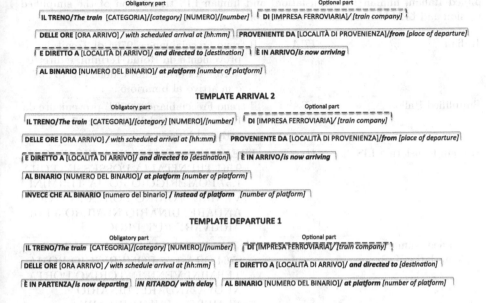

Fig. 2. The templates *Arrival 1*, *Arrival 2* and *Departure 1*. Fixed lexical entries are indicated in bold. The square parenthesis indicate variable lexical entries. The dotted lines indicate the optional parts, while solid lines indicate the mandatory parts.

5. a coordination of two reduced relative clauses encoding origin and final destination of the train (e.g., "proveniente da Roma Termini" / *"from Roma Termini"* and "diretto a Torino Porta Nuova" / *"directed to Torino Porta Nuova"*);

6. a prepositional phrase encoding the scheduled time (e.g., "delle ore 13:57" / *"with scheduled arrival at 13:57"*).

The MAS manual specifies what parts of the template are obligatory or optional, respectively. The optional parts are the first intersective adjective, the name of the company, and the final destination of the train. Both obligatory and optional parts are composed of fixed parts, invariable lexical items, and variable parts that depend upon specific features of the train (e.g., the name of the final destination of the train). For example, in the template *Arrival 1* (see Fig. 2), "Il treno' / *"The train"* is a mandatory part composed of fixed lexical items ("Il" + "treno"), while "diretto a [località di arrivo]" / *"directed to [destination]"* is an optional part composed of fixed lexical items (e.g., "diretto" + "a") and variable lexical items (e.g., "località di arrivo"" / *"destination"*, in square brackets).

By analyzing a corpus of messages produced within 24 h of a random day at the Torino Porta Nuova Station (5014 messages total), we found that a small number of templates cover the majority of announcements, while others are virtually absent. The three most frequent templates are *Arrival 1*, which covers

Table 1. Example of a railway station announcement from Arrival 1 in: Italian, simplified Italian, human LIS translation, and human LIS translation of the simplified version and LIS4ALL automatic translation.

Italian	ITA	Il treno Frecciabianca, 9764 di Trenitalia, proveniente da Roma Termini, e diretto a Torino Porta Nuova, delle ore 13 : 57, è in arrivo al binario 5
Simplified Italian	ITA'	Il treno Frecciabianca, 9764, proveniente da Roma Termini, delle ore 13 : 57, è in arrivo al binario 5
Human translation LIS	H_{LIS}	TRENO FRECCIABIANCA NUMERO 9764 TRENITALIA POSSESSIVO ORA 1.57 POMERIGGIO ROMA TERMINI VENIRE, TORINO PORTA NUOVA ANDARE, BINARIO NUMERO 5 LUI ARRIVARE FUT_PROG
Simplified Human Translation LIS	H'_{LIS}	TRENO FRECCIABIANCA NUMERO 9764 ORA 1.57 POMERIGGIO ROMA TERMINI VENIRE, TORINO PORTA NUOVA ANDARE, BINARIO NUMERO 5 LUI ARRIVARE FUT_PROG
System Translation	$LIS4ALL$	TRENO FRECCIABIANCA NUMERO 9764 ORA 1.57 POMERIGGIO ROMA TERMINI VENIRE_PROVENIRE BINARIO NUMERO 5 ARRIVARE FUT_PROG

36 %, *Departure 1* that covers 26 %, and *Arrival 2* that covers 14 %; altogether, they cover about 80 % of the total number of announcements. Therefore, we focused on the translations of the railway station announcements that feature these three templates. All these templates are exemplified in Fig. 2.

Analyzing the corpora of the announcements, we built three regular expressions that match the three templates above. Specifically, for each template, we designed a sequence of semantic slots that are filled, during the translation process, with lexical elements (e.g., scheduled time, platform, station name, destination, place of departure, train category). Each slot corresponds to a variable part of the template. However, considering the high complexity of the nominal subjects in the source language and the fact that nominal modification is highly understudied of the LIS grammar [9], we could not address all the types of nominal modifiers omitted in the templates. So, we limited the development of the automatic translation to the mandatory components of the templates (including both fixed and variable parts, i.e. bold and square parenthesis parts in Fig. 2), by introducing a pre–processing module that simplifies a sentence by deleting the optional components.

Table 1 reports an example of a railway station announcement belonging to the *Arrival 1* template. The first row reports the original announcement in Italian (ITA), the second row reports the simplified announcement in Italian (ITA'), the third row reports the LIS human translation (H_{LIS}), the fourth row reports the human translation of the simplified announcement (H'_{LIS}), the (last) fifth row reports the machine translation output (LIS4ALL). Specifically, the name of the train enterprise and the second conjunct of the reduced relative clause (the one specifying the final destination of the train) have been removed.

Without entering the details of the syntactic structure of the human translation, one important aspect to notice is that the human translation includes a pronominal pointing (i.e., Italian third person singular pronoun "LUI"/ "IT"), that is missing from the automatic translation. This pronominal pointing corresponds to a sort of subject clitic doubling, which is required by the LIS grammar when the subject is too complex. In general, a number of relevant aspects of the LIS grammar are not accounted for by the LIS4ALL project, namely: non-manual "articulators", classifier constructions, grammatical use of the signing space, and prosodic structuring of the message. We are planning a thorough evaluation to identify the priority of each construct to be addressed; in the rest of this paper, we describe a preliminary evaluation that takes into account the components implemented so far through accuracy measures that allow to compare the human, with respect to the automatic Italian–to–LIS translation.

4   Evaluation

The evaluation of the structural components of our Italian–to–LIS translation adopts the BLEU-RAC4 metric [17], a variant of BLEU (BiLingual Evaluation Understudy) [6,13], a common evaluation metrics in machine translation, also for the case of sign languages [12,15,16]. The BLEU-RAC4 score is a measure based on the correspondence of n-grams (sequence of adjacent lexical items) between a reference translation (in our case, the Italian–to–LIS human translation) and a candidate translation (the LIS4ALL automatic translation). The BLEU result is a measure of precision p_n that ranges from 0 to 1 (often reported as a percentage from 0 to 100 %). This measure reflects the accuracy of the candidate translation relative to the temporal order of the sequence of signs. While the classical BLEU metric considers the *precision* based on n-grams and combines each n-gram precision through a geometric mean, the BLEU-RAC4 considers *recall* to yield a better performance at the sentence level and relies on the arithmetic mean [17]. Similarly to BLEU, BLEU-RAC4 assigns a score between 0 and 1 as a measure of the quality of the machine translation. We adopted the BLEU-RAC4 metric rather than BLEU, because our domain of application is made of single sentences and not of concatenated sentences.

The aim of the experiment is to assess the correspondence between the LIS4ALL translation output, which does not account for the optional parts, and the human translation, which does account for the optional parts. In particular, given a fixed number of optional parts, we selected a sample of sentences that uniformly contain such parts; then, we built a modified sample consisting of the same sentences lacking the optional parts; both samples were translated manually by the human interpreters (H_{LIS} and H'_{LIS} translation, see above); both samples were also translated through the LIS4ALL system (LIS4ALL translation, see above); for each pair of translated samples, the one with the optional parts and the one without the optional parts, we computed the BLEU-RAC4 score that measures the difference between the human and the system translation, respectively; finally, we applied a statistical t–test to measure the distance between the two scores.

Each sample of sentences in Italian contains 21 tokens for each of the three templates above, 63 announcements total (21 for Arrival 1, 21 for Arrival 2, and 21 for Departure 1, see Sect. 3). The number 21 comes out of a combinatory calculation that takes into account two specific optional components (the train company and destination/delay, respectively, see below) and the possible lexical gaps due to incompleteness of the sign repository (in turn due to uncertainty in the definition of the individual signs in such a niche domain). Tokens from the first sample contained a selection of the optional components, concerning the phrases corresponding to the train company (e.g., "di [Impresa ferroviaria]" / "[train company]") and either the destination of the train (for arrivals only, e.g., "diretto a [località di arrivo]" / "directed to [place of arrival]") or the amount of delay (for departures only, e.g., "in ritardo" / "with delay"). In addition to these two optional components, we included the problem of lexical gaps for the case of train categories missing in the lexicon (which numbered three). The combination of multiple optional parts together with lexical gaps leads to a sample of 21 sentences per template. These parts were removed from the second sample, which only consisted of sentences with components implemented in LIS4ALL, which could only contain accidental lexical gaps.

Then, on the one hand, the two samples were manually translated by following the set of rules elaborated by a team of interpreters and a linguist (one of the authors of this paper), on the other, the two samples were automatically translated by the LIS4ALL system (i.e., they were the output of the open CCG realizer – see Fig. 1). An example of the announcements with the optional parts, a simplified version, and their human and automatic translations in LIS, respectively, are given in Table 1. For the purpose of this paper, we only focus on the comparison between the sequences of glosses produced by the human and the automatic translations, respectively. Section 4.1 illustrates how the BLEU-RAC4 score is computed, Sect. 4.2 reports the discussion of the results.

4.1   Computing the BLEU-RAC4 Score

The *BLEU-RAC4* is defined as follows:

$$BLEU - RAC4 = \left(\frac{1}{4} \sum_{n=1}^{4} r_n \right) \tag{1}$$

where the recall r_n is defined as:

$$r_n = \frac{Shared}{Total} \tag{2}$$

Shared is the number of n-grams shared by the candidate translation and the reference translation, *Total* is the total number of n-grams in the reference translation. For example, given the *LIS4ALL* translation compared to the H_{LIS} translation, the *2-gram* "Treno Frecciabianca"/*"Train Frecciabianca"* finds a match in the H_{LIS} translation, and the same is for the *3-gram* "Ora 1.57 pomeriggio" *"1.57 p.m."*. Since the 2-gram "Treno Frecciabianca" and the 3-gram "Ora 1.57 pomeriggio" appear both in the H_{LIS} and in the LIS4ALL translations, so both increase the *Shared* counter. The computation of the total score of the *LIS4ALL* translation compared to the H_{LIS} translation is given in Fig. 3. Notice that this system does not penalize for lexical items that for some reason appear in the candidate but do not appear in the reference translation.

n-gram	Shared n-gram between H-LIS and LIS4ALL Translator announcement	Total n-gram in H-LIS announcement	$r_{n\text{-}gram}$
1	15	22	15/22
2	11	21	11/21
3	7	20	7/20
4	4	19	4/19
BLEU-RAC4 SCORE		44,15% (0, 4415)	

Fig. 3. An example for computing the BLEU-RAC4 score.

4.2 Results and Discussion

For each announcement, we computed the BLEU-RAC4 score, comparing the *LIS4ALL* translation against the human translation of the full announcement, H_{LIS}, and its simplified version, H'_{LIS} (see Sect. 3). The prediction is that the *LIS4ALL* automatic translations have a better performance, compared with the human translation of the simplified announcements than compared with the translation of non-simplified announcements. Mean and standard deviation for each template are given in Table 2.

Paired sample t-tests reveal that the difference between the two series of scores is significant (Arrival 1: $t_{20} = -5.72$, $p < .001$; Arrival 2: $t_{21} = -4.30$, $p < .001$, Departure 1: $t_{21} = -6.90$, $p < .001$). Significance is also maintained at the global level ($t_{63} = -9.35$, $p < .001$). As expected, *LIS4ALL* translations better match H'_{LIS} than H_{LIS}. Despite the fact that the simplified Italian version of the announcements is better handled by our system, a degraded performance with respect to human translations is still observed (overall BLEU-RAC4

Table 2. Mean and the standard deviation for LIS4ALL translation of templates A1, A2 and P1.

Result	Arrival 1	Arrival 2	Departure 1	Mean
H_{LIS}	0.55 (sd = 0.09)	0.62 (sd = 0.07)	0.58 (sd = 0.09)	0.58 (sd = 0.09)
H'_{LIS}	0.66 (sd = 0.09)	0.70 (sd = 0.08)	0.66 (sd = 0.09)	0.67 (sd = 0.09)

score = 0.67). This is partly due to the fact that our system is currently not able to manage the subject pronominal doubling observed in the H'_{LIS} translations and partly to accidental lexical gaps.

In addition to this, lexical gaps have unexpected outcome orders on the output of the open CCG realizer. This can be shown by looking at the boldfaced constituents in the two examples below:

1. H'_{LIS}: treno/*train* [**intercity notte**/*intercity notte*] numero/*number* [9 6 1 0] ora/*with scheduled arrival at* [5.02] mattina/*a.m.* [**napoli centrale venire**]/ *directed to [napoli centrale]* [**binario numero 16**]/*platform number [16]* ix3 arrivare fut_prog/ */is arriving*;
2. *LIS4ALL*: treno/*train* [**napoli centrale venire**]/*directed to [napoli cen- trale]* [**binario numero 16**]/*platform number [16]* numero/*number* [9 6 1 0] ora/*with scheduled arrival at* [5.02] mattina / *a.m.* arrivare fut_prog. / *is arriving*.

The effect of lexical gap on the order of signs in the LIS4ALL automatic translation scores 0.71. The subject modifiers referring to train origin and platform number are displaced to second and third position, right after the subject in the LIS4ALL automatic translation. This error correlates with lexical gaps on the train category ("Intercity notte" is missing in the LIS4ALL translation). The result is that the order of higher level constituents (larger n-grams) is disrupted, and the final score of the automatic translation is lower than expected.

5   Conclusion

The LIS4ALL prototype is a system that translates railway station announce- ments from Italian into LIS. The paper described its architecture, the domain of application, and the preliminary evaluation of its output. Currently, the system has been developed to handle a simplified version of three templates used in Italian stations. Recognition is done by a parser based on regular expressions, while generation is left to a filler/slot based semantic interpreter and to an open CCG realizer. The output is then sent to an animation interpreter which pro- duces the translation into sign language. In this paper, we evaluated the output of the open CCG realizer module by comparing the temporal order of the glosses of the signs as produced by human and automatic interpreter, respectively. The temporal sequence of the glosses for 63 announcements (21 for each template) has been evaluated by using the BLEU-RAC4 metric. Results showed a mean score of 0.67. Three sources of errors have been identified: (1) the inability to handle subject doubling, (2) lexical gaps, (3) displacement of some subject modifiers (possibly due to lexical gaps in parts of the sentence). While the field of automatic translation into Sign Languages is still in its infancy and several aspects of the human sign language production are still to be implemented in the automatic translation pipeline (especially those concerning the non-manual component), projects such as LIS4ALL show that the automatic translation into sign languages is a worth endeavor.

Acknowledgments. This work has been partially supported by the project LIS4ALL partially funded by Regione Piemonte, Innovation Hub for ICT, 2011–2014, POR-FESR 07–13. Part of the research leading to these results also received funding from the European Research Council under the European Union's Seventh Framework Program (FP/2007–2013) / ERC Grant Agreement n. 324115-FRONTSEM (PI: Schlenker). Research was partially conducted at Institut d'Etudes Cognitives (ENS), which is supported by grants ANR-10-IDEX-0001-02 PSL and ANR-10-LABX-0087 IEC.

References

1. Acoustic Announcements Manual - MAS, Rete Ferroviaria Italiana (RFI) (2011). http://www.rfi.it/cms-file/allegati/rfi/MAS.pdf (in Italian)
2. Cox, S., Lincoln, M., Tryggvason, J., Nakisa, M., Wells, M., Tutt, M., Abbott, S.: Tessa, a system to aid communication with deaf people. In: Proceedings of the Fifth International ACM Conference on Assistive Technologies, pp. 205–212. ACM (2002)
3. Foster, M.E., White, M.: Techniques for text planning with xslt. In: Proceedings of the Workshop on NLP and XML (NLPXML-2004): RDF/RDFS and OWL in Language Technology, pp. 1–8. Association for Computational Linguistics (2004)
4. Geraci, C., Mazzei, A.: Last train to "rebaudengo fossano": the case of some names in avatar translation. In: Proceedings of the 6th Workshop on the Representation and Processing of Sign Languages, pp. 63–66 (2013)
5. Huenerfauth, M.: Generating American Sign Language classifier predicates for English-to-ASL machine translation. Ph. D. thesis, University of Pennsylvania (2006)
6. Koehn, P., Monz, C.: Manual and automatic evaluation of machine translation between european languages. In: Proceedings of the Workshop on Statistical Machine Translation, pp. 102–121. Association for Computational Linguistics (2006)
7. Lombardo, V., Battaglino, C., Damiano, R., Nunnari, F.: An avatar-based interface for the Italian sign language. In: International Conference on Complex, Intelligent and Software Intensive Systems, CISIS 2011, June 30 - July 2, 2011, Korean Bible University, Seoul, Korea, pp. 589–594 (2011)
8. Lombardo, V., Nunnari, F., Damiano, R.: A virtual interpreter for the Italian sign language. In: Allbeck, A., Badler, N., Bickmore, T., Pelachaud, C., Safonova, A. (eds.) IVA 2010. LNCS, vol. 6356, pp. 201–207. Springer, Heidelberg (2010)
9. Mantovan, L., Geraci, C.: The syntax of cardinal numerals in LIS. In: Presented at the 45th Annual Meeting of the North Esta Linguistic Society (NELT), October 31 - November 2. MIT, Cambridge (2014)

10. Mazzei, A., Lesmo, L., Battaglino, C., Vendrame, M., Bucciarelli, M.: Deep natural language processing for Italian sign language translation. In: Baldoni, M., Baroglio, C., Boella, G., Micalizio, R. (eds.) AI*IA 2013. LNCS, vol. 8249, pp. 193–204. Springer, Heidelberg (2013)
11. Morrissey, S., Way, A., Stein, D., Bungeroth, J., Ney, H.: Combining data-driven mt systems for improved sign language translation. In: Proceedings of Machine Translation Summit XI (MT 2007) (2007)
12. Morrissey, S., Way, A.: Lost in translation: the problems of using mainstream mt evaluation metrics for sign language translation. In: Proceedings of the 5th SALTMIL Workshop on Minority Languages, May 23, 2006, Genoa, Italy (2006)
13. Papineni, K., Roukos, S., Ward, T., Zhu, W.-J.: Bleu: a method for automatic evaluation of machine translation. In: Proceedings of the 40th Annual Meeting of the Association for Computational Linguistics, pp. 311–318. Association for Computational Linguistics (2002)
14. Reiter, E., Dale, R., Feng, Z.: Building Natural Language Generation Systems. MIT Press, Cambridge (2000)
15. San-Segundo, R., Montero, J.M., Córdoba, R., Sama, V., Fernández, F., D'Haro, L.F., López-Ludeña, V., Sánchez, D., García, A.: Design, development and field evaluation of a Spanish into sign language translation system. Pattern Anal. Appl. 15(2), 203–224 (2012)
16. Segundo, R.S., Pérez, A., Ortiz, D., Fernando, D.L., Torres, M., Casacuberta, F.: Evaluation of alternatives on speech to sign language translation. In: INTER-SPEECH, pp. 2529–2532. Citeseer (2007)
17. Song, X., Cohn, T., Specia, L.: Bleu deconstructed: designing a better mt evaluation metric. In: Proceedings of the 14th International Conference on Intelligent Text Processing and Computational Linguistics (CICLING) (2013)
18. Steedman, M.: The Syntactic Process. MIT Press, Cambridge (2000)
19. White, M.: Efficient realization of coordinate structures in combinatory categorial grammar. Res. Lang. Comput. 4(1), 39–75 (2006)

User Friendly Interfaces for Sign Retrieval and Sign Synthesis

Eleni Efthimiou[✉], Stavroula-Evita Fotinea, Theodore Goulas,
and Panos Kakoulidis

Institute for Language and Speech Processing/ATHENA RC, Athens, Greece
{eleni_e, evita, tgoulas, panosk}@ilsp.gr

Abstract. In this paper we touch upon the request for dynamic synthetic signing by discussing requirements for accessibility via Sign Language for information retrieval and dynamic composition of new content. The key issues remain the option for reuse of pre-existing signed "text" along with the exploitation of basic editing facilities similar to those available for written text. We present an approach to the development of intuitive HCI interfaces for dynamic synthetic signing, while synthetic sign content is presented to the user by means of a signing virtual agent (i.e. avatar).

Keywords: Web access · HCI for dynamic sign language synthesis · Deaf communication · Deaf education

1 Introduction

The development of Web 2.0 technologies has made the WWW a place where people constantly interact with each other, by posting information (e.g. on blogs or discussion forums), by modifying and enhancing other people's contributions (e.g. in Wikipedia), and by sharing information (e.g., on Facebook and social news websites).

Unfortunately, these technologies are not easily accessible to sign language (SL) users, because they require the use of written language. On the other hand, sign language videos have two major problems: first, they are not anonymous and second, they cannot be easily edited and reused in the way written texts can.

As recently verified by the proof of concept demonstrator of the Dicta-Sign project[1] [1, 2], the advanced scenario that makes Web 2.0 interactions in sign language possible may incorporate real time recognition and dynamic production of sign language where sign utterance presentation is made available via a signing avatar (Fig. 1).

Within the Dicta-Sign sign-Wiki demonstrator environment, the end user had the option –among other functionalities–of both creating and viewing signed content by exploiting pre-existing lexical resources (Fig. 2) [3]. One of the options demonstrated was the possibility for slight modifications of the stored resources and previously created utterances in order to convey a new message. In all cases, stored and new content was presented to the user by means of a signing avatar [4].

---

[1] http://www.dictasign.eu/ .

© Springer International Publishing Switzerland 2015
M. Antona and C. Stephanidis (Eds.): UAHCI 2015, Part II, LNCS 9176, pp. 351–361, 2015.
DOI: 10.1007/978-3-319-20681-3_33

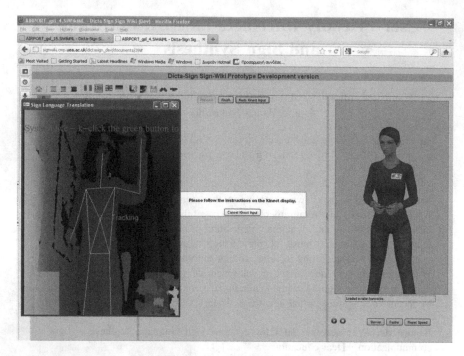

Fig. 1. Kinect input to sign representation

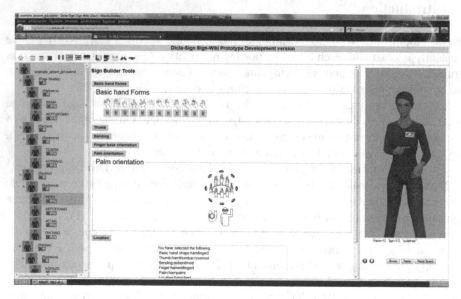

Fig. 2. Sign building and representation environment in the sign-Wiki Dicta-Sign demonstrator

As much freedom as a given system may give the user to create and view synthetic signing, signing avatar performance still remains a challenging task within the domain of sign language technologies. In the rest of the paper, we will discuss the issues of creation and maintenance of sign language resources for synthetic signing, as well as development of sign synthesis interfaces for non-expert users in view of the implementation of synthetic signing in education and communication.

2   Language Resources for Sign Synthesis

For decades, the video has been widely acknowledged among deaf individuals as the only option for transferring signed linguistic utterances. However, although the video remains the only means for SL message transmission that preserves naturalness of expression, it poses a number of serious restrictions as regards the on-the-fly composition of new "text" or the modification of previously created text. These actions are so common in everyday human communication and educational practice, that it is considered trivial for written text to be copied, modified and reused regardless of whether it was originally located on a web page or a local computer.

The limitations in composing, editing and reusing sign language utterances, as well as their consequences for Deaf education and communication have been systematically mentioned in SL studies literature since the second half of the 20th century. Researchers such as Stokoe [5] and more recently the HamNoSyS team [6, 7] and Neidle [8] have proposed different systems for sign transcriptions in an attempt to provide a writing system for SLs in line with the systems available for oral languages [9]. However, the three-dimensional properties of SLs have prevented wide acceptance of such systems for incorporation by Deaf individuals in everyday practice.

In lab environment, however, the possibility of phonetic decomposition of signs and the association of each component of sign articulation with a set of possible features enabled experimentation on synthetic signing performed by signing avatars. Therefore, it is clear that synthetic signing technology heavily depends on two equally significant parameters: (i) an effective sign synthesis engine and (ii) the availability of language resources adequate for sign synthesis.

2.1   Resources Creation and Maintenance

Availability of adequately annotated resources is a necessary condition for synthetic signing. However, creating resources for sign synthesis is not a trivial task since the annotator must be aware of the formation of the reference sign and also able to verify his/her annotations by constantly viewing the synthetic performance of stored annotations. To facilitate the creation and maintenance of lexical resources for synthetic signing the Internet based tool SiS-Builder[2] was developed [10] on the basis of the architecture schematically depicted in Fig. 3.

---

[2] http://speech.ilsp.gr/sl

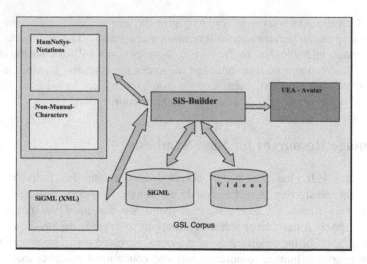

Fig. 3. The SiS-Builder architecture

In the SiS-Builder environment, the author manually creates SL lemmas by providing phonetic transcriptions of signs. The tool accepts as input any sequence of HamNoSys notations and automatically transforms it to a corresponding SiGML script. SiGML transcripts that are so generated can be executed by the avatar, which performs SL content presentation.

In the course of its implementation, SiS-Builder was enriched with a number of functionalities that have provided a complete environment for creating, editing, maintaining and testing lexical resources of, appropriately annotated for sign synthesis and animation. The environment currently allows for the assignment of both manual and non-manual features to signs utilizing the HamNoSys notation system and a drop-down menu for non-manual features (Fig. 4).

SiS-Builder enables multiple users to create and test their own data sets. It may accommodate video files of SL lemmas and associate them with a complex structure of data which include lemma coding for manual and non-manual articulation elements, visualization of the coded items via sign performance by an avatar and conversion of HamNoSys to SiGML files and vice versa allowing for easy coding of corrections and modifications where necessary. As regards Greek Sign Language (GSL) resources, SiS-Builder currently entails approximately 5,500 entries appropriately annotated for synthetic signing.

Furthermore, SiS-Builder has been subject to both classification and initial evaluation in respect to its accessibility features and use in the educational environment at European level [11] in the framework of the ENABLE network (http://www.i-enable.eu/).

2.2   On Signing Avatar Technology and Acceptance

Sign synthesis developed by utilizing sign formation features in order to provide 3D synthetic representations of natural signing.

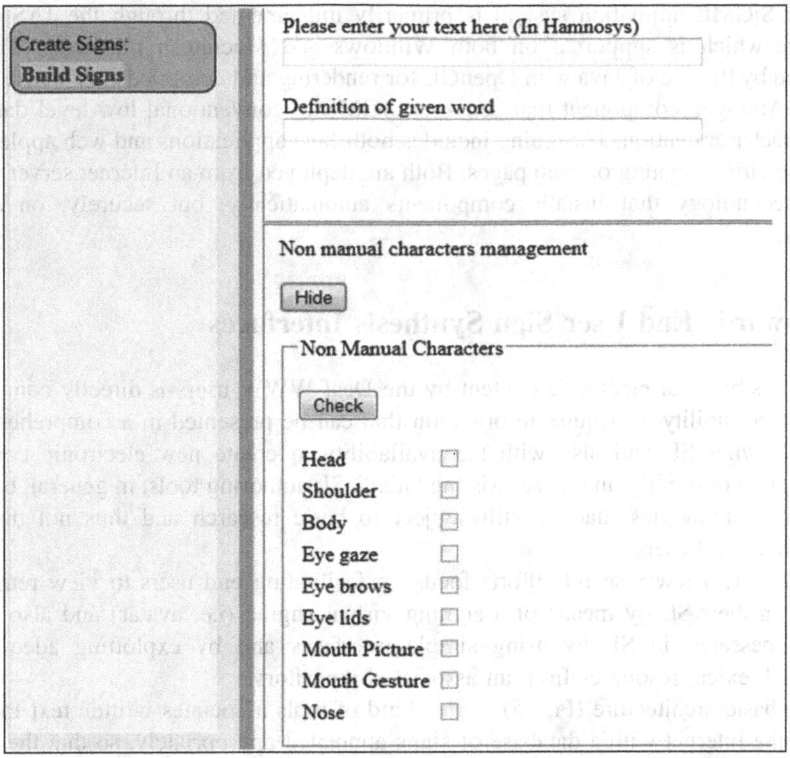

Fig. 4. The SiS-Builder drop-down menu for the assignment of non-manual features to sign lemmas coding.

As far as the Deaf user communities are concerned, avatars have been received with scepticism, since the naturalness of the video was not possible for early synthetic signing. During the last decade, signing avatar technology has developed to the point to allow representation of more complex motion including simultaneous performance of the hands, the upper body and the head, also including a number of facial expressions [12, 13]. Technological enhancements allowed for a higher score of acceptance among end users of synthetic signing engines, which paved the way towards considering the development of complete editing environments for sign language.

The avatar currently used to perform GSL signs in the SiS-Builder environment is the signing avatar developed by the University of East Anglia (UEA).[3] Some of the recent enhancements of this specific avatar were verified by results of extensive testing and evaluation by end-user groups as part of the user evaluation processes that took place in the framework of the Dicta-Sign project [14].

Synthesis, in this context, is based on the use of SiGML (Signing Gesture Markup Language) which is an XML language based heavily on HamNoSys transcriptions which can be mapped directly to SiGML.

---

[3] http://vh.cmp.uea.ac.uk .

The SiGML animation system is primarily implemented through the JASigning software which is supported on both Windows and Macintosh platforms. This is achieved by the use of Java with OpenGL for rendering and compiled C++ native code for the Animgen component that converts SiGML to conventional low-level data for 3D character animation. JASigning includes both Java applications and web applets for enabling virtual signing on web pages. Both are deployed from an Internet server using JNLP technology that installs components automatically, but securely, on client systems.

3   Towards End User Sign Synthesis Interfaces

The accessibility of electronic content by the Deaf WWW users is directly connected with the possibility to acquire information that can be presented in a comprehensible way in his/her SL and also with the availability to create new electronic content, comment on or modify and reuse existing "text". SL authoring tools, in general, belong to rising technologies that are still subject to basic research and thus not directly available to end users.

However, a few research efforts focus on facilitating end users to view retrieved content in their SL by means of a signing virtual engine (i.e. avatar) and also composing messages in SL by using simple interfaces and by exploiting adequately annotated lexical resources from an associated repository.

The basic architecture (Fig. 5) of this kind of tools associates written text located e.g. on the Internet with a database of signs annotated appropriately, so that the latter can be displayed via synthetic signing performed by an avatar.

Unknown lexical content may be checked against the lexicon of signs by means of a simple input search box (Fig. 6). End users usually follow a "copy-paste" procedure

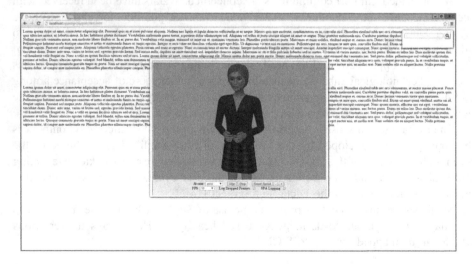

Fig. 5. Association of written text on the Internet with a database of appropriately annotated SL lexicon presented by means of a signing avatar applet.

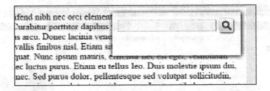

Fig. 6. SL lexicon search box for association of "unknown" words in a text with their equivalent signs.

to enter their queries. The task to be executed, however, is by no means trivial, since in many cases the morphological form of a word in a text differs considerably from the form associated with a headword in a common dictionary. Thus, the successful execution of a query demands an initial processing step invisible to the user. This step is the morphological decomposition of the selected word prior to its correct association with the corresponding lemma entry.

Nevertheless, such an application needs considerable infrastructure from the domain of Language Technology, which may overload a system that needs to provide real time responses. This kind of Language Technology may even not be available for a specific language.

In order to overcome this problem a number of approaches have been tested. Queries in electronic dictionaries may allow a degree of fuzziness with respect to matching the string which the user enters in the search box with the available entries in the lexicon database. This is the case in the NOEMA multimedia dictionary for the language pair GSL-Greek in which a search option in written Greek is incorporated in the environment [15]. The search result provides a list of candidate lemmas for the user to choose the one he/she is interested in. A similar approach to search by keywords was implemented in the Dicta-Sign sign-Wiki environment (Fig. 7). Again, partial match is also foreseen here, allowing for more than one search results, and thus facilitating the interaction of Deaf users with the Wiki.

Popular user interfaces, especially with deaf end users, suggested the use of a search mechanism based on the handshape (primary and/or secondary) in the lemma formation. This mechanism is present both in the NOEMA multimedia dictionary as well in the DIOLKOS Trilingual terminology environment: GR/ENG/GSL [16] (Fig. 8).

Another approach to the search mechanism, which is more appropriate for video databases of signs is often present in educational or e-government internet based applications. This approach is selecting the alphabetical ordering of the written concept and then choosing the appropriate lemma on those ordered lists (Fig. 9). This method prevents the delay in the system response caused by the searching within the entire content of a video database [17].

As far as sign synthesis interfaces are concerned, the composition of synthetic signing phrases may facilitate communication over the Internet, and it can also be crucial for education and group work, since it allows direct participation and dynamic linguistic message composition, which is similar to what hearing individuals do when writing.

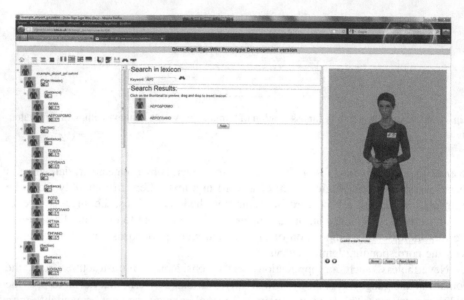

Fig. 7. Search via keywords and display of results in the Dicta-Sign sign-Wiki; the avatar performs the user's choice from the list of results.

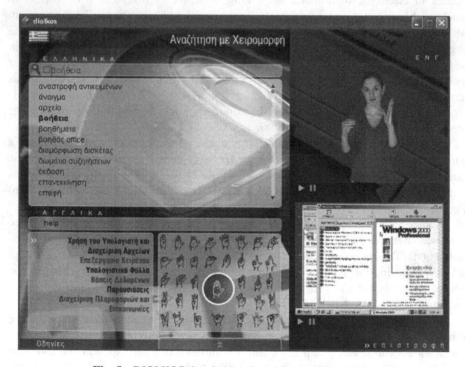

Fig. 8. DIOLKOS: hand shape-based retrieval mechanism

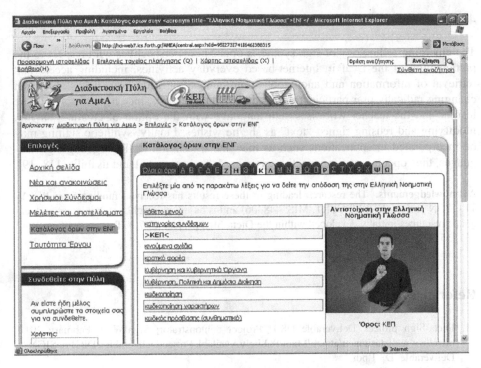

Fig. 9. Bilingual terminology lists

The composition of new synthetic phrases results by selecting the desired phrase components from a list of available, appropriately annotated lexical items.

End users interact with the system via a simple search-and-match interface to compose their desired phrases. Verifying user choices is important at any stage of this process, so that they can be certain about the content they are creating. When the structuring of the newly built signed phrase is completed (Fig. 10), this phrase is performed by a signing avatar for final verification. The user may select to save, modify of delete each phrase she/he has built. Users may reuse the entire phrases or part of the phrases they save depending on their communication needs.

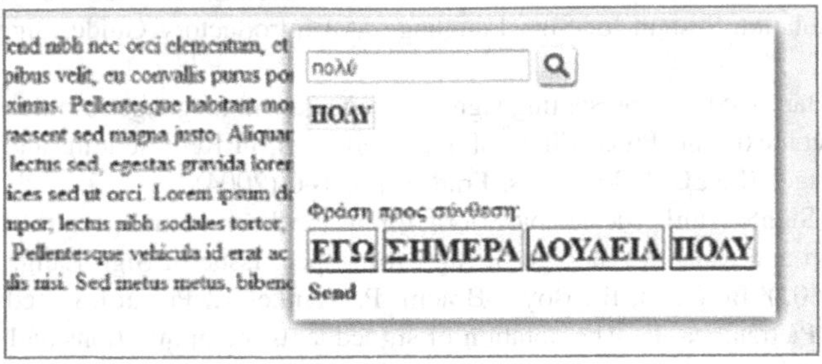

Fig. 10. Synthetic phrase building components by selection from a list

4   Conclusion

The emerging technology of sign synthesis opens new perspectives with respect to the participation of the Deaf in Internet-based everyday activities, including access and retrieval of information and anonymous communication. Moreover, it has also been changing radically user participation in educational practice, since it provides both the learner and the teacher who uses sign language with the option of creating, saving, modifying and reusing signed "text" as she/he wishes. Finally, synthetic signing may be incorporated in applications such as machine translation (MT) targeting sign languages, thus opening new perspectives as regards their potential and usability [18, 19].

Acknowledgements. The research leading to these results has received funding from POLY-TROPON project (KRIPIS-GSRT, MIS: 448306) and is based on insights, technologies and language resources initially developed within the Dicta-Sign project (FP7-ICT, grant agreement n°: 231135).

References

1. Dicta-Sign project, Deliverable D8.1: Project demonstrator: Sign-Wiki, February 2012. http://www.dictasign.eu/attach/Main/PubliclyAvailableProjectDeliverables/DICTA-SIGN_Deliverable_D8.1.pdf
2. Efthimiou, E., Fotinea, S.-E., Hanke, T., Glauert, J., Bowden, R., Braffort, A., Collet, C., Maragos, P., Lefebvre-Albaret, F.: The Dicta-Sign Wiki: enabling web communication for the deaf. In: Miesenberger, K., Karshmer, A., Penaz, P., Zagler, W. (eds.) ICCHP 2012, Part II. LNCS, vol. 7383, pp. 205–212. Springer, Heidelberg (2012)
3. Efthimiou, E., Fotinea, S.E., Hanke, T., Glauert, J., Bowden, R., Braffort, A., Collet, C., Maragos P., Lefebvre-Albaret, F.: Sign language technologies and resources of the dicta-sign project. In: Proceedings of the 5th Workshop on the Representation and Processing of Sign Languages: Interactions between Corpus and Lexicon (LREC-2012), Istanbul, Turkey, pp 37–45 (2012)
4. Elliott, R., Glauert, J.R.W., Jennings, V., Kennaway, J.R.: An overview of the sigml notation and sigml signing software system. In: Proceedings of 1st Workshop on Representing and Processing of Sign Languages (LREC-2004), Lisbon, Portugal, pp. 98–104 (2004)
5. Stokoe, W.C.: Sign language structure, 2nd edn. Linstock Press, Silver Spring MD (1978)
6. Prillwitz, S., Leven, R., Zienert, H., Hanke, T., Henning, J.: HamNoSys Version 2.0. Hamburg Notation System for Sign Language: An Introductory Guide. Signum, Hamburg (1989)
7. Hanke, T.: HamNoSys - representing sign language data in language resources and language processing contexts. In: Proceedings of 1st Workshop on Representing and Processing of Sign Languages (LREC-2004), Paris, France, pp. 1–6 (2004)
8. Neidle, C.: SignStream™: a database tool for research on visual-gestural language. Sign Transcription and Database Storage of Sign Inf., Spec. Issue of Sign Lang. Linguist. 4(1), 203–214 (2002). Bergman, B., Boyes-Braem, P., Hanke, T., Pizzuto, E. (eds.)
9. Pizzuto, E., Pietrandrea, P.: The notation of signed texts: open questions and indications for further research. Sign Lang. Linguist. 4(1/2), 29–45 (2001)

10. Goulas, T., Fotinea, S.E., Efthimiou, E., Pissaris, M.: SiS-Builder: a sign synthesis support tool. In: Proceedings of 4th Workshop on Representation and Processing of Sign Languages: Corpora and Sign Language Technologies. (LREC-2010), Valletta, Malta, pp. 102-105 (2010)
11. Fotinea, S-E., Efthimiou, E., Goulas, T., Pissaris, M., Dimou, A-L.: SiS-builder: a tool to support sign synthesis and sign language resources maintenance - the end user perspective. In: Proceedings of 2nd Enable Conference – Using New Technologies for Inclusive Learning, York, UK, pp. 26–36 (2014)
12. Glauert, J., Elliott, R.: Extending the SiGML notation - a progress report. In: Second International Workshop on Sign Language Translation and Avatar Technology (SLTAT-2011), Dundee, UK (2011)
13. Schnepp, J., Wolfe, R., McDonald, J.: Synthetic corpora: a synergy of linguistics and computer animation. In: Proceedings of 4th Workshop on Representation and Processing of Sign Languages: Corpora and Sign Language Technologies, (LREC-2010), Valletta, Malta, pp. 217–220 (2010)
14. Dicta-Sign project, Deliverable D7.4: Prototype Evaluation, April 2011. http://www.dictasign.eu/attach/Main/PubliclyAvailableProjectDeliverables/D74d.pdf
15. Efthimiou, E., Dimou, A.-L., Fotinea, S.-E., Goulas, T., Pissaris, M.: SiS-builder: a tool to support sign synthesis. In: Proceedings of the Second International Conference on the Use of New Technologies for Inclusive Learning, York, UK, pp. 26–36 (2014)
16. Efthimiou, E., Katsoyannou, M.: Research on the greek sign language (GSL): vocabulary study and lexicon creation. In: Studies in Greek Linguistics, pp. 42–50 (2001) (in Greek)
17. Efthimiou, E., Fotinea, S-E.: An environment for deaf accessibility to educational content. In: Proceedings of the first International Conference on Information and Communication Technology and Accessibility (ICT & Accessibility-2007), Hammamet, Tunisia, pp. 125–130 (2007)
18. Fotinea, S.-E., Efthimiou, E.: Tools for deaf accessibility to an eGOV environment. In: Miesenberger, K., Klaus, J., Zagler, W.L., Karshmer, A.I. (eds.) ICCHP 2008. LNCS, vol. 5105, pp. 446–453. Springer, Heidelberg (2008)
19. Efthimiou, E., Fotinea, S.-E., Goulas, T., Dimou, A.-L., Kouremenos, D.: From grammar based MT to post-processed SL representations. In: Universal Access in the Information Society (UAIS) journal. Springer. doi:10.1007/s10209-015-0414-3

Using Computational Resources on Bilingual Deaf Literacy: An Analysis of Benefits, Perspectives and Challenges

Marta Angélica Montiel Ferreira[1], Juliana Bueno[2($\boxtimes$)], and Rodrigo Bonacin[1,3]

[1] FACCAMP, Rua Guatemala, 167, Campo Limpo Paulista
SP 13231-230, Brazil
zmontefer@gmail.com,

[2] Informatics Department, Federal University of Paraná, Centro Politécnico,
Jardim Das Américas, Curitiba, PR, Brazil
juliana@inf.ufpr.br

[3] Center for Information Technology Renato Archer, Rodovia Dom Pedro I,
Km 143, 6, Campinas, SP 13069-901, Brazil
rodrigo.bonacin@cti.gov.br

Abstract. Various educational strategies have been explored on deaf literacy education. In bilingual deaf literacy, students learn two languages: first a sign language followed by a written language. This paper investigates the use of computational resources to improve bilingual deaf literacy. A study was performed in the context of the Literacy Project of the Baptist Church in Santana, Amapá, Brazil. It explored the use of technological resources in four activities with students from public schools. Results highlight the difficulties that arise from a lack of knowledge of written language. The article also presents design recommendations for Web projects that focus on learning activities and discusses perspectives and challenges.

Keywords: Accessibility · Computational resources · Deaf · Brazilian sign language

1 Introduction

Many people with hearing loss have serious difficulties learning a second language [1] due to teaching strategies that do not properly explore visual experiences to enhance learning. Some authors (e.g., [3] and [7]) emphasize the importance of taking into account cultural artifacts in studies of deaf education, in particular their visual experiences...

In the context of this work, we understand visual experiences as the use of vision (visual perception) instead of hearing (auditory perception) as a means of communication [6]. The deaf culture is based on visual experiences that influence their mode of being, expressing and experiencing the world. Usually, visual experiences are expressed by means of a sign language [2]. Consequently, it is necessary to provide

© Springer International Publishing Switzerland 2015
M. Antona and C. Stephanidis (Eds.): UAHCI 2015, Part II, LNCS 9176, pp. 362–372, 2015.
DOI: 10.1007/978-3-319-20681-3_34

deaf learners with educational strategies that recognize linguistic differences in the way that deaf people access knowledge.

Bilingual (and bicultural) deaf literacy education is highly recommended because it promotes learning in two languages: a sign language (L1) as the first and highest proficiency language, and a written language as a second language (L2). For example, in the Brazilian context, the L1 is Libras (Brazilian Sign Language) and the L2 is Portuguese (written) language.

Studies in education point out that the use of pictures is a valuable pedagogical resource for both hearing and deaf students. Visual resources are even more important for deaf students by the fact that they require many images to learn their first language [4], and to understand the context of the world around them. Thus, professional training and teaching materials must be supported by images/pictures. They can serve as a direct reference to the meaning of words and concepts [7].

The hypothesis of this study is that by providing design solutions that are able to explore visual resources through interaction models, computers can effectively support deaf bilingual (and bicultural) literacy education. These solutions can also associate textual content with representative images. According to Marschark et al. [5], the combination of verbal/writing information with visual resources substantially improves learning and content retention.

In this context, we analyzed the importance of computational resources for supporting bilingual literacy education. This analysis included how the resources contributed to student learning performance, as well as teacher training. In particular, we focused on alternatives to encourage the autonomy of deaf students in the use of computational artifacts and to explore the Web as an educational resource. The paper also points out the difficulties raised during a set of activities performed with deaf students.

This study was performed in the context of the Literacy Project (*Projeto de Letramento*) of the Baptist Church in Santana, Amapá, Brazil. It used technological resources available in the computer labs of public schools in the state of Amapá-Brazil.

During the sessions, a researcher was responsible for assisting a teacher in the preparation of each activity. This researcher monitored the activities by observing the students' achievements and their main difficulties. The teacher reported on the students' performance during each activity, as well as the difficulties in accessing the Web and using the text editor.

This article also presents a tabulation of the researcher and the teacher observations according to key categories that identify the main student achievements, their difficulties, and the role of the computational resources employed during the performed tasks. The paper ends with a discussion about perspectives and challenges related to the use of computational resources for supporting deaf literacy courses and other disciplines.

This paper is structured as follows: the second section presents important facts about deafness and bilingualism in Brazil; the third section reports how the study was designed and executed; the fourth section discusses the results and challenges, and presents a set of design recommendations; and the fifth section concludes the paper.

2 Deafness and Bilingualism in Brazil

According to official statistics, there are approximately 350 thousand (totally) deaf citizens in Brazil.[1] However, even after the publication of the law 10.436/200,[2] Brazil is still a monolingual country regarding sign language [1]. This law recognizes Libras (Brazilian Sign Language) as a national language with the same status as Portuguese (the national oral language).

In recent years, deaf education in Brazil has been progressing from oral based education to bimodal bilingual education [1], where Libras is the L1 and Portuguese is the L2. Despite Libras' legal status, as well as its importance to deaf communities, there are still recurrent problems regarding deaf literacy in L2. These problems result in rudimentary skill acquisition in L2, so that bilingualism in Brazil is far from ideal. This situation is associated with many factors, one of which is the way both languages are presented to deaf students. Many educators argue that the bilingual learning process should occur at the proper age, presenting L1 and L2 at the same time [1].

In addition, current research highlights the importance of deaf students' contact with technology on all levels. In accordance with [8, 9], among other studies, we argue that information technology can be used to support the deaf students' learning process. The main contribution of our paper is to present an experimental study with deaf students that leads to a set of high level interface design recommendations.

3 Study Design and Execution

This section details how the study was planned and performed. Section 3.1 presents the context of study and the profile of the participants, and Sect. 3.2 describes the practices and activities performed with the students.

3.1 Context and Subjects

The activities with the students were performed during two months within the context of the Literacy Project, however the entire project took a year to complete. All the activities with the users were performed in groups: two groups of 8 students and one group of 7 students. The activities were assisted by a researcher and a teacher. The teacher selected the groups according to the education level of the participants in order to provide a better understanding of the students.

The activities were selected by the researcher in consonance with the teacher's lesson plans in order not to interfere with the pedagogic content. The teacher had the role of evaluator, taking into consideration the students' previous knowledge and adjusting the expectations accordingly. Table 1 presents the basic profile of the participants in the study.

---

[1] http://www.ibge.gov.br/home/estatistica/populacao/censo2010/default.shtm.

[2] http://www.planalto.gov.br/ccivil_03/LEIS/2002/L10436.htm.

Table 1. Participants of the study

No.	Name	Age	Education level	Leave of hearing loss	Use Libras	LIP reading
01	T. E. S. P.	27	Secondary	Profound	Yes	No
02	J. L. C. O.	19	Secondary	Profound	Yes	Yes
03	A. S. N.	29	Secondary	Profound	Yes	No
04	M. P. R.	13	Primary School Student	Profound	Yes	No
05	J. K. S. O.	15	Secondary	Profound	Yes	No
06	R. S. O.	14	Secondary	Profound	Yes	Yes
07	R. C. A. S.	18	Secondary	Profound	Yes	Yes
08	A. V. C. S.	12	Primary School Student	Profound	Yes	Yes
09	R. A. S.	16	Primary School Student	Profound	Yes	Yes
10	E. S.	15	Primary School Student	Profound	Yes	No
11	H. F. R.	18	Secondary	Profound	Yes	Yes
12	D. S.	27	Secondary	Profound	Yes	No
13	A. O. B.	29	Graduate	Profound	Yes	Yes
14	D. R. C.	29	Secondary	Profound	Yes	Yes
15	J. C. S. B.	21	Secondary	Profound	Yes	Yes
16	A. A. C.	20	Graduate	Profound	Yes	Yes
17	N. S. P.	17	Secondary	Profound	Yes	Yes
18	E. S. S.	20	Secondary	Profound	Yes	Yes
19	M. M. C.	29	Secondary	Profound	Yes	Yes
20	A. J. S. B.	29	Secondary	Profound	Yes	Yes
21	R. S. C.	30	Graduate	Listener	–	–
22	R. C.	29	Graduate	Listener	–	–
23	C.A.B	29	Graduate	Profound	Yes	Yes
24	T. A.G	19	Secondary	Profound	Yes	Yes
25	A. D. R	21	Secondary	Profound	Yes	Yes

A total of four literacy activities were performed with the users. During these activities the students answered questions written in the Portuguese language (L2) by searching the Web and using a text editor. Each lesson was based on activities that magnify language barriers, including: fill out a form, shop online, read a text and search for unknown words/concepts, interpret a text on a blog, and write a summary review.

The researcher provided support for the teacher during the execution of each group activity. The researcher also observed and reported on the students' major difficulties from both her own point of view and that of the teacher. The report included Web accessibility problems, problems using the text editor, and teacher *feedback* about the performance of the students during the development of the activities.

3.2   Execution of the Practices

This section briefly describes the four practices performed with the students including the main results and important remarks.

First Practice: syllabic separation.

The objective of this lesson was to explore the phonology of L2. This aspect of language is difficult for the majority of deaf people to understand. Phonology is the study of how words are formed, how the speech sounds are structured in L2, and how to classify the phonemes in units capable of distinguishing meaning.

This activity was performed using a web site for teaching Portuguese[3] which includes interactive games. The rationale was to make use of existing Web resources that are not especially designed for the deaf, exploring visual aspects that facilitate the improvement of the deaf students' vocabulary and also as a way to present new words and concepts.

During this activity each task was presented and explained using Libras. Then, the students classified the words according to their own understanding. The software tool allowed three attempts based on multiple choice questions, after which the students were shown the right and wrong answers. The student's progress was presented at the end of the activity. Table 2 presents a summary of activity 1, including the context, answers and remarks.

Table 2. Summary of practice 1

Activity 1	Syllabic separation (Grammar)
Objective	To answer correctly the separation of syllables.
No. of participants	25
No. of sessions	Three (3) groups selected according to the education level (*c.f.*, Sect. 3.1) participated of three sessions with two activities each.
When	The sessions took place on different days.
Duration	One (1) minute for each word, when they went to the next participant.
Task to be performed	Each PARTICIPANT answered a word, but everyone observed the answers. It was carried out as a test format.
Qty. of right answers	9
Qty. of wrong ans.	14
Equipment usage	They answered on a computer and the others observed. The teacher had to explain the meaning of the words in Libras before they use the computer.

Important remarks: they made more mistakes in long words and in situations where they did not know the word beforehand.

Figure 1 presents an example of a Web application used during the first activity. In Fig. 1a students were asked to divide the word into syllables; Fig. 1b presents the feedback for a correct answer; and Fig. 1c presents the feedback for an incorrect answer. In this application the words were randomly selected. Some words were

---

[3] http://www.soportugues.com.br.

simple, and others more complex. The teacher supplemented the learning activity by exploring visual resources available on the Web.

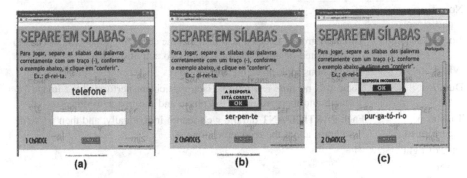

Fig. 1. Example of Web application used in the first practice (The entire set of tools can be accessed at: http://www.soportugues.com.br/secoes/jogos.php)

Second Practice: exploring writing

The second activity focused on exploring the Web using images to develop writing capabilities. During this task the participants searched for images and constructed phrases to describe them. The objective was to verify the deaf student's ability to compose sentences and to use the correct vocabulary. In this activity the participants had the support of a thesaurus integrated into the text editor. Table 3 presents a summary of activity 2, including the context, answers and remarks.

Figure 2 presents an example of student work during the second activity. Figure 2a[4] presents a picture from the Web selected by a student, and Fig. 2b presents the phrase constructed by the student to describe the picture. This Figure shows a common problem in deaf literacy, which is the absence of connectives.

Third Practice: reading and interpretation

During the third activity the students elaborated a briefly summary of a text posted on a blog. First, the teacher explained how to correctly use connectives to give meaning to the sentences. Then, the students navigated on web blogs and wrote summaries of the posted texts. This task required knowledge about the grammar structure of L2. The teacher also emphasized the need to use and understand synonyms. Table 4 presents a summary of activity 3, including the context, answers and remarks.

Figure 3 presents an example of text written by a student during the third activity. This Figure shows the common Portuguese expression "Pérolas Gramaticais"/ "Grammatical Pearls" used to denote inadequately used vocabulary in language constructions. The most common difficulties were related to the limited vocabulary and misunderstanding of the meaning of the words when grouped in phases.

---

[4] This picture was recovered from: http://www.osvigaristas.com.br/imagens/criancas/.

Table 3. Summary of practice 2

Activity 2	Exploring writing
Objective	Check writing and the use of connectives.
No. of participants	25
No. of sessions	Three (3) groups selected according to the education level (*c.f.,* Sect. 3.1) participated of three sessions, with two activities each.
When	The sessions took place on different days
Duration	There was no time restriction. Each participant performed the image search and then presented the phase and the image to others.
Task to be performed	Each PARTICIPANT did the web search individually, and then wrote up a phrase about the recovered ima-ges.
Qty. of right resp.	1
Qty. of wrong resp.	23
Equipment usage	Each participant used a computer, after that they shared the results with others.

Important remarks: the most frequent difficulty was the wrong application of the connectives. Only one student made the correct use of connectives in all sentences.

 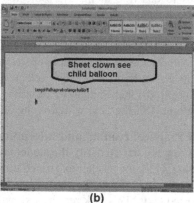

(a)   (b)

Fig. 2. Example of activity on the second practice

3.2.1   Fourth Activity: Writing and Understanding

In the fourth activity the students were asked to complete a register on the Web. Each participant searched a website and tried to fill in the required fields. The teacher explored the use of a dictionary integrated into a text editor and web search scenarios. Table 5 presents a summary of activity 4, including the context, answers and remarks.

The majority of the students managed to complete the register, however all of them had difficulties filling out the form. None of the students were able to complete the

Table 4. Summary of practice 3

Activity 3	Exploring the reading and interpretation
Objective	Check text understanding and writing skills.
No. of participants	25
No. of sessions	Three (3) groups selected according to the education level (*c.f.*, Sect. 3.1) participated of three sessions, with two activities each.
When	The sessions took place on different days.
Duration	There was no time restriction, everyone did the reading and wrote the text and then presented the activity to the others.
Task to be performed	Each PARTICIPANT navigated on a web blog. After that they drew up a short text. It was an individual task, however after each participant shared the result with the group.
Qty. of right resp.	1
Qty. of wrong resp.	23
Equipment usage	Each participant used a computer, after that they shared the results with others.

Important remarks: they had frequent difficulties in the words they did not know the meaning in Libras.

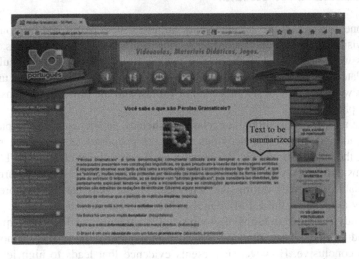

Fig. 3. Example of activity on the third practice (http://www.soportugues.com.br/secoes/perolas/)

entire process without teacher support. However, the researcher noticed that sites with easier questions and good field descriptions were easier for the participants. All the websites used in this practice were constructed according to accessibility principles.

Table 5. Summary of practice 4

Activity 4	Exploring writing and understanding
Objective	Verify understanding of words and text writing on web form fields.
No. of participants	25
No. of sessions	Three (3) groups selected according to the education level (*c.f.*, Sect. 3.1) participated of three sessions, with two activities each.
When	The sessions took place on different days
Duration	There was no time restriction, everyone did a search on a site of interest and then performed a registration with no time restrictions.
Task to be performed	Each PARTICIPANT explored sites of (s)he personal interests and then performed a registration.
Qty. of right resp.	16
Qty. of wrong resp.	8
Equipment usage	Each participant used a computer.

Important remarks: the most frequent difficulty was is related to the interpretation of polysemous words. The students usually knew only a single meaning for each word.

4   Discussions Over Results

As mentioned above, all the activities with the users were performed in groups, under the supervision of a teacher. According to our results and teacher remarks, the main difficulties were not related to the use of the technology itself. The difficulties were mostly related to poor understanding of L2 including: the difficulty to understand words that were not previously presented in Libras, and the difficulty to construct well structured phases.

Despite the observed difficulties related to literacy deficiencies, all the participants were able to perform all the activities using the proposed technological resources. Therefore, the study pointed out the possibility of using the Web to teach L2. Simple mechanisms and tools, which were not necessarily designed to support learning, provided valuable resources during the activities. These tools can be explored by the teachers by associating the L2 to images and visual representations.

This study is limited in terms of group size (24 students and 1 teacher), quantitative results, and number of activities performed. Consequently the results cannot be considered as conclusive. However, it presents evidence that leads to high level design recommendations for Web projects that focus on supporting learning activities in L2, as those presented in this work:

- Simple design with straightforward information;
- Minimalist design focused on the information need to solve a problem;
- Use images to contextualize the problems;
- Game-based tools can be explored to teach L2.

The recommendations aim to produce accessible interfaces for deaf users, where the technology can support and improve the attractiveness of L2 education. In addition, the teacher and researcher noticed that all the participants frequently use mobile technology to communicate using text messages in L2 (despite their limitations). Thus, mobile technology should be also explored in further applications.

This work contributed to verifying the potential of computational resources in support of bilingual deaf education. However, a challenge remains to design pedagogical studies to improve the use of these tools, for example, to contribute to teacher education, to encourage student autonomy, and to better explore the nature of WEB imagery as a teaching resource.

Visual literacy should also be explored more deeply as, unlike the hearing, the deaf first interprets the visual aspects of words and then associates meaning. Computational resources can be important tools in this process if explored at the "ideal age". Tools specially designed for children learning at "ideal age" can potentially represent important advances in the deaf literacy rates. However this demands expressive efforts on both pedagogical and interaction design studies.

5 Conclusion

Proponents of deaf bilingual education advocate learning two languages simultaneously, a sign language as the first language and a written language as the second. As an additional learning tool, technological resources can potentially serve as an inductor of deaf bilingual education. In this paper, we explored the use of computational tools (including Web tools and text editors) in educational activities with deaf students. The activities explored syllabic separation, phrase construction/writing, reading and interpretation, and writing/understanding of L2.

Results highlighted that deaf students made good use of the technological resources during the execution of the activities. The results pointed out that the difficulties arose from lack of knowledge of L2, and, consequently, new learning processes as well as design strategies should be explored in future work. As next steps, we propose to conduct detailed studies to determine the influence of design issues on students' performance, explore new pedagogical strategies using technological resources, produce a detailed design recommendation set, and construct and evaluate prototypes based on these recommendations.

References

1. Fernandes, E., Silva, A.C., Correia, C.M.C., Santos, K.R.O.R.P., Karnopp, L.B., Pereira, M. C.C., e Quadros, R.M.: Surdez e Bilinguismo, 4ª edn. Editora Mediação, Porto Alegre (2011)
2. Gesser, A.: Libras? Que língua é essa? Crenças e preconceitos em torno da língua de sinais e da realidade surda. Parábola Editorial, São Paulo (2009)
3. Ladd, P.: Understanding Deaf Culture: In Search of Deafhood. Multilingual Matters, Clevedon (2003)

4. Zafrulla, Z., Brashear, H., Yin, P., Presti, P., Starner, T., Hamilton, H.: American sign language phrase verification in an educational game for deaf children. In: IEEE International Conference on Pattern Recognition, pp. 3846–3849 (2010)
5. Marschark, M., Sapere, P., Convertino, C.M., Mayer, C., Wauters, L., Sarchet, T.: Are deaf students' reading challenges really about reading? Am. Ann. Deaf **154**, 357–370 (2009). http://www.rit.edu/ntid/cerp/marc
6. Bianchini, C.S., Borgia, F., De Marsico, M.: SWift - A signwriting editor to bridge between deaf world and e-learning. In: 12th IEEE International Conference on Advanced Learning Technologies, pp. 526–230 (2012)
7. Ulbricht, V.R., Vanzin, T., Villarouco, V.: Ambiente Virtual de Aprendizagem Inclusivo. Ed. Pandion, Florianópolis (2011)
8. Kourbetis, V., Boukouras, K.: Accessible open educational resources for students with disabilities in greece: they are open to the deaf. In: Stephanidis, C., Antona, M. (eds.) UAHCI 2014, Part II. LNCS, vol. 8514, pp. 349–357. Springer, Heidelberg (2014)
9. Kourbetis, V.: Design and development of accessible educational and teaching material for deaf students in greece. In: Stephanidis, C., Antona, M. (eds.) UAHCI 2013, Part III. LNCS, vol. 8011, pp. 172–178. Springer, Heidelberg (2013)

The Low Use of SignWriting Computational Tools from HCI Perspective

Carlos E.A. Iatskiu$^{(\boxtimes)}$, Laura Sánchez García, Rafael Dos Passos Canteri, and Diego Roberto Antunes

Federal University of Paraná,
Curitiba, PR, Brazil
{ceaiatskiv,laurag,rpcanteri,diegor}@inf.ufpr.br

Abstract. There are several ways of communication, however, these are considered volatiles, i.e. passed from people to people, there is the risk of having changed meaning and significance. But the writing stays intact and that's why comes the need of the written record of languages, even of sign languages. Several tools exists to provide support for the written record of sign languages, however which are not used by these communities, especially the Brazilian. This paper supported in the HCI literature, has the objective point out the reasons from no or low use of these tools by an analytical inspection.

Keywords: Human-computer interaction · Deaf culture · Social inclusion · Computational tools for citizenship · SignWriting

1 Introduction

The deaf community in Brazil and worldwide uses sign language for communication between the deaf and the society in general. When the members of this community need to write their language using computing devices, they need to rely on the written representation of an oral language not used by their, in the case of Brazil, the Portuguese language [16].

There are various forms of communication between humans, such as speech and gestures, but these are volatile ones, in the sense that they can change when they are passed among people at high risk of meaning modification. Writing is a nonvolatile form of communication, the preservation of records in written form allows for the storage and spreading of information by individuals that are distanced geographically and also between generations, emerges naturally relevance of the written form of sign language [1].

The use of the country's oral language as the only option for the language written record interferes with the deaf culture, because the communication between individuals must be mediated or adapted in a process between the sign languages and the oral language in question [3].

The existence of sign language writing is a reality since many years ago, as researchers have created different writing systems, like Stokoe's System [22],

M. Antona and C. Stephanidis (Eds.): UAHCI 2015, Part II, LNCS 9176, pp. 373–382, 2015.
DOI: 10.1007/978-3-319-20681-3_35

the François Neve's Notation [23], the HamNoSys's Notation [15] and SignWriting [24], the latter being the most comprehensive and the most used, although not taken advantage, by deaf communities around the world.

SignWriting is a notation for writing the visual language of signs. Its components allow for any sign language to be visually represented, i.e., they allow for the representation of the grammatical structure of sign languages in graphical form. SW was developed by Valerie Sutton in 1981 and is part of a larger system of movement notation, the Sutton Movement Writing & Shorthand, able to systematically record any movement, whether in dance, sign language, mime, sports, physiotherapy, among others [24]. In Brazil, the use of SignWriting is still very limited, being the hypothesis of to come from the fact that most of the information and knowledge legacy is recorded in other written languages, such as Portuguese [23].

There are some tools that have been developed in order to assist these communities in regards to learning, documentation and record of sign languages through SignWriting. These artifacts do not address the needs of deaf, so they are not adopted by the deaf as communication, interaction and learning resources.

The first sign languages have emerged around 1755 and was brought to Brazil in 1856. The LIBRAS was recognized as the National Sign Language in the Brazilian Constitution of 2002. Stokoe created the first writing system for sign languages in 1960. Nowadays there are several tools for the graphic recording of sign languages, and a question arises: Why these tools have not been taked advantage of by Deaf Communities?

A detailed study on several existing tools in literature, helps to understand the reasons why deaf communities have not adopted these tools in their daily life. Human Computer Interaction literature is full with sets of principles, guidelines and heuristics, that lead designed systems to be quickly and easily learned by users [14]. However, the misuse of these criteria leads to systems that are not suitable for the target audience and this may be the primary response to the low (non) use of these tools.

From this study that indicated the reasons for the low usage of the tools of LIBRAS graphic record and after having worked together and identified the needs of this community, this paper present literature based evaluation of existing SignWriting Computational Tools and also reports mistakes found in these softwares. This way, it is expected that new tools do not repeat the same mistakes, have greater acceptance and meet the need for information access by the deaf communities. Therefore, it won't be necessary to appeal to the oral language graphic record of the country only for lack of inner writing system. Additionally documentation of sign languages worldwide will be facilitated.

Section 2 describes Deaf Community: characteristics ans needs, Sect. 3 presents SignWriting Computational Tools and Evaluation, Sect. 4 shows The Low Use of SignWriting Computational Tools from HCI Perspective. Finally, Sect. 5 discusses Conclusions and Future Works.

2   Deaf Community: Characteristics and Needs

People with special needs are generally excluded in society, and among them, are the Deaf and their communities. The prejudices faced by the deaf community are many, for example, the mistaken ideas of society, which are seen as politically correct. The definitions of deafness like "hearing impaired Deaf" and/or "deaf and dumb" are examples of this erroneous conception which tend to create stereotypes. The deaf has its own language, which disqualifies the term "dumb", for example [18].

At the same time, members of the Deaf community do not want to be defined by their deafness. They want to be included in society acting naturaly in their universe. For this, the deaf require a tool to help them in the communication with each other and with other members of society. After all, more and more the world is based on information and knowledge, and who is not included in this circle, is excluded from the society [11].

For communicating, the Brazilian Deaf using the Brazilian Sign Language (LIBRAS), which is a legitimate and natural language system that enables the social and intellectual development, favoring their access to cultural and scientific knowledge, as well the integration to the social group to which it belongs. LIBRAS express feelings, psychological states, concrete and abstract concepts and reasoning processes [17]. Its form of representation guard specificities that differentiates it from other languages, such as Portuguese, yet at the same time, it allows the expression of any concept of reality or reference data [7].

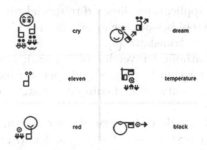

Fig. 1. Examples of SignWriting. Adapted from [3] and [9]

Even though they use the LIBRAS for communication, the deaf still have difficulty as the registration of knowledge in written form. When it happens, it is still mediated by written Portuguese and in this way, the knowledge and culture is unsatisfactorily reported since they are not represented by the sign language [24]. Many written systems for sign languages have emerged to try to solve the spelling of the signs, but this did not solve the problem for the community.

The SignWriting Writing System is the most used by the communities. It was developed by the American researcher Valerie Sutton, in the 70s, to spell the footsteps of traditional ballet. Its components permit any sign language words visually represented, allowing the writing system represent the graphically grammatical structure [3]. In Brazil, the use of the system is restricted, however, many authors defend that their use is necessary for increasing the documentation of LIBRAS [23]. Figure 1 shows examples of SignWriting.

3   SignWriting Computational Tools

There are some initiatives whose purpose is to assist those communities with respect to the learning of sign languages and record of languages through Sign-Writing. Often the developed tools although they have the objective of helping the Deaf, are produced for a very specific audience (Deaf that dominate the reading and writing the main language of their country) and, in this way, are not adopted in the daily lives of the Deaf as communication resources, interaction and learning.

Many of these artifacts do not address the needs of the deaf, among which we can mention language issues (e.g. the information is represented mostly in a language other than LIBRAS in case the Portuguese on the understanding that all the deaf has the domain of this language) and interaction (e.g. most of the tools for user interaction with the interface is not mediated by LIBRAS). The computational support tools for SignWriting were studied:

- AGA-Sign (UFRGS - Federal University of Rio Grande do Sul / UCPel - Catholic University of Pelotas): is a gesture animator applied to sign language,developed for applications directed to special education, particularly for Deaf education. The tool besides the animator, includes among other modules SignWriting editor and translator [5].
- SignNet (UCPel - Catholic University of Pelotas): is intended to adapt the Internet technology for sign languages and special education of the Deaf. Its goal was to implement software and computer systems oriented towards writing of sign languages [23].
- SW-Edit (UCPel - Catholic University of Pelotas): this system has the main functionality, editing text in sign languages, based on SignWriting writing system. Their data base is expandable and has a sign dictionary, which is available as a file on the web [26].
- SignTalk, SignSim e SignEd (UCPel - Catholic University of Pelotas): has the objective interaction through LIBRAS and Portuguese via chat, semi-automatic translator between sign language and a editor for writtin signs [2].
- SignWriter (USA - Deaf Action Committe): is a text editor in SignWriting signs. Arrived until the 4.4 version and has been discontinued, despite having support for multiple languages, no success, mainly by the precariousness of their interface, destined for MS-DOS [8]. Figure 2, presents the Interface of SignWriter.
- SignPuddle (SignWriting.org): has several online tools, such as dictionary, maker for written signs, search for symbols or explanations, signs of maker in

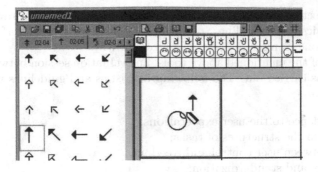

Fig. 2. SignWriter interface adapted from [8]

the mail and simple editor. Has online help with a single click, multilingual support with unique code and storage of texts in various versions [20]. Figure 3, shows the interface of SignPuddle Online.

- SignWebMessage (UFRGS - Federal University of Rio Grande do Sul): is the development of a prototype software, similar to a webmail, where messages may be exchanged through the writing of Brazilian Sign Language - LIBRAS, based on SignWriting system [21].
- SignWriter Studio (Jonathan Duncan - FreeWare): was developed to provide an easier starting point for beginners who are learning SignWriting and a faster way for everybody to write and share sign languages [6].

Fig. 3. SignPuddle online interface adapted from [20]

3.1 Evaluation of SignWriting Computational Tools

To make it possible to identify the reasons from low or no use of computational tools to support SignWriting, by the deaf community in general and especially the Brazilian, an analytical review of these (users are not directly involved) was held.

This inspection was carried out by three specialists in HCI, provided with a set of heuristics and guidelines, performing a check that the interfaces of each tool violates one or more heuristics, where and why.

For each of the mentioned above tools, an evaluation session between one and two hours was carried out. The following heuristics and guidelines were used in the evaluation:

- Correspondence to the user expectations;
- Simplicity in the structures of tasks;
- Balance between user control and freedom;
- Consistency and standardization;
- Stimulus for the user efficiency;
- Anticipation of user needs;
- Visibility and recognition;
- Relevant content and adequate expression;
- Design for errors;
- Usability;
- Communicability.

The evaluation was considered satisfactory by the evaluators, because it raised several hypotheses for the low use of the tools.

4   The Low Use of SignWriting Computational Tools from HCI Perspective

The HCI literature is replete with sets and principles, guidelines and heuristics. The proper application of many of the principles and guidelines depends on the designer's knowledge of the users of the problem domain and its activities in this area [10].

For the deaf community use an interactive system, that is interact with its interface to reach goals in a particular context of use, in this case written signs through SignWriting, the interface must be adequate for these users, in particular to make the most of computational support offered by the system.

These people expect that the computational potential offered through the support SignWriting tools, is simple, fast and easy to learn. Employing information and communication technologies every day is justified to facilitate the implementation of activities, and not make them more difficult and complex. In the following subsections will be presented the guidelines and heuristics IHC, which held by inspection, were not covered by tools.

4.1   Simplicity in the Structures of Tasks

To facilitate user interaction, it is recommended to simplify the structure of the tasks, reducing the amount of planning and problem solving that they require. Unnecessarily complex tasks can be restructured using technological innovations [13].

The SignWriting already has an extremely complex structure, because of the wide number of classification groups and large number of primitives used for the spelling of the signs. The way, that the tools organize these primitive, often ends up, despising this criterion of simplicity, so hampering interaction. Figure 4, presents the complex groups of SignWriting.

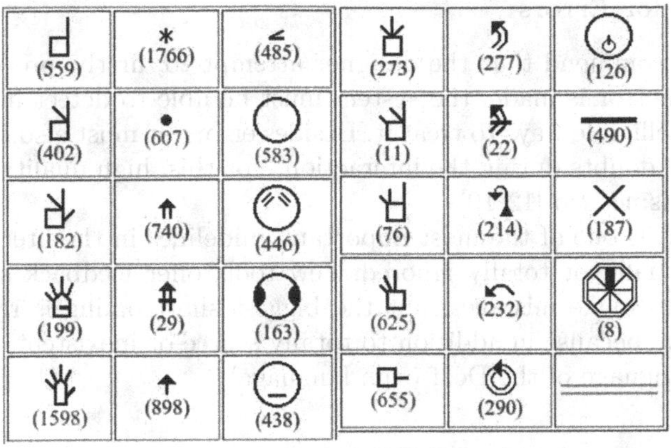

Fig. 4. Examples of SignWriting. Adapted from [9]

4.2 Anticipation of User Needs

Applications should try to predict what the user wants and needs rather than wait which they seek or collect information on tools. The software should take initiative and provide useful information, instead of just answer the question precisely what the user does. Is important to carefully define the values and the default setting (default) also defaults should be easily replaced by more specific values appropriate to the current situation [4, 25].

Neither of tools has functionality to meet the anticipation criteria, that is, no action to facilitate user interaction, for example, offer motion-local options or movement, after the user enters the hand configuration, or withdraw the options of facial expression, after it's inserted. These are small details that can increase user affinity with the tool.

4.3 Relevant Content and Adequate Expression

For a simple interaction is required following four maxims: quality, quantity, relevance and clarity. Dialogues should not contain information which is irrelevant or rarely needed. The instruction and help messages must be concise and informative about problems that occur. The labels on menus and buttons should be clear and free of ambiguity. Besides taking care of the content, the designer must make sure that the text is also readable [4, 12, 25].

This is a criterion that is ignored by virtually all SignWriting support tools, because the information is represented in the oral language of the country for which it was developed and not the primary language of the deaf. To follow this guideline,Textual information, menus, documentation, and among others should present the information in SignWriting too.

4.4 Design for Errors

Researchers recommend that the designer attempt to, firstly, prevent errors, if possible. If an error is made, the system must be able to detect it and provide simple and intelligible ways to treat it. Besides errors, it must also support users to clarify their doubts during the interaction. For this, high quality documentation and help is needed [12,19].

Although it is one of the most important guidelines in the literature, in the tools it is partially or totally ignored. Few tools offer feedback so that users do not come to make mistakes, but the biggest shortcoming is related to the documentation, because in addition to totally scarce or inexistent, they are not in the main language of the Deaf (sign language).

4.5 Stimulus for the User Efficiency

The system should be sensitive to what the user is doing and should not interrupt him unnecessarily while the user is working on something. In order to promote efficiency of frequent users, it is recommended to provide shortcuts and accelerators. As the frequency of use increases so the desire of users to reduce the number of interactions and accelerate the pace of interaction. For frequent operations, the designer can also provide the default configuration values, individually or in groups, forming on which such transactions profiles [4,12,19].

This criterion was the most ignored by all the tools and possibly coming to cause more aversion from the community. None of the tools promotes user efficiency, on the contrary, makes that it has to spend considerable effort and time to perform a high writing a single signal, practically making it impossible to write long texts.

4.6 Correspondence to the User Expectations

It is recommended to structure the dialogue form following a line of thought and provide a closure, the sequences of actions must be organized into groups with a beginning, middle and end. Designers must follow the real-world conventions, making the information appear in a natural and logical order [12,19].

The tools do not follow a reasoning logic with real-world conventions, they have no order and even less logic in the order of inclusion of the primitives to the composition of the signs.

Several other guidelines were partially or totally ignored by some tools,but there were no problems found in unanimity among them, such as: consistency and standardization, visibility and recognition, usability and communicability.

5 Conclusions and Future Works

As previously mentioned in the introduction, sign languages are old in the world, including Brazil, which is a law of the national constitution, systems for writing sign languages have existed for more than 50 years and the high number of computational tools to assist the communities in their day-to-day, in this case in particular to the deaf community in access to information. Why still the community do not use these tools that are extremely important?

The present study in this papper, where an analytical assessment was performed on the main existing tools, may at the same time give us an answer and in the future a solution for this serious problem. The guidelines and heuristics must be followed so that the interfaces from any tool have quality, especially when you are developing something that is intended for a community which have special needs such as the Deaf community.

Tools created to offer accessibility, that do not consider HCI guidelines are not alternative to information access for this community, on the contrary, they cause aversion to the tools. To resolve this, designers must reproject existing interfaces and design new interfaces considering the guidelines and heuristics mentioned in this work.

To eliminate this aversion and to enable access the information through the graphical record of sign languages, as future guidelines and specific HCI heuristics will be created (derived from existing) to the development of interfaces intended for deaf community, thus seeking a final order to solve this problem.

Acknowledgments. We would like to thank the students and teachers that collaborated to this research. This work is funded by Coordenação de Aperfeiçoamento de Pessoal de Nível Superior - CAPES and Fundação Araucária.

References

1. Azevedo, D.: A importância da escrita na sociedade contemporânea. Universidade Estácio de Sá (2010)
2. Campos, M.B.: Editor de línguas de sinais. Pontifícia Universidade Católica do Rio Grande do Sul (2008)
3. Capovilla, F, Raphael, W.: Dicionário Enciclopédico Ilustrado Trilíngue da Língua de Sinais Brasileira, vol. I. Sinais de A á L. Editora da Universidade de São Paulo, São Paulo (2001)
4. Cooper, A.: The Inmates are Running the Asylum: Why High-Tech Products Drive Us Crazy and How to Restore the Sanity. Sams Publishing, Indianapolis (1999)
5. Denardi, R.M., Menezes, P.B., Rocha Costa, A.C.: AGA-Sign: Animador de Gestos aplicado á Língua de Sinais UFRGS - Universidade Federal do Rio Grande do Sul (2010)
6. Duncan, J.: SignWriter Studio - The ultimate Program for writing sign languages (2009)
7. Fernandes, S.F.: Os sotaques dos sinais. Língua Portuguesa (2007)
8. Glaves, R.: Editor de texto em sinais em signwriting. Deaf Action Committe, USA (2004)

9. Iatskiu, C.E.: Serviço Web para a Interpretação do Modelo Fonológico da LIBRAS para os Símbolos Gráficos do SignWriting. Dissertação de Mestrado - UFPR (2014)
10. Mayhew, D.: The Usability Engineering Lifecycle: A Practitioner's Handbook For User Interace Design. Morgan Kaufmann Publishers Inc., San Francisco (1999)
11. Monteiro, M.S.: Historia dos movimentos dos surdos e o reconhecimento da libras no Brasil. ETD Educação Temática Digital (2006)
12. Nielsen, J.: Usability Engineering. Academic Press, New York (1993)
13. Norman, D.A.: Psychology of Everyday Things. Basic Books, New York (1988)
14. Norman, D.A.: The Designg of Everyday Things. Currrency Doubleday, New York (1990)
15. Prillwitz, S., Leven, R., Zienert, H., Hanke, T.: Hamnosys version 2.0: Hamburg notation system for sign languages: an introductory guide. In: International Studies on Sign Language and the Communication of the Deaf, pp. 195–278 (1989)
16. Quadros, R.M.: Aquisição de l1 e l2: o contexto da pessoa surda. Divisão de Estudos e Pesquisas INES, editor, Seminário Desafios e Possibilidades na Educação Bilíngue para Surdos, Rio de Janeiro (1997)
17. Quadros, R.M., Karnopp, L.B.: Língua de sinais brasileira: estudos linguísticos. Artmed, Porto Alegre (2004)
18. Santos, B.S.: Um discurso sobre as ciências. Porto, Afrontamento (1987)
19. Shneiderman, B.: Designing the User Interface. Addison-Wesley, Reading (1998)
20. SignWriting.org.: Oficializado alfabeto internacional do signwriting (2013)
21. Souza, V.C.: Pesquisa - Sign WebMessage Unisinus (2015)
22. Stokoe, W.C.: Sign Language Structure. Linstok Press, Silver Spring (1978)
23. Stumpf, M. R.: Língua de sinais: escrita dos surdos na internet. V Congresso Ibero americano de Informática Educativa (2000)
24. Stumpf, M.R.: Aprendizagem de Escrita de Língua de Sinais pelo Sistema Sign-Writing: Línguas de Sinais no Papel e no Computador. Universidade Federal do Rio Grande do Sul, Tese de Doutorado (2005)
25. Tognazzini, B.: A Quiz Designed to Give You Fitts. Ask Tog (1999)
26. Torchelsen, A.C.R., Costa, R.P.: Aquisição da escrita de sinais por crianças surdas através de ambientes digitais. Universidade Catóolica de Pelotas, Escola de Informática (2002)

The Effect of Rendering Style on Perception of Sign Language Animations

Tiffany Jen and Nicoletta Adamo-Villani(✉)

Purdue University, West Lafayette, USA
tiffanyjenny66@gmail.com, nadamovi@purdue.edu

Abstract. The goal of the study reported in the paper was to determine whether rendering style (non-photorealistic versus realistic) has an effect on perception of American Sign Language (ASL) finger spelling animations. Sixty-nine (69) subjects participated in the experiment; all subjects were ASL users. The participants were asked to watch forty (40) sign language animation clips representing twenty (20) finger spelled words. Twenty (20) clips were rendered using photorealistic rendering style, whereas the other twenty (20) were rendered in a non-photorealistic rendering style (e.g. cel shading). After viewing each animation, subjects were asked to type the word being finger-spelled and rate its legibility. Findings show that rendering style has an effect on perception of the signed words. Subjects were able to recognize the animated words rendered with cel shading with higher level of accuracy, and the legibility ratings of the cel shaded animations were consistently higher across subjects.

Keywords: Sign language · Animation · Non photorealistic rendering · Cel shading · Deaf education

1   Introduction

Computer animation provides a low-cost and effective means for adding signed translation to any type of digital content. Despite the substantial amount of ASL animation research, development and recent improvements, several limitations still preclude animation of ASL from becoming an effective, general solution to deaf accessibility to digital media. One of the main challenges is low rendering quality of the signed animations, which results in limited legibility of the animated signs.

This paper investigates the problem of clearly communicating the ASL handshapes to viewers. With standard rendering methods, based on local lighting or global illumination, it may be difficult to clearly depict palm and fingers positions because of occlusion problems and lack of contour lines that can help clarify the palm/fingers configuration. *"Interactive systems that permit the lighting and/or view to be controlled by the user allow for better exploration, but non-photorealistic methods can be used to increase the amount of information conveyed by a single view"* [1]. In fact, it is common for artists of technical drawings

© Springer International Publishing Switzerland 2015
M. Antona and C. Stephanidis (Eds.): UAHCI 2015, Part II, LNCS 9176, pp. 383–392, 2015.
DOI: 10.1007/978-3-319-20681-3_36

or medical illustrations to depict surfaces in a way that is inconsistent with any physically-realizable lighting model, but that is specifically intended to bring out surface shape and detail [1].

The specific objective of this experiment was to answer the research question of whether the implementation of a particular non-photorealistic rendering style (e.g., cel shading) in ASL fingerspelling animations can improve their legibility. The paper is organized as follows. In Sect. 2 (Background) we discuss computer animation of sign language, we define cel shading, and we explain the importance of ASL fingerspelling. In Sect. 3 (Study Design) we describe the user study, and in Sect. 3.5 (Findings) we report and discuss the results. Conclusion and future work are included in Sect. 4 (Conclusion).

2   Background

2.1   Computer Animation of Sign Language

Compared to video, animation technology has two fundamental advantages. The first one is scalability. Animated signs are powerful building blocks that can be concatenated seamlessly using automatically computed transitions to create new ASL discourse. By comparison, concatenating ASL video clips suffers from visual discontinuity. The second advantage is flexibility. Animation parameters can be adjusted to optimize ASL eloquence. For example, the speed of signing can be adjusted to the ASL proficiency of the user, which is of great importance for children who are learning ASL. The signing character can be easily changed by selecting a different avatar, hence the possibility of creating characters of different age and ethnicity, as well as cartoon characters appealing to young children.

Several groups have been focusing on research, development and application of computer animation technology for enhancing deaf accessibility to educational content. The ViSiCAST project [2], later continued as eSIGN project [3], aims to provide deaf citizens with improved access to services, facilities, and education through animated British Sign Language. The project is developing a method for automatic translation from natural-language to sign-language. The signs are rendered with the help of a signing avatar. A website is made accessible to a deaf user by enhancing the website's textual content with an animated signed translation encoded as a series of commands. Vcom3D commercializes software for creating and adding computer animated ASL translation to media [5,6]. The SigningAvatar®software system uses animated 3-D characters to communicate in sign language with facial expressions. It has a database of 3,500 English words/concepts and 24 facial configurations, and it can fingerspell words that are not in the database.

TERC [5,6] collaborated with Vcom3D and the National Technical Institute for the Deaf (NTID) on the use of SigningAvatar software to annotate the web activities and resources for two Kids Network units. Recently, TERC has developed a Signing Science Dictionary (SSD) [7,8]. Both the Kids Network units and the science dictionary benefit deaf children confirming again the value of animated ASL. Purdue University Animated Sign Language Research Group, in collaboration with the Indiana School for the Deaf (ISD), is focusing on research, development, and evaluation of 3-D animation-based interactive tools for improving math and science education for the Deaf. The group developed Mathsigner, a collection of animated math activities for deaf children in grades K-4, and SMILE, an educational math and science immersive game featuring signing avatars [9,10].

Many research efforts target automated translation from text to sign language animation to give signers with low reading proficiency access to written information in contexts such as education and internet usage. In the U.S., English to ASL translation research systems include those developed by Zhao et al. [11], Grieve-Smith [12] and continued by Huenerfauth [13]. To improve the realism and intelligibility of ASL animation, Huenerfurth is using a data-driven approach based on corpora of ASL collected from native signers [14]. In France, Delorme et al. [15] are working on automatic generation of animated French Sign Language using two systems: one that allows pre-computed animations to be replayed, concatenated and co-articulated (OCTOPUS) and one (GeneALS) that builds isolated signs from symbolic descriptions. Gibet et al. [16] are using data-driven animation for communication between humans and avatars. The Signcom project incorporates an example of a fully data-driven virtual signer, aimed at improving the quality of real-time interaction between humans and avatars. In Germany, Kipp et al. [17] are working on intelligent embodied agents, multimodal corpora and sign language synthesis. Recently, they conducted a study with small groups of deaf participants to investigate how the deaf community sees the potential of signing avatars. Findings from their study showed generally positive feedback regarding acceptability of signing avatars; the main criticism on existing avatars primarily targeted their low visual quality, the lack of non-manual components (facial expression, full body motion) and emotional expression. In Italy, Lesmo et al. [18] and Lombardo et al. [19] are working on project ATLAS (Automatic Translation into the Language of Sign) whose goal is the translation from Italian into Italian Sign Language represented by an animated avatar. The avatar takes as input a symbolic representation of a sign language sentence and produces the corresponding animations; the project is currently limited to weather news.

Despite the substantial amount of ASL animation research, development and recent improvements, several limitations still preclude animation of ASL from becoming an effective, general solution to deaf accessibility to digital media. One of the main problems is low visual quality of the signing avatars due to unnatural motions and low rendering quality of the signed animations, which results in limited legibility of the animated signs.

2.2   Rendering of Sign Language Animations

The visual quality of the ASL visualization depends in part on the underlying rendering algorithm that takes digital representations of surface geometry, color, lights, and motions as input and computes the frames of the animation. With

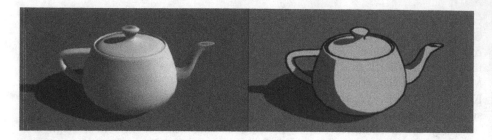

Fig. 1. Teapot model rendered by a photo-realistic rendering algorithm (left) and by a cel shading algorithm (right) [20]

photorealistic rendering methods, based on local lighting or global illumination, it may be difficult to clearly depict palm and fingers positions because of occlusion problems and lack of contour lines that can help clarify the palm/fingers configuration. Non-photorealistic methods, such as cel shading, could be used to increase the amount of information conveyed by a single view.

Cel shading is a type of non-photorealistic rendering in which an image is rendered by a computer to have a "toon" look that simulates a traditional hand-drawn cartoon cel. The toon appearance of a cel image is characterized by the use of areas selectively colored with a fill, a highlight, shading, and/or a shadow colors. Contour lines can be used to further define the shape of an object and color lines may be used to define the different color areas in the colored image. The contrast of the color lines and the thickness of the contour lines can be adjusted to improve clarity of communication. The type of cel shading used in this study produced images that have a stylized hand drawn look, with constant-size outlines and uniformly colored areas. Figure 1 shows a simple 3D model rendered by a photo-realistic rendering algorithm and by a cel shading algorithm with contour lines, one level of shading and shadows.

2.3   ASL Finger Spelling

Learning finger spelling is important, as it is very difficult to become fluent in ASL without mastering fingerspelling. Finger spelling is essential for four reasons. It is used in combination with sign language for (1) names of people, (2) names of places, (3) words for which there are no signs and (4) as a substitute when the word has not yet been learned. It is generally learned at the beginning of any course in sign language also because the hand shapes formed in finger spelling provide the basic hand shapes for most signs [21]. In spite of its importance and its apparent simplicity, high fluency in finger spelling is not easy to acquire, mainly for the reasons outlined. Achieving fingerspelling proficiency requires the visual comprehension of the manual representation of letters and one reason students experience difficulty in fingerspelling recognition is its high rate of handshape presentation. Most signs in ASL use no more than two hand shapes [22], but fingerspelling often uses as many handshapes as there are letters in a word.

3 Study Design

The objective of the study was to determine whether cel shading allowed the subjects to better recognize the word being signed to them. The independent variable for the experiment was the implementation of cel shading in ASL animations. The dependent variables were the ability of the participants to understand the signs, and their perception of the legibility of the finger-spelled words. The null hypothesis of the experiment was that the implementation of cel shading in ASL animations has no effect on the subjects' ability to understand the animations presented to them and on the perception of their legibility.

3.1 Subjects

Sixty-nine (69) subjects age 19–64, thirty-five (35) Deaf, thirteen (13) Hard-of-Hearing, and twenty-one (21) Hearing, participated in the study; all subjects were ASL users. Participants were recruited from the Purdue ASL club and through one of the subject's ASL blog (johnlestina.blogspot.com/). The original pool included 78 subjects, however 9 participants were excluded from the study because of their limited ASL experience (less than 2 years). None of the subjects had color blindness, blindness, or other visual impairments.

3.2 Stimuli Animations

Forty animation clips were used in this test. The animations had a resolution of 640×480 pixels and were output to Quick Time format with Sorensen 3 compression and a frame rate of 30 fps. Twenty animation clips were rendered with cel shading and twenty animation clips were rendered with photorealistic rendering with ambient occlusion. Both sets of animations represented the same 20 finger-spelled words. Camera angles and lighting conditions were kept identical for all animations. The animations were created and rendered in Maya 2014 using Mental Ray. Figure 2 shows a screenshot of one of the animations in Maya; Fig. 3 shows 4 frames extracted from the photorealistic rendering animation and 4 frames extracted from the cel shaded animation.

3.3 Web Survey

The web survey consisted of 1 screen per animated clip with a total of 40 screens (2×20). Each screen included the animated clip, a text box in which the participant entered the finger-spelled word, and a 5-point Likert scale rating question on perceived legibility (1 = high legibility; 5 = low legibility). The animated sequences were presented in random order and each animation was assigned a random number. Data collection was embedded in the survey; in other words, a program running in the background recorded all subjects responses and stored them in an excel spreadsheet. The web survey also included a demographics questionnaire with questions on subjects' age, gender, hearing status and experience in ASL.

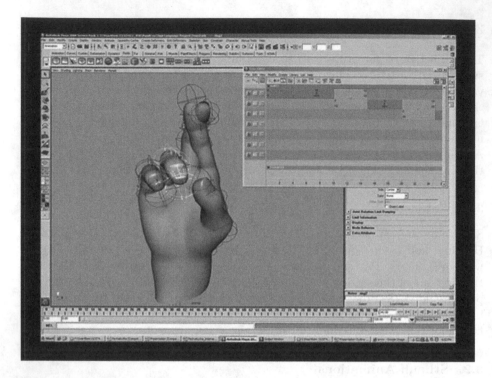

Fig. 2. The twenty words shown in the animations were: "cracker," "heavy," "can," "drain," "fruit," "milk," "Kyle," "child," "movie," "awesome," "axe," "bear," "voyage," "kiosk," "wild," "adult," "year," "duck," "love," and "color." The words were selected by a signer with experience in ASL. The choice was motivated by two factors. The words include almost all the letters of the manual alphabet (20/26), and the majority of these words present challenging transitions between hand-shapes. Since finger-spelling does not rely on facial expressions or body movements, the animations showed only the right hand.

3.4   Procedure

Subjects were sent an email containing a brief summary of the research and its objectives (as specified in the approved IRB documents), an invitation to participate in the study, and the http address of the web survey. Participants completed the on-line survey using their own computers and the survey remained active for 2 weeks. It was structured in the following way: the animation clips were presented in randomized order and for each clip, subjects were asked to (1) view the animation; (2) enter the word in the text box, if recognized, or leave the text box blank, if not recognized; (3) rate the legibility of the animation. At the end of the survey, participants were asked to fill out the demographics questionnaire.

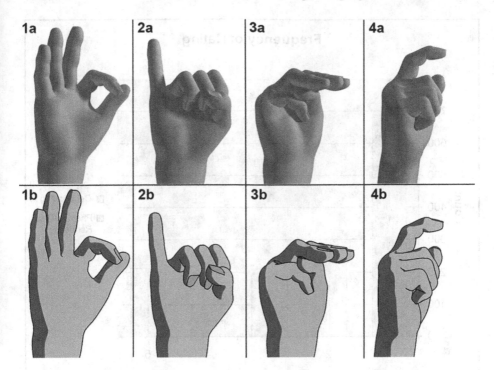

Fig. 3. Handshapes rendered with photorealistic rendering method (top, 1a–4a); handshapes rendered with cel shading (bottom, 1b–4b)

3.5   Findings

For the analysis of the subjects' legibility ratings a paired sample T test was used. With twenty pairs of words for each subject, there were a total of 1,380 rating pairs. The mean of the ratings for animations rendered with photorealistic rendering was 2.21, and the mean of the ratings for animations rendered with cel shading was 2.12. Using the statistical software SPSS, a probability value of .048 was calculated. At an alpha level of .05, the null hypothesis that cel shading had no effect on the user's perceived clarity of the animation was therefore rejected. Perceived legibility was significantly higher for the cel shaded animations than for the photorealistic rendered animations. Figure 4 shows the breakdown of the subjects' ratings of the animations.

For the analysis of the ability of the subjects to recognize the words, the McNemar test, a variation of the chi-square analysis, was used. Using SPSS once again, a probability value of .002 was calculated. At an alpha level of .05, a relationship between cel shading and photorealistic rendering and the subject's ability to identify the word being signed was determined. Word recognition was higher with cel shading across all subjects.

Two extraneous variables that were not considered during the design phase were revealed by the feedback provided by the subjects at the end of the survey:

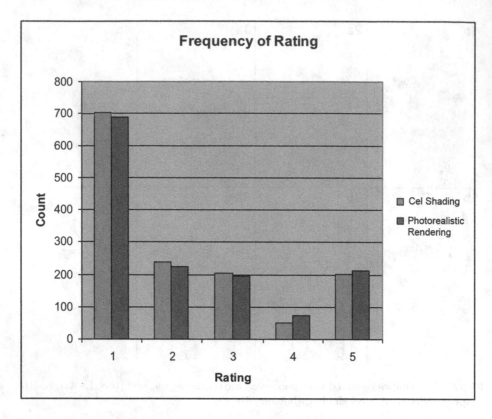

Fig. 4. A graph showing the breakdown of the subjects' ratings of the animations. Lower ratings, which indicate higher legibility, were more frequent with cel shaded animations, whereas higher ratings were more common for animations with photorealistic rendering.

(1) variation in subjects' computer screen resolution and (2) variation in subjects' internet connection speed. (1) Some subjects had a low screen resolution, which forced them to scroll down to see each animation. This might have caused the subjects to miss a part of the word being signed. (2) Since the survey was posted online, connection speed was also a problem. Several subjects mentioned that the animations were choppy and jumpy at times and caused them to miss some letters. In both cases, since the results from the survey were being compared within the subjects, that is, one subject's responses in one category were being compared to his/her responses in the other category, those extraneous variables did not have a substantial impact on the results.

4   Conclusion

In this paper we have reported a user study that aimed to determine whether rendering style has an effect on subjects' perception of ASL fingerspelling animations. Findings from the study confirmed our hypothesis: rendering style has an effect and non-photorealistic rendering (specifically, cel shading) improves subjects' recognition of the finger-spelled words and perceived legibility of the animated signs. Although the study produced significant results, it was limited to ASL finger spelling and the animations showed only the 3D model of the right hand. In future work we will extend the study to full-body avatars and complex 2-handed signs that involve body movements and facial expressions. As mentioned in the introduction, the authors believe that sign language animation has the potential to improve deaf accessibility to digital content significantly. The overall goal of this study, and other previous studies [23–25], is to advance the state-of-the-art in sign language animation by improving its visual quality, and hence its clarity, realism and appeal.

Acknowledgement. This research is supported in part by a grant from the Dr. Scholl Foundation

References

1. Rusinkiewiz, S., Burns, M., De Carlo, D.: Exaggerated shading for depicting shape and detail. ACM Trans. Graph. **25**(3), 1199–1205 (2006). (Proc. SIGGRAPH)
2. Elliott, R., Glauert, J.R.W., Kennaway, J.R., Marshall, I.: The development of language processing support for the ViSiCAST project. In: Proceedings of ASSETS 2000, pp. 101–108 (2000)
3. eSIGN (2003). http://www.visicast.cmp.uea.ac.uk/eSIGN/index.html
4. Vcom3D (2007). http://www.vcom3d.com
5. Sims, E.: SigningAvatars. In: Final Report for SBIR Phase II Project, U.S. Department of Education (2000)
6. TERC (2006). http://www.terc.edu/
7. Vesel, J.: Signing science. Learn. Lead. Technol. **32**(8), 30–31 (2005)
8. Signing Science (2007). http://signsci.terc.edu/
9. Adamo-Villani, N., Wilbur, R.: Two novel technologies for accessible math and science education. IEEE Multimedia **15**(4), 38–46 (2008). Special Issue on Accessibility
10. Adamo-Villani, N., Wilbur, R.: Software for math and science education for the deaf. Disabil. Rehabil. Assistive Technol. **5**(2), 115–124 (2010)
11. Zhao, L., Kipper, K., Schuler, W., Vogler, C., Badler, N.I., Palmer, M.: A machine translation system from English to American sign language. In: White, J.S. (ed.) AMTA 2000. LNCS (LNAI), vol. 1934, pp. 54–67. Springer, Heidelberg (2000)
12. Grieve-Smith, A.: SignSynth: a sign language synthesis application using web3D and perl. In: Wachsmuth, I., Sowa, T. (eds.) Gesture and Sign Language in Human-Computer Interaction. LNCS, vol. 2298, pp. 134–145. Springer-Verlag, Berlin (2002)
13. Huenerfauth, M.: A multi-path architecture for machine translation of English text into American sign language animation. In: Student Workshop at the Human Language Technology Conference/North American Chapter of the Association for Computational Linguistics (HLTNAACL) (2004)
14. Huenerfauth, M.: Cyclic data-driven research on American sign language animation. In: Proceedings of SLTAT 2011, University of Dundee, UK (2011)

15. Delorme, M. Braffort, A., Filhol, M.: Automatic generation of French sign language. In: Proceedings of SLTAT 2011, University of Dundee, UK (2011)
16. Gibet, S., Courty, N., Duarte, K.: Signing avatars: linguistic and computer animation challenges. In: Proceedings of SLTAT 2011, University of Dundee, UK (2011)
17. Kipp, M., Heloir, A., Nguyen, Q.: A feasibility study on signing avatars. In: Proceedings of SLTAT 2011, University of Dundee, UK (2011)
18. Lesmo, L., Mazzei, A., Radicioni, D.: Linguistic processing in the ATLAS project. In: Proceedings of SLTAT 2011, University of Dundee, UK (2011)
19. Lombardo, V., Nunnari, F., Damiano, R.: The ATLAS interpreter of the Italian sign language. In: Proceedings of SLTAT 2011, University of Dundee, UK (2011)
20. Decaudin, P.: Cartoon-looking rendering of 3D-scenes. In: Syntim Project INRIA, p. 6 (1996)
21. Flodin, M.: Signing Illustrated: The Complete Learning Guide. Berkley Publishing Group, New York (1994)
22. Battison, R.: Lexical Borrowing in American Sign Language. Linstok Press, Silver Spring (1978)
23. Adamo-Villani, N.: 3D rendering of American sign language finger-spelling: a comparative study of two animation techniques. In: Proceedings of ICCIT 2008 - 5th International Conference on Computer and Instructional Technologies, vol. 34, pp. 808–812 (2008)
24. Adamo-Villani, N., Wilbur, R., Eccarius, P., Abe-Harris, L.: Effects of character geometric model on the perception of sign language animation. In: IEEE Proceedings of IV 2009 - 13th International Conference on Information Visualization, Barcelona, pp. 72–75 (2009)
25. Adamo-Villani, N., Kasenga, J., Jen, T., Colbourn, B.: The effect of ambient occlusion shading on perception of sign language animations. In: Proceedings of ICCEIT 2011, Venice, Italy, pp. 1840–1844 (2011)

Comparison of Finite-Repertoire and Data-Driven Facial Expressions for Sign Language Avatars

Hernisa Kacorri[1] and Matt Huenerfauth[2(✉)]

[1] Doctoral Program in Computer Science, The Graduate Center, City University of New York (CUNY), 365 Fifth Ave, New York, NY 10016, USA
hkacorri@gc.cuny.edu
[2] Golisano College of Computing & Information Sciences, Rochester Institute of Technology (RIT), 152 Lomb Memorial Drive Rochester, New York, NY 14623, USA
matt.huenerfauth@rit.edu

Abstract. To support our research on ASL animation synthesis, we have adopted and enhanced a new virtual human animation platform that provides us with greater fine-grained control of facial movements than our previous platform. To determine whether this new platform is sufficiently expressive to generate understandable ASL animations, we analyzed responses collected from deaf participants who evaluated four types of animations: generated by our old or new animation platform, and with or without facial expressions performed by the character. For animations without facial expressions, our old and new plat-forms had equivalent comprehension scores; for those with facial expressions, our new platform had higher scores. In addition, this paper demonstrates a methodology by which sign language animation researchers can document transitions in their animation platforms or avatar appearance. Performing such an evaluation enables future readers to compare published results over time, both before and after such a transition in animation technology.

Keywords: American sign language · Accessibility technology for people who are deaf · Facial expression · Animation · Evaluation · User study

1 Introduction

Many people who are deaf have difficulty reading information content in the form of written language text, due to limitations in spoken language exposure and other educational factors. For example, in the U.S., standardized testing has revealed that many deaf adults graduating from secondary school (age 18) perform at or below fourth-grade English reading level (typically age 10) [10, 25]. Thus, if the text on online media is too complex, these adults may not comprehend the message. However, many of these users have sophisticated fluency in American Sign Language (ASL), which is a distinct language from English and is the primary mean of communication for more than 500,000 people in the U.S. [19]. Technology that can synthesize ASL animations from written text has accessibility benefits for these individuals.

© Springer International Publishing Switzerland 2015
M. Antona and C. Stephanidis (Eds.): UAHCI 2015, Part II, LNCS 9176, pp. 393–403, 2015.
DOI: 10.1007/978-3-319-20681-3_37

While incorporating videos of real human signers in websites and other media would make information accessible to deaf users, this approach is not ideal: the recordings are difficult and often prohibitively expensive to update, leading to out-of-date information. Further, there is no way to support dynamically generated content from a query. For these reasons, we investigate computer-synthesized animations (from an easy-to-update script as input), which allow for frequent updating, automatic production of messages (via natural language generation or machine translation techniques), wiki-style applications in which multiple authors script a message in ASL collaboratively, or scripting of messages by a single human author.

In ASL, a signer's facial expressions and head movements are essential to the fluency of the performance; these face and head movements convey: emotion, variations in word meaning, and grammatical information during entire sentences or syntactic phrases. This paper focuses on this third use, which is necessary for expressing questions or negation. In fact, a sequence of signs performed on the hands can have different meanings, depending on the syntactic facial expression that co-occurs [20]. E. g., a declarative sentence (ASL: "MARY LIKE BOOK" / English: "Mary likes the book.") can become a Yes-No question (English: "Does Mary like the book?"), with the addition of a Yes-No Question facial expression. This is performed by the signer raising their eyebrows and tilting their head forward during the sentence.

Similarly, the addition of a Negation facial expression (the signer shakes their head left and right while furrowing their eyebrows somewhat) during the verb phrase "LIKE BOOK" can change the meaning of the sentence to "Mary doesn't like the book." It is important to note that the word NOT is actually optional, but the facial expression is required [28]. For interrogative questions (with a WH word like "what, who, where"), a WH-Question facial expression (head tilted forward, eyebrows furrowed) is required during the sentence, e.g., "MARY LIKE WHAT."

There is variation in how these facial expressions are performed during a sentence, based on the length of the phrase when the facial expression occurs, the location of particular words during the phrase (e.g., NOT or WHAT), the facial expressions that precede or follow, the overall speed of signing, and other factors. Thus, in order to build our ASL animation synthesis system, we cannot simply record a single version of this facial expression and replay it whenever needed. We must be able to synthesize the natural variations in the performance of a facial expression, based on these complex linguistic factors, in order to produce understandable results. The production of grammatical facial expressions and head movements, which must be time-coordinated with specific manual signs, is crucial for the interpretation of signed sentences and acceptance of this technology by the users [13, 18].

In order to support our research on facial expressions, our laboratory has recently adopted and enhanced a new animation platform (details in Sect. 3), which provides greater control over the face movements of our virtual human character. Since we had conducted several years of research using a previous platform, we needed to compare the new avatar to the old avatar, in regard to their understandability and naturalness. This paper presents the results of experiments with deaf participants evaluating animations from both of these platforms. This comparison will enable future researchers to compare our published results before and after this platform change, and it will allow us to evaluate whether our new avatar is sufficiently understandable to support our future work. Further, this paper demonstrates a methodology by which sign language animation researchers can empirically evaluate alternative virtual human animation platforms to enable more specific comparisons between systems.

2 Related Work

Sign language avatars have been adopted by researchers that seek to make information accessible to people who are deaf and hard-of-hearing in different settings such as train announcements (e.g. [3]) and education (e.g., [2, 6]). While authoring by non-experts is one of the research focuses when designing a new animation platform (e.g. [1, 9, 26]), typically these platforms are seen as the output medium for machine translation tools that will allow text-to-signing, e.g. [4, 7, 11]. There has been recent work by several groups (e.g. [5, 22, 27]) to improve the state-of-the-art of facial expressions and non-manual signals for sign language animation, surveyed in [16].

Other researchers are also studying synthesis of facial expressions for sign language animation, e.g., interrogative (WH-word) questions with co-occurrence of affect [27], using computer-vision data to produce facial expressions during specific words [22], etc. However, few researchers have conducted user studies comparing different avatars with facial expressions. A user study by Smith and Nolan [24] indicated that the addition of emotional facial expressions to a "human-looking" avatar was more successful than a caricature avatar when comparing native signers' comprehension scores. Still, both avatars were created within the same sign language animation platform. Kipp et al. [18] asked native signers' feedback on 6 avatars, created either by an animation synthesis platform or by a 3D artist, with a varying level of facial expressions each. However, the stimuli used in the assessment were not the same, they differ in content and sign language.

3 Finite-Repertoire Vs. Data-Driven Facial Expressions

This section explains how our lab has recently made a major change in the avatar platform that is used to synthesize virtual humans for ASL animations. After explaining both platforms, this section will outline our research questions and hypotheses that motivated our comparison of both platforms in experiments with deaf participants.

3.1 Finite-Repertoire Facial Expressions in Our Old Avatar Platform

Our prior animation platform was based on a commercially available American Sign Language authoring tool, VCOM3D Sign Smith Studio [26], which allows users to produce animated ASL sentences by arranging a timeline of animated signs from a prebuilt or user-defined vocabulary. The software includes a library of facial expressions that can be applied over a single sign or multiple manual signs, as shown in

Fig. 1. While this finite repertoire covers adverbial, syntactic, and emotional categories of facial expressions, the user cannot modify the intensity of the expressions over time, nor can multiple facial expressions be combined to co-occur. Because such co-occurrences or variations in intensity are necessary for many ASL sentences, we were motivated to investigate alternative animation platforms for our research.

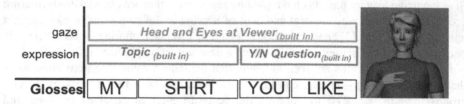

Fig. 1. This graphic depicts a timeline of an ASL sentence consisting of four signs (shown in the "Glosses" row) with co-occurring facial expressions from the software's built-in repertoire as specified by the user (shown in the "expression" row). The creator of this timeline has specified that a "Topic" facial expression should occur during the first two words and a "Yes No Question" facial expression during the final two.

3.2 Data-Driven Facial Expressions in Our New Avatar Platform

In order to conduct research on synthesizing animations of facial expressions for ASL, our laboratory required an animation platform that exposed greater control of the detailed aspects of the avatar's face movement. Further, we wanted an approach that would allow us to make use of face-movement data recorded from human ASL signers in our research. Our new animation platform is based on the open source tool EMBR [8], which has been previously used for creating sign language animations. Our lab extended its 3D avatar with ASL handshapes and detailed upper-face controls (eyes, eyebrows, and nose) that are compatible with the MPEG-4 Facial Animation standard [14]. As shown in Fig. 2, as part of our enhancements to EMBR, a professional artist designed a lighting scheme and modified the surface mesh to support skin wrinkling, which is essential to perception of ASL facial movements [27].

The MPEG-4 face parameterization scheme allows us to use recordings from multiple human signers, who may have different face proportions, to drive the facial expressions of the avatar. In particular, we implemented an intermediate component that converts MPEG-4 facial data extracted from facial movements in videos of human signers to the script language supported by the EMBR platform. To extract the facial features and head pose of the ASL human signers in the recordings, we use Visage Face Tracker, an automatic face tracking software [21] that provides MPEG-4 compatible output.

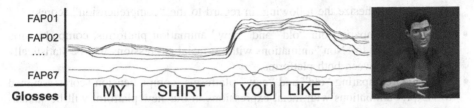

Fig. 2. A timeline is shown that specifies an ASL sentence with four words (shown in the "Glosses" row), with additional curves plotted above, each of which depicts the changing values of a single MPEG-4 parameter that governs the movements of the face/head. For instance, one parameter may govern the height of the inner portion of the signer's left eyebrow.

3.3   Comparison of New Vs. Old Avatar Platform

To compare the naturalness and understandability of the ASL facial expressions synthesized by the two animation platforms, we analyzed data from prior studies [15, 17] in which native signers evaluated animations from each. The multi-sentence stimuli shown and the questions asked were identical: Specifically, the hand movements for both avatars in those sentences are nearly identical (differences in avatar body proportion contributes to some hand movement differences). Thus, we present in Sect. 4 data from "Old" vs. "New" animations. Further, for each platform, the stimuli were shown in two versions: with facial expressions ("Expr.") and without facial expressions ("Non"), where the hand movements for both versions were identical. Thus, there were a total of four varieties of animations shown to participants. Participants were asked to report whether they noticed a particular facial expressions being performed by the avatar and to answer comprehension questions about the stimuli.

Clearly, we are interested in comparing results across the two platforms ("old" v. "new"). Further, we are also interested in our ability to see a difference between the animations with facial expressions ("Expr.") and those without facial expressions ("Non") in each case. (If we can't see any difference in "notice" or "comprehension" scores when we animate the face of the character, this suggests that the platform is not producing clear sign language facial expressions.) We hypothesize:

- H1: When comparing our "new" and "old" animation platforms, we expect the "notice" scores will be statistically **equivalent** to the corresponding scores ("Expr." or "Non") between both platforms.
- H2: When comparing "Expr." animations with facial expressions and "Non" animations without facial expressions, we expect that our new platform will re-veal differences in "notice" scores **at least as well as** our earlier platform.

To explain our reasoning for H1 and H2: For the "Non" case, there is no reason to think that the change in virtual human platform should affect the scores since the face does not move during these animations. For the "Expr." case, while the new platform may have more detailed movements, there is no reason to think that people would notice face movements more in our new character, even if they were more detailed.

We also hypothesize the following, in regard to the "comprehension" scores:

- H3: When comparing our "old" and "new" animation platforms, comprehension scores assigned to "Non" animations without facial expressions will be statistically **equivalent** between both platforms.
- H4: When comparing "old" and "new" platforms, comprehension scores assigned to "Expr." animations with facial expressions in our new platform will be statistically **higher** than those for the old platform.
- H5: When comparing "Expr." animations with facial expressions and "Non" animations without facial expressions, we expect our new platform to reveal differences in comprehension scores **at least as well as** our old platform.

To explain our reasoning: When comparing the "Non" versions (no face movements), we expect the comprehension scores to be similar between both platforms because the hand movements are similar. However, we expect the animations with facial expressions created in the new platform to be more comprehensible, given that the new platform should be able to reproduce subtle movements from human signers.

4 Experiment Setup and Results

While different animation platforms were used to generate the animations shown to participants, the "script" of words in the stimuli was identical. We previously published a set of stimuli for use in evaluation studies of ASL animations [12], and we used stimuli codenamed N1, N2, N3, W2, W3, W5, Y3, Y4, and Y5 from the set in this study. These nine multi-sentence stimuli included three categories of ASL facial expressions: yes/no questions, negation, and WH-word questions.

A fully-factorial design was used such that: (1) no participant saw the same story twice, (2) order of presentation was randomized, and (3) each participant saw half of the animations in each version: (i) without facial expressions ("Non") or (ii) with facial expressions ("Expr"). All of the instructions and interactions for both studies were conducted in ASL by a deaf native signer, who is a professional interpreter. Part of the introduction, included in the beginning of the experiment, and the comprehension questions of both studies were presented by a video recording of the interpreter.

Animations generated using our old animation platform were shown to 16 native signers [17]. Of 16 participants, 10 learned ASL prior to age 5, and 6 attended residential schools using ASL since early childhood. The remaining 10 participants had been using ASL for over 9 years, learned ASL as adolescents, attended a university with classroom instruction in ASL, and used ASL daily to communicate with a significant other or family member. There were 11 men and 5 women of ages 20–41 (average age 31.2). Similarly, animations generated using our new animation platform were shown to 18 native signers [15], with the following characteristics: 15 participants learned ASL prior to age 9, The remaining 3 participants learned ASL as adolescents, attended a university with classroom instruction in ASL, and used ASL daily to communicate with a significant other or family member. There were 10 men and 8 women of ages 22–42 (average age 29.8).

After viewing each animation stimulus one time, the participant answered a 1-to-10 Likert scale question as to whether they noticed a facial expression during the animation; next, they answered four comprehension questions about the information content in the animation (using a 1-to-7 scale from "Definitely Yes" to "Definitely No").

Figures 3 and 4 display the distribution of the Notice and Comprehension scores for the "Expr." and "Non" types of stimuli in the studies. (Box indicates quartiles, centerline indicates median, star indicates mean, whiskers indicate 1.5 inter-quartile ranges, crosses indicate outliers, and asterisks indicate statistical significance. To aid the comparison, mean values are added as labels at the top of each boxplot.) Labels with the subscript "(OLD)" indicate animations produced using our prior animation plat-form, and labels with the subscript "(NEW)" indicate animations produced using our new animation platform.

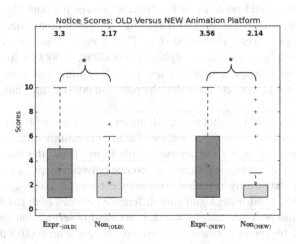

Fig. 3. Notice scores for OLD and NEW animation platform

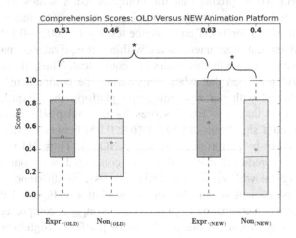

Fig. 4. Comprehension scores for OLD and NEW animation platform

Since hypotheses H1 and H3 require us to determine if pairs of values are statistically equivalent, we performed "equivalence testing" using the two one-sided test (TOST) procedure [23], which consists of: (1) selecting an equivalence margin theta, (2) calculating appropriate confidence intervals from the observed data, and (3) determining whether the entire confidence interval falls within the interval (-theta, +theta). If it falls within this interval, then the two values are deemed equivalent. We selected equivalence margin intervals for the "notice" and comprehension scores based on their scale unit as the minimum meaningful difference. This results intervals of (-0.1, +0.1) for the 1-to-10 scale "notice" scores and (-0.14, +0.14) for the 1-to-7 scale comprehension scores. Having selected an alpha-value of 0.05, confidence intervals for TOST were evaluated using Mann-Whitney U-tests for Likert-scale data and t-tests for comprehension-question data. (Non-parametric tests were used for the Likert-scale data because it was not normally distributed.)

Hypothesis H1 would predict that the "notice" scores for both "Non" and "Expr." stimuli would be unaffected by changing our animation platform. The following confidence intervals were calculated for TOST equivalence testing: (-0.00002, +0.00003) for $Non_{(OLD)}$ vs. $Non_{(NEW)}$ and (-0.000008, 0.00006) for $Expr._{(OLD)}$ vs. $Expr._{(NEW)}$. Given that these intervals are entirely within our equivalence margin interval of (-0.1, +0.1), we determine that the pairs are equivalent. Thus, hypothesis H1 is supported.

Hypothesis H2 would predict that evaluations conducted with our new animation platform are able to reveal with-vs.-without facial expressions differences in "notice" scores at least as well as our old animation platform. Thus, the statistical test is as follows: If there is a pairwise significant difference between $Expr._{(OLD)}$-$Non_{(OLD)}$, then there must be a statistically significant difference between $Expr._{(NEW)}$-$Non_{(NEW)}$. In support of H2, Fig. 3 illustrates significant difference between both pairs on the basis of Kruskal-Wallis and post hoc tests ($p < 0.05$). We also observed that the magnitude of this difference is bigger in our new platform (d: 33, p-value: 0.001) than it is in our prior animation platform (d: 24, p-value: 0.02). Thus, hypothesis H2 is supported.

Hypothesis H3 would predict that the comprehension scores for "Non" stimuli would be unaffected by changing our animation platform. The following confidence intervals were calculated for TOST equivalence testing: (+0.002, +0.119) for $Non_{(OLD)}$ vs. $Non_{(NEW)}$. Given that these intervals are within our equivalence margin interval of (-0.14, +0.14), we determine that the pairs are equivalent. Thus, H3 is supported.

Hypothesis H4 predicted that when considering the comprehension questions in evaluations conducted with our new animation platform the "Expr." stimuli would receive higher scores than the "Expr" scores for our old platform. As illustrated in Fig. 4, we observed a significant difference ($p < 0.05$) between $Expr_{(OLD)}$-$Expr_{(NEW)}$ comprehension scores by performing one-way ANOVA. Thus, H4 is supported.

Hypothesis H5 predicted that evaluations conducted with our new animation platform would reveal with-vs.-without facial expressions differences in comprehension scores at least as well as our old animation platform. Figure 4 illustrates a significant difference when comparing $Expr._{(NEW)}$-vs.-$Non_{(5EW)}$ comprehension scores for our new animation platform but not for the prior platform. Significance testing was based on one-way ANOVA and post hoc tests ($p < 0.05$). Thus, H5 is supported.

5 Discussion and Future Work

This paper has demonstrated a methodology by which sign language animation researchers can directly compare the understandability and expressiveness of alternative animation platforms or avatars, through the use of experimental studies with deaf participants evaluating stimuli of identical ASL messages and responding to identical sets of comprehension questions. Such a comparison is valuable for ensuring that a new animation platform is able to produce human animations that are sufficiently expressive, and it also allows readers to understand how the results and benchmark baselines published in prior work would compare to results that are published using the new platform. In this case, we found that our new platform was able to produce animations that achieve similar scores to our old platform (when no facial expressions are included) or higher scores (when facial expressions are included). We also found that our new platform was able to produce animations with facial expressions that achieved significantly higher scores than animations without facial expressions.

Now that we have determined that this new animation platform is suitable for our research, in future work, we will investigate models for automatically synthesizing facial expressions for ASL animations, to convey essential grammatical information.

Acknowledgments. This material is based upon work supported by the National Science Foundation under award numbers 1506786 and 1065009. We acknowledge support from Visage Technologies AB. We are grateful for assistance from Andy Cocksey, Alexis Heloir, Jonathan Lamberton, Miriam Morrow, and student researchers, including Dhananjai Hariharan, Kasmira Patel, Christine Singh, Evans Seraphin, Kaushik Pillapakkam, Jennifer Marfino, Fang Yang, and Priscilla Diaz.

References

1. A-V, N., Popescu, V., Lestina, J.: A non-expert-user interface for posing signing avatars. Disabil. Rehabil: Assistive Technol. **8**(3), 238–248 (2013)
2. Adamo-Villani, N., Wilbur, R.: Software for math and science education for the deaf. Disabil. Rehabil. Assistive Technol. **5**(2), 115–124 (2010)
3. Ebling, S., Glauert, J.: Exploiting the full potential of JASigning to build an avatar signing train announcements. In: 3rd International Symposium on Sign Language Translation and Avatar Technology (2013)
4. Elliott, R., Glauert, J., Kennaway, J., Marshall, I., Safar, E.: Linguistic modeling and language-processing technologies for avatar-based sign language presentation. Univ. Access Inf. Soc. **6**(4), 375–391 (2008). Springer, Heidelberg
5. Filhol, M., Hadjadj, M.N., Choisier, A.: Non-manual features: the right to indifference. In: 6th Workshop on the Representation and Processing of Sign Language (LREC) (2014)
6. Fotinea, S.-E., Efthimiou, E., Dimou, A.-L.: Sign language computer-aided education: exploiting GSL resources and technologies for web deaf communication. In: Miesenberger, K., Karshmer, A., Penaz, P., Zagler, W. (eds.) ICCHP 2012, Part II. LNCS, vol. 7383, pp. 237–244. Springer, Heidelberg (2012)

7. Gibet, S., Courty, N., Duarte, K., Naour, T.L.: The SignCom system for data-driven animation of interactive virtual signers: methodology and evaluation. ACM Trans. Interact. Intell. Syst. **1**(1), 6 (2011)
8. Heloir. A., Nguyen, Q., Kipp, M.: Signing avatars: a feasibility study. In: 2nd International Workshop on Sign Language Translation and Avatar Technology (2011)
9. Heloir, A. Nunnari, F.: Towards an intuitive sign language animation authoring environment for the deaf. In: Proceedings of the 2nd Workshop in Sign Language Translation and Avatar Technology (2013)
10. Holt, J.A.: Stanford achievement test - 8th edition: reading comprehension subgroup results. Am. Ann. Deaf **138**, 172–175 (1993)
11. Huenerfauth, M.: Spatial and planning models of ASL classifier predicates for machine translation. In: The 10th International Conference on Theoretical and Methodological Issues in Machine Translation (2004)
12. Huenerfauth, M., Kacorri, H.: Release of experimental stimuli and questions for evaluating facial expressions in animations of American sign language. In: Proceedings of the 6th Workshop on the Representation and Processing of Sign Languages (LREC) (2014)
13. Huenerfauth, M., Lu, P., Rosenberg, A.: Evaluating importance of facial expression in American sign language and Pidgin signed english animations. In: The Proceedings of the 13th International ACM SIGACCESS Conference on Computers and Accessibility, pp. 99–106 (2011)
14. ISO/IECIS 14496-2 Visual (1999)
15. Kacorri, H., Huenerfauth, M.: Implementation and evaluation of animation controls sufficient for conveying ASL facial expressions. In: Proceedings of the 16th International ACM SIGACCESS Conference on Computers and Accessibility, pp. 261–262 (2014)
16. Kacorri, H.: TR-2015001: A Survey and Critique of Facial Expression Synthesis in Sign Language Animation. Computer Science Technical Reports. Paper 403 (2015)
17. Kacorri, H., Lu, P., Huenerfauth, M.: Effect of displaying human videos during an evaluation study of american sign language animation. ACM Trans. Accessible Comput. **5**(2), 4 (2013)
18. Kipp, M., Nguyen, Q., Heloir, A., Matthes, S.: Assessing the deaf user perspective on sign language avatars. In: The Proceedings of the 13th International ACM SIGACCESS Conference on Computers and Accessibility, pp. 107–114. ACM Press, New York (2011)
19. Mitchell, R., Young, T., Bachleda, B., Karchmer, M.: How many people use ASL in the United States? Why estimates need updating. Sign Lang. Stud. **6**(3), 306–335 (2006)
20. Neidle, C., Kegl, D., MacLaughlin, D., Bahan, B., Lee, R.G.: The Syntax of ASL: Functional Categories and Hierarchical Structure. MIT Press, Cambridge (2000)
21. Pejsa, T., Pandzic, I.S.: Architecture of an animation system for human characters. In: Proceedings of the 10th International Conference on Telecommunications, pp. 171–176 (2009)
22. Schmidt, C., Koller, O., Ney, H., Hoyoux, T., Piater, J.: Enhancing gloss-based corpora with facial features using active appearance models. In: Proceedings of the 2nd Workshop in Sign Language Translation and Avatar Technology (2013)
23. Schuirmann, D.J.: A comparison of the two one-sided tests procedure and the power approach for assessing equivalence of average bioavailability. J. Pharmacokin Biopharm **15**, 657–680 (1987)
24. Smith, R., Nolan, B.: Manual evaluation of synthesised sign language avatars. In: Proceedings of the 15th International ACM SIGACCESS Conference on Computers and Accessibility, pp. 57 (2013)

25. Traxler, C.: The Stanford achievement test, 9th edition: national norming and performance standards for deaf and hard-of-hearing students. J. Deaf Stud. Deaf Educ. **5**(4), 337–348 (2000)

26. VCOM3D.: Homepage (2015). http://www.vcom3d.com/

27. Wolfe, R., Cook, P., McDonald, J.C., Schnepp, J.: Linguistics as structure in computer animation: toward a more effective synthesis of brow motion in American sign language. Sign Lang. Linguist. **14**(1), 179–199 (2011)

28. Zeshan, U.: Interrogative and Negative Constructions in Sign Languages. Oxford University Press, Oxford (2006)

Assessing the Efficiency of Using Augmented Reality for Learning Sign Language

Ines Kožuh[1(✉)], Simon Hauptman[1], Primož Kosec[2], and Matjaž Debevc[1]

[1] Faculty of Electrical Engineering and Computer Science,
University of Maribor, Maribor, Slovenia
{ines.kozuh,simon.hauptman,matjaz.debevc}@um.si
[2] Nuimo, Kamnica, Slovenia
primoz@nuimo.si

Abstract. In this study we examined whether the success rate regarding accuracies of signing particular words differs when the signs for the words are acquired either from (a) a picture symbolizing a sign, (b) an Augmented Reality mobile application, or (c) a physically present sign language interpreter. We analyzed whether any differences would appear between the 25 people included in an experiment. We used three pairs of words and the participants were accordingly classified into three groups. Each group was asked to sign one pair of words based on acquiring signs either from pictures, the Augmented Reality mobile application or a sign language interpreter. When the participants signed single words, their accuracies (=success rates) were evaluated by two sign language interpreters. The results revealed the lowest success rates when watching pictures, while the success rates improved by 35 % when using the Augmented Reality mobile application. When a sign-language interpreter signed words the participants' success rates in signing increased by an additional 9 %. No differences were found between D/HH signers and hearing non-signers. Generally, participants were the least successful when signing the words "break" and "claw".

Keywords: Deaf · Hard of hearing · Augmented reality · Sign language

1 Introduction

Augmented reality (AR) is one of the recent popular technologies which can be used for simplifying people's lives by bringing virtual information to their environments. It can be defined as a real-time direct or indirect view of a physical real-world environment that has been augmented by adding virtual computer-generated information to it [1].

A number of recent studies have examined the applicability of AR within various areas of life and showed that it can help people with disabilities [1–6]. These studies mostly investigated potentials for using AR from different points of view in regard to educational purposes for the d/Deaf and hard of hearing (D/HH).

© Springer International Publishing Switzerland 2015
M. Antona and C. Stephanidis (Eds.): UAHCI 2015, LNCS 9176, pp. 404–415, 2015.
DOI: 10.1007/978-3-319-20681-3_38

For instance, some studies emphasized the use of AR for vocabulary acquisition [2, 3] since learning how to read and write can pose several challenges for deaf persons, especially when they perceive sign language as a first language and written language as the second language. Moreover, Carmigniani et al. [1] pointed out the importance of using AR as a substitute for users' missing senses, i.e. when they need a sensory substitute like augmenting hearing by the use of visual cues. Similarly, the University of Applied Sciences in Düsseldorf developed a "Deaf Magazine" [5] where mobile AR application helps sign-language users understand written content by providing additional audio-video material.

The above-mentioned studies mainly focused on examining the purposes AR can be used for. However, to the best of our knowledge, there has been a lack of investigative efficiency in D/HH people's usages of AR mobile applications where paper-based written information is augmented with a virtual sign-language interpreter (SLI) video. Moreover, there is a lack of D/HH users' perceptions of the concepts of using AR for the purposes mentioned above. Such investigation may be crucial when addressing e-inclusion in terms of implementing the use of AR in education.

The main purpose of the current study was to meet this deficiency by conducting an experiment where we evaluated the efficiency of using AR when learning how to sign particular words in sign-language and participants' perceptions of the augmented content. In line with that, a mobile AR application was developed and used to augment paper-based pictures, symbolizing signing words, and with SLI videos displayed on a mobile phone. Thus, the following hypotheses were examined:

RQ1: Are there statistically significant differences in the success rates of signing between different ways of acquiring signing words (a picture symbolizing signing words, the AR mobile application and a SLI) for D/HH and hearing people?

We would expect to find significantly higher success rates in the accuracy of signing words when using the AR mobile application compared to using a picture symbolizing signing words in both D/HH and hearing people (=signers and non-signers). In contrast, success rates in accuracy regarding performed signing words when acquiring signing from the AR mobile application would not be expected to be significantly higher than when watching a SLI personally.

RQ2: Are there statistically significant differences in success rates between signing different words within the same level of difficulty and when using the same ways of acquiring signing words (a picture symbolizing signing words, the AR mobile application or a SLI)?

It would not be expected to find that success rates would vary significantly when signing different words within the same level of difficulty.

The paper is organized as follows. We start by presenting the AR application for learning sign language. Next, the research method is presented by describing the design and procedure of the experiment. Then participants' characteristics, data analyses and results are shown. Finally, discussion and conclusion with study limitations follow.

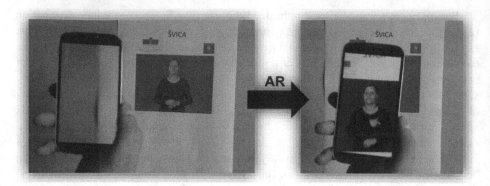

Fig. 1. The concept of AR application for augmenting an object in a physical real-world environment with a SLI video.

2   AR Application for Learning Sign-Language

Figure 1 shows the concept of our designed mobile AR application. A photo of SLI was used as a reference image for augmentation. When the user of a mobile AR application positions his/her phone above the photo, a camera captures it and a SLI video appears within the photo frame. Some general requirements for recording SLI videos were followed when preparing the SLI video [8, 9].

3   Methods

3.1   Design and Procedure of the Experiment

Table 1 shows the design of the experiment which sought to identify whether the use of AR significantly contributed to the learners' success rates when signing specific words.

Table 1. Design of the experiment

Introduction to the test	Training session	Experimental and evaluation session							Final evaluation session
		Test A							
			Phase 1		Phase 2		Phase 3		
Information sheet for participants	Training for phase 1, 2 and 3	Picture 1a → Picture 2a →	Success rate in signing	AR 1b AR 2b	Success rate in signing	SLI 1c → SLI 2c →	Success rate in signing		
		Test B							Final questionnaire (written and sign language)
			Phase 1		Phase 2		Phase 3		
Consent form		Picture 1c → Picture 2c →	Success rate in signing	AR 1a AR 2a	Success rate in signing	SLI 1b SLI 2b →	Success rate in signing		
	Training for SLIs	**Test C**							
Initial questionnaire (written and sign language)			Phase 1		Phase 2		Phase 3		
		Picture 1b → Picture 2b →	Success rate in signing	AR 1c AR 2c	Success rate in signing	SLI 1a SLI 2a →	Success rate in signing		

Used words: 1a-now, 1b-break, 1c-listen, 2a-butterfly, 2b-claw, 2c-to exploit

The experiment was divided into four sessions: (a) introduction to the test, (b) training session, (c) experimental and evaluation session, and (d) final evaluation session.

3.1.1 Introduction to the Test

Prior to starting the training session, the participants were informed about the experiment in written form and in sign-language. Next, they were asked to sign a written consent form. Filling out an initial questionnaire followed, where participants provided information about their genders, ages, types of hearing loss if any, skills at using smartphone, as well as estimations about sign and written language competencies. The competencies were measured using questions developed on the basis of the adjusted Deaf Acculturation Scale [7]. The questionnaire was put online and all questions were entirely presented in both Slovenian written and sign-language.

3.1.2 Training Session

One picture symbolizing a signing word served for the training session. After watching a single picture for six seconds, participants were asked to sign the word by themselves and two SLIs evaluated its accuracy. Next, a smartphone with AR mobile application was given to them and they were asked to position the phone above a new picture, so that the SLI video appeared within the photo frame on the phone. After six seconds, they were asked to sign the word, which was again evaluated by two SLIs. Finally, a SLI was given six seconds to sign the word and participants were asked to sign it. Once again, two SLIs evaluated its accuracy. The results from the training sessions only served for acknowledgement of the procedure and were excluded from the data analysis.

3.1.3 Experimental and Evaluation Session

This session was conducted in three main steps. During each step, participants were asked to sign two different words, which were six words in total in this session.

In the first step, the participants were given six seconds to view a picture symbolizing a sign for one word. Then, the picture was taken away and participants were asked to sign the word. Two SLIs evaluated them. The same procedure was repeated for the second word.

In the second step, the participants were given the smartphone with the AR application installed on it. Once again, they were asked to capture the picture and were given six seconds before being asked to sign one word. Afterwards, two SLIs evaluated them. The same procedure was repeated for one additional word.

In the third step, the participants were given six seconds to look at the SLI standing in front of them when signing another word. Afterwards, they were asked to sign the word by themselves and two SLIs evaluated them. The same procedure was repeated for the second word.

The above-mentioned procedure was performed during three different tests: A, B and C. Table 1 shows the distributions of words within these tests for training, experimental and evaluation sessions. SLIs evaluated the participants' signings on a scale from 1 (fail) to 10 (excellent).

3.1.4   Final Evaluation Session

Participants were asked to fill out the final questionnaire, where they reported whether they had known the signs for all the included words before participating in the experiment. In addition, they were asked how difficult it was for them to sign the words. Again, the questionnaire was put online and was entirely presented in both Slovenian written and sign-languages.

3.1.5   Further Conditions

Besides the above-mentioned points, some additional criteria were followed regarding the design and procedure of the experiment. Firstly, we selected the words from a nationally recognized set of three books for learning Slovenian sign-language – the Visual dictionary of Slovenian sign-language. This set of books provides explanations of written words in sign-language both in pictures, symbolizing signing words, and in SLI videos.

While these books provided sign language interpretations for a large number of words, we asked one deaf person, one hard of hearing person and one SLI to consensually choose the words for the experiment. The main criteria for selection of words were frequency of using signing gestures among signers and complexity of gestures. Additionally, a precondition told to these persons was that one word and its signing version would be used in the training session and the additional six words would be used in the main experimental session.

These six words were of two different levels of difficulty. Accordingly, three pairs of words were created, where the first word was of lower and the second word was of higher levels of difficulty. Each pair of words was then used once during each of three steps in the experimental session.

Secondly, two SLIs participated in the experiment as evaluators. The main criterion for their selection was that they were certified SLIs on the national level. We involved two of them in order to increase the reliability of evaluating signed words.

Thirdly, the accuracies of the signed words were evaluated by two SLIs based on their mutually agreed criteria, where consistency of their evaluation was to be assured. In addition, both SLIs were chosen strictly from the surroundings of the town in the north-eastern part of Slovenia where the experiment took place and where participants who were sign-language users came from. Consequently, we tried to avoid possible errors in evaluating the signing due to unpredicted variations in sign-language which might occur when SLIs were used to sign some words in different ways than the participants.

By following the above-mentioned criteria, we tried to avoid the inconsistency in evaluating signing which was also the case in a previous study [10] where the authors emphasized the problem of assessing signing on SLIs' personal knowledge leading to inconsistency in evaluating the signing.

Fourthly, the times of viewing pictures, SLI videos and SLI were defined according to the longest time needed by a SLI for signing any word among predefined sets of words. Accordingly, the durations of all SLI videos, times of viewing pictures and SLI were the same. In this way, our aim was to meet the same conditions for all three steps of the experimental session.

3.2 Participants

The sample for this study was recruited from the D/HH and hearing populations in Slovenia. The participants were personally invited to participate. The majority of hearing participants were students at the University of Maribor and most D/HH participants who responded were members of the Association of the Deaf and Hard of Hearing Podravje, Maribor.

In total, 34 people participated. Out of these, 12 were d/Deaf or hard of hearing and 20 were hearing; two persons reported that they do not know what level of hearing loss if any they had. Twenty-six participants were male and 8 participants were female. On average, they were 30.38 years old (age range: 21–61, SD = 12.03). Nineteen participants were signers and 15 participants were non-signers.

For the purpose of the current study we classified participants in two groups, while other participants were not subjects of this study:

- Group 1: D/HH signers ($n = 11$),
- Group 2: hearing non-signers ($n = 14$).

3.3 Data Analyses

A two-way mixed-design between-within subjects analyses of variance (ANOVA) [11] was conducted in order to assess the effect of the mode of presenting signing words on the accuracies of the participants' signing of these words across groups having different hearing status and status of using sign-language. Statistically significant differences between the three independent groups were checked with a one-way ANOVA [12]. All analyses were performed with SPSS version 21.0.

4 Results

4.1 Results on Research Questions

The first research question sought to identify whether success rates regarding accuracy when performing signing words would be significantly better when using the AR mobile application compared to acquiring signing words from viewing a picture and a SLI personally.

We conducted an analysis for hearing non-signers and D/HH signers. In both groups, evaluations of signing gestures for two words in each category, i.e. picture, AR and a SLI, from two different SLIs were summed. Accordingly, a maximum score in evaluation of a single category was 40. Table 2 shows rounded values for the mean values, standard deviations and standard errors of mean values.

We conducted a two-way mixed-design ANOVA to compare success rates in accuracy of performing signing words between hearing non-signers and D/HH signers when using three different ways when articulating particular signs: a picture, an AR mobile application and a SLI.

Table 2. Level of success rate in accuracy of signing the words when using a picture only, AR application and a SLI.

		Mean	Std. deviation	Std. error of mean
Both groups	Picture	22.80	9.92	1.98
	AR	30.84	8.22	1.64
	SLI	33.68	6.65	1.33
Group 1 (hearing)	Picture	21.64	8.92	2.38
	AR	29.36	8.04	2.15
	SLI	31.79	6.97	1.86
Group 2 (D/HH)	Picture	24.27	11.34	3.42
	AR	32.73	8.44	2.54
	SLI	36.09	5.61	1.69

The results showed a significant effect on success rates when using different ways of displaying signing words: *Wilks' Lambda* = .50, $F(1, 23) = 11.15$, $p < .001$, $\eta p^2 = .50$, with both groups together (hearing non-signers and D/HH signers) showing an increase of success rate when signing words were shown with the second and third ways compared to the first way (see Table 2 and Fig. 2). This indicates that when the signing words were acquired by using the AR mobile application and by watching a SLI's signing, the success rates increased in both groups. We calculated the increment by using the following equation:

$$increment = \frac{\overline{x_2}}{\overline{x_1}} * 100 - 100 \tag{1}$$

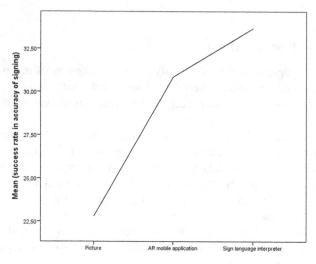

Fig. 2. Success rate in accuracy of signing when acquiring signing words from pictures, the AR mobile application and a SLI.

An increment of 35 % was achieved in success rate when using the AR mobile application instead of a picture. The increment in success rate was 9 % when acquiring a signing word from a SLI personally instead of using the AR application. The most obvious increment is evident in the success rate when watching a SLI compared to using a picture −48 %.

However, no statistically significant interaction was found between the success rate in different ways of acquiring signing words and hearing loss groups: *Wilks' Lambda* = .992, F (1, 23) = .09, p > .05, ηp^2 = .008.

What is more, the main effect for the two groups was not statistically significant, F (1, 23) = 3.10, p > .05, ηp^2 = .12. It indicated that there was no significant difference in success rate regarding accuracies of signing certain words for hearing non-signers and D/HH signers.

In order to find an answer on the second research question, we conducted a one-way ANOVA in order to inspect statistically significant differences between different tests (A, B and C) in success rates for each way of acquiring signing words (a picture, the AR application and a SLI). For each word we summed the evaluation marks from both SLIs that evaluated participants' signings. Thus, each word could be evaluated in total up to a score 20.

The results showed statistically significant differences between the three tests in the following ways of acquiring signing words:

- Picture 1, $F(2, 22) = 9.16$, $p < .01$, $\eta p^2 = .45$,
- Picture 2, $F(2, 22) = 9.05$, $p < .01$, $\eta p^2 = .45$,
- The first video in the AR mobile application (AR 1), $F(2, 22) = 5.60$, $p < .05$, $\eta p^2 = .34$,
- The first word signed by a SLI (SLI 1), $F(2, 22) = 4.54$, $p < .05$, $\eta p^2 = .29$.

In order to discover whether the differences occurred within or between the groups, we conducted post hoc comparisons with a Tukey HSD test. For picture 1, significant differences in success rates were found between the first and third words, as well as between the second and third words. Table 3 shows mean values, standard deviations and standard errors of means for the success rates in the accuracy of signing for the words across ways of acquiring signing words and types of tests.

Our result thus indicated that the success rates when signing the word "now" were significantly better than those for the word "break". Likewise, the success rates for the word "listen" were significantly better than those for the word "break".

Post hoc comparisons of success rates for picture 2 showed that the differences among all three words were significant, except the differences between the words "to exploit" and "claw".

In addition, in AR 1 the post hoc comparisons showed that signing the word "break" was evaluated with significantly lower scores than signing the words "now" and "listen". Similarly, when acquiring the signing word from a SLI (see SLI 1 from Table 3), participants' signing the word "now" were evaluated as significantly better than signing the word "break".

Table 3. Descriptive statistics on different ways of acquiring signing words and specific words

	Test	Words	Mean	Std. deviation	Std. error of mean
	A	now	15.11	6.31	2.10
Picture 1	B	listen	17.33	2.18	.73
	C	break	7.29	5.06	1.91
	A	butterfly	15.00	4.69	1.56
Picture 2	B	to exploit	5.56	6.23	2.08
	C	claw	6.00	4.36	1.65
	A	break	12.11	5.33	1.78
AR 1	B	now	17.44	3.68	2.23
	C	listen	17.71	.49	.18
	A	claw	13.44	5.27	1.76
AR 2	B	butterfly	16.33	5.66	1.89
	C	to exploit	16.15	4.06	1.53
	A	listen	17.56	2.79	.93
SLI 1	B	break	14.67	3.74	1.25
	C	now	18.86	1.21	.46
	A	to exploit	17.11	3.30	1.10
SLI 2	B	claw	15.00	4.39	1.46
	C	butterfly	18.71	2.63	.99

4.2 Further Analysis

Further analysis showed no significant differences in the success rates when signing for participants' prior knowledge of signs. Table 4 shows the results for participants' skills of using smartphone, as well as skills of using sign and written language. The results are presented for both groups together (hearing and D/HH) and for each group separately.

5 Discussion

In this study we found significant effects regarding the different ways of acquiring signing words on the success rates in the accuracies of signing these words. When using the AR mobile application, the success rate was significantly better compared to using a picture symbolizing the same word. When participants were watching a SLI, signing specific words, they achieved significantly higher scores in accuracy of signing compared to using a picture or the AR mobile application.

This finding suggests that AR can be understood as a supportive technology not only to the hearing but also to D/HH users. Our study showed that both groups significantly benefited from using it, which is complementary to the finding by Carmigniani et al. [1] who pointed out the benefit of AR in a way that D/HH users can receive visual cues instead of missed audio information.

Our findings, however, also imply that the role of a SLI is still important, since participants achieved the highest scores when a SLI interpreted signs personally when

Table 4. Descriptive statistics on participants' skills

		Mean	Std. deviation	Std. error of mean
Both groups	Skills of using smartphone	4.16	.63	.13
	Skills of using sign language	1.85	2.15	.43
	Skills of using written language	3.89	.71	.14
Group 1 (hearing)	Skills of using smartphone	4.29	.61	.16
	Skills of using sign language	0.00	.00	.00
	Skills of using written language	4.26	.49	.13
Group 2 (D/HH)	Skills of using smartphone	4.00	.63	.19
	Skills of using sign language	4.21	.43	.13
	Skills of using written language	3.42	.68	.21

standing in front of them. It may indicate that AR cannot replace a SLI but could be understood as a complementary tool, especially when the physical presence of a SLI is impossible. Naturally, an additional precondition is also that the content which needs to be interpreted into sign-language is previously known and the SLI video could thus be pre-recorded.

The next finding of our study was that the success rates did not significantly differ between hearing non-signers and D/HH signers when signing by taking different ways of acquiring signs (a picture symbolizing signing words, the AR mobile application or a SLI). This finding may indicate that the AR technology has a potential in learning sign-language not only for beginners but also for those who already use sign-language and have a need to expand their vocabulary by learning new signs.

Our next findings were the significant differences between signing specific words within each way of acquiring signs. Accordingly, we analyzed the differences in success rates for signing the words with lower levels of difficulty and when acquiring a signing word by using a picture symbolizing a sign. The same analysis was performed for using the AR mobile application and watching a SLI personally. Generally, we found higher scores for the success rates when signing the word "now" compared to signing the words "listen" and "break".

For higher level of difficulty we found a significant difference in performance when signing different words only for a situation when using a picture. Signing the word "butterfly" had significantly better scores in success rates than signing the words "to exploit" and "claw". This finding can be understood through the frequencies of using certain signs in everyday communication and the complexity of gesture to be accurately shown.

6 Conclusion

The findings suggest that AR has the potential to be used for learning sign language not only among the hearing but also among D/HH people, regardless of their proficiencies in using sign-language. Our study showed that the success rate in the accuracy of performing signs increased by 35 % when acquiring signs from the AR mobile application instead of a picture symbolizing signs. When a SLI was physically present and showed the sign directly to participants, the success rate increased by an additional 9 %, compared to acquiring signs from the AR mobile application. These findings can thus contribute to increasing the awareness of how beneficial AR technology for acquiring signs can be, when learning sign-language.

This study had two main limitations. Firstly, there were small numbers of D/HH and hearing participants included within the study. However, it is important to consider that only a relatively small number of D/HH people are available in Slovenia who could be included in the study [13]. In order to address this limitation, we suggest repeating the study on a larger sample in Slovenia, as well as in other countries.

Secondly, participants' written and sign language skills were not objectively measured but were rather self-reported. Consequently, we could not know how skilled the participants really were and thus we had to rely on participants' self-estimations of their competencies.

Acknowledgements. We thank D/HH and hearing people for participating in the study, sign-language interpreters and representatives of the Association of the Deaf and Hard of Hearing Podravje, Maribor. Special thanks go to the Slovenian Association of the Deaf and Hard of Hearing for their permission to use the material from the Visual dictionary of Slovenian sign-language during our experiment. The study was supported by the Slovenian Research Agency [no. 1000-11-310140] under The Young Researcher Programme.

References

1. Carmigniani, J., Furht, B., Anisetti, M., Ceravolo, P., Damiani, E., Ivkovic, M.: Augmented reality technologies, systems and applications. Multimed. Tools Appl. **51**, 341–377 (2011)
2. Fecich, S.: The use of augmented reality-enhanced reading books for vocabulary acquisition with students who are diagnosed with special needs. The Pennsylvania State University (2014)
3. Jones, M., Bench, N., Ferons, S.: Vocabulary acquisition for deaf readers using augmented technology. In: 2nd Workshop on Virtual and Augmented Assistive Technology, 30 March, Minneapolis, Minnesota, USA (2014)
4. Lange, B.S., Requejo, P., Flynn, S.M., Rizzo, A.A., Cuevas, F.J., Baker, L., Winstein, C.: The potential of virtual reality and gaming to assist successful aging with disability. J. Phys. Med. Rehab. Clin. North America **21**(2), 339–356 (2010)
5. Project Das Deaf Magazine (2014). http://www.deafmagazine.de/
6. Zainuddin, N.M., Zaman, H.B.: Augmented reality in science education for deaf students: preliminary analysis. In: Regional Conference on Special Needs Education, Faculty of Education, Malaya University (2009)

7. Maxwell-McCaw, D., Zea, M.C.: The deaf acculturation scale (DAS): development and validation of a 58-item measure. J. Deaf Stud. Deaf Educ. **16**, 325–342 (2011)
8. Debevc, M., Kosec, P., Holzinger, A.: Improving multimodal web accessibility for deaf people: sign language interpreter module (SLIM). Multimed. Tools Appl. **45**(1), 181–199 (2010)
9. Kožuh, I.: The Deaf and Hard of Hearing on Social Networking Sites: Identities, Community Building and Connections between Communities. [Gluhi in naglušni na spletnih družbenih omrežjih: identiteta, grajenje skupnosti in povezave med skupnostmi.]. Doctoral Dissertation (2015, in press)
10. Lee, S., Henderson, V., Hamilton, H., Starner, T., Brashear, H., Hamilton, S.: A gesture-based American sign language game for deaf children. In: CHI 2005 Extended Abstracts on Human Factors in Computing Systems, pp. 1589–1592 (2005)
11. Tabachnick, G.G., Fidell, L.S.: Experimental Designs Using ANOVA. Duxbury, Belmont (2007)
12. Howell, D.: Statistical Methods for Psychology. Duxbury, Pacific Grove (2002)
13. Kožuh, I., Hintermair, M., Holzinger, A., Volčič, Z., Debevc, M.: Enhancing universal access: deaf and hard of hearing people on social networking sites. Univers. Access Inf. Soc., 1–9 (2014)

Smart and Assistive Environments

Virtual Interactive Space (VIS): Creating a Unique Dynamic HCI Ludic Engaging Design (Apparatus/Method) for Human Performance and (Re)Habilitation

Anthony Lewis Brooks[(✉)]

Aalborg University Esbjerg, Niels Bohrs Vej 8, 6700 Esbjerg, Denmark
tb@create.aau.dk

Abstract. This paper shares code that enables the making of a Virtual Inter-active Space (VIS) where the *skin* of the invisible active sensor area is dynamically responsive to the velocity of a limb e.g. hand. Used in proprioception training of movement the patch is at the core of the author's *Reafferentation* concept, which takes advantage of human natural and unconscious capacity. The mapping of the patch to a sound (e.g. drum, thus realizing an 'air-drum') resulted in increased client engagement in physiotherapist-led movement training sessions. The paper also reflects on how a cable-less physical environment augments the research.

Keywords: Virtual interactive space · Performance art · Movement training · Rehabilitation · Motivation · Auditory · Multimedia feedback · Reafferentation

1 Introduction

Virtual Interactive Space (VIS) was first published in 1999 at the World Congress of Physical Therapy (WCPT) in Yokohama, Japan [1]. The VIS concept is subject of ongoing research focused on rehabilitation. Recently, adoption of such sensors and multimedia/games as responsive content in healthcare and rehabilitation has been more widespread and continues to grow. Importantly, the size of the game industry has resulted in affordable access to sensor-based game-control peripherals, which are used to source human input. Pervasiveness of sensor-rich smart phones adds to such accessibility to game and creative-expressive feedback to human gestures. The patch herein detailed illustrates such sensor-based opportunities to engage participants who are undergoing a movement treatment program as well session facilitators.

This paper first presents a background and overview of the research that resulted in the emergence of the patch and its use in rehabilitation. Following this introduction, the need for a wireless environment is stated to contextualize the intervention and end-users that have been involved in the studies. The patch is then presented within the graphical programming environment where it was created. This is cross-referenced to a compressed text format shared in the appendix, which enables others to copy and paste into the software. Specific results from the patch use are subject of prior publications

© Springer International Publishing Switzerland 2015
M. Antona and C. Stephanidis (Eds.): UAHCI 2015, LNCS 9176, pp. 419–427, 2015.
DOI: 10.1007/978-3-319-20681-3_39

where the patch was not detailed but rather acting as an aspect of the intervention as a whole. Thus, this paper focuses on the detailing of the patch within a rehabilitation context. Use of the bespoke system in performance (stage) and installation art (e.g. Museums of Modern Art), including the presented patch, is not detailed in this paper. However, for interested readers, HCI cross-informing learning that emerged from VIS system experimenting and improvising within the arts is presented in the author's prior publications e.g. [2–4].

1.1   Background

A focus of the VIS research has been on augmenting rehabilitation intervention via apparatus and method development. Bespoke systems that enabled exploration of human performance plasticity and digital media plasticity emerged. Closure of the afferent-efferent neural feedback loop where human gestures are mapped to multimedia to stimulate sequential gestures has been at the core of the work (biofeedback).

The mature body of work that realized VIS began around 1985 following explorative studies of the author having been born into an artistic family with members with profound impairment. Simple music mapped pedal-based weight adjusted systems were initially explored. The work included exploring commercial worn bio signal sensor systems, held and non-worn/held devices. Early research evidenced the need for a simple system where a participant could just enter a space and immediately begin manipulating media through unencumbered gesture. This was effective when compared to worn sensor systems where a preparation of a participant involved the application of conductive gel and precise positioning of sensors.

Bespoke hardware resulted in the form of a volumetric infrared sensing device developed for invisibly interfacing a human with a music synthesizer via MIDI communication (Musical Instrument Digital Interface). Later, as technology evolved, the human input data was mapped to computer software programs that enabled manipulation of multimedia (sounds, images, games, and robotic devices). The media selective opportunities of input (feed forward) and mapping (feedback) enabled the tailoring to individual preference, needs and desires, which was found to optimize participation of both client and facilitator.

The created adaptive VIS systems enabled motion data to be sourced and mapped to immediate and direct feedback stimuli that informs both the participant and observers (e.g. therapist, carer, and family). The concept thus empowers engaging, fun and playful interactions in interventions that are otherwise reported as boring and mundane where repeated movement exercises give no feedback to the participant (client/patient). As well as acting as an entertaining human performance instrument, the system can record the movement data for post-session analysis. The analysis informs of patient progress and the iterative design session-to-session within a program of treatment.

The dynamics of such motion activities involve proprioceptive and kinematic sensibilities. However, the early systems were lacking in translating that sense into dynamic feedback so that for example a high velocity movement gave a louder sound that a lower velocity movement. This was conceptualized as offering an interactive dynamic response to consciously driven movement in movement training. An analogy is in the physical world where a drum is struck with increased force whereby the drummer consciously desires a louder response/sound.

The detail of this patch is presented in Sect. 2. The next sections present the scope of the work as applied in the field, and, specifically, how latest advances in wireless technologies aid this work through addressing the need for a cable-less physical environment.

1.2   Wireless Environments – a Need and Recent Solution

The sensing space being infrared is beyond what the eye can register. However, such systems have historically necessitated the use of cables to transfer the data from the sensing apparatus to the computer or synthesizer. Typically, in this work, multiple sensing devices that constitute a testing setup usually surround a participant to source multidimensional input (e.g. left/right arm/hand, head, right/left leg/foot). The participant often would be wheelchair bound. In such physical environments, the cables were found to be a hindrance and often led to accidents or incidents of damage to cables and thus signal degradation or loss. Recent developments in data transfer efficiency and effectiveness include opportunities for building wireless systems in context of this research.

Stepping back for a moment and reflecting the history in the field of device-to-device communication, this body of work took advantage of the MIDI communication protocol shortly after it was introduced in the 1980s. MIDI opened the possibilities to connect various devices to other devices each with suitable MIDI input/output/through capabilities. In order to communicate, unscreened cables with male 5-pin din plugs on each end are typically used. For more robust signal transfer two 5-pin din to 3-pin XLR adapters are used to take advantage of screened, thus reduced noise, XLR cabling. Thus enabling increased distance design between sensors and robust signal i.e. reduced SNR (Signal to Noise Ratio). However, no matter robustness of signal, cables are rarely immune to abuse such as being rolled over by a fully laden wheelchair and/or the wear and tear imparted by incorrect system dismantling, wrongly winding of cables, and/or improper storage under weighted equipment.

Contemporary advances in hardware and software around 2006 resulted in wireless MIDI transfer systems – so cable-less communication became available and tested in this work. The system used was the M-Audio MidAir Wireless MIDI Transmitter and Receiver System. This was a 2.4 GHz wireless device that enabled interfacing MIDI hardware at distances up to 30 feet where a MIDI cable would connect a controller to a battery-powered transmitter. The transmitter sent the data to a receiver positioned adjacent to the system computer. The receiver with its USB computer connection functioned as a class-compliant cross-platform Windows XP and Mac OS X, 1 × 1 MIDI interface. In tests, this system exhibited limitations on data dropouts. Thus, it was not a true success and whilst offering wireless communication, data dropouts were found to confuse participants as feedback was interrupted with constant resets.

Latest computer and smart device system developments around 2014 include Mac OS Yosemite and Apple iOS that have opened the door for more robust and non-latency wireless MIDI communication over Bluetooth e.g. MIDI LE, a free app for iOS 8 that's designed to bring low-latency MIDI over Bluetooth LE to CoreMIDI compatible iOS-Synths and applications. If controllers are battery-powered in line with tablets (iPad etc.) the combination results in a clear space and no floor cabling to protect from wheelchairs. Testing is ongoing on the wireless system as of writing.

1.3 Emergent Modalities of Use from Created Apparatus and Methods

The scope of the research involves two modalities unique to the research apparatus and methods that have emerged and been investigated in the field. The first of these modalities of use is the means of extending the active range of sensor-emitted infrared light (IR) for the sourcing of motion data. This is where prism-based versus ball-based reflective materials were found from research to intensify the IR reflections back in the same direction as received [3]. In the case of the SoundScapes system IR sensors, the infrared emitter and receiver are mounted next to each other to take advantage of this. The method enables a typical 150 cm active IR range to be extended to approximately 14 meters, so a rough factor of 10x is possible with this material. Additionally, the material can be worn (as in MoCap system tracking); hand manipulated (data changed according to occlusion manipulation); or mounted (e.g. as a window blind) to enable whole body or limb occlusion to generate data e.g. for balance, kinematic, proprioception training sessions as an element of a physical dysfunction treatment program as reported in the author's previous publications [e.g. 1–5].

The second embodiment of IR sensor investigation is the creation of a dynamic air patch as an element of the VIS and this is the focus of this contribution in the field of Human Computer Interaction. This is introduced in the next section.

2 Dynamic Air Patch

Around 1996 the original patch shared in this paper was created in the Opcode MAX software (Opcode is now Cycling74.com). MAX is a visual programming environment that is easily accessible and thus widely used for multimedia and music. It is modular, with most routines existing in the form of shared libraries. The MAX API (application programming interface) is a set of routines, protocols, and tools that enables third-party development of new routines (called "external objects"). Because of the API, it requires no line coding unless one wishes to create new objects that are not in the extensive and growing library. An analogy to the use of guitar pedals (as in the author's initial work) exemplifies how MAX enables an input (guitar) to be processed (e.g. distortion, delay, reverb circuitry) and delivered (e.g. via an amplifier and speakers). The player responds to the delivered sound with next input (Fig. 1).

The Max software has evolved over approximately twenty-five years and since Max 5 (version as of writing is Max 7) there has been a compressed text format that enables more effective and efficient sharing of patches. Thus, the MAX patch used to create dynamic air is shown in Fig. 2 with the appendix having the same patch as a shared compressed text format for interested readers to copy and reuse by copy-pasting within the MAX environment to realize the patch as shown in Fig. 2.

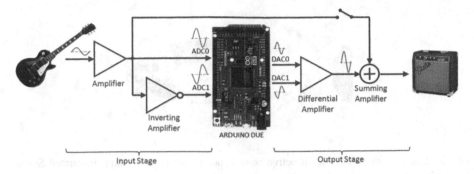

Fig. 1. Analogy of signal input, processing effect pedal (Arduino), delivery (amp) source http://www.electrosmash.com/pedalshield.

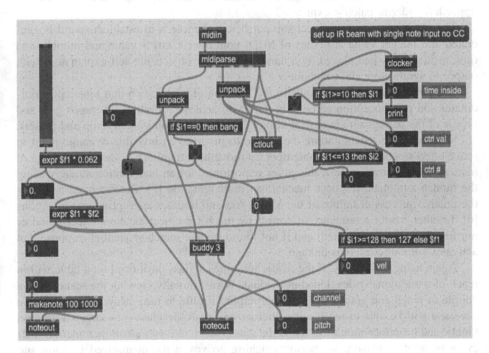

Fig. 2. Cycling74 Max 7 Dynamic Air Patch (see appendix for text code)

2.1 Patch and Use Detail

Knowing the attributes of MIDI the patch was created to use both discrete/binary and the continuous attributes of the MIDI protocol combined. Thus, a single note number corresponding to a musical pitch is programmed to an infrared sensor-activated free air space with a volumetric profile (VIS) (Fig. 3 – see also [3]). An interference velocity at the specified point in space (representing the volumetric 'skin') triggers this note such that the "Attack" attribute of the ASRD envelope (attack, sustain, release, decay) is

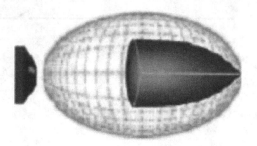

Fig. 3. Sensor with volumetric IR active zone – outer matrix green 'skin' illustrated Source: Interactive Light.

affected with 'aftertouch' active as an adjustable sensitivity expression attribute i.e. upper left slider in patch < expr > .

The patch contains test object sub-patch < makenote > to establish sound is generated and integer value attributes of MIDI controller < ctrl > value and number and time inside (e.g. when played by a hand). The other objects are self-explanatory with output to synthesizer via < noteout > .

The point in space corresponds to the location of a user such that kinematic coordinates and proprioception correlation matrix to achieve operation. Therapist goal and profile of the participant are crucial design factors of session system setup and presets.

Specifically in rehabilitation, the ability to program an invisible dynamic point in space offers opportunities for contemporary movement training e.g. increasing range of motion/reach. In this context, this gives opportunity for an intervention strategy using the human automatic response mechanism reafferentation [5]. Reafferentation gauges the relative success or failure of the Motor Act and initiates appropriate modifications [6]. In other words, a sequence of conscious reach for object location/object found or not found feedback (expected) and if not found initiate search sequential response that activates without conscious linkage.

Again using an analogy, if the reader imagines a glass positioned on a table within reach of a traditionally developed individual. Whilst initially viewing the scene, after a couple of reach and grab actions the participant is able to turn away and/or close the eyes and still be able to reach out as before and grab the glass – as targeted through kinetic and proprioception memory. If the glass is then moved a small increment further away by another person, the person reaching arrives at the memorized location and finding the glass not where it was expected there is an automatic response to search for the glass. Upon locating the glass in its new position, i.e. a little further away, the body sense is that its memory sensing was not accurate and a compensatory sensing mechanism activates to brain-body program the new location as the previous position. This relates to afferent-efferent neural feedback loop closure as previously presented in [7]. However, a big difference in this example is that the glass is a physical object and realistically any movement of the glass away from the reaching person will likely be detected. This makes the invisible sensing spaces (VIS) an ideal vehicle for Reafferentation due to the fact that each increment can be a pre-programmed preset that can be triggered without the participant knowing.

3 Proprioception and Kinesthetic Sense – Interoception and Exteroception

Simply put, proprioception is the sense of the relative position of the body, its constituent parts, and the related effort of movement. The brain senses the proprioceptive body position, its motion and acceleration. Kinesthetic sense is a related term referring to locomotion and physiological muscle sense, here including skin, joints, and structures such as tendons etc. Also related are the terms "interoception" and "exteroception" whereby these are in turn providing information about the internal organs, and the providing of information originating outside the body, via the eyes, ears, mouth, and skin. Central to proprioception are the body's muscle spindles that inform of limb position and movement, so for example in reaching as outlined in the reafferentation example earlier introduced in this paper. In line with this, therapist experts have evaluated hand-eye coordination outcomes from the studies as a key improvement for participants with profound impairment(s).

4 Conclusions

This paper has presented emergent modalities from the author's mature body of research. The two foci herein align with emergent models for in-action and on-action intervention and evaluation in contemporary rehabilitation that are subject of the author's previous publications [1–5, 7]. Additionally, the same system in the arts, specifically in stage performance and in realizing interactive installations and exhibitions at Museums of Modern Art, has proven to be an invaluable learning vehicle for the author in applying the digital media system in rehabilitation.

Evaluations overall have been positive. This despite early doubts by institutes, therapists and carers to the introduction of interactive technology with profoundly disabled. Third party investigation is also generally positive, which includes a randomized intervention study reporting outcomes of the commercial product realized from the research showing a marked improvement of 400 % in training specific performance benefit [8]. Experts in the field – including occupational and physical therapists, neuropsychologists, psychologists - have positively evaluated outcomes from the studies over the years. However, this is the tip of the iceberg as increasingly new authoring tools to enable adaptation of systems more accessible for carers, family members and therapists to tailor for the person that they are attached to. More than ever the opportunities for motivated ludic engagement design for all abound. What is needed, according to these researches findings, is a funding infrastructure that enables specific classes and courses, as well as time to learn such ICT systems for therapists and others involved in the care system. In this way a contribution to future predictions of demographic health care service shortcomings, where there are increased aged where the incidences of impairment are highest, is made. Alongside, reflections on how such art-based performances contribute to opportunities in communication; possibly non-verbal and utilizing ICT should be considered beyond the traditional linear way of thinking when one considers assistive technology.

Future studies include a more thorough study of reafferentation via clinical analysis of joint position matching tests that measure a subject's ability to detect an externally imposed passive movement, as well as the ability to reposition limbs to predetermined positions without vision to guide. Through the apparatus and method presented herein, multimedia feedback offers a means to not only entertain and engage the participant and give data for the therapist, but also it acts as a direct feedback to retrain the proprioception and kinetic senses of the participant in instances of e.g. an acquired brain injury (e.g. stroke) where a sense of body-in-space is damaged (e.g. balance, gait, etc.) and intervention strategies use alternative processing to retrain.

A potential of the ongoing work are new ICT baselines for analysis and improved design of interventions that take advantage of sourcing information data from inside and outside a human and from the space surrounding that person, which is anticipated as cable-less and robust in signal to provide direct and immediate stimuli to human input.

Appendix

– Cycling74 Max compressed text (dynamic air patch)

```
<pre><code>
----------begin_max5_patcher----------
1544.3oc6a98bbZCDG+4y+UvP8Sct5QqD+rScmoSdpu1WyzICGHaqXN3FPmi
Syj+2KnErO6XDxmIJfievbb5.wpOZ0puZQ9KmrxcS4s7ZWme248NqV8kSVsR
UTaAq599J2sI2llmTqtL2s755jK4tqweSxuUpJulKc1uy4u+GmM7jsNeRHux
oVTbYN2onTxcDE61KaN04cuq+dK2Ky4R4m2wQCv004e69ocIxzqZt6OTwSk3
u5E4cFYsCKp8H0yW8A8Lxc2iHSYHka93uA98OiZ4myUUuaeIE62JJZdtplC8
9BQqQUJzV3WO4j1CqMjKE7O07j+Frz11apYWMsqvy7W63wTMHePWyxi0WOWT
VHKR1hsr+pRjjaXClcPETK9O0UBMOtmjCjigC62tgWMbW7ZG2MIEWpuqVgDV
XnBIDsHgNNR1kT0TtjW8AdQxFjNDyvE7bvEc5ba1lbMWMrAHj1+HCBzKxKSj
sTEOYbr5QTii.HTKWA65pcLrqoE2TIuPWMJFNI1.WMxLxU6tKtZahpoDLcNe
2vy0DuxORgLluxMhFnCYr3WrWD46d.qmFBRw11IspEYbMvHvO.GLohdGDoEF
QKVXrqRTnaNr.hZjC3onAySKFBewX.9Aggz7xzq0L413gf6.UnxQAC5LHmBd
wbh9b3zDJ5IUVk6bSRtACbhTBdzqli4u.F3LAxd7Yn5OVv3SFw7V15d1rWJK
KFjWiOuMN3AX372j9iOIqXOy3JeeGX7KiOrfRYp.oZknwnK14SRuJonPqJCu
Hj.w3Z.XZAArbmXUzzxcGcQud3TpL8hsH+bDlziFd.SzGljFsvWd3zwq9gR5
4Uva7Jf3cPL3Q3U3a7pW7OJkaDd4+Fu54EtlwQ3E6Md4i4XnKgCivqWmoCTb
gyoB3OOGnQNxq3EMOzPGddM24zKfiKc58TEPczAZWAFEr6Z1goFc+w4.CI2o
B5w99GP03DEo.h1EuSIK1EuemuFoGXvKBX.t3rQ.FDuX8vRk45eCOrXFNAIp
aUqHdHZA7JddZNruXWR50C5qnxfH9gNuFFlQdPYwijhLvxoRbBinuYeV1mcX
ZmYT8mVVgJIXznwWjLDXWGK1Qvpgd2xmdjQffXbrF9ptXz1W+0f7wfDp0ZPo
k4kUX0qf+8GfCp3IM1dWoat7BQdt54+gdB3dYURlfeex4O7hTGgNTflIDwBh
aOgxHQgAOzn+l6k12NCh7W+nOzdi82GMlzzGzdOLRbDwCOqoHX3JHocOCnfT
H4Nhb3ErqpbWYkTTVnBfcFK9opk8xx6Xi5xBi+AjlRZLJuJNZ7zTB1OMkCMf
ibbi25lniFBFLditXUHM9d5fgqsqOEUZ2TG.rXmwGkJd94cJEUiFNJGGZ.JU
```

L.EJA5mIir.jJNAq6E5fBthW8q6M9U4xdmFEkTDc.tfW8JJiVrBJ2JxDMcw0
7wkTt9Anas4RywnZXzcfn0gzxJyCmVPJJz5zY.jvsoX2tKZ.FE7yQbrtcyW2
hTz503+pLLF+1cUsIpy4WaNdjYeJxSIlBywdjV2Ju4uvp5bQlN2JsoOOtkDA
j6ETCdCnnlNgNMe2TSdf2QSyHf9RnBknjLDqeyQ+iKrixbbyEEOdOmqZQsk+
P9UWtuJsu82M+ry8MpLdsTTjzuTv2emVnCtlqDYY7hC6vyD0s9.YCKFdJsl1
7tLmLGOqZNvXlCwZlSnAzIxpVSvXvo0bnVybniYNgyK5DXM5DXfqi8fS6+xC
iZNs6eeaYOfl1Cyt1CXh8.1wdL.O91iNFXMTXVYNpQ51ouhYxPcp87kMxd.6
o34QM8m1dX1KVH0jXOT57xd.vZ9yThIwlsGdLwbXVzdLo2xZVyiFGO.cXyK6
gZOE7JAniMwNKvt1yn7IbdwGp+LydHVKXnQ8WPjcsGvD6wR8WFI9wx1yXqJk
FLu3CXw4K7lY1Cadk.JyrG6INDnyKwgfIpw.Kp2vDspj4k4bjcVXhvS1s6Fd
UcWUpLD2sIeD2+TgqUeUTfeUUitU7aD8WuJK7tIUoWIj7T49JLi82FguWQ2s
kY7ph8htjv27j+5I+OPWCnOO
------------end_max5_patcher------------
</code></pre>

References

1. Brooks, A.L.: Virtual interactive Space (V.I.S.) as a movement capture interface tool giving multimedia feedback for treatment and analysis (1999). http://www.researchgate.net/publication/257536829
2. Brooks, A.L.: Body electric and reality feedback loops: virtual interactive space & entertainment potentials. In: Proceedings of the 14th International Conference on Artificial Reality and Telexistence – ICAT2004, Korean Advanced Institute of Science and Technology (KAIST) and the Virtual Reality Society of Japan (VRSJ), pp. 93–98 (2004)
3. Brooks, A.L.: Enhanced gesture capture in virtual interactive space. Digit. Creat. 16(1), 43–53 (2005)
4. Brooks, A.L.: SoundScapes/ArtAbilitation - evolution of a hybrid human performance concept, method & apparatus where digital interactive media, the arts, & entertainment are combined. In: Furht, B. (ed.) Handbook of Digital Media in Entertainment and Arts, pp. 683–711. Springer, Berlin (2009)
5. Brooks, A.L.: Intelligent decision-support in virtual reality healthcare and rehabilitation. In: Brahnam, S., Jain, L.C. (eds.) Advanced Computational Intelligence Paradigms in Healthcare 5. Studies in Computational Intelligence, pp. 143–169. Springer, London (2010). vol. 326
6. Ackermann, U.: Essentials of human physiology (1992). http://thjuland.tripod.com/descending-tracts.html
7. Brooks, A.L., Camurri, A., Canagarajah, N., Hasselblad, S.: Interaction with shapes and sounds as a therapy for special needs and rehabilitation. In: Sharkey, P. (ed.) Proceedings of the 4th International Conference Disability, Virtual Reality & Associated Technology, Veszprém, Hungary, pp. 205–212 (2002)
8. Hagedorn, D.K., Holm, E.: Effects of traditional physical training and visual computer feedback training in frail elderly patients. A randomized intervention study. Eur J Phys Rehabil Med. 46(2), 159–168 (2010)

Knowledge, Technology and Intelligence for eInclusion

Laura Burzagli and Pier Luigi Emiliani[✉]

Institute of Applied Physics "Nello Carrara", National Research Council of Italy,
Sesto Fiorentino, Italy
{l.burzagli,p.l.emiliani}@ifac.cnr.it

Abstract. In eInclusion, the main interest has traditionally been in granting interaction with ICT, i.e. the accessibility of interfaces. Due to the developments toward an AmI (Ambient Intelligence) information society, the technology of interest in accessibility and its integration in multimedia interfaces matched to the user requirements and preferences are becoming of interest for the general customers. Therefore, the point made in the paper is that the concept of eInclusion, as it already happened at the political level, should be generalized to include actions able to guarantee well-being. Therefore, it becomes necessary to collect knowledge about activities necessary for living comfortably and enjoyably, to identify and implement an ICT environment offering the functionalities to carry them out and to make available the quantity and quality of intelligence necessary to adapt the environment to different users and contexts of use.

Keywords: eInclusion · Ambient intelligence · Design for All · Artificial intelligence · Technology forecast

1 Introduction

The continuous development of ICT technology has been considered both a possible risk and a potential opportunity in offering people the possibility of accessing information, communicating, and being in control of the environment. From an ethical and conceptual perspective, the reported definition of eInclusion as a right of any person to be included in any human activity is a recent very important development at the social and political levels: *"eInclusion" means both inclusive ICT and the use of ICT to achieve wider inclusion objectives. It focuses on participation of all individuals and communities in all aspects of the information society. eInclusion policy, therefore, aims at reducing gaps in ICT usage and promoting the use of ICT to overcome exclusion, and improve economic performance, employment opportunities, quality of life, social participation and cohesion*[1]. This implies that all citizens have the right to be granted availability of all information and communication facilities in the Information Society and, when necessary and possible, to be supported by ICT for achieving their goals in all environments.

---

[1] Pt. 4 Ministerial Declaration Approved Unanimously on 11 June 2006, Riga.

© Springer International Publishing Switzerland 2015
M. Antona and C. Stephanidis (Eds.): UAHCI 2015, Part II, LNCS 9176, pp. 428–436, 2015.
DOI: 10.1007/978-3-319-20681-3_40

One of the aspects of eInclusion is to obtain inclusiveness by making systems and services accessible to all citizens, but this is not enough. For example, when people are supported by ICT functionalities for independent living at home, particularly if they are have some cognitive impairment, this requires more than accessibility to systems and services. The environment should be able to support them with specific functionalities.

The reality is far from this principle. Ideally, everyone agrees on the fact that life should be comfortable and enjoyable. However, if people are old, comfortable and enjoyable is downgraded to independent. Enjoyment is supposed to come from the happiness they should feel because society can save money if they are independent. Moreover, if people have some lack of ability, irrespective of their age, the main perceived problem is that the human/technology interface of ICT systems, services and applications should be accessible by them. Subtitling for deaf people and/or a screen reader for blind people is what is considered satisfactory for helping them.

The paper aims to make the point that technology is mature enough for being exploited as a support to construct environments where people can live independently in a comfortable and enjoyable way, irrespective of the lack of abilities due to age, impairment or context. This is possible using the knowledge about necessary activities of people in the different living environments, integrating the right technology and introducing enough intelligence in the control of the environment.

In order to make discussion more understandable with practical example reference is made to the AAL FOOD[2] Project (Framework for Optimizing the prOcess of FeeDing). In the project, under the responsibility of the Italian Company Indesit, a kitchen environment has been developed with interconnected appliances, an Internet link and services and applications dealing with all aspects of feeding (e.g. from accessing databases of recipes and getting ingredients for cooking to socializing around food topics with friends). Activity and results are reported elsewhere [1]. In this paper, the FOOD project is used from one side as a source of practical and concrete examples to support the discussion and from the other as a case study for pointing out remaining problems to be considered in future developments.

2 Supporting Knowledge

As asserted in the introduction, from the perspective of eInclusion, the main concern should not be about accessibility, but about the possibility of granting people an independent, but also comfortable and enjoyable life. A lot of knowledge is necessary to cope with the corresponding problems. It is necessary to know:

- Activities to be carried out in order to live (e.g. feeding, going around, socializing, entertaining …)
- ICT functionalities necessary to support people in these activities (e.g. being able to communicate by voice or video, to access information for buying goods, to pay for them)[3];

---

[2] http://www.food-aal.eu.

[3] In the paper, functionality is used as a synonym of service.

- Preferences of people for the implementation of the functionalities and the interaction with them;
- Technology that can be used to implement the functionalities and the interfaces;
- Level of intelligence to be used to control the entire living environment. This must include the possibility of a Design for All [2] technical approach, defined as the possibility of introducing adaptability to the single user and adaptivity to her behavior.

Moreover, since in an intelligent environment the knowledge is supposed to be used not only by human designers during set up but also by the system control during use, it must be available in a formal representation.

For what concerns activities and functionalities a lot of knowledge already exists. One classical example is the International Classification of Functioning and Disabilities, produced by the World Health Organization (WHO) in 2001 [3]. It presents a classification of Body Functions, Body Structures, Activities and Participation, and Environmental Factors. The classification can also be expanded, and a few modifications have already been approved by the WHO [4]. Moreover, the ICF classification is now also available as an ontology. ICF allows the connection of activities and sub-activities with functionalities and with possible limitations to their performance due to lack of personal abilities and contextual factors. As an example, with reference to the FOOD project, in the ICF classification feeding is obviously listed as one of the fundamental activities for living and it is clearly stated what people must be able to do for feeding: they must decide what to eat, collect the food, know how to cook it, cook it without danger[4]. More specifically, the following relevant activities are considered: Acquisition of goods and services (d620), Preparing meals (d630), Doing housework (d640), Caring for household objects (d650), Complex interpersonal interactions (d720), and Informal social relationships (d750). It is interesting to note that human relationships are considered relevant in this context.

However, the situation is much more complex, since food can interfere with the health situation of people. With reference to a specific example such as diabetes, not only the health aspects are considered, but also the more general aspects related to well-being. The ICF classification has been extended to consider the impact of food on health, e.g. on the diabetes disease [5, 6]. Fourteen ICF categories of the "Activity and Participation" components are considered influential from the patient's perspective. Moreover, lot of additional knowledge is also available. An example of food ontology for diabetes control is presented in [7] within the domain of nutritional and health care. This ontology has been produced in the context of the PIPS (Personalized Information Platform for Health and Life Services) international project [8], to manage heterogeneous knowledge coming from different source.

These are only some examples of the available knowledge about activities to guarantee well-being to people. It is interesting that most of it (as ICF) is formalized (normally as ontologies) and therefore usable with reasoning techniques.

---

[4] This may appear trivial, but many projects still conduct user needs analyses to rediscover these simple facts.

An enormous amount of knowledge also exists about available or foreseen technology of interest for the creation of inclusive environments and/or for the support of people in them. The main problem is that information is too much and varying too fast to be efficiently organized in a form (e.g. with semantic components), useful to reason about its usefulness in situations of interest. Moreover, a structured information critical for granting easy interoperability of different components is normally lacking.

Knowledge about the user is of fundamental importance. From this perspective, it is crucial to consider two aspects. The first is "what" (i.e. what activities people should be able to carry out for a satisfactory life), the second is "how" (i.e. how people like to carry out them). For the first aspect, since the main goal is to consider the variety of users, it is important to utilize international classifications that are produced and approved by a wide range of stakeholders, as the already cited WHO ICF document, produced through the agreement of people around the world and therefore widely accepted. Users should be involved in defining the how component, e.g. if they like to buy food in a shop or on the network, to get recipes from books or for friends and so on. Therefore, the real implementation must be made in a continuous cooperation with end users.

Finally, it is important to take into account that people, even if they live independently, should be considered part of the society. Complex interpersonal interactions and informal social relationships are considered important by ICF also for feeding. Many investigations are being carried out about the possible impact on and use by old people of emerging social networks. The collected knowledge should be taken into account when the selection of functionalities for supporting people in their daily activities is made.

3 Technology

The living environments are now changing in a fundamental way with the development of the information society as an intelligent environment as foreseen by ISTAG [9]. Technology and correspondingly its individual human-technology interface is supposed to disappear for the user consciousness and to be embedded in appliances and in the living environment. According to most technological forecasts, computers, as the ones we are using today, will only remain in some professional environments. All objects (not only home appliances, TV sets, telephones or hifi systems, normally perceived as technological objects, but also e.g. lamps, furniture and so on) will have computers embedded and will exhibit some intelligence.

Correspondingly, interfaces as the ones available today, based on screens with windows and allowing interactions through the manipulation of objects (textual, auditory, and graphical) on them, are supposed to disappear. Interaction will be with the objects in the environment and based on media and metaphors automatically adapted to what is available, the user and the context of use. A migration is foreseen from a model where the user interacts with a computer or a terminal, to a model where the user interacts using (disembodied) natural interfaces with functionalities made available by single intelligent objects, by their cooperation under the supervision of a control center, and by the cooperation through external networks, as depicted in Fig. 1.

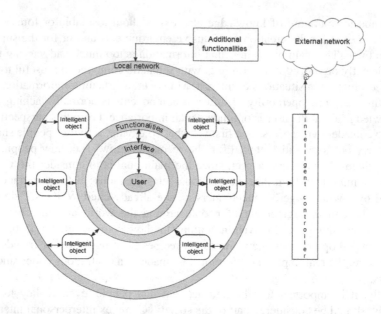

Fig. 1 The Ambient intelligent environment

An intelligent environment, through its Ambient User Interfaces (AmUIs) [10], should be able to:

- Take advantage of the available infrastructure, in order to support seamless, high-quality, unobtrusive, and fault-tolerant interaction that is tailored to the current needs and characteristics of a particular user and context of use;
- Allow multimodal interaction distributed in space (e.g., employ the TV screen and stereo speakers to provide output, and get input through both speech and gestures);
- Monitor and use behavior patterns extracted from the interaction itself: in a pro-active way (e.g. comparing user's routine with an optimal routine and suggesting activities), in preventive way (checking the status of appliances and monitoring actions left unfinished such as cooking in order to prevent accidents), and in assisting way (e.g. by analyzing and extracting the user's path patterns outside the house, the system could make suggestions and issue reminders).

Considering the present situation, it is clear that the main developments have been in the "ambient" component, meaning that a lot of sensors and systems with on board computers and possibilities of interconnections have been made available, without an in depth analysis of how the acquired information can be integrated and used to support people. Less effort has been devoted to the "intelligence" that should lead to components as the one listed by the ISTAG experts:

- Media management and handling, including presentation languages that support "produce once" and "present anywhere", methods and tools to analyze content and enrich it with metadata, and tools for exploiting the Semantic Web;

- Natural interaction that combines speech, vision, gesture, and facial expression into a truly integrated multimodal interaction concept. This should allow human beings to interact with virtual worlds through physical objects and to navigate the available information;
- Computational intelligence: natural language search and dialogue systems, systems that can adapt to human behavior, and computational methods to support complex search and planning tasks;
- Contextual awareness, to support navigation in public environments and to support context-aware control and surveillance systems;
- Emotional computing that models or embodies emotions in the computer, systems that can respond to or recognize the moods of their users, and systems that can express emotions.

The consideration of these intelligence components is supposed to help in constructing an environment that according to ISTAG should be able to:

- Facilitate human contacts;
- Be oriented towards community and cultural enhancement;
- Help to build knowledge and skills for work, better quality of work, citizenship and consumer choice;
- Inspire trust and confidence;
- Be consistent with long-term sustainability – personal, societal and environmental - and with life-long learning;
- Be controllable by ordinary people.

4 Intelligence

In conclusion, designing for eInclusion is not only a problem of accessibility, but it implies the re-design of entire living environment that needs to be in control of a reasoning system. This must be able:

- To identify needs (activities to be carried out) from available formalized knowledge and preferences about the way of implementing them from single users;
- To select and implement the functionalities necessary for carrying them out within the limitations and preferences of the single person;
- To select the technology and develop interfaces for its interoperability;
- To make available the suitable interactions.

From the users' perspective, the main perceived features of an AmI environment are probably its adaptability to their requirements and preferences and adaptivity to the changes in their behavior or in the context, as already claimed by Design for All. However, the situation is more complex. Adaptability and adaptivity should not only be limited to the interaction and based on simple deterministic rules as: if the user is blind then use voice and sound interaction. Instead, AmI needs real reasoning capabilities for identifying the goals of the users and helping users in fulfilling them using the available resources.

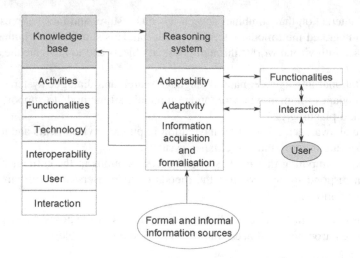

Fig. 2 The intelligent control

The quality and quantity of intelligence necessary can be assessed considering the requirements expressed in the ISTAG document, where the main high-level design requirements of an ambient intelligence environment are listed. It must be:

- Unobtrusive (i.e. many distributed devices are embedded in the environment, and do not intrude into our consciousness unless we need them);
- Personalized (i.e. it can recognize the user, and its behavior can be tailored to the user's needs);
- Adaptive (i.e. its behavior can change in response to a person's actions and environment)
- Anticipatory (i.e. it anticipates a person's desires and environment as much as possible without the need for mediation).

It is evident that these necessary features require real intelligence and the core of an AmI system can be described with reference to Fig. 2.

The control part is made of two main blocks. The first is a knowledge base where information is available in a formal representation about:

- Activities to be carried out in the environment;
- Functionalities, whose individual use or cooperation with other functionalities in complex applications is necessary to carry out the activities;
- Technology, whose basic functionality and embedded intelligence can be used to implement the functionalities;
- Interoperability, i.e. description of interfaces and communication protocols to use technology in an integrated form
- Users: abilities of individual users and their requirements and preferences about functionalities to be used to support them in carrying out the necessary activities with the preferred interaction;
- Interactions: available interaction capabilities and possibility of integration.

Information is made available to a reasoning system able to:

- Enrich the knowledge base acquiring and integrating information already received in a formal representation and/or extracting it from informal information (for example expressed in natural language);
- Use the information in the knowledge base to construct in an unobtrusive and anticipatory way adaptability and adaptivity in the functionalities made available and in their interactions.

Considering examples from the same FOOD project, the fridge in the kitchen should be aware of its contents, suggesting recipes based on what is available or what to buy, according to the identified habits of the owner. It should be able to connect with the supermarkets to order the necessary goods, select the one where the quality/price ratio is maximized, and pay them in compliance with a predefined limit. If the user want to choose personally, it should show the products on the supermarket shelves, with information about their characteristics. The oven should remind people that it is time to start cooking or automatically start it, using cooking cycles built in by the producer or previously generated by the owner. The entire kitchen should guarantee the safety of the person in any situation. Moreover, and this is the level where accessibility needs to be considered, the environment should be able to interact with the person in the form that s/he likes.

Finally, applications that appear trivial to most people instead require a lot of intelligence. Let assume that a person is diabetic. In the Applications markets, hundreds of applications are available aimed to suggest a correct diet. But, this does not simply depends on knowing if some ingredient is present in the available food as in the case of allergies, but on a set of conditions: the type of diabetes, the real time measurement of the present status, what the person ate the previous day, what will probably be available today and tomorrow, the activities to be carried out. The problem is so complex that an expert system is necessary to decide about the diet [11]. The expert system uses a lot of knowledge about the illness, the characteristics of food and the interrelations between the illness and the food, fortunately already available in a formalized form.

5 Conclusions

ICT can potentially be useful to all citizens including users with activity limitations (due to an impairment, or age or the context), who often require to be "assisted" to reach well-being in their independent life. In order to take advantage of the new possibilities offered by the technological developments it is necessary:

- To exploit existing sensorial, computing and networking technology and their integration in an ambient infrastructure transparent to the user;
- To produce intelligent human machine interfaces based on the modalities of natural human interaction;
- To develop designed-for-all services and applications that will assist the user to cope with their possible activity limitations;

- To take advantage of research in the fields of cognitive systems, computer vision, monitoring and event recognition, reasoning, natural human-computer interaction, data and media collection, handling and presentation;
- To integrate sensors and services/applications in an intelligent control system.

As a conclusion, a careful integration of knowledge, technology and intelligence is necessary.

References

1. Allen, J., Boffi, L., Burzagli, L., Ciampolini, P., De Munari, I., Emiliani, P.L.: FOOD: discovering techno-social scenarios for networked kitchen systems. In: Encarnação, P., Azevedo, L., Gelderblom, G.J. (eds.) Assistive Technology From Research to Practice. Assistive Technology Research Series, pp. 1143–1148. IOS press, Amsterdam (2013). vol. 33
2. Emiliani, P.L., Stephanidis, C.: Universal access to ambient intelligence environments: opportunities and challenges for people with disabilities. IBM Syst. J. **44**(3), 605–619 (2005)
3. WHO International Classification of Functioning, Disability and Health (ICF). World Health Organization, Geneve. http://www.who.int/classifications/icf/en
4. List of Official ICF Updates. http://www.who.int/classifications/icfupdates/en/
5. Ruof, J., Cieza, A., Wolff, B., Angst, F., Ergeletzis, D., Omar, Z., Kostanjsek, N., Stucki, G.: ICF core sets for diabetes mellitus. J. Rehabil. Med. Suppl. **44**, 100–106 (2004)
6. Kirchberger, I., Coenen, M., Hierl, F.X., Dieterle, C., Seissler, J., Stucki, G., Cieza, A.: Validation of the International Classification of Functioning, Disability and Health (ICF) core set for diabetes mellitus from the patient perspective using focus groups. Diabet. Med. **26**, 700–707 (2009)
7. Cantais, J., Dominguez, D., Gigante, V., Laera, L., Tamma, V.: An example of food ontology for diabetes control. In: Proceedings of the International Semantic Web Conference 2005 Workshop on Ontology Patterns for the Semantic Web, pp. Galway (2005)
8. PIPS project. http://www.hon.ch/Global/pdf/pips_sanna.pdf
9. Ducatel, K., Bogdanowicz, M., Scapolo, F., Leijten, J., Burgelman, J.C.: Scenarios for ambient intelligence in 2010, Technical report (2001). http://cordis.europa.eu/fp7/ict/istag/reports_en.html
10. Streitz, N., Magerkurth, C., Prante, T., Rocker, C.: From information design to experience design: smart artefacts and the disappearing computer. Interact. **12**(4), 21–25 (2005)
11. Snae, C., Brückner, M.: A Food-oriented Ontology-driven system. In: Second IEEE Conference on Digital Ecosystems and Technologies, pp. 168–176 (2008)

Brain Neural Computer Interface
for Everyday Home Usage

Christoph Hintermüller[1], Eloisa Vargiu[2], Sebastian Halder[3],
Jean Daly[4], Felip Miralles[2], Hannah Lowish[5], Nick Anderson[6],
Suzanne Martin[4], and Günter Edlinger[1,7(✉)]

[1] Guger Technologies OG, Herbersteinstrasse 60, 8020 Graz, Austria
[2] Barcelona Digital Technology Center, Barcelona, Spain
[3] Institute of Psychology, University of Würzburg, Würzburg, Germany
[4] The Cedar Foundation, Belfast, UK
[5] Telehealth Solutions, Medvivo Group, Wiltshire, UK
[6] Cortech Solutions, Inc.,
1409 Audubon Blvd, Unit B1, Wilmington, NC 28403, USA
[7] G.Tec Medical Engineering GmbH,
Sierningstrasse 14, 4521 Schiedlberg, Austria
edlinger@gtec.at

Abstract. In the last years, Brain Neural Computer Interfaces (BNCIs) have been investigated and several applications have been proposed. Those systems have been explored almost exclusively in laboratories with developers and researchers. Home usage has been demonstrated, though only with on-going expert supervision. In this paper, we present a BNCI for everyday home usage. The proposed system is aimed at supporting the autonomy and independence of people living at home with a disability. The overall system is currently installed in three end-users' home in Belfast.

1 Introduction

Research efforts have improved Brain Neural Computer Interface (BNCI) technology in many ways and numerous applications have been prototyped. With the hope of restoring independence to the disabled individual, the focus of such applications [7] is on communication [6], environmental control [1], as well as neuro-rehabilitation [11]. Until recently, such BCI systems have been explored almost exclusively in laboratories primarily with developers and sympathetic, enthusiastic populations for example researchers. Home usage has been demonstrated, though only with on-going expert supervision. A significant advance on BNCI research and its implementation as a feasible assistive technology is therefore the migration and easy set up of BNCIs into people's homes to provide new options for communication and control that increase independence, autonomy and reduce social exclusion. In this paper, a new BNCI system is presented which combines a wireless EEG recording unit, which sets new standards of lightness, autonomy, comfort and reliability, with easy-to-use software, tailored to people's needs, within a platform of everyday applications, i.e. twitter and support services. The BackHome BNCI platform also moves beyond the individual to

M. Antona and C. Stephanidis (Eds.): UAHCI 2015, Part II, LNCS 9176, pp. 437–446, 2015.
DOI: 10.1007/978-3-319-20681-3_41

the space where they live bringing in a sensor-based telemonitoring and home support system. This work is part of the European BackHome project (GA no: 288566) and the overall system is installed at end-users' facilities for testing. The results achieved by the end-users are presented.

Section 2 illustrates the system architecture of the developed system together with the description of its components. Section 3 presents the results coming from the system validation which are briefly discussed in Sect. 4.

2   System Architecture

Within the BackHome platform, the end user interacts and communicates with her/his environment through the Primary User Interface (PUI) of the User Station (see **Fig.** 1) with the electrodes as harvesting brain signals as the actuator. The User Station includes the BNCI component with the PUI providing including a user interface for visual stimulation and feedback. The AmI block, which is the central control unit interlinks all the services with the BNCI system and thereby provides control over these systems to the user.

The User Station is connected to a remote Therapist Station, as shown in **Fig.** 1. A web-based easy-to-use service, which allows a therapist from her base of work to deliver tele-assistance service or professional to access information stored in the cloud and gathered from users and sensors around them: users' inputs, activities, selections and sensor data, as well as planning and remote coordination of the users BNCI based rehabilitation tasks. This service was developed based on request from target end users, i.e. people with acquired brain injury who have a desire for prolonged engagement with therapist post discharge from acute rehabilitation services following an acquired brain injury.

As **Fig.** 1 also shows, the system provides a number of services that can be grouped as follows: Smart Home control, cognitive stimulation, and Web access.

2.1   User Station

The BCI user interface is based upon the Screen Overlay Control Interface (SOCI) library [4], which allows embedding the BCI stimuli on top of the native interface of any user application and communicates with the BCI hardware via a network connection.

Along with the integration of SOCI, the PUI has been designed following the recommendations expressed by target end users, according to a user-centred design approach. The number of lines, columns, the spaces in between and thus the display size of the individual icons are defined depending upon users' capabilities and do not change depending the dimension of the matrix and number of icons displayed. Masks which are smaller are automatically centred by SOCI within the visible area. The Application ConTrol and Online Reconfiguration (ACTOR) protocol [3] allows the application to explicitly position its masks on the screen.

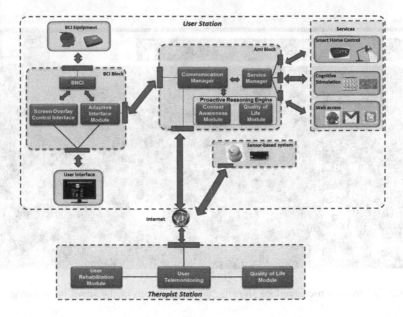

Fig. 1. BackHome architecture overview

Figure 2 above shows the PUI, which is split into three sections. On top of the screen a history bar shows the last selections made. On the top right side the current time of the day is displayed along with the quality of the EEG signal recorded. The middle section displays the active P300 matrix for the currently selected service or service group, for example the Smart Home group for interaction with user's environment and the multimedia player. The bottom row of the screen displays the menu which allows switching between the different services and service groups (i.e., Smart Home control, Web access, Cognitive Rehabilitation Games, Brain Painting, and Speller). When the user selects one of the icons on the screen, the system automatically activates the selected service group and displays the corresponding masks.

The user interface for the caregiver (see **Fig.** 3) allows starting the system with just one-click, to create the classifier (in training mode) and to shutdown (Quit) the BCI system. Furthermore, when the system is started it automatically activates the check signals mode and starts the signal acquisition. This simplifies the mounting of the electrode cap as the signal quality display is visible during the whole procedure.

The Wireless EEG Recording System. Based upon the user feedback, a new biosignal acquisition system called g.Nautilus[1] was developed. Its biosignal amplifier uses wireless technology to transmit the EEG signals with 24 bit resolution. The signal of each EEG channel is highly oversampled in order to keep the signal to noise ratio (SNR) high at the offered rates of 250 Hz and 500 Hz. Furthermore, it is capable of

---

[1] http://www.gtec.at/Products/Hardware-and-Accessories/g.Nautilus-Specs-Features

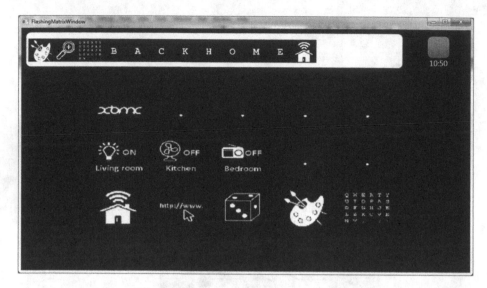

Fig. 2. Primary user interface showing the main screen of the smart home service

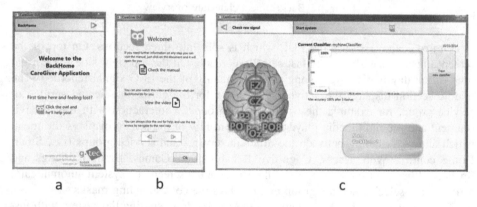

Fig. 3. Care giver interface. The interface has been designed to optimally guide the care giver through the setup process step by step (a) and provide access to help and support information (b) on every screen. Only those information and controls are shown which are necessary to accomplish the current step (c) or advance to the next one when finished or go back to the previous one.

measure the electrode-skin impedance at each electrode position for both gel based and dry electrodes (see **Fig.** 4).

A base station which is connected to the host system through USB is used to receive the recorded and digitized EEG signals. The biosignal amplification unit consists of the headset including the wireless biosignal amplifier electrodes, an EEG cap and the base station including a USB cable for connecting it to the host computer and a QI compatible wireless charging station. The 10 electrodes including reference

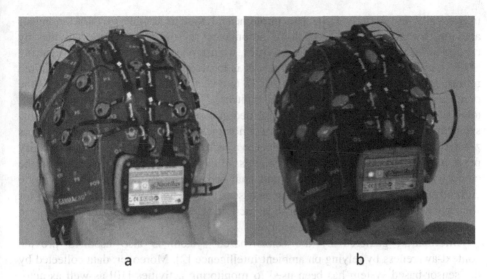

a   b

Fig. 4. g.Nautilus headset with gel based (a) and dry elecectrodes (b)

channel and ground are pre-connected to the amplifier with their positions preconfig-
ured for recording visual P300.

The user interface of the headset consists of the power switch and the status LED.
Both are located on the top face of the head set. The electrodes are connected to two
groups of monopolar amplifiers. The first group is connected to the ground electrode
and the first 16 EEG channels and the second group is connected to the electrode
positions 17-to 32 and the reference channel.

The Implemented Services. As mentioned earlier, the system provides a number of
services grouped as follows: Smart Home control, cognitive stimulation, and Web
access [5]. Smart Home control service is aimed at giving control over the environment, as well as over useful devices. The ultimate aim is to facilitate the user to exert
control home devices (e.g., a light, a fan, a radio) as well as to interact with the XBMC
multimedia player. Cognitive stimulation services allow users to improve their cognitive capabilities by performing cognitive rehabilitation tasks assigned by a therapist
[12] or by using their creative skills through Brain Painting [9]. Web access services
enable participation and inclusion by offering users the possibility to engage in social
interaction through the Web, such as Web browsing, emailing and tweeting.

All those services, and in particular, those related to Web access, rely on a P300
spelling and control system. In the adopted speller, the highlighting happens with freely
selectable images (famous faces) instead of just changing the colour of the background.

Sensor-based Telemonitoring and Home Support. Community based living, often
alone with intermittent care creates possible scenarios of risks for all individuals. When
cognitive changes are likely to have taken place it is crucial to understand what the
risks may be and monitor these. To monitor users at home, we develop a sensor-based
system [8] which is able to gather data and report on the stability and evolution of the

user's daily life activity [14]. The implemented system is able to monitor indoor activities by relying on a set of home automation sensors and outdoor activities by relying to MOVES.[2] As for indoor activities, we use presence sensors (i.e., Everspring SP103), to identify the room where the user is located (one sensor for each monitored room); a door sensor (i.e., Vision ZD 2012), to detect when the user enters or exits the premises; electrical power meters and switches, to control leisure activities (e.g., television and pc); pressure sensors (i.e., bed and seat sensors), to measure the time spent in bed and wheelchair. From a technological point of view, we use wireless z-wave sensors that send the retrieved data to a central unit located (based on Raspberry pi) at user's home. That central unit collects all the retrieved data and sends it to the cloud where it is processed, mined, and analysed. As for outdoor activities, we are currently using the user's smartphone as a sensor by relying to MOVES, an app for smartphones able to recognize physical activities (such as walking, running, and cycling) and movements by transportation.

Information gathered by the sensor-based system is also used to provide context-awareness by relying on ambient intelligence [2]. Moreover, data collected by the sensor-based system has been used to monitoring activities [10] as well as automatically assess quality of life of people [13].

2.2   Therapist Station

The Therapist Station[3] is a Web based application providing clinicians/therapists tools for user management, cognitive rehabilitation task management, quality-of-life assessment, statistics on BCI usage, as well as for communication between therapist and user. Therapists are able to interact with the users remotely in real time or asynchronously and monitor the use and outcomes of the cognitive rehabilitation tasks and quality-of-life assessment. A therapist can prescribe, schedule, telemonitor and personalize cognitive rehabilitation tasks and the assessment of the users quality-of-life through questionnaires and adopt those tasks to the users therapeutic range (i.e. motivating and supporting their progress), in order to help to attain beneficial therapeutic results.

As for the cognitive rehabilitation sessions, using the Therapist Station, healthcare professionals can remotely manage a caseload of people recently discharged from acute sector care. They can prescribe and review rehabilitation. Through the Therapist Station, game sessions can be configured, setting the type of games that the user will execute, their order within the session the difficulty level and game specific parameters. Once the session is scheduled, users will see their BCI matrix updated on the User Station the day the session is scheduled. Through that icon, the user will start the session. The user can then execute all the games contained in it in consecutive order. Upon completion of the game session execution on User Station, results are sent back to the Therapist Station for review. A notification indicating that the user has completed

---

[2] http://www.moves-app.com/

[3] https://station.backhome-fp7.eu:8443/BackHome/

the session, will be posted on the dashboard of the concerned healthcare professionals involved. Healthcare professionals with the right credentials can browse user session results once they are received. The Therapist Station provides session results in a summary view for each person and an overview of completed sessions to map progress, which shows session parameters and statistics along the specific results.

The results and statistics about the quality of life coming from the telemonitoring and home support system are sent to the Therapist Station to inform the therapist about improvement and worsening of user's quality of life (**Fig. 5**). Moreover, the therapist may directly ask the user to fill a questionnaire, either once or on a regular basis. Once scheduled, the user receives an update in the BCI matrix indicating that a questionnaire has to be filled. After the user has completed the questionnaire with the help of the caregiver its results are sent to the therapist who may revise them.

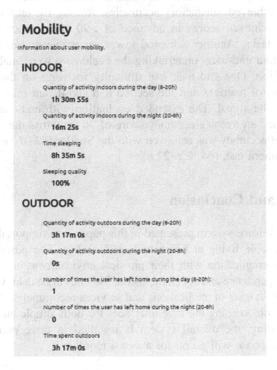

Fig. 5. An example of data coming from the sensors as shown to the therapist

Finally, through the Therapist Station, therapists may consult a summary of activities performed at home by the user; e.g., visited rooms, sleeping hours and time elapsed at home. Moreover, also the BCI usage is monitored and high-level statistics provided. This information includes BCI session duration, setup time and training time as well as the number of selections, the average elapsed time per selection and a breakdown of the status of the session selections. Therapists have also the ability to browse the full list of selections executed by a user, such as context information as application running, selected value, grid size and selected position.

3 System Validation

The development and validation of BackHome has gone through three main iterative stages of design and work directly with target end users, i.e. people with acquired brain injury and therapists working in neurology. In preparation for the installation of the system at the end users homes for long term evaluation of half a year, a pre-evaluation phase of the services in the overall system was undertaken by a control group of fourteen healthy users (9 females, M = 28.1 years ± 8.6, range: 21-46) [5]. Subsequently a total of nine end-users, four users with muscle impairments (f, 80 years; f, 58 years; m, 42 years; m, 51 years) and five users (1 female, M = 37 years, ± 8.7) who are living with acquired brain injury (Post ABI M = 9.8 yrs, ± 3.7) operated the system. All of them completed the protocol on three different occasions.

Seven of the nine end users involved in the evaluation were able to gain control over the BCI and achieved satisfactory accuracies. Among the end-users with muscle impairments, one achieved scores in advance of >90 % accuracy for the spelling, games and twitter tasks. Another achieved lower accuracies scores averaging 75 %. Two of the initial four end-users undertaking the evaluation were unable to operate the BCI on one occasion. One end user had difficulty focusing on the relatively small symbols in the control matrices and the second had significant muscle spasticity that caused artifacts in the signal. The extended evaluation with end-users with acquired brain injury recorded an average accuracy score of 76 % across the four applications. The highest overall accuracy was achieved with the Speller (82.07 % ± 13.34) and the lowest with the camera task (64 % ± 22.8).

4 Discussion and Conclusion

The aim of the BackHome system presented in this paper is to support the autonomy and independence of people living at home with a disability. The purpose is to support interaction and communication with their physical environment and social networks, thereby regain independence and social inclusion. This has been achieved by integrating the BNCI system with a set of applications and services recommended by the users and their care givers while keeping the user interfaces for both simple and easy to use.

At time of writing, the overall system is installed in three end-users' home in Belfast and the test phase will go on for about 4 months.

Acknowledgments. The research leading to these results has received funding from the European Community's, Seventh Framework Programme FP7/2007-2013, BackHome project grant agreement n. 288566.

References

1. Aloise, F., Schettini, F., Aric, P., Salinari, S., Guger, C., Rinsma, J., Aiello, M., Mattia, D., Cincotti, F.: Validation of an asynchronous P300-based BCI with potential end users to control a virtual environment. In: Proceedings of 5th International Brain-Computer Interface Conference (2011)

2. Casals, E., Cordero, J.A., Dauwalder, S., Fernández, J.M., Solà, M., Vargiu, E., Miralles, F.: Ambient Intelligence by ATML - Rules in BackHome. Emerging ideas on Information Filtering and Retrieval. DART 2013: Revised and Invited Papers; C. Lai, A. Giuliani and G. Semeraro (eds.) (2015)
3. Hintermüller, C., Kapeller, C., Edlinger, G., Guger, C.: BCI Integration: Application Interfaces, Brain-Computer Interface Systems - Recent Progress and Future Prospects, Dr. Reza Fazel-Rezai (ed.), ISBN: 978-953-51-1134-4, InTech (2013). doi:10.5772/55806. http://www.intechopen.com/books/brain-computer-interface-systems-recent-progress-and-future-prospects/bci-integration-application-interfaces
4. Kapeller, C., Hintermuller, C., Abu-Alqumsan, M., Pruckl, R., Peer, A., Guger, C.: A BCI using VEP for continuous control of a mobile robot. In: 35th Annual International Conference of the IEEE Engineering in Medicine and Biology Society (EMBC), pp. 5254–5257 (2013)
5. Käthner, I., Daly, J., Halder, S., Räderscheidt, J., Armstrong, E., Dauwalder, S., Hintermüller, C., Espinosa, A., Vargiu, E., Pinegger, A., Faller, J., Wriessnegger, S.C., Miralles, F., Lowish, H., Markey, D., Müller-Putz, G.R., Martin, S., Kübler, A.: A P300 BCI for e-inclusion, cognitive rehabilitation and smart home control. In: Müller-Putz, G.R., Bauernfeind, G., Brunner, C., Steyrl, D., Wriessnegger, S., Scherer, R. (eds.), Proceedings of the 6th International Brain-Computer Interface Conference, September 16–19, 2014, pp. 60–63. Graz University of Technology, Austria: Verlag der Technischen Universität Graz (2014). doi:10.3217/978-3-85125-378-8-15
6. Kübler, A., Neumann, N., Kaiser, J., Kotchoubey, B., Hinterberger, T., Birbaumer, N.P.: Brain-computer communication: self-regulation of slow cortical potentials for verbal communication. Arch. Phys. Med. Rehabil. **82**(11), 1533–9 (2011)
7. Mak, J.N., Wolpaw, J.R.: Clinical applications of brain-computer interfaces: current state and future prospects. IEEE Rev. Biomed. Eng. **2**, 187–199 (2009)
8. Miralles, F., Vargiu, E., Dauwalder, S., Solà, M., Fernández, J.M., Casals, E., Cordero, J.A.: Telemonitoring and home support in BackHome. In: DART 2014 - 8th International Workshop on Information Filtering and Retrieval - co-located with AIxIA 2014 (2014)
9. Münßinger, J.I., Halder, S., Kleih, S.C., Furdea, A., Raco, V., Hösle, A., Kübler, A.: Brain Painting: first evaluation of a new brain–computer interface application with ALS-patients and healthy volunteers. Frontiers in Neuroprosthetics, **4**(182) (2010). doi:10.3389/fnins.2010.00182
10. Rafael-Palou, X., Vargiu, E., Serra, G., Miralles, F.: Improving activity monitoring through a hierarchical approach. In: The International Conference on Information and Communication Technologies for Ageing Well and e-Health, May, 20–22 2015, Lisbon (2015)
11. Ramos-Murguialday, A., Broetz, D., Rea, M., Läer, L., Yilmaz, Ö., Brasil, F.L., Liberati, G., Curado, M.R., Garcia-Cossio, E., Vyziotis, A., Cho, W., Agostini, M., Soares, E., Soekadar, S., Caria, A., Cohen, L.G., Birbaumer, N.: Brain–machine interface in chronic stroke rehabilitation: A controlled study. Ann. Neurol. **74**, 100–108 (2013). doi:10.1002/ana.23879
12. Vargiu, E., Dauwalder, S., Daly, J., Armstrong, E., Martin, S., Miralles, F.: Cognitive rehabilitation through BNCI: serious games in BackHome. In: Müller-Putz, G.R., Bauernfeind, G., Brunner, C., Steyrl, D., Wriessnegger, S., Scherer, R. (eds.), Proceedings of the 6th International Brain-Computer Interface Conference,September 16–19, 2014, pp. 36–39. Graz University of Technology, Austria: Verlag der Technischen Universität Graz (2014). doi:10.3217/978-3-85125-378-8-9

13. Vargiu, E., Fernández, J.M., Miralles, F.: Context-Aware based Quality of Life Telemonitoring. Distributed Systems and Applications of Information Filtering and Retrieval. Lai, C. et al. (eds.), Distributed Systems and Applications of Information Filtering and Retrieval, Studies in Computational Intelligence 515, Springer-Verlag, Berlin Heidelberg 2014. doi:10.1007/978-3-642-40621-8_1 (2014)
14. Vargiu, E., Fernández, J.M., Torrellas, S., Dauwalder, S., Solà, M., Miralles, F.: A sensor-based telemonitoring and home support system to improve quality of life through BNCI. In: Assistive Technology: From Research to Practice, AAATE 2013. Encarnação, P., Azevedo, L., Gelderblom, G.J., Newell, A., Mathiassen, N.-E. (eds.), September 2013. ISBN 978-1-61499-303-2 (2013)

Design and Design Thinking to Help the Aged People in Fallen Situations

Jeichen Hsieh(✉)

Tung Hai University, Taichung, Taiwan
jeichen@thu.edu.tw

Abstract. Falling down is a serious problem for the aged people since they are degenerated in the physical and psychological. In some areas, when aged people is fallen it will be nobody around and will be dead in a painful situation. The research focuses on developing a carry on device by mobile technique connected with cloud computing by some emergency departments to help them. The design thinking and the protocol device is developed and expected to be simulated. The research expects to implement the real device at economic price for the needed people to save their lives.

Keywords: Aged people · Fallen situation · Design · Design thinking

1 Introduction

World Health Organization definition of the elderly population is aged 65 and over [1]. Taiwan, the US Census Bureau estimated the population in 2020 more than 14 % of the elderly, into an Aged Society. And even more rapidly than the rate of aging in Japan, will reach 20 % in 2029, to enter the Super Aged Society [2].

For this social phenomenon, the government also launched a related academic re-search. In a period of three years project, Silver Health Care Research and Development Community Habilitation in Taiwan, research selects two regions and involves architecture, landscape departments to the fields. After development of design thinking, specific output of useful products attempt to help the two regions' elderly people.

In the study conducted last year, took place on a real case, an elderly woman living alone with ability to have independent living alone in the mountains. In the backyard garden after fall tillage, she keeps conscious but unable to move and stood. It causes anxiety and helplessness more than two hours. Fortunately one of research member wants to do in-depth interviews again, find her and give emergency relief. This case reflects low birth rate, social change, living alone, and no proper support, could not immediately notice the plight of medical injuries caused by the accident.

Lack of manpower, the use of technology may be to choose a program to solve. How to apply network technology, sensing components, communication technology, and mobile phone functions to prevent falls is the research topic.

M. Antona and C. Stephanidis (Eds.): UAHCI 2015, Part II, LNCS 9176, pp. 447–454, 2015.
DOI: 10.1007/978-3-319-20681-3_42

2 Literature Review

Elderly research in recent years is more and more. Since design thinking in the re-search is application. The literature review focuses on in the range of fall detection system:

2.1 Sensing System

Fall protection mechanism, the primary protection can reduce possibility but it is difficult to avoid. The previous proposal [3–5] focused on secondary prevention, harm reduction and shorten response time. Benny [8] proposed to do with wisdom camera motion analysis to determine the status and send message rescue. But technology, costs are high, to be more restrictions on the development of privacy. Majd [10] places vibration sensor to detect the main floor, but the group is difficult to fully construct and cost is also high. Karantonis [6] uses ZigBee transmission on belt with two rows of triaxial acceleration detector operates motion analysis then transfer information to backend computer to operate help analysis, although the action recognition rate, fall detection rates are up to 90.18 % and 95.6 %, but the reaction time is too long (happened to inform 60 s). If the situation is urgent, there is still considerable risk. Wang C. [7] axis accelerometer will postharvest ear hearing aid, detection time can be shortened to two seconds. According to that research, Chang improves it by ear hook to solve transmission line constraints and inconvenience [9].

2.2 Wireless Technology

Bandwidth and transmission speed is shown in Fig. 1 [12].

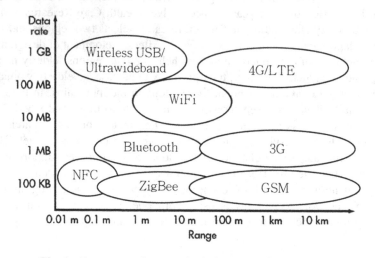

Fig. 1. Data rate and range of wireless network applications

Table 1 Compares weaknesses and good points of ZigBee and Bluetooth [11].

Table 1. Pros and cons between ZigBee and Bluetooth

Comparison project \Technology	ZigBee	Bluetooth
Target market	Monitoring applications or wireless sensor networks	Replace the transmission line
Costs	<4USD	5USD
Typical current	<20 mA	<30 mA
maximum bandwidth	250 kbit/s	201 Mbit/s
maximum number of nodes	65536	7
Transmission distance (ft)	30 ~ 100(Indoor) 150 ~ 300(Outdoor)	30 ~ 300
Main application	Low duty cycle equipment ex: 8-bit, battery-powered control center	PDA Mobile phone handheld device

3 Methodology

Observation method is used to understand the community elderly, their environment, behavior and reaction events, and interactive scenarios. Through notes and photos, record videos, and to observe the structural formula of the locking system environment and behavioral elements clear case definition to look for patterns of everyday life or physical psychological trend. After obtaining a large number of audio and video records, it attempts to identify the mode of photo analysis among elderly peoples dress, behavior, reactions and interpersonal contact. Finally, the empirical design life requirement (EBD) expands the design and user experience to converge preset gap between design alternatives.

4 Implementation

4.1 Field Investigation

The first year of fieldwork focuses in the mountains (Skun). The second year field-work launches on seaside (Chinsui) areas. The reason is that geographic, cultural relativity of the two major ethnic groups in Taiwan. Photos, interviews questionnaire are the main record. Some representatives of the photo shown as Figs. 2 and 3:

After the photo analysis, elderly person's behavior and the scope of their activities are observed:

Skun District simple family contacted more consistent, daily meal is also consistent, and fruit farming, mountain farming are the main daily jobs

Chinsui District is high degree of commercialization, and involves the military com-munity, quite different in other regions.

Skun District

Fig. 2. Photos of Skun area

Chinsui Distict

Fig. 3. Photos of Chinsui area

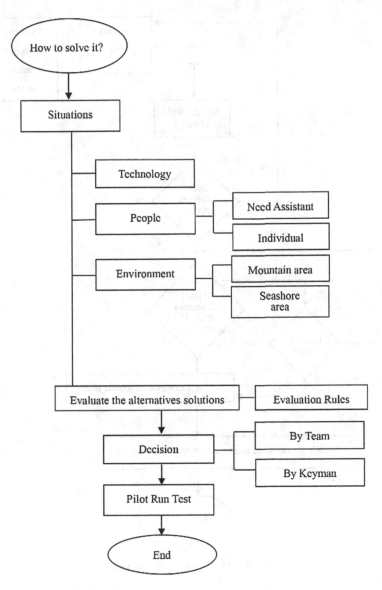

Fig. 4. Flowchart of development and final stages

United military community area, aging people meals are mostly pasta. Elderly person has been in a long and mutually support by the next generation or neighborhood.

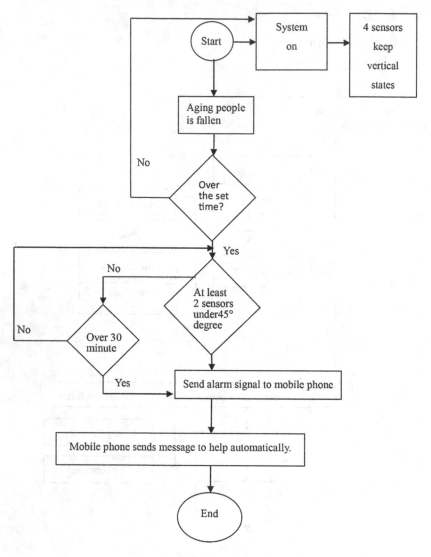

Fig. 5. Algorithm of the System

The other areas are heavy personal ideology, high commercial value and protect their own interests first. The aged present similarities in two areas also are:

(a) Physical body and routine daily schedule is the same. By organizing specific events in the two regions in the characteristics of the interior space (puzzles, dough, body dance) with all free food, observation finds that all will be early arrived at the appointed time. It seems all of them look forward to participating in the reaction of pleasure. In the process, just one or two leave when they feel tired.

(b) Respect for the food presentation is consistent. Generally they will be willing to pack extra food back. Appetite is no different from ordinary people.

(c) Clothing, apparel, aids also show consistency.

4.2 Design Thinking

Design thinking on the development and final stage is as Fig. 4.

The algorithm of the system is as Fig. 5.

5 Conclusion

After long-term care for the elderly subjects, selecting the mountain stages, two Tai-wan seaside communities, conduct fieldwork and import design thinking, expand the essence of the design. Because of the resources, early in the fieldwork, and propose specific outputs active notification for the two regions after an elderly person fell habit wearable button-type design.

In addition, to specific design thinking to research an attempt to simulate the future entity is suggested to adjust the user experience.

This product design features some single parts [12–16], effectively evoke the wireless network equipment and contact the community support is expected to avoid the fall tragedy.

References

1. International database (IDB) of the U.S. Census Bureau Population Division. http://www.census.gov/ipc/www/idb/informationGateway.php
2. Department of Health Statistics News. http://www.doh.gov.tw/statistic/index.htm
3. Brewer, K., Ciolek, C., Delaune, M. F.: Falls in community dwelling older adults: introduction to the problem. In: APTA Continuing Education Series, pp.38–46 (2007)
4. King, M.B., Tinetti, M.E.: Fall in community dwelling older person. J. Am. Geriatr. Soc. **43** (10), 1146–1154 (1995)
5. Alwan, M., Fleder, R.A.: Eldercare Technology for Clinical Practitioners, 1st edn, pp. 187–201. Humana Press, Totowa (2007)
6. Karantonis, D.M., Narayanan, M.R., Mathie, M., Lovell, N.H., Celler, B.G.: Implementation of a real-time human movement classifier using a triaxial accelerometer for ambulatory monitoring. IEEE Trans. Inf. Technol. Biomed. **10**, 156–167 (2006)
7. Wang, C.C., Chiang, C.Y., Lin, P.Y., Chou, Y.C., Kuo, I.T., Huang, C.N., Chan, C.T.: Development of a fall detecting system for the elderly residents. In: The 2nd International Conference on Bioinformatics and Biomedical Engineering, ICBBE 2008, pp.1359–1362 (2008)
8. Benny, P.L., Jeffrey, LW., Guang-Zhong, Y.: From imaging networks to behavior profiling: ubiquitous sensing for man-aged homecare of the elderly. In: Adjunct Proceedings of the 3rd International Conference on Pervasive Computing, pp. 101–104 (2005)

9. Hong, Z.H.: U-life Is coming: the rise of short-range wireless integrated fashion. The New Communications, 85 (2008)
10. Majd, A., Siddharth, D., Steve K., Robin F.: Derivation of basic human gait characteristics from floor vibrations. In: 2003 Summer Bioengineering Conference, pp. 25–29 (2007)
11. Chang, L.S.: Location-aware study of fall detection system. National Yang-Ming University, Institute of Biomedical Engineering Master's Thesis, unpublished (2009)
12. Yu, Z.C., Pan, M.H., Lin, Z.: Unlimited Personal Area Network – casual Technology and Application of Sensor Networks, 1st edn. Z-Chen Press (2007)
13. Blumenthal, J., Grossmann, R., Golatowski, F., Timmermann, D.: Weighted centroid localization in ZigBee-based sensor networks. In: IEEE International Symposium Intelligent Signal Processing, WISP 2007, pp.1–6, 3-5 October 2007
14. Zan, M.: Biomedical Technology. http://www.aescutechnology.com
15. Lindemann, U., Hock, A., Stuber, M., Keck, W., Becker, C.: Evaluation of a fall detector based on accelerometers: a pilot study. Med. Biol. Eng. Comput. 43(5), 548–551 (2005)
16. Leadtek: http://lpc.leadtek.com/cht/Products.aspx?pid=C351.1M%E7%84%A1%E7%B7%9APT%E7%B6%B2%E8%B7%AF%E6%94%9D%E5%BD%B1%E6%A9%9F.html&fo=Products/%E7%B6%B2%E8%B7%AF%E6%94%9D%E5%BD%B1%E6%A9%9F/amor%20%E5%B1%85%E5%AE%B6%E9%98%B2%E8%AD%B7%E7%B3%BB%E5%88%97

Automatic Analysis of Speech and Acoustic Events for Ambient Assisted Living

Alexey Karpov[1,2(✉)], Alexander Ronzhin[1], and Irina Kipyatkova[1]

[1] St. Petersburg Institute for Informatics and Automation of the Russian
Academy of Sciences, St. Petersburg, Russia
{karpov,ronzhinal,kipyatkova}@iias.spb.su
http://www.spiiras.nw.ru/speech
[2] ITMO University, Saint-Petersburg, Russian Federation

Abstract. We present a prototype of an ambient assisted living (AAL) with multimodal user interaction. In our research, the AAL environment is one studio room of 60 + square meters that has several tables, chairs and a sink, as well as equipped with four stationary microphones and two omni-directional video cameras. In this paper, we focus mainly on audio signal processing techniques for monitoring the assistive smart space and recognition of speech and non-speech acoustic events for automatic analysis of human's activities and detection of possible emergency situations with the user (when an emergent help is needed). Acoustical modeling in our audio recognition system is based on single order Hidden Markov Models with Gaussian Mixture Models. The recognition vocabulary includes 12 non-speech acoustic events for different types of human activities plus 5 useful spoken commands (keywords), including a subset of alarm audio events. We have collected an audio-visual corpus containing about 1.3 h of audio data from 5 testers, who performed proposed test scenarios, and made the practical experiments with the system, results of which are reported in this paper.

Keywords: Ambient assisted living · Assistive technology · Multimodal user interfaces · Universal access · Human-Computer interaction · Automatic speech recognition · Acoustic event detection

1 Introduction

Ambient Assisted Living (www.aal-europe.eu) [1–3] is a new special area of assistive information technologies [4–6] that is focused on designing smart spaces, rooms, homes and intelligent environments to support and care some disabled and elderly people. At present AAL domain includes several International projects, for example, DOMEO, HAPPY AGEING, HOPE, SOFTCARE, Sweet Home, homeService, We-Care, etc. Arrays of microphones, video cameras and other sensors are often installed in assistive smart spaces [7].

In this study, we also analyze audio and video modalities for automatic monitoring of activities and behavior of single elderly persons and people with physical, sensory or mental disabilities. In our previous recent work [8], we presented a prototype of a

© Springer International Publishing Switzerland 2015
M. Antona and C. Stephanidis (Eds.): UAHCI 2015, Part II, LNCS 9176, pp. 455–463, 2015.
DOI: 10.1007/978-3-319-20681-3_43

multimodal AAL environment with main focus on video-based methods for space and user behavior monitoring by omni-directional (fish eye) cameras, mainly for detection of accidental user falls. In this article, we focus mainly on audio-based techniques for monitoring the assistive smart space and recognition of speech and non-speech acoustic events for automatic analysis of human's activities and detection of possible emergency situations (when some help is needed to the person). The use of audio-based processing additionally to video analysis makes many multimodal systems more accurate and robust [9, 10]. Acoustic events in AAL environments can be such as human's speech / commands as well as artificial sounds directly or indirectly produced by a human being (for example, cough, cry, chair movements, knocking at the door, steps, etc.). Spoken language is the most meaningful acoustic information; however other auditory events give us much information too. In scientific literature, there are some recent publications on automatic detection of individual acoustic events such as cough, sounds of human fall, cry, scream, distress calls or other events, for example in works [11–15].

In our research, the AAL environment is one room of 60 + square meters. We developed a software-hardware complex for audio-based monitoring of this AAL environment during the Summer Workshop on Multimodal Interfaces eNTERFACE in Pilsen. The room (physical model of the AAL environment) has 2 tables, 2 chairs and a sink, as well as it is equipped with 2 omni-directional video cameras and 4 stationary microphones in a grid. One Mobotix camera is placed on the ceiling and the second one is on the side wall; camera's frame resolution is 640 × 480 pixels at 8 fps rate. 4 dynamic condenser microphones Oktava MK-012 of the smart environment are connected to a multichannel external sound board M-Audio ProFire 2626. Each microphone has the cardioid diagram of direction and can capture audio signals in a wide sector below the microphone with almost equal amplification. All the microphones are placed on the ceiling (about 2.5 m above the floor) in selected locations. The scheme of the physical model of our AAL environment is shown in Fig. 1.

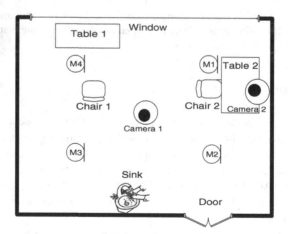

Fig. 1. Scheme of the physical model of the Ambient Assisted Living environment

The paper below describes the architecture and implementation issues of the automatic recognition system in Sect. 2, as well as presents some experimental results and analysis of its evaluation in Sect. 3.

2 Architecture of the Automatic Recognition System

The recognition vocabulary includes 12 non-speech acoustic events for different types of human activities plus 5 possible spoken commands. We defined also a set of alarm audio events X = {"Cough", "Cry", "Fall" (a human being), "Key drop" (a metal object), "Help", "Problem" (commands)}, which can serve as a signal on an emergency situation with the user inside the AAL environment. Figure 2 presents a tree classification of audio signals in the AAL environment including speech commands and acoustic events, which are modelled in the automatic system.

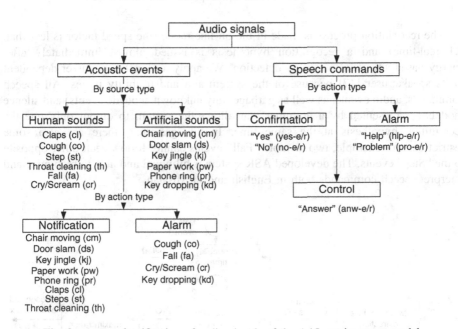

Fig. 2. A tree classification of audio signals of the AAL environment model

Figure 3 shows the software-hardware architecture of the automatic system for recognition of speech and non-speech acoustic events. Acoustic modeling in the system is based on single order Hidden Markov Models (HMM) with Gaussian Mixture Models (GMM) as many modern automatic speech recognition systems [16]. Our system extracts feature vectors consisting of 13 Mel-frequency cepstral coefficients (MFCC) with deltas and double deltas from the multichannel audio signals.

The system uses HMM-based Viterbi method and software algorithm for finding an optimal model for input audio signal (Fig. 4). HMMs having a unique topology with different number of states (from 1 to 6 states per one model) represent all acoustic events and phonemes of speech commands depending on duration.

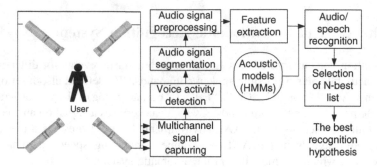

Fig. 3. Architecture of audio event/speech recognition system

The recognition process is made in the on-line mode (the speed factor is less than 0.1 real-time) and a recognition hypothesis is issued almost immediately after energy-based voice/audio activity detection. We apply a speech recognizer dependent to its speaker/user [17] because of the system aim and usability issues. All speech commands, audio events, as well as garbage (any unknown acoustic events) and silence models are presented by a grammar that allows the system to output only one the recognition hypothesis at the same time. In this grammar, there are also some restrictions; for example, two or more "Fall" events cannot follow each other opposite to the "Step" events. The developed ASR system is bilingual and able to recognize and interpret speech commands both in English and in Russian.

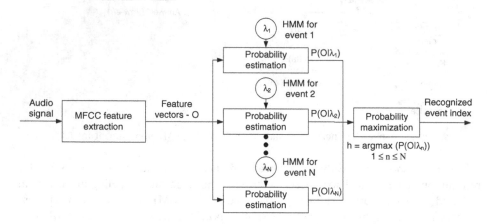

Fig. 4. HMM-based method for automatic recognition of audio signals

In order to train probabilistic HMM-based acoustic models of the recognizer, a new audio corpus has been collected in normal room conditions with an acceptable level of background noise (SNR > 20 dB). In total, we have recorded over 1.3 h of audio data from several potential users performing certain scenarios. Above 2 K audio files were recorded; almost half of which are non-speech audio events. Approximately 2/3 audio data of each subject we used for the training and development purpose and the rest data were employed during the evaluation.

3 Results of the Experiments with the AAL Model

We have developed some scenarios for modeling basic actions performed by people in a living room (studio). The first scenario involves one person and simulates an emergency situation (drop of a metal object and fall of a human on the floor in the end). The second scenario involves up to 3 subjects, who can interact each other, and subjects may occlude each other at some frames (it is used for testing the video-based user monitoring sub-system) [8]. The main scenario involving audio-visual data supposes the following actions of a tester:

(1) Enter the room from the door side (open & close the door).
(2) Walk to the table 1.
(3) Take a glass with water from the table 1.
(4) Walk to the chair 1.
(5) Sit on the chair 1.
(6) Drink water.
(7) Long cough after drinking.
(8) Stand up.
(9) Walk to the table 1.
(10) Release the glass (it drops).
(11) Walk to the sink.
(12) Wash hands in the sink.
(13) Exit the room (open & close the door).
(14) Enter the room again.
(15) Walk to the chair 2.
(16) Sit on the chair 2.
(17) Telephone rings on the table 2.
(18) Say "Answer phone".
(19) Talk by the telephone.
(20) Say "Hello".
(21) Say "I'm fine".
(22) Say "Don't worry".
(23) Say "Good bye".
(24) Stand up.
(25) Walk to the table 1.
(26) Take a metallic cup on the Table
(27) Free walk (several steps).
(28) Drop the cup on the floor.
(29) Make a step.

(30) Fall on the floor.
(31) Cry.
(32) Ask for "Help"

During the multimodal database collection we have recorded audio-visual samples of the presented first Scenario from 5 different subjects (potential users). They were free to perform the fall (on the hard floor that produces a sound) as it was comfortable for them. Also a training part of the audio database has been recorded in the same room, where a factor of entering new people into the room during the recording session was avoided that allows removing major external noises. 5 check points have been defined in the room for collecting the training audio data; 4 of them were located on the floor under each microphone and the last one was in the centre of the room. Each of 5 testers performed the following sequence of user's actions:

(1) Come to a checkpoint.
(2) Give a speech command or simulate a non-speech audio event.
(3) Move to the following checkpoint (1).

All the speech commands and acoustic events were simulated many times by different testers. In total, we have recorded above 2800 audio files (in the PCM WAV format); 44 % of them contain non-speech events and the rest – speech commands. 70 % recordings for each subject were used for system's training and the rest of the data were used in the experiments. This corpus (SARGAS DB) has been registered in the RosPatent (№ 2013613086 on 25/03/2013).

Table 1. Confusion matrix for speech command recognition (accuracy, %)

Speech command	Num.	ans -e	hlp -e	no -e	pro -e	yes -e	yes -r	no -r	ans -r	hlp -r	pro -r
ans-e	388	100	0	0	0	0	0	0	0	0	0
hlp-e	100	0	85	0	0	0	0	0	0	0	15
no-e	120	0	0	100	0	0	0	0	0	0	0
pro-e	249	0	0	0	94	0	0	0	0	0	6
yes-e	104	0	0	0	0	100	0	0	0	0	0
yes-r	100	0	0	0	0	0	100	0	0	0	0
no-r	100	0	0	0	0	0	0	100	0	0	0
ans-r	118	0	0	0	0	0	0	0	100	0	0
hlp-r	155	0	0	0	2	0	0	0	0	95	3
pro-r	151	0	0	0	9	0	0	0	0	0	91

The automatic system for recognition of speech commands and audio events was evaluated using audio recordings including the audio corpus part containing data of the first Scenario made in the ambient assisted living environment. Table 1 shows the confusion matrix with the accuracy rates (in %) for recognized speech command.

Table 2. Confusion matrix for acoustic event recognition (accuracy, %)

Acoustic event	Num.	cl	cm	co	cr	ds	fa	kd	kj	pw	pr	st	th
cl	112	100	0	0	0	0	0	0	0	0	0	0	0
cm	152	0	100	0	0	0	0	0	0	0	0	0	0
co	72	0	0	100	0	0	0	0	0	0	0	0	0
cr	108	0	0	0	100	0	0	0	0	0	0	0	0
ds	111	0	0	0	2	98	0	0	0	0	0	0	0
fa	108	0	0	1	0	0	63	0	0	0	0	36	0
kd	129	15	0	0	0	0	0	75	0	10	0	0	0
kj	44	0	0	0	0	0	0	0	100	0	0	0	0
pw	68	4	0	0	0	0	0	0	0	96	0	0	0
pr	32	0	0	0	0	0	0	0	0	0	100	0	0
st	166	0	0	6	0	0	0	0	0	0	0	94	0
th	124	0	0	0	0	0	0	0	0	0	0	0	100

Presented results show that the most of speech commands were recognized with a high accuracy over 90 %, however still there were some recognition errors during test scenarios.

Table 2 shows another confusion matrix with the accuracy rates (in %) for recognized acoustic events in the AAL environment model. The presented results show that the lowest accuracy was observed for the non-speech audio event "Fall". In the third of such cases this acoustic event was recognized as "Step".

In average, the recognition accuracy for acoustic events was 93.8 % and 96.5 % – for speech commands.

4 Conclusion

We presented a software-hardware complex for audio-based monitoring of the AAL environment model. Audio signals in AAL environments can be human's commands/speech and artificial sounds produced by a human directly or indirectly (for example, chair movements, cough, cry, knocking at the door, steps, etc.). The system uses Viterbi-based algorithm for finding an optimal model for input audio signal. HMMs having a unique topology with different number of states (1-6) model each acoustic event and command depending on its duration. The recognition is performed in on-line mode (speed factor < 0.1 real-time) and a hypothesis is issued almost immediately after energy-based voice/audio activity detection. We apply the speaker-dependent recognizer because of the system aim and usability issues. The vocabulary includes 12 non-speech acoustic events for different types of human activities plus 5 user's spoken commands including a set of some alarm events, which can serve as a signal about an emergency situation inside the AAL environment. To train acoustic models, we have collected an audio corpus in quiet room conditions with a low level of background noise (SNR > 20 dB). Above two thousand audio files were recorded; almost half of which are non-speech audio events. Approximately 2/3 audio data of each subject we used for the training and development purpose and the rest data were employed during the evaluation. In the experiments, the best recognition accuracy for the acoustic events was 93.8 % in average and 96.5 % – for speech commands.

Acknowledgements. This research is partially supported by the Council for Grants of the President of Russia (Projects No. MD-3035.2015.8 and MK-5209.2015.8), by the Russian Foundation for Basic Research (Projects No. 15-07-04415 and 15-07-04322), and by the Government of the Russian Federation (Grant No. 074-U01).

References

1. Burzagli, L., Di Fonzo, L., Emiliani, P.L.: Services and applications in an ambient assisted living (aal) environment. In: Stephanidis, C., Antona, M. (eds.) UAHCI 2014, Part III. LNCS, vol. 8515, pp. 475–482. Springer, Heidelberg (2014)
2. Sacco, M., Caldarola, E.G., Modoni, G., Terkaj, W.: Supporting the design of AAL through a SW integration framework: the D4All project. In: Stephanidis, C., Antona, M. (eds.) UAHCI 2014, Part I. LNCS, vol. 8513, pp. 75–84. Springer, Heidelberg (2014)
3. Mora, N., Bianchi, V., De Munari, I., Ciampolini, P.: A BCI platform supporting AAL applications. In: Stephanidis, C., Antona, M. (eds.) UAHCI 2014, Part I. LNCS, vol. 8513, pp. 515–526. Springer, Heidelberg (2014)
4. Karpov, A., Ronzhin, A.: A Universal assistive technology with multimodal input and multimedia output interfaces. In: Stephanidis, C., Antona, M. (eds.) UAHCI 2014, Part I. LNCS, vol. 8513, pp. 369–378. Springer, Heidelberg (2014)
5. Argyropoulos, S., Moustakas, K., Karpov, A., Aran, O., Tzovaras, D., Tsakiris, T., Varni, G., Kwon, B.: A Multimodal framework for the communication of the disabled. J. Multimodal User Interfaces 2(2), 105–116 (2008). Springer
6. Karpov, A., Ronzhin, A., Kipyatkova, I.: An assistive bi-modal user interface integrating multi-channel speech recognition and computer vision. In: Jacko, J.A. (ed.) Human-Computer Interaction, Part II, HCII 2011. LNCS, vol. 6762, pp. 454–463. Springer, Heidelberg (2011)
7. Portet, F., Vacher, M., Golanski, C., Roux, C., Meillon, B.: Design and evaluation of a smart home voice interface for the elderly: acceptability and objection aspects. Pers. Ubiquit. Comput. 32(1), 1–18 (2011)
8. Karpov A., Akarun L., Yalçın H., Ronzhin Al., Demiröz B., Çoban A., Zelezny M.: Audio-visual signal processing in a multimodal assisted living environment. In: Proceedings of the 15th International Conference, INTERSPEECH-2014, Singapore, pp. 1023–1027 (2014)
9. Karpov, A.: An automatic multimodal speech recognition system with audio and video information. Autom. Remote Control 75(12), 2190–2200 (2014). Springer
10. Karpov, A., Ronzhin, A.: Information Enquiry Kiosk with Multimodal User Interface. Pattern Recogn. Image Anal. 19(3), 546–558 (2009). Springer
11. Drugman T., Urbain J., Dutoit T. Assessment of audio features for automatic cough detection. In: Proceedings of the 19th European Signal Processing Conference, EUSIPCO-2011, Barcelona, Spain, pp. 1289–1293 (2011)

12. Zigel, Y., Litvak, D., Gannot, I.: A method for automatic fall detection of elderly people using floor vibrations and sound - proof of concept on human mimicking doll falls. IEEE Trans. Biomed. Eng. **56**(12), 2858–2867 (2009)
13. Miao, Yu., Naqvi, S.M., Rhuma, A., Chambers J.: Fall detection in a smart room by using a fuzzy one class support vector machine and imperfect training data. In: Proceedings of the 36th International Conference, ICASSP-2011, Prague, Czech Republic, pp. 1833–1836 (2011)
14. Huynh, T.H., Tran, V.A., Tran, H.D.: Semi-supervised tree support vector machine for online cough recognition, In: Proceedings of the 12th International Conference, INTERSPEECH-2011, Florence, Italy, pp. 1637–1640 (2011)
15. Aman, F., Vacher, M., Rossato S., Portet, F.: In-Home Detection of Distress Calls: The Case of Aged Users. In: Proceedings of the 14th International Conference, INTERSPEECH-2013, Lyon, France, pp. 2065–2067 (2013)
16. Levin, K. et al.: Automated Closed Captioning for Russian Live Broadcasting. In: Proceedings of the 15th International Conference, INTERSPEECH-2014, Singapore, pp. 1438–1442 (2014)
17. Matveev, Y.: The Problem of voice template aging in speaker recognition systems. In: Železný, M., Habernal, I., Ronzhin, A. (eds.) SPECOM 2013. LNCS, vol. 8113, pp. 345–353. Springer, Heidelberg (2013)

Improving Speech Intelligibility in Classrooms by Decreasing Sound Energy of Low Frequency

Wei Lin[1(✉)], Hsuan Lin[2], and Kung-Huang Huang[3]

[1] Department of Interior Design, Hwa Hsia University of Technology,
Taipei, Taiwan
weilin@cc.hwh.edu.tw
[2] Department of Product Design, Tainan University of Technology,
Tainan, Taiwan
te0038@mail.tut.edu.tw
[3] General Manager, Shang You Construction Co. Ltd., Kaohsiung, Taiwan
sf.land@msa.hinet.net

Abstract. Speech intelligibility is one of the sound field quality evaluation criteria, class-room space needed to create a low-noise and clear listening environment. In addition to the reverberation time (sec), chamber volume (m3) and speech clarity (dB) can tolerate higher use of space and other influencing factors of critical sound energy at low frequency, the spatial frequency factor for indoor conversation came the noise amplification effect will affect listening clarity. Evaluative standard of Rapid Speech Intelligibility (RASTI) for an indoor sound field has been studied for a long time, only 500 Hz and 2 K-Hz cannot be precisely estimated the impact of low frequency noise. After making a Chinese phase and sentence questionnaire for the test, studies will be conducted objective and subjective verification verified statement containing the real class-room space by physical quantities (Reverberation time (RT30, sec) and Signal to noise ratio (S/N ratio, dB) of low-frequency sound energy is correlated be-tween with objective measurement, and subjective test of virtual classrooms is also be made in anechoic chamber to correspond with the low frequency impact factor of speech intelligibility index.

Keywords: Speech intelligibility · Low frequency of sound energy · Virtual sound field · Subjective test

1 Introduction

Classroom acoustics is the research point for room acoustics filed, effective factors of analysis for speech intelligibility and improvement of environment for the classroom acoustic is another subjective sense of current studies. The objective parameters influence speech intelligibility which included chamber's volume, the reverberation time, the signal to noise ratio, the speaker's voice level and talker-to-listener distance. Although the Reverberation time and signal to noise ratio are the most commonly discussed, low frequency sound energy range correspondence with signal to noise ratio

© Springer International Publishing Switzerland 2015
M. Antona and C. Stephanidis (Eds.): UAHCI 2015, Part II, LNCS 9176, pp. 464–473, 2015.
DOI: 10.1007/978-3-319-20681-3_44

and the reverberation time in the classroom assessment may not have consistent results [1, 2].

Impulse response of the signal are obtained through by processing software and can also be produced by changing the actual sound impulse response. By the signal processing of the different adjustments, resulting in the ideal value of the parameter corresponding to a combination of low-frequency factors, and further the sound field to discuss the proper signal to noise ratio and reverberation time. Many studies have found that the impulse response of the sound field are adjusted the reflection density through the differences of room volume, and then achieve a different reverberation time by adjusting the amplitude and attenuation rate [3, 4]. Even if reverberation time are the same, the density of amplitude reflection are the difference [5]. Current assessment parameter (RASTI) at indoor sound field for speech intelligibility is a comprehensive physical evaluation which is mainly discussed at the band of 500 Hz and 2000 Hz. It may not clearly show contours at the low frequency band of sound field conditions. Through digital signal processing, correlation between the subjective experiment and the objective evaluation of the results on the current trend may also be conducted by tuning the low frequency elements.

1.1 Effect of Low Frequency's Element on Theory of Speech Signal

Low frequency impact on speech signals in a voice message expression is a critical issue, since the high-frequency elements on the voice pronunciation have been concentrated as the main octave band, high frequency octave band have been discussed more than low frequency. This leads to interference noise suppression efforts in the high-frequency band, but to ignore the low-frequency band caused by a more serious factor of the shadowing effect. By German linguist Slawin [6] studies, f1 effect will be generated a multi-level sense of hearing additional harmonics in strong signal frequency, as shown by the following Eq. 1.

$$f = (n+1)\,\text{Fi}; \quad n = 1, 2, 3, \ldots \tag{1}$$

When multiple strong signals f1 and f2 simultaneously act, in addition to the respective homophonic will occur, it will also produce a "Aggregate homophonic": as shown by the following Eq. 2.

$$fK = nf1 \pm mf2; \quad m = 1, 2, 3, \ldots \tag{2}$$

The auditory organs get additional sounds, calling the "subjective homonym", it is interesting a sense of hearing homonym that cannot be presented by the measurement in a real environment. The numbers of homophonic sense of hearing increase the energy of the sound field with the actual sound level which are also in disproportionate. In subjective sense of hearing, when the low frequency of sound energy is higher than 80 dB, the sense of hearing harmonics of phonics articulation at high frequency feel strongly than the fundamental ones. As in the bass strings when toggle, the sense of hearing of harmonics sound is more active than fundamental sound energy. When powerful tone or noise sound caused by echoes of sound energy of nonlinear super-position, listening masker of high frequency acoustic energy may occur, especially for speech intelligibility, masking effects in high frequency band is more severe. The University of Göttingen professor Hellbrueck's study [7] found that, strong low-frequency acoustic masked the feeling of the high-frequency hearing, and despite the high-frequency sound enhance, it is not easy to improve the intelligibility of subjective judgments due to the low frequency sound energy shaded. Furthermore, if the obscured low-frequency and obscured high-frequency signals arrive simultaneously in one ear, unintelligibility of hearing can be more severe. It also shows that if the hearing-impaired friends are in the crowded reception space, even if wear the func-tional hearing aids, they are still extremely uncomfortable [8]. By German National Research Center IBP acoustic researcher [9] further confirmation, subjective experi-ments of German syllable intelligibility, experiments results may have a severe inter-ference through 20 Hz–20 kHz broadband pink noise. In all evaluation of the results of those tests, if the frequency of the sound-absorbing material considerations as low as 50 Hz are installed in the test chamber while scores of its higher speech intelligibility may occur, and listening comfort may also improve.

1.2   Control Background Noise in Classroom

Control of self-generated noise in the classroom is an important issue, and requirements of general use of language-based indoor background noise is 40 dB (A) or less. High relative quiet background noise in the classroom, talking to each other in the process (at 1 m distance) can be achieved in the state of relaxed conversation and achieve good speech intelligibility. When the increase or enlarge classroom speakers voice happen, it also means that the noise criteria of sound field move to a noisy indication. In terms of direct experience of the listeners receive the average loudness of sound energy and stability of sound source, classroom sound power level Lw as shown in Eq. 3:

$$Lw = Lw - 10\lg V + 10\lg T + 14 dB \tag{3}$$

Lw is stand for sound power, V is stand for chamber volume (m3), T is for the reverberation time (s)

When a single talker speak in the classroom (sound power Lw), speaker himself feel volume boost due to noise factor, subjective perception of speaker think that listeners can clearly hear his voice words, and thus understand its discourse content, then Lw as shown in Eq. 4:

$$Lw = Lw + 10\lg n - 10\lg V + 10\lg T + 14 dB \tag{4}$$

In the Formula 4, 10 lg n stand for multiple noise sources and amplification, the hearing threshold of entire spectrum will cause increase. In Reverberation time formula (RT), the same acoustic energy in the corresponding multiples enlarge chamber vol-ume, due to the secondary path of the reflection sound energy also will multiply, with increasing reverberation time. Appropriate reverberation time in the chamber can improve speech intelligibility, however, due to the height of 3.5 m ~ 4 m Classroom restrictions and noise will amplify sound energy at low frequency, and high frequency shadowing effects become more significant. If the speech sound power increase, as Lw = 80 dB (A), and assuming that the direction of the sound source characteristics of 10 lg v = 3 dB, r indicates the distance the sound source, the following equation (Eq. 5) can be expressed in sound power Lw:

$$Lw = \text{Lw} + 10\lg V - 20\lg r - 11 \text{dB} \tag{5}$$

For the speech transmission, listeners need to perceive speech intelligibility, which is generated by the sound energy of increasing talker sound level higher than the background noise. Within the corresponding German Standards Institute [10] for speech intelligibility, difference of interference level (12 dB to -6 dB), the sound power level and the distance between the sound source, the proposed space allow sound level shown as in Table 1.

Table 1. DIN 18041–2004 (German Standards Institute [10]) proposed space allow sound level as function which are evaluated by speech intelligibility, difference of interference level (12 dB to − 6 dB), the sound power level and the distance between the sound source.

Talker sound power, Lw dB (A)	Speech Intelligibility											
	Excellent (12 dB)			Good (6 dB)			Fair (0 dB)			Bad (-6 dB)		
	0.5 m	1 m	2 m	0.5 m	1 m	2 m	0.5 m	1 m	2 m	0.5 m	1 m	2 m
	Allowed sound level dB(A)											
62	48	42	36	54	48	42	60	54	48	66	60	54
68	54	48	42	60	54	48	66	60	54	72	66	60
74	60	54	48	66	60	54	72	66	60	78	72	66
80	66	60	54	72	66	60	78	72	66	84	78	72

High quality classroom space is the creation of high-definition voice environment, for the theory of the influence of the voice signal can be seen from the low-frequency, high frequency sound energy as if by a powerful low-frequency interference signals can affect the sound, the subjective high frequency sound energy will be obscured due to the superposition of the hom-onym. Under consideration of the self-generated noise control in classroom, the usage of speech-based indoor background noise control requirement is at 40 dB (A) or less.

The purpose of this study is to establish the low-frequency factor for understanding the in-fluence of speech intelligibility in classroom, based on objective parameters of the sound field data, effect factors of subjective evaluation and corresponding with multi-dimensions of con-sistency would have discussion. Research steps are divided into three parts, the first phase of the field measurement of parameter performance on the space of the classroom have been collected, and the classroom located at the National Taitung University which is as the proto-type of virtual sound field for next stage. The second phase will be the impulse response of field classroom has been collected, through a subjective assessment to discuss the degree of obscured sound at low frequency band for the sense of hearing for speech intelligibility. Dry source are accomplished with phonics list which is using by a digital signal recording in ane-choic chamber, modification using the digital impulse response of different chamber volume are been conducted, and then create multiple sets of different classroom sound field by taking into consideration the different combinations of signal to noise ratio and reverberation time. After completion of convolution with read paragraph (Dry source) in different groups of sound source, subjective test samples with different conditions of the sound field are also obtained. The third phase is to take a subjective hearing test which the test segments is made of many groups of sound field voice, and compared with the actual filed subjective test consistency.

2 Previous Research Works

Standard classroom type at National Taitung University is as the verification space, renovation in the original open classroom is also be conducted in order to modify the effect of sound energy at low-frequency band which may meet the room acoustical design as the main tar-get. The picture image of renovated classroom at National Taitung University is shown in Fig. 1. Total area of interior floor was 100 m^2 and the basic conditions for classroom space are shown in Table 2. The performance of the reverberation time yielded by adjusting the use of sound-absorbing material, and consider the full frequency high sound absorption rate, especially for the absorption properties of low-frequency is the main choice direction. The micro perforated plates and melamine foam are used as a broadband application of sound absorption material, each absorption coefficient of 1/1 center octave band is shown in the Table 3.

Table 2. Construction conditions of real classroom space

Function	Classroom
Room type	Rectangular shape
Room size	Width × Length × High: 12.9 m × 7.8 m × 3 m
Volume	100 M^3
Absorption material	Melamine foam and micro perforated plates

Table 3. Table of material absorption coefficient of 1/1 center octave band are listed

Material (Thickness)	125 Hz	250 Hz	500 Hz	1 K Hz	2 K Hz	4 K Hz
Melamine foam (2 M)	0.14	0.17	0.42	0.68	0.88	0.92
Melamine foam (5 M)	0.25	0.65	1	1	1	1
Micro perforated plates (10CM)	0.15	00.45	0.78	0.90	0.57	0.58
Micro perforated plates (20CM)	0.25	0.71	0.92	0.56	0.58	0.56
Micro perforated plates (30CM)	0.53	0.78	0.65	0.70	0.60	0.55

Fig. 1. Renovated Standard classroom type at National Taitung University

3 Methodology

The first phase of the field measurement of classroom performance on the parameter has been collected. As a result of the physical quantity measured objectively in the classroom, RASTI shows a little significant difference between the original mode and renovated mode. If the evaluation results of speech intelligibility determined by the RASTI directly, it will ignore the impacts caused by the low frequency of sound. In order to effectively understand the impact of low frequency factor of speech intelligibility, investigation of differences of correspondence between the subjective evaluation and the objective measurement were also con-ducted. And in the previous phase measurement of classroom space (prototype) for the second phase of the modified one was the virtual sound field. Finally, the third stage explored a consistency and comparisons a sense of subjective tests between the virtual field and real field were considered.

3.1 Syllable Table for Subjective Test

Preliminary study, based on the Chen's [11] research, the production of speech syllable table of Chinese words and sentences (meaningful) were completed. Due to the 1198 syllables in the actual application of testing, avoid to lead to the difficulties by utilizing a stratified probability sample (stratified sampling) way was conducted, and the computer "random" the same amount of sampling six syllables was also yielded, made a total of 108 syllables as a single sample of the sound which might consist sort of a sets of words and sentences table.

3.2   Reproducibility of Virtual Sound Field

The actual collection of the impulse response of the classroom were placed through the sound effect system with ambient noise, the impulse response of the classroom field measurement was collected by the digital signal station, the reverse function integration of Schroeder's proposed use of function [12] was also obtained integral curves of the reverberation time.

3.3   Completion of Subjective Test with Virtual Classroom

The Chinese continuous speech of continuous meaningful female voice of test table (maskee1) table have been accomplished which were recorded in the anechoic chamber, then recorded test tables were edited by using by FFT signal processing software, Sound forge7.0 version. Dry source voice sample convolution (Convolution) was placed the classroom sound field which got a different sound field conditions such as three groups of signal to noise ratio of, three groups of low-frequency and three group of sound reverberation time in combination with a segment group of 27 field samples were available. To make sense of hearing the result of differences effectively, avoid to excessive combinations of subjective test caused by invalid, re-downsizing the number of combinations to 9 samples formed is listed in the Table 4. With the results shown in Table 4, three groups of reverberation time (0.55 s, 0.85 s and 1.15 s) and three groups of signal to noise ratio (0 dB, +6 dB and +15 dB) combination of different sound field environment, explore the results of impacts by the three groups of low frequency sound (125 Hz, 63 Hz and 50 Hz). Sample of a subjective test track is shown in Fig. 2, speech convolution with signal to noise ratio (+ 6 dB) is calculated which explore sound at low frequency band (63 Hz) of hearing response in virtual classroom of the reverberation time of 1.15 s sound field.

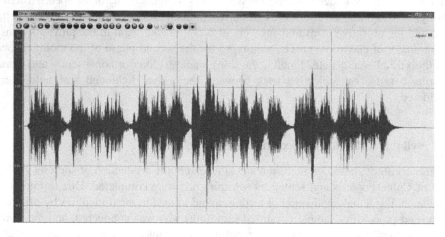

Fig. 2. The subjective test tracks with signal to noise ratio (+ 6 dB) are calculated which explore sound at low frequency band (63 Hz) of hearing response in virtual classroom of the reverberation time of 1.15 s sound field.

Table 4. Combination with a segment group of 9 field samples were available

		Reverberation Time T30 (s)		
		0.55 s	0.85 s	1.15 s
S/N ratio(dB)	0 dB	125 Hz		
	+6 dB		63 Hz	
	+15 dB			50 Hz

4 Discussion

The purpose of this study is to establish the low-frequency factor for understanding the in-fluence of speech intelligibility in classroom, based on objective parameters of the sound field data, effect factors of subjective evaluation and corresponding with multi-dimensions of con-sistency would have discussion. Research steps are divided into three parts, the first phase of the field measurement of parameter performance on the space of the classroom have been collected, and the classroom located at the National Taitung University which is as the proto-type of virtual sound field for next stage. The second phase will be the impulse response of field classroom has been collected, through a subjective assessment to discuss the degree of obscured sound at low frequency band for the sense of hearing speech intelligibility.

4.1   Field Verification with Measurements

Acoustical measurements using an aural tone speaker were followed by a objective study comparing future subjective test with recorded sound in classroom (Code 105), National Tai-tung University. The 100-m2 of floor area provided a space for listeners. The location of a microphone receiver at the audience seats have to be placed average distribution in class-room. Acoustical measurements were taken using the B&K Dirac software package, from which ISO standard measures were also conducted. An e-sweep sine signal was emitted from at a height of 1.5-m Auratone 4-inch speaker aimed at an elevation angle of 0 °. Di-rectivity of characteristics for the Auratone 4-inch speaker was measured in anechoic chamber in National Taiwan University of Science and Technology. The speaker was placed on central axis at 2 m from the stage platform line was supported on a tripod at 1.5 m above the floor.

4.2   Results on the Field Verification

Figure 3 shows T30 (Reverberation time) taken the 0 ° azimuth angles with the speaker aimed frontally. The data from the original mode and from renovated mode are averaged. The difference of T30 between the original mode and renovated mode of classroom was 30 % decreases for frequency bands 31.5 Hz through 63 Hz. The value was close to 1.0 s at the renovated mode after the absorption material installed. There was a little difference be-tween the 2 Modes when evaluated the parameter of speech intelligibility (RASTI), which was close 0.65 corresponding with the subjective evaluation indicate (Good).

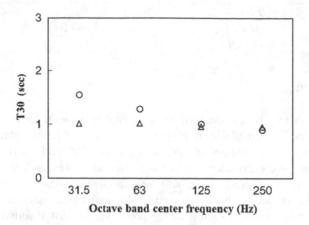

Fig. 3. Reverberation time (T30) as a function of frequency bands 31.5 Hz through 250 Hz comparing original mode (O) to renovated mode (△).

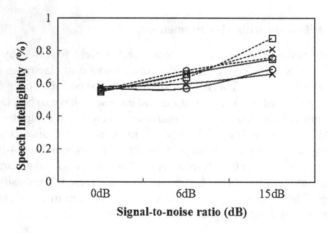

Fig. 4. Two groups reverberation time (0.55 s(—) and 1.15 s(____)) and three groups of signal to noise ratio (0 dB, +6 dB and +15 dB) combination of different sound field environment, explore the distribution of subjective test (speech intelligibility)by the three groups sound at low frequency band (125 Hz(O), 63 Hz(✗) and 50 Hz(□)).

Subjective experiment was carried out through headphones at acoustical laboratories of Hwa Hsia Institute of Technology, simulation the scene of fidelity was also be conducted which the scenario image of classroom of National Taitung University might been projected during the test. Surveying the questionnaire tests were evaluated which the content of words and sentences are meaningful. Three groups of reverberation time

(0.55 s, 0.85 s and 1.15 s) and three groups of signal to noise ratio (0 dB, +6 dB and +15 dB) combination of different sound field environment, explore the results of impacts by the three groups sound at low frequency band (125 Hz, 63 Hz and 50 Hz). It was found that the high value of signal to noise ratio (S /N ratio) may effectively enhance the results of subjective evaluation, however, the difference among combination of reverberation time (T30) is not significant difference (correlation coefficient r = 0.28). Test results on speech convolution with signal to noise ratio (+ 15 dB) and low frequency band (50 Hz) of hearing response in virtual classroom of the reverberation time of 0.55 s sound field may obtain the highly scores. See the Fig. 4.

Acknowledgements. The authors wish to thank Huang Kung Huang, Natural Acoustic for the helps of filed measurements, and Professor Wei-Hwa Chiang, Dep. of Architecture, National Taiwan University of Science and Technology the kindly assistances during the measurement phase.

References

1. Shield, B.M., Dockrell, J.E.: The effects of noise on children at school: a review. Build. Acoust. **10**(2), 97–116 (2003)
2. Maria, L.G., da Oiticica, R., Moura, M.B., da Silva, L.B.: Assessment of acoustics quality in a public school building-case report. The 2005 congress and exposition on noise control engineering, pp. 1792–1783 (2005)
3. Allen, J.B., Berkley, D.A.: Image method for efficiently simulating small-room acoustics. J. Acoust. Soc. Am. **65**(4), 943–950 (1979)
4. Lee, H., Lee, B.-H.: An efficient algorithm for the image model technique. Appl. Acoust. **24** (2), 87–115 (1988)
5. Chiang, W.H., Lin, W., Yu, Y.J.: Subjective assessments of acoustical environments for un-assisted traditional peking opera performances. J. Acoust. Soc. Am. **123**(5), 3097 (2008)
6. Slavin, I.I.: Industrielarm und Seine Bekampfung. Verlag Technik, Berlin (1960)
7. Hellbruck, J., Ellermeier, W.: Horen (2004)
8. Reichardt, W.: Grundlagen der technischen Akustik. Geest and Portig, Leipzig (1968)
9. Rau, C.: Einfluss tieffrequenter Str-orgerausche auf die Sprachverstandlichkeit. Diplomarbeit am Fraunhofer IBP, Stuttgart (2004)
10. DIN 18041: Horsamkeit in kleinen bis mittelgroBen Raumen (2004)
11. Chen, C., Chen, L., Lin, W.: A study on evaluation method of Chinese articulation standard of speech intelligibility for sound field in Taiwan. J. Archit. Soc. Tw **43**, 27–36 (2002)
12. Schroeder, M.R.: New method of measuring reverberation time. J. Acoust. Soc. Am. **37**(3), 409–412 (1965)

CanIHelp: A Platform for Inclusive Collaboration

Hugo Paredes[1]([⊠]), Hugo Fernandes[1], André Sousa[1], Renata Fortes[2],
Fernando Koch[3], Vitor Filipe[1], and João Barroso[1]

[1] INESC TEC and Universidade de Trás-os-Montes E Alto Douro,
Vila Real, Portugal
{hparedes,hugof,andresousa,vfilipe,jbarroso}@utad.pt
[2] Computer Science Department (SCC), University of Sao Paulo (USP),
São Carlos, SP, Brazil
renata@icmc.usp.br
[3] SAMSUNG Research Institute, Campinas, SP, Brazil
fernando.koch@samsung.com

Abstract. Technology plays a key role in daily life of people with special needs, being a mean of integration or even communication with society. By built up experience, we find that support tools play a crucial part in empowerment of persons with special needs and small advances may represent shifts and opportunities. The diversity of solutions and the need for dedicated hardware to each feature represents a barrier to its use, compromising the success of the solutions against, among others, problems of usability and scale. This paper aims to explore the concept of inclusive collaboration to enhance the mutual interaction and assistance. The proposed approach combines and generalizes the usage of human computation in a collaborative environment with assistive technologies creating redundancy and complementarity in the solutions provided, contributing to enhance the quality of life of people with special needs and the elderly. The CanIHelp platform is an embodiment of the concept as a result from an orchestrated model using mechanisms of collective intelligence through social inclusion initiatives. The platform features up for integrating assistive technologies, collaborative tools and multiple multimedia communication channels, accessible through multimodal interfaces for universal access. A discussion of the impacts of fostering collaboration and broadening from the research concepts to the societal impacts is presented. As final remarks a set of future research challenges and guidelines are identified.

Keywords: Accessibility · Collaboration · Inclusion · Interaction · Blind · Elderly · Mobile technologies · Wearable computing · Smart environments · Ambient assisted living

1 Introduction

Recent advances achieved in the fields of information and telecommunications technologies shape a paradigm change, characterised by a synergistic trend of

M. Antona and C. Stephanidis (Eds.): UAHCI 2015, Part II, LNCS 9176, pp. 474–483, 2015.
DOI: 10.1007/978-3-319-20681-3_45

basic supporting technologies, targeting a new generation of communication devices and access to information. The World Wide Web is currently an environment for sharing and collaboration, promoting the foundations of social life and mutual support. Proliferation of mobile devices and the increasingly widespread use of wearable technologies, accelerate the changes, anticipating innovative ways of interaction and the growing pervasiveness of technology in the daily live. Technology plays a key role in daily life of people with special needs, being a mean of integration or even communication with society. By built up experience [6,10,12,14,16], we find that support tools play a crucial part in empowerment of persons with special needs and small advances may represent shifts and opportunities. The diversity of solutions and the need for dedicated hardware to each feature represents a barrier to its use, compromising the success of the solutions against, among others, problems of usability and scale. Therefore, there has been the need for developing a comprehensive environment to support the daily life of people with special needs, which is not limited to the availability of technological tools, but combines technological support with people interaction, fostering the social integration, ensuring a higher level of trust and, consequently, autonomy and freedom to its users. This papers proposes and discuss the concept of inclusive collaboration as a possible solution to this problem.This concept advocates a model to boost the mutual interaction and assistance.

The proposed approach aims to combine and generalised the use of human computation in a collaborative environment with assistive technologies creating redundancy and complementarity in the solutions provided and contributing to enhance the quality of life of people with special needs and the elderly. The concept can be demonstrated in the scenario where an elderly helps the blind to recognise an expiration date of a product when the technological solutions cannot, or guiding a blind man in a museum with the reciprocity of the blind showing the exhibition to the bedridden elderly in a first-person view. The CanIHelp platform is an embodiment of the concept as a result from a orchestrated model using mechanisms of collective intelligence through social inclusion initiatives. The platform features up for integrating assistive technologies, collaborative tools and multiple multimedia communication channels, accessible through multimodal interfaces for universal access. For this, sets up a decision triangle of users, context, and devices, governed by a model of interface adaptation fed by a cross-platform meta-language for representation and integration of information. Additionally, strategies for user participation, based on their routines and taking advantage of the ubiquity of technology are introduced. The core of this proposal is the aim to foster collaboration, broadening from the research team to the society.

The future development of the CanIHelp platform has several research challenges to be discussed by the community. A key challenge is related to the privacy the trust of system users'. Somehow associated with this challenge is also the usability of the solution, which requires the use of specific hardware (or at least be able to provide the data required for the operation of the system). Another aspect that has raised in this discussion is the integration and interoperability

ability with different assistive solutions, benefiting the user experience and the richness of information provided and processed.

The structure of the remaining paper is as follows: Sect. 2 describes background and related work. In Sect. 3, the CanIHelp platform is introduced highlighting the concept of inclusive collaboration, and discussing its major requirements. The fourth section focuses on presenting some application scenarios of inclusive collaboration, using the CanIHelp Platform. A discussion is presented in Sect. 5, followed by some final remarks on Sect. 6.

2   Background

Assistive technologies based on computer vision can provide to the blind a remarkable autonomy. Recently, systems have been developed which use Computer Vision to extract information about the surrounding environment. The simplest vision systems to support the guidance of blind users extract this type of information analysing the characteristics of the objects present in the captured image, using classical image-processing techniques [4,8]. Other works explore a multi-sensory approach combining computer vision with location technologies to provide orientation and mobility to the blind [3,24]. These systems typically try to address the problems of user location, navigation and environment recognition in one global solution [2,11,15,20].

However, most of them fail in assisting pedestrian navigation, especially for the blind, because they try to adapt vehicle navigation techniques. Moreover, current image recognition systems are highly specialised constrained by the environment and require expensive expert knowledge restricting its usage. Human-powered services can provide a complementary help needed for filling these gaps.

According to ITU, in 2013, 2.7 billion people, almost 40 % of the world's population, were online. Moreover, the same source predicts 2.1 billion active mobile-broadband subscriptions by the end of 2013. These can represent a huge labour force if technological pervasive solutions can be embedded in their usual online activities. "The rise of crowdsourcing", triggered in 2006, awoke the companies and the research community for this opportunity. The crowdsourcing tenders feature a bidirectional strand when applied to social inclusion. As ageing societies require measures for preventing social isolation, the participation in crowdsourcing initiatives can be motivated by socialisation and avoid elder isolation. The "human computations" performed may be in the scope of social intervention, such as describing a square (as Times Square) with several advertising displays constantly changing, recognise certain obstacles which may pose a hazard to the blind, such as a dog of a dangerous race or even warn blind navigation systems for a car parked in a sidewalk. Moreover, collective intelligence can be explored in many ways as human computation, crowdsourcing and social computing.

Previous studies on human computation and crowdsourcing have been focused on complex cognitive tasks such as accurate text translation, social business process management, fast data collection through "human sensors", disease control, sentiment polarity analysis, image tagging, questions and answers, OCR correction, video and audio classification, city maintenance and civil protection, and digital repositories using citizen scientists' contributions [13].

Human computation can provide real-time information with extreme accuracy for real problems [9,19]. Collaborative accessibility improvement has been seen as a critical approach to improving the Web navigation experience for humans with special needs [22]. Friendsourcing is a way of having remote friends answer visual questions for the approximately 39 million of blind users worldwide [7]. Design issues, cognitive barriers, accessibility problems, and accurate metadata authoring are some variables that should be analysed including people with disabilities since the early stage of social computing development process [21]. Collaborative book scan and transcription by volunteers show a research possibility for improving blind users? experience (e.g., Bookshare[1]). Moreover, recent community services, such as Be My Eyes[2] allow volunteers all over the world to help blind people through a live video stream using their mobile phones.The mobile computing ecosystem presents several opportunities for crowd labour (work as a service on demand). Ubiquitous use of smartphones and tablets by nomadic and mobile humans in a diversified set of work settings include requirements that vary continuously. In this kind of settings, human crowds can act as cognitive operators performing computation tasks anytime and anywhere, sharing knowledge facts quickly and efficiently. Viz Wiz [5] is an application that lets blind users ask questions to the "crowd" or their friends. More applications of this nature are needed to support blind-world interaction.

WHO [18] defines active ageing as *"the process of optimising opportunities for health, participation and security in order to enhance quality of life as people age"*. Information and communication technologies (ICT) have been explored to assist and support active ageing. The new dimensions of communication made possible by ICT reduce the barriers, either physical or geographical, that often intrude among the elderly and their families [23]. This communication enables older people to participate in social life and thus avoiding loneliness and isolation [17].

3   The CanIHelp Platform

The CanIHelp platform is an embodiment of the concept of inclusive collaboration, promoting integration and mutual aid among people regardless of their special needs or limitations and adding human computing to the latest advances in information and computing technologies. The system results from a orchestrated model using mechanisms of collective intelligence through social inclusion initiatives. The platform features up for unifying assistive technology coupled with a set of collaborative tools associated with multiple multimedia communication channels (image, video, audio, text) and accessible through multimodal interfaces for universal access. It incorporates three real time operating modes:

---

[1] https://www.bookshare.org/.

[2] http://www.bemyeyes.org/.

automatic (assistive technologies); assisted (human computation); and manual (groupware). These three modes are complemented by an asynchronous mode, for platform refinement, evolution and learning. The automatic operating mode autonomously addresses the needs of users, helping them in most situations, using a high degree of "intelligence" of the supporting tools, enhanced with algorithms developed for specific situations. Using computer vision techniques the platform is provided with algorithms for automatic text reading, recognition of bar and QR codes (for example, medications or packaged foods), recognition of specific objects, for which it will be trained in advance, both in indoor and outdoor environments. The CanIHelp is also a digital assistant for its users, reminding them, for example, tasks that must necessarily perform as taking the medication. In this mode the platform still uses algorithms to search the Internet to provide additional information on a particular product or subject, which the user wishes to gain further knowledge.

In situations where the results obtained by assistive tools are not sufficiently accurate and reliable to help the user, the platform switches to the assisted mode, combining the mechanisms in use with collaboration and communication tools. The result of this switching is the direct mutual assistance between users and the possibility of the system learning with the results of human computation. Therefore, CanIHelp platform features skills of machine learning and advanced embedded technologies resulting from the interaction with users, particularly in the operating modes with alternative mechanisms (assisted and manual). Additionally, the system can learn and evolve based on the validation of the results of interactions with users in automatic mode, being made a post-validation using the same mechanisms of human computation. As an example, one or more users can validate asynchronously the result obtained in the recognition of an object. Thereby the recognition algorithms can have feedback and converge for optimizing results.

In everyday life there are situations in which technology plays only a facilitating role, promoting the person-person computer-mediated interaction. The CanIHelp platform in manual mode allows overcoming these communication barriers and intervening as mediator in this interaction, providing users the means and mechanisms tailored to their needs to overtake the obstacles.

The CanIHelp aims to be a platform that integrates the latest technologies, taking advantage of the latest developments, both in terms of use of mobile devices and wearable devices and sensors, such as miniature cameras (Google glasses, smartphones) and smart watches (Samsung Gears), and the digital platform, using the programming capabilities for cloud computing as well as integration of robust and efficient computer vision algorithms. Users' security and privacy issues are considered of utmost importance and treated as early as the design of CanIHelp. The participants must be registered in the platform and the interaction is only allowed between these persons previously selected and authorised by the users.

The interaction with the CanIHelp platform is available through a non-invasive natural interface, to allow a usage adapted to the characteristics and limitations of users without the need to change their habits and routines. The main purpose is that CanIHelp is a mutual assistance smart platform that fights digital divide making its users feeling perfectly integrated in the digital society. The user interface is one the system's major challenges. Current diversity of mechanisms and interaction devices allow exploring alternative modes of interaction adapted to each user and situation. Linked to this, is also the ubiquitous use of technology, introducing the contextual factor to the interface requirements. The purposes of the platform and its role of social integration, still require the interface to be universal access, ensuring any person to use and enjoy its inclusive capabilities.

4   Application Scenarios

The blind face major difficulties in their day-to-day needing constant help either in indoor environment with their activities of daily life, whether in outdoor environment, when they want to move from one location to another. On the other hand, older people have sometimes a lot of free time and can use it to help the blind in various day life activities, contributing to enhance their autonomy. These interactions can be computer mediated through the CanIHelp platform, where blind can apply for help and elderly reply to the aid requested and provide remote assistance. These groups represent a wide range of special needs given their physical (vision, hearing, mobility) and cognitive (memory deficits, depression, dementia) limitations. They also represent a universe of users for whom the platform is an asset both in their daily autonomy, either in social integration. The CanIHelp platform behaviour can be illustrated through the presentation of different contexts: the application scenarios. These scenarios allow the evaluation and discussion of the users requirements and their accessibility and usability needs. Moreover, aspects as the social integration and autonomy provided by te platform should also be evaluated, as well as the intrusion of the systems in the daily habits of their potential users. There are two application scenarios of the CanIHelp platform, one indoor and other outdoor, respectively: teaching cooking recipes; and visit to a museum.

The first application scenario is an indoor case combines the knowledge and experience of elderly and cultural heritage, with the inclusion and collaborative potential offered by CanIHelp platform. The cuisine features a culture and is passed from generation to generation. The making of a cooking recipe is linked to a set of activities associated with innate vision that become a challenge for a blind. This scenario can be seen as a distance class for assisted cooking, where an elderly prepares and teaches a particular recipe to a blind, assisting him/her in the work. Finding him/her in a known environment (at home), the scenario is familiar, allowing the blind recognising most of the locations and ensuring a high degree of autonomy. In turn it is intended that the scenario is not technologically intrusive to users, i.e., that the technology used is ubiquitous. Therefore, several possibilities are used to interact with the system using multiple devices and interfaces. Among the devices stands out the usage of a SmartTV (with custom application and using its videoconferencing voice recognition and gestures capabilities), tablets (Samsung Galaxy 10' as an alternative to SmartTV to increasing mobility) and wearable consumer devices, in particular the Samsung Gears (using various location sensing and object recognition by Near Field Communication – NFC) and Google Glasses (using the integrated camera to allow video streaming for the elderly in a first person perspective, and the elderly as option of augmented reality to provide contextual information in task execution). The interaction is driven to achieve of a set of tasks that serve as a demonstration and testing of the functionality of the CanIHelp platform. The system operates in automatic mode in the tasks of object and text recognition, such as the distinction between a package of flour and a packet of sugar, or reading the weight displayed by the scale. As defined, when the values are not trustworthy, the system switches to assisted mode and the blind is aided by the elderly. In the tasks for implementing the cooking recipe, the system works in manual mode, promoting direct interaction and socialisation between the blind and the elderly. To perform the tasks described CanIHelp object and text recognition assistive tools are used, complemented by collaboration tools, including video streaming (to allow the elderly to see and help the blind) and audio conferencing.

The second application scenario is a visit to a museum. The exterior scenario presents different challenges for the blind user, starting with the navigation and orientation in the environment. Meanwhile, to the elderly who find themselves in their homes, deprived of mobility the interaction is limited, and only the SmartTV is used taking all necessary support functions and communication with the blind. The blind uses the same devices used in the first scenario, i.e., wearable devices to meet the mobility needs. During the visit to the museum, the elderly using audio conferencing and video streaming tools guides the blind. The platform works mostly in manual mode, once during the visit and focusing on a specific piece, can switch to automatic or assisted mode to recognise a piece and provide additional information.

5   Discussion

The user interface and its usability are a major research topics in this domain and associated with the platform development. According to the specifications of the CanIHelp platform, users can interact with the system through contextual multimodal interfaces. The participation model and the natural integration of technology in the daily lives of users, by mechanisms for inclusive collaboration is a key research topic. The success of such a platform and model depends on the reciprocal benefits of both groups of users and their motivation to participate.

The assessment of users' needs proves to be a requirement. Currently, several studies reflect the requirements analysis and evaluation of user needs following different methodologies. One of the most common is the User Centred Design (UCD)[1]. Conceptually, it is clear that requirements analysis and specification of user requirements does not constitute a challenge to the scientific and technological level, existing, however, implications at the system design level.

The challenge itself is the system's ability to respond to needs and requirements that are different to different users and the context in which they are. To meet this challenge, it will be essential to define a model that allows adapting the interface and transforming data to meet user specific requirements and the context. The process can be defined based on a set of rules that take into account issues of context, availability of interaction modes and special needs of the user. If, from the point of view of the user there is the need to ensure the satisfaction of their needs, from the point of view of platform there is the requirement of ensuring the evolution and learning of the system, particularly in modes of assisted and manual operating modes. The ability to represent information so that it may be exchanged between the various processes of the platform and that it can be transformed and adapted to be communicated to the user is another of the technological challenges. This representation of the information should be cross-platform, ensuring interoperability between all components.

The collaborative capabilities of the system and its capacity for social inclusion also present some scientific and technological challenges that have been of interest to these communities. User participation and adherence to technology, as well as online socialising has been the subject of study in recent decades. Several possibilities have been explored, from the clarification of the role of the users in virtual environments and mechanisms of popularity, to gamification techniques. However, despite the numerous contributions, there is no model that can be considered a reference in this field. A natural approach should be followed trying to integrate the participation in daily activities of the user while not breaking their routines, and taking advantage of the ubiquity of technology.

6   Final Remarks

In the work presented in this paper we highlight the need to combine human computation and assistive technologies to enhance the daily life of the blind. We introduce the concept of inclusive collaboration to promote the interaction and assistance in a collaborative assisted environment. The CanIHelp platform is an embodiment of the concept introducing several research challenges that will be addressed in the implementation of the conceptual platform presented.

Therefore, the work presented intends to be a further step to the implementation of the concept of inclusive collaboration. Primarily it is expected that this paper contributes to a more solid and sustained knowledge about the state of the art in domains of assistive technologies for the blind and collaboration.

The paper proposes a conceptual platform for addressing inclusive collaboration. A major research challenge of its future implementation is the adaptation model and the meta-language for representing information. The adaptation model will allow CanIHelp platform to adapt by means of the user needs, context and interaction mechanisms and devices available. The integration between the platform components, data flow and representation freedom (transparency) will be ensured by the meta-language. This representation is also essential to enhance the mechanisms of human computation and machine learning of the platform.

Beyond this contribution, it is expected that the development of the CanIHelp platform produces results and impacts into related scientific areas, and related with the presented challenges, namely: universal access, social inclusion and collaboration.

Acknowledgements. This work is financed by the FCT – Fundação para a Ciência e a Tecnologia (Portuguese Foundation for Science and Technology) within project UID/EEA/50014 /2013 and research grants SFRH/BD/89759/2012 and SFRH/BD/87259/2012.

References

1. Abras, C., Maloney-Krichmar, D., Preece, J.: User-centered design. In: Bainbridge, W. (ed.) Encyclopedia of Human-Computer Interaction, vol. 37(4), pp. 445–456. Sage Publications, Thousand Oaks (2004)
2. Adao, T., Magalhaes, L., Fernandes, H., Paredes, H., Barroso, J.: Navigation module of blavigator prototype. In: World Automation Congress (WAC), pp. 1–6. IEEE (2012)
3. Alghamdi, S., van Schyndel, R., Khalil, I.: Accurate positioning using long range active rfid technology to assist visually impaired people. J. Netw. Comput. Appl. **41**, 135–147 (2014)
4. Ancuti, C., Ancuti, C., Bekaert, P.: Colenvison: color enhanced visual sonifier a polyphonic audio texture and salient scene analysis (2009)
5. Bigham, J.P., Jayant, C., Ji, H., Little, G., Miller, A., Miller, R.C., Miller, R., Tatarowicz, A., White, B., White, S., Yeh, T.: Vizwiz: nearly real-time answers to visual questions. In: Proceedings of the 23rd Annual ACM Symposium on User Interface Software and Technology, UIST 2010, pp. 333–342. ACM, New York (2010). http://doi.acm.org/10.1145/1866029.1866080
6. Bittar, T.J., Fortes, R.P., Lobato, L.L., Watanabe, W.M.: Web communication and interaction modeling using model-driven development. In: Proceedings of the 27th ACM International Conference on Design of Communication, pp. 193–198. ACM (2009)
7. Brady, E.L., Zhong, Y., Morris, M.R., Bigham, J.P.: Investigating the appropriateness of social network question asking as a resource for blind users. In: Proceedings of the 2013 Conference on Computer Supported Cooperative Work, CSCW 2013, pp. 1225–1236. ACM, New York (2013). http://doi.acm.org/10.1145/2441776.2441915
8. Capp, M., Picton, P.: The optophone: an electronic blind aid. Eng. Sci. Educ. J. **9**(3), 137–143 (2000)
9. Cardonha, C., Gallo, D., Avegliano, P., Herrmann, R., Koch, F., Borger, S.: A crowdsourcing platform for the construction of accessibility maps. In: Proceedings of the 10th International Cross-Disciplinary Conference on Web Accessibility, W4A 2013, pp. 26:1–26:4. ACM, New York (2013). http://doi.acm.org/10.1145/2461121.2461129
10. Du Buf, J.H., Barroso, J., Rodrigues, J.M., Paredes, H., Farrajota, M., Fern, H., José, J., Saleiro, T.M., Fernandes, H., Teixeira, V., et al.: The smartvision navigation prototype for blind users. In: JDCTA: International Journal of Digital Content Technology and Its Applications (2011)

11. Faria, J., Lopes, S., Fernandes, H., Martins, P., Barroso, J.: Electronic white cane for blind people navigation assistance. In: World Automation Congress (WAC), pp. 1–7. IEEE (2010)
12. Fernandes, H., Conceição, N., Paredes, H., Pereira, A., Araújo, P., Barroso, J.: Providing accessibility to blind people using gis. Univ. Access Inf. Soc. **11**(4), 399–407 (2012)
13. Fraternali, P., Castelletti, A., Soncini-Sessa, R., Ruiz, C.V., Rizzoli, A.E.: Putting humans in the loop: social computing for water resources management. Environ. Model. softw. **37**, 68–77 (2012)
14. Grillo, F.D.N., de Mattos Fortes, R.P.: Accessible modeling on the web: a case study. Procedia Comput. Sci. **27**, 460–470 (2014)
15. Kammoun, S., Parseihian, G., Gutierrez, O., Brilhault, A., Serpa, A., Raynal, M., Oriola, B., Macé, M.M., Auvray, M., Denis, M., et al.: Navigation and space perception assistance for the visually impaired: the navig project. Irbm **33**(2), 182–189 (2012)
16. Affonso de Lara, S.M., Watanabe, W.M., dos Santos, E.P.B., Fortes, R.P.: Improving wcag for elderly web accessibility. In: Proceedings of the 28th ACM International Conference on Design of Communication, pp. 175–182. ACM (2010)
17. Lö fqvist, C., Granbom, M., Himmelsbach, I., Iwarsson, S., Oswald, F., Haak, M.: Voices on relocation and aging in place in very old age-a complex and ambivalent matter **53(6)**, 919–927 (2013). http://dx.doi.org/10.1093/geront/gnt034
18. World Health Organization: Active ageing: a policy framework (2002)
19. Shigeno, K., Borger, S., Gallo, D., Herrmann, R., Molinaro, M., Cardonha, C., Koch, F., Avegliano, P.: Citizen sensing for collaborative construction of accessibility maps. In: Proceedings of the 10th International Cross-Disciplinary Conference on Web Accessibility, W4A 2013, pp. 24:1–24:2. ACM, New York (2013). http:// doi.acm.org/10.1145/2461121.2461153
20. Stephanidis, C.: The Universal Access Handbook. CRC Press, Boca Raton (2014)
21. Takagi, H., Kawanaka, S., Kobayashi, M., Itoh, T., Asakawa, C.: Social accessibility: achieving accessibility through collaborative metadata authoring. In: Proceedings of the 10th International ACM SIGACCESS Conference on Computers and accessibility, pp. 193–200. ACM (2008)
22. Takagi, H., Kawanaka, S., Kobayashi, M., Sato, D., Asakawa, C.: Collaborative web accessibility improvement: challenges and possibilities. In: Proceedings of the 11th International ACM SIGACCESS Conference on Computers and accessibility, pp. 195–202. ACM (2009)
23. Taylor, A.: Social media as a tool for inclusion. Retrieved from Homelessness Resource Center website: http://homeless.samhsa.gov/Resource/View.aspx (2011)
24. Wang, S., Pan, H., Zhang, C., Tian, Y.: Rgb-d image-based detection of stairs, pedestrian crosswalks and traffic signs. J. Vis. Commun. Image Represent. **25**(2), 263–272 (2014)

Smart Remote Control Design for Seniors

António Pereira[1,2(✉)], Fernando Silva[1], José Ribeiro[1],
Isabel Marcelino[1], and João Barroso[3,4]

[1] School of Technology and Management, Computer Science
and Communication Research Centre,
Polytechnic Institute of Leiria, Leiria, Portugal
{apereira, fernando. silva, jose. ribeiro,
isabel. marcelino}@ipleiria. pt
[2] Information and Communications Technologies Unit, INOV INESC
Innovation-Delegation Office at Leiria, Leiria, Portugal
[3] Universidade de Trás-os-Montes e Alto Douro, Quinta de Prados,
5000-801 Vila Real, Portugal
[4] INESC TEC (formerly INESC Porto), Porto, Portugal
jbarroso@utad. pt

Abstract. Technology is present in almost all aspects of our modern lives, and technological advances have been more and more prevalent. One would expect this to facilitate everybody's life, rendering common tasks more practical and easier to perform, but that is often not the case – at least not for the elderly. Older people have significant difficulties in using technological equipment due to the visual, physical, cognitive and hearing limitations associated with the natural aging process; these aspects must be taken into account if the intention is that of integrating technology in the lives of the elderly.

In order to improve the quality of life of the elderly, as well as to prevent their social isolation, a mobile device application was developed to act as an intelligent remote control. This mobile application deals with data from two different platforms that were previously developed for improving the quality of life of the senior population: HbbTV and +Social. The features built into this virtual remote control include the integration with the +Social platform, as well as a speech recognition mechanism, and the possibility of making and receiving video calls with an integrated contacts list.

A comprehensive study was carried out, focusing on recommendations and rules for graphical interfaces for the elderly, so as to allow equipping the application with adequate usability standards. The most relevant result was the definition of a list of guidelines used to steer the development of the interface. An investigation of mechanisms and technologies for enabling the implementation of the required functionalities was also carried out in order to define methodologies for freeing the user from the need of possessing any level of computer literacy.

A series of usability tests was also performed to validate the viability of the remote control application. These tests allowed assessing the quality of the application, especially concerning the Graphical User Interface, as well as to receive feedback from potential end users. Based on the data collected during the test phase we conclude that this product is useful and that it responds to a current need.

Keywords: Remote control · Elderly · Graphical user interface · Android

© Springer International Publishing Switzerland 2015
M. Antona and C. Stephanidis (Eds.): UAHCI 2015, Part II, LNCS 9176, pp. 484–495, 2015.
DOI: 10.1007/978-3-319-20681-3_46

1 Introduction

Statistics indicate a growing elderly population and this trend is expected to continue in the coming years [1]. It is also evident that older people are becoming increasingly isolated, both geographically and socially; many live alone in their homes and in need of specialized treatment.

It is necessary to find solutions to prevent feelings of isolation and insecurity, and technology can play a key role in this. The problem is that most existing technology is quite complex and is designed to achieve high levels of elegance and intuitiveness. For younger users, this is not problematic; however, for the elderly, these conditions may not be the most favorable and, in fact, hinder their use of technological devices.

The need to create systems adapted to this particular audience, which are simple and easy to use, is paramount; however, developing such a system can be challenging. It is necessary to find solutions that take into account all the limitations that the elderly may have, whether they are visual, cognitive or mobility-related, so that the final product is able to mitigate these limitations and provide a pleasant user experience.

+Social [2] is a multi-service platform aiming to provide the elderly population with a range of services to introduce technology in their daily routines, so as to improve their quality of life and to increase their sense of security – both their own and that of their caregivers. One of the services integrated in the +Social platform is a SmartBox responsible for the transmission of television channels to a monitor, which provides some advanced and customized features, including full integration with the platform. The contents provided by SmartBox must be controllable, so there is a need for developing a remote control that can, for practical purposes, transform this platform into a SmartTV.

The objective of this project is, therefore, the development of a Smart Remote Control that allows control of the SmartBox; to differentiate this remote control from traditional models, it will be designed as an Android-based touch-enabled device, and its development will take into account the common limitations of the elderly. In order to do so, a preliminary study was carried out on interfaces for the elderly to ensure that the developed product complies with existing standards.

This paper is organized as follows. The following section provides background on the +Social platform and the technologies involved in the implementation of this project, while overviewing and contextualizing related work. Section 3 details the architecture of the platform. The process of defining the set of guidelines gathered for steering the development of the Smart Remote Control is explained in Sect. 4, while Sect. 5 details the design specifications adopted and used for developing this device. In Sect. 6, the tests carried out for validation are detailed and discussed. The final section summarizes the main contributions of this paper and sets ground for future work.

2 Background and Related Work

The main objective of this project is the development of a Smart Remote Control with elderly targeted functionalities for integration in the myPhoneOnTV application [2]. The myPhoneOnTV application runs on a SmartBox developed in the context of the

+Social platform and incorporates the several features, such as the streaming of television channels, content display in full and reduced screen modes, access to the television channels' programming and phone contacts.

Fig. 1. The myPhoneOnTV application.

Other applications and solutions targeting an elderly audience already exist. TVKiosk [3] is a project that aims to simulate social interaction in order to avoid the isolation of the elderly. This platform uses a Virtual Private Ad Hoc Network so that information can be shared among the system's users, e.g. the elderly, their family and caregivers. The elderly typically interact with the television using a remote control designed for this purpose, while other participants may opt to use a computer.

The TVKiosk shares several similarities with the +Social platform; the crucial difference is the means of communication with the television set. Instead of using a traditional remote control, our proposal suggests the use of a Smart Remote Control command which supports more functionality and, therefore, offers greater possibilities in terms of accessibility and integration.

One of the great advantages of the Android operating system is the potential for customization, e.g. by means of custom-tailored application Launchers. Launchers are programs that aid the user in finding and using other applications, and also allow changing the graphical aspect of the system and the navigational approach employed. Several Launchers have been developed with the objectives of simplifying and adapting the operating system for usage by the elderly, such as Phonotto [4], Big-Launcher [5] and the Protege SOS Launcher [6]. These typically focus on the graphical aspect and on exposing the most important features of a smartphone so that its use is direct, simple and effective, but do not include remote control capabilities. There is, nevertheless, a wide variety of applications which enable Android smartphones to act as remote controls, such as Able Remote [7], Iris Remote [8] and the MEORemote [9]. However, these applications, had no proper graphical interface for the elderly, with their interfaces being too complex. To the best of our knowledge, no remote control applications exist for Android-based smartphones which target elderly users.

3 Architecture

This section depicts the architecture of the +Social platform, showcasing its distributed nature and the way in which its components are connected, and focusing on the way in which the Smart Remote Control developed will be integrated.

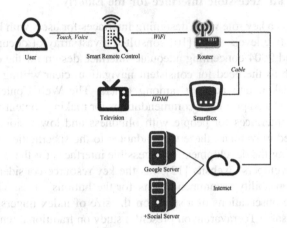

Fig. 2. General architecture.

The Smart Remote Control is the Android device in which the Remote Control application will run; the user interacts directly with this device by touch, voice and video captures. In general terms, its objectives are those of controlling the my-PhoneOnTV application and making/receiving calls. The Smart Remote Control needs to communicate with the Google server to use the voice recognition feature.

The SmartBox is where myPhoneOnTV application is executed; the television is the device used by the SmartBox to output graphical content. The +Social server hosts and provides a range of services related to +Social platform, including the IP Multi-media Subsystem for making video calls.

4 Interface Guidelines

The elderly are especially prone to having specific physical and cognitive difficulties that hinder their perception of graphical interfaces. Vision loss, in particular, impacts the elderly at different levels, including: the ability to concentrate on the tasks; perception and sensitivity to color; pupil reduction, meaning that more light is required and there is a reduced ability to adapt to changing light; visual field reduction; a decrease in sensitivity to contrast. Additionally, there are common diseases that may occur and further affect vision, the most common being cataracts and macular degeneration.

It is important to understand the main adaptations that must be made at the interface level, in order to target an elderly public. With this in mind, a set of guidelines for steering the development of graphical user interfaces for the elderly on Android-based touch-enabled devices was assembled.

4.1   Designing an Accessible Interface for the Elderly

Accessibility plays a key role when designing interfaces for users with limitations at the physical or cognitive levels. Arch [10] consulted a vast array of documents published between 2000 and 2004 concerning adequate interface design for the elderly; relevant conclusions, such as the need for consistent navigation, clear writing, and short texts with lists were taken into account, among others. The Web Content Accessibility Guidelines 2.0 [11] also provide recommendations for making content more accessible, specifically web interfaces for people with blindness and low vision, cognitive limitations and limited movement; these were adapted to the specificities of this particular project. Concerning the development of accessible interfaces for the Android platform, the "Android Developers" website [12] was the key resource considered; namely, the accessibility and usability recommendations for the buttons' sizes. These were complemented by the observations of a study on the size of index fingers [13].

In [14], Poonsak e Teeravarunyou present a study on traditional remote controls for television, with the objective of reaching a set of guidelines suitable for the elderly, comprising criteria ranging from form, function, layout and grouping to user feedback. Problems identified with traditional remote controls include: the command format (usually too big), the function keys (many of the elderly make mistakes when using remote controls for television by pressing the wrong button), the arrangement and number of buttons (in general, elderly patients need to memorize the layout of approximately 19 to 30 buttons) and the lack of button groups (older people require groupings of buttons in order to see and/or memorize them). It was also stressed that older people do not usually know the result produced by theirs actions when using a traditional remote control.

4.2   Interface Guidelines for a Smart Remote Control

The following list contains a set of guidelines which aim to provide guidance for developing interfaces and applications that target the elderly public, and are applicable in the context of the Android-based touch-enabled Smart Remote Control device proposed; they were compiled based on current literature on the subject, as detailed in the previous section.

1. Symbols and Images
   (a) Graphics should be relevant and not used as decoration.
   (b) Icons should be simple and should translate concrete meaning.
2. Text
   (a) Changing the position of the text should be avoided.
   (b) The main body of text should be written in *sentence case.*

(c) *Sans serif* fonts, such as Helvetica or Arial, should be used and font types with effects should be avoided.

(d) The font size should be between 12 and 14 points.

3. Navigation

(a) Deep hierarchies should be avoided.

(b) Ample time should be provided for reading information.

(c) The repetition of actions should be avoided.

4. Screens

(a) Scroll bars should be avoided.

(b) Only one screen should be exhibited at a time; overlapping screens should be avoided.

5. Content

(a) Irrelevant information should be omitted from the screen.

(b) Important information should be concentrated at the center of screen.

(c) The screen's layout and navigation should be simple, clear and consistent.

(d) The effort to recall should be reduced by showing as few options to the user as possible.

(e) It should be obvious which components are selectable (and vice versa).

6. Color

(a) Colors should be employed in a conservative manner.

(b) Pure white color should be avoided for the background.

(c) When switching screens, brightness should not change abruptly.

7. Contrast

(a) The contrast between the elements of the foreground and the background should be strong.

8. Touch

(a) Multi-touch interactions should be avoided.

9. Space and size of buttons

(a) Touch targets should have a width and height greater than 14 mm.

10. Remote Commands

(a) Group the buttons "Channel Up" and "Channel Down".

(b) Group the buttons "Volume Up" and "Volume Down".

11. Buttons Grouping

(a) For grouping buttons, the edge of the buttons should be used.

12. Feedback

(a) Feedback that eliminates the need to look at the remote control, such as a verbal response, should be preferred.

5   Interface Design

This section presents the design options followed in order to develop the Smart Remote Control. Firstly, the application requirements are presented. These were used in order to project and determine each screen of the remote control. With that in mind, several prototypes were built for each screen, which eventually lead to the final interface design. It is important to have in mind that the perception of the interface by the elderly is quite different from that of the general public. This is mainly related to the specifics of this particular age group.

5.1 Requirements

In order to better serve the purpose of the application, a list of functional and non-functional requirements was produced. The most important functional requirements are presented below.

1. The user must be able to: turn the SmartBox on and off; request an emergency call to the myPhoneOnTV application; change the channel on the remote my-PhoneOnTV application; change the volume; and use context buttons to interact with the myPhoneOnTV application by touching the corresponding action button.
2. The user may change the channel of the remote application myPhoneOnTV by voice command.
3. The user must be able to access his contacts list.
4. The user must be able to perform a video call to any of the contacts present in his contacts list.
5. The user must be able to accept or decline incoming video calls.

The following list presents the most important non-functional requirements of the Smart Remote Control application.

1. The application must be able to operate in Android devices that run Android 2.2 or above [12].
2. The application must run on devices that have a minimum screen size of 3.2 in. or above.
3. The target public of the application must be 65 or more.
4. The application must be ready to be operated by illiterate people.

5.2 Interface Design Specifications

When developing the interface, several aspects were taken into consideration for all of the screens. Almost all of the interface buttons use symbols that represent their actions, allowing for an easier association between the symbol and its function. There are textual descriptions for the symbols in the screen and for describing the function of a button or a group of buttons. For the text information, a sans serif font is used. The text size was also maximized; however, the size of the text may vary with the type of device that is running the application. Regarding the buttons, several measures were taken to assure the best possible compromise in size and spacing. Despite the fact that the size of the buttons depends on the size of the device, the interface is designed for assuring that each button has at least 14 mm in height and width. The size of the buttons is also maximized in order to fit the available screen size. The spacing between buttons is never smaller than 1.5 mm, regardless of the size of the device. The Android guidelines

[15] for defining button sizes and spacing according to the screen size of the device were also adopted. The shape of the buttons is rectangular, allowing a better use of the available space without compromising usability. By touching any button of the application, the device produces three different feedback signals: a small sound, a vibration and a change in the visual aspect of the button. This allows the user to perceive that an action is being performed.

Specifically with the elderly in mind, some of the design guidelines for touch-based interfaces for the elderly [16] were taken into consideration, namely those regarding symbols and images, text, navigation, content, colors and contrast, touch, buttons spacing and size, grouping buttons and feedback.

With the application requirements in mind, five different screens were built for operating the remote control. The specifications for each one of the screens are presented next.

Remote Control Main Screen. This screen contains all of the functionalities that allow for controlling the remote myPhoneOnTV application and that provide access to the contacts list. It is also on this screen that it is possible to use voice recognition for remotely operating the myPhoneOnTV application. Figure 3 shows the final version of this screen. The top four buttons allow the existing TV channels in myPhoneOnTV to be changed. The group "CANAL" allows the TV channel number to be changed (zapping). In the same manner, the "VOLUME" group allows the sound volume to be increased or decreased. There is a group of four buttons with different colors and no images that are called "service buttons". These will depend on different services that can or not be active through the myPhoneOnTV application. The final group of buttons of the screen allows the user to make a video call through the contact list (first button), to make an emergency call to the myPhoneOnTV application (second button), to activate the voice control of the myPhoneOnTV application (third button), and the last button allows to turn off the SmartBox device (see Figs. 2 and 3).

Contact List Screen. This screen shows a contacts list. It also allows a video call to be made to any of the contacts present at the list. The navigation scheme of the contact list is organized in page style. This screen also allows returning to the remote control main screen.

Fig. 3. Remote control main screen

Outgoing Video Call Screen. This screen is used whenever a user starts a video call from the contact list screen. It shows the name and photo of the contact and it allows the current call to be turned off. This screen switches to the Video Call screen when the contact answers the call, or switches to the Contact List screen if the call is refused or unanswered.

Incoming Video Call Screen. Whenever the user is requested to a video call, this screen is showed by the application. The screen shows the name and photo of the incoming call contact, and it allows the call to be received by redirecting the user to the Video Call screen, or to reject the call by navigating to the previous screen.

Video Call Screen. This screen appears whenever a video call is established. It shows the name and the video feed of the other user that is communicating through the system in real time. It also allows the current call to be cancelled.

6   Testing and Results

This section presents the usability tests made to the Smart Remote Control application. It starts by presenting the users testing group, as well as with the tests that were used to validate the application's ease of use. After that, the result analysis is done, where the strengths and weaknesses are identified, including some observations made by the test group.

6.1   Test Scenario

In order to test the usability of the application, a group of senior people was selected to evaluate it. This group was composed of seven different users from a nursing home in Memória County, in Portugal, with ages between 77 and 91, and an average of 83 years old. All of the users were literate.

A task guide for performing when testing the Smart Remote Control was made, as well as an evaluation questionnaire for registering the tasks' results (errors, execution times and the ability to perform the task) and users' opinions. These were provided to the test group after a brief explanation on how to operate the Smart Remote Control.

Table 1 presents the usability tests task guide. Each task represents one action that the remote control can perform for controlling the myPhoneOnTV application. The questionnaire used for obtaining the opinion and evaluating the satisfaction of the users with the application is presented in Table 2.

6.2   Test Results

Figure 4 shows the results of the average execution time for the tasks presented in Table 1. We focus on the analysis of the tasks that present higher execution times. Task number 4 proved to be a challenge to the users. This task is related to the content currently available on the myPhoneOnTV, therefore the users were looking for a symbol on the remote control, but that symbol was only present on the TV display. Even though tasks 5 to 7 make use of the same strategy, the users were faster at these

Table 1. Usability tests task guide

Number	Task
1	Change to the next TV channel
2	Lower the volume of the TV broadcast
3	Change to the previous TV channel
4	Change to full screen (yellow context button)
5	Access the TV guide (green context button)
6	Answer incoming call (red context button)
7	List contacts (blue context button)
8	Press emergency button
9	Change to channel "SIC"
10	Change to channel "RTP1" using voice control
11	Change to channel "RTP2" using voice control
12	Perform a video call to a contact
13	Accept an incoming call
14	Stop a video call
15	Turn TV off

Table 2. Evaluation questionaire

Number	Question
1	The vibration on touch, was it useful?
2	The sound on touch, was it useful?
3	Do you prefer the direct channel access buttons over the zapping buttons?
4	Do you think that the remote control would be useful in your daily life?
5	Would you use the voice commands present in the remote control?
6	Would you change anything in the product?
7	Would you use the product for video calls?
8	Would you use the product again in the future?

operations, since they were now aware of that particularity of the system. Tasks 10 and 11 were the ones where the users needed more time to perform the required operations. This was mainly due to two reasons: difficulty in understanding how the voice command operates and errors in audio recognition. Nevertheless, several of the tasks present an execution time of less than 7 s, which appears to be very reasonable, considering that this was the first contact of the test group with the application.

Figure 5 presents the results of the questionnaire previously shown on Table 2. The Smart Remote Control received a very positive evaluation from the test group. The whole test group found that the remote control is useful in their daily life and it would use it again in the future. Questions 5 and 7 were mainly evaluated in a negative way. The majority of the test group thinks that the voice recognition system is not practical and they would rather use other tools that they are more familiar with for doing video calls (e.g., Skype or Google Hangouts). Concerning question 6, when the users who answered "yes" were asked what they would change on the remote, all of them focused on the fact that the context buttons of the remote should use a subtitle or symbol to indicate their function, instead of only showing it on the television's display.

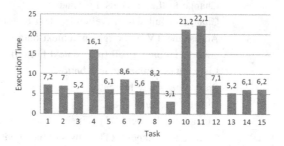

Fig. 4. Average execution times for the tasks presented in Table 1

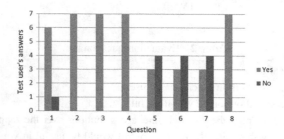

Fig. 5. Test user's answers to the questionnaire presented in Table 2

7 Conclusions and Future Work

The Smart Remote Control for Seniors is an Android application that aims to allow the elderly to control the myPhoneOnTV application. It uses data from two different platforms that were previously developed for improving the quality of life of the senior population: HbbTV and +Social. This work focuses on the development and evaluation of a user interface for the senior population, which has particular characteristics and needs. A study of the existing literature on this subject was carried out to support the development of the interface. In addition, a prototype of the Smart Remote Control was built and tested in a nursing home in order to draw conclusions and gather ideas for future developments.

There was very positive feedback from the test group, namely regarding the following aspects: the pleasant appearance of the graphic user interface; the use of vibration and sound feedback when touching the command buttons; the usefulness of the system and the desire to use it again in the future; and the usefulness of the buttons that enable direct access to television channels. It was nevertheless possible to observe that some of the execution times were excessively long, mainly due to two distinct situations: the use of context dependent buttons on the remote control and the use of the voice commands for controlling the remote. These are two major issues that should be worthy of our attention in the future.

Although some improvements are required to optimize the interface, we believe that this product is useful and that it responds to a current necessity of the elderly and, in particular, to the users of the myPhoneOnTV application.

References

1. RAND Corporation: Preparing for an Aging World. http://www.rand.org/pubs/research_briefs/RB5058/index1.html
2. Correia, L., Costa, N., Pereira, A.: Fighting elders' social and technological exclusion: the TV based approach. In: Ramos, C., Novais, P., Nihan, C.E., Rodríguez, J.M.C. (eds.) Advances in Intelligent Systems and Computing. AISC, vol. 291, pp. 209–216. Springer, Heidelberg (2014)
3. Steenhuyse, M., Hoebeke, J., Ackaert, A., Moerman, I., Demeester, P.: TV-kiosk: an open and extensible platform for the wellbeing of an ageing population. In: Rautiainen, M., Korhonen, T., Mutafungwa, E., Ovaska, E., Katasonov, A., Evesti, A., Ailisto, H., Quigley, A., Häkkilä, J., Milic-Frayling, N., Riekki, J. (eds.) GPC 2011. LNCS, vol. 7096, pp. 54–63. Springer, Heidelberg (2012)
4. Phonotto. http://www.phonotto.com/
5. BigLauncher. http://biglauncher.com/
6. Protege Launcher SOS. https://play.google.com/store/apps/details?id=pt.protegeipl.launcher
7. Able Remote. http://ableremote.com/
8. Iris Remote. https://play.google.com/store/apps/details?id=pt.zon.remote
9. Meo Remote. https://play.google.com/store/apps/details?id=pt.ptinovacao.iad.meoremote
10. Arch, A.: Web Accessibility for Older Users: A Literature Review. W3C Working Draft, W3C (2008)
11. Caldwell, B., Cooper, M., Reid, L.G., Vanderheiden, G., Chisholm, W., Slatin, J., White, J.: Web Content Accessibility Guidelines (WCAG) 2.0. W3C Recommendation, W3C (2008)
12. Android Developers. http://developer.android.com/index.html
13. Design Brother: Touch screen design: the ideal button size. http://designbrother.com/2013/04/29/touch-screen-design-the-ideal-button-size/
14. Poonsak, T., Teeravarunyou, S.: Accessibility design guideline for the elderly: a case study of TV remote control. In: The Eighth Pan-Pacific Conference on Occupational Ergonomics (PPCOE 2007), Bangkok, Thailand (2007)
15. Android Developers: Supporting Multiple Screens. http://developer.android.com/guide/practices/screens_support.html
16. Boustani, S.: Designing Touch-Based Interfaces for the Elderly. University of Sydney, Sydney (2010)

An IR View on Lifelogging

Till Plumbaum[(⊠)] and Sahin Albayrak

Technische Universität Berlin, Berlin, Germany
{till, sahin}@dai-lab.de

Abstract. Lifelogging has recently found its way into public consciousness. More and more devices, sensors and applications become available for the end-user. Data is collected from a whole lot of different sensors. The wealth of data is overwhelming. Suddenly, we know more about a single user than ever before. This data allows us to approach new use cases allowing applications to be more useful to a user then previously possible. In this paper, we want to discuss what implications, challenges and opportunities arise for research in the area of information retrieval (IR). We present use cases for lifelogging that go beyond the Quantified Self use case. We also present an application that collects various lifelogging data and discuss what of the presented use cases is feasible with the given data.

Keywords: Lifelogging · Information retrieval · Quantified self

1 Introduction

Lifelogging has recently found its way into public consciousness. More and more devices, sensors and applications become available for the end-user. In this paper, we want to discuss what implications, challenges and opportunities arise for research in the area of information retrieval (IR). Lifelogging is the process of automatically capturing and storing every possible piece of information about a person's life. A good definition comes from Dodge and Kitchin [1]. They define lifelogging as "…a form of pervasive computing consisting of a unified digital record of the totality of an individual's experiences, captured multimodally through digital sensors and stored permanently as a personal multimedia archive". Furthermore, they define the goal of lifelogging to have "…a record of the past that includes every action, every event, every conversation, every material expression of an individual's life; all events will be accessible at a future date because a life-log will be a searchable and recallable archive". The amount of collected data differs depending on the used sensors. An Autographer[1] camera is making up to 1 million photos every day, which sums up to 480 GB per year per person. This is only one example for data collection. Data is collected from a whole lot of different sensors. Activity tracking for instance is possible using Fitbit One[2], Withings Pulse[3] or various other tracking devices. There are numerous Apps like Moves[4] or the Sony LifeLog app

---

[1] http://autographer.com/.
[2] http://www.fitbit.com/one.
[3] http://www.withings.com/withings-pulse.html.
[4] https://www.moves-app.com.

© Springer International Publishing Switzerland 2015
M. Antona and C. Stephanidis (Eds.): UAHCI 2015, Part II, LNCS 9176, pp. 496–504, 2015.
DOI: 10.1007/978-3-319-20681-3_47

that are tracking what you did and where you've been. The wealth of data is overwhelming. Suddenly, we know more about a single user than ever before. Instead of only getting information such as ratings for items, we know the context a user made a decision in. This data allows us to approach new use cases allowing applications to be more useful to a user then previously possible.

The paper is structured as followed: In the following we will outline the general application areas of lifelogging, the use cases for lifelogging. Based on this, we will discuss in-depth lifelogging and how information retrieval can support lifelogging. Therefore, we present a web application, DailyMe, developed at our university that allows connecting different tracking applications and get a personal diary for every day. We describe the data collected and outline what can be done and what is still a problem for an IR system. Based on this we will discuss what needs to be done to enable IR systems to make full use of lifelogging data and enable users to benefit from it.

2 Use Cases for Lifelogging

While a lot of current discussions center around what is technically possible, we want to examine feasible use cases for lifelogging. In their book Total Recall, Bell and Gemmell, identify four main areas for lifelogging use cases:

- Work
- Health
- Learning
- Everyday life (social)

Correspondingly, Sellen and Whittaker describe five use cases where lifelogs can be beneficial, the so-called 5 Rs:

- Recollecting: Recalling a specific moment in life (episodic memory).
- Reminiscing: Recalling a specific moment for emotional or sentimental reason, this can be seen as a special case of Recollecting.
- Retrieving: Retrieve a previously encountered digital item or information, such as documents, email, or Web pages.
- Reflecting: A more abstract representation of personal data to facilitate reflection on Reviewing of, past experience.
- Remembering intentions: Remember to do, e.g. remembering to show up for appointments.

These use cases come along with some challenges for IR, which are described in the book LifeLogging: Personal Big Data by Gurrin et al.:

- Data gathering: Data collection is time consuming and requires different sensors and manual effort. Also, the data is private and thus only data from the user itself can be used.
- Data analysis: Understanding data from heterogeneous sources, e.g., multimedia, text and sensors and extract meaning out of it (semantic extraction/semantic organization).

- Search & retrieval: The heterogeneous data makes searching for information more complicated. We have not well understood retrieval requirements and use-cases coming with lifelogging. Instead of using text queries to find documents, we can now find for instance events based on context information we remember.
- Evaluation: Datasets seem be a problem. As the data is private by nature, public datasets will be hard to get.
- Summarization and data mining: Pre-step to a good and helpful presentation allowing the user to take advantage of the collected data. Supporting quantified-self style analysis and narrative/story-telling presentation.
- User interaction and presentation: Lifelogging will produce a big amount of data. We need to define likely usage scenarios, potentially omnipresent and even how to support query formulation for many of the use-cases. This is currently poorly understood.

All of these different use cases and challenges will be problems for some time to come. A lot of effort is already put into some of these challenges for certain use cases but we are just at the beginning and it is exciting what will come. Admittedly, one major real world challenge is filtering out noisy or meaningless data. Data collected by an Autographer camera so far produced mostly pictures (the ones not blurred) showing a person during daily activities like driving, drinking coffee and sitting in front of a computer.

Driving   Getting Coffee   Working

What also needs to be remembered is that the data belongs to the user. This implies that services in the context of lifelogging should leave the user in full control over the data. The user must be able to decide what the data is used for. The full data must be accessible, e.g., by an API. And of course, the user must be allowed to delete the data.

3 Lifelogging in the Field

In this section, we will discuss lifelogging applications and their usage. We concentrate on the use cases presented by Sellen and Whitaker – the 5 Rs. We argue that a person itself mainly drives the motivation for lifelogging, and especially the 5 Rs. While there are approaches by companies for equipping their customers, e.g. car insurances tracking the driving behavior of their customers, these approaches are restricted to a limited number of people. The main driver for lifelogging today is still the idea to gain information about oneself and learn from this data. We also argue that the uses cases presented by Bell and Gemell are covered by the 5 Rs as the approach from an IR view is similar, only the context differs. 'Recollecting' for example is relevant for work, learning and the every day life. A user wants to revisit a certain moment to either remember the outcome of a work discussion, an example from a school lesson or an event with friends. From an IR view, the task is similar. Based on the available information, such as people who were also there, a IR system allows to search for this data. In the next section, we present a web application, DailyMe, developed at our university that allows connecting different tracking applications, collecting data and get a personal diary for every day.

3.1 DailyMe – A Daily Diary

DailyMe is a web-based application, which allows connecting external applications from Fitbit, Foursquare, Flickr and Moves and also allows making notes and tags. By using the external applications, we come close to the general lifelogging goal that the daily behavior is tracked without much manual assistance. It allows us to track what we did, where we have been and collects photos taken. Figure 1 shows the start page of DailyMe where the user gets an overview of the activities of the last 7 days compared to the overall statistics.

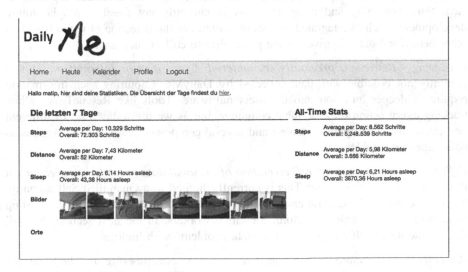

Fig. 1. Dailyme - startpage showing the statistics for the last 7 days and the overall statistics

Figure 2 shows the overview of a single day of a typical DailyMe user. In the upper left, it shows the type of activities and the proportional distribution for the day. Next to it, it shows a map view visualizing the places a user has visited and the routes the user has taken that day. Below, the photos taken on that day are shown, followed by an overview of the places. This information describes the day of the user in form of behavioral and location based patterns. DailyMe also collects data about the sleep duration and efficiency and the users' weight. This information is collected automatically using external apps. To better describe the day, or to allow users to make notes about memorable events not captured before, DailyMe also allows tagging the day or writing down notes.

This describes the data foundation of DailyMe and is similar to other applications such as Day One. In the next section, we revisit the 5 Rs and discuss how they can be approached with the currently available data based on the DailyMe scenario.

3.2   The 5 Rs and DailyMe

Recollecting - Recalling a specific moment in life: With the data available, we can search for places and with the right image processing capacity, e.g. detecting persons in a picture, we can also search for multimedia information. By adding context information such as weather data a basis for searching and retrieving a specific moment in life is possible.

Reminiscing - Recalling a specific moment for emotional or sentimental reason: This use case is currently only possible when the user enters emotions or sentiments by hand. As stated in the beginning, the goal for lifelogging is the automatic capturing of data, thus, collecting and using emotions is currently not feasible. Maybe future developments such as integrated sensors in watches or the detection of mood based on other behavioral data [7] gives us the possibility to collect such data.

Retrieving - Retrieve a previously encountered digital item or information: This is currently not possible with data collected by DailyMe. Capturing such information requires a deeper intrusion into the users hardware. Tools like RescueTime[5] allow tracking every action on a personal computer, but as we use today a set of different devices such as smartphones, tablets and several computers, we face a heterogeneous data collection problem.

Reflecting - A more abstract representation of personal data to facilitate reflection on Reviewing of past experience: This is currently limited to a Quantified Self scenario. Thus, we can learn behavioral patterns and remind users to e.g. walk more or stand up from time to time, which is helpful for office workers. In the next section, we will discuss the data itself and present the "Data Problem" with lifelogs.

Remembering intentions - Remember to do, e.g. remembering to show up for appointments: A main benefit for users would be an IR system that is capable to learn from past behavior and alert users to do something, e.g. remember the user to pick up the kid after soccer. The problem with the currently collectable data is, that is does not allow us to do sophisticated forecasts. What is achievable is that we predict normal paths for users based on daily routines. This means that we can forecast the way to

---

[5] https://www.rescuetime.com.

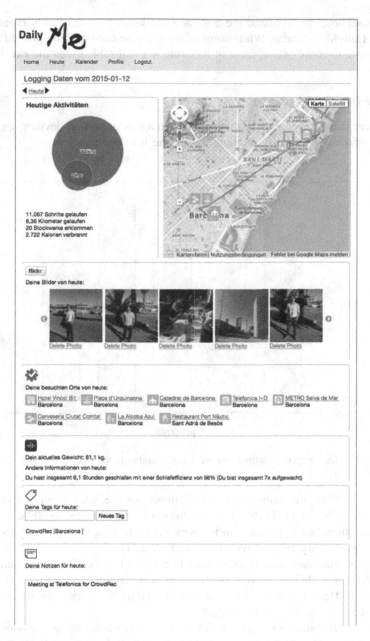

Fig. 2. DailyMe - view for a single day - showing the type of activities, places visited, photos, sleep and weight information, tags and text.

work for a user, based on typical patterns on weekdays. This is used for instance by Google Now and on Apple iOS to give users information about their way to work. But if the users have other destinations, we cannot predict or forecast this.

In this section, we discussed the 5 Rs and discussed their feasibility based on the presented DailyMe scenario. While some of the use case can be accomplished with the given sensors, to some extent, most of them are not realizable given the existing data.

3.3   The Data Problem

With the currently collectable data using external applications and devices, we still get a limited amount of information about a user and his intentions.

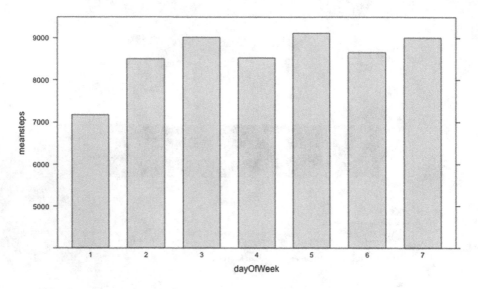

Fig. 3. Mean step distribution per weekday. Sunday is the first day of the week

Figure 3 shows the normal step distribution per weekday from a typical user working in an office at TU Berlin. The distribution is computed using 600 days of data. We see that there are only small differences between most days of the week. Only Sunday seems to varying a bit with fewer steps than usual.

We observe the same data distribution when we look at the sleeping patterns of the same user, see Fig. 4. The sleep is almost a uniform distribution with a bit more sleep on Saturdays. The efficiency, which takes into account how often the users' sleep is interrupted, is also uniformly distributed.

From an information retrieval point of view, this data holds not many opportunities to detect and learn different intentions of the user. We can learn typical patterns like the users' way to way to work, but not much more. Especially when we take into account that the 5 Rs are closely related to sentiments and emotions, we observe a lack of data and information.

This becomes even more visible when we visualize the data as points with distances describing the dissimilarities between the points, see Cox et al. and Gower [5, 6]. We see that most points are similar to each other, see Fig. 5. Only few outlier exist, which

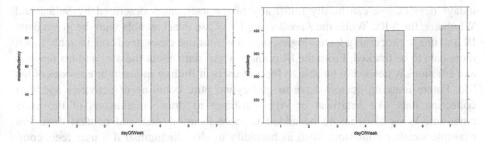

Fig. 4. Mean distribution of the sleep efficiency and the minutes of sleep per weekday. Sunday is the first day of the week.

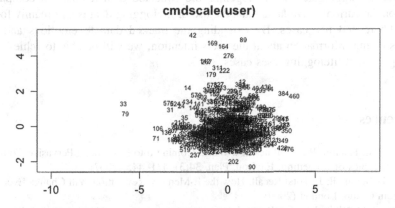

Fig. 5. Data points of the example user. Each point describes a day

are days with very few sleep (points above the point cloud), and days with very few steps (left of the cloud).

We can detect these outliers and data-wise understand why their outliers. But we cannot detect or understand the reason from the data. We still need information from the user, e.g. tagging or describing the reason manually. Another real world problem we face is the tracking of users with different devices and comparing their behavior. If we for instance compare results from users tracking with a FitBit One compared to a Jawbone Up[6] bracelet, results for steps differ around 10–15 percent.

4   Conclusion

In this paper, we described lifelogging use cases that go beyond the ideas of Quantified Self and connected these use cases to a real world application, DailyMe, which aggregates and collects different types of data from users. What we see is that with

---

[6] https://jawbone.com/up.

todays devices, we can hardly fulfill any of the uses cases described by Sellen and Whittaker, the 5 Rs. While the *Recollecting* Use Case is achievable with the given data, IR and image processing technologies, the other four use cases need considerably much more data to be tracked. From the IR point of view, data about the user and his feelings and emotions is needed to be able to support users in finding moment or episodes of his life. Future tracking devices have to go beyond pure counting of activities and start collecting data like heartbeat or skin resistance to draw conclusions of the users emotions. What also has to be added is more location data and context data. For example weather conditions such as humidity to also distinguish if a user feels comfortable because of the activity he is doing or of the weather condition.

Beside the missing data, the problem of heterogeneous data becomes more urgent in the near future. As more and more devices become available, lifelogging applications need to aggregate and homogenize the collected data to make it comparable. Based on the currently available data, the use of lifelogging data is still mainly focused on health related use cases. By extending the tracked data to emotions and other features giving information about the users intention, we will be able to achieve more of the presented lifelogging uses cases.

References

1. Dodge, M., Kitchin, R.: 'Outlines of a World Coming into Existence': Pervasive Computing and the Ethics of Forgetting. Environ. Plan. **34**(3), 431–445 (2007)
2. Bell, G., Gemmell, J.: Total Recall: How the E-Memory Revolution Will Change Everything. Penguin Group, London (2009)
3. Sellen, A.J., Whittaker, S.: Beyond total capture: a constructive critique of lifelogging. Commun. ACM **53**(5), 70–77 (2010)
4. Gurrin, C., Smeaton, A.F., Doherty, A.R.: Lifelogging: personal big data. Found. Trends Inf. Retrieval **8**(1), 1–125 (2014)
5. Cox, T.F., Cox, M.A.A.: Multidimensional Scaling, 2nd edn. Chapman and Hall, London (2001)
6. Gower, J.C.: Some distance properties of latent root and vector methods used in multivariate analysis. Biometrika **53**, 325–328 (1966)
7. Wang, R., Chen, F., Chen, Z., Li, T., Harari, G., Tignor, S., Zhou, X., Ben-Zeev, D., Campbell, A.T.: StudentLife: assessing mental health, academic performance and behavioral trends of college students using smartphones. In: Proceedings of the 2014 ACM UbiComp 2014, pp. 3–14 (2014)

Biologically Inspired Vision for Human-Robot Interaction

Mario Saleiro[(✉)], Miguel Farrajota, Kasim Terzić, Sai Krishna,
João M.F. Rodrigues, and J.M. Hans du Buf

Vision Laboratory, LARSyS, University of the Algarve, 8005-139 Faro, Portugal
{masaleiro,mafarrajota,kterzic,jrodrig,dubuf}@ualg.pt,
saikrishnap2003@gmail.com

Abstract. Human-robot interaction is an interdisciplinary research area
that is becoming more and more relevant as robots start to enter our
homes, workplaces, schools, etc. In order to navigate safely among us,
robots must be able to understand human behavior, to communicate,
and to interpret instructions from humans, either by recognizing their
speech or by understanding their body movements and gestures. We
present a biologically inspired vision system for human-robot interaction
which integrates several components: visual saliency, stereo vision, face
and hand detection and gesture recognition. Visual saliency is computed
using color, motion and disparity. Both the stereo vision and gesture
recognition components are based on keypoints coded by means of cortical V1 simple, complex and end-stopped cells. Hand and face detection
is achieved by using a linear SVM classifier. The system was tested on a
child-sized robot.

Keywords: Hand gestures · Human-robot interaction · Biological
framework

1 Introduction

It is expected that, in the future, robots will employ a growing number of roles
in society. Currently robots are mainly used in factory automation, but they
are also deployed in service applications, medical assistance [1], schools [2] and
entertainment, among other application fields. As they start to roam among us,
there will be a need to interact with them in easy and natural ways. Human-
robot interaction (HRI) research is therefore attracting more and more attention.
Researchers are trying to develop new, easy and natural ways of programming
robots, either by teaching them by manipulating a robot's hardware manually [3]
or by creating programming interfaces so simple that even children can use them
at school [2]. However, programming a robot still requires some skill that must
be learned. In a world where robots navigate next to us, it will be necessary to be
possible to interact with them effortlessly, using voice commands or gestures. In
an ideal situation, robots should even be able to perceive some of our intentions
by analysing the motions of our body.

© Springer International Publishing Switzerland 2015
M. Antona and C. Stephanidis (Eds.): UAHCI 2015, Part II, LNCS 9176, pp. 505–517, 2015.
DOI: 10.1007/978-3-319-20681-3_48

The analysis and recognition of static hand gestures for HRI has been an interesting research area for some time and there have been many approaches. Some are intrusive, requiring the user to use specially designed gloves [4], while others are less intrusive, but still require specific hardware like Leap Motion [5] or Microsoft Kinect [6]. Other approaches rely on simple cameras and computer vision methods. A simple solution can be based on skin color segmentation and matching of previously stored gesture templates [7]. More complicated is to extract the skeleton of the hand [8] and use this for matching. For dynamic gestures there are methods that perform tracking and motion detection using sequences of stereo color frames [9], or gestures are characterized by using global properties of trajectories described by a set of keypoints [10]. Although many solutions may work quite well for a specific type of application, they are too simple for more complex gestures. In addition, they are often limited by fixed hardware devices or lighting conditions. In order to use gesture analysis and recognition for human-robot interaction, a system that is able to work under most lighting conditions and almost anywhere is needed.

In our previous work [7] we developed a biological and real-time framework for detecting and tracking both hand and head gestures. In this paper we present an extension of the system and also add new features to improve the system for human-robot interaction. The previously developed framework is based on multi-scale keypoints detected by means of models of cortical end-stopped cells [11,12]. We have improved the previous annotation of keypoints by using a fast binary descriptor that allows for fast and robust matching. We also added a combined disparity and motion saliency process so that the robot can initially focus on the hands of the user and track them. Gesture recognition is performed by matching the descriptors of the detected keypoints with the descriptors of previously stored templates. We also integrated a head and hand detector based on a linear SVM classifier.

The robot uses stereo vision for navigation, which also allows it to detect obstacles. Every time it finds an obstacle in front of it, it looks up and searches for the user's head in order to start the interaction. The robot attempts to center its own camera on the user's face, and then starts performing hand detection and gesture recognition. To detect a face/hand we employ a modified HOG (Histogram of Oriented Gradients) descriptor combined with responses of complex cells and a linear SVM to code the shape. The face and hand detectors were trained and evaluated on the FaceScrub dataset [13] and the Oxford hand dataset [14], respectively. The developed HRI system does not need any prior calibration and has been designed to run in real time.

2   Biologically Inspired HRI System

In this section we describe all components of the developed system: (a) keypoint descriptor, (b) stereo vision for navigation and obstacle detection, (c) visual saliency, (d) face and hand detection, and finally (e) gesture recognition.

2.1 Keypoint Descriptors for Gesture Recognition

In cortical area V1 there are simple, complex and end-stopped cells [12], which are thought to be responsible for part of the process of coding the visual input: they extract multi-scale line, edge and keypoint information (keypoints are line/edge vertices or junctions and also blobs). In this section we briefly describe multi-scale keypoint detection and the fast binary descriptor that we designed for matching keypoints. The descriptor is also based on V1 cell responses.

Keypoint Detection: Responses of even and odd simple cells, which correspond to the real and imaginary parts of a Gabor filter [12], are denoted by $R_{s,i}^{E}(x,y)$ and $R_{s,i}^{O}(x,y)$, i being the orientation (we use $4 \leq N_\theta \leq 12$). The scale s is defined by λ, the wavelength of the Gabor filters, in pixels. We use $4 \leq \lambda \leq 12$ with $\Delta\lambda = 4$. Responses of complex cells are obtained by computing the modulus $C_{s,i}(x,y) = [\{R_{s,i}^{E}(x,y)\}^2 + \{R_{s,i}^{O}(x,y)\}^2]^{1/2}$. The process of edge detection is based on responses of simple cells: a positive or negative line is detected where R^E shows a local maximum or minimum, respectively, and R^O shows a zero crossing. In the case of edges the even and odd responses are swapped. Lateral and cross-orientation inhibition are used to suppress spurious cell responses beyond line and edge terminations, and assemblies of grouping cells serve to improve event continuity in the case of curved events. On the other hand, keypoints are based on cortical end-stopped cells [11] and they provide important information because they code local image complexity. Since keypoints are caused by line and edge junctions, they are usually located at interesting locations of the image. When combined with a proper descriptor, they can be very useful for object categorization [15]. There are two types of end-stopped cells, single and double. These are applied to $C_{s,i}$ and are combined with tangential and radial inhibition schemes to obtain precise keypoint maps $K_s(x,y)$. For a detailed explanation with illustrations see [11,15].

Binary Keypoint Descriptors: Creating a biological descriptor for keypoints is not a trivial task, mainly because responses of simple and complex cells, which code the underlying lines and edges at vertices, are not reliable due to response interference effects [16]. Therefore, the responses in a neighbourhood around a keypoint must be analyzed, the neighbourhood size being proportional to the scale of the cells. In our approach we developed a 128-bit binary keypoint descriptor based on the responses of simple cells, each bit coding the activation level of a single cell. Also, from a computational point of view, a binary descriptor is much faster to compute and to match than a floating-point one. This method is an improvement of the previous method [17]. We start by applying maximum pooling in a circular region around each keypoint, followed by zero-mean normalization and extraction of the maximum cell responses in 8 filter orientations. Then we combine the extracted values by a weighted sum, using a weight matrix previously learned using LDAHash [18] on the Notredame dataset [19]. Finally, we apply a threshold vector, also previously trained on the Notredame dataset, to set each of the 128 bits to 1 or 0. The resulting descriptor is a huge improvement of the previous one [17]. It is comparable to the SIFT-based LDAHash descriptor in terms of performance when tested on the Yosemite dataset [19]. The developed descriptor significantly outperforms other biologically-inspired descriptors. In terms of processing time, the descriptor is also very fast to compute and to match. Figure 1 (left) shows one example of matching using the present descriptor. The right graph shows a comparison between our descriptor(128 bits), BRISK(512 bits) and BRIEF(128 bits) and LDAHash (128 bits) over 200,000 patches of the Yosemite dataset.

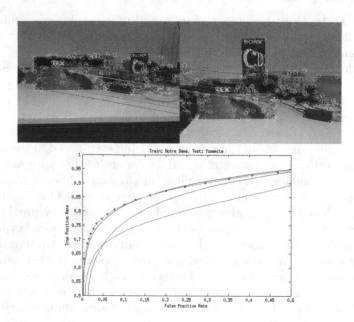

Fig. 1. Top: Example of matching. Bottom: comparison between our descriptor(blue), BRISK(green), BRIEF(red) and LDAHash(pink) over 200,000 patches (Colour figure online).

2.2   Stereo Vision for Robot Navigation and Obstacle Detection

Stereo vision is a fundamental process for robot navigation: it allows the robot to detect open spaces, obstacles on its path and estimate the distance to those obstacles. It can also be useful for computing visual saliency. The algorithm we used to generate the disparity maps is the same as previously used in [17]: (a) resize the left and right images to a small size (160×120); (b) extract complex cell responses on circles around each pixel; (c) compare each pixel P in the left image to the next K pixels in the right image on the same line and starting from the same position P as in the left image (we used $K = 35$); (d) use the Hamming distance to find the best-matching pixels; and (e) apply median filtering (5×5 kernel) to reduce noise due to wrong matches. The computed disparity maps are then thresholded to find nearby obstacles ($t_d = 70$). Whenever the robot detects an obstacle by using the thresholded disparity maps, it looks up and evaluates if it is a person by trying to find a human face using a linear SVM classifier, as described in Sect. 2.4. Figure 2 (top) row shows one example of an image acquired by the robot and the respective disparity map.

2.3   Visual Saliency

Visual saliency is also an important component of the real-time vision system, since by using it the robot can select important regions to process instead of processing entire images. The generated saliency maps are also useful to segregate hands from the background, to reduce clutter and to improve gesture recognition rates. The visual saliency algorithm we developed is an improvement of the one described in [17] and combines three different features: color, disparity and motion. The three features are processed separately and then merged into a single saliency map with equal weights. The top row of Fig. 2 shows an image of a person in front of the robot (left and right frames), the resulting disparity map, and the middle row shows the motion (left), color (middle) and disparity(right) saliency maps. The bottom row shows the resulting saliency map the thresholded map and the selected regions. Details are explained below.

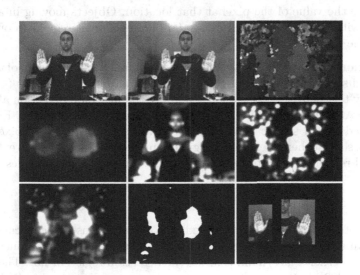

Fig. 2. Top row: stereo images acquired by the robot camera and the disparity map. Middle row, from left to right: motion saliency, color saliency and disparity saliency. Bottom row, from left to right: resulting saliency map, thresholded saliency map ($t_f =$ 200) and selected regions after blob detection and region growing (Color figure online).

Color Saliency: We build a stack of 6 retinotopic maps representing different channels in CIE L*A*B color-opponent space, which is based on retinal cones and provides a standard way to model color opponency. The first three channels code white, green and blue. The remaining three channels complement the first ones and represent black, red and yellow. After computing the maps, a stack of bandpass Difference-of-Gaussians (DoG) filter kernels with $\sigma_+ \in \{5, 10, 20\}$ and $\sigma_- = 2\sigma_+$ are used for blob detection. Since a saliency map does not need to be detailed, we compute them using subsampled color images for faster processing.

Disparity Saliency: To generate the disparity-based saliency map, we use the disparity and map computed in Sect. 2.2, and extract a single disparity layer where pixels with disparity $d = 100$ get the maximum value $M = 20$ and pixels bigger or smaller than d get smaller values according to their difference from d. After this step we apply the same filtering used for the colour-based saliency maps.

Motion Saliency: To compute the motion-based saliency map, we first calculate the optical flow using Farneback's method for every pixel [20]. Then we process the flow's magnitude and direction separately, creating a feature stack of magnitudes and orientations of motion. The feature stack has 3 maps representing the magnitude (speed) of motion and also has 8 maps representing 8 different directions of motion with either 0 or the value itself. In practice, 0 occurs when a pixel is not moving in the preferred direction or with preferred speed. When a pixel is moving in the preferred direction or with preferred speed we consider the value to be the value of the pixel at that location. Objects moving in a certain direction with certain speed will thus cause large coherent regions in one of the maps of the stack.

Final Saliency Map: The final saliency is the equally-weighted sum of the three normalized saliency maps. After computing this map we threshold it ($t_f = 200$) to get only the nearest regions and then apply the fast blob detection algorithm from [21]. After blob detection, only the two biggest blobs are kept. Each blob is converted into a square region that afterwards is grown by 15 pixels in all directions, so that there is enough margin to apply the Gabor filters to extract the simple cell responses used to extract keypoints and build keypoint descriptors.

2.4   Face and Hand Detection

Detection of faces and hands is achieved by coding responses of cortical complex cells within a region into a feature vector and by using a classifier (linear SVM) to predict whether a face/hand is inside the detection region or not. The process is similar to [22], but in our case the detection process employs a single Gabor filter scale ($\lambda = 6$) and 8 orientations ($N_\theta = 8$) for the complex cells (see Sect. 2), but also in combination with several scales of the HOG-like features (several sizes) over the entire image, and then a sliding window (6×6 blocks) to scan all blocks inside the sliding window's region. At each layer, the pooling cell size is increased, but the detection window size and the block's size remain the same. To this purpose, we use between 6×6 and 10×10 pixels per cell with a stride of 1 pixel. Finally, non-maximum suppresion is applied to eliminate multiple detections of the same face/hand (see below). We used the FaceScrub dataset [13] and the Oxford Hand dataset [14] to train and evaluate our face and hand detectors. For each detector we train an initial classifier using the positive and a random set of negative examples, then we use it to scan over images not containing faces or hands and collect false positives, and then we do a second round of training by including these hard false positives into the negative training set. The FaceScrub dataset consists of 107,818 face images of 530 celebrities (265 male and 265 female), although only 80,659 faces could be downloaded successfully and a few samples being unusable for training. For negative samples we took 100,000, 42 × 42 pixel patches from random images of the SUN database [23]. For training our hand classifier we used the Oxford hand dataset which contains 13,050 annotated hand instances (26,100 mirrored samples). Again, we took 30,000 random 42 × 42 pixel patches from the SUN database as negative samples.

Fig. 3. (Left to right) a person in front of the robot in gray scale (left) coded by HOG-like features (middle) with detected face and hands (right).

HOG-like Features: A modified version of the Dalal and Triggs HOG features is used here for person detection. In their implementation [22] they use the RGB colour space with no gamma correction, 1D gradient filters, linear gradient voting into 9 orientation bins, 16 × 16 pixel blocks of four 8 × 8 pixel cells, a Gaussian spatial window with $\sigma = 8$ pixels, L2-Hys block normalization, a block spacing stride of 8 pixels, and a 64 × 128 detection window for training the linear SVM classifier for pedestrian detection. Here we use an adapted and slightly modified version of the previous procedure for face and hand detection: (a) we use only grayscale information for speed purposes, (b) complex cell responses are used as gradient information, (c) no Gaussian window is applied, (d) the L2-norm is used instead of L2-Hys and (e) a 42 × 42 detection window for training. Complex cell responses provide a good alternative for gradient information since they are also robust to noise. In addition, linear gradient voting can be skipped because of the cells' oriented responses. We use 12 × 12 pixel blocks of four 6 × 6 pixel cells with 50 % block overlap; see below for parameter assessment and evaluation. Our selection ensures optimal performance while also complying also with Dalal and Triggs' recommendations [22] of having many orientation bins in combination with moderately sized, strongly normalized and overlapping descriptor blocks. See Fig. 3 (middle) for the bio-inspired HOG-like features.

Classification: To detect a face or a hand, features in a detection window are classified using a linear SVM. The face and hand classifiers are trained using the FaceScrub dataset and the Oxford hand dataset, respectively, with a soft linear SVM (C=0.01) using LIBLINEAR [24]. As mentioned above, we used a 42×42 pixel detection window for training both classifiers, since the sizes of hands and faces in the image relative to the robot are similar. This results in 6×6 blocks to be used by the classifiers across the image at all scales. We found that a detection window of 42×42 pixels for training constitutes a good trade-off between performance and running speed. Increasing the detection window's size beyond 42×42, although increasing detection performance, has a significantly higher computational cost due to more features being used for classification.

Non-maximum Suppression: The detection window is applied to salient image regions using a sliding window approach where multiple detections of the same head or hands often occur. To remove multiple detections due to the sliding window, a non-maximum suppression technique is applied to discard overlapping windows: when two windows overlap at least 50 %, the window with the weakest classification response is discarded. To this purpose, we use the unsigned SVM classification output in order to determine a window's classification response. Figure 3 (right) shows detected regions of face and hands after non-maximum suppression.

Concerning performance evaluation and optimization, several factors have been evaluated in the classifier training stage, namely Gabor filter scale (λ), number of orientations (N_θ), cell size, block size and overlap. Smaller sets of 2000 positive and 2000 negative random samples for training, and 1000 positive and 1000 negative random samples for testing were used for cross-validation and parameter optimization for both classifiers. We used detection error trade-off (DET) and miss rate (better: 1.0 - Recall) measures to quantify the performance.

First, the scale of the cortical cells was analyzed in order to determine the optimal λ. Figure 4 (top-left) shows the overall performance of seven different scales $\lambda = [4, 10]$. Smaller scales yield better performance than bigger scales, mainly due to lines and edges being better encoded by smaller filters. Moreover, by choosing a smaller λ the processing time decreases. Here, $\lambda = 4$ performed best. Figure 4 (top-middle) shows the performance impact of the number of orientations used ($N_\theta \in [4, 12]$) in the HOG-like feature bins. Increasing the number of orientations beyond 8 does not improve performance significantly. Therefore, for the final classifier we chose $N_\theta = 8$ orientations which gave a 1.4 % and 8.03 % miss rates for face and hand detection, respectively. Three other key factors taken into account were the block size vs. cell size vs. block overlap. Figure 4 (middle and bottom) shows three graphs with 0 % (left), 25 % (middle) and 50 % (right) block overlap, with block sizes ranging from 1×1 to 4×4 and pooling cell sizes from 4×4 to 10×10 for faces (middle) and hands (bottom). From all tested combinations, block sizes of 2×2 with 6×6 pooling cells and 50 % overlap, gives the best performance with a 1.1 % miss rate for face and 8.6 % for hand detection. Figure 4 (top-right) shows the overall performance of the two detectors.

2.5   Gesture Recognition

In order to be able to recognize gestures, the robot keeps in its memory a small set of templates of different hand gestures. These templates have been prepared prior to robot operation, and by applying exactly the same processing as done during real-time robot operation. At the moment we use a set of 7 different gestures for both hands, with several samples for each gesture with different backgrounds and sizes. After finding the hand regions, the robot then processes those regions for keypoint extraction and their descriptors. Descriptor matching is based on the 128-bit Hamming distance: when the distance between two keypoint descriptors is smaller than 30, a match is accepted. When at least 4 matches between the acquired hand region and a template are found, the robot assumes that the gesture that corresponds to the matched template has been detected. For faster

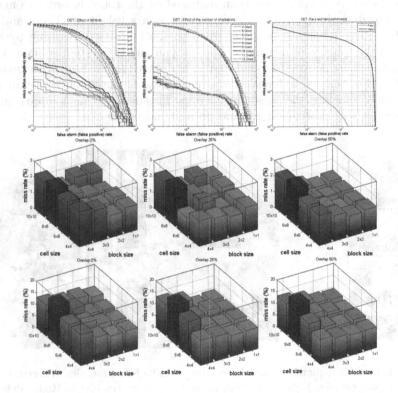

Fig. 4. HOG-like feature parameter performance. Top row: effects of λ (left) and the number of orientations (middle-left) in face (full lines) and hand (dot lines) detection. The mid-right and right plot shows the overall performance of our face and hand detectors. Middle and bottom rows, left to right: block vs. cell size combinations with 0 %, 25 % and 50 % block overlap, and with block size from 1×1 to 4×4 and cell size from 4×4 to 10×10 (bluer is better) for face (middle) and hand (bottom) detectors. The best result is given by 2×2 blocks with 6×6 cell size and 50 % overlap with 1.1 % miss rate for face and 8.6 % for hand detection

computation time and higher reliability of the system, we extract keypoints at scale $\lambda = 12$ and use simple cell responses at scale $\lambda = 6$ for the descriptors. By extracting keypoints at a coarser scale, they become more stable. By using scale $\lambda = 6$ on extracted keypoint locations, more detail is available to describe the keypoints.

3   Tests and Results

To test the developed system we used a child-sized Pioneer 3DX robot, equipped with a Bumblebee-2 stereo camera, a PhantomX robot turret for pan and tilt movement of the camera, and ultrasonic and laser rangefinder sensors (see Fig. 5 left). The Bumblebee-2 camera captures images at a resolution of 1024×768 pixels. The range sensors are only used for emergency collision avoidance, not for navigation. A structure has been mounted on the robot in order to make it taller, providing the point of view of a child with a height of $115\,cm$ and eyes at $110\,cm$. The robot has been set up with ROS (Robot Operating System). Although the robot is of mecanoid type, its pan and tilt system combined with the stereo camera convey the idea that it has a neck and a head with two eyes. Since it is programmed to focus on a person's head in the center of the image, it seems like it is looking the person in the eyes. This makes it much more engaging than a robot with static cameras and no neck movements.

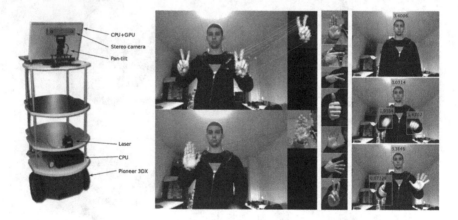

Fig. 5. Left: robotic platform used for testing. Middle left: examples of recognition of two different gestures. Middle Right: some of the gesture templates. Right: detection of heads and hands using the SVM classifiers.

Figure 5 right shows some results: on the left we can see the mobile robot platform used for testing; on the middle left column we show two examples of gesture recognition using the extracted keypoints and their descriptors; on the middle right column we show some of the gesture templates; and on the right we show some examples of head and hand detection using the SVM classifiers.

The system proved to work quite well, being able to recognize the 7 different gestures for both hands in most situations. At start it failed to recognize some of them but as we added more gesture templates with different sizes and backgrounds the gesture recognition was improved.

As usual with most vision systems, we noticed that under bad illumination the system can sometimes fail to detect hands or head and thus may not be able to recognize gestures. Failure in detection of hands and recognizing gestures could also happen during fast hand movements, since in these cases the image of the hands is blurred.

4 Discussion

In this paper we presented a biologically inspired vision system for human-robot interaction. It allows the robot to navigate and to evaluate if an obstacle is, in fact, a person by trying to find a human face whenever it encounters an obstacle. The system also allows the robot to direct its attention to important visual areas using an attention model which is based on color, disparity and motion. The presented methods allow the robot to identify human hands in salient regions and then recognize the gestures being made by using keypoints and keypoint descriptors based on V1 cell responses. Although biologically inspired methods usually require a high computational power and long computation time, due to the many filter kernels at several orientations and scales, by choosing only a few scales the system is able to run in real time. The SVM classifiers showed to be fast in detecting faces and hands in an image using a sliding window. Faces had the best performance overall with few false negatives, while hands had less performance in detection mainly due to the large intra-class variability. The keypoints and their descriptors proved to be quite robust and work quite well for recognizing the gestures previously stored as templates. Although sometimes few keypoints were matched to wrong keypoints, most of them were matched to the correct ones. These wrong matches can easily be eliminated by using some geometry between groups of keypoints to validate or invalidate matches. Experiments showed that the system can now be programmed to execute different actions according to specific hand gestures.

As future work we plan to add more gestures to the system, increase the precision such that individual fingers can be detected, and integrate facial expression recognition in order to allow the robot to act according to a person's mood. We also plan to use the ability of recognizing gestures and facial expressions as a way to teach the robot simple tasks through reinforcement learning: by using different gestures or facial expressions it will be possible to tell the robot that it is doing the right or the wrong thing. Another part of future work consists of integrating the binary keypoint descriptor into the GPU implementation of the keypoint extractor in order to free the CPU for other future developments. Future work will also address motion prediction, a process that occurs in cortical area MST.

Acknowledgements. This work was partially supported by the Portuguese Foundation for Science and Technology (FCT) projects UID/EEA/5009/2013 and SparseCoding EXPL/EEI-SII/1982/2013; and by FCT PhD grants to MS (SFRH/BD/71831/2010) and MF (SFRH/BD/79812/2011).

References

1. Messias, J., Ventura, R., Lima, P., Sequeira, J., Alvito, P., Marques, C., Carrio, P.: A robotic platform for edutainment activities in a pediatric hospital. In: Proceedings of IEEE International Conference Autonomous Robot Systems and Competitions, pp. 193–198 (2014)
2. Saleiro, M., Carmo, B., Rodrigues, J.M.F., du Buf, J.M.H.: A low-cost classroom-oriented educational robotics system. In: Herrmann, G., Pearson, M.J., Lenz, A., Bremner, P., Spiers, A., Leonards, U. (eds.) ICSR 2013. LNCS, vol. 8239, pp. 74–83. Springer, Heidelberg (2013)
3. Kronander, K., Billard, A.: Learning compliant manipulation through kinesthetic and tactile human-robot interaction. IEEE Trans. Haptics **7**(3), 367–380 (2014)
4. Kumar, P., Verma, J., Prasad, S.: Hand data glove: a wearable real-time device for human-computer interaction. Int. J. Adv. Sci. Technol. **43**, 15–25 (2012)
5. Han, J., Gold, N.: Lessons learned in exploring the leap-motion(tm) sensor for gesture-based instrument design. In: Proceedings New Interfaces for Musical Expression, pp. 371–374 (2014)
6. Qian, K., Niu, J., Yang, H.: Developing a gesture based remote human-robot interaction system using Kinect. Int. J. Smart Home **7**(4), 203–208 (2013)
7. Saleiro, M., Farrajota, M., Terzić, K., Rodrigues, J.M.F., du Buf, J.M.H.: A biological and real-time framework for hand gestures and head poses. In: Stephanidis, C., Antona, M. (eds.) UAHCI 2013, Part I. LNCS, vol. 8009, pp. 556–565. Springer, Heidelberg (2013)
8. Ionescu, B., Coquin, D., Lambert, P., Buzuloiu, V.: Dynamic hand gesture recognition using the skeleton of the hand. EURASIP J. Appl. Sig. Proc. **13**, 2101–2109 (2005)
9. Ghaleb, F., Elmezain, M., Dewdar, F.: Hand gesture spotting and recognition in stereo color image sequences based on generative models. Int. J. Eng. Sci. Innovative Technol. **3**(1), 78–88 (2014)
10. Suk, H., Sin, B., Lee, S.: Hand gesture recognition based on dynamic Bayesian network framework. Pattern Recogn. **43**(9), 3059–3072 (2010)
11. Rodrigues, J., du Buf, J.: Multi-scale keypoints in V1 and beyond: object segregation, scale selection, saliency maps and face detection. BioSystems **2**, 75–90 (2006)
12. Rodrigues, J., du Buf, J.: Multi-scale lines and edges in V1 and beyond: brightness, object categorization and recognition, and consciousness. BioSystems **95**, 206–226 (2009)
13. Ng, H., Winkler, S.: A data-driven approach to cleaning large face datasets. In: Proceedings of IEEE International Conference on Image Processing (ICIP), vol. 265(265), p. 530 (2014)
14. Mittal, A., Zisserman, A., Torr, P.H.S.: Hand detection using multiple proposals. In: British Machine Vision Conference (2011)
15. Terzic, K., Rodrigues, J., Lam, R., du buf, J.: Bimp: a real-time biological model of multi-scale keypoint detection in V1. Neurocomputing **150**, 227–237 (2015)

16. du Buf, J.: Responses of simple cells: events, interferences, and ambiguities. Biol. Cybern. **68**, 321–333 (1993)
17. Saleiro, M., Terzic, K., Lobato, D., Rodrigues, J., du Buf, J.: Biologically inspired vision for indoor robot navigation. Image Anal. Recogn. Part II **8815**, 469–477 (2014)
18. Strecha, C., Bronstein, M., Fua, P.: Ldahash: Improved matching with smaller descriptors. IEEE Trans. Pattern Anal. Mach. Intell. **34**(1), 66–78 (2012)
19. Brown, M.: Learning local image descriptors data (2011) (Accessed 17-February-2015]
20. Farnebäck, G.: Two-frame motion estimation based on polynomial expansion. In: Bigun, J., Gustavsson, T. (eds.) SCIA 2003. LNCS, vol. 2749, pp. 363–370. Springer, Heidelberg (2003)
21. Saleiro, M., Rodrigues, J., du Buf, J.: Automatic hand or head gesture interface for individuals with motor impairments, senior citizens and young children. In: Proceedings International Conference Software Device for Enhancing Accessibility and Fighting Info-Exclusion pp. 165–171 (2009)
22. Dalal, N., Triggs, B.: Histograms of oriented gradients for human detection. In: Proceedings IEEE Computer Society Conference on Computer Vision and Pattern Recognition vol. 1 pp. 886–893 (2005)
23. Xiao, J., Hays, J., Ehinger, K.A., Oliva, A., Torralba, A.: Sun database: Large-scale scene recognition from abbey to zoo. In: IEEE conference on Computer vision and pattern recognition (CVPR), 2010 pp. 3485–3492 (2010)
24. Fan, R., Chang, K., Hsieh, C., Wang, X., Lin, C.: LIBLINEAR: a library for large linear classification. J. Mach. Learn. Res. **9**, 1871–1874 (2008)

Engaging Users in Self-Reporting Their Data: A Tangible Interface for Quantified Self

Federico Sarzotti[1], Ilaria Lombardi[1], Amon Rapp[1(✉)],
Alessandro Marcengo[2], and Federica Cena[1]

[1] Computer Science Department, University of Torino,
C.so Svizzera, 185, 10149 Turin, Italy
{sarzotti,lombardi,cena}@di.unito.it,
amon.rapp@gmail.com
[2] Research and Prototyping, Telecom Italia,
via Reis Romoli, 274, 10148 Turin, Italy
alessandro.marcengo@telecomitalia.it

Abstract. Personal Informatics systems allow users to self-track a variety of states and behaviors. However, not all these data are suitable to be automatically collected. This is especially true for emotions and mood. These data require to be self-reported by the users and this activity can be very cumbersome, requiring an high compliance to be effective: instead users often fail in reporting their data due to forgetfulness, lack of time and motivation. To overcome these problems, we propose to exploit Tangible User Interface for relieving the task of self-reporting. In particular, we present a Personal Informatics Tangible Interface able to support users in self-reporting their mood. This solution allows the collection of emotional states in an amusing, simple and appealing way by means of a physical object.

Keywords: Tangible interfaces · Personal informatics · Quantified self · Behavior change · Self-tracking · Ubicomp technologies

1 Introduction

Technological advances in sensors, ubiquitous technologies and mobile devices open new horizons for Personal Informatics (PI). Personal Informatics systems have the goal of exploiting technology for gathering data on different aspects of people daily lives. Nowadays, a large variety of data can be somehow collected by means of PI technologies: from the mood or the glucose level in the blood, to performance values, habits and actions. Collecting these data allows users to self-monitor their behaviors in a way inconceivable without such technological means.

The first PI systems were conceived mainly for clinical purposes, to help patients in tracking dysfunctional behaviors. They then started to be used outside the clinical setting by researchers and technology enthusiasts, such as the members of the Quantified Self movement [1]. Today, we assist to their commercial diffusion at consumer level, widening the possibility of their widespread adoption and their integration in everyday life. This nonetheless poses a double problem. First, common users are unfamiliar with PI

© Springer International Publishing Switzerland 2015
M. Antona and C. Stephanidis (Eds.): UAHCI 2015, Part II, LNCS 9176, pp. 518–527, 2015.
DOI: 10.1007/978-3-319-20681-3_49

tools and may have a misperception of their limits and potentialities. Second, we believe that current PI tools are not designed with enough understanding of common users' needs, desires and problems they may encounter in their everyday lives [2].

In particular, manually collecting data with actual PI tools is cumbersome. Although it is possible to imagine that many behavioral data in the future will be tracked automatically thanks to the advancement of ubiquitous and wearable technologies, many aspects of people's behavior, such as emotions and mood, will continue to rely on self-reporting, since they involve cognitive and interpretative components that cannot be automatically collected. In fact, even if it can be possible to obtain physiological measurements and objective measures of the behaviors expressed by the emotions, it is not possible to measure the way in which the subject experiences the physiological and behavioral changes other than through self-report [3]. However, the act of self-reporting requires an high compliance to be effective, while common users often fail in reporting their data due to forgetfulness, lack of time and motivation [2].

Tangible User Interfaces (TUIs) is a new type of user interface that exploits physical affordances for connecting the digital world with the physical one [4]. TUIs seem to be more inviting than Graphical User Interfaces (GUIs) when a given task is not appealing [5], providing a more involving experience that may enhance the number of actions performed by users [6]. Using TUIs for self-reporting can make users more physically engaged, providing richer feedback during the interaction [7]. The act of self-reporting, from this point of view become a sort of "physical activity", in which users "play" with objects giving, at the same time, information about their behaviors.

Thus, we propose a Personal Informatics Tangible Interface able to support users in self-reporting their mood. This solution, built on an Arduino board, allows for self-reporting of emotional states in an amusing, simple and appealing way by means of a physical object. The data gathered by our TUI could be then analyzed, correlated with other personal data and fed back to the user in meaningful visualizations, in order to provide user with a picture of her states. To this aim, we integrated our TUI in an existent framework, Specch.io,[1] a quantified self platform for seamless data collection, mash-up, visualization and exploration of personal data. The Specch.io's goal is to raise awareness on individual life patterns and about aspects of the "self" that can be hardly captured from a subjective point of view [8]. In this paper, however, we will focus on describing our solution's architecture as a stand-alone system, even if the Specch.io's context is useful to fully understand our solution's potentialities.

The paper is structured as follow. Section 2 provides the most relevant related work in relation of technologies for self-tracking of mood and emotions. Section 3 provides a usage scenario that describes a possible context of use for our solution. Section 4 describes the general architecture of the system, and delves into the implementation details both from server and client point of view. Finally, Sect. 6 concludes the paper providing the future directions of the work.

---

[1] http://specch.io.

2 Related Work

Emotion tracking is a widely-studied topic and several applications, research works and technological tools addressed to this aim, either self-reported or automatic, have been developed so far. In this section, we only provide an overview of the most relevant in comparison with our solution, focusing on self-reporting of emotions.

There are a lot of systems with the aim of collecting user's emotions for therapeutic and rehabilitation purposes. For example, we can cite, Mobile Mood Diary [9], a mobile and online symptom tracking tool for adolescents with mental problems, and MoodTracker [10], an online tool for manage depression, bipolar disorder, or anxiety.

There are also a lot of commercial applications and devices with the goal of promoting a self-knowledge through a visual exploration of the gathered data. In fact, beside the data collection, they are able to suggest patterns, trends and correlations between emotions changes and habits or occurred events. For example, we can cite T2 Mood Tracker [11], an app designed to help users in tracking emotional experiences over time and sharing these data with an health care provider, and MedHelp Mood Tracker [12], that tracks general mood, as well as symptoms and treatments related to specific mood disorders.

Other apps, like Mood Panda [13], add the social component to the tracking and visualization of data: users can share their mood with friends in order to be supported by them and support them.

All these apps require the user to suspend her current activity to interact with the phone and this makes the tracking burdensome and annoying, with the risk that in the long term the user could give up.

Our solution supports users in self-collecting emotions by providing a tangible interface able to motivate her to report her data. This is different from other systems presented above that make use of a traditional GUI on the screen of mobile device. Our aim is to overcome such limitations in using these tools and facilitate this task for the user, by making it straightforward with a tangible interface.

3 Usage Scenario

In order to better understand the motivation of our work, we provide a usage scenario for our TUI integrated in the Specch.io framework.

Peter is a 35 years old programmer who lives in a big city. He has a sedentary lifestyle, even if he enjoys walking. He uses several personal computers during the day: of course for his job and also at home to be informed and to keep in touch with friends. Generally, he is very anxious and he would like to live a more relaxing life. He decides to use a personal informatics tool in order to gain awareness of some aspects of his everyday life that sometimes prevents him from truly relaxing. The TUI positioned on Peter's desk (both at home and at workplace) reminds him (with a light jingle or only with its presence) to periodically track his mood. Thus, Peter, rotating the object, reports his data every evening.

To increase his self-awareness, he also decides to install, in his home entrance, the Specch.io system. It identifies Peter when he reflects himself and shows all the information and correlations gathered about his habits and his moods, without the use of a personal computer. Thanks to a tangible/gestural interface, Peter can interact with the mirror and he is able to explore his mood in the last weeks and months and correlations among data. He can see the aggregated data about emotions and other contextual and behavioral data (e.g., other physical parameters collected with other PI devices, such where he has been, what he has done, who he has met, etc....). This allows him to discover an unexpected correlation among his lunch habits and his mood: every time he does not make sport at lunch, he feels anxious. Thus, he considers to change his habits in order to take a break at lunch and make some sport.

4 Our Solution

The idea is to create a portable, entertaining and, above all, not burdensome platform that can support users in self-collecting their mood states in several moments of the day.

Fig. 1. The TUI Object

Our solution is based on a client-server architecture (see Fig. 2) where the client is a tangible user interface (TUI), i.e. a physical smart object that the user can manipulate in order to communicate her mood, while the server has the aim to store the received information in a database, to enable other platforms (such as Specch.io) to integrate them. The client and the server communicate each other with a Wi-Fi connection.

We implemented our TUI by means of a wooden cube with each face representing a specific mood state (see Fig. 1). It has been decided to monitor six different mood levels. Users can communicate their mood by moving the cube and positioning it on the table/desk so that the relevant face is the top one. The TUI is able to store these data since it is built on an Arduino board [14]. Arduino is an open-source platform for building digital devices and interactive objects that can sense and control the physical world. When the TUI recognizes the chosen face (Mood Manager), the information about the mood state and the time (Time Manager) are managed by the Data Manager and saved into a storage device, possibly with other information gathered from some sensors such as temperature and barometric pressure. Later, these data are read from the storage device and are wirelessly sent to the remote server by the Communication Manager. On the server side, the data received by the Communication Manager are sent to the Data Manager that saves them into a storage device. Then some checks are performed and if the data are considered valid, they are stored also into a database.

Then the user, through her PC/device or Specch.io, can be notified of specific conditions, patterns and correlations (e.g. every time she meets a particular person, she gets happy).

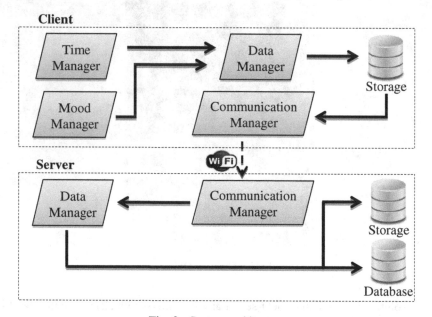

Fig. 2. System architecture

5 Implementation Details

In this section, we provide a technical description of our solution, both for the client and the server sides.

5.1 Client Side: TUI Implementation

To support users in self-collecting their mood states, we have to recognize the TUI face, matching it with an event or a specific time, gather some data from several sensors, send this information to a remote server and save it in a database. In order to accomplish these tasks, we chose to realize a TUI based on an Arduino platform.

Hardware architecture. We created a first prototype using an Arduino Uno board. Several parts have been added to the platform:

- an *inertial measurement unit (IMU)* is used to recognize which face of the TUI the user selects. We used an IMU with 10 degrees of freedom (SEN0140 by dfRobot[2]). It integrates an accelerometer, a magnetometer, a gyro and a barometric pressure and temperature sensor. To communicate with this sensor, we use a dedicated free library, FreeIMU [15];
- a *Real Time Clock* is necessary to get the current date/time and allow for associating the emotional state to a particular event or time. It holds a battery;
- an *SD card* reader stores data before they are sent to the remote server and some initialization parameters used by the platform, such as Wi-Fi network name and passphrase and server IP and port;
- a *Wi-Fi shield* enables the wireless connection to the remote server. We used a WizFi250 shield by Seeedstudio[3];
- a *buzzer* is used to alert the user that the platform is waiting for her input;
- some RGB *LEDs* show the state of the platform to the user.

While the Wi-Fi shield is plugged directly into the Arduino Uno board, the remaining parts are mounted on a breadboard and then connected to the board. After some test, we need to move to the Arduino Mega board that provides more memory space for the firmware.

Finally, we designed the physical object to contain the platform. We had to satisfy some constraints: (i) internal dimension should be at least 15 × 10 cm in order to contain the Arduino Mega platform[4] and all the other components, (ii) metal case is not appropriate due to the wireless activity, and (iii) we had to detect 6 different states. The simplest object that satisfies these constraints is a cube. We decided to build the cube in wooden material with six faces as shown in Fig. 1.

---

[2] http://www.dfrobot.com/wiki/index.php/10_DOF_Sensor_%28SKU:SEN0140%29.
[3] http://www.seeedstudio.com/wiki/Wifi_Shield_%28Fi250%29.
[4] The TUI could be powered using a 9 V power supply or 6 AA batteries, with, at least, 1000 mAh.

Software modules. We envisaged a scenario where the user tracks her mood at home or in the workplace with our TUI. We can take for granted that, in such contexts, the TUI is always on and placed in an area covered by a Wi-Fi network. The user can interact with the TUI at any time during the day: it selects a face of the cube that represents her mood (the one facing upward), then some parameters are automatically gathered and all the data are stored into the SD card. Then, those data are read and sent to a remote server. Every interaction is temporarily stored on the SD card, marked with a timestamp. The SD card also contains some files used to configure the platform:

- *Wi-fi.txt* contains a list of known Wi-Fi networks (SSID, passphrase, authentication type, BSSID, channel);
- *Server.txt* contains information related to the remote server: IP address and TCP port where information is to be sent.
- *Request.txt* contains the times of the day when the device has to remind the user that it is waiting for an input.
- *Param.txt* contains some parameters described below.

The overall behavior of the client is modeled by the finite state machine shown in Fig. 3. In the following, we shortly describe the client side software modules.

Time Manager. The platform alerts the user that it is waiting for its input (depending on the times stored in the file *Request.txt*) by activating a buzzer which plays a jingle for one minute: if in the meanwhile the user interacts with the TUI, the song stops; otherwise, after one minute, the buzzer stops anyway not to burden the user.

Mood Manager. The system identifies as "user interaction" any handling of the TUI (detected by the IMU) that lasts for at least X seconds (the value is stored in the file *Param.txt*). Once a user interaction is detected, the procedure that recognizes the face of the cube selected by the user will start: if the system is not able to recognize the face (if, for example, the TUI is not properly placed on a face), a red LED is turned on intermittently and if it keeps failing to identify a face within a specified timeout (whose value stored in the file param.txt), it aborts the "user interaction" operation and reverts to wait for a new user input. Otherwise, once the face has been identified, a blue LED is turned on intermittently for Y seconds (the value is stored in the file *Param.txt*) as a feedback for the user that her choice was identified. During this period, the user has the possibility to change the selected face: in this circumstance, the blue LED is turned off, and will be turned on when the device will correctly detect the new selected face. Once the registration process has started (i.e. the detected movements last for more than X seconds), it cannot be stopped and the device, once identified the face, will necessarily save the data.

Data Manager. When the system is ready to store the data, the blue LED is turned off and a green one is turned on, alerting the user that it starts to save the data. To grant privacy and data security, every TUI has a unique identifier (TUI ID, i.e. its Wi-Fi MAC address), and every user has a username and password. This information is stored into the SD card and can be changed by the user. All the data both gathered from the sensors (the cube face, time, etc.) and others (TUI ID, username and password) are saved in a file on the SD card in a JSON string.

Communication Manager. Once the information is stored on the SD card, the device tries to send it to the remote server, using a known Wi-Fi network. The system will attempt to connect to any Wi-Fi network whose parameters are written in the file *Wi-fi. txt.* Once connected, it tries to establish a TCP connection to the remote server using the parameters stored in the file *Server.txt.* All data stored into the SD card will be then transferred to the server, including any other data that have not been previously transferred, due, for example, to a temporary Wi-Fi connection loss. If the transmission is successful, the data on the SD card are deleted and the system returns to its initial state (all LEDs off), waiting for the future user input.

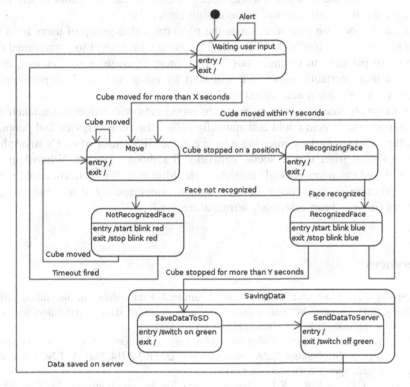

Fig. 3. Finite state machine describing the TUI behavior

5.2   Server Side Implementation

On the server side, there are two modules working together in order to manage the data gathered from the TUI: the Communication Manager and the Data Manager.

Communication Manager. It receives JSON data from the TUI Communication Manager and send it to the Data Manager.

Data Manager. It checks if the identifier, the username and the password contained in the incoming JSON string are correct, valid and exist in the central database.

If so, the data are stored in files on the server and sent to a document database (MongoDB); otherwise, data are only stored as files on the server for logging purposes and future checks but no data will be sent to the database.

6 Conclusion and Future Works

In this paper we propose a TUI which allows users to self report their mood. This tangible interface is intended to make the task of tracking the mood amusing, simple and immediate. We described a possible usage scenario motivating our work integrating it with an existent framework, Specch.io, the technical details of the implementation and the motivations of some design choices.

As future work, we plan to evaluate the platform with a group of users for a long period to collect their feedbacks about the TUI usage with respect to a traditional GUI. We are also planning to optimize our TUI, in order to create a smaller and, consequently, a more portable object. We will start by using Arduino Yun platform that integrates a Wi-Fi shield and an SD card reader.

On the other side, we want to integrate mood data with information taken from other sources: the system could automatically collect the context (place and people) in which the mood state arises, inferring it from e.g. the GPS sensor of user's smartphone, events gathered from user's social networks (Facebook, Twitter, WhatsApp, Google +), shared calendars (Google calendar), etc. Moreover, the platform could receive further information from other devices able to automatically detect physiological indicators (such as heart rate, body temperature, etc.).

References

1. Marcengo, A., Rapp, A.: Visualization of human behavior data: the quantified self. In: Huang, L.H., Huang, W. (eds.) Innovative approaches of data visualization and visual analytics, pp. 236–265. IGI Global, Hershey (2013)
2. Rapp, A., Cena, F.: Self-monitoring and technology: challenges and open issues in personal informatics. In: Stephanidis, C., Antona, M. (eds.) UAHCI 2014, Part IV. LNCS, vol. 8516, pp. 613–622. Springer, Heidelberg (2014)
3. Wallbott, H.G., Scherer, K.R.: Assessing emotion by questionnaire. In: Plutchik, R., Kellerman, H. (eds.) Emotion: Theory, research and experience, vol. 4 The measurement of emotions, pp. 55–82. Academic Press Inc, San Diego (1989)
4. Shaer, O., Hornecker, E.: Tangible user interfaces: past, present, and future directions. Found. Trends Hum.-Comput. Interact. 3(1–2), 1–137 (2010)
5. Horn, M.S., Crouser, R.J., Bers, M.U.: Tangible interaction and learning: the case for a hybrid approach. Pers. Ubiquit. Comput. 16(4), 379–389 (2012)
6. Xie, L., Antle, A., Motamedi, N.: Are tangibles more fun? comparing children's enjoyment and engagement using physical, graphical and tangible user interfaces. In: Proceedings of TEI 2008, pp. 191–198 (2008)
7. Zuckerman, O., Gal-Oz, A.: To TUI or not to TUI: Evaluating performance and preference in tangible vs. graphical user interfaces. Int. J. Hum.-Comput. Stud. 71(78), 803–820 (2013)

8. Marcengo, A., Buriano, L., Geymonat, M.: Specch.io: a personal QS mirror for life patterns discovery and "self" reshaping. In: Stephanidis, C., Antona, M. (eds.) UAHCI 2014, Part IV. LNCS, vol. 8516, pp. 215–226. Springer, Heidelberg (2014)
9. Matthews, M., Doherty, G.: In the mood: engaging teenagers in psychotherapy using mobile phones. In: Proceedings of CHI 2011, pp. 2947–2956. ACM, New York (2011)
10. Mood tracker. https://www.moodtracker.com/
11. T2 Mood Tracker. http://www.t2.health.mil/apps/t2-mood-tracker
12. Med Help Mood Tracker. http://www.medhelp.org/user_trackers/gallery/mood
13. Mood Panda. http://www.moodpanda.com/
14. Arduino. http://www.arduino.cc
15. Varesano, F.: FreeIMU: An open hardware framework for orientation and motion sensing, CoRR abs/1303.4949 (2013)

An Electrooculography Analysis in the Time-Frequency Domain Using Morphological Component Analysis Toward the Development of Mobile BCI Systems

Balbir Singh[1], Guangyi Ai[1], and Hiroaki Wagatsuma[1,2]($\boxtimes$)

[1] Graduate School of Life Science and Systems Engineering, Kyushu Institute of Technology, 2–4, Hibikino, Wakamatsu-ku, Kitakyushu 808-0196, Japan
[2] RIKEN BSI, 2-1 Hirosawa, Wako-shi, Saitama 351-0198, Japan
{awana-balbir-singh,ai-kouitsu}@edu.brain.kyutech.ac.jp,
waga@brain.kyutech.ac.jp

Abstract. Morphological Component Analysis (MCA) extended the traditional concept of signal decomposition and reconstruction by using "basis." The use of a basis not only guarantees accuracy in the reconstruction process but also requires the uniqueness of the representation using the basis. By admitting a redundancy in representations of a signal *i.e.* as a way of decomposition, MCA introduced the concept of a "dictionary", which includes mixtures of traditional basis. This method is frequently applied to biological signals and natural and complex image processing. In the present study, we applied MCA to decompose real electrooculography (EOG) in the time-frequency domain, which includes the electroencephalogram (EEG) signal, noise originating from measurement tools and cables for signal transmission and amplification, power-supply instability, biological fluctuations and so on. In our analysis using MCA, the EOG was decomposed into separate signal sources that could be represented using a linear expansion of waveforms from redundant dictionaries: DIRAC, UDWT and DCT. MCA was performed over several iterations to reduce the error in reconstruction. During this process; decomposed signals exhibited different characteristics in the time-frequency domain. By stopping the iteration when the correlation coefficient between the original and reconstructed signals reached a maximum (0.989 as the average), the DIRAC, UDWT and DCT represent irregular spikes, smooth curve in both the frequency and time domains and high-pass filtered components,respectively. Our results demonstrate successful decomposition via MCA and, consequently, authenticate it as an effective tool for the removal of artifacts from raw EOG signals.

Keywords: EOG · Blind Source Separation(BSS) · ICA · Artifacts and Morphological Component Analysis (MCA)

© Springer International Publishing Switzerland 2015
M. Antona and C. Stephanidis (Eds.): UAHCI 2015, Part II, LNCS 9176, pp. 528–537, 2015.
DOI: 10.1007/978-3-319-20681-3_50

1   Introduction

An electrooculogram (EOG) is the recording of electrical activity originating from blinking as the movement of the eyeball itself, which is obtained by using electrodes placed on the skin around eyes. The an electrical potential difference is created between the cornea and the ocular fundus and the time course of the potential subsequently monitored with typical values ranging from 250 to 1000 μV [1,2]. Both blinking and movement of the eye is a source of noise when neuronal activity is recorded via EEG. This is largely due to the fact that the EEG potential is less than one tenth of the EOG, typically ranging from 5 to 100 μV. The estimation of pure EOG and EEG signals is essential for parallel verification of changes in visual attention and event related neuronal activities. Both signals are generated from the same biological systems and interfere with each other as a result. To separate these two types of signals, identification of the individual characteristics of each signal in the time-frequency domain is key. Once these characteristics are identified, the unique shape of EOG and EEG signals under various conditions can be determined.

Signal feature extraction methods using linear analysis in time-frequency domains include Fast Fourier transform, wavelet transform, eigenvectors and so on [3]. For signal source separation, blind source separation (BSS), independent component analysis (ICA),the principal component technique (PCA) and many other methodologies have been used to extract independent signal features. However every technique has advantages and disadvantages and we have yet to reach the stage in which real time analysis can be employed as a single method. For example, PCA is known as a sophisticated technique to suppress artifacts. It specifies principal components (PC) to reconstruct the overall data structure and to remove components with small amplitudes and irregular changes. However, there are cases involving signals that have very low amplitudes as compared to those from other sources that are, nevertheless, necessary for reconstruction of the signals. It is difficult to specify that any or more PCs represent the artifacts as the identification of PCs requires prior knowledge of the artifacts [4,5]. Therefore research trends have shifted towards decomposition by ICA with higher order statics to determine independence in signals. Since ICA is based on the measurement of signal independence, the noise of the input is amplified by ICA, inhibiting the detection of true EOG components by the spread of Gaussian noise over the components, the method is not recognized as a complete solution to discriminate between artifact components and signal components [6–9].

Morphological Component Analysis, however is not restricted by the concept of independence, which was recently developed and has attracted attention in sparse signal processing as a means to decompose signals and images [10]. Due to the sparseness in bio-signal representation provided by various signal sources, the signal are decomposed with a redundant basis or a mixed overcomplete dictionary [11]. An overcomplete dictionary is described as a collection of different types of mathematical basis functions representing evoked potentials and their associated background noise respectively. Yong et al. [14] demonstrated the removal of artifacts from EEG signals using MCA with a Dirac δ function basis (DIRAC), discrete wavelet transform with a Daubechies filter (DWT) and a discrete cosine transform (DCT). The results were subsequently compared with other traditional methods of blind source separation such as AMUSE and EFICA.

In this paper, we focused on a decomposition method for EOG signals using Morphological Component Analysis with DIRAC, UDWT (undecimated discrete wavelet transform) and DCT basis, which was inspired by the approach of Yong et al. [14]. EOG and EEG are similar biological signals and their interference with each other induces the appearance of similar components in both signals. In principle, artifacts are derived from measurement equipment, cables used for signal transmission and amplification, power-supply instabilities, and so on. When biological signals are contaminated, it is difficult to define the signal/noise ratio or to identify artifacts. The proposed method in this has the advantages of facilitating the separation of different types of signals, including the measurement of artifacts from the desired signal(EOG), thereby making analysis of EOG possible.

This paper in organized into the following sections: the concept of MCA is explained in Sect. 2, the EOG measurement is explained in Sect. 3, experimental results are given in Sect. 4 and finally the conclusion and discussion are described in Sect. 5.

2   Morphological Component Analysis Concepts

Biomedical signal decomposition has been performed using various methods such as PCA, Wavelets, ICA and so on [3]. Blind Source Separation (BSS) like ICA relies on the independence of signals, this concept can be extend to a sparse representation in linear analysis to treat bio-medical signals and time course of natural phenomena. BSS algorithms estimate the vector m under the condition that the underlying sources is $X \in \mathbb{R}^{m*N}$ and the observed signal is taken from the k channel or sensor, $S \in \mathbb{R}^{k*N}$. The vector length N is the number of samples taken during the entire recording time T, which is given by $T = N \cdot f_s$ where f_s is the sampling rate. Assuming that the relevant signals are recorded from channels as independent sources, the mixing of each independent source can be classified by

$$Signal(amplitude) = electrical coupling \cdot electrical potential \qquad (1)$$

and can then be written as:-

$$S = BX + W \qquad (2)$$

where B is the $k \times m$ coefficient mixing matrix the sources X and W is assumed to be noise, which is generated from power supply, electronic devices for amplification and so on. B and X are the unknown values to be estimated by this method. Various algorithms are organized in the context of different assumptions. The MCA is recently established as a general form to use various combinations of such dictionaries, depending on target applications [10].

We assume that the target EOG signal can be represented by a linear super-position of several signal sources with a time constant [12]. According to the sparsity and morphological diversity of the EOG signal, *i.e.* the assumption that each of the m sources $\{S_1, \cdots, S_m\}$ is sparse in an overcomplete dictionary D, the raw vector S_i is modeled by a linear combination of p morphological components:

$$S_i = \sum_{k=1}^{p} S_{i,k} = \sum_{k=1}^{p} \beta_k^i \phi_k \qquad (3)$$

where S_i is ith source, $S_{i,k}$ is the time series of the kth morphological component and the β_k^i are the coefficients corresponding to dictionary ϕ_k.

The dictionary D is a collection of mathematical basis functions represent-ing parameterized waveforms ϕ_m with parameter number m. The parameter m determines a set of indexing frequencies, such as time-frequency dictionaries [13,14]. ϕ_m plays a role in discriminating between different signal components. For instance, a morphological component might be categorized as sparse in one particular dictionary but not in another. To find the sparsest of all signals within an augmented dictionary containing all values of ϕ_m , we use the following equa-tion:

$$\{\beta_1^{opt}, \ldots, \beta_m^{opt}\} = \arg \min_{\{\beta_1, \ldots, \beta_m\}} \sum_{i=1}^{m} \parallel \beta_i \parallel_1 + \lambda \parallel S - \sum_{i=1}^{m} \beta_i \phi_i \parallel_2^2 . \qquad (4)$$

To solve this equation(4), we used a numerical solver called the Block-Coor-dinate Relaxation Method [10] with an appropriate value of λ.

We hypothesized that the EOG signal could be decomposed into three cate-gories: irregular spike activities, slow EOG changes and EEG related activities with multi-frequency components. We used the DIRAC, UDWT and DCT dic-tionaries respectively.

3   Experiment and Measurements

3.1   Experiments Procedure

In our experiment, electrodes were placed on the skin around eyes and designated as channels $\{V_z, V_u^R, V_d^R, V_u^L, V_d^L, H^R, H^L\}$. The suffixes u and d represents the upper and lower sides of the eye respectively and suffixes R and, L represents the right and left eyes respectively. The electrode for channel Vz is placed between the eyebrows. All potentials were recorded with a resolution of 0.1 μV, a sam-pling interval of 1 microsecond, *i.e.* and a sampling rate of $1/1000\,$s. The subjects were instructed to see a fixed point in the screen and spontaneous eye blinks were monitored.

3.2   EOG Signal Decomposition Using MCA

The MCA concept used for modeling of the EOG signal. The decomposition of EOG signal S as

$$S = \sum_{i=1}^{m} \beta_i \phi_i \qquad (5)$$

Here the EOG signal can be classified by linear combination of morphological components. It is described by

$$S = \sum_{i=1}^{m_1} \beta_i^{DIRAC} \cdot \phi_i^{DIRAC} + \sum_{i=1}^{m_2} \beta_i^{UDWT} \cdot \phi_i^{UDWT} + \sum_{i=1}^{m_3} \beta_i^{DCT} \cdot \phi_i^{DCT} \qquad (6)$$

where β_{DIRAC}, β_{UDWT} and β_{DCT} are the coefficient vectors corresponding to the complete dictionaries of ϕ_d, ϕ_{UDWT} and ϕ_{DCT}, denoting respectively the Dirac basis, Undecimated discrete wavelet transform and discrete cosine transform. $m = m_1 + m_2 + m_3$.

4   Results

In the experiment, EOG signals were obtained to identify the high-amplitude baseline changes attributed to blinking. In this analysis, we constructed a dictionary that included information from the DIRAC, UDWT and DCT dictionaries. This dictionaries were selected according the characteristics of signal. The categorization of morphological components depends on the particular dictionary used, as many dictionaries do not agree on whether a component should be labeled sparse. Consequently these components represent only one type of signal feature. By applying the proposed MCA method with the DIRAC, UDWT and DCT basis, we were able to successfully decompose the EOG signal into it's separate features. Figure 1 shows that the original signal was successfully decomposed into three parts. This signal was then reconstructed with a high correlation coefficient(0.9841) following 450 iteration of the Block-Coordinate Relaxation Method [10], the numerical method used to apply MCA. The DIRAC components represent spike-like activities, UDWT represent components that change shape slowly, which are believe to correspond to pure EOG signals and the DCT components represent EEG signals mixed with cyclic background noise. As shown in Fig. 2, the correlation coefficient between the original and reconstructed signal monotonically increases, reaching a maximum value and then drastically decreases, thereby upsetting the balance between the three parts.

The power spectrum of the individual parts, shown in Fig. 3, indicates that the UDWT portion is closely correlated with the slowest components and decreases smoothly from the beginning of the measurement. DIRAC portion starts to be a flat line, which develops a bumping distribution over frequencies. A hill-like distribution in the lower (1–9 Hz) frequency ranges appears in the DCT portion of the spectrum, representing alpha, delta and theta rhythms. However noise generated by electronic devices, power lines and other type of noise cannot easily be singled out in spectrum. It is possible that baseline changes arising from power supply instability of the power supply are embedded in the UDWT components causing an overshoot for measurement devices relying on an AC amplifier. This would explain spiking activity as being a mixture of biological artifacts and device-driven artifacts. Higher frequency EEG signals such as gamma, which ranges between 25 to 100 Hz, do not appear in DCT components but may however, be accounted for in the DIRAC results. Specific tendencies will be clarified

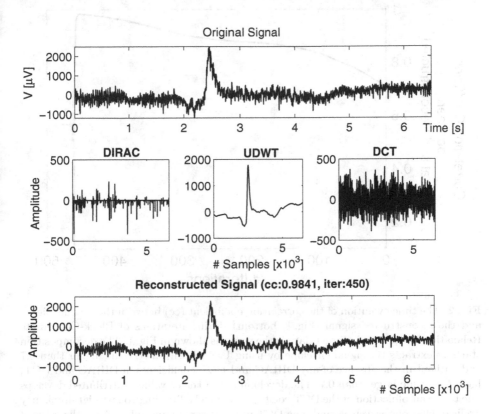

Fig. 1. An example of the MCA decomposition. The original signal is obtained from V_u^L, 6.5 s (6500 samples), including a eye blink. In Block-Coordinate Relaxation Method, we used 3 as λ to be the noise removal condition according to the result of Starck et al. [10]. The top, middle and bottom panels represent the original signal, coefficients of three dictionaries (DIRAC, UDWT and DCT) and the reconstructed signal from the three components. UDWT clearly pursuits reproduces the envelop of the target signal by showing the a large of amplitude change around 2.5 s to be an envelop and there is no after the removal of spike-like activities. The EOG potential is known to change slowly rather than EEGs [1,2]. This result indicates the combination of DIRAC, UDWT and DCT dictionaries provides an effective method to extract pure EOG signals from artifacts with multi timescales. cc and iter represent respectively correlation coefficient and the number of iterations.

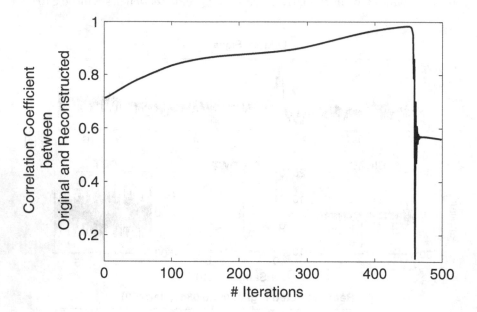

Fig. 2. The time evolution of the correlation coefficient (cc) between the original signal and the reconstructed signal (Fig. 1; bottom) during iterations of Block-Coordinate Relaxation Method [10]. Target data is the same as shown in Fig. 1. The decomposition starts to extracts the signal envelope by using UDWT with a cc value higher than 0.7 and without in the absence of any DIRAC and DCT coefficients in DIRAC and DCT, having cc value larger than 0.7. The development of the cc value is attributed develops due to the amplification of the DCT coefficients in DCT fitteding to fast high-frequency cyclic oscillations as well as, and then DCT pursuits remaining spikes. After the value of cc reached a maximumthe peak point of cc, the DIRAC components represent become an over-fitting curve to pursuit the original signal. Once it exceeds the maximum cc, the time evolution goes down drastically.

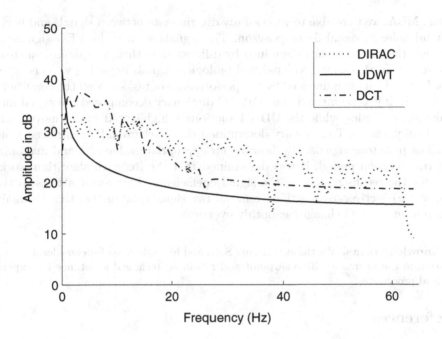

Fig. 3. The resultant frequency distribution of for each part, which is obtained from the reconstructed signals in the individual DIRAC, UDWT and DCT dictionaries of DIRAC, UDWT and DCT and itstheir respective coefficients (Fig. 1; middle) In the power spectrum, UDWT corresponds to the slowest component, DIRAC spreads over all the frequencies with bumps and DCT corresponds to lower frequencies. The DCT frequency range is from the 1- to 9 Hz and, which is covers the ranges of the alpha, delta and theta rhythms of EEG signals.

536   B. Singh et al.

in further analysis, whcih will include detail analyses of EEG channels. The correlation coefficient between the original and reconstructed signals was measured at 0.989 as averaged over channels $\{V_z, V_u^R, V_d^R, V_u^L, V_d^L, H^R$ and $H^L\}$. This demonstrates that decomposition via the MCA method ia an effective tool to analyze various features of biological signals and further, to remove artifacts from the target signal.

5 Conclusion

Using MCA, we were able to successfully discriminate between signals and background noise in signal decomposition. The signals seem to be EEG signals as well as other artifacts, as determined by differences in their morphological characteristics. In this paper, we analyzed biological signals involving various types of affects, which are influenced by the performance of tasks as well the conditions under which it is performed. The DIRAC dictionary decomposed the signal into spike-like activities, while the UDWT dictionary highlighted slower movements and finally, the DCT dictionary determined that background signals arise from EEG or pure tone signals. By choosing an appropriate value of λ and maximizing the iteration period, it was determined that the iterative algorithm works well for the reconstruction of the signal coefficients. This result attests to the respective effectiveness of artifact removal raw signals and further that the main component of EOG changes smoothly overtime.

Acknowledgments. We thank Naoyuki Sato and his colleagues for considerable suggestion in the neuroscientific viewpoint and advanced technical assistance for experimental procedures.

References

1. Berg, P., Scherg, M.: Dipole models of eye movements and blinks. Electroencephalography and Clinical Neurophysiology **79**(1), 36–44 (1991)
2. Brown, M., Marmor, M.: Vaegan, Zrenner, E., Brigell, M., Bach, M.: ISCEV Standard for Clinical Electro-oculography (EOG) 2006. Documenta Ophthalmologica **113**(3), 205–212 (2006)
3. Al-Fahoum, A.S., Al-Fraihat, A.A.: Methods of EEG signal features extraction using linear analysis in frequency and time-frequency domains. Int. Sch. Res. Notices 2014 **730218**, 1–7 (2014)
4. Berg, P., Scherg, M.: A multiple source approach to the correction of eye artifacts. Electroencephalogr. Clin. Neurophysiol. Suppl. **90**(3), 229–241 (1994)
5. Sadasivan, P.K., Dutt, D.N.: SVD based technique for noise reduction in electroencephalographic signals. Sign. Proces. **55**(2), 179–189 (1996)
6. Vigário, R.N.: Extraction of ocular artefacts from EEG using independent component analysis. Electroencephalogr. Clin. Neurophysiol. Suppl. **103**(3), 395–404 (1997)
7. Joyce, C.A., Gorodnitsky, I.F., Kutas, M.: Automatic removal of eye movement and blink artifacts from EEG data using blind component separation. Psychophysiol. **41**(2), 313–325 (2004)

8. Zhou, W., Gotman, J.: Automatic removal of eye movement artifacts from the EEG using ICA and the Dipole Model. Prog. Nat. Sci. **19**(9), 1165–1170 (2009)
9. Sameni, R., Gouy-Pailler, C.: An iterative subspace denoising algorithm for removing electroencephalogram ocular artifacts. J. Neurosci. Methods **225**, 97–105 (2014)
10. Starck, J.-L., Moudden, Y., Bobin, J., Elad, M., Donoho, D.L.: Morphological Component Analysis. In: Proceedings of the SPIE conference wavelets, vol. 5914 (2005)
11. Mallat, S.G., Zhang, Z.: Matching pursuits with time-frequency dictionaries. IEEE Trans. Signal Process. **41**(12), 3397–3415 (1993)
12. Zeng, H., Song, A.: Removal of EOG artifacts from EEG recordings using stationary subspace analysis. Sci. World J. 2014 **259121**, 1–9 (2014)
13. Chen, S.S., Donoho, D.L., Saunders, M.A.: Atomic decomposition by basis pursuit. SIAM J. Sci. Comput. **20**(1), 33–61 (1998)
14. Yong, X., Ward, R. K., Birch, G. E.: Generalized morphological component analysis for EEG source separation and artifact removal. In: Proceedings of the 4th International IEEE EMBS Conference on Neural Engineering, pp. 343–346 (2009)

State-of-the-Art and Future Concepts for Interaction in Aircraft Cockpits

Peter Thomas$^{(\boxtimes)}$, Pradipta Biswas, and Patrick Langdon

University of Cambridge, Cambridge CB2 1PZ, UK
prt32@cam.ac.uk

Abstract. Aircraft cockpits have substantially increased in complexity over the last 60 years. Whilst the additional instrumentation and systems have improved operational performance and certain aspects of situational awareness, they have also substantially increased the cognitive skills needed of pilots. A pilot interacts with the modern cockpit displays through cursor control devices (CCD), and the implementation and type of CCD has an impact on the quality, performance, and workload experienced by the pilot. This paper highlights the direction of research and development in pilot human-computer interaction (HCI) for both civilian and military aircraft, with regards to CCDs. Particular focus is placed on unconventional interaction methods that are being developed to provide more intuitive, naturally perceptive interfaces. Preliminary work by the authors in contribution to the evaluation of these new input modalities is also briefly presented.

1 Introduction

From the humble cockpit of the Wright Flyer in 1905 to the spacious flight decks of today's civil transport jet airliners, the growth in the complexity in the cockpit has been enormous. By the 1970s a single-seat jet fighter accommodated up to 300 instruments, indicators, and control switches [37]. This was mainly in support of increasingly more capable aircraft, with more instrumentation and controls needed to regulate more flight parameters and performance systems. The significant mental effort required of the pilot to keep track of the number of displays and instruments necessitated the development of a new display concept.

1.1 Multi-function Displays

The tradition of using one dedicated display for a single flight instrument was put aside when Electronic Flight Instrument Systems or 'glass cockpits', were introduced. The important benefit of this display ideology was the ability to declutter the cockpit by reducing the number of individual display instruments by compiling flight data into an integrated, easily understood picture of the aircraft. Furthermore, using soft keys (configurable buttons) the pilot can configure the displays to show the different types of information on the same multi-function display (MFD) further reducing the space requirements for physical instruments.

© Springer International Publishing Switzerland 2015
M. Antona and C. Stephanidis (Eds.): UAHCI 2015, Part II, LNCS 9176, pp. 538–549, 2015.
DOI: 10.1007/978-3-319-20681-3_51

The multi-functionality of a single display provided an unprecedented amount of flexibility to both cockpit display designers and pilots, and was a timely solution of the need for pilots to exhibit short-term flexibility while maintaining long-term adaptability [6]. A good example of the benefits of the MFD is the evolution of the F-15 cockpit. The F-15A variant, operational in 1975, housed 28 electromechanical instruments, two cathode ray tube (CRT) displays and a multifunction HUD. By the mid 1980s the F-15E variant possessed half the number of dedicated instruments, a HUD, and three fully multi-function CRT displays [44]. This permitted the pilot to arrange the data required for each mission in the most convenient position in the cockpit. The other significant 'benefit' from glass cockpits has been to obviate the role of the flight engineer by allowing the pilot and co-pilot to monitor and interact with the aircraft's systems themselves via the displays.

1.2 Display Interaction

One of the biggest challenges in the glass cockpit is to comprehensively understand and successfully interact with flight systems through the MFDs. Even with the increased automation and data reduction the current cockpit still constrains the transfer of information to the pilot as they must assimilate all the data from the panel displays to build a three-dimensional mental model of the aircraft and the external environment. With this in mind, MFDs should be designed to provide intuitive interfaces for ease of learning and ease of use as well as to support the information decoding process. This is true of both the interaction method and the graphical user interface design [32]. With fewer displays there are increasing demands on effective cursor control devices (CCDs) which act as the primary interface technology with the display-driven cockpit.

Existing CCDs do not necessarily best match with pilots' basic cognitive and psychomotor capabilities or, more generally, are slow and overly complex ways of controlling a specific function. The result of this is more training time required for efficient use, and increases the potential risk of cognitive overloading in high workload situations. As one older pilot is reported to have said regarding the use of cockpit automation: "Thus far, my mind/hand/feet combination is faster than my monitoring/programming capabilities" [47]. Whilst this could be argued as a factor of experience, it is true that current cockpit architectures are fast reaching a limit on the number of systems that can be efficiently operated by pilots, necessitating different design approaches based on the principles of natural and direct hands-on interaction [45]. Consequently, effective pilot interaction with MFDs in accessing the data or programming flight plans plays an important role in reducing cognitive load, better enabling the pilot to generate the mental model of the aircraft and thus improving flight safety.

Many of these limitations in pilot-cockpit interaction were originally recognised at least three decades ago by the United States Air Force which idealised solving all of these problems in one 'Super Cockpit' [25]; a generic crew station that would conform to operators' natural perceptual, cognitive, and motor capabilities. Technologies were envisaged that would provide the means to create virtual worlds with visual and auditory fidelity, and perceive operators interactions using cognitively simpler, 'biocybernetic' control inputs. Other facilities of similar goals were concerned with the civilian sphere of aviation [14], examining the possibilities of keyboards, touch panels, and voice controls. Interestingly, Furness also predicted many of the solutions being implemented or proposed today. The envisaged Super Cockpit made use of the following five input modalities: (1) Head-aimed control, (2) Voice-actuated control, (3) Touch sensitive panels, (4) Virtual hand control, and (5) Eye gaze control. The first of these (head-aiming) had just been introduced in Apache gunships, though not for the functionality that Furness envisaged. The next two (voice and touch control) are only now being introduced into the 5th generation of military jet fighter aircraft. Recent developments in eye-tracking technology is looking promising as the next interesting development in pilot-cockpit interaction.

2   Cursor Control Devices

Table 1 identifies the types of existing CCDs found in various aircraft types. There is some commonality within aircraft types but increasingly there is divergence based on manufacturers' preferences. Thumbsticks are typical of rotorcraft and business jets, tending to be mounted on the control yoke or arm rests respectively. Trackballs and touchpads in integrated hand rests are also used in business jets, and Thales' new TopDesk design for helicopters features a trackball hand rest. The newly designed flight management system (FMS) on the Airbus A380 uses the same style of hand rest with integrated trackball and buttons, in addition to a QWERTY keyboard and trackpad for the on-board information system.

In fighter jets fingersticks are common, positioned on the throttle lever and forming part of the hands-on-throttle-and-stick (HOTAS) system that is common-place in this type of aircraft. Modern fighters from the turn of the century also provide direct voice input (DVI) systems. In the Eurofighter Typhoon it can be used to control a wide range of functions from weapons system management, to format selection and manipulation, to alphanumeric data entry [28]. The combination of DVI and throttle and stick controls (voice, throttle and stick; VTAS system) means that the pilot can manipulate the vast majority of controls while keeping their hands on the throttle and stick. It was originally considered for the F-22 but was ultimately judged too technically risky and not included. In a study by Zon and Roerdink [51] airline pilots reported that the current usability of DVI may be a bit too unpredictable for high workload situations. Were it more reliable it would be a very useful tool for emergency situations.

Some recent fighters (such as the Dassault Rafale and Lockheed Martin F-35) also integrate a touchscreen display in the cockpit. Touchscreen displays have also been retrofitted into older F-18 aircraft still in service, and are increasingly being used in modern business jets. Research in such tactile touch displays shows promising benefits in situational awareness and quicker access of information [1,32], though there remains work to be done to better understand the ergonomic factors and robustness under vibration [4].

Table 1. Types of cursor control devices (CCD) in various aircraft

	Aircraft	Type	Year	Thumbstick	Fingerstick	Trackpad	Trackball	Touchscreen	Voice
Civil	Boeing 777	Jet airliner	1995		•				
	Gulfstream G150	Business jet	2001	•					
	AugstaWestland AW139	Utility helicopter	2003	•					
	Airbus A380	Jet airliner	2007			•	•		
Military	A-10 Thunderbolt II	4th gen. jet fighter	1977	•					
	AH-64 Apache	Attack helicopter	1986	•					
	Dassault Rafale	4.5th gen. jet fighter	2001	•				•	•
	Eurofighter Typhoon	4.5th gen. jet fighter	2003	•					•
	Boeing KC-767	Refuelling tanker	2005			•			
	F-35 Lightning II	5th gen. jet fighter	2015	•				•	•

There have been many studies on the performance of various CCDs in a general context and for the office environment (e.g. [20,23]), often proving the enduring performance of the mouse. However the high vibration and high acceleration environment of cockpits eliminates it as a viable option. More unconventional, but intuitive interaction methods such as eye tracking or gesture control are being actively pursued in human-computer interaction (HCI) research. Some of these modalities, at various points in the last 30 years, were proposed for the cockpit but were held back by the state of technology at the time. Continuing developments in these modalities are making their use more and more viable.

2.1 Head-Aiming

Helmet-mounted displays (HMD) have been the mainstay of military fixed and rotary wing aircraft since the 1970s. It is now slowly migrating to commercial aviation where lower cost head-worn displays (HWDs) are being developed. They revolutionised targeting with 'off-boresighting' launching - the ability to aim and target objects with short range missiles by looking at them, rather than navigating the aircraft's nose to face it.

The significance of these systems is in the migration away from head down displays, where a pilot would have had to use a CCD to pick targets from a display, which would compromise situational awareness. Furness [25] envisaged such systems to also enable the pilot to place a stabilised reticle over a virtual switch in the cockpit and press an enabling switch to activate that particular function. Some research into the physicality of such a system showed promising results, and when combined with other modalities [8]. Advances in the fidelity of augmented reality [15,16,27] are certain to make this a more viable system, though cockpit stabilisation from turbulence, vibration, and G-forces will be needed [43,46] for both the augmented visuals and cursor control in the form of biodynamic and vibration compensation [35,36].

2.2   Eye Gaze Aiming

Eye tracking, and subsequently point of gaze cursor control, has been a keen topic in general HCI research (consider [10,21], or [42] for a survey). Eye tracking techniques have also been extensively used to examine both pilot's and air traffic controller's instrument scanning techniques (e.g. [7,19,22,33,34]). In a series of experimental investigations Calhoun *et. al.* [11–13] and Borah [8] examined the possibility of utilising eye gaze for selection of switches in a cockpit environment. These studies concluded that selecting switches with eye gaze was both intuitive and as fast as selecting switches manually with a hand. The same proposition for eye gaze control was made a few years later, but in the context of the civilian flight deck [39]. Eye control would be a promising interface control for operations under acceleration when arm and hand movement is difficult, if not impossible. It is however important to consider the viability of eye-tracking in a variety of task-loaded conditions involving concurrent visual tasks [12] (e.g. tracking tasks, target searching, visual monitoring) and whether interference can occur.

Modern eye trackers are small, accurate and their output can be processed in real time, making the way towards the inclusion of such an eye tracking system embedded into the HMD viable. Such a system would then enable a pilot, using a colour-capable display, to lock targets and guide weapons solely with his eye [18]. This also brings the potential of combined head movement and eye gaze selection in the cockpit [30] or eye gaze with voice activation [26,29]. However, current (especially commercial) eye tracking systems must be improved with regards to reliability and robustness to external motions. Pilots involved with the research in [18] frequently had issues with degrading calibration, and alignment drift due to shifting helmets. The authors' own experience using eye trackers has been similar, encountering differing accuracy and precision between individual users likely due to the effectiveness and robustness of the calibration process. In the presence of such issues eye gaze control with switching to another, fine-tuning modality is a promising strategy, especially when targets are small [8,38].

2.3   Hand/Gesture Control

Of the possible CCD concepts discussed here hand/arm or gesture control is the least developed, with little research to-date being conducted in the area of aircraft cockpits. It is however being actively pursued for cars [2,49,50], whilst some have proposed gesture-based flight control of unmanned systems [24,41]. Furness' idea of a virtual hand controller in a fighter cockpit [25] would involve a tracking system able to sense a pilot's hand position and orientation with six degrees-of-freedom. When the hand is put into a pre-determined volume or region within the cockpit, a three-dimensional virtual control panel appears, allowing the pilot to activate functions or make vernier adjustments by moving his hand or placing a finger over a virtual switch.

Recent attempts and ideas at gesture control in a cockpit environment extol the primary benefits of natural and intuitive control and, consequently, of lower cognitive overhead [3]. Technically this kind of system could easily be achieved using existing tracking methods for helmets, but tailored for the pilot's gloves. However the practicality of such a system will have to deal with effective feedback (auditory, visual, or tactile feedback), and the issues already discussed regarding vibration compensation in the virtual displays. Such a system may become more desirable the further the piloting task moves away from the HOTAS paradigm. With current technology it may be easier to implement in the more benign environments of unmanned and air traffic control stations.

3 Experimental Work

The authors' research is motivated by a modern evaluation of conceptual designs for future cockpit interaction systems. Technology has improved since the original ideas were born in the 1980s, and recent systems may have sufficiently matured to provide more viable solutions. In order to evaluate the performance of intuitive 'bio-cybernetic' control devices a repeated measures dual task experiment involving a flight monitoring task was designed and carried out.

3.1 Experiment Design

Ten participants, with a mean age of 32.4 years and ranging between 24 and 51 years, were asked to complete a point-and-selection task based in a MFD simulation whilst monitoring an aircraft's changing heading on a HUD from a flight simulator. An audio cue with randomised interval was used to instruct the subjects to report the heading value into a microphone whilst completing the MFD task. The flight path and turn rate, $\dot{\psi}$, from the simulator was randomised. The subjects were screened only for normal visual and auditory acuity; specifically, they were screened on their ability to read the HUD parameter from the seating position and to detect the audio cue. The experimental setup is shown in Fig. 1.

Four different CCDs were investigated: (1) a HOTAS pointer, (2) an eye tracker, (3) a head tracker, and (4) a hand tracker. The HOTAS pointer is a standard CCD of modern fighter jets – the particular one used here is part of a Thrustmaster A10-C Warthog replica throttle box. The pointer itself is a pressure sensitive pointing stick with integrated button. The Tobii X2-60 eye tracker consists of two infrared emitters and two 60 Hz IR cameras. The IR light reflected by the subject's cornea and the detected centre of the pupil by image processing software are used to calculate the three-dimensional rotation of each eyeball, and hence the gaze direction. The Emotiv EPOC incorporates a two axes gyro-based inertial measurement system which can be used to detect a subject's head movement. Lastly, the Leap motion hand recognition tracking system was used to detect and output hand motion. For each device specific software was used to map their output to movement of the display screen cursor.

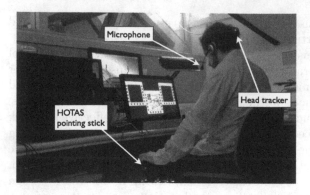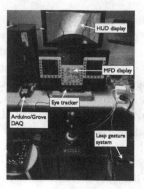

Fig. 1. Experimental setup

3.2 Preliminary Results and Observations

Figure 2 shows the task completion times for each device where a repeated measures ANOVA showed a statistically significant difference, $F(1.14, 10.25) = 4.89$, $p < 0.05$, with the head tracker performing the best and significantly better than the HOTAS following a Tukey-Kramer multiple comparison analysis ($p < 0.05$). The issues discussed above concerning the accuracy and precision of the eye tracker were experienced here. Note that in the initial, ballistic phase of cursor movement the eye tracker can perform faster than the other methods (evident from the steeper gradient in Fig. 3); the larger task completion times are due to the accuracy and drift issues for some participants in completing

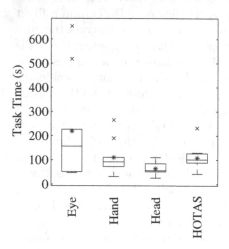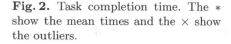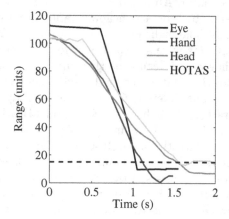

Fig. 2. Task completion time. The *
show the mean times and the × show
the outliers.

Fig. 3. Typical example of cursor
movements towards a target.

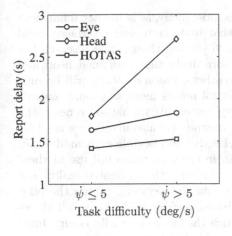

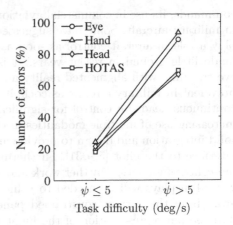

Fig. 4. Report delay between task difficulty. Hand tracker results are excluded due to inconclusive data.

Fig. 5. Percentage of errors between task difficult.

the final, corrective phase of cursor movement. Therefore the provision of finer control from another modality, or an adaption technique (e.g. magnetic cursor), still seems necessary for implementing an eye tracking solution. Also noticeable from Fig. 3 is a significant latency (approximately 300 ms) in the eye tracker's response.

In the interactions shown in Fig. 4 a small (a mean of approximately half a second) difference in the reporting delays using the different devices was obtained. The delay report is taken as the time from when the audio cue is made, to when the participant speaks in the voice recording. The interaction in Fig. 5 shows the effect of device and task difficulty on the errors in the reported values. An error is counted when the value reported by the participant was greater than 3 degrees from that of the flight simulator. As the task difficulty (the turn rate) was randomised due to limitations in the flight simulator, distribution of samples across task difficulty was not balanced and a percentage ratio of errors against the sample size is shown. Of note from these results a greater increase in the number errors for the eye and hand trackers, but an apparent larger influence of the head tracker on reporting delay (Fig. 4), though neither of these effects were found to be statistically significant from the current data.

4   Future Trends

Touch displays are currently being deployed in some aircraft and research is likely to continue on improving their reliability and performance, integrating them with particular systems (such as the FMS [32]), or in developing larger projection displays [17]. Given the recent developments and improving fidelity of voice commands, its use in commercial aviation is most likely, as is further refinement in military aircraft. Some have suggested that brain computer interfaces could play a role in aircraft control as soon as 2020 [40,48], though this research has made little ground in recent years. It is more likely that combined head and eye tracking, with augmented reality and synthetic vision displays, will become prevalent in military aircraft as cockpit control moves more and more towards continuous heads-up control for significantly better situational awareness. The increasing use of multiple modalities in the cockpit will also mandate a need for solid integration and design to provide an effective and flexible multimodal user interface to the pilot [5,9,31]. Furthermore, in order to make full use of these bio-centric modalities, further work and integration with augmented reality and virtual displays will be needed to achieve a complete system, taking the pilot away from the current constrained panel-based cockpit and into a full three-dimensional representation of the flight which the pilot can easily comprehend and interact with in a more naturally perceivable fashion.

5   Conclusions

In this paper a brief summary of the current state and future developments in aircraft cockpit interaction has been presented. Initial experimental work has looked into some of these in the form of 'bio-cybernetic' CCDs, where the benefits and limitations with regards to performance, cognitive load, and interference with flight tasks need to be considered. Initial results favour head tracking, though if the calibration and drift issues with eye tracking technology can be overcome they would provide a significant capability to pilots in interacting with cockpit controls and displays. Current research in the field is focusing on developing and evaluating touch displays, whilst direct voice input is also likely to play an increasing role in both civilian and military flight. Coupled eye and head tracking in HMDs will not only provide pilot's with a significant improvement in off-boresighting, but could also provide an effective interface with virtual cockpit controls in a wholly heads-up cockpit.

References

1. Alapetite, A., Fogh, R., Zammit-Mangion, D., Zammit, C., Agius, I., Fabbri, M., Pregnolato, M., Becouarn, L.: Direct tactile manipulation of the flight plan in a modern aircraft cockpit. In: International Conference on Human-Computer Interaction in Aerospace, Brussels, Belgium, September 2012
2. Alpern, M., Minardo, K.: Developing a car gesture interface for use as a secondary task. In: CHI 2003 Extended Abstracts on Human Factors in Computing Systems, Ft. Lauderdale, Florida, USA, pp. 932–933, April 2003
3. Amit, K., Shivangi, R.: Avionics control using 3D gestures. In: Proceedings of the 7th IRF International Conference, Goa, India, pp. 25–30, October 2014
4. Barbe, J., Wolff, M., Mollard, R.: Human centered design approach to integrate touch screen in future aircraft cockpits. In: Proceedings of the 15th International Conference on Human-Computer Interaction: Interaction Modalities and Techniques Part IV, Las Vegas, Nevada, USA, pp. 429–438, July 2013

5. Bastide, R., Nigay, L., Bazalgette, D., Bellik, Y., Nouvel, C.: The INTUITION design process: structuring military multimodal interactive cockpits design according to the MVC design pattern. In: Proceedings of the International Conference on Human-Computer Interaction, Las Vegas, Nevada, USA, July 2005

6. Baty, D.L., Watkins, M.L.: An advanced cockpit instrumentation system: The coordinated cockpit display. NASA Techincal Memorandum, vol. 78559. Imprint, Washington, DC (1979)

7. Bjorklund, C.M., Alfredson, J., Dekker, S.W.A.: Mode monitoring and call-outs: an eye-tracking study of two-crew automated flight deck operations. Int. J. Aviat. Psychol. 16(3), 257–269 (2006)

8. Borah, J.: Investigation of eye and head controlled cursor positioning techniques. Air Force Materiel Command Report AL/CF-SR-1995-0018, September 1995

9. Bouchet, J., Nigay, L., Ganille, T.: The ICARE component-based approach for multimodal input interaction: application to real-time military airraft cockpits. In: Proceedings of the 11th International Conference on Human-Computer Interaction, Las Vegas, Nevada, USA, July 2005

10. Bulling, A., Gellersen, H.: Toward mobile eye-based human-computer interaction. IEEE Pervasive Comput. 9(4), 8–12 (2010)

11. Calhoun, G.L., Arbak, C.J., Boff, K.R.: Eye-controlled switching for crew station design. In: Proceedings of the Human Factors and Ergonomics Society 28th Annual Meeting, Santa Monica, California, USA, vol. 28, pp. 258–262, October 1984

12. Calhoun, G.L., Janson, W.P.: Eye line-of-sight control compared to manual selection of discrete switches. AFSC Technical Report AL-TR-1991-0015, April 1991

13. Calhoun, G.L., Janson, W.P., Arbak, C.J.: Use of eye control to select switches. In: Proceedings of the Human Factors and Ergonomics Society 30th Annual Meeting, Dayton, Ohio, USA, vol. 30, pp. 154–158, September 1986

14. Chappell, S.L., Sexton, G.A.: Advanced concepts flight simulation facility. Appl. Ergonomics 17(4), 252–256 (1986)

15. Chinthammit, W., Seibel, E.J., Furness, T.A.: Unique shared-aperture display with head or target tracking. In: Proceedings of the IEEE Virtual Reality Conference 2002, Orlando, Florida, USA, pp. 235–242, March 2002

16. Chinthammit, W., Seibel, E.J., Furness, T.A.: A shared-aperture tracking display for augmented reality. Presence 12(1), 1–17 (2003)

17. Cuypers, D., Smet, H.D., Hugel, X., Dubroca, G.: Projection technology for future airplane cockpits. In: Proceedings of the International Display Workshops, Kyoto, Japan, vol. 19, pp. 1995–1998, December 2012

18. de Reus, A.J.C., Zon, R., Ouwerkerk, R.: Exploring the use of an eye tracker in a helmet mounted display. National Aerospace Laboratory Technical report NLR-TP-2012-001, November 2012

19. Di Nocera, F., Camilli, M., Terenzi, M.: A random glance at the flight deck: pilots' scanning strategies and the real-time assessment of mental workload. J. Cogn. Eng. Decis. Making 1(3), 271–285 (2007)

20. Doyon-Poulin, P., Routhier, N.: Use of throughput to evaluate a cursor control device (ccd) performance. In: 31st Conference of Applied Statistics in Ireland, Galway, Ireland, May 2011

21. Duchowski, A.T.: A breadth-first survey of eye tracking applications. Behav. Res. Methods Instrum. Comput. 34(4), 455–470 (2002)

22. Dunn, R.S., Haspel, D.L.: Development of a low-cost helmet mounted eye gaze sensor. Technical report TM 88–46 SY, Naval Air Test Center, October 1988

23. Epps, B.W.: Comparison of six cursor control devices based on fitts' law. In: Proceedings of the Human Factors and Ergonomics Society 30th Annual Meeting, Dayton, Ohio, USA, vol. 30, pp. 327–331, September 1986
24. Fong, T., Thorpe, C.: Vehicle teleoperation interfaces. Auton. Robots 11(1), 9–18 (2001)
25. Furness, T.A.: The super cockpit and its human factors challenges. In: Proceedings of the Human Factors and Ergonomics Society Annual Meeting, Dayton, Ohio, USA, vol. 30, pp. 48–52, September-October 1986
26. Glenn, F.A., Iavecchia, H.P., Ross, L.V., Stokes, J.M., Weiland, W.J., Weiss, D., Zakland, A.L.: Eye-voice-controlled interface. In: Proceedings of the Human Factors and Ergonomics Society 30th Annual Meeting, Dayton, Ohio, USA, vol. 30, pp. 322–326, September 1986
27. Haas, M.W.: Virtually-augmented interfaces for tactical aircraft. Biol. Psychol. 40(1–2), 229–238 (1995)
28. Hartley, K.: The eurofighter development programme. Air Space Eur. 1(3), 46–50 (1999)
29. Hatfield, F., Jenkins, E.A., Jennings, M.W.: Eye / voice mission planning interface (EVMPI). Technical report AL/CF-TR-1995-0204, Air Force Materiel Command, December 1995
30. Janson, W.P.: Eye and head response to peripheral targets. USAF Technical Report AAMRL-TR-89-033, August 1989
31. Jovanovic, Mladjan, Starcevic, Dusan, Obrenovic, Zeljko: Designing aircraft cockpit displays: borrowing from multimodal user interfaces. In: Gavrilova, Marina L., Tan, CJKenneth (eds.) Transactions on Computational Science III. LNCS, vol. 5300, pp. 55–65. Springer, Heidelberg (2009)
32. Kaber, D.B., Riley, J.M., Tan, K.W.: Improved usability of aviation automation through direct manipulation and graphical user interface design. Int. J. Aviat. Psychol. 12(2), 153–178 (2002)
33. Karsten, G., Goldberg, B., Rood, R., Sulzer, R.: Oculometer measurement of air traffic controller visual attention. Federal Aviation Administration Interim Report FAA-NA-74-61, February 1975
34. Kasarskis, P., Stehwien, J., Hickox, J., Aretz, A., Wickens, C.: Comparison of expert and novice scan behaviors during VFR flight. In: 11th International Symposium on Aviation Psychology, Columbus, Ohio, USA, March 2001
35. Lifshitz, S., Merhav, S.J.: Adaptive suppression of biodynamic interference in helmet-mounted displays and head teleoperation. J. Guidance Control Dyn. 14(6), 1173–1180 (1991)
36. Lifshitz, S., Merhav, S.J., Grunwald, A.J., Tucker, G.E., Tischler, M.B.: Suppression of biodynamic interference in head-tracked teleoperation. NASA Technical Memorandum 103833, January 1991
37. Lovesey, E.J.: The instrument explosion - a study of aircraft cockpit instruments. Appl. Ergonomics 8(1), 23–30 (1977)
38. McMillan, G.R., Eggleston, R.G., Anderson, T.R.: Nonconventional controls. In: Hanbook of Human Factors and Ergonomics, 2nd edn., pp. 729–771. Wiley (1997)
39. Merchant, S., Schnell, T.: Applying eye tracking as an alternative approach for activation of controls and functions in aircraft. In: Proceedings of the 19th Digital Avionics Systems Conference, Philadelphia, Pennsylvania, USA, vol. 2, October 2000
40. Nayak, S.: Technologies enabling the cockpit of the future: User-friendly UI and seamless connectivity driving next-gen cockpit. Frost and Sullivan Technical Insights Webinar, August 2014

41. Nelson, W.T., Anderson, T.R., McMillian, G.R.: Alternative control technology for uninhabited aerial vehicles: Human factors considerations. In: Virtual and Adaptive Environments: Applications, Implications, and Human Performance Issues, ch. 14, pp. 303–324. Taylor and Francis (2008)

42. Raynor, K.: Eye movements in reading and information processing: 20 years of research. Psychol. Bull. **124**(3), 372–422 (1998)

43. Smith, S.D., Smith, J.A.: Head and helmet biodynamics and tracking performance in vibration environments. Aviat. Space Environ. Med. **77**(4), 388–397 (2006)

44. Sokol, T.C., Stekler, H.O.: Technological change in the military aircraft cockpit industry. Technol. Forecast. Soc. Chang. **33**, 55–62 (1988)

45. Thales: Thales unveils Avionics 2020 the cockpit of the future. now. Press Release (June 2013)

46. Tung, K.A., Miller, M.E., Colombi, J.M., Smith, S.: Eye movement in a vibrating HMD envrionment. In: Proceedings of the 2014 Industrial and Systems Engineering Research Conference, Montreal, Canada, May-June 2014

47. Wiener, E.L.: Human factors of advanced technology ("glass cockpit") transport aircraft. NASA Contractor Report 177528, NASA Ames Research Center, June 1989

48. Wourms, D.F., Mansfield, L., Cummingham, P.H.: Status update of alternative control and display technologies, Volume I: Final report. US Army Reserach Laboratory HSIAC-RA-2001-001, May 2001

49. Zobl, M., Geiger, M., Bengler, K., Lang, M.: A usability study on hand gesture controlled operation of in-car devices. In: Proceedings of the SIGCHI Conference on Human Factors in Computing Systems. Seattle, Washington, USA, March 2001

50. Zobl, M., Geiger, M., Schuller, B., Lang, M., Rigoll, G.: A real-time system for hand gesture controlled operation of in-car devices. In: Proceedings of the IEEE International Conference on Multimedia and Expo, San Jose, California, USA, vol. 3, pp. 541–544, July 2003

51. Zon, G.D.R., Roerdink, M.I.: Using voice to control the civil flightdeck. National Aerospace Laboratory Technical report NLR-TP-2006-720, March 2007

Applying Universal Design Principles to Themes for Wearables

Vladimir Tomberg[1(✉)], Trenton Schulz[2], and Sebastian Kelle[3]

[1] Institute of Informatics, Tallinn University, Tallinn, Estonia
vtomberg@tlu.ee
[2] Norwegian Computing Center, Oslo, Norway
Trenton.Schulz@nr.no
[3] Stuttgart Media University, Stuttgart, Germany
kelle@hdm-stuttgart.de

Abstract. Wearable computing offers new opportunities for technology to help us in many different contexts. Yet, it is important that designers of wearable devices take into account Universal Design principles to ensure that as many people as possible can benefit. We discuss the possible advantages of applying universal design principles to different themes that wearable technologies address. We use six themes that are driving wearable enhancements. These themes cut across industry and use cases; most wearable technologies will use at least one of these themes. We take each of the universal design principles and see how they apply to each theme and what advantages can be expected from such an application. The study shows that a balance needs to be achieved to the accessibility, usability, and general use of a wearable device.

Keywords: Wearables · Wearable computing · Design · Universal design

1   Introduction

Wearables, also known as wearable computers, became widely known because of the popularity of activity trackers. A wearable is a fully functional, self-powered, self-contained computer that is worn on the body, providing access to and interaction with information anywhere and at anytime [1]. Wearables are not a new trend: experiments from the 1960 s [2] helped pave the way for wearables. According to BI Intelligence, the market of wearables has grown by 50 millions of units from 2010 to 2015 [3].

While wearable tracking devices are becoming popular, the problem of technology acceptance is still remains. According to Moti & Caine [4], more than half of U.S. consumers who have owned an activity tracker no longer use it. A third of U.S. consumers who have owned one stopped using the device within six months of receiving it. Moti & Caine argue that human factors need to be addressed during the early design stage of wearable applications. To accomplish this, we need to identify principles that are relevant for designing a human-centered wearable application. Moti & Caine propose a set of principles; other authors proposed their own design principles for wearables with different focus and degree of granularity [5–8].

© Springer International Publishing Switzerland 2015
M. Antona and C. Stephanidis (Eds.): UAHCI 2015, Part II, LNCS 9176, pp. 550–560, 2015.
DOI: 10.1007/978-3-319-20681-3_52

Instead of proposing our own framework, we examine the well-known and mature Universal Design (UD) principles, which were approved by community of designers during the last 17 years. We aim to understand what impact does Universal Design have to designing wearables?

We apply UD principles to themes that drive wearable enhancements instead of dividing the area of research to sectors, products, applications and functions [9]. First, the themes are general: they can drive design of wearables that do not exist today. Themes are good triggers that include the main motivation for a design. A theme is not limited to a specific application domain and one wearable device can be driven by several themes at once. For example, the same wearable may be used by someone to track their accuracy in performing an action, while another may use it to test the progression of rehabilitation. Since themes represent more general concepts, they can be separately examined on compliance with specific design approaches. The results of such examination can be then emphasized in the inherited domains and applications.

2   From the Internet of Everything to Wearables

The Internet of Everything (IoE) has its beginning in the Internet of Things (IoT). The Internet of Things was originally introduced as a concept for describing a world where RFID chips would be used for tracking different objects [10]. Though these chips were not on the Internet, their movement and exchanging of information among themselves mimicked exchange of data. It was a literal network of things. Yet, other definitions exist [11], and a more common understanding now is to think of an object or thing that is on the Internet, but not a traditional computer. For example, Busch et al. [12] present an idea for a medicine cabinet that can help people remember to take their medicine; it accomplishes this by keeping track of the pill boxes and knowing the medicine schedule for the person. Over time, radios and sensors have become smaller, and more things can contain them. It is now possible for a home to have many different devices that are using the Internet. The addition of objects and services using the Internet brings its own set of trust and UD issues [13].

As the popularity of the idea of the Internet of Things moved from beyond research into consumer consciousness, Cisco [14] introduced the idea of the IoE to highlight that only a small subset of things are connected to the Internet, and adding more objects would result in better use of data and connections. If wearable computing devices (or wearables) have some sort of connection and are able to talk to each different object, we have wearables as good candidates for making better use of data and connections.

Wearables allow people to do different types of computing in new contexts, basically wherever the person is, without having to involve the person's hands or another device. The idea behind wearables is to make making computers small enough and energy efficient enough so they can be used in different articles of clothing or other accessories. The most popular forms are items that can be put around your wrist, worn around the body, worn as eyeglasses, or something small that can fit into a pocket. Many of the current devices help in recording fitness data. Most of these devices do not offer a traditional interface as found on a PC. Many require little or no input from the wearer at all; all information is gathered automatically. The collected data is sent to servers where it is analyzed and interpreted by semantic engines. Others provide a voice-driven interface. Some of these devices do not have a direct connection to the Internet, but instead piggyback off another device (for example, connecting to a smartphone through Bluetooth and pushing heavy processing off to the phone).

Since wearables (like clothes) can be with us in multiple contexts, it makes sense to not categorize wearables by industry or product type, but to look at themes driving wearable enhancements. That is, what sort of goals or uses a person may have for a wearable. A wearable may also be composed of different themes, so it we don't have to be strict about where a wearable belongs. PSFK Labs [15] defines six themes:

- **Bio-Tech Fusion**: technologies quickly evolve by creating a closer relationship between wearable devices and the human body. Examples include wearable devices that a person will seldom remove such as medical devices or activity tracking.
- **Synced Lifestyle**: ability to sync with a broader ecosystem of connected technologies. Many of the current fitness tracking devices aim to make it easier to keep track of activity done during the day and synchronize it with different cloud services.
- **Organic Computing**: opening the door for a more natural form of communication and computing by introducing wider range of human inputs from gestures to biometrics; for example using touches and hugs to transmit affection and care between people, especially when they are separated by a great distance.
- **Human Enhancement**: appearance of assistive technologies that are capable of both restoring and augmenting existing senses and abilities. This can work for security and safety, for example, detecting hazardous substances to indicating security levels to being assistive technology for helping someone with a disability to be more independent.
- **Health Empowerment**: empowering people to take a more active role in the management of their personal well-being. This goes beyond your typical fitness tracking to also include helping keep track of a medical condition or helping someone regulate a disease.
- **Personalized Context**: situated within a given context, self-aware devices and platforms can facilitate connected experiences that deliver greater meaning and relevancy into people's lives. For example, devices and wearables communicating to reduce lighting and play calming music at the end of a stressful day.

3   Principles of Universal Design

There are several terms that are simultaneously used for description of design that intended to include as much as possible wide target audience: Universal Design, Exclusive Design, and Design for All. While all three have different origins and different ways of individual evolution, they have similar goals and concepts and often are used as interchangeable ones [16, 17].

The term *Universal Design* comes from U.S., where the moving force for design for disabled influenced by the demographic change of the aging population. The huge population of veterans from several wars increased this need. The origin of the

Universal Design concept was proposed by Ronald L. Mace [18], program director of The Center for Universal Design in Carolina University. As a wheelchair user himself, Mace was focused on issues of accessibility in buildings. In his book, Mace outlined distinction of universal design to other types of design for people with special needs: "While accessible or adaptable design requirements are specified by codes or standards for only some buildings and are aimed at benefiting only some people (those with mobility limitations), the universal design concept targets all people of all ages, sizes, and abilities and is applied to all buildings" [19, p. 3].

While Mace was the first researcher who defined UD concept, his works were influenced by early ideas of UK researcher Goldsmith, which were published in his book Designing for the Disabled [20]. Also a wheelchair user, Goldsmith had professional roots in architecture. His attention was focused on accessible buildings, e.g., public toilets for users with special needs, steps and stairs, and tactile pavings [17].

In 1998, Mace with his colleagues extended definitions and described in detail UD guidelines in book, *The Universal Design File*, where they first time defined seven principles applicable to environmental accessibility [21]. UD was defined in the book as the design of products and environments to be usable to the greatest extent possible by people of all ages and abilities. Titles and descriptions of seven UD principles are as shown in Table 1.

Table 1. Principles for Universal Design and their definitions

Principle	Description
Equitable Use	The design is useful and marketable to people with diverse abilities
Flexibility in Use	The design accommodates a wide range of individual preferences and abilities
Simple and Intuitive Use	Use of the design is easy to understand, regardless of the user's experience, knowledge, language skills, or current concentration level
Perceptible Information	The design communicates necessary information effectively to the user, regardless of ambient conditions or the user's sensory abilities
Tolerance for Error	The design minimizes hazards and the adverse consequences of accidental or unintended actions
Low Physical Effort	The design can be used efficiently and comfortably and with a minimum of fatigue
Size and Space for Approach and Use	Appropriate size and space is provided for approach, reach, manipulation, and use regardless of user's body size, posture, or mobility

4   Applying UD Principles to Wearable Technologies

As Story et al. [22] suggested, besides educating designers and consumers about the characteristics of more usable products and environments, UD principles could be applied to *evaluate* existing designs and *guide* the design process.

Universal Design principles can be applied in different ways and to the different domains. There are three examples of applying of Simple and Intuitive principle proposed by Story:

- For architecture — methods of creating clear environmental way-finding features;
- For products — methods of applying the concepts of correspondence and cognitive mapping to user interfaces;
- For software — methods of supporting broadly accessible user interaction modes [23].

For the study where wearables are a subject of research both the second and third methods are relevant.

Why it is important to use UD principles? Developing countries have advantages over industrialized countries, as they can avoid mistakes that the industrialized countries have committed. For these countries, Balaram proposed four areas of design intervention, where UD principles can be applied [24]:

- *Educating for the future*: as fostering positive attitudes toward people with different abilities as part of their regular education in schools, colleges, and universities;
- *Positive thinking by user groups*: people with disabilities should be seen as people with *different* capabilities rather than people with lesser capabilities;
- **Increasing the usability range**: universally designed products and environments can foster equality by adding universal features into usual products;
- *Bridging the gap between people*: there is a need for products that act as a bridge between different people and their needs, whether that difference is cultural or physical.

How do UD principles influence assistive technology? Designers who use UD principles [21] attempt to create solutions that are usable by as many people as possible instead of trying to create special solutions for a specific disability. As more services are being offered as digital-only, universal access and quality of use for the broadest possible user population is a requirement for citizens of an information society [25]. In this case, non-traditional interfaces can help people with disabilities live more independent and better lives or they can exclude them from any benefit and leave them as second-class citizens.

The importance of UD principles becomes apparent when taking a look at the flipside of things. Design can potentially become subject of abuse. According to Clarkson and Coleman, "we live in a world increasingly shaped by human intervention where design can enable or disable people" [17].

It is important to mention that the *Human Enhancement* theme has the same roots in accessibility as UD: UD and its close cousin, Accessible Design continue to gain popularity and their influence spreads; this causes society to change its collective conceptions about human functioning [26]. Therefore we can talk about two directions: applying UD principles to assistive design (which always will be relevant) and to other kinds of design, which do not aim improving accessibility.

In the following subsections we apply UD principles to different themes, and speculate on these applications.

4.1 Equitable Use

Equitable Use principle is transcending, integrating principle. Equitability imposes constraints on the other design principles and forces the integration of the other universal design principles [26].

For that principle, the following recommendations are defined: to provide the same means of use for all users, to avoid segregating or stigmatizing any users, to make provisions for privacy, security, and safety equally available to all users; make the design appealing to all users.

It seems natural that wearables can help in multiple contexts, but wearables also can be a way forward for achieving equality by including people with different abilities into use of modern services that improve quality of life. For example, the same heart rate sensors could be used by athletes for tracking their training and the elderly or infants for tracking their health. It is hard to imagine any area of use of the wearables, which does not aim the equality or the safety. Recommendation to test any wearables idea to *Equitable Use* principle could be considered as the first and essential activity when design process starts. Such testing could be useful for understanding that the idea does not contradict to equality and at the same time may provide prompts for use of the same wearables by diverse groups of people. Each theme that is introduced in the Sect. 2 is affected by *Equitable Use* principle.

The *Equitable Use* principle promotes such aspects as privacy, security, and safety, which can make designers examine ethical questions. *Human Enhancement, Health Empowerment, Personalized Context* themes seem as the most sensible for testing these aspects. The themes of *Human Enhancement* and *Health Empowerment* are all about *Equitable Use* assuming that they are helping to bridge gaps in human capacity or make it so someone can be more independent. The *Personalized Context* theme is also about *Equitable Use* since the idea is that the wearable fits a person (perhaps literally) and can be used in the context a person chooses.

Bio-Tech Fusion allows more people to participate in society. An automated syncing implied in the *Synched Lifestyle* allows information to be synced to multiple devices or presented on a device that works better for a particular person. *Organic Computing* implies new ways of interaction open up possibilities for others that cannot use other forms of communication. Of course, if they are dependent on average human skills, they may still limit their use.

4.2 Flexibility in Use

In contrast to the *Equitable Use* principle, the *Flexibility in Use* is the process-related principle. According to this principle, the design should accommodate a wide range of individual preferences and abilities. The principle can be applied to the design of wearables to provide choice in methods of use, facilitate the user's accuracy and precision, and provide adaptability to the user's pace. Flexibility is the common principle. Following it can hypothetically enhance user experience with any known wearable device. However, at first it could be considered for application to the themes that are the most rich by user-interactions like *Human Enhancement*. This theme aims restoring and augmenting existing senses and abilities that exactly requires taking into account the wide range of individual preferences and abilities. Adaptability looks like a challenging issue when it is applied to a body. Glasses, 3D printed exoskeletons, and embedded sensors should provide greater amount of flexibility and help users to adapt for different tasks and situations.

Another way to think of flexibility is the environments where it will be used. Like clothes, wearables may be used in a variety of conditions (e.g., rain, snow, extreme heat, extreme cold). They could also be under differing levels of stress and atmospheric pressure. The different wearable themes imply that a wearable will likely be used in multiple places in different conditions, indicating a need for flexibility.

4.3 Tolerance for Error

Tolerance for Error principle implies the design that minimizes hazards and the adverse consequences of accidental or unintended actions. While purely recreational wearable technology is less critical with respect to error-tolerance, assistive technology puts forth a higher requirement in this aspect. Assistive devices need to be dependable and reliable, especially during use in potentially hazardous situations, such as public transit. These qualities are the most important for *Human Enhancement* theme as it is mainly focused on the assistive technologies.

The second theme that is important for application of *Tolerance for Error* principle is *Bio-Tech Fusion*. As this theme aims for creating a closer relationship between the wearable and the human body, errors in such bio-tech products like implants can be risky for one's life.

When looking at the themes for wearables, one can hope that the wearable itself has some tolerance for error. For example, putting the device on backwards should not cause the wearable to suffer a catastrophic malfunction. It likely should be able to give some sort of indication about which ways is correct, but it might be possible to use it while worn incorrectly.

The more difficult issue is dealing with the computing the wearable does. If the wearable is part of the *Synced Lifestyle*, then the solution should allow for synchronization errors and corrections. If the wearable is providing *Health Empowerment* or a *Personalized Context*, it should avoid presenting data in a way that could cause the user to make a bad decision. *Organic Computing* wearables should tolerate errors in their input, especially since organic input is likely to be fuzzier than digital input. Finally, if the wearable is part of *Human Enhancement*, it should allow for human errors and corrections in daily use.

4.4 Simple and Intuitive Use

Simple and intuitive use principle is the third process-related principle. It promotes usability and simplicity of use. Design that follows this principle is easy to understand, regardless of the user's experience, knowledge, language skills, or current concentration level. Applying this idea to wearables is quite natural: one does not notice one's clothes, footwear, or glasses after dressing. The distinction of the wearables to other smart things is that the wearables, in many cases, should be imperceptible by the user. Often wearables have very simple user interfaces, sometimes with very small or even no screens at all. Designing of such interfaces requires use of non-standard design approaches [27]. Wearable that requires a lot of attention from the user will produce negative user experience and finally will be dropped.

If we examine the themes, the need for interfaces that are simple and easy to learn is almost baked into the themes themselves. *Bio-Tech Fusion, Organic Computing, Human Enhancement,* and *Health Empowerment* all require the wearable to work seamlessly with the wearer. This can only be accomplished if the wearable is easy to learn and simple to use. If the wearable is communicating with other devices as part of the *Synced Lifestyle*, this communication should be seamless and easy to set up. Alternatively, if the user wishes not allow communication, it should be possible to easily disable the communication. A *Personalized Context* implies that the interface should be tailored to the wearer and the context the wearer is in. Having an easy to learn and simple to use wearable would help in making this experience personal.

4.5 Perceptible Information

The aim of this principle is to communicate necessary information effectively to the user, regardless of ambient conditions or the user's sensory abilities.

Wearables that are addressing the themes of *Bio-Tech Fusion, Organic Computing, Human Enhancement,* or *Health Empowerment* may need to be in a form or worn in a location that makes using a display impractical, but other modalities are available. For example, the texture of the wearable could change resulting in different information based on the touch. Vibration could also be an effective way of providing information via touch. One could even examine creating different smells based on different situations. If the wearable is part of the *Synchronized Lifestyle*, it should be possible to export the information to a device or system that can present the information in the most accessible way for a person. Perceptible information is also a feature of personalization that would be needed for a wear's *Personalized Context*.

4.6 Low Physical Effort

The design can be used efficiently and comfortably and with a minimum of fatigue.

This is especially important when dealing with devices that have high requirements on ergonomics, such as custom-molded prosthetics or other gear that is in constant physical contact to the user.

Since most of the current wearables, such as sports trackers are designed to be worn for extended periods of time, they need to have a low amount of physical effort involved in their use. Any wearable that is addressing the themes in § 2 should not require much physical effort. If a wearable will be in everyday activities, it should not cause extra strain or be tiring itself. Wearables addressing the theme of *Human Enhancement*, *Health Empowerment*, or *Bio-Tech Fusion* may be worn by people who may have limited physical strength. A feature of the *Organic Computing* theme may be that it requires less effort than other forms of interaction. Looking at the theme of a *Synced Lifestyle*, synchronization with other devices should not cause great physical effort.

4.7 Size and Space for Approach and Use

This principle promotes an appropriate size and space, which should be provided for approach, reach, manipulation, and use regardless of user's body size, posture, or mobility.

This concept relates to the spatial dimensions of an appliance that typically should be adapting to the user's characteristics. We differentiate between the "one size fits all" and the "one size fits one" approach [28]. While the first approach is typically cheaper and simpler to achieve it yields a margin of users that are excluded, steepening the cost at a later point of time when they have to be included anyway. Using adaptive design patterns, the latter approach can be targeted at additional cost and effort with the cost curve flattening over time, e.g. during the maintenance phase.

In most cases, wearables abide by this principle regardless of the themes from Sect. 2. Wearables are on the person and eliminate their need for approach and use. If wearables are abiding by the other principles, then they are normally not getting in the way of the wearer. Even if a wearable is big and bulky, it's more an issue that the environment needs to be universally designed to accommodate the person wearing the wearable.

5 Discussion

This study shows that applying UD principles to the themes that drive wearable enhancements can provide interesting ideas that can be discussed in a framework of design process. The themes help generate concepts for wearables. At the same time, examining design concepts against UD principles offer designers constraints for equality, inclusion, and accessibility.

UD principles can be applied to products and architectures in a wide scope. If a product or a building meets all or some of the associated requirements, it is considered to be universally designed. One condition for success is mutual benefit—the design should benefit both users and the manufacturers [29]. On the other hand, universal design is not only a result (e.g. the wearable), but also a process. If a designer wants to know if something is universally designed, including people with disabilities is an important way to evaluate the wearable [30].

Overall, the question of balance between accessibility, usability and wearability of devices remains a complex problem, which we tried to soften by illuminating different dimensions and themes that are related to the issues at hand. On the one hand, a wearable device can be empowering, providing assistive technology to a user where and when needed. On the other hand, certain additional risks of failure emerge proportionally with the technical complexity of such devices.

An interesting point that puts emphasis on a critical viewpoint [4] is the observation that, ironically, wearables often have a low wearability, that is, they are not worn long periods of time. An example for this could be Google's Glass, which had two main reasons for failure. First, the battery life was too short—a problem that remains yet to be solved due to weight and size restrictions. The second factor was social acceptance; people were concerned about their privacy upon encountering a Glass wearer, because of the Glass's built-in camera. The latter effect sheds insight on the potential for wearables to cause unexpected effects that are not directly related to inherent design features — a challenge that hints at the assumption that Universal Design should not just focus on a single individual in user-centered design, but also consider wider environmental factors, e.g. social context.

This study shows that the application of UD principles to the themes that drive wearable enhancements may provide additional ideas that can have impact on design of the wearables. Such the application can be recommended on the earliest phases of wearables design process to discuss possible features, opportunities, restrictions, and risk. Also, the application can improve accessibility and adaptability of wearables that could broaden the base of potential users of the product.

References

1. Watier, K.: Marketing Wearable Computers to Consumers: An Examination of Early Adopter Consumers' Feelings and Attitudes Toward Wearable Computers (2003). http://www.watier.org/MarketingWearableComputerstoConsumers.pdf
2. Kieffner, T.: Wearable Computers: An Overview
3. Danova, T.: The Wearables Report: Growth trends, consumer attitudes, and why smartwatches will dominate. http://www.businessinsider.com/the-wearable-computing-market-report-2014-10
4. Motti, V., Caine, K.: Human Factors Considerations in the Design of Wearable Devices. In: Proceedings Human Factors …. (2014)
5. Lyons, K., Profita, H.: The multiple dispositions of On-Body and wearable devices. IEEE Pervasive Comput. 13, 24–31 (2014)
6. Weller, M.: 10 Top Wearable Technology Design Principles. http://www.designprinciplesftw.com/collections/10-top-wearable-technology-design-principles
7. Johnson, W.: Web Design Principles in Wearable Technology. http://www.business2community.com/tech-gadgets/web-design-principles-wearable-technology-0937461
8. Kitagawa, K.: 7 rules for designing wearable devices. http://embedded-computing.com/articles/7-rules-designing-wearable-devices-2/
9. Beecham Research Ltd., Wearable technologies: Wearable Technology Application Chart. http://www.beechamresearch.com/article.aspx?id=20

10. Ashton, K.: That internet of things thing. RFID J. **22**, 97–114 (2009)
11. Bassi, A., Horn, G.: Internet of Things in 2020: A Roadmap for the Future (2008)
12. Busch, M., Hochleitner, C., Lorenz, M., Schulz, T., Tscheligi, M., Wittstock, E.: All in: targeting trustworthiness for special needs user groups in the internet of things. In: Huth, M., Asokan, N., Čapkun, S., Flechais, I., Coles-Kemp, L. (eds.) TRUST 2013. LNCS, vol. 7904, pp. 223–231. Springer, Heidelberg (2013)
13. Schulz, T.: Creating universal designed and trustworthy objects for the internet of things. In: Zaphiris, P., Ioannou, A. (eds.) LCT. LNCS, vol. 8524, pp. 206–214. Springer, Heidelberg (2014)
14. Bradley, J., Barbier, J., Handler, D.: Embracing the Internet of Everything To Capture Your Share of $ 14.4 Trillion (2013)
15. Fawkes, P.: The Future of Key Trends Driving The Form and Function of Personal Devices. New York (2014)
16. Coleman, R.: The Case for inclusive design-an overview. In: Proceedings of the 12th Triennial congress international ergonomics association Human Factors Association Canada (1994)
17. John Clarkson, P., Coleman, R.: History of Inclusive Design in the UK. Appl. Ergon. **46**, Part B, 235–247 (2013)
18. Mace, R.: Universal Design, Barrier Free Environments for Everyone. Designers West, Los Angeles (1985)
19. Mace, R.: Universal design: housing for the lifespan of all people (1988)
20. Goldsmith, S.: Designing for the disabled (1967)
21. Connell, B., Jones, M., Mace, R., Mullick, A., Ostroff, E., Sanford, J., Steinfeld, E., Story, M., Vanderheiden, G.: About UD: Universal Design Principles. Version 2.0. Raleigh: The Center for Universal Design., Raleigh, NC (1997)
22. Story, M., Mueller, J.L., Mace, R.L.: The universal design file: designing for people of all ages and abilities. Des. Res. Methods J. **1**, 165 (2011)
23. Story, M.F.: Maximizing usability: the principles of universal design. Assist. Technol. **10**, 4–12 (1998)
24. Balaram, S.: Universal design and the majority world. In: Preiser, W.F.E., Smith, K.H. (eds.) Universal Design Handbook, pp. 50–55. McGraw-Hill, New York (2001)
25. Stephanidis, C., Jenkins, P., Karshmer, A.I., Murphy, H.J., Vanderheiden, G.: Toward an information society for all : an international R & D agenda session chairs. Int. J. Hum. Comput. Interact. **10**, 107–134 (1998)
26. Erlandson, R.F.: Universal and accessible design for products, services, and processes. CRC Press, Boca Ratonc (2010)
27. Kohl, J.: Designing For Smartwatches And Wearables To Enhance Real-Life Experience. http://www.smashingmagazine.com/2015/02/10/designing-for-smartwatches-wearables/
28. Edwards, A.D.N.: Extra-ordinary Human-Computer Interaction: Interfaces For Users with Disabilities. CUP Archive, Chapman (1995)
29. Choi, S.: Strategic Use of Universal Design as a Business Tool for 21st Century. Strategic Use of Universal Design as a Business Tool for 21st Century (2005)
30. Fuglerud, K.S., Sloan, D.: The link between inclusive design and innovation: some key elements. In: Kurosu, M. (ed.) HCII/HCI 2013, Part I. LNCS, vol. 8004, pp. 41–50. Springer, Heidelberg (2013)

A Method to Evaluate Intuitive Sense by Using a Robotic Tool: Towards Engineering for Assistive Technology and Accessibility

Gyanendra Nath Tripathi[1], Hiroaki Wagatsuma[1,2]([✉]),
Maya Dimitrova[3], Maria Vircikova[4], and Peter Sinčák[4]

[1] Graduate School of Life Science and Systems Engineering, Kyushu Institute
of Technology, 2-4 Hibikino, Wakamatsu-Ku, Kitakyushu 808-0196, Japan
tripathi-gyanendra-nath@edu.brain.kyutech.ac.jp
[2] RIKEN BSI, 2-1 Hirosawa, Wako, Saitama 351- 0198, Japan
waga@brain.kyutech.ac.jp
[3] Institute of Systems Engineering and Robotics, Bulgarian Academy
of Sciences, Acad. G. Bonchev str., bl. 2, P.O. Box 79, 1113 Sofia, Bulgaria
dimitrova@iser.bas.bg
[4] Center for Intelligent Technologies, Technical University of Kosice,
Letna, 9, 04001 Kosice, Slovakia
{maria.vircikova,peter.sincak}@tuke.sk

Abstract. The evaluation of subjective feelings of discomfort is a serious problem in the field of ergonomics, environment engineering and human-robot interactions. It is difficult to measure them by using objective quantifications in a traditional sense. We have hypothesized that the unpleasant feeling emerges caused by deviating from the autonomy, which exists in the perception-action cycle, the convective flow in two layers of intuition and perception and continuity in the dialogue. The present paper discusses the issue with respect to two examples; an unexpected breaking of balance in the trained motion and irritation at the lack of progress by discontinuity in the dialogue, and attempts to build a theoretical framework to detect a deviation from ongoing autonomy. This paper discusses a way of the theoretical modeling and explores possible implementations into the robotic experiment that reproduces human behaviors in need of supervision by the central nervous system. This preliminary report can contribute to an extension of the coupling between the central and peripheral nervous systems to social communications which is supported by assistive technologies and accessibility improvements.

Keywords: Assistive robots · Principle component analysis · Dynamical systems approach · Emotion · Levels of cognitive involvement

1 Introduction

A sensation of danger is happening even in well-accustomed motions in daily life such as slipping of the toe in running, mismatch of the chair's height at the last moment while sitting and uncomfortable feeling when entering to a broken escalator [1].

© Springer International Publishing Switzerland 2015
M. Antona and C. Stephanidis (Eds.): UAHCI 2015, Part II, LNCS 9176, pp. 561–569, 2015.
DOI: 10.1007/978-3-319-20681-3_53

The nervous and the musculoskeletal systems can provide an autonomy especially in repeated motion after motor learning, which is considered as a feedback control system to pursuit the desired trajectory on a rapid time scale [2]. On the other hand, the central nervous system monitors such motions globally, serving as a supervisor to know what the ideal schedule of segmented motions is and to connect them smoothly on a slow time scale. A possible interpretation is that the happening of mismatch between the two levels startles us and we feel some kind of danger [2].

Physiotherapists practically recognize that the degree of the remaining peripheral sensation determines the effect of rehabilitation, which traditionally focuses on the afferent input from the body to the brain [3, 4]. Recently the contribution of "aware-ness" of what is happening is highlighted [5, 6] and provides a clue to consider how the reality comes and what mechanism maintains it to be an appropriate coordination between the implicit perception-action cycle and the explicit perceiving process with a low temporal granularity [7, 8].

We have hypothesized that the control range of the implicit perception-action cycle - without any supervisor – changes, depending on the complexity of the behavior espe-cially on how much (to what extent) the unstable (uncontrollable) states are involved. In typical motion like walking stable and unstable states appear alternatively (alter-natingly) in the standing and swing phases of locomotion. The sitting motion on a chair is unstable at the last moment to release all the power of the body. The predictor knows how fast it comes back to the stable state, while it alerts if there is a large gap with the estimated time to stay in the unstable domain.

In the human-computer (assistive device) interaction, we consider that the com-fortable feeling is obtained (achieved) by the reduction of such a gap between the two types of cycles in automation and awareness. In the present study, as the preliminary result, we explore a way to visualize the stable and unstable states during motion by using a humanoid robot to reproduce the target motion.

For example, a target motion pattern can be described by the series of ideal positions of individual joints of the body. Autonomy is designed to follow such temporal sequences as a feedback control system to pursuit the ideal trajectory. However it is a passive system to minimize the error and there is no guarantee to exceed a certain maximum range of the error. If it is possible to introduce the supervision for the guarantee and the system is "aware" of the excess. The concept of the coupling between the central (aware system) and peripheral (autonomy) systems can apply to analyses investigating how social communications are smoothly maintained, and enlarge the possibility of supports by assistive technologies and accessibility improvements.

2 Why Autonomy?

We focus on the existence of a meeting point between the subconscious and conscious levels. According to Sigmund Freud's theory of human mind, which is remodeled by Ledoux [9] and Damásio [10] in neurological sense, the conscious state is represented by the tip of the iceberg of a whole entity of the mind, consisting of three levels such as conscious, preconscious and unconscious. Ledoux classified feelings and emotions, into subconscious and conscious levels respectively, in the viewpoint of dual neural pathways i.e. rapid limbic pathway from the thalamus to the amygdala and slow bypass routes through sensory cortices. The question of whether or not "physiological and behavioral responses precede subjective experience in emotions" was presented by William James [11–13], which is motivated by alternative hypotheses, (1) stimulus $\rightarrow$ feelings $\rightarrow$ responses and (2) stimulus (event) $\rightarrow$ responses (reactions) $\rightarrow$ subjective feelings (emotions). He noted that a physical response fight or flight when encountering a bear precedes a feeling of fear and concluded the cascade process as stimulus $\rightarrow$ physical responses $\rightarrow$ feedbacks to the cognitive system $\rightarrow$ emotions, conducted on the existence of the emotion-specific autonomic nervous system (ANS). In the viewpoint of "emergency responses" like fight or flight, Cannon [14] investigated functions of the sympathetic nervous system, which is one of the two main divisions of the autonomic nervous system, criticized the James's theory because that physical responses such as sweaty palms and a racing heart mainly governed by the sympathetic nervous system is too slow to be read out by the cognitive system to express emotions. Our emotions arise before exhibiting sweaty palms and a dry throat. This conflict of two hypotheses originated from the description of block diagrams, which force to determine which is first, but as Ledoux [9, 15] discussed, these two are inconsistent in their views of which emotion is labeled by which and consistent in a view that emotions associated with emotion-specific physical responses are different from other mind states. It implies the limitation of block diagram based modelings and flowcharts of functional blocks. Zajonc [11] presented a positive evidence to prove that inferences and reasoning are not necessary for the preference formation. In his experiment, subjects are not conscious of the presentation of stimuli but clearly determine a specific stimulus according to the presentation order as their own preference, which means the preference can be controlled on the subconscious level by the presentation order, i.e. a kind of subliminal effects. Similar experiments support affective functions without any conscious states, such as stereotype threat that triggers arousal [16]. Therefore, there is no doubt that we can not deal with emotions as vectors even in multidimensional spaces, like the extreme simplification known as Plutchik's diagram [17]. Once an emotion is represented by a vector representation to be an engineering approximation and then it is no longer possible to compare with biological and realistic emotions. As a clue to solve this duality in processes of unconscious feelings and subjective experiences like emotions, Ledoux [9, 15] suggests to consider the diversity and parallel processing of affective nervous systems. The amygdala, the core of affective nervous system to access the hormonal system, receives multiple resources from the sensory thalamus (characteristics of stimuli), sensory cortex (object recognition), entorhinal cortex (spatial and non-spatial associations), hippocampus (elimination of conditional memory), having different time scales for information processing. As he suggested, a possible interpretation of this complex network into a functional modeling is to describe a conjunction of the amygdala-centered surval circuit, the sensory system, the cognitive system modulatory systems, explicit memory systems, motivational system, in the assumption that innate, behavioral, ANS and hormonal responses are controlled by the surval circuit as rapid reactions and the motivational system governs goal-directed and purpose-oriented behaviors. The purpose in this paper is to find a meeting point between automated motion (stereotyped or learned) reactions and subjective feelings and build a method to measure a moment of interacting/uninteracting of the two processes. In other words, it can contribute for education of how the body feedback and CNS arousal access to the "Cognitive Workspace" which Ledoux illustrated [15].

3 Theoretical Frameworks for Implementation

In considering of the theoretical framework of autonomy and its supervision in the brain information processing, Tani [18] have emphasized the function of the actitipation, which can be considered as a consequence of the memory retrieval process involving the hippocampal episodic memory and the prefrontal decision-making process. Weng [19–22] consistently propose a possible framework for implementing such an automatic and predictable system into robots (Fig. 1). As Vernon et al. [22, 23] discussed, three types of modeling have been proposed; Characteristic, Cognitivist and Emergent types. The characteristic type is represented by computational operations, vector representations (presumably, traditional fuzzy logic implementation is in this type), data clustering, which seems to be convenient for treatments in discrete time models. For example, the typical system is described by $q_t = f(t, q_t; \gamma)$ where q_t and γ respectively denote state-vectors of time t and a set of parameters as a constant. The cognitivist type is represented by semantic manipulation of symbols or abstract symbolic representations, procedural or probabilistic reasoning, which is related to semantic network modeling and ontology database structure. For example, if it is probabilistic, the occurrence of the states is given by $Pr(q_t) = L(q_t|q_{t-1}, q_{t-2}, \cdots; \gamma)$. The emergent type is categorized in dynamical systems approaches, which deal with concurrent self-organization, global systems states,

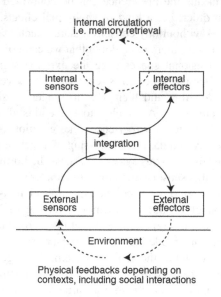

Fig. 1. A schematical illustration of a possible theoretical modeling to reproduce autonomy and its supervision in the brain information process that is proposed by Tani [18] and consistently presented by Weng [19–22].

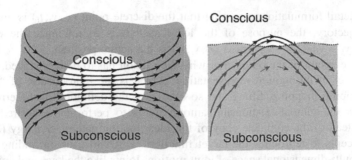

Fig. 2. A schematical illustration of a possible interpretation of the "integration" part in Fig. 1, as a metaphor of the tip of the iceberg of the Freud's mind theory. (Left) "Cognitive Workspace" [15] and Global Workspace theory [24] suggested a concentration of various types of information into a space in which the top-down system monitors and interferes, as is illustrated "Conscious" (white area in the center). (Right) The side view of the information flow. The preprocessed sensory information comes up from the bottom and some parts exceed the threshold level.

synchronous real-time entrainment, developing of new dynamics and increasing the space of interaction. i.e. Cognition itself implies autonomy. Tani [18] and Weng [19–22] approaches are considered as models of the third type. In dynamical systems approaches, time evolution of variables is the central issue and then the process is described by dynamical models such as $\dot{q} = f(q, \dot{q}, \ddot{q}, \cdots; \gamma)$ where $\dot{q}$ and $\ddot{q}$ respectively denote first and second derivations. Assuming that the system is an automatic control of car driving to keep the same distance q from the car in front, the system do not change q directly and change the speed $\dot{q}$ as the first derivation by pushing pedals of the brake and accelerator as $\ddot{q}$. In this sense, the integration part of the model as is illustrated in Fig. 1 may not be a mixture of two types of signals on the same time scale, like a matrix transformation of patters. This can be the key to consider this problem.

For bridging between the discussion in Sect. 2 and those possible theoretical frameworks, the important point is that we should focus on information flow instead of the detail of information representation as Tani [18] suggested. The concept is schematically illustrated in Fig. 2.

4 Autonomy and Supervision in the Behavior Control

In the case of the reproduction of a specific motion, the ideal motion is determined by a set of desired trajectories of individual joints of the body. i.e. temporal sequences of ideal positions of the individual joints. Figure 3 represents that ideal trajectory and the acceptable limit of the error. Since the local system is designed to pursuit the desired trajectory, if once the actual trajectory is out of bounds, the system performs the best effort to come back and there is no guarantee of the strict prohibition and returning within a certain time period. In addition, if it is a dynamical motion like jumping, hopping and lifting in a short moment, the actual trajectory easily exceeds the limitation during a short moment; but we intuitively know that it can perform safely, which means the trajectory comes back to the designed trajectory.

In the detail formulation, assuming that the discrete point (x_i, y_i, t_i) is given as the desired trajectory, the purpose of the local system is to minimize the error $d = |x_i - \hat{x}_i| + |y_i - \hat{y}_i| + |t_i - \hat{t}_i|$ where $(\hat{x}_i, \hat{y}_i, \hat{t}_i)$ is the actual position.

In the viewpoint of the purpose of why the motion has to be reproduced, we reach the meta level of the motion representation, which is the reproduction of "function" such as jumping, hopping, lifting and so on. Thus, the definition of the error can be extended as the mutual relationship among joints to perform the desired function (action) instead of the complete copy of the ideal motion pattern. Synergy [25, 26] is one of concepts to reproduce the target function, which focuses on finding coupling factors in multi-dimensional space of joint motion. Joints like the knee and ankle in one side of the body change synchronously during walking, but the head may not be synchronize together with the leg's movement. If such a coupling movement preserves, the whole system can admit to exceed for an individual joint the limit defined independently (Fig. 3(3)). The concept of Synergy can be implemented properly if the combination of the coupling or synchronous factors are determined as a fixed relationship. Possible implementations are (1) strong assumption by using a fixed relationship (i.e. walking in a stable way), (2) weak assumption by using a piecewise fixed relationship (i.e. standing rapidly), (3) assumption with a dynamics, which has to analyze the kinetics and dynamics (i.e. sitting slowly). In the first case, the relationship can be obtained from the average over the whole relationship. In the second case, the

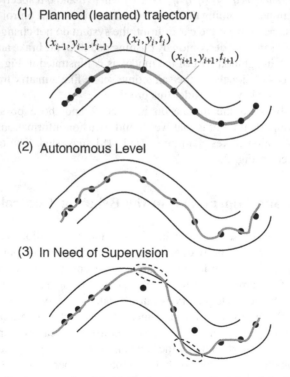

Fig. 3. An example of the desired trajectory of a joint of the body

important point is to find the transition point to change the relationship against the past tendency. The piecewise fixed relationship can be defined by the transition time point and the next transition point. In the last case, the key to solve this problem not only consider the level of approximations but also analyze the structure of attractors controlling the factors to pull together for keeping the same relationship. The mixture of stable and unstable attractors are embedded in the case [27].

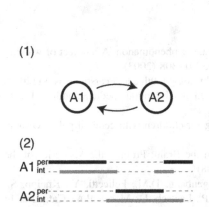

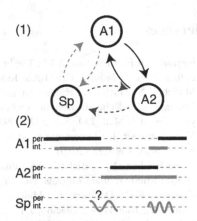

Fig. 4. (1) A situation of a coupling interaction (dialogue) between persons (A1 and A2). (2) time courses with two levels (per: perception (conscious) and int: intuition (subconscious) levels).

Fig. 5. (1) A supporter (human, robot, assistive devices and so on; Sp) participate a established coupling interaction (dialogue) (A1 and A2). (2) time courses with two levels (per: perception (conscious) and int: intuition (subconscious) levels). It is unclear what happens in Sp.

5 Concluding Remarks

In this paper, we discussed a way of the theoretical modeling and explored possible implementations that reproduces human behaviors in need of supervision by the central nervous system. In considering of an extension as is illustrated in Figs. 4 and 5, a coupling in social communications exhibits some disconnection during dialogue frequently but they are connected in the intuitive level. According to Dimitrova [28], Intuition is a process under the baseline of cognitive adaptation to the ever-changing environment of the surrounding world, which suggest the supporting system to keep a connection when disconnection is happing in the perceptual level.

For applying the functional implementation to be the social communication accompanied with a supporting person, robot and assistive devices, further analyses are necessary by monitoring individual intra-communication in the person (per vs. int) and inter-communications among persons.

An important point is to visualize stable and unstable states in motion/communication and to evaluate the time scale of the transition between those factors. If the timescale is in predictable range and acceptable range of the system, the person can be accustomed and accept the change preventing the occurrence of a discomfort feeling and enhancing a comfortable feeling.

Acknowledgments. This work was supported in part by the FY2014 JSPS Invitation fellowship Program for Research in Japan ID S-14156 at Kyushu Institute of Technology (KYUTECH).

References

1. Reynolds, R.F., Bronstein, A.M.: The broken escalator phenomenon. Aftereffect of walking onto a moving platform. Exp. Brain Res. **151**(3), 301–308 (2003)
2. Marieb, E.N., Hoehn, K.: Human Anatomy and Physiology, 9th edn. Pearson, Boston (2012)
3. Molnar, G.E.: Rehabilitation in cerebral palsy. In rehabilitation medicine-adding life to years. West J. Med. **154**, 569–572 (1991)
4. Mattern-Baxter, K.: Locomotor treadmill training for children with cerebral palsy. Orthop. Nurs. **29**(3), 169–173 (2010)
5. Ramachandran, V.S., Blakeslee, S.: Phantoms in the Brain: Probing the Mysteries of the Human Mind. William Morrow, New York (1998)
6. Cicerone, K.D., Dahlberg, C., Malec, J.F., Langenbahn, D.M., Felicetti, Y., Kneipp, S., Ellmo, W., Kalmar, K., Giacino, J.T., Harley, J.P., Laatsch, L., Morse, P.A., Catanese, J.: Evidence-based cognitive rehabilitation: updated review of the literature from 1998 through 2002. Arch. Phys. Med. Rehabil. **86**(8), 1681–1692 (2005)
7. van Wassenhove, V.: Minding time in an amodal representational space. Philos. Trans. R. Soc. Lond. B Biol. Sci. **364**(1525), 1815–1830 (2009)
8. Wagatsuma, H., Tomonaga, Y.: Problems of temporal granularity in robot control: levels of adaptation and a necessity of self-confidence. In: Proceedings of International Joint Conference on Neural Networks (IJCNN 2011), pp. 2670–2675 (2011)
9. Ledoux, J.E.: The Emotional Brain: The Mysterious Underpinnings of Emotional Life. Simon and Schuster, New York (1998)
10. Bechara, A., Damasio, H., Damasio, A.R.: Emotion, decision making and the orbitofrontal cortex. Cereb. Cortex **10**(3), 295–307 (2000)
11. Zajonc, R.B.: Feeling and thinking: preferences need no inferences. Am. Psychol. **35**, 151–175 (1980)
12. Reisenzein, R., Meyer, W.-U., Schützwohl, A.: James and the physical basis of emotion: a comment on Ellsworth. Psychol. Rev. **102**(4), 757–761 (1995)
13. Friedman, B.H.: Feelings and the body: the Jamesian perspective on autonomic specificity of emotion. Biol. Psychol. **84**, 383–393 (2010)
14. Cannon, W.: Bodily changes in pain, hunger, fear, and rage. Appleton, New York (1929)
15. LeDoux, J.E.: Rethinking the emotional brain. Neuron **73**(4), 653–676 (2012)
16. Ben-Zeeva, T., Feinb, S., Inzlichtc, M.: Arousal and stereotype threat. J. Exp. Soc. Psychol. **41**, 174–181 (2005)
17. Plutchik, R.: Emotion: A Psychoevolutionary Synthesis. Harper and Row, New York (1979)
18. Tani, J.: Autonomy of 'self' at criticality: the perspective from synthetic neuro-robotics. Adapt. Behav. **17**(5), 421–443 (2009)
19. Weng, J.: Developmental robotics: theory and experiments. Int. J. Human. Rob. **1**(2), 199–236 (2004)

20. Weng, J.: A theory of developmental architecture. In: Proceedings of the 3rd International Conference on Development and Learning (ICDL 2004), La Jolla (2004)
21. Weng, J.: A theory for mentally developing robots. In: Proceedings of the 2nd International Conference on Development and Learning (ICDL 2002), pp. 131–140. IEEE Computer Society (2002)
22. Vernon, D., Metta, G., Sandini, G.: A survey of artificial the cognitive system: implications for the autonomous development of mental capabilities in computational agents. IEEE Trans. Evol. Comput. 11(2), 151–180 (2007)
23. Vernon, D.: Cognitive vision: the case for embodied perception. Image Vis. Comput. 26(1), 127–140 (2008)
24. Baars, B.J., Franklin, S.: An architectural model of conscious and unconscious brain functions: global workspace theory and IDA. Neural Netw. 20(9), 955–961 (2007)
25. Aubry, M., Julliard, F., Gibet, S.: Modeling joint synergies to synthesize realistic movements. In: Kopp, S., Wachsmuth, I. (eds.) GW 2009. LNCS, vol. 5934, pp. 231–242. Springer, Heidelberg (2010)
26. Latash, M.L.: Synergy. Oxford University Press, New York (2008)
27. Fu, C., Suzuki, Y., Kiyono, K., Morasso, P., Nomura, T.: An intermittent control model of flexible human gait using a stable manifold of saddle-type unstable limit cycle dynamics. J. R. Soc. Interface 11(101), 20140958 (2014)
28. Dimitrova, M.: The educational media of the web: levels of cognitive involvement. In: Proceedings of SOLON – Sofia Lectures of Ontology, October 2007

BioCyberUrban ParQ: Brasilia's Smart National Park as an Extension of Our Senses

Suzete Venturelli$^{(\boxtimes)}$ and Francisco de Paula Barretto

Computer Art Research Lab, University of Brasilia, Brasilia,
Federal District, Brazil
{suzeteventurelli,kikobarretto}@gmail.com,
http://midialab.unb.br

Abstract. Brasilia Smart National Park as an extension of senses is the second stage of a project entitled parQ prepared in the Computer Art Research of the University of Brasilia (Midialab). The project was started in 2011 and aims to transform the National Park of Brasilia into a bio-cybernetic artwork. We introduced smart technologies that can scan signals/information issued by living beings, objects and the environment, to be used as parameters and variables of a Computational System of Senses Extension (CSSE), which will generate in real-time a multimedia concert based on gathered information from the park. The goal of BioCyberUrban parQ project is to connect the living things, objects and environment in order to enable their cybernetic communication/coexistence in Sarah Kubitschek Park (Brasilia's city park). Art and society context aim the processes of physical, intellectual and moral users consciousness development, along with all living beings in the City Park. Therefore we seek for a better ecosystem coexistence, integration and communication through the crowd-collected data as the foundation of this cyber community.

Keywords: Biocybernetic art · Multimodal interaction · Computer art · Pervasive computing

1 Introduction

The BioCyberUrban parQ project was developed at the Computer Art Research Laboratory (Midialab) in collaboration with laboratories from the Faculty of Technology and the Scientific Technology Development Center (CDTC), both from the University of Brasilia. It started in 2011 and was designed to be developed in stages, as raising funds for its development. Undergraduate, graduate and post-graduate students from the University of Brasilia and the Community College of Brasilia (IESB) are involved[1].

---

[1] The main students involved are Guilherme Shimabuko, Marcelo Rios, Juliana Hilário, Ana Lemos, Bruno Braga, Sidney Medeiros, Camille Venturelli Pic, Claudia Loch, Roni Ribeiro, Fábio Fonseca, Hudson Bomfim and Eber Felipe Oliveira.

© Springer International Publishing Switzerland 2015
M. Antona and C. Stephanidis (Eds.): UAHCI 2015, Part II, LNCS 9176, pp. 570–581, 2015.
DOI: 10.1007/978-3-319-20681-3_54

ParQ was be implemented in Sarah Kubitschek Park, which is the largest urban park in the world, with 1.62 square miles, overcoming the Central Park in New York. This park allows on foot or cycling activities for both amateurs and professional athletes. There is a 2.5 miles route for beginners and two longer routes for more experienced athletes, with 3.7 and 5 miles. Besides sport practices, there are several restaurants, a large woodland with picnic tables, an amphitheater, a kart track, playgrounds, an amusement park and an equestrian center. It is signed by three important people in the art, architecture and urbanism fields: the architectural design is by Oscar Niemeyer, the landscaping work was done by Roberto Burle Marx and urban area was developed by Lcio Costa (all of them have participated on the concept and construction of Brasilia).

Fig. 1. ParQ social network interface (2014).

The development the parQ system [1] was separated in two distinct stages: The first one is composed by a social network [2], (Fig. 1), an android app to explore the park (parQ), pedParQ android app for counting footsteps, a cyber-object bench with a scale for measuring weight (Fig. 2), QRCode signposts (Fig. 3) and an ambient sound for plants and humans composed by sensors (further explained in Sect. 3). All these components aim to encourage coexistence among living things, objects and environment, to enable the coexistence and cybernetic communication in the City Park of Brasilia.

The social network parQ was implemented in 2011, adapting functions such as the graphical user interface and the database server itself from Wikinarua [3], integrating the park's security cameras with the social network, a web-radio, network communication implementation and data interaction visualization between living beings, objects and the environment. The second stage aims to develop and install cyber objects in the park, with a function to communicate and feed the social network and mobile devices by sending different types of information. That is, while being used by the public, these objects are build up according to their interests.

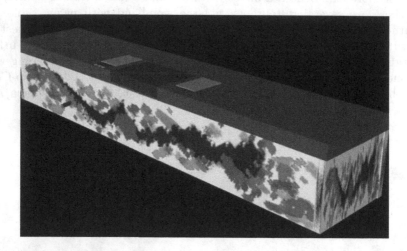

Fig. 2. Exact 3D model of the implemented bench-scale.

The system has three main principles: the first one is knowledge about the operating environment, the second is reproduction quality and the third is presence metaphor. By definition, it is a social network as a social entities set, such as individuals or social organizations connected by relationships built from their social interactions. With the advent of Web2.0, new possibilities and paradigms have emerged. Between these newborn paradigms the most relevant for this social network is the content and modeling construction of its final shape been made through user interactions. With this new user provided content there might be the rise and formation of new social groups.

The main features of parQ are:

- Computational open platform;
- Collaborative Mapping/Data crowdsourcing;
- Interaction between members;
- Data Sharing;
- Construction of Identities;
- Augmented Reality Application;
- Distribution and communication of applications, games, cyber objects and widgets;

The project assumes that currently one of the most important subjects in the urban context addresses the reshape of the infrastructure in the urban centers to become intelligent, self-sustainable and humane. This project is moving along

Fig. 3. 3D simulation of QRCode signpost and smart trash can final design.

this line of questioning, reflecting that this idea can extend the social relations and allow people to participate deeply in the life of the city to maintain the balance between the natural and the artificial elements. In this context, the methodology applied considers that it is vital to develop interfaces for natural interaction human- computer, which in this project, the search for a practical way to connect the living beings, the environment and the objects of the City National Park, in a aesthetic perspective.

The connection, occurs whereas the theories of sustainability, as well as the computational art, the calm computer technology, ubiquitous computing and pervasive, Augmented Reality, the design, among other studies, which can contribute to structuring the poetry of an artistic computational ecosystem.

2   Theoretical Framework

In parQ's theoretical context Art, Computer Science and Engineering fields are involved in order to develop objects whose characteristics are derived from ubiquitous and pervasive computing. Giving continuous communication and computer technical progresses, it seems that we're riding in complete computing activities integration into human everyday.

The creative process in this project involves clear notions of pervasive computing where computers are within the objects. Moreover, the project uses the ubiquitous computing in which computers are scattered and hidden in the environment of the Brasilia's City Park, an ubiquitous art inclusion into everyday life. According to Luigi Carro and Flvio Rech Wagner [4], there are currently great demand for mobile computing, ubiquitous and high computational power.

This proposal has also been inspired particularly by the autopoietic mechanisms of life and the reflection of how living things are organized, developed, evolved and adapted to the environment. The concept of autopoiesis, as the organization of the living, originated in the Chilean biologists Humberto Maturana and Francisco Varela work in 1970s [5]. This idea was developed in the theoretical biology context and was early associated with artificial life simulation long before the term artificial life was introduced in the late 1980 s in [6]. Pier Luisi presents a good concept review in [7]. Besides we are influenced by the work of Garnet Hertz [8] and Stocker and Schopf [9].

When items are organized in a system, the interactions between components cause a qualities set, which is not owned by any isolated component. For example a given capacity of a living being, like running, cannot be expressed by any of its isolated organs. In the same way a machine like a computer has higher qualities levels than the sum of its parts. Some the objects we're developing aim to use living being knowledge to solve problems. They represent knowledge, data gather or rules like any other computer. These rules and data might be triggered when necessary by digital devices. These objects possess a software layer that allows them to execute some tasks which might involve a decision making process. This knowledge is some times incorporated by some snippet code in order to reflect a knowledge change in the code itself.

The ParQ project presents a systemic approach, since it's being developed in the context of pervasive and ubiquitous computing, which thus is required. We recur to Weiser and Brown's concept of calm technology in order to project information systems able to perform in the outskirt of our attention, based on cognitive psychology studies about attention mechanisms [10].

All computers and intelligent machines as we know today are cybernetic applications. Cybernetics has also provided powerful methods to control two main systems: society and economy. A cybernetic system may be identified as an element set, which interact with each other. These interactions set might be based on substance information or energy exchanges. The elements of this compound system react and change according to these exchanges, changing itself or the possible interactions set with other compounds. Communication, signal, information and feedback are main concepts of the cybernetic field, fitting all criteria to also be an autopoietic system.

Ubiquitous computing will let the user visit the park without paying too much attention to the fact that there is a computer system allowing a more natural and transparent human-computer interaction. On the other hand, pervasive computing enables this natural interaction since the gathering and interaction data been made through everyday objects, embedded with computing devices. This mix of ubiquity and pervasiveness enable a cybernetic communication fluid among living beings, environment and cyber objects [10]. Mark Weiser in 1988 proposed this new idea with the phrase ubiquitous computing, when he was Xerox Palo Alto Research Center (PARC) Chief Technologist.

At the same time one aim to dilute the devices medley that surrounds computer technologies, parQ seeks to make unnecessary too much cognitive effort from the users to perceive the motivation behind the artistic proposal, using ubiquitous computing. By adopting unexceptional objects and expanding some of their original functions with computing devices that can process information and communication with other systems, like our social network.

It also involves an environment information system, containing the data visualization gathered from animals and environment. In order to achieve it we do recur to biosensors, which are sensorial devices used to determine the concentration of substances and other parameters that might be interesting from the biological point of view. These biosensors might communicate wirelessly, like smart sensors to enable the digitalization of such environmental data. The correspondence between the system and the real world considers that the information is truly relevant also from an aesthetic point of view.

Finally this research considers the Soundscape concept, as invented by Murray Shafer and the World Soundscape Project (WSP) [11], in order to understand the intersections between art and science in a transdisciplinary ambient acoustic project. We aim to find out which are the main aesthetical principles that regulate the sonic environment of the City Park, including the connected devices, people and the park itself.

3   Our Senses in Landscape

In some countries the parks are important areas of transformation. For example, architects, artists, private sector and public authorities of Rotterdam, the second largest city of the Netherlands, came together to create a green space that is both recreational and garbage recycler at the same time, called Recycled Island [12].

This garbage island is about floating space that helps to troubleshoot a major challenge faced worldwide: ocean pollution by plastic artifacts. They intend to create an artificial island that will recover waste plastic from the Nieuwe Maas river before reaches the Northern Sea. Nevertheless this island is meant to be also a park where people can have recreational activities.

According to creators, this is possible because the garbage collected is relatively "fresh" and therefore has a higher potential for recycling. Furthermore, the building blocks are designed in a way that plants can grow. The bottom platform has a rough rustic finishing where plants may have sufficient surface to grip and fish will have a place to lay eggs.

In a similar way, The "Noah's Ark" [13] project is another interesting example. Based on the biblical legend, this dashing space that floats amid the ocean will provide food through the agriculture in fertile lands, filter rainwater and use solar, wind and waves clean energy. The project was created by a couple of architects from Serbia, Aleksandar Koksimovic and Jelena Nikolic, has the shape of a buoyant and sustainable space that aims to harbor the survivors of natural disasters.

Designed to be itinerant, this structure has rings and underwater towers, responsible for the Ark stability. Noah's Ark is a self-sustainable floating city that is able to support a wide series of living species, from aquatics to terrestrial beings that might have been evicted from homeland by natural disasters or even war.

These floating buildings are also able to connect to other floating structures or ships and boats through a submarine cable network, as well as to dock on land - particularly in order to rescue of the survivors.

Another important work we are studying relates to the urban water sources and is called Nascentes Urbanas, which aims to restore and preserve existing water sources, springs and streams in urban and rural environments. It aims to maintain the natural underground water supply network in order to extend its reach, contributing to effective preservation of groundwater. They aim to maintain and preserve the riparian areas through reforestation and mitigate the causes and effects of pollution, which causes flooding, droughts, soil erosion and siltation of waterways.

The riparian reforestation associated with a fauna and flora protection plan aims to enable the creation of ecological corridors, preserving biodiversity, harmonizing the management of water resources with regional development and environmental protection. It might also encourage the protection of waters against actions may compromise the current and future use.

Socio-educational activities on rational use of water, prevention of soil erosion, promotion and integration of actions in defense against critical hydrological events that offer health risks, public safety, economic and social losses are of extreme interest. Such actions will be possible through a network of partners and project staff through social technologies. Community participation in such actions is possible through distributed work centers.

4   Human-Computer-Nature Interaction

The users of the city park are an active part of the artwork, because they can collaborate with its extension or not. To achieve and facilitate this collaboration we are currently working with wireless sensor networks. Those networks, at our current development stage, presents the most appropriate technology for the creation of a pervasive and ubiquitous computing system that allows the user to listen a multimedia concert composed in real-time by the sensor gathered information (Fig. 4).

In our approach, the constituent elements of the park can communicate and therefore provide feedback information to the CSSE. For example, a user can track its path while running in the park and, at the same time, warn about any infraction against the environment or it's living beings by sending messages through the CSSE, Through their mobile devices, these data are supplying the aesthetic component of multimedia concert composer.

We are also considering the creation of a multimodal Human-Computer-Nature Interaction related to a connection between the virtual and physical environments through natural modes of communication [14]. In this sense, we

Fig. 4. 3D simulation of QRCode signpost and smart trash can final design (2013).

understand that the natural and the digital environments might be represented as cooperation between emotional and intelligent machines, thus creating and emotional and intelligent environment with living species.

In order to explore this multimodal interaction some artists are currently transforming signals emitted by nature, as signs of plants, animals or the environment, to show the possibility of coexistence between different species, causing changes in our own perception about the meaning of life.

One example of this interaction is a game-art (Fig. 5), developed during the first stage of this project and currently under extension that aims to connect the park users with our parQ network through the use of mobile devices. The game entitled PedparQ [1] (ped stands for feet in Portuguese) aims to avoid user sedentarism. Therefore, when activated, PedparQ counts the footsteps and if it doesn't reach a minimum, will consider the user as sedentary and in this case an alert sound is played on the mobile device. This game art will be connected to parQ social network and will send automatically this data.

For the second CSSE development stage, there are trash bins that send an alarm signal when they are almost full. Bikes can transmit real-time images of the environment; a park bench may have a function of weight balance; a fitness bar extends its function and monitors users physiological signals; a totem displays and sends information about the air quality.

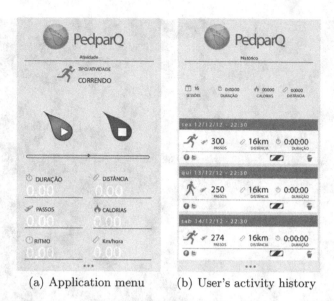

(a) Application menu   (b) User's activity history

Fig. 5. PedParq application running in an android phone (2013).

Through this multimodal signals, the CSSE will allow the visualization of data variation that later will be analyzed though data mining algorithms in order to detect whether the park is in harmony or not. Then it can respond by turning the lights on, generating sounds, flash messages in led panels installed in the park or around the lake, compose a multimedia concert with images and sounds. Then, the whole park becomes a live element, starring the scene, in constant aesthetic transformation.

In addition to user-dependent interfaces we are designing a sensor wireless network involving specific data-gathering devices distributed along the park. Those connected nodes are able to pre-process, store and send sensing data to adjacent nodes. Through the analysis of each node we can measure various parameters for a more effective management of the park network.

Those independent sensors are a subsystem that feeds a collaborative online data management platform, which stores the information to an open database. Open data can be interpreted and visualized by third-part applications, like the Wikisensing [15] platform.

Other services allows developers to incorporate real-time graphics and widgets on third-part web sites, as well as analyze and process historical data taken from data feeds and send real-time alerts from any data flow to control scripts, devices and environments. We highlight in this proposal the sensors relevance as a fundamental part of the new interfaces that promote more natural interactions to the user.

Sharing this approach, the artist Victoria Vesna, created an acoustic networks of birds [16], this three-year research project is led by evolutionary biologist Charles Taylor. This project has helped to expand our acoustic senses in our daily environment and called our attention the Santa Monica Mountains where they went on songbird recording and tracking. It is quite a challenge, since this research aims to go beyond the territorial and mating aspects of bird communication. They aim to discover semantic and lexical data in bird singing.

Another interesting art project that dialogues with our main concepts is entitled Telebiosfera [17], developed by Carlos Nobrega (2014). He aims to build a hybrid environment (composed of natural and artificial elements), in which an immersive experience is possible through telematics bio-communication between distinct geo-located ecosystems (Fig. 6). This telematics communication occurs between two small domes that allow the visitor to view and interact with a remote peer environments. Each Telebiosfera is meant to receive and transmit ecosystem images and data in real-time.

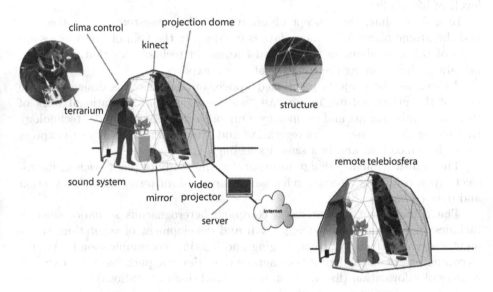

Fig. 6. Telebiosfera architectural diagram (2014).

Artists Sabrina Maia and Lasaro Camargos developed an artwork entitled eSYLPH [18] that allows the user to experience a electronic presentation of elsewhere blowing wind. Each time a user presents itself in front of the camera sensor a geographical position is randomized and then is presented as digital sylphs based on weather forecast application programming interface (API).

Those mutant sound clouds are audio-visually rendered in real-time and materialize according to the weather API data such as wind speed and direction that controls its virtual clouds chromatic variation, dispersion and movement.

Common features appear in the three mentioned artistic projects. First the multimodal interaction occurs between humans, machines and nature. Second, the technologies are not really suitable for this interaction, because the proposals go beyond what machines are able to process. Finally, the interaction generates visual and sound based on the perceived signals, causing new emergent aesthetic perceptions, dissolving the boundary lines between culture and nature.

5 Conclusion

The real - and most important - challenge in our project is to transform the traditional Brasilia City Park in a smart environment artwork, considering art as a major factor of social and ecological transformation. The concept of intelligent park is related to the proposal for shaping smart cities, which until recently was subject treated only in science fiction. The idea is to create sustainable and efficient environments with a high degree of connectivity and hence with better levels of life quality.

In a short time, the concept of smart cities has overstepped the academy and the utopic plane. What nowadays is included in the field of smart cities are ways of thinking about urban life and the use of technologies that, somehow, has always been among the concerns of urban experts.

As well as the projects mentioned above, our project was designed to be part of the urban nature. In our case, was designed for the National Park of Brasilia, combining art and technology. Our project uses multimodal technology that allows the ecosystem - its vegetation and the park environment - to express through sounds that are, in a sense its feelings.

The transdisciplinary design incorporates the study of plant science, microelectronics, computer interaction human nature, and software design, integration and data communication.

The management system has a complex, heterogeneous scenario, since it includes: closed and open space, growth and development of vegetation; treatment systems such as irrigation, fogging and lighting; communication tools such as computers, personal digital assistants, mobile devices, park users and external sources of information (like forecast and natural disaster stations).

The whole system consists of sub-systems set and these elements provide connection/communication and delivery real-time information between/to phones and databases. The social network, parQ.unb.br, can be considered itself a complex autopoietic living system since it is able to self regulate through human interaction, reflecting the changes in it's inside configuration and database, according to these interactions and data gathering.

parQ software can be set to a parallel universe, in which each biological entity culture is considered/represented as digital one. Thus, for example, a tree becomes an e-Tree, assuming a technological system layer, other layers other living beings are visiting the park itself and the environment, its climate, its architectural objects. This way, we hope that it might provoke human self-expression among with human integration with the environment.

References

1. Venturelli, S., Barretto, F., de Freitas, A.: BioCyberUrban parQ: an ubiquitous and pervasive computing system for environmental integration. In: Constantine, S., Margherita, A. (eds.) UAHCI 2013, Part III. LNCS, vol. 8011, pp. 116–124. Springer, Heidelberg (2013)
2. parQ (2013). www.parq.unb.br
3. Venturelli, S.: Wikinarua. Texto Digit. 8(1), 206 (2012)
4. Carro, L., Wagner, F.R.: Desafios para a computação pervasiva no futuro cenário tecnológico. In: PPGC - UFRGS (2012)
5. Maturana, H., Varela, F.: Autopoiesis and Cognition: the Realization of the Living. Volume 42 of Boston studies in the philosophy of science, 1st edn. D. Reidel Publishing Company, Dordrecht (1980)
6. Langton, C.: Artificial Life: Proceedings of an Interdisciplinary Workshop on Synthesis and Simulation of Living Systems, pp. 1–47. Addison-Wesley, Redwood City (1989)
7. Luisi, P.L.: Autopoiesis: a review and a reappraisal. Naturwissenschaften 90(2), 49–59 (2003)
8. Hertz, G.: Cockroach Controlled Mobile Robot. Gizmodo, Redwood City (2008)
9. Stocker, G., Schöpf, C.: Hybrid: living in paradox. Ars Electronica (2005)
10. Wieser, R.M., Brown, J.S.: The coming age of calm technology. Xerox PARC (1996)
11. Schafer, R.M.: The Soundscape: Our Sonic Environment and the Tuning of the World. Destiny Books, New York (1977)
12. Recycled-Island-Foundation. http://www.recycledisland.com
13. Joksimovic, A., Nikolic, J.: http://goo.gl/wjepby
14. Goodman, E.: Three environmental discourses in human-computer interaction. In: CHI 2009 Extended Abstracts on Human Factors in Computing Systems, CHI EA 2009, pp. 2535–2544. ACM, New York (2009)
15. Silva, D., Ghanem, M., Guo, Y.: Wikisensing: an online collaborative approach for sensor data management. Sensors 12(10), 13295–13332 (2012)
16. Taylor, C., Cody, M., Vesna, V.: (2014). http://artsci.ucla.edu/birds
17. Nobrega, C.A.: (2014). http://www.nano.eba.ufrj.br/?portfolio=telebiosfera
18. Maia, S., Camargos, L.: esylph: Por uma tecnoatmosfera da terra. In: Venturelli, S. (ed.) Anais do 12 Encontro Internacional de Arte e Tecnologia, University of Brasília (2013)

Adaptive Sensor Data Fusion for Efficient Climate Control Systems

Matthias Vodel[1][✉], Marc Ritter[2], and Wolfram Hardt[1]

[1] University Computer Centre, Chemnitz, Germany
marc.ritter@informatik.tu-chemnitz.de
[2] Junior Professorship Media Computing, Technische Universität Chemnitz,
09107 Chemnitz, Germany
{matthias.vodel,wolfram.hardt}@hrz.tu-chemnitz.de

Abstract. Thousands of data centres are using traditional air-conditioned cooling concepts for the entire payload. Most of these data centres include multiple hardware generations and different types of IT-infrastructure components, i.e. storage, compute, and network devices. In the context of Green-IT, an efficient and safe parameterization of the air-conditioning-system is essential - keep the temperature as low as necessary, but not too low. Usually, only a few amount of temperature sensors are available to handle these important control cycles. But in order to optimise the cooling capacity, several scenario-specific parameters have to be considered, including the shape of the room, air flow, or component placements. In this context, the TU Chemnitz develops novel concepts to improve this process. We are using local sensor capabilities within the hardware components and combine these information with actual system loads to create an extended knowledge base, which also provides adaptive learning features. First measurement scenarios show huge optimisation potential. The respective trade-off between power consumption and cooling capacity results in significant cost savings.

Keywords: Data centre · Air conditioning · Adaptive · Sensor · Data fusion

1 Introduction

The optimisation of traditional air-cooled data centre environments regarding energy- and cost-efficiency is one of the central challenges for hundreds of institutions in the public and educational domain. Multiple hardware generations over several decades are running side-by-side. New hardware components provide a significantly higher energy density and accordingly, the respective cooling capacity becomes a critical issue. Due to physical limitations regarding cooling power and energy density per rack, a large amount of space capacity inside the air-cooled server racks is wasted (see Fig. 1). In order to improve this situation, we have to analyse the key parameters, which have a direct impact on the cooling efficiency.

M. Antona and C. Stephanidis (Eds.): UAHCI 2015, Part II, LNCS 9176, pp. 582–593, 2015.
DOI: 10.1007/978-3-319-20681-3_55

Fig. 1. Key issue within traditional, air-cooled data centre environments – optimising the rack efficiency by maximising the filling level.

2 Problem Description

There are two major problems for usual air-cooled data centres: *Inhomogeneous air temperature* and the *inhomogeneous air flow* inside the data centre. These parameters are strongly dependent on the server rack location within the room and even on the position of each individual server component inside the rack. These two challenges are shown in Fig. 2 based on measurements in our TU Chemnitz data centre.

With focus on an entire data centre with multiple server racks and hundreds of server systems, an additional issue becomes critical: Turbulences and interferences between different air flows around the individual racks. These effects have a huge impact on the cooling efficiency.

Facing these efficiency challenges from an administrative perspective, the monitoring and measuring of the respective values appears in a very basic manner [1,2]. Usual data centre environments only provide a few global temperature sensors for the entire room. Accordingly, the control loop for the air conditioning is very simple. Besides the global room temperature, no further information are available.

3 Related Work

Due to these issues, several professional solutions try optimise this situation regarding monitoring capabilities, sensor data sources, management & control processes as well as cost- and energy savings.

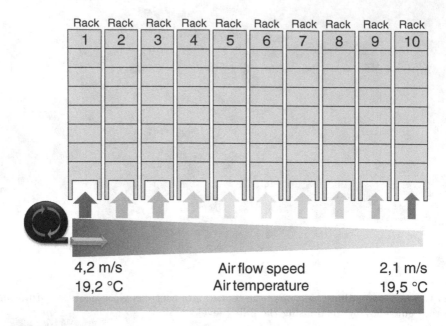

Fig. 2. Key problems for traditional, air-cooled data centre environments. Inhomogeneous air temperature and air flow speed dependent on the positioning of the server rack. Starting from the air intake on the left side, the cooling capacity shrinks from rack to rack

3.1 Cold Aisle Containment and Air Boosters

One of the most efficient optimisation steps for traditional air-cooled data centres represents *cold aisle containments*, which allows us to concentrate the cooling capacity directly to the server hot spots within the room. Accordingly, we reduce the effective volume from the entire room space to single enclosures with a significant smaller capacity. Figure 3 shows the three realised cold aisle containments of the TU Chemnitz data centre.

Each containment provides individual temperature sensors and is equipped with optional *booster* elements. The booster technology is shown in Fig. 4. As one can see, the boosters allow us to modify the air flow individually for each zone. In order to establish such cold aisle containments, each hardware component has to be re-organised regarding the direction of the air flow. Air intakes have to be located inside the containment, air offtakes outside the enclosures. Accordingly, the installation of these containments is very time-consuming, requires a detailed timeline and is critical with respect to system downtimes or failures.

But anyway, the control cycles as well as the information database for adapting the boosters and the air conditioning system are still the same. The control loops only operate in a static, reactive approach, based on single temperature measurements inside the containment. No further information are available.

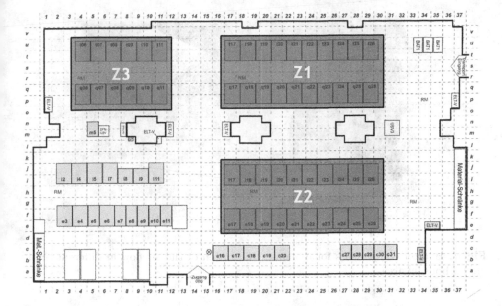

Fig. 3. TU Chemnitz data centre with three cold aisle containments, which represent operational zones Z1, Z2, and Z3.

3.2 Genome Project

In order to provide a better sensor data knowledge base, Microsoft Research starts the *Genome project* [3,4], which adds dedicated wireless sensor nodes to each server rack. These nodes (called *Genomotes*) are organised in a master-slave chained sensor network design (*RACNet*), based on the IEEE 802.15.4 low-power, low-data rate communication stack [5]. The RACNet infrastructure provides several information sets about the environmental status, including heat distribution, hot spots, and facility layout. Each node sends its data to a pre-defined data sink, which creates a global view regarding the health status. The entire raw data is merged together for different data representation tasks (analysis, prediction, optimisation, and scheduling).

3.3 SynapSense

Another company, which also uses such kinds of sensor nodes is *SynapSense* [6]. Here, several node classes with different types of information are available, e.g. *Therma Nodes*, *Pressure Nodes*, or *Constellation Nodes*. The data sets from the nodes are processed in a centralised manner by a special software tool, which is able to adapt and to steer the air conditioning system.

All of these approaches possess two critical disadvantages. The first one deals with additional hardware costs for the different sensors. This includes costs for installation, configuration, operation, and maintenance. For large-scaled data

Fig. 4. Booster components for dynamic adaptation of the air flow in different, individual housing areas.

centre environments, the required financial resources are very high [7]. The second disadvantage represents the type of data. All of these systems are measuring external parameters from the current point in time, thus providing no learning capability from the past. In addition, there are no server-internal data sources like the system load or any kind of hardware health status as well.

Nevertheless, all of these solution offer the same benefits, which are equal to the objectives of our research work:

- Enabling real-time monitoring & control
- Optimised change management
- Optimised capacity planning
- Optimised server positioning and provisioning
- Optimised fault diagnostics
- Optimised energy- & cost-efficiency (TCO)

4   TU Chemnitz Adaptive Cooling Approach

Based on the related research projects and products, we developed a more flexible, more cost-efficient and smarter solution for heterogeneous, air-cooled data centre environments. *TUCool* denotes our adaptive cooling approach at TU Chemnitz. Instead of using dedicated measurement hardware, we decided to use the already available hardware components inside the data centre. Accordingly, each single server system, each network core switch, each storage system becomes an additional sensor source for environmental data.

4.1 Knowledge Base Extension with Sensor Data Fusion

The idea is simple but quite efficient. With the TUCool monitoring and control approach, we include different sensor plugins. Each plugin represents a class module for a specific kind of sensor data. A given server system typically provides several temperature sensors, located at the mainboard, the CPUs, and the cooling fans (illustrated in Fig. 5).

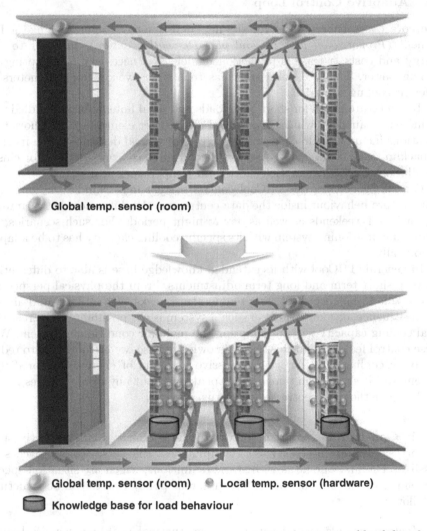

Fig. 5. Extension of the knowledge base by using additional sensors and load data from the individual server systems.

Further information modules are monitoring and learning the system load values of physical/virtual server entities and the respective impact on the data centre temperature behaviour. Accordingly, TUCool is able to map temperature and system load information for an efficient adaptation of the cooling capacity. Different sensor data sources are merged together to more abstract information sets. The fusion results indicate the actual health status of the data centre as well as a prediction trend for the future. Past monitoring data represents a continuous input for the machine learning capabilities.

4.2   Adaptive Control Loop

The core control mechanism for the air conditioning is operating like a PID element (*Proportional plus Integral plus Derivative action*). In order to save energy and costs, a feasible prediction model [8] is necessary for adapting the cooling power. The TUCool system has to handle two control parameters for different cooling scenarios.

Temperature peaks for short term loads and local hot spots are handled with an increased air flow, which means local air booster elements. Such short term situations include hundreds of boot processes of virtual desktops in the morning or backup tasks in the night. Also small- and mid-size compute jobs for cluster installations may result in such short term temperature peaks.

On the other side, the TUCool control system must handle the long term temperature behaviour inside the data centre, e.g. the differences between working days and weekends as well as day & night periods. For such scenarios, the entire air conditioning system with its specific cooling capacity has to be adapted periodically.

In general, TUCool with its extended knowledge base is able to differentiate between short term and long term adjustments. From the physical perspective, we are able to balance short term temperature peaks with an increased airflow. In consequence, one key benefit of such a system is the possibility to increase the local cooling capacity without adapting the main air conditioning system. With these control features and this sensor knowledge base, we are now able to reduce the basic cooling level for saving massive amounts of energy. The prediction system avoids short term temperature peaks without any disadvantages for the hardware or the data centre health status.

Static Constraints. In order to control the cooling system, respective policies or rule sets are necessary. For defining these rule sets, two approaches are possible. The first one deals with static definitions, which are situation-specific predefined by the administrator. The different policy classes can be structured as follows:

- *Temperature hot spot* (local short term thermal peak) → increase booster level
- *System load peak* (local behaviour of a server bay or rack) → increase booster level
- *Average zone temperature* (cooling zone hits a predefined thermal value) → increase cooling capacity

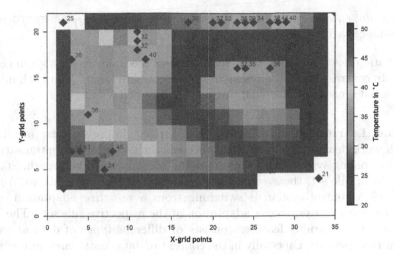

Fig. 6. TU Chemnitz data center heat map. Hot spots without cold aisle containment in the bottom left corner are clearly visible.

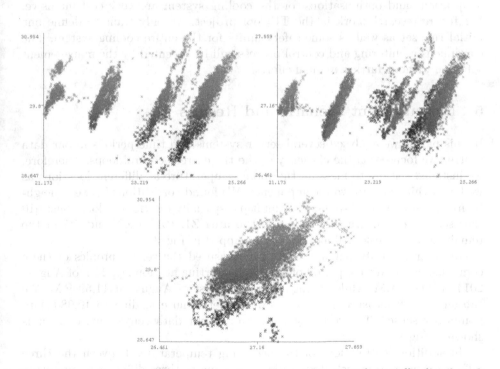

Fig. 7. Co-occurrences of temperatures from three different and spatially distributed sensor groups: q10 vs. i05 (top left), q10 vs. t21 (top right), and t21 vs. i05 (bottom).

– *Time slot entered* (predefined, time-specific behaviour) → increase/decrease
cooling capacity / booster level

These static rules represent a basic set of control mechanisms for a given cooling
system. In contrast to related research projects, we are focusing on both internal
and external sensor data for adapting the cooling behaviour.

Machine Learning Capabilities. For further improvements, our future
research work deals with automated processes for a continuous optimisation of
the entire cooling system. This represents the second control approach. Starting
from a static rule set, the system has to provide self-learning features. Accordingly, such a control system is switching from a *re-active* adaptation of the
cooling capacity to a *pro-active* adaptation of the respective rule sets. The input
for the machine learning features consists of different types of data as well as
different time periods. Especially in the context of data centre environments, the
knowledge about frequently repeating event in time is very helpful for optimising
the energy-efficiency of the cooling system.

Another key benefit deals with the efforts for maintenance and the adaptation processes. Time resources of IT administrators are limited and accordingly,
adaptations and optimisations for the cooling system are very cost-intensive.
For future research work in the TUCool project, we only want to define one
initial rule set as well as some safety limits for the entire cooling system. The
continuous monitoring and control process will be executed by the management
software without further manual efforts.

5   Measurement Scenario and Results

In this paper, we analysed several server systems and time periods in our data
centre. We focused on the efficiency of the the current control loops. Therefore,
we installed sensors to measure the room temperature at different locations as
well as within the hardware components. We found correlations between neigh-
boured sensors areas. We focus on multiple spatially distributed locations: q10
represents the temperature output in the area Z1, t21 in Z2, and i05 in the
remaining warm aisle. All locations are mapped in Fig. 3.

In order to verify our approach, we measured the sensor profiles of these
components over a time period of one week, starting at Monday, 25th of August
2014 at 00:00 A.M. while ending at Sunday, 31st of August at 11:59 P.M. We
subsampled all measurements to 1 sample per minute leading to 10,080 data
points per sensor. The resulting heat map of our data centre environment is
shown in Fig. 6.

In addition, correlations of the occurring temperatures between the three
different sensors are illustrated in Fig. 7, yielding to three different temperature
distributions. The combination with the time series plot of these sensor values
in Fig. 8 confirms a certain degree of dependency between those areas leading

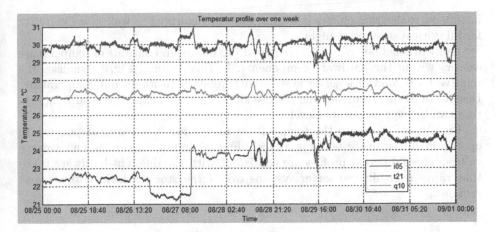

Fig. 8. The one week temperature profile shows three sensors in three locations from above yielding to distinct temperature zones. These were controlled by using the proposed adaptation scheme thus being capable of stabilizing the interconnections of the varying temperature gradients.

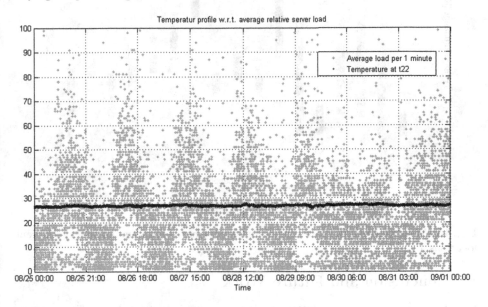

Fig. 9. The relative average CPU load per minute of a DeLL 2960 server located at position t22 (grey dots) does not affect the overall cooling temperature in the region at t21 (black line).

to similar gradients. A globally small but locally noticeable change in the temperature (represented by some spikes) is visible. This results from periodically executed tasks like server maintenance, software distribution processes, virtual desktop management, and storage deduplications. Further relevant processes

include virtualization cluster boot-up tasks each morning as well as backup task
for all critical services at night.

As mentioned before, we also recorded the inputs and outputs of temperature
sensors within the hardware components. In this context, Fig. 9 visualises the
relative CPU load of a server system with relation to its output temperature.
Despite different, recurring and intense shifts in work loads, the local temperature can be kept at a stable level.

Finally, we illustrate the temperature ranges for hardware components in
operation during the tests in Fig. 10 including minimum, maximum, and average
values. These different profiles are consistent with the different hardware types
that range from diverse server systems over large storage devices to network
switches.

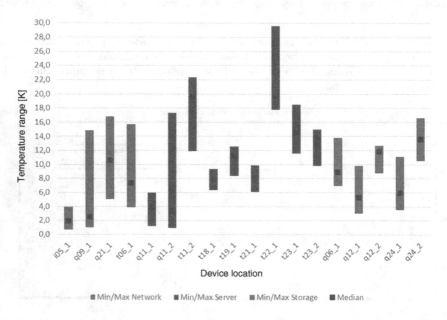

Fig. 10. Measured temperature ranges for several hardware components at different
locations.

6   Conclusion and Future Work

In this paper, we presented TUCool, an innovative approach for optimising heterogeneous data centre environments with traditional air cooling systems. In
contrast to other professional solutions and research projects, TUCool does not
require any further hardware components or installation efforts. The system uti-
lizes given sensor sources from each hardware system and aggregates these data
sets into one single knowledge base. Accordingly, based on this sensor data fusion
approach, TUCool is capable of controlling and optimising the entire cooling system automatically and continuously over the time. This results in massive energy
and cost savings.

In the next project steps, we want to use these measurements and results to develop a detailed simulation model for heterogeneous data centre environments. The research goal deals with the vision of optimising an entire data centre environment based on extensive simulation processes without trial-and-error approaches using real hardware. Critical optimisation parameters might include energy- and cost-efficiency as well maintenance efforts and load balancing.

Acknowledgement. This research work is supported by the *RenewIT* project, which is co-financed by the 7th Framework programme of the Eu ropean community (FP7) under grant agreement number 608679. Furthermore, the work was partially accomplished within the InnoProfile-Transfer-Initiative *localizeIT* under grant number 03IPT608X, funded by the *Federal Ministry of Education and Research* (BMBF, Germany) in the program of *Entrepreneurial Regions*. All measurements were done within the data centre environment of the *Technische Universität Chemnitz*.

References

1. Liu, J., Terzis, A.: Sensing data centers for energy efficiency. Philos. Trans. R. Soc. A **370**, 136–157 (2012)
2. Vodel, M.: Energy-efficient communication in distributed, embedded systems. Ph.D thesis, TU Chemnitz, Chemnitz, February 2014. ISBN 978-3-941003-18-7
3. Microsoft Research. DC Genome Project (2009). http://research.microsoft.com/en-us/projects/dcgenome/. [Accessed: 2015/02/18]
4. US Department of Energy. Wireless sensors improve data center energy efficiency. Technical report CSO 20029, USA, September 2010
5. Liang, C-J.M., Liu, J., Luo, L., Terzis, A., Zhao, F.: RACNet: a high-fidelity data center sensing network. In: Proceedings of the SenSys (ACM Conference on Embedded Network Sensor Systems). ACM, November 2009
6. SynapSense. Active Control (2015). http://www.synapsense.com [Accessed: 2015/02/18]
7. Rodriguez, M.G., Ortiz Uriarte, L.E., Jia, Y., Yoshii, K., Ross, R., Beckman, P.H.: Wireless sensor network for data-center environmental monitoring. In: Proceedings of the 5th International Conference on Sensing Technology (ICST), pp. 533–537, November 2011
8. Li, L., Liang, C-J.M., Liu, J., Nath, S., Terzis, A., Faloutsos, C.: Thermocast: a cyber-physical forecasting model for data centers. In: Proceedings of the SIGKDD (Conference on Knowledge Discovery and Data Mining). ACM, August 2011

Subjective Ratings of Biological Effective Light in Seminar Rooms and How to Handle Small Sample Sizes of Ordinal Data

Manuel H. Winkler[1]([⊠]), Herbert Plischke[2], and Werner Jensch[1]

[1] Department of Building Services Engineering, Munich University of Applied Sciences, Munich, Germany
manuel.winkler@hm.edu
[2] Department of Applied Sciences and Mechatronics, Munich University of Applied Sciences, Munich, Germany

Abstract. Our field study was conducted to examine the influence of biologically effective lighting in students' natural environment. A group of 21 regular master students were exposed to two different lighting scenarios. A developed questionnaire was used to collect subjective ratings according to overall indoor environmental quality. Data produced with questionaires are ordinal data. To analyse this type of data, especially with small sample sizes, an adequate statistical method is needed. This paper uses selected data from the field study to introduce one method based on rank data. Three questions were analysed to compare the subjective ratings of our probands according to the new biologically effective lighting. German seminar rooms or classrooms are built with a high daylight factor. Daylight is a strong confounder for field studies in rooms like that, which can't be controlled in a very good way. We know from other studies that the concentration of carbon dioxid is a second very strong confounder which must be considered. Typical classrooms with 60 - 80 m^2 furthermore limit the sample sizes. As well as know from other lab and controlled field studies that there can be measurable effects in the protection of health. Further testing with classrooms with a less daylight factor or in regions of less daylight might promise a better advantage to students.

Keywords: Seminar room · Artificial lighting · Blue-enriched white light · Illuminance · Indoor environmental quality · Small sample size · Ordinal data · Statistical method

1 Introduction

Light is more powerful than most of us would have recognized until the early nineties of the last century. Light with a high illuminance level and daylight-white coloured leads to an increased alertness [1]. Light is able to increase the performance of night shift workers [2–4]. And Fleischer showed that light could be used to increase the vigilance [5]. Especially since Brainard et al. [6] and

© Springer International Publishing Switzerland 2015
M. Antona and C. Stephanidis (Eds.): UAHCI 2015, Part II, LNCS 9176, pp. 594–603, 2015.
DOI: 10.1007/978-3-319-20681-3_56

Thapan et al. [7] in 2001 independently published that the exposure of light, especially the blue spectra, could cause melatonin suppression in humans; a new field of research for different groups of interest was born. Besides medical scientists, psychologists and biologists, engineers and architects are also involved in answering questions about how light influences humans [1].

Very interesting is the fact that in the world of science only two studies has been known up until January 2008 dealing with modern artificial lighting systems; they are neon tubes and their effects at schools [1]. The first study took place in Sweden. Two objectives were declared: how light effects the production of stress hormones and classroom performance. The authors used observational techiques to operationalize the ability to concentrate. They found out, that there must be a systematic seasonal variation of stress hormones (with higher levels in summer than in winter). Moderate or low levels of stress hormones appeared to increase individual concentration, they concluded [8].

Secondly an elemantary school in Manchester was equipped with dynamic lighting. No effects could be found, [9] cited in [1]. In the meantime since 2008, more results were published in this context. The effects of variable lighting (variable in illuminance and colour temperature) on students' performance and attitude were investigated at the University Medical Center Hamburg-Eppendorf. Barkmann et al. found out, that students "made fewer errors, particularly fewer errors of omission", by using a standardized test of attention [10] and a special light program called "Concentrate" (very bright, cold light: 1.060 lx, 5.800 K) [11]. The "reading speed" (...) "rose significantly" and "students and teachers rated" the new light "positively and found it useful" [ibidem]. This study was done with neon tubes as well.

A current paper investigated effects of light in two German high schools. To prove their hypotheses, they equipped two classrooms in each of the two schools with an LED lighting system. The system consisted of a direct part (OSRAM Siteco Quadrature II LED, CCT: 4.000 K) and an indirect part (customized LED modules, CCT: 14.000 K). Vertical illuminance levels, measured at the eye-level in sitting position, were about 300 lx and the correleted colour temperature (CCT) was about 5.500 K. Compaired with two standard classroom illuminations (First: 3.000 K and second: 3.500 K (at the eye-level)) the results show "beneficial effects of blue-enriched white light on students' performance". Keis et al. wrote that "in comparison to standard lighting conditions, students showed faster cognitive progressing speed and better concentration" [12]. Keis et al. [ibidem] used the same standardized test of attention [10] as Barkmann et al. [11]

Our objectives are increasing the rare knowledge about effects of dynamic light (variate illuminance and colour temperature by time) of students at universities (ages between 21 and 35) and adding the technical component of concentration of carbon dioxide into account, which seems to have been forgotten as a covariate in previous studies. We also used the standardized test of attention [10] mentioned above to be comparable, which is not part of this paper. Secondly, we used a questionaire to investigate students' subjective ratings of different indoor environmental quality parameters; they are lighting and carbon dixode, for example. By using questionaires (results are most of the time rank data at the ordinal level), one challenge is to find the right statistical method which is able to offer mathematically correct answers. We want to introduce a method based on rank data for small sample sizes of dependent groups to find in [15] and present some first results of our study according to subjective ratings of students corresponding to dynamic blue-enriched LED light in a seminar room in Munich.

2   Method

2.1   The Test Environment

At the Munich University of Applied Sciences, a typical German seminar room was rebuilt in summer of 2012. With the technically new equipped seminar room, it shall be possible to answer research questions according to biologically effective light on the one hand and, at the same time, indoor environmental quality parameters. The room is now equipped with 32 different types of sensors and measuring points. Besides the indoor air temperature, the indoor humidity and the concentration of carbon dioxide (all of them measured at three different spots), the illuminance inside (at each light band) and outside (in front of the facade) is measured. Some relevant dimensions are documentated as follows: ground area: $77,9 \, m^2$, room depth: $9,0 \, m$ and percentage of transparent surface: $55,3 \, \%$, orientation: south-western. One of the aims was to create a test environment, in which the students do not feel like being in a lab. The study was set as a field study with all its difficulties. The subjects are real master students, using the seminar room the entire time for their readings. Figure 1 shows the rebuilt seminar room with two different types of lights switched on.

2.2   Light Sources

The seminar room is now equipped with a direct light part using 18 Lumilux T5 HE 35 W neon tubes with a correlated colour temperature of 3.000 K and an indirect part using 144 white and 72 blue light emitting diods (LED) with the possibility to scale the correlated colour temperatur from 6.500 K up to 13.000 K (at the ceiling). The whole system was built by OSRAM GmbH; Munich, Germany. Two different scenarios were programmed. The first curve is called "baseline". According to the former light system, the seminar room was equipped with an illuminance of 300 lx horizontal [16] and a correlated colour temperature of 3.000 K was programmed without any variation by time. A second curve called "dynamic light" starts with 100 lx (vertical at eyelevel) and goes up to nearly 300 lx. The correlated colour temperature starts at the level of 3.000 K and goes up to 5.000 K (also measured vertically at eyelevel). This level of correlated colour temperature equates to [17] which was released after the design of experiments was done. Figure 2 shows the two different light curves measured with Jeti Spectro-Radiometer specbos 1211 and closed blinds in February 2013.

Fig. 1. Photographic picture of the Munich seminar room with the biologically effective light system, the picture consists of two different parts: left: 100 % blue LEDs and 0 % white LEDs are switched on, right: 100 % white LEDs and 0 % blue LEDs are switched on. Between these two stages, the software calculates the dynamic curve which will be shown below (see: Fig. 2)

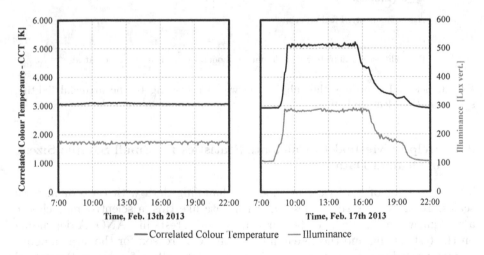

Fig. 2. Comparison of the two different light scenarios presented in the lecture hall, left: baseline, right: dynamic curve, all of them measured between two light bands at 1,20 m and a Jeti Spectro-Radiometer specbos 1211

2.3   Chosen Questions

We chose three questions out of the survey instrument to show some first results out of the Munich field study regarding subjective rating of biologically effective light in seminar rooms. To evaluate the data a special method is needed, we want to use this paper to demonstrate a predestined method as well. First of all, we asked the students to rate the importance of indoor air quality for their well-being. Within same question, they were able to rate the importance of artificial light. We asked them to rate how they like the different light settings and, finally, to rate their subjective performance efficiency. (cf. Figure 3)

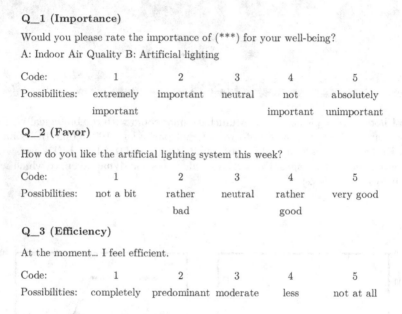

Q_1 (Importance)

Would you please rate the importance of (***) for your well-being?

A: Indoor Air Quality B: Artificial lighting

Code:	1	2	3	4	5
Possibilities:	extremely important	important	neutral	not important	absolutely unimportant

Q_2 (Favor)

How do you like the artificial lighting system this week?

Code:	1	2	3	4	5
Possibilities:	not a bit	rather bad	neutral	rather good	very good

Q_3 (Efficiency)

At the moment... I feel efficient.

Code:	1	2	3	4	5
Possibilities:	completely	predominant	moderate	less	not at all

Fig. 3. Selected questions the subjects answered according to the artificial lighting system in their lecture hall

2.4   Helpful Method to Calculate Statistics for Small Sample Sizes of Ordinal Data

There are a lot of statistical methods for handling data with ratio or interval scales. To answer research questions with data like this, a scientist may choose a well-known method like a t-test or multifactorial tests like ANOVA depending on the test setting and the research questions. One reason for the large amount of test procedures is that ratio and interval data allow for all mathematical operations with raw data because of the degree of information given by the data. One classic method for testing hypotheses of nonparametric dependent data is the well known Wilcoxon-test. Bortz and Lienert indicate that this method demands at least cardinal scale level (interval or ratio scale) and the test *should* not be used for ordinal scaled data [13]. At page 200 [ibidem] they claim that the Wilcoxon-test used with ordinal data could lead to wrong conclusions. An example for that possibility could be found in [14]. Brunner et al. wrote more concretly that the application of the Wilcoxon-test is *not allowed*, because of calculating differences in using raw data [15]. The authors introducing some different methods for different settings in their book, based on *Nonparametric Marginal Models*. For the exact derivations and further details please look into [ibidem].

Estimation of Relative Treatment Effects (short: RTE). The so called relative treatment effect $p_i = \int H dF_i$ for the group i is estimated after some mathematical conversions Brunner et al. [ibidem] did, by $\hat{p}_i$ as follows

$$\hat{p}_i = \int \hat{H} d\hat{F}_i = \frac{1}{n_i} \sum_{k=1}^{n} \hat{H}(X_{ik}) = \frac{1}{N}\left(\overline{R}_i - \frac{1}{2}\right) \tag{1}$$

Here, $\overline{R}_i = \frac{1}{n_i} \sum_{k=1}^{n} R_{ik}$ is the arithmetic mean of the ranks in the ith experimental group and R_{ik} is the rank of X_{ik} among all $N = \sum_{i=1}^{a} n_i$ observations $X_{11}, ..., X_{an_a}$. [ibidem]

The Hypothesis $H_0^F : F_1 = F_2$
  In what follows, R_{ks} denotes the rank of $X_{ks}, k=1, ..., n, \ s=1,2,$ among all $N = 2n$ observations and $\overline{R}.s = n^{-1} \sum_{k=1}^{n} R_{ks}$ the mean of the ranks, $s = 1, 2$. The ranks used for the computation of the statistics are taken from a special layout you will find in [15] at page 25. Let

$$S_{n,0}^2 = \frac{1}{n-1} \sum_{k=1}^{n} (R_{k2} - R_{k1} - \overline{R}_2 + \overline{R}_1)^2 \tag{2}$$

denote the empirical variance of the rank differences $R_{k2} - R_{k1}, k = 1, ..., n$. Then, for large samples, the statistic

$$T_n^F = \sqrt{n}\frac{\overline{R}_2 - \overline{R}_1}{S_{n,0}} \tag{3}$$

has a standard normal distribution $N(0,1)$ under the hypothesis H_0^F. [ibidem] "For small sample sizes, one approximates the distribution of the statistics T_n^F under H_0^F with a central t_{n-1}-distribution. Simulation studies show that this approximation is fairly accurate for $n \geq 7$ and continuous distributions. For discrete distributions, the quality of the approximation naturally depends on the number of ties. For $n \geq 15$, however, the approximation is satisfactory if not too many ties are present". [ibidem]

3   Results

3.1   Answers of the Subjects, Coded into Rank Data

In the winter semester 2013/14 our questionaire was presented each week for 12 weeks. All required indoor environmental quality parameters were measured per minute and the lighting scenarios alternated each week according Fig. 2. Each Thursday between 9 am and 12 am, the questoinaire was given to the students. For this paper, we chose one week (*base*) in October 2013 (21st until 25th, Baseline light) and one week (*dynamic*) in November 2013 (11th until 15th, Dynamic light). The remaining data show nearly the same results as it will be pointed out below (cf. Table 1). The corresponding rank values (R_1 and R_2) are calculated according to [13] page 41.

Table 1. Ordinal data given from the questionaire (x_1 and x_2), the results of the calculation of the corresponding rank postions (R_1 and R_2) and the rank means. IAQ means Indoor Air Quality

| Subject | Q_1 (Importance) | | | | Q_2 (Favor) | | | | Q_3 (Efficient) | | | |
| | Baseline IAQ | | Baseline Light | | Baseline | | Dynamic | | Baseline | | Dynamic | |
	x_1	R_1	x_2	R_2	x_1	R_1	x_2	R_2	x_1	R_1	x_2	R_2
1	2	25,5	2	25,5	2	3	4	23,5	3	23,5	2	8
2	2	25,5	1	8	1	1	3	10	4	33	3	23,5
3	2	25,5	2	25,5	5	32	4	23,5	2	8	3	23,5
4	2	25,5	2	25,5	3	10	4	23,5	2	8	3	23,5
5	2	25,5	2	25,5	4	23,5	3	10	3	23,5	3	23,5
6	1	8	2	25,5	4	23,5	4	23,5	2	8	3	23,5
7	1	8	2	25,5	3	10	4	23,5	4	33	3	23,5
8	2	25,5	1	8	4	23,5	4	23,5	4	33	3	23,5
9	1	8	2	25,5	3	10	4	23,5	3	23,5	2	8
10	1	8	3	39	4	23,5	2	3	2	8	2	8
11	1	8	3	39	4	23,5	2	3	3	23,5	2	8
12	1	8	2	25,5	3	10	3	10	2	8	2	8
13	1	8	1	8	3	10	3	10	2	8	3	23,5
14	1	8	3	39	4	23,5	4	23,5	2	8	3	23,5
15	1	8	3	39	3	10	3	10	2	8	2	8
16	2	25,5	3	39	4	23,5	4	23,5	3	23,5	3	23,5
17	1	8	2	25,5	-	-	-	-	3	23,5	2	8
18	2	25,5	3	39	-	-	-	-	-	-	-	-
19	1	8	2	25,5	-	-	-	-	-	-	-	-
20	2	25,5	3	39	-	-	-	-	-	-	-	-
21	1	8	2	25,5	-	-	-	-	-	-	-	-
Rank means:	15,50		27,50		16,28		16,72		17,88		17,12	

3.2   Statistical Results

Brunner et al. offer a macro to calculate the statistics via computer in [15]. The macro is called "LD_F1" (corresponding to the introduced model above) and can be downloaded at http://www.ams.med.uni-goettingen.de/sasmakr-ord-de.shtml. The macro has to be used in the statistics software SAS, but with the formulas above, comparable experiments could be calculated by hand. The results are shown in Table 2.

Table 2. Statistical parameters, computed by the statistics software SAS and a special macro called "LD_F1" [15] (IAQ means Indoor Air Quality, RTE means Relative Treatment Effect, see Eq. 1)

Subject	Q_1 (Importance)		Q_2 (Favor)		Q_3 (Efficient)	
	Baseline IAQ	Baseline Light	Baseline	Dynamic	Baseline	Dynamic
n_{sub}	21	21	16	16	17	17
n_{obs}	42		32		34	
Rank means	15,50	27,50	16,28	16,72	17,88	17,12
RTE (*eq. 1*)	0,357	0,643	0,493	0,507	0,511	0,489
Statistics:						
H_0^F (*eq. 3*)	3,830		0,146		-0,256	
t(n-1)	0,00105**		0,885		0,801	

** p < 0,01

4   Discussion

Küller and Lindsten concluded from their study in classrooms that "windowless classrooms should be avoided for permanent use" [8]. The tested seminar room within the present study has a percentage of transparent surface of more than 50 %, which is wonderful for getting enough daylight in. If the main focal point of a study is to determine effects of biologically effective light, however, it must be realized that **daylight** (in winter times as well) is a **strong confounder**. The outside illuminance in the direction of the south reached a maximum of 2.400 lx in week *base* (Thursday forenoon, by the time the questionaire was filled out). The mean illuminance inside was nearly 1.800 lx. In week *dynamic*, the outside illuminace reached 2.300 lx (Thursday forenoon), and the mean illuminance inside could be retained as nearly 1.500 lx. These values may influence the effects of artificial light in a strong way. A **second strong confounder** in school studies is the concentration of **carbon dioxide** indoors. Several studies showed that a high level of carbon dioxid reduce students performance [18]. The performance measured with the d2-test [10] is significant dependent on carbon dioxd, too [19]. Further light studies should consider that, as we did.

Barkmann et al. rudimentally described the building relevant to the parameters of their tested classrooms; they are the sizes of the used classrooms, the directions the windows face (school one: one to north and one to south, school two: both to west), school one has "standard window shapes" and in both schools the relevant windows "were equipped with simple curtains, which could be drawn during normal lessons when the sunlight coming in was especially intense" [11]. Keis et al. didn't write about building relevant parameters [12]. Both of the recent studies [11] and [12] didn't mention any results from measurements of outside conditions or real inside illuminance confounded by sunlight. Our experience is that in the special case of rooms (classroom, seminar rooms), daylight influences the experience of artifical light. How much the effects are actually confounded must be shown in future studies.

Nevertheless, we found a highly significant difference within the question about the importance of two different aspects of indoor environmental quality. The indoor air quality is "extremely important" said 57 % and 43 % said at least "important". Compared to only 14 % who answered that light is "extremly important" and nearly one third gave a "neutral" answer to the question. This may mean that the real importance of the influence of light is not really common. No significant differences could be found within the question about students preferences between baseline and dynamic light. This may mean that they dont prefer a scenario and that significant differences within the students' subjective ratings of their own performance efficiency cannot be found within this data. Although 59 % aswered to feeling "moderately" efficient and 41 % felt "predominantly" efficient during the week of dynamic light, whereas 18 % said they felt "less" efficient, 35 % "moderate" and 47 % ticked "predominant".

5   Conclusion

Within this paper, we introduced a statistical method for calculating nonparametric dependent ordinal rank data with small sample sizes. The method is well known in the field of medical scientists and biologists, but not really in engineering science, as we had to realise. To offer engineers a possibility to evaluate subjective ratings of their building's industry projects was one of our aims. Further publications will show our results of the standardized test of attention [10] we did as well, corresponding to the main building-physical covariates we determined: light scenario (daylight) and concentration of carbon dioxide indoors.

Acknowledgements. The authors would like to thank the German Federal Ministry for Economic Affairs and Energy (BMWi) for supporting the research project "Energy Efficient Schools" (support code: 03ET1075A) in which this study was embedded. We also want to thank project management Jülich. Special thanks to OSRAM AG for supporting us with knowledge and to Seebacher ISYGLT for supporting the project with their knowledge and automation equipment. Finally, we wish to thank the students for their collaboration.

References

1. Wessolowski, N.: Wirksamkeit von Dynamischem Licht im Schulunterricht. Universität Hamburg (2014)
2. Campbell, S.S., Dawson, D.: Enhancement of nighttime alertness and performance with bright ambient light. Physiol. Behav. **48**, 317–320 (1990)
3. Boyce, P., Beckstead, J.W., Eklund, N.H., Strobel, R., Rea, M.S.: Lighting the graveyard shift: the influence of a daylight-simulating skylight on task performance and mood of nightshift workers. Lighting Res. Technol. **29**(3), 105–134 (1997)
4. Figueiro, M.G., Rea, M.S., Boyce, P., White, R., Kolberg, K.: The effects of bright light on day and night shift nurses' performance and well-being in the NICU. Neonatal. Intens. Care **14**(1), 29–32 (2001)
5. Fleischer, S. E.: Die psychologische Wirkung veränderlicher Kunstlichtsituationen auf den Menschen. TU Berlin (2001)
6. Brainard, G.C., Hanfin, J.P., Greeson, J.M., Byrne, B., Glickman, G., Gerner, E., Rollag, M.D.: Action spectrum for melatonin regulation in humans: evidence for a novel circadian photoreceptor. J. Neurosci. **21**, 6405–6412 (2001)
7. Thapan, K., Arendt, J., Skene, D.J.: An action spectrum for melatonin supression: evidence for a novel non-rod, non-cone photoreceptor system in humans. J. Physiol. **535**(1), 261–267 (2001)
8. Küller, R., Lindsten, C.: Health effects of work in windowless classrooms. Swedish Council for Building Research, Stockholm (1992)
9. Knoop, M.: Dynamic Lighting at schools. Investigation at Green End Primary School. Philips Lighting, Eindhoven (2008)
10. Brickenkamp, R.: Test d2: Aufmerksamkeits-Belastungs-Test, 9th edn. Hogrefe Verlag, Göttingen (2002)
11. Barkmann, C., Wessolowski, N., Schulte-Markwort, M.: Applicability and efficacy of variable light in schools. Physiol. Behav. **105**, 621–627 (2011)
12. Keis, O., Helbig, H., Streb, J., Hille, K.: Influence of blue-enriched classroom lighting on students' cognitive performance. Trends Neurosci. Educ. **3**, 86–92 (2014)
13. Bortz, J., Lienert, G.A.: Kurzgefasste Statistik für die klinische Forschung - Leitfaden für die verteilungsfreie Analyse kleiner Stichproben. Springer, Heidelberg (2008)
14. Bortz, J., Lienert, G.A., Boehnke, K.: Verteilungsfreie Methoden in der Biostatistik. Springer, Heidelberg (2008)
15. Brunner, E., Domhof, S., Langer, F.: Nonparametric Analysis of Longitudinal Data in Factorial Experiments. Wiley, New York (2002)
16. DIN Deutsches Institut für Normung e. V.; Beuth Verlag GmbH Berlin DINEN 12464-1 (August 2011): Light and lightig - Lighting of work places - Part1: Indoor work places; German version EN 12464-1 (2011)
17. DIN Deutsches Institut für Normung e. V.; Beuth Verlag GmbH Berlin DIN SPEC 67600. Biologically effective illumination - Design guidelines, April 2013
18. Mendell, M.J., Heath, G.A.: Do indoor pollutants and thermal conditions in schools influence student performance? A Crit. Rev. Lit. Indoor Air **15**, 27–52 (2005)
19. Ribic, W.: Schulstudie. Ziel: Keine Beeinträchtigung der Leistungsfähigkeit durch schlechte Luft an Österreichs Schulen. Unser Weg, 62. Jahr, Heft 5 (2007)

Author Index

Printed in the United States
By Bookmasters